13. Entrepreneurs generally enjoy their activities so much that they move from one project to another without stopping. When you complete a project successfully, do you immediately begin another? Yes, plus two. No, minus two.
14. Would you be willing to spend your savings to start a business? If so, add two—and deduct that many if you are not.
15. Add two more if you would be willing to borrow from others to supplement your own funds. If not, you lose two points.
16. If you failed, would you immediately work to start again? Yes gives you four, no takes that many away.
17. Subtract another point if failure would make you look immediately for a good paying job.
18. Do you believe entrepreneurs are risk-takers? Yes, minus two. No, plus two.
19. Add a point if you write out long-term and short-term goals. Otherwise, subtract a point.
20. You win two points if you think you have more knowledge and experience with cash flow than most people. You lose them if you think you do not.
21. If you are easily bored, add two. Deduct two points if you are not.
22. If you are an optimist, add two. If you are a pessimist, subtract two.

Total

Scoring:

If you score 35 or more you have everything going for you; between 15 and 35 suggests you have the background, skills, and talents to succeed; zero to 15 indicates you ought to be successful with application and skill development.

Zero to minus 15 does not rule you out, but it indicates you would have to work extra hard to overcome a lack of built-in advantages and skills; if you score less than minus 15, your talents probably lie elsewhere.

Source: © 1985, 1987 adapted from the Northwestern Mutual Life Insurance Company, Milwaukee, Wisconsin. Reprinted with permission.

THIRD EDITION

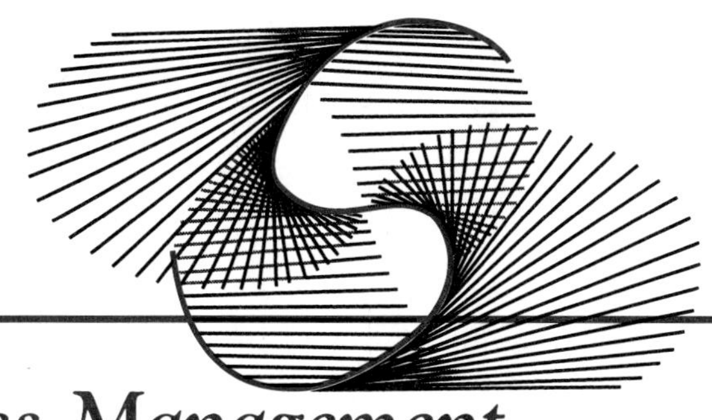

Small Business Management

RALPH M. GAEDEKE
DENNIS H. TOOTELIAN
California State University at Sacramento

ALLYN AND BACON

Boston London Toronto Sydney Tokyo Singapore

Series Editor: Jack Peters
Senior Editorial Assistant: Carol Alper
Production Administrator: Peter Petraitis
Editorial-Production Service: Karen Mason
Copy Editor: Karen M. Stone
Text Designer: Karen Mason
Cover Administrator: Linda K. Dickinson
Manufacturing Buyer: Louise Richardson

A Division of Simon & Schuster, Inc.
160 Gould Street
Needham Heights, Massachusetts 02194

Library of Congress Cataloging-in-Publication Data

Small business management / Ralph M. Gaedeke, Dennis H. Tootelian.
—3rd ed.
p. cm.
Includes bibliographical references and index.
ISBN 0-205-12729-0
1. Small business—Management. I. Tootelian, Dennis H.
II. Title.
HD62.7.G33 1990
658.02'2—dc20 90-20494
CIP

Printed in the United States of America
10 9 8 7 6 5 4 3 2 1 95 94 93 92 90

Brief Contents

Contents

PART TWO STARTING A NEW VENTURE

COMPREHENSIVE CASES

Preface

As with previous editions, the purpose of *Small Business Management* is to provide students with a realistic orientation to starting and successfully managing a small business. The focus throughout the book is to give students a fundamental understanding of small business management and an appreciation for the role and challenges faced by entrepreneurs.

Based on the thoughtful comments and recommendations from both instructors and students who had firsthand experience using the previous editions of the book, as well as suggestions from the many reviewers who made significant contributions to the current edition, we added several new features to the text, including:

Integration of CNN's Inside Business and Pinnacle Interviews

Twenty-five current, informative interviews from the popular programs *Inside Business* and *Pinnacle* are integrated into examples throughout the text. They feature successful entrepreneurs, as well as chief executives of relatively large companies, and provide immediate reinforcement of information and concepts. Interviews of decision makers from large companies illustrate how their practices can sometimes be the best medicine for smaller companies.

ENTREPRENEURS AND CHIEF EXECUTIVES INTERVIEWED

Company	*Chapter References*
Arthur Young and Company	14, 22
Black Enterprise Magazine	5, 19
The Blackstone Group	7
Compaq Computer Corporation	5, 9, 11, 12, 16, 18, 19, 21
Cray Research	8, 12, 13
Custom Shop	3, 11, 21
Della Femina, McNamee, Inc.	5, 17
Golden Door	1, 6, 10, 14, 15
Häagen Dazs	1, 2, 3, 4, 8, 9, 16
Joseph Baum, Restaurateur	3, 7, 18
Lenox China and Crystal	2, 16, 20
Lillian Vernon Corporation	1, 7, 9, 11, 16, 17, 19
Lotus Development Corporation	8, 13
Nike Inc.	9, 13, 15, 16, 18
Primerica	18

Robert Mondavi Winery	4, 21
Rouse Company	10, 22
Six Flags Theme Park	12, 14, 18, 19
Southeast Banking Corporation	8
Taylor Energy Company	4
Thermo Electron Corporation	12, 22
The Timberland Company	1, 7, 9, 10, 11, 16, 17, 18, 21
U.S. Playing Card	4, 13, 15, 20
Wally "Famous" Amos Cookies	1, 9, 11
Whittle Communications	1, 13, 16, 19

New Coverage of Current Small Business Developments

To ensure that the text's coverage of small business topics is comprehensive and up-to-date, developments such as the significant increase of women entrepreneurs, overseas opportunities for small business, and the computerization of small firms are highlighted.

Self-Test Review

Each chapter includes a self-test consisting of multiple choice questions and true/false statements. By answering these exercises, students actively focus on and review key material.

HOW THE TEXT IS ORGANIZED

The organization of the text follows the logical development of a small business. Part One provides a perspective of small business and entrepreneurship in the economy, together with a discussion of the advantages and disadvantages of operating a small business.

Part Two proceeds to develop the process involved in starting a new venture. Emphasis is given to the personal decision-making process, ways to enter a business, franchising, and legal ownership considerations.

Part Three focuses on fundamental preoperating decisions that are essential to launching a business on a sound basis. Consideration is given to developing a business plan, assessing the market, selecting a business location, financing the business, insuring the firm, and organizing and staffing the firm.

Part Four emphasizes the basic management functions that keep a business solvent and operating profitably. The focus is on management practices and strategies pertaining to accounting, finance, marketing, promotion, credit, employee training, personnel relations, purchasing, inventory control, operations management, and computerization. The last chapter includes a discussion on government and small business.

NOTEWORTHY FEATURES

Chapter 1, Small Business and Entrepreneurship

- Differences in gender characteristics of entrepreneurs
- 22-item entrepreneurial quiz (The Northwestern Mutual Life Insurance Co., Milwaukee, WI)

- Globalization of small business (export opportunities)
- Small business in the year 2000

Chapter 2, Advantages and Disadvantages of Operating a Small Business
- Common characteristics of successful small businesses [1989 study commissioned by American Express "Small Business Services" and the NFIB (National Federation of Independent Business)]
- Small business performance based on most recent Dun and Bradstreet studies

Chapter 3, Small Business and Industry
- Increased emphasis on services
- Coverage of manufacturing

Chapter 4, The Personal Decision-Making Process
- Revised checklist on how to assess personal readiness to become an entrepreneur
- Expanded consideration of the advantages and disadvantages of a family-owned business

Chapter 5, Starting or Buying a Business
- Steps in starting a new venture
- Determining the value of an established business

Chapter 6, Franchising
- Examples of "hot" franchise opportunities
- Trends and outlook of franchising

Chapter 7, Legal Forms of Ownership
- Advantages and disadvantages of sole proprietorships
- Advantages and disadvantages of partnerships
- Advantages and disadvantages of incorporating

Chapter 8, Developing Business Plans and Policies
- New outline of a business plan
- How policies and procedures are developed for key areas

Chapter 9, Marketing Research and Market Assessment
- Convincing skeptics on why and how research can be a powerful tool
- A step-by-step approach of the marketing research process
- How to collect primary and secondary data
- How to conduct a market analysis

Chapter 10, Selecting a Location
- Factors to consider in retail and service locations
- Meaning and implication of trading area analysis

Chapter 11, Financing the Business
- Revised sample loan package
- Description of the types of loans and their sources
- The role of government in financing small businesses

Chapter 12, Risk and Insurance Management
- Types of risks faced by small businesses and how they can be protected against
- How to balance risk and return
- How to determine the small business's needs for insurance

Chapter 13, Organizing and Staffing the Firm
- Revised discussion of the types of organizational structures
- Steps in the hiring process

Chapter 14, Accounting and Financial Records
- In-depth discussion of the bookkeeping process
- Understanding how key financial statements are created

Chapter 15, Use of Accounting and Financial Records
- How to evaluate the key financial statements
- Revised description of how to assess the financial capabilities of the firm

Chapter 16, Marketing Considerations
- Emphasis on customer service
- How to implement the marketing concept
- Increased emphasis on buyer behavior, target marketing, and the "4Ps"

Chapter 17, Promotion and Credit Policies
- Deciding how much to spend on promotion
- How to measure advertising effectiveness
- Revised framework for improving personal selling
- Ways to improve credit control

Chapter 18, Employee Orientation, Training, and Compensation
- Methods of training personnel
- Expanded discussion of wage and benefit packages

Chapter 19, Personnel Relations
- How to develop a leadership style
- Monetary and nonmonetary means of motivating personnel

Chapter 20, Purchasing and Inventory Control
- Relationship between purchasing and inventory control
- Discussion of material requirements planning
- Discussion of just-in-time inventory management

Chapter 21, Operations Management and Computerizing the Small Business
- Condensed discussion of designing production work flows
- Revised consideration of the components of a computer system
- Expanded description of the process of selecting a computer system

Chapter 22, Government and Small Business
- Expanded consideration of the regulatory process
- Government as a purchaser of goods and services from small businesses
- Revised discussion of the financial and managerial support services available from government entities

Comprehensive Cases
- Two (new) comprehensive cases

LEARNING AIDS IN THE TEXT

The following learning aids are provided to aid in understanding the material:

- **Chapter Outline.** Each chapter is introduced with a chapter outline. These outlines can help students keep chapter content in perspective and help them preview chapter material.

- **Learning Objectives.** Each chapter lists major learning objectives. These objectives direct the student to key study areas and provide a framework for self-learning.
- **Summary.** Each chapter includes a point-by-point summary of the important material that has been covered.
- **Key Terms and Concepts.** A list of key terms and concepts is included at the end of each chapter following the summary to help ensure that students note important topics.
- **Questions for Discussion.** Each chapter ends with several questions to provide students an opportunity to test knowledge of factual and conceptual material.
- **Self-Test Review.** A series of multiple choice questions and true/false statements are included in each chapter to focus on and review key material.
- **Concluding Case.** A short case is included for each chapter for write-up and/or discussion in class.
- **Comprehensive Cases.** Two comprehensive cases appear at the end of the text. They focus on key decisions faced by managers.
- **Index.** A thorough subject and company name index is included to provide easy access to topics discussed in the text.

ACKNOWLEDGEMENTS

We are grateful to our colleagues and students for providing critical comments during the preparation of this third edition. We also appreciate the useful feedback provided by adopters of the previous editions.

Special thanks are in order to the following professors for their extensive reviews, suggestions, and comments: Yohannan Abraham, *Southwest Missouri State University;* Michael Cicero, *Highline Community College;* Walter Green, *University of Texas;* Edward Hamburg, *Gloucester County College;* Homer Saunders, *University of Central Arkansas;* and Jonnie Williams, *Grand Rapids Junior College.*

We appreciate the generous support and encouragement provided by the dedicated professionals at Allyn and Bacon throughout the revision process. John D. Peters, Senior Editor; Karen Stone, copy editor; Karen Mason, graphic design and production service; and Carol Alper, senior editorial assistant deserve special recognition. Their careful attention to the content of the book was most important.

We also want to acknowledge all the organizations that granted permission for us to use their materials. A special thanks to CNN for participating in the joint venture of creating the CNN/Allyn and Bacon video program to accompany Gaedeke and Tootelian, *Small Business Management,* Third Edition.

CHAPTER ONE

Small Business and Entrepreneurship

CHAPTER OUTLINE

WHAT IS A SMALL BUSINESS?
- Small Business Administration Standards
- Committee for Economic Development Definition

THE PROFUSION OF SMALL BUSINESSES

WOMEN-OWNED BUSINESSES

CONTRIBUTIONS OF SMALL BUSINESS
- Social Contributions
- Economic Contributions

ENTREPRENEURSHIP

MINORITY BUSINESS AND ENTREPRENEURSHIP

SMALL BUSINESS IN THE YEAR 2000
- Demographic Changes
- Technological Changes
- The Internationalization of the American Economy

SUMMARY

LEARNING OBJECTIVES *The objectives of this chapter are to assist you in understanding:*

1. The meaning of small business.
2. The profusion of small business establishments and women's participation therein.
3. The social and economic contributions of small business.
4. The characteristics of entrepreneurs and meaning of entrepreneurship.
5. The impact of demographic and technological changes and the internationalization of the American economy on small business between now and the year 2000.

Interest in small business and entrepreneurship is flourishing today, as evidenced by current media exposure and the success of entrepreneurs. A proliferation of books, magazines, regular newspaper features, and special televised programs focus on entrepreneurship and small business. Thousands of small business owners and would-be entrepreneurs who want to learn how to start and successfully manage a business are finding that colleges and other institutions offer a wide array of night and weekend courses aimed specifically at the entrepreneur. Among community colleges, for example, more than 90 percent have small business courses.[1] Public and private universities offer programs leading to degrees in small business management or certificates in entrepreneurship.

The interest in entrepreneurship is encouraging more students to start careers in business. The Association of Collegiate Entrepreneurs, a national organization for students interested in entrepreneurial activities, has seen its membership increase from only 200 in 1983, its first year, to 4,500 in 1989.[2] While some members want to become entrepreneurs after they graduate, many are not waiting until graduation. Instead, they start their first businesses while still in college.

Chris Whittle, chairman of Whittle Communications, started the company while he was still in college. He began publishing in 1970 as a student at the University of Tennessee. His first publication, *Knoxville in a Nutshell,* was a survival guide for college freshmen. From this beginning, he successfully launched a career that resulted in about 42 publications. His latest project is in television: Channel One, a 12-minute news program beamed daily into various secondary schools.[3]

The dream of starting, owning, and operating a small business is durable and widespread. This desire is repeatedly stated in surveys and opinion polls, which show that nearly one out of every two Americans would like to run his or her own business and intends to try someday. Among the motivating factors that contribute to this desire are the potential financial rewards or profits, independence or being one's own boss, and doing what one likes to do. For those who say, "If this were my business, I would . . ." or "If I only had a chance to do it my way . . . ," owning a small business is a way to make wishes become reality. In short, small business ownership provides opportunities for those who value individuality, freedom, variety, and challenge.

Of the individuals who start small businesses, surprisingly few conform to the stereotype of the profit-oriented entrepreneur. Thousands of new business ventures are started each year because people become frustrated with working hard for someone else. To

The key to Chris Whittle's success from the beginning has been his development of targeted publications. His first publication, Knoxville in a Nutshell, *was designed for University of Tennessee college freshmen. He continues to target specific audiences with such projects as Channel One, a 12-minute news program for high school students.* (Photograph courtesy of Whittle Communications)

these people, being an independent owner-operator of a business is more important than anything else. To be sure, some hope to turn a new idea into a major enterprise. Milton Hershey (candy business), J.C. Penney (department stores), David Packard (calculators, personal computers, electronics), Ray Kroc (McDonald's), Colonel Sanders (Kentucky Fried Chicken), Mary Kay Ash (cosmetics), Stephen Wozniak (Apple computers), and Deborah Fields (chocolate chip cookies) are examples of people whose small business ventures became extremely successful. Most entrepreneurs, however, would be content to earn a decent living while enjoying not having to answer to anyone.

To the classic small business operator, there is nothing like being independent. It is true that the odds against success are high, that the financial risks are great, that the average earnings of the self-employed fall below earnings of those who are on someone else's payroll, and that the hours worked are long. In a recent survey, the National Federation of Independent Business found that 53 percent of small business owners work more than 60 hours a week and 25 percent work more than 70 hours a week.[4] Nevertheless, independent small business operators may fare better than people who work for someone else because of nonmaterial benefits their businesses can provide them. There is great personal satisfaction in having the freedom to be deliberately involved in all business decisions and in fulfilling that great American dream of entrepreneurship.

WHAT IS A SMALL BUSINESS?

Most people would agree that their neighborhood hairdresser, dry cleaner, flower shop, restaurant, and pizza parlor are small businesses, while automobile manufacturers, defense contractors, and professional football organizations are large businesses. Between these extremes, there is little agreement about what is small or large, because size is a relative concept. What is considered small in one industry in terms of revenue, assets, or employment might be large in another industry.

The conceptual definition of a **small business** is one that is independently owned and operated and not dominant in its field of operation. Based on their experience, a number of small business operators would add other characteristics when defining a small business, including:

- A small business is small enough to be exempt from the government regulations its owner knows about, but large enough that government agencies cite it for violating regulations its owner never heard of.
- A small business has at least three fewer employees than it really needs to get the job done.
- A small business has missed at least one payroll.

Several different standards have been applied to fit particular governmental assistance programs, legislation, or research studies. "Small business" is actually a gross oversimplification. The term means many things.

According to a survey of 218 small business leaders, owners of companies with fewer than 500 employees prefer to describe their companies as a small business. When asked what they like to call their kind of business, small business ranked first, followed by entrepreneurs, closely held companies, growing companies, family business, self-employed, and emerging business.[5]

Small Business Administration Standards

The Small Business Administration (SBA), created by the Small Business Act of 1953 to provide assistance to small business firms, specifies that a small business is one that is independently owned and operated and that is not dominant in its field of operations. The SBA has established size standards that determine eligibility for its financial, procurement, management, and other assistance programs. In 1984, the SBA issued a revised set of size standards, some of which are stated in terms of number of employees and others of which are stated in terms of annual sales revenue. Some of these standards are shown in Exhibit 1–1. As illustrated in this exhibit, size standards vary for industry groups (manufacturing, wholesaling, retailing, service) and selected industries within these groups.

Committee for Economic Development Definition

The Committee for Economic Development (CED) provides a somewhat different concept for defining a small business by stressing qualitative rather than quantitative

EXHIBIT 1–1 ***SBA Size Standards of Industry Groups and Selected Industries***

Industry Group	Number of Employees	Yearly Sales ($ millions)
Manufacturing	50–1,500	—
Wholesaling	500	—
Retailing	—	3.5–13.5
Services	—	3.5–14.5

Selected Industries

Manufacturers:	*Employing fewer than:*
Furniture and fixtures	500 persons
Electronic computers	1,000 persons
Petroleum refining	1,500 persons
Wholesalers:	*Employing fewer than:*
Automotive parts and supplies	500 persons
Dairy products	500 persons
Sporting goods	500 persons
Retailers:	*Earning sales of less than:*
Bakeries	$13.5 million/year
Restaurants	10.0 million/year
Grocery stores	13.5 million/year
Services:	*Earning sales of less than:*
Beauty shops	$ 3.5 million/year
Computer processing services	7.0 million/year
Passenger car rental and leasing	12.5 million/year

Source: Small Business Administration: Small Business Standards, *Federal Register,* Vol. 49, No. 28 (Washington, D.C.: February 9, 1984), 5024–5048.

criteria that distinguish small firms from large ones. The CED, composed of leading business people and educators, suggests that a small business has at least two of the following features:[6]

1. Management is independent. Generally the managers are also the owners.
2. Capital is supplied by an individual owner or a small group.
3. The area of operation is local. Employers and owners reside in one home community, although markets served need not be local.
4. The size of the firm is small relative to the industry. The size of the top bracket varies widely, so that what might seem large in one field would definitely be small in another.

THE PROFUSION OF SMALL BUSINESS

For several reasons, there are numerous answers to the question of how many small businesses exist.[7] First, there is no standard size definition of a small business. As pointed out previously, the size of a business may be measured in terms of employment or in terms of receipts (sales). For most statistical purposes, the Office of Advocacy of the Small Business Administration defines small businesses as those having either under 500 employees or under 100 employees.

The definition used may depend on the policy issue or question being analyzed, or the industry being studied. When examining retail sales, for example, an upper limit of 100 employees may be most useful, since most retail establishments have only a few employees, and most retail firms have few establishments. An **establishment** is defined as any single physical location where business is conducted, while an **enterprise** is a business organization consisting of one or more establishments under the same ownership or control. The average entity in the industry, whether establishment or enterprise, is small, and that smallness is captured within a lower size limit. In some industries, such as automobile manufacturing, the typical establishment may be much larger than 100 employees, and the limit of less than 500 employees accurately captures the fact that a firm with 300 or 400 employees may be small relative to the industry average.

Once agreement is reached on an upper boundary for the size of small businesses, the question of a lower boundary becomes an issue. Many people implicitly define a business as an organization having one or more employees. But most small businesses have no employees other than the owner (who may or may not be counted as an employee, depending on the federal agency that does the counting), and many business owners work only part time at their business.

Statistics published by the Internal Revenue Service provide the broadest measure of nonfarm businesses in the United States. An estimated 18.1 million business tax returns were filed in the tax year 1987. Returns were filed by 3.7 million corporations, 1.9 million partnerships, and 12.6 million sole proprietorships. Fewer than 7,000 of these businesses qualify as large businesses if an employment cutoff of 500 employees is used to define small- and medium-sized businesses.

It should be noted that the statistical counting procedure is hindered by the fact that many small businesses operate illegally in the sense that they are not registered with the IRS and State Department of Taxation, and they do not have the required local business licenses. This is unfortunate in at least one respect—there may be no way to

EXHIBIT 1–2 **Enterprises by Industry and Firm Size, 1986**

Industry	Total	Employment Size by Firm 1–4	5–19	20–99	100–499	500+
Total, U.S. Enterprises	3,805,982 (100.0%)	1,967,806 (51.7%)	1,350,788 (35.5%)	401,143 (10.5%)	71,607 (1.9%)	14,638 (0.4%)
Retail Trade	1,046,302	53.2%	36.4%	9.1%	1.0%	0.2%
Services	906,562	53.2%	33.6%	10.1%	2.6%	0.6%
Construction	527,058	61.3%	30.1%	7.6%	0.9%	0.1%
Wholesale Trade	419,441	47.3%	41.4%	10.0%	1.2%	0.1%
Manufacturing	359,039	32.0%	40.7%	21.1%	5.0%	1.2%
Finance, Insurance, Real Estate	271,863	56.5%	31.2%	9.8%	1.9%	0.5%
Transportation, Communication, Public Utilities	137,112	42.1%	40.5%	14.4%	2.4%	0.6%
Agriculture, Forestry, Fishing	104,764	61.3%	32.6%	5.4%	0.7%	0.1%
Mining	33,841	48.7%	37.0%	12.0%	1.9%	0.5%

Percentages may not add up to 100 due to rounding.

Source: Small Business Administration, Office of Advocacy, Small Business Data Base, USEEM file, version 8, 1987.

assess the worth of the business when it becomes available for sale and many years of building equity may be lost to the owner. The value of complying with the laws is to avoid serious problems and to reduce the anxiety one may have about business life.

The Small Business Administration's Small Business Data Base (SBDB) covers only businesses with employees, and accounts for approximately 93 percent of private employment. As shown in Exhibit 1–2, there were 3.8 million businesses (enterprises) in the SBDB in 1986, of which 51.7 percent had 1–4 employees and 97.7 percent had fewer than 500 employees. Exhibit 1–3 illustrates the percentage of enterprises by employment size, while Exhibit 1–4 illustrates the composition of small business.

EXHIBIT 1–3 **Percentage of Enterprises by Employment Size, 1986**

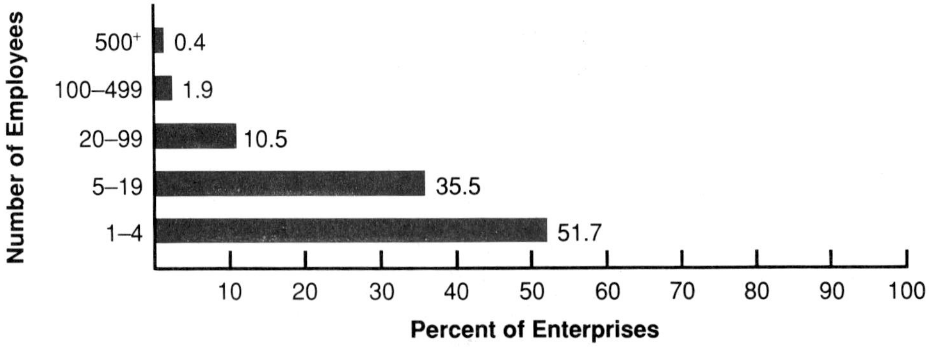

Source: Adapted from Small Business Administration, Office of Advocacy, Small Business Data Base, USEEM file, version 8, 1987.

EXHIBIT 1–4 **Composition of Small Businesses Employing Fewer than 100 Employees**

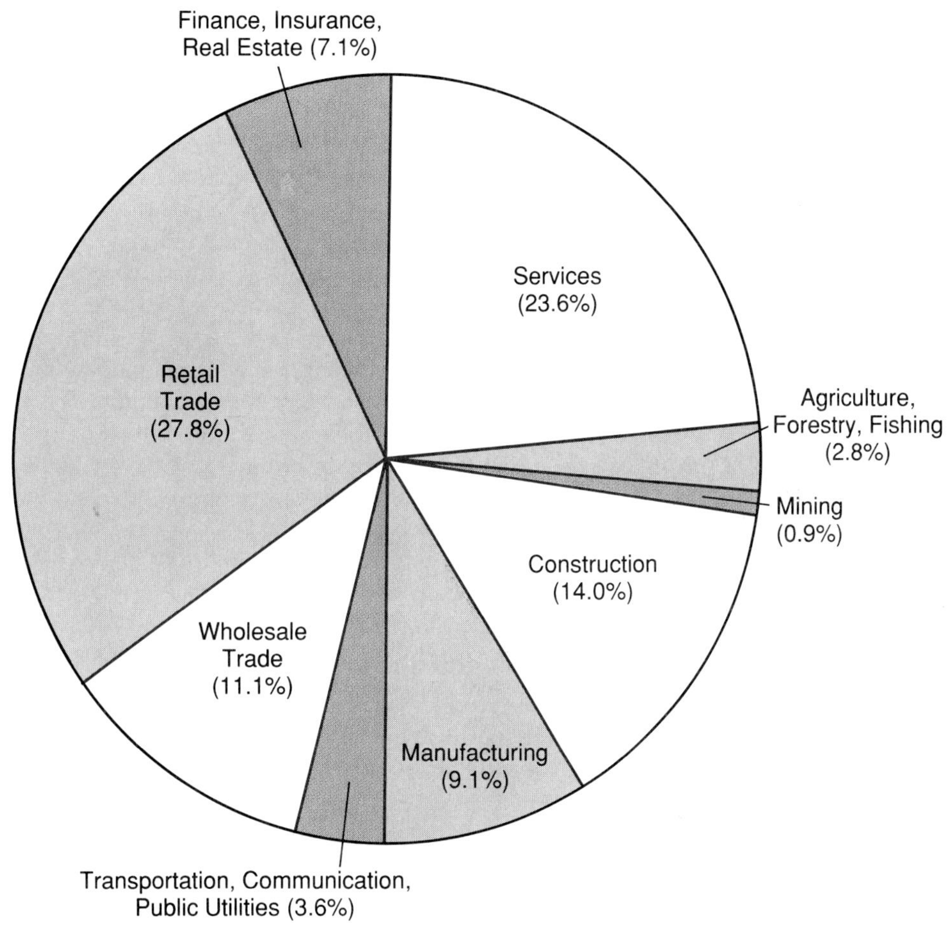

Source: Small Business Administration, Office of Advocacy, Small Business Data Base, USEEM file, version 8, 1987.

WOMEN-OWNED BUSINESSES

Test

Businesses owned by women—already more than four million strong—are proliferating.[8] Today, women are starting their own businesses at about twice the rate of men.[9] The growth rate of women-owned businesses, both in number and in average receipts, exceeds comparable statistics for businesses owned by men. Furthermore, because of the recent more intense proliferation of women-owned businesses in nontraditional industries, the group of women-owned businesses is becoming more industrially diverse.

GOLDEN DOOR®
RANCHO LA PUERTA®

Women-owned businesses have been primarily located in the services and retail trade industries. For example, Deborah Szekely founded the model health spa, Rancho Lapuerta. Some call it a mecca for fitness, one that attracts the likes of William Buckley and Elizabeth Dole. Her determination has earned her the title of the Grand Dame of Fitness, but she prefers to call herself an innkeeper. Her inns, Rancho Lapuerta in Mexico and the Golden Door in California, are privately owned and family run. According to Szekely, the difference between a man and a woman in business is that a man has to have it all and a woman knows when she is content.[10]

LILLIAN VERNON®

Another successful woman entrepreneur is Lillian Vernon, founder and chief executive officer of Lillian Vernon Corp. She is a leader in the catalogue industry, with a customer base of about 11 million and 1989 sales of $150 million. The company was founded in 1951, with a $500 advertisement in *Seventeen* magazine. The advertisement generated $32,000 in sales, and the company has been growing ever since.[11]

In recent years, more women business owners have been venturing into industries not traditionally occupied by women. For example, between 1980 and 1985, women-owned nonfarm sole proprietorships increased by 124.2 percent in the transportation industry, and by 116.3 percent in mining, construction, and manufacturing combined. Except in finance, women-owned businesses are expanding into all industrial sectors more rapidly than those owned by their male counterparts.

Although the population of women business owners is rapidly expanding, women are still relative newcomers to the business ownership arena. Compared to businesses owned by men, women-owned businesses tend to be newer and smaller in size for both employment and receipts. The relative youth and modest size of the average woman-owned business largely reflects the recent growth in the number of women-owned businesses.

There are other differences in the characteristics of male and female business owners and their businesses. For example, compared to men and their businesses,

- Women start or acquire their businesses with less financial capital,
- Women business owners tend to have less work and managerial experience,
- Among sole proprietors, a larger percent of women tend to be less than forty-five years old.

Many of the differences in the characteristics of women-owned businesses, especially the average age of the business and size of receipts, are directly traceable to the higher rate of formation of women-owned businesses. The relatively large inflow of new women-owned businesses tends to lower the average age of the business and receipts size of the entire population of these firms. Certain characteristics of women business owners,

After eighteen years as a homemaker, Sheila West was at what she called the empty vision time of her life. She had shot competitive archery in high school and her husband was a hunter, so at his suggestion she bought a compound-bow store. "I'd learned how to cook, how to be a wife, how to be a parent, so I figured, why can't I learn how to sell archery equipment? At first it was hard to accept that I was a CEO (Chief Executive Officer). I mean CEOs are people who run major companies. But I decided CEO stands for catch every obstacle and create endless opportunities, and I said OK, that's me." (*Source: Inc.*, December 1989, p. 94; photograph courtesy of President/CEO ACI Consolidated, Inc. and Archery Center International, Inc., an ACI Company)

especially their average level of work and managerial experience, are legacies of their labor market disadvantages.

The motivation for starting their own business is different for women owners than for men. A recent survey of more than 450 female entrepreneurs found that only 9 percent of them said they started their own companies "to earn more money." Instead, most indicated they were motivated by such factors as wanting more control over their careers or by encouragement from friends and relatives.[12] Female entrepreneurs indicate that the most satisfying aspects of business ownership are producing a quality product or providing a quality service, having more control over their lives or more flexibility in their lifestyles, and interacting with clients. Furthermore, most female entrepreneurs define success by either happiness or self-fulfillment, by the challenge and achievement of entrepreneurship, and by helping others.[13] Only a minority measure success by sales growth or profit.

Several sources of help and information are available to women planning to start or expand their businesses, including:

- Office of Women's Business Ownership, U.S. Small Business Administration, 1441 L St., N.W., Room 414, Washington, D.C. 20416. A current program called "Meet the Lenders," available through district SBA offices, offers information about obtaining credit and enables women to meet local lenders.
- National Federation of Business and Professional Women's Clubs, 2012 Massachusetts Ave., N.W., Washington, D.C. 20036. The organization has 120,000 members in nearly 3,500 chapters. Activities include lobbying and sponsoring scholarships for women over 25.
- American Women's Economic Development Corp., 60 E. 42nd St., Suite 405, New York, N.Y. 10165. AWED offers programs on starting and managing a business.
- National Women's Economic Alliance Foundation, 1440 New York Ave., N.W., Washington, D.C. 20005. The organization offers advanced management programs for women who have been in business at least five years, and it identifies qualified women to serve on corporate boards.
- National Association of Women Business Owners, 600 S. Federal St., Suite 400, Chicago, IL 60605. The organization is helping novice business owners and their veteran counterparts by providing how-to seminars, counseling on such basics as obtaining commercial credit, finding international trading partners, and lobbying Congress. Recently, it helped ensure passage of the federal Women's Business Ownership Act of 1988. Among other provisions, the law reduced barriers to commercial credit that have traditionally confronted women and established a panel to develop goals for aiding women entrepreneurs.

CONTRIBUTIONS OF SMALL BUSINESS

The contributions of American small business to economic prosperity and social well-being cannot be overstated.

- More than half of all private-sector employees now work for companies with fewer than 100 employees.
- Over 37 percent of the gross national product is generated by small business.
- Most new ideas and product innovations come from new and small ventures.

- Nearly two out of every three jobs are created by small business.
- Small businesses account for over 99 percent of all U.S. firms.

In short, it is the entrepreneur, the small business owner, who is the cornerstone of our economy.

Social Contributions

There has always been a close parallel between the aspirations of the American people as a group and the hopes of individual Americans who sought a livelihood through entrepreneurship. The paramount American ideal has always been freedom—freedom to live, speak, work, worship, or otherwise exist with as little interference and as much individual fulfillment as possible.

For about one century after the signing of the Declaration of Independence, small business had no rival in the economic sphere. The situation could hardly have been otherwise, because there were many opportunities for growth as the United States struggled from infancy toward its eventual status as a world power. During this formative century, small business produced the bulk of the gross national product. Thousands of creative, adventurous, and industrious entrepreneurs realized the American dream. They not only enjoyed upward social and economic mobility because of their personal successes, but they made substantial contributions to the quality of life throughout the United States through their inventions, production, and services. Even today, millions of Americans aspire to follow their example.

Looking back, one finds a tradition established by small entrepreneurs. This heritage contains elements of social service and consciousness that play an important role in contemporary American life, exemplifying the compatibility that exists between small enterprise and American ideals. Every year, several hundred thousand more Americans seek the prosperity and independence that success has already brought to so many entrepreneurs.

Today, these opportunities are especially important in efforts to incorporate new immigrants and the disadvantaged, primarily members of this nation's racial and ethnic minorities, into the mainstream of national life. Hence, the tradition of small business has become a valuable contributor to social progress and upward mobility. At the same time, small business continues to play a vital role in the economy. If every small business closed its doors today, the economy would be seriously impaired: More than half the work force would be unemployed; construction would virtually cease; more than 90 percent of all businesses would halt their operations; and before long, larger businesses

Entrepreneurs such as this video store owner are the cornerstone of our economy. Small businesses account for over 99 percent of all U.S. firms and provide nearly two out of every three jobs. (Photograph © Ann M. Mason)

would be affected too, because in many cases they are heavily dependent on small businesses as suppliers or customers. Most important would be the decline in diversity and competition that would accompany such an event.

Economic Contributions

Small businesses are the single most important element in the economy. They are manufacturers, processors, distributors, and customers. They serve the consumer and meet the needs of other businesses, large and small. They buy from other producers, creating a vast market within the economy. They provide an important part of the market for banks and financial institutions. In short, they are everywhere and of every type, as a quick glance in the yellow pages or a walk down Main Street, U.S.A., would reveal. They are downtown. They line commercial streets, fill up industrial parks, provide the stores in shopping malls, and enrich people's lives with a variety of food, drink, music, games, entertainment, and other pleasures. They build and repair homes; sell and service cars, trucks, televisions, computers, and appliances; cater weddings; and sell gifts for all occasions—the list is endless.

Perhaps most important, small business contributes significantly to the theory and practice of free enterprise. **Free enterprise** refers to a business firm privately owned and operated for a profit motive. In the free-enterprise system, most of the goods and services are provided by the private sector. (The means of production and distribution are privately owned and operated for a profit.) Small firms provide much of the competition that characterizes free enterprise. Their number, variety, and geographic dispersion are all consistent with dominant economic values. Even their failures are functional in that such failures provide a continuous flow of information on what will not work in the marketplace. This kind of information is vital to maintaining a dynamic, expanding economy.

When one considers the new products and new processes of the past 30 to 50 years, it is extraordinary how many of them were introduced by aggressive entrepreneurs or small business firms. A variety of studies conducted at different times, by different people, over different products, indicates that small firms and individual inventors produced anywhere from 20 percent to 100 percent of the important innovations; the 50 percent range was the most common result.[14] The Xerox copier, the Polaroid camera, the personal computer, stereo recordings, frozen foods, permanent-press clothing, and so on—the list is long and most impressive.

Small business also rates high for conceptual innovation, for coming up with new ways of organizing older services. Containerization, the discount store, the warehouse store, the motel, franchising the sale of fast-food products (hamburgers, fried chicken, tacos, pizzas, and so on) and services (home improvements, house cleaning, drycleaning, diet and exercise training, and so on) are among ideas first conceptualized and tested by small entrepreneurs.

Being entrepreneurial, small business fills market gaps and fills them quickly. Small business fills gaps by serving highly specialized markets and/or markets with limited demand, new markets which will eventually become mass markets, and markets affected by new economies of scale.[15]

A major advantage of large firms is their capacity to mass produce for mass markets. It is the type of activity in which economies of scale accrue very quickly. **Economies of**

scale refers to the effects on unit costs of a firm as it increases its scale or plant size over the long run. Economies of scale imply decreasing unit costs as plant size increases.

However, there are numerous markets too small or too specialized for large firms—markets in which economies of scale reach maximum efficiency points very quickly. This is one area of dominance for small business. Examples include various service and retail industries for which quality and personal relationships are integral parts of a sale—the boutique in contrast to Wal-Mart, the French restaurant in contrast to Denny's. Examples also include machine tool and metalworking machinery industries that are made up mostly of small firms. Each of these industries has a limited or specialized market in which few economies of scale exist.[16]

An important recent economic contribution of small business has been the growth of small manufacturing firms. Over the 1976–1986 decade, small manufacturers' net employment increased by 1.3 million workers, while large manufacturers showed a net loss of 100,000 jobs. The gains by small business in manufacturing reflect a number of factors, including technological advances, changes in the work force, the relative costs of various factors of production, the emergence of independent business firms, deregulation, and changes in procurement practices by large firms.[17]

As major job generators in the American economy, small firms are also important sources of training for the nation's work force. Recent studies of training in small firms find that it is more general, informal, and diversified than training in large firms. Workers in small firms receive less formal on-the-job training than those in larger firms, but they are more likely to obtain training from other sources, such as vocational and apprenticeship programs or university-sponsored programs. When on-the-job training is provided in small firms, it is as extensive as that provided in large firms.[18]

Because small firms are the first employers of a large proportion of workers—they provide two out of three workers with their first jobs—they are more likely to encounter problems related to lack of experience and illiteracy. Many small firms must spend substantial resources to teach basic or remedial work habits, such as timely and regular attendance.[19]

Congress has repeatedly confirmed its conviction that small business is essential to our nation's well-being. The importance of small business in a free enterprise system has been recognized by all Presidents and Congresses, dating to the time of George Washington and Thomas Jefferson. If one believes in private initiative, one must acknowledge the right of small business to exist. Also, it must be admitted that the destruction of opportunity for the small businessperson in any given industry to compete inexorably follows the concentration of control of such industry into a small number of dominating corporations.[20] In summary, the social and economic contributions of small business is vital to free enterprise and competition.

ENTREPRENEURSHIP

Today, the meaning of entrepreneur and entrepreneurship is taken for granted. Trying to define these terms, however, is problematic, because there are no standard definitions. An entrepreneur is not identified by formal rank or title, but retrospectively, after the successful practice of innovation.[21]

An **entrepreneur** can be defined as a person who organizes and manages a business or enterprise, usually with considerable initiative and risk. In this text, the term *entre-*

EXHIBIT 1–5 **Formal Education of New Business Owners and the Adult Public**

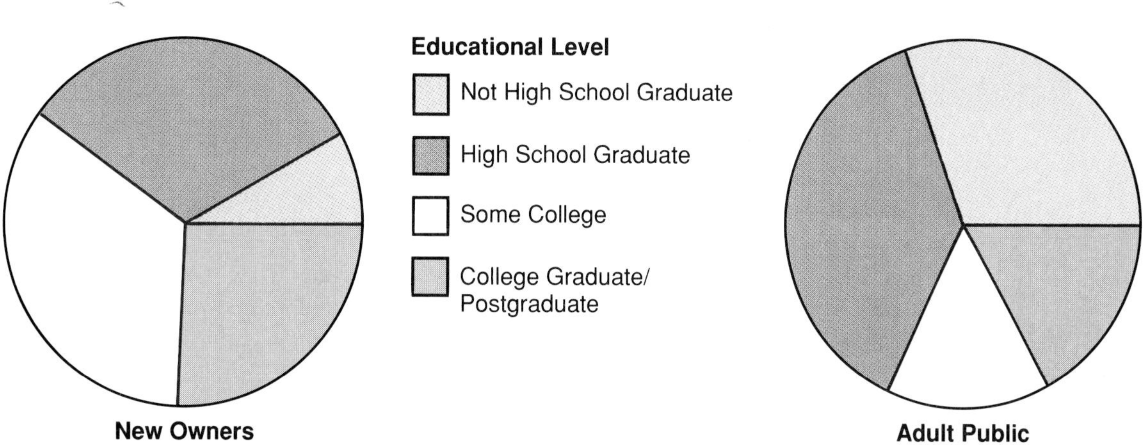

Source: Data developed and provided by The NFIB Foundation and sponsored by the American Express Travel Related Services Company, Inc.

preneur includes the innovator, founder, and all active owner-managers of a business firm. Entrepreneurs are distinguished from the rest of society by their desire for independence and their unwavering belief that their ventures will succeed.[22] **Entrepreneurship** can be defined as "purposeful and successful activity to initiate, maintain, or develop a profit-oriented business."[23]

As shown in Exhibits 1–5 and 1–6, research studies indicate that entrepreneurs as a group have more formal education than does the general population, and they often

EXHIBIT 1–6 **Additional Courses/Training of New Owners by Course/Training Type**

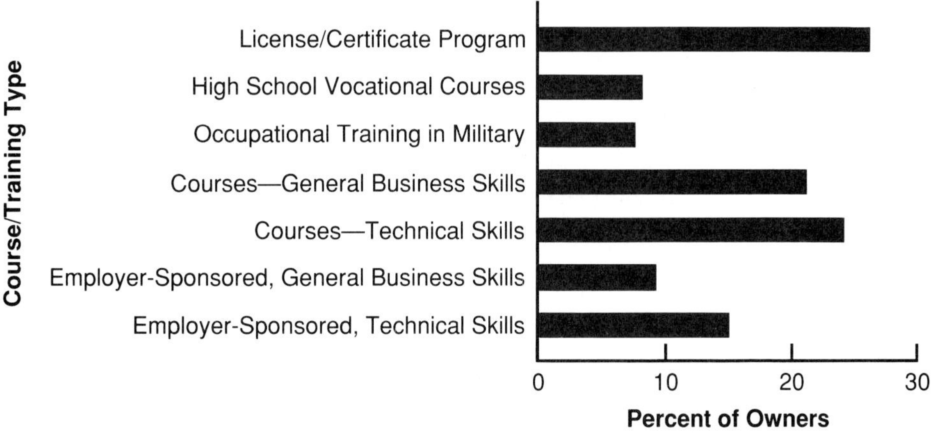

Source: Data developed and provided by The NFIB Foundation and sponsored by the American Express Travel Related Services Company, Inc.

attend courses and workshops once they are out of school. Nearly 60 percent of new business owners have taken at least one specialized course to supplement their formal education prior to business entry. Studies also indicate that nearly 60 percent of small business owners start their companies at a relatively young age (25–40), as illustrated in Exhibit 1–7.

From the entrepreneur's perspective, small business represents an opportunity to achieve economic independence. People who own or operate small businesses might not be completely independent, but they are freer than most individuals to earn a living by testing their skills and ideas in the marketplace. Even though this success depends on many factors that are beyond their control, they still have more influence over their own economic well-being than almost anyone else in society. They have an opportunity to express themselves in economic terms, although they cannot do so without incurring substantial risk. They usually get their ideas for a new business from a previous job or from a hobby, as shown in Exhibit 1–8.

Wally Amos's entrepreneurial recipe for success is stores selling chocolate chip cookies. The business Amos started in 1975 has grown into a company with over $20 million in sales. This high school dropout sampled several careers before he helped create a $350 million-a-year gourmet cookie market. Now that Famous Amos's face smiles on grocery shelves from coast to coast, it is hard to imagine when this walking cookie commercial was not famous.[24]

EXHIBIT 1–7 **Owner Age When Business Formed**

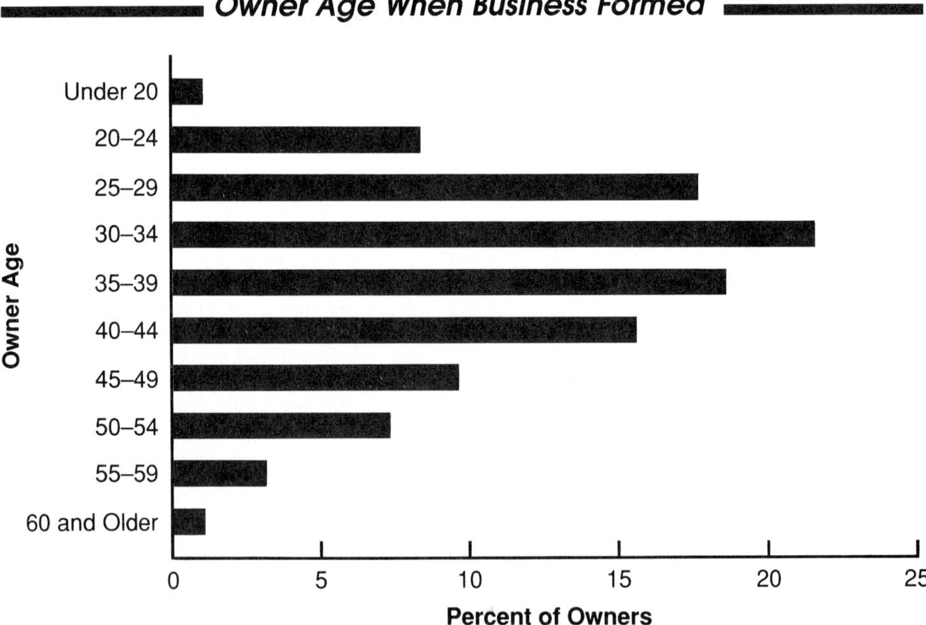

Source: Data developed and provided by The NFIB Foundation and sponsored by the American Express Travel Related Services Company, Inc.

EXHIBIT 1–8 **Sources of Business Ideas**

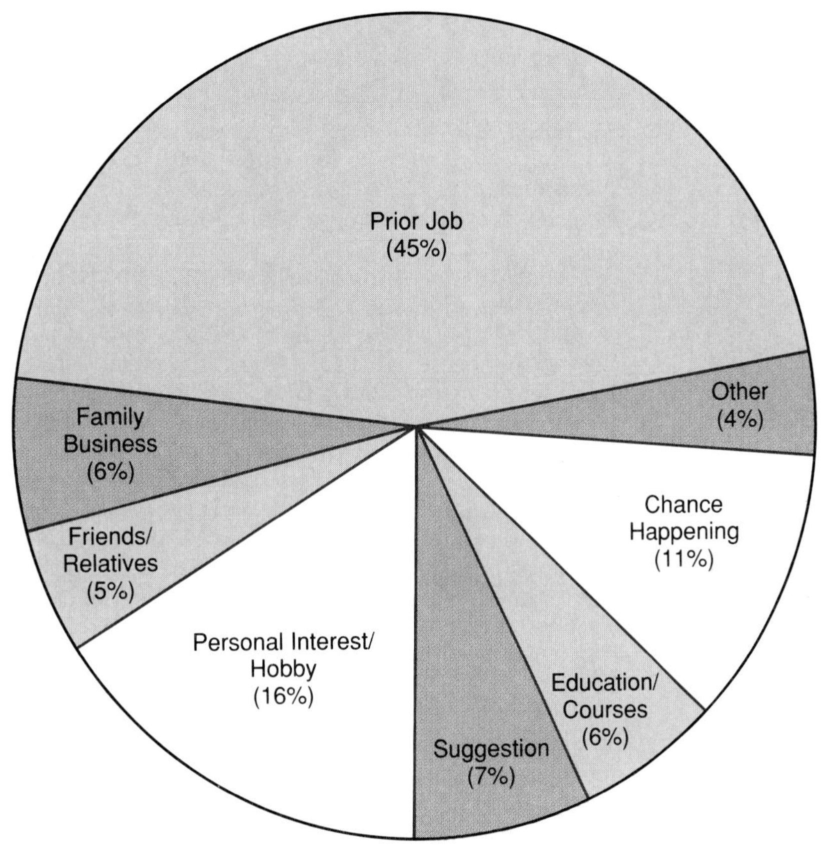

Source: Data developed and provided by The NFIB Foundation and sponsored by the American Express Travel Related Services Company, Inc.

Although a great deal of research about the personal qualities and behavior of entrepreneurs has been conducted, there is no agreement on universal entrepreneurial characteristics. They are as varied as the businesses they operate. Studies have shown, however, that the role requirements of entrepreneurs are significantly different from those who choose salaried employment. Such findings are useful for a realistic self-appraisal to determine one's own suitability for entrepreneurship.

Although a definitive profile of entrepreneurs does not exist, a number of dominant characteristics of successful entrepreneurs have been identified.[25]

1. Entrepreneurs have a great deal of personal energy and drive.
2. Successful entrepreneurs have a high level of self-confidence and are achievement-oriented.
3. Entrepreneurs attach a special meaning to money—it is a way of keeping score.
4. Entrepreneurs who successfully start new businesses possess intense levels of determination and desire to solve problems and complete jobs.

EXHIBIT 1–9 Entrepreneurial Quiz

Are you equipped with the qualities to be a successful entrepreneur? Do you have what it takes to start up your own business? The quiz below might clarify your own understanding.

1. Significantly high numbers of entrepreneurs are children of first-generation Americans. If your parents were immigrants add one to your score. If not, subtract one. ____
2. As a rule, successful entrepreneurs were not top achievers in school. If you were a top student deduct four. If not, add four points. ____
3. Entrepreneurs were not especially enthusiastic about group activities in school. If you enjoyed such activities subtract one. If not, add it. ____
4. Studies show that as youngsters, entrepreneurs often preferred to be alone. Did you prefer solitude? If so, add one. Otherwise, subtract it. ____
5. Those who started childhood enterprises, such as lemonade stands, or who ran for elected office at school, can add two, because enterprise is easily traced to an early age. Those who were not enterprising must subtract two. ____
6. Stubbornness as a child seems to translate into determination to do things one's own way—a hallmark of proven entrepreneurs. If you were stubborn enough to learn the hard way, add one. Otherwise, subtract it. ____
7. Caution can involve unwillingness to take risks. Were you a cautious child? If so, drop four points. If you were not cautious, you can add them. ____
8. If you were more daring than your playmates, add four. ____
9. If the opinions of others matter a lot to you, subtract one. Add one otherwise. ____
10. Weariness with daily routine is sometimes a motivating factor in starting a business. If this would be a factor in your own desire to go out on your own you have earned yourself two points. Otherwise, you have lost them. ____
11. If you really enjoy work, are you willing to work overnight? Yes, add two. No, deduct six. ____
12. Add four more if you would be willing to work as long as it takes with little or no sleep to finish a job. No deductions for failing to fit this pattern. ____

5. Successful entrepreneurs have the ability and commitment to set clear goals.
6. Entrepreneurs prefer to take moderate, calculated risks.
7. Effective entrepreneurs let their failures teach them how to avoid similar problems in the future.

8. Entrepreneurs use feedback to improve performance.
9. Successful entrepreneurs take initiative and seek personal responsibility.
10. Entrepreneurs who are successful know when, where, and how to seek help.
11. High-performing entrepreneurs continuously compete against self-imposed standards.
12. Successful entrepreneurs are able to tolerate modest–to–high levels of uncertainty concerning job security.

While few entrepreneurs possess all these characteristics to a high degree, the absence of several of them implies low or marginal suitability for successful entrepreneurship.

The quiz in Exhibit 1–9 is intended to help the would-be entrepreneur evaluate his

Entrepreneurial Quiz (continued)

13. Entrepreneurs generally enjoy their activities so much that they move from one project to another without stopping. When you complete a project successfully, do you immediately begin another? Yes, plus two. No, minus two. _____
14. Would you be willing to spend your savings to start a business? If so, add two—and deduct that many if you are not. _____
15. Add two more if you would be willing to borrow from others to supplement your own funds. If not, you lose two points. _____
16. If you failed, would you immediately work to start again? Yes gives you four, no takes that many away. _____
17. Subtract another point if failure would make you look immediately for a good paying job. _____
18. Do you believe entrepreneurs are risk-takers? Yes, minus two. No, plus two. _____
19. Add a point if you write out long-term and short-term goals. Otherwise, subtract a point. _____
20. You win two points if you think you have more knowledge and experience with cash flow than most people. You lose them if you think you do not. _____
21. If you are easily bored, add two. Deduct two points if you are not. _____
22. If you are an optimist, add two. If you are a pessimist, subtract two. _____

Total _____

Scoring:

If you score 35 or more you have everything going for you; between 15 and 35 suggests you have the background, skills, and talents to succeed; zero to 15 indicates you ought to be successful with application and skill development.

Zero to minus 15 does not rule you out, but it indicates you would have to work extra hard to overcome a lack of built-in advantages and skills; if you score less than minus 15, your talents probably lie elsewhere.

Source: © 1985, 1987 Adapted from The Northwestern Mutual Life Insurance Company, Milwaukee, Wisconsin. Reprinted with permission.

or her potential. Although this quiz is not scientific, it can help clarify one's own understanding of whether or not one possesses the qualities characteristic of successful entrepreneurs. While this survey can be a first step in developing self-awareness, it should not serve as the only assessment tool for evaluating one's entrepreneurial potential, since there is no universally accepted entrepreneurial profile.

The current media exposure and success of entrepreneurs can be threatening to established corporations, with smaller, aggressive, entrepreneurially driven firms developing new products and becoming dominant in certain markets. This presents opportunities to employees of large firms who catch the entrepreneurial fever. In response to this, some of these companies are attempting to create the same spirit, challenges, and rewards of entrepreneurship in their own organizations.[26] This practice of entrepreneurship within a large firm is called **intrapreneurship.** In some companies intrapreneurship requires that the entrepreneurial unit be segregated or isolated from the others, thus providing a corporate culture supportive of an entrepreneurial style of management. This is illustrated in the case of Häagen-Dazs.

Häagen-Dazs In 1962 Häagen-Dazs was founded in New York City by Ruben Mattus. Mattus sold the ice cream company to Pillsbury in 1983. Pillsbury hired "Ice Cream Emperor" Mark Stevens to maintain the entrepreneurial excellence of Häagen-Dazs. Stevens is responsible for continuing that entrepreneurial—or rather, intrapreneurial—zeal at Häagen-Dazs. He does so by encouraging teamwork, building a commitment around the idea that Pillsbury has a set of values—a constitution that all believe in, a Pillsbury-style democracy. In short, Stevens is Pillsbury's intrapreneur for Häagen-Dazs ice cream.[27]

MINORITY BUSINESS AND ENTREPRENEURSHIP

In recent years, there has been considerable growth and change in both the number of minority-owned firms and their industry types.[28] The number of firms more than doubled between 1972 and 1982, and has probably passed the one million mark since the last economic census was taken in 1982. There are now also more firms in wholesaling, business services, and other industries with higher potential for employment and wealth creation than the more traditional firms owned by minorities.

While the number of racial and ethnic minority business owners in the United States has increased steadily in recent years, the rate of business participation is still far lower for some minority groups than for the nonminority population. Research studies completed during the past eight years indicate that the relatively small number of minority-owned firms is a result of lower business formation rates and not high closure rates.

The causes of low business formation rates in some minority communities are not yet fully understood. It appears, however, that an important factor is the availability of three interdependent sources of capital—human, social, and financial. **Human capital** includes such individual characteristics as education, business experience, psychological and cultural attitudes, and risk-taking. **Social capital** can be defined as the social resources available from group support networks. **Financial capital** is the debt and equity financing available to a business owner. These resources historically have played a role in business development within all racial and ethnic communities. Where one or more of these resources is inadequate to support business development, the rate of business formation is usually low.

The distribution of social capital varies among minority groups. Black business owners have fewer entrepreneurial role models in firms operated by close relatives than do Asian, Hispanic, or nonminority male owners. Asians rely more than the other groups on relatives or friends for business start-up loans. Black entrepreneurs are more likely to sell

The number of minority business owners in the United States has increased steadily in recent years. The efforts of such minority entrepreneurs as this flower arranger contribute greatly to the U.S. economy. (Photograph © Ann M. Mason)

to minority customers and hire more minority employees than Asian, Hispanic, or nonminority male-owned enterprises.

Access to financial capital also differs by ethnic group. Asian businesses raise considerable debt and equity capital from both commercial financial institutions and the previous business owners. Hispanic businesses also obtain some debt and equity capital from Hispanic communities and from conventional financial institutions. Black-owned businesses, which face greater constraints, are relatively undercapitalized and raise relatively little capital (debt or equity) from their communities or from conventional financial institutions.

As pointed out, the three capital resources—human, social, and financial—are very much interdependent. The individual entrepreneur—the human element—is a critical factor in a business's success. The business owner, based on his or her experience, education, and skills, must choose where to seek financial resources and how to use the social resources available.

But the reverse is also true. The availability of financial institutions and group resources within the minority community can contribute to the individual's interest and ability to become an entrepreneur. An understanding of the capital resources available to various minority ethnic groups can assist business owners as well as public and private institutions seeking to increase minority business ownership.

SMALL BUSINESS IN THE YEAR 2000

Small businesses have done very well during the decade of the 1980s.[29] As pointed out earlier in this chapter, employment growth in small firms has been exceptionally strong, and proprietorship earnings have gained each year. What is the outlook for small business in the last decade of the twentieth century? At least three major trends are expected to affect small firms and markets in which they operate: demographic changes, technological changes, and the internalization of the American economy.

Demographic Changes

Two major demographic changes will affect small business between now and the year 2000. First, the overall population will become older, with the greatest growth occurring in the prime working age population between the ages of 35 and 54. Second, the rate of population growth is expected to decline to nearly its lowest level in the twentieth century, from an average annual growth rate of 1.14 percent during the 1980s to 0.73 percent between 1990 and 2000.

The Aging of the Population and the Labor Force

The age distribution of the population will have significant effects on the demand for goods and services in the economy. As the population ages, the demand for goods and services will be more a function of income growth than of population growth, so that demand for income-sensitive goods will increase more rapidly. Examples of such goods are restaurant meals, travel and tourism, and luxuries such as more expensive automobiles and high-quality consumer durables. The demand for hospital care, medical services, and related services should also increase significantly as the population ages.

The restaurant industry will produce the most new jobs between now and the year 2000; health practitioners will produce the second-largest number of new jobs. The relative decline in the proportion of younger people in the population will have a negative effect on the demand for housing and consumer durables related to housing, such as kitchen equipment.

The age structure of the labor force is important to small business for a number of reasons. Small businesses tend to hire relatively more younger and older workers than large businesses. Because the labor force is expected to decline in both of these age groups, small businesses may find it more difficult to recruit a work force like that which they have employed in the past. Consequently, they can expect to employ relatively more people in the prime age groups between 35 and 54. This age group is harder to recruit and demands more money and fringe benefits than younger or older workers.

The Declining Rates of Population and Labor Force Growth

The declining rate of population growth implies a significant decline in the labor force growth rate and, consequently, a decline in the ability of the economy to increase the output of goods and services between now and the year 2000. The total work force is expected to grow by only 1.2 percent per year from 1986 through the year 2000, down from an average annual growth rate of 2.7 percent between 1972 and 1979 and 1.7 percent between 1979 and 1986.

Women continue to constitute the fastest-growing portion of the labor force. The labor force participation rate for women between the ages of 25 and 54 will increase from 70.8 percent in 1986 to an expected level of 80.8 percent in the year 2000.

Other groups experiencing relatively large increases in the labor force during the next decade will include Asians and Hispanic Americans. A third source of growth will be net immigration. Projections by the U.S. Census Bureau call for net immigration of roughly 450,000 people per year through the year 2000—approximately the same level of legal immigration as during the recent past.

The declining rate of overall population growth, the relatively greater population growth of blacks, Hispanics, and Asians, and the increasing participation rate of women in the labor force will affect small firms in a number of ways.

The growing number of women in the work force may push small businesses toward providing more child care benefits, which also may be added to the menu of cafeteria-style benefits. (These are plans that allow employees to choose several benefits from a large selection.) There will be louder demands that governments at all levels increase subsidization of child care and preschool education. By the year 2000, it is almost certain that the total share of GNP devoted to child care and related educational activities will have increased significantly. Part of this increased spending will come from small and large businesses, and part will continue to come from government expenditures, financed by tax receipts. Small business will be faced with a greater challenge than ever before in providing the same level of goods and services with fewer employees who are receiving higher levels of income.

Technological Changes

Technological change is a second major factor likely to affect small business success between now and the year 2000. Changes in technology have always played an important role in the economy. The mix of outputs produced in the American economy has shifted continuously with technological advances.

The introduction and utilization of the microcomputer has been one of the most significant technological changes affecting business. It has led to the development of entirely new classes of industries in which information generation and manipulation are the primary activities. A prime example is in finance, where many small, specialized companies have been formed to provide information about particular classes of markets.

But small business has lagged behind somewhat in introducing computers to the production process. As of 1985, the over 3 million businesses with fewer than 20 employees were, on average, far behind larger firms in computer use. Of businesses with fewer than five employees, only 26 percent reported using computers, compared to 95 percent of businesses with 100 or more employees. It seems clear that small businesses will face increasingly difficult competition from their larger rivals unless they increase their computer use.

To date, smaller businesses have reported that computers are used primarily for word processing and accounting. In the future, small firms can be expected to increase their use of computers for planning, scheduling, and extensive inventory and process control. The ordering of materials and the tracking of goods-in-process will be tied into computers that also produce and track bills, produce shipping documents, and provide analytical or progress reports as needed. Small businesses will, in many cases, be able to match some of the distributional economies once enjoyed only by large companies utilizing mainframe computers.

Small business will use computers more intensively between now and the year 2000. The expected outcome will be more efficient and therefore more competitive small businesses. Businesses that vigorously explore the potential of computers and invest in the training needed to effectively use their capabilities will be more successful.

The Internationalization of the American Economy

If small business is to participate fully in the development of the American economy between now and the year 2000, the third major area of engagement must be in the international economy. International trade is already an important element of American life. In 1987, the United States imported roughly $547 billion worth of goods and services from foreign suppliers and exported approximately $428 billion in goods and services to overseas destinations. Combined, exports and imports in 1987 were roughly 21.7 percent of GNP. In comparison, in 1967, exports and imports were slightly less than 14 percent of GNP. By the year 2000, the value of exports and imports is expected to increase to approximately 38 percent of GNP.

Specialists say that small exporters already constitute a larger part of the export trade than is often supposed, and their portion is growing. Indeed, small businesses far outnumber large companies in the export arena. A recent Commerce Department study shows that 80 percent of the 100,000 American exporters in 1987 had shipments totaling less than $25,000. Most of the firms making such limited shipments are probably small companies. Another study, conducted by the Small Business Administration, estimated that manufacturers with fewer than 500 employees accounted for half of the value of American-made goods exported by manufacturers in 1985.[30]

What do exports and imports mean to small business? Traditionally, many small businesses have ignored the international marketplace. On the import side, small retail and wholesale businesses welcome imports. Many of the goods imported into the United States, particularly goods such as automobiles and high-technology consumer goods such as stereos, compact disc players, televisions, and videocassette recorders are important to small business. Most of these goods are imported, distributed, serviced, and sold primarily by small businesses. Small firms make good profit margins on these imports, in many cases better margins than they could on similar American products. Small businesses are a minority of total manufacturing businesses, and few small manufacturing businesses are hurt directly by imports.

Timberland®

Except for a minority of small businesses that choose to specialize in overseas markets, relatively few small firms export their products or services. One exception is The Timberland Company. Timberland, which makes those rugged outdoor boots, shoes, apparel and accessories, has the ingredients of a classic American success story. About one third of the total company revenues come from overseas sales. Timberland is selling its products in Japan, Hong Kong, and almost all of Europe. According to Sidney Swartz, chairman, chief executive officer, and president of The Timberland Company, quality American products are in great demand all over the world. Swartz emphasizes that "we specially go out of our way to have 'Made in the USA' put on our product. It is an enormous selling vehicle. People say manufacturing is dead in the United States. I don't believe it."[31]

For the most part, small businesspeople appear to find the American marketplace so large that they need not venture beyond the nation's borders. In fact, many small businesses will never export; they offer services intended only for local markets. The corner valet, for example, who specializes in cleaning clothes and repairing and shining shoes, is unlikely to become an exporter. But many small manufacturing and service firms can find valuable opportunities in overseas markets if they choose to look for them. Today, much of the small business interest focuses on the prospects for expanding in Western Europe, anticipating the removal of nearly all trade barriers there in 1992. In addition, the reunification of Germany and the democratic processes evident in Eastern Europe will provide new business growth opportunities for Western business.

Reasons to Market Overseas

There are numerous reasons for small businesses to consider foreign markets. First, the dollar's real exchange rate is down significantly from its peak in February of 1985. A decline in the price of the dollar makes American goods less expensive in terms of foreign currency. Manufactured products in the United States, including the products of small businesses, are thus much less expensive than they were in early 1985.

Second, the world economy is expected to expand at an annual rate of 3.3 percent for the next 10 years—slightly higher than the annual 3 percent growth rate over the past 11 years and considerably higher than projected U.S. domestic growth rate of 2.4 percent. The relatively strong growth of income in foreign countries will also expand market opportunities for American business.

Third, the globalization of small business underscores corporate America's belief that in the future most companies, including small ones, must compete internationally to succeed. Already, a number of small American companies are taking the next step after exporting to becoming global businesses. They are setting up their own operations overseas, not just shipping their goods abroad.[32]

Some smaller companies are building factories in foreign markets, but most are initially making less costly moves, such as arranging joint ventures, partnerships, and licensing agreements in Western Europe, Japan, and elsewhere. For example, at a time when American shoe companies are under stiff competition from foreign manufacturers, an American shoe company in Port Washington, Wisconsin, recently opened concept stores in Paris and Brussels for its celebrated new women's shoes. And that is not all. Allen–Edmonds Shoe Corporation is selling its top-quality dress shoes in 33 foreign countries. Included among them is Japan, where in 1987 company owner John Stollenwerk, after being denied access to a Tokyo shoe fair, set up a booth outside the hall and took orders for 300 pairs of his high-priced shoes! In October, 1988, Allen–Edmonds signed a distribution agreement with Otsuka Shoe Co., a firm with annual sales of $64 million. That is determination![33]

Resources for Small Exporters

Successful participation in international trade begins with a competitively priced product or service in the home market, complemented by the knowledge, skill, and resources necessary to sell and maintain the product or service in foreign markets. Small businesses with a strong productivity focus can and will develop the basic products and services. In most circumstances, these productive businesses will find it more efficient to turn to outside specialists for help with foreign market research and marketing, for distributive support, and for necessary maintenance and repair support. Many small businesses will find it difficult to support their products overseas unless they enter into contracts with foreign businesses willing to act as product distributors or product maintenance and service contractors.

There are many sources that provide assistance for the small- or medium-sized business seeking to export. Small business exporters can benefit from a variety of services provided by the SBA and U.S. Department of Commerce. Types of services include export counseling, workshops and training conferences, publications, and financial assistance.

Special services provided by SBA include the Service Corps of Retired Executives (SCORE), Small Business Development Centers (SBDCs), the Export Legal Assistance Network (ELAN), and the Export Revolving Line of Credit (ERLC) Program. SCORE, with over 730 chapters and 13,000 members throughout the country, offers one-on-one counseling by retired executives, who provide small businesses with access to years of business and international experience. SBDCs, operating in cooperation with local universities and colleges, also offer in-depth business counseling and training. Through ELAN, a small business can receive a free one-time legal consultation with export-knowledgeable attorneys.

SBA's financial assistance programs are also available to small business exporters. The ERLC program provides guarantees on short-term, preexport working capital through commercial bank lines of credit. In addition, through its Export Information System, the SBA can provide an initial market study. Export Information System identifies the primary importing and exporting countries for a particular product.

The Department of Commerce offers a wide range of information on export potential, overseas markets, trade leads, and overseas contacts. The Department also conducts trade missions and catalogue exhibitions, and assists firms participating in overseas trade shows.

Entrepreneurs interested in international trade can look to state and local agencies for additional information and programs. Small business owners can also take advantage of assistance available through chambers of commerce. Some chambers are active in promoting exports, providing training programs, counseling, referrals, trade missions, and publications.

Assistance is also available through domestic exporting representatives. Export management and export trading companies, for example, manage exports for other firms. These companies serve as export sales intermediaries and representatives for manufacturers. They act essentially as external exporting departments for companies whose exporting volume or experience is too limited to justify in-house export departments. Although the main responsibilities of export management and export trading companies are to locate foreign markets for their clients' products and to arrange for sales in these markets, they may also be involved in promotions, financing, and transportation for overseas shipment.[34]

Given the wide range of resources available to help small businesses export, the relatively strong rate of growth projected for foreign countries, and the expected favorable value of the dollar, small business will have real opportunities to increase exports in goods and services between now and the year 2000.

SUMMARY

1. Interest in entrepreneurship is flourishing today, as evidenced by its media exposure and college curricula.
2. Entrepreneurs value independence and being their own boss.
3. The conceptual definition of a small business is one that is independently owned and operated and not dominant in its field of operation.
4. The large majority of enterprises in the United States are small-sized businesses. Approximately 52 percent employ between one and four people; less than .5 percent employ more than 500.
5. The growth rate of women-owned businesses, in both number and average receipts, continues to exceed comparable statistics for businesses owned by men.
6. Small business has been a vital contributor to social progress and upward mobility in the United States.
7. Millions of small businesses contribute significantly to the theory and practice of free enterprise in the United States.
8. An entrepreneur is distinguished from the rest of society by a desire for independence and an unwavering belief that the business will succeed.
9. Entrepreneurs are also characterized by such attributes as their high levels of self-confidence, achievement, energy, and initiative.
10. Entrepreneurship can be defined as purposeful and successful activity to initiate, maintain, or develop a profit-oriented business.
11. The relatively small number of minority-owned firms is a result of lower business formation rates and not high closure rates.
12. Low business formation rates in some minority communities are due to insufficient human, social, and financial capital.
13. The three major trends expected to affect small firms and markets in which they operate between now and the year 2000 are demographic changes, technological changes, and the internationalization of the economy.
14. Two major demographic changes that will affect small business between now and the year 2000 are the aging of the population and the labor force, and the declining rates of population and labor force growth.
15. The introduction and utilization of the microcomputer has been one of the most significant technological changes affecting business. Small business will use computers more intensively

between now and the year 2000, and thus become more efficient and therefore more competitive.

16. If small business is to participate fully in the development of the American economy between now and the year 2000, it must serve overseas markets by exporting goods and services.
17. The increasing attraction of overseas markets is due to the decline in the price of the dollar and the favorable growth rate in the world economy.
18. Several resources are available to help small exporters, including federal government programs to support small business, assistance programs provided by state and local economic development agencies, and assistance offered by export marketing companies and export trading companies.

KEY TERMS AND CONCEPTS

Small business
Establishment
Enterprise
Free enterprise
Economies of scale
Entrepreneur
Entrepreneurship
Intrapreneurship
Human capital
Social capital
Financial capital

QUESTIONS FOR DISCUSSION

1. Why is entrepreneurship so popular today?
2. What is the conceptual meaning of small business?
3. How do the Small Business Administration and the Committee for Economic Development define small business?
4. What is the difference between an enterprise and an establishment?
5. In what industries does small business dominate in terms of employment?
6. What are some gender differences in the characteristics of business owners?
7. Why and how does small business contribute to the social well-being of the United States?
8. Perhaps the most important economic perspective on small business is that the nation's millions of small businesses contribute significantly to the theory and practice of free enterprise. Explain.
9. What distinguishes an entrepreneur from the rest of society?
10. Name ten dominant characteristics of successful entrepreneurs.
11. Why is the rate of business participation for some minority groups far lower than that of the nonminority population?
12. How do human, social, and financial capital contribute to small business success?
13. What are the major demographic changes that will affect small business between now and the year 2000?
14. Why is it necessary for small business to increase the utilization of computers?
15. What is the impact of the internationalization of the American economy on small business?

SELF-TEST REVIEW

Multiple Choice Questions

1. Which of the following is most important to the small business person?
   a. Having a lot of status.
   b. Making a maximum profit.
   c. Having short working hours.
   d. Being one's own boss.

2. According to the Small Business Administration, which of the following is a characteristic of small business?
   a. Number of owners does not exceed a standard.
   b. Markets served are local.
   c. Number of employees does not exceed a standard.
   d. Owner and employees live in one community.
3. Which of the following is not a dominant characteristic of successful entrepreneurs?
   a. Drive.
   b. Self-confidence.
   c. Authoritativeness.
   d. Initiative.
4. Which of following factors is not a cause for the low business formation rates in some minority communities?
   a. Human capital.
   b. Social capital.
   c. Financial capital.
   d. None of the above.
5. Which of the following is not a major trend expected to affect small firms between now and the year 2000?
   a. Aging of the U.S. population.
   b. Expansion of the young labor force.
   c. Utilization of microcomputers.
   d. Internationalization of the economy.

True/False Statements

1. There is general agreement as to what constitutes small business.
2. Small business only dominates certain discrete sectors of the U.S. economy.
3. Congress tends to discourage small business in favor of larger concerns.
4. The growth rate of women-owned businesses exceeds that of businesses owned by men.
5. Small business is not a major source of conceptual innovations.
6. In order to maintain their businesses, small business entrepreneurs must continually take substantial risks.
7. Entrepreneurs have more influence over their own economic well-being than almost everyone else in society.
8. The relatively small number of minority-owned firms is a result of high closure rates.
9. Computers are primarily used for word processing and accounting in small business.
10. Due to the favorable growth rate of the U.S. economy, small business does not have to worry about overseas markets between now and the year 2000.

ROBERTO'S GOURMET ICE CREAM AND DESSERTS

Roberto Florentelli, owner of Roberto's Gourmet Ice Cream and Desserts, had a hunch five years ago and acted on it. Today Roberto's is one of the fastest-growing businesses in a midwestern metropolitan area. Florentelli's idea for making and distributing premium ice cream and frozen desserts through selected outlets in the three largest cities in the state materialized and enjoyed phenomenal growth. Sales of $1,645,000 were generated at the end of the fifth fiscal year, up from $155,000 the first year.

Florentelli decided to go into the ice cream and frozen dessert business because he believed that excellent opportunities existed for small manufacturers in this line of business. He was aware that consumer preference had shifted in recent years to premium ice creams and frozen desserts, and that regional as well as national manufacturers were enjoying booming sales. Statistics indicate that ice cream and frozen dessert consumption will continue to grow, especially for premium products. Roberto's uses all natural ingredients—fresh fruits, fresh cream, liquid egg yolks, cane sugar, and pure flavor extracts.

"I find being my own boss very rewarding," says Florentelli. "It's not the money. It goes beyond that. Money is merely a way of keeping score. If there is something I want to do, I can do it. I have the flexibility to pursue whatever hunches I might have."

Florentelli says that his business administration studies provided him with an overview, the tools, and the confidence to start his own business. A course in small business management reinforced his desire to pursue the American dream of independence and being his own boss. He attributes his company's success to several factors: his background and high level of achievement, his willingness to take moderate risks, good timing, outstanding employees, help from the outside, and the growing public demand for quality products made with natural ingredients.

Four weeks after Florentelli became aware that

he had a stomach ulcer and high blood pressure, he asked his sales manager, David House, "How would you like to buy my business?" At first House simply shrugged his shoulders and went about his work. Two weeks later, however, Florentelli asked House, "Have you given any further thought to buying my business?"

House worked for Roberto's Gourmet Ice Cream and Desserts since its beginning five years ago. During the first two years, he was responsible for the initial contact and delivery of products to retailers and restaurants. His enthusiasm and success in obtaining between one and three new accounts per week led to his promotion to sales manager in the third year.

House enjoys both being sales manager and the bonus he receives at the end of each year for exceeding his sales quota. In addition to his base salary of $34,000, House earned a bonus of $6,450 three years ago, $11,500 two years ago, and $15,750 last year. A high school dropout, House is proud that he has earned almost twice as much as his older brother, a recent college graduate. Now House asks himself, "Am I really suited to be owner-manager of Roberto's Gourmet Ice Cream and Desserts?"

QUESTIONS

1. What are the dominant characteristics of Florentelli that make him a successful entrepreneur?
2. Do you believe David House is suited to be the owner-manager of Roberto's Gourmet Ice Cream and Desserts?

NOTES

1. Roger Ricklefs, "Schools Increase Courses to Help Entrepreneurs," *The Wall Street Journal,* February 6, 1989, B1.
2. Suzanne Alexander, "Student Entrepreneurs Find Road to Riches on Campus," *The Wall Street Journal,* June 23, 1989, B1.
3. Based on Cable News Network's "Pinnacle," March 4, 1989. Guest: Christopher Whittle, Whittle Communications.
4. NFIB Foundation, *Small Business Primer* (Washington, D.C.: The NFIB Foundation, 1988), 17.
5. " 'Small Business' Isn't So Bad After All," *The Wall Street Journal,* April 19, 1989, B1.
6. *Meeting the Special Problems of Small Business* (New York: Committee for Economic Development, 1957), 14.
7. Excerpted from *The State of Small Business: A Report of the President* (Washington, D.C.: U.S. Government Printing Office, 1988), 19–21.
8. Excerpted from Small Business Administration, *Small Business in the American Economy* (Washington, D.C.: U.S. Government Printing Office, 1988), 117–144.
9. Different Motivation for Women Owners," *The Wall Street Journal,* July 7, 1989, B1.
10. Based on Cable News Network's "Pinnacle," April 22, 1989. Guest: Deborah Szekely, Golden Door.
11. Based on Cable News Network's "Pinnacle," December 18, 1988. Guest: Lillian Vernon, Lillian Vernon Corp.
12. *Ibid.*
13. *Ibid.*
14. *The State of Small Business: A Report of the President* (Washington, D.C.: U.S. Government Printing Office, 1983), 121–128.
15. John Sloan, "The Present and Future Contributions of American Small Business," paper presented at a seminar at the Center for Constructive Alternatives, Hillsdale College, February 6, 1984.
16. *Ibid.*
17. Excerpted from Small Business Administration, *Small Business in the American Economy* (Washington, D.C.: U.S. Government Printing Office, 1988), v.
18. *Ibid.*
19. *Ibid.*
20. U.S. Congress, House Committee on Small Business, *Summary of Activities,* 94th Congress, November 1976, Report 1738, 292.
21. Albro Martin, "Additional Aspects of Entrepreneurial History," in Calvin A. Kent, Donald L. Sexton, and Karl H. Vesper, *Encyclopedia of Entrepreneurship* (Englewood Cliffs, N.J.: Prentice–Hall, 1982), 16.
22. Roger Thurow, "Scholars Identify Qualities that Make Entrepreneurs," *The Wall Street Journal,* April 4, 1980, 28.

23. Harold C. Livesay, "Entrepreneurial History," in Kent *et al.*, 10.
24. Based on Cable News Network's "Pinnacle," September 24, 1988. Guest: Wally Amos, Famous Amos.
25. Adapted from J. A. Timmons *et al.*, *New Venture Creation* (Homewood, IL: Richard D. Irwin, 1977), 77–83.
26. Robert D. Hisrich and Michael Peters, *Entrepreneurship* (Homewood, IL.: BPI/Irwin, 1989), 10.
27. Based on Cable News Network's "Pinnacle," November 14, 1987. Guest: Mark Stevens, Häagen-Dazs.
28. Excerpted from Small Business Administration, *Small Business in the American Economy* (Washington, D.C.: U.S. Government Printing Office, 1988), 165–191.
29. Excerpted from Small Business Administration, *Small Business in the American Economy* (Washington, D.C.: U.S. Government Printing Office, 1988), 1–30.
30. Barbara Marsh, "Small Business Isn't So Little in Export Trade," *The Wall Street Journal,* August 18, 1989, B1.
31. Based on Cable News Network's "Pinnacle," August 30, 1987. Guest: Sidney Swartz, Timberland Co.
32. Louis Uchitelle, "Small Firms Push to Go Global or Lose Out," *Sacramento Bee,* December 4, 1989, D1.
33. "An American Shoe Designer in Paris," *Network,* September 10, 1989, 12.
34. Brian Toyne and Peter G. P. Walters, *Global Marketing Management* (Needham, MA: Allyn and Bacon, 1989), 516.

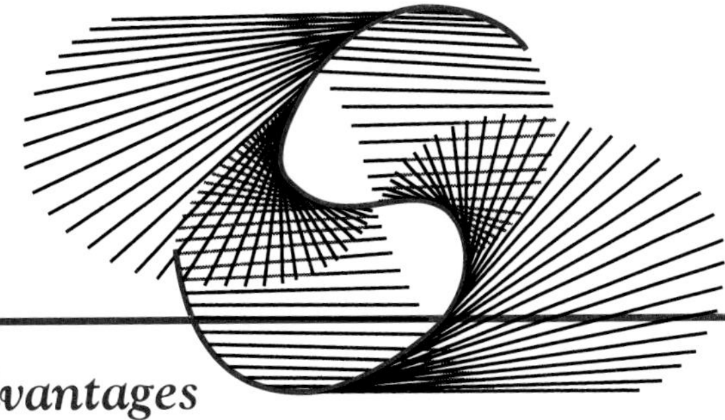

Chapter Two

Advantages and Disadvantages of Operating a Small Business

Chapter Outline

Learning Objectives *The objectives of this chapter are to assist you in understanding:*

1. The areas in which the small business entrepreneur enjoys distinct advantages.
2. The disadvantages facing small business operators.
3. The major pitfalls of managing a small business.
4. The financial performance of small business.
5. The rate of business dissolutions and primary causes of business failures.

The predominance of small firms in the U.S. economy suggests that these establishments and their owners enjoy many distinct advantages. However, small businesses also encounter numerous problems, many of which are directly related to their size of operation.

SUCCESS IN A NEW BUSINESS

An overwhelming majority of new businesses succeed, according to a recent nationwide study of nearly 3,000 new firms tracked from 1985 to 1987. The study, commissioned by American Express Small Business Services and the National Federation of Independent Business, found that 77 percent still were going concerns after three years, the study's criterion for success. Three years after starting their business, more than 90 percent said they would do it again, and 64 percent said their level of personal satisfaction equaled or exceeded their original expectations.[1]

The study found six common characteristics among successful new businesses. The key characteristics are:

- *Self-confidence*—of those who initially believed their chance of success was at least nine out of 10, 82 percent remained in business after three years, compared to 67 percent for entrepreneurs who had estimated their chances at six out of 10.
- *Size, measured in capital and employees*—the survival rate was 84 percent for businesses whose start-up capital exceeded $50,000, compared to 74 percent for those starting with less than $20,000. Of firms that began with six or more employees, 82 percent survived, compared to 71 percent of firms starting with two or fewer.
- *Emphasis on service rather than price*—the survival rate was 82 percent for firms that said better service comprised more than 51 percent of their business strategy, compared with 70 percent for firms relying mostly on lower prices.
- *Working hard, but knowing when to stop*—entrepreneurs who worked 60 to 69 hours per week had a business survival rate of 80 percent. The rate was 76 percent for those working fewer hours and 75 percent for those working more.
- *Devoting full time to the business*—the survival rate was 78 percent for entrepreneurs who said their business was their only job, compared to 70 percent who held another job.
- *Product knowledge*—the survival rate was 80 percent for entrepreneurs who said they had worked with the same products or services in their prior employment, compared with 72 percent for those who had not.

While no single factor meant the difference between success or failure, the more of these characteristics a firm had, the better its chance of succeeding.

ADVANTAGES OF BEING SMALL

There are several areas in which the small business entrepreneur enjoys distinct advantages that are the direct result of being small. These advantages make it possible to compete effectively with large firms.

Personalized Customer Service

Personalized customer service provided through direct contact is a dimension customers very much desire and small business owners find most satisfying about their business. A small business provides an environment in which management is close to its customers. This closeness and acquaintance with customers, often on a first-name basis, makes it possible to better serve the specific needs of customers, to respond to their suggestions and complaints, and to provide a personal, friendly atmosphere. Surveys show that such personalized service is not only highly valued by customers but is often the single major reason for patronizing a business. While large businesses also attempt to provide the personal touch, they are usually not as successful as small firms, because employees may not be sufficiently motivated to cultivate close, personal customer relationships.

Safford Sweatt, president of Lenox China and Crystal, believes that developing personal relations with customers is the real key to success. He learned how to deal in the real world environment with people. Ultimately, all business connections boiled down into personal relations. He learned how to do that successfully by organizing and adapting products to meet the needs of customers. That, according to Sweatt, was really the key to success.[2]

The continued survival of the neighborhood hardware store provides testimony to the importance of customer service. While discount stores, membership wholesale clubs, and chain stores account for the dominant portion of total hardware retail sales, the independent neighborhood hardware store continues to survive. Consider these comments from the book *The Modern Hardware Store,* published in 1929:

> We have a more discriminating public to serve—one in which the woman buyer with all her whims and fancies is playing a larger part. . . . The hardware dealer has more competition from other lines. The drugstore has added hardware specialties . . . the department stores are pushing hardware sales with vigor. . . . Chain stores have developed to the point that the consumer even in the hinterlands has access to them.

Now, more than 60 years later, when nuts, bolts, washers, paint, and so on, can be picked up while shopping for groceries or ordered through the mail, the battle to win and keep customers continues.

How does the independent neighborhood hardware store survive among competitors charging lower prices and/or providing greater shopping convenience? The key to its

Safford Sweatt's diverse background and experience has been instrumental in transforming Lenox into a comprehensive and sophisticated marketing driven company. Lenox flourishes through the careful union of modern manufacturing and merchandising techniques with the steadfast commitment to "old world quality" and value, and service to the customer. (Photograph courtesy of Safford P. Sweatt)

survival is personalized service. The biggest reason that customers keep coming back is the personal service provided: finding out how to fix a leaky faucet or repair a screen door, or being able to buy just the one screw they need instead of a blister pack of a dozen or more.

The authors of *The Modern Hardware Store* counseled the independent merchant in 1929 that he "has in his favor a long list of factors that influence the purchase of the consumer. He has personality, sympathy, friendliness, and an understanding of his local problems." Those traits continue to be the single major advantage not only of the neighborhood hardware store, but other small businesses as well.

Detailed Knowledge of Customer Needs

Small companies frequently specialize on the basis of products carried, services provided, and customers served. Such specialization makes it possible to acquire detailed knowledge of customer characteristics and needs, and emerging trends. This information is of particular importance in reviewing current marketing efforts and planning marketing strategies. Whereas large firms conduct costly market research studies to determine changing customer and market characteristics, the small entrepreneur is generally in a unique position to sense and recognize changes as they occur and to respond to them quickly.

Keeping merchandise on hand that will satisfy changing customer needs is a constant challenge to every store owner. In the case of hardware store owners, new products are picked up at the hardware shows and others are stocked as a result of customer requests. Although sales of products stocked as a result of customer suggestions may not turn out to be best sellers, customers reward the business that responds to their changing needs with repeat business. For the small business owner there is considerable pride in offering the products and services desired by customers.

Close Ties to the Local Community

Being part of the local community is a distinct advantage. Smaller firms are customarily managed by local residents of the community, and this means that they have an intimate knowledge of the community's needs and characteristics. Residents of a community recognize this and tend to prefer to support local firms.

Local news media typically provide more publicity for locally owned and operated

There are many areas in which the small business entrepreneur holds an advantage over larger firms. This businessperson's commitment to the local community is recognized by residents who will support his small business. (Photograph courtesy of Westinghouse)

businesses than for others. They focus on local entrepreneurs and small firms through special-interest stories and news features. As a result, the desire in a community to support local business is enhanced.

Personalized Approach with Employees

The personal approach of the small entrepreneur attracts many employees who want to be thought of and treated as individuals. Many employees value close supervision and the personal relationship with the manager brought about by direct, face-to-face communication. Similarly, many small business owners rank employee contact among the most satisfying aspects of operating their business.

Unlike larger firms, small businesses have short and direct lines of communication, increasing operating efficiency, and decreasing communication distortion. For example, an employee in a large firm generally finds that corporate policies require that suggestions and complaints pass through specified levels in the chain of command before reaching the decision maker. In the process, time is lost, the message may become distorted, and various people in the organization will have access to the information. This tends to inhibit or even prevent the communication process from taking place. In smaller firms these problems are greatly reduced. Employees often appreciate the manager or owner's interest in and commitment to sharing and communicating similar feelings.

Flexibility in Management

Another fundamental advantage of small firms is that management is not so formalized. Management has greater flexibility to implement new strategies in production, marketing, and so on. This ability to change direction quickly is seldom found in big companies. Managers of large businesses are generally characterized by their inability to make decisions quickly or to implement them rapidly once they are made.

The entrepreneur is relatively free to enter or leave a business, to grow or contract, and to succeed or dissolve the business. Management's relative flexibility to meet changing market, production, and overall business conditions allows the firm to adapt quickly to the ever-changing environment in which it operates. Small business owners indicate that such flexibility is among the most important sources of satisfaction about their business.

Carol Russell, owner of Russell Personnel Services recognizes that her most precious resource is the human resource. That is why she pays her people better than the industry standard, trains them constantly, empowers them to make their own decisions, and gives them credit for a job well done. (Photograph courtesy of Russell Personnel Services, Inc.)

Government Procurement Preference

Government procurement offices at the municipal, state, and federal levels often give preference to small businesses. Indeed, legislation may require that a certain portion of government contracts be awarded to small business firms. At the federal level, the Small Business Administration uses so-called "set-aside" contracts, which are strictly for small business. Such contracts specify that a minimum percent of the contract is to be awarded to small firms.

Other Advantages

Small businesses also enjoy the advantage of special tax rates and/or incentives. Furthermore, they operate with lower overhead costs. As indicated in Chapter 1, small business owners are individuals with the freedom and independence to do as they please, provided their actions are consistent with government rules and regulations and creditor requirements. They usually have the choice to remain small and to retain personal control over all business decisions, or they can attempt to join or be affiliated with larger businesses.

In reference to the neighborhood hardware store example discussed previously, independent store operators might choose to be affiliated with major suppliers such as ACE, True Value, or Sentry. The advantages of such affiliation are to buy merchandise on a cost-plus basis, to participate in promotion programs, and to obtain management assistance in operating the business.

DISADVANTAGES OF BEING SMALL

All businesses, regardless of size, are vulnerable to failure arising from various causes. The frustrations of small business owners, however, are particularly noteworthy. For example:

- Bankers often look at small business owners as if to say, "Who needs them?" For the same amount of paperwork they can arrange a bigger transaction.
- Inflation hits small business owners hard, yet they balk at raising prices too fast because they deal with customers they know on a first-name basis.
- They face cash flow problems more frequently than large firms do, and they may not meet every payroll period on time.
- Many establishments are in deteriorating high-crime urban neighborhoods that have been abandoned by other stores and middle-class customers.
- Owners would like to retire but cannot find a suitable replacement willing to put in the long hours.
- After the fears and self-doubts they faced when starting their companies, entrepreneurs often find that the demands of business can lead to neglect of their families.
- Letting go of the businesses that have been the focus of their lives for decades can lead to an intolerable sense of loss.
- Like Rodney Dangerfield, many home businesses, estimated at 14.6 million full-time establishments, get no respect. Typically, they are not viewed as bona fide businesses.[3]

Besides risking money and working long hours, entrepreneurs gamble with their careers, their places in the world, and their egos. Once they get started, they find it hard to stop. Small wonder that entrepreneurs often feel panic, and that businesses take over people's lives.[4]

Specific disadvantages of small business firms include lack of management expertise, capital shortages, high interest rates, inability to absorb losses, product liability, personnel recruiting difficulties, rural location handicaps, government regulations and paperwork, and psychological conflicts. These obstacles require great initiative, ingenuity, and sometimes luck to overcome.

Lack of Management Expertise

The caliber and experience of management are the most important factors influencing business success. Small business management's vulnerability to failure is often attributable to the entrepreneur's incompetence and lack of previous operating and managerial experience. An owner of a small business must be an expert in many areas, whereas large companies can afford to employ experts in procurement, production, finance, marketing, and other functional areas of business.

The American Express study mentioned earlier found, however, that the factor that did not appear to influence the chances of success included an owner's *prior management experience.* In fact, after controlling for other factors such as education and the type of business, companies whose owners had such experience grew at a slower rate than companies whose owners did not.[5] The same study noted that having a graduate degree in business does not affect an entrepreneur's probability of success.

Capital Shortages

Various obstacles reduce business's access to sufficient capital, and some work to the detriment of small business especially. In recent years, consumer savings have been depressed for a variety of reasons. As a result, small business has suffered not only from the general lack of saving but also because entrepreneurs have historically looked to family and friends to supply the equity investment funds used as seed capital to form new businesses. When saving becomes difficult, these sources are materially diminished. Studies indicate that surviving companies are likely to have started with higher levels of capital than businesses that fail.

Small business also operates under a handicap in the competition for business funds. Small size translates into greater vulnerability, thus raising the risk associated with any given investment in a small business. In addition, economies of scale (see Chapter 1) tend to preclude small business participation in the more impersonal mechanisms of our financial system. For example, registration requirements associated with the public issuance of stock can be afforded only if the cost is spread over a large number of shares. Similarly, loans from insurance companies, banks, and other major sources of investment capital are rendered less economical by the costly information requirements of the prospective lenders. Access of small business to investment capital is therefore frequently limited to individuals and small lending institutions that have a personal relationship with the entrepreneur.

High Interest Rates

Interest rates can also be a special problem for small business. High interest rates cause severe cash flow problems that are particularly threatening to small businesses. Because many small businesses tend to be undercapitalized and/or require substantial capital to finance growth, they have a heightened sensitivity to high and volatile interest rates. The volatility of interest rates associated with the higher levels also creates hardship by raising the risk associated with investment and growth.

The cost of capital is a significant portion of production and marketing expenses, and wide swings in interest rates can produce ruinous cost structures for small businesses. Moreover, the deductibility of interest expense is of less help to small businesses because they frequently generate insufficient income—especially new ventures—to take full advantage of the tax deduction.

Inability to Absorb Losses

One disadvantage unique to small business is the inability to absorb losses or errors of any significant proportion. A small firm may find that a $15,000 to $25,000 loss arising from obsolete inventory or internal theft can be mortal, or at minimum can restrict working capital so severely as to curtail operations and expansion plans. This same kind of loss would be relatively inconsequential for large businesses. Similarly, the personally owned company is frequently too small to be diversified in products, personnel, and markets; one large lawsuit, a bad account, or the loss of a key employee can do irreparable damage to the business.

Product Liability

Few recent issues have mobilized the small business community as rapidly as the issue of product liability. Dramatic changes in product liability law have made it easier to bring, and win, lawsuits. Product liability law holds that a firm is legally responsible for any bodily injury or property damage incurred by the user of any product manufactured, processed, or sold by the firm. With the judicial adoption of the theory of strict liability, liberal requirements for the proof of a product's defect have displaced negligence as the criterion for assessing liability for product-related injuries.

The concept of **strict liability** is based on the proposition that losses from injuries caused by defective products should not be placed upon the victims, regardless of negligence. The rationale is that those who produce (manufacturers) and sell (wholesalers and retailers) products are in a better position to insure against a loss and to distribute the cost equitably to all consumers of the product through higher prices.

High defense costs and large damage awards in product liability cases have caused many insurers to withdraw coverage or dramatically increase premiums. As a result, many firms are not able to spread the risk or pass the added costs to customers. This is especially true for small businesses that do not have the financial resources to assume the risk of potentially costly litigation and court verdicts.

Personnel Recruiting Difficulties

Small business owners frequently mention the difficulty or even impossibility of hiring competent employees as one of their major disadvantages vis-à-vis large firms.

This is particularly the case during periods of prosperity and full employment. College recruiting is especially difficult for smaller businesses because they cannot match the training programs, fringe benefits, and starting salaries of large firms.

As a small business grows, it needs to hire additional managerial personnel, but many entrepreneurs find it difficult to attract qualified talent. Management professionals cite the lack of benefit programs, low salaries, and the reputation of small business for ignoring modern management techniques as reasons for not considering employment in a small business.

Rural Location Handicap

The difficulties facing small business operators in rural areas are even more pronounced than those faced by entrepreneurs in urban areas. In general, rural areas do not provide an environment that is very conducive to a small business for these reasons:

1. Management problems facing the rural entrepreneur include the lack of managers with management skills, the steady emigration of the young-to-middle aged group to cities, and the lack of management training facilities.
2. Local financial institutions are often undercapitalized or are parts of larger banking chains, which affects their policies on lending to small business. Large outside institutions find it financially unrewarding to handle small loans to entrepreneurs in rural areas.
3. The assistance needed to deal with government regulations, paperwork, and taxes is lacking in rural areas.
4. The type of environment in which a business can thrive is usually not found in rural areas. Hospitals, libraries, schools, housing, and transportation may be inadequate. The local population may not provide an adequate market. Supplies and suppliers are not nearby. Business services provided by accountants, lawyers, engineers, and consultants may be lacking.

Government Regulations and Paperwork

The functions of government that have an impact on small business have multiplied and expanded beyond the average businessperson's control and comprehension. It is becoming increasingly costly and time consuming to comply with a never-ending stream of government rules and regulations.

In a recent study it was reported that the time required for a small business to compute withholding for federal income and Social Security taxes, to post employee records, to prepare W-2 and 1099 forms, and to prepare quarterly and annual reports required considerably more hours per year per employee than is the case for firms with a large number of employees. Paperwork required by the Department of Labor, OSHA, the Equal Employment Opportunity Commission, Environmental Protection Agency, and other bureaucratic agencies is also costly and very time consuming.

Psychological Conflicts

Women business owners may face additional disadvantages in operating a business. Many women state that they start their own business with certain handicaps:

- Fear of accounting and math frequently discourages women from properly diagnosing the conditions of their business and from planning their direction.
- A dislike for asserting themselves sometimes keeps women from confronting employees who should be disciplined or fired.
- Worries about neglecting their other responsibilities as wives and/or mothers sometimes become a harmful preoccupation.[6]

As women are increasingly exposed to the information and training required to run a successful business, these disadvantages are likely to diminish.

PITFALLS OF MANAGING A SMALL BUSINESS

The major pitfalls of managing a small business as reported to Dun and Bradstreet by people who are actually in business are:

- Lack of experience,
- Lack of money,
- The wrong location,
- Inventory mismanagement,
- Too much capital going into fixed assets,
- Poor credit-granting practices,
- Taking too much out for yourself,
- Unplanned expansion, and
- Having the wrong attitude.

While it is impossible to avoid all the pitfalls of starting and operating a business, knowing and anticipating the pitfalls can help you minimize them. Indeed, one of the best ways to learn management skills is to study one's own mistakes and those of others.

Häagen-Dazs

Mark Stevens, chief executive officer of Häagen-Dazs, admits to having made lots of mistakes. However, he has always learned from such mistakes. According to Stevens, "The interesting thing I've learned in business is that the only time you learn anything is when you've made a mistake. I never learned a thing from success. Mistakes are groveling, humiliating, annoying, angering kinds of things that just really teach you a lot."[7]

Lack of Experience

Business owners both large and small agree that one of the greatest pitfalls of managing a small business is lack of experience. Everyone says, "Sure, you have to have experience." To be successful in textiles, you need to work in textiles. To be successful in construction, work in the building trades. To be successful in retailing, have varied experience in sales. But the problem is more complex. It is not only the time spent but also, and more important, what was learned. What duties were performed? What responsibilities were discharged? The amount of experience required for success varies with the type of operation.

Business owners report that what is needed is not just experience but **balanced experience.** They say you need:

- Knowledge of buying,
- Knowledge of your products or services,

- Knowledge about how to get customers,
- Knowledge about handling finances,
- Knowledge about motivating employees, and
- Knowledge about responding to competition.

Varied experience in business helps one acquire these types of knowledge.

Lack of Money

Inadequate starting capital is the second major pitfall. In the 1950s it was not uncommon for the new business owner to start with $3,000. Some still cling to the old idea that you can start a business with nothing and work your way up, but experience shows that this is merely wishful thinking.

A paint retailer notes, "I have only been in business about seven months, but my main concern has been the lack of working capital." A women's wear retailer says, "Anyone going into business now without plenty of capital in back of her should have her head examined."

That it may take years to overcome lack of capital is apparent here:

> The first pitfall I encountered was simply not having enough money. For the first several years I was forced to resort to borrowing money from banks and friends, with the resulting loss of profits through interest rates. I progressed from borrowed funds to special terms with my suppliers, but still sacrificed profits through loss of discounts. It was many years before I finally reached the position where I could operate on my own money and earn my discounts.[8]

When lack of money afflicts a business, there is little time for anything but the struggle to appease creditors and worry about paying the bills. "You don't know what pressure is until you go to bed with $200 in the bank and you have a $4,000 payroll in the morning," says an owner of a troubled concrete drilling and cutting business who had plenty of nights like that. "I'd decide who was the debtor with the greatest chance of paying, and when he opened in the morning, I'd be there. I wouldn't leave until I had a check," he adds.[9]

The Wrong Location

In planning a business, location is very important. The cost of that location is rent. While everyone tells you, "Don't pay too much for rent," many business owners make a mistake because they do not pay enough rent! One experienced business owner says:

> I've been associated with some businesses where we rented stores at very low rates. Volume was poor. Almost always a low rent location is a poor bargain for the retailer. The additional rent needed at a more active location is more than paid for by the increased volume.

One manufacturer says, "As a business grows, it should be able to expand, physically speaking, on the land on which it started. It might be well for someone starting in business to put a little more money in land in the beginning."

The importance of location, today and in the future, is explained this way by one entrepreneur: "We're boxed in. We built up our sales, but now we are gradually losing

In planning a business, location is an important consideration. Although a low rent may appear to be advantageous to the entrepreneur, this out-of-the-way location may not be the best one for drawing customers. (Photograph © Ann M. Mason)

customers. They just can't reach us anymore. There's no way to park a car. Do we move or do we give up?"

Rent is a problem for all business owners. It must be figured carefully, not only for what it costs but also for the revenue the location will produce.

Inventory Mismanagement

Carrying an improper amount of inventory is a common pitfall. You hear, "Let's not get too much inventory," but it is not too much inventory per se that can be a problem; it is usually too much of the wrong kind of inventory.

One business owner comments: "They were good salesmen, I'll admit, but they put me in the hole because I didn't buy right." Many businesses are stuck with slow-moving, outdated, or excessive inventory. Carrying this inventory not only adds to costs but ties up money that could be employed more effectively elsewhere.

Too Much Capital Going into Fixed Assets

If you put capital into fixtures or into real estate, chances are the money is going to come out of your working capital or be borrowed. When your plant or store becomes larger and you need more working capital, it is just the time you have less of it. Some business owners get into trouble because they do not anticipate this. They fail to realize that when a second plant or store is opened, there are twice the employees and largely expanded receivables, payables, and inventory requirements.

Poor Credit-Granting Practices

Pressure to sell on credit terms is strong. If other stores are granting credit, it is difficult not to follow suit. If competition comes from a low-margin, big-volume cash competitor, the urge to grant a credit service not offered by the cash house is strong.

A credit business can be handled profitably, but before you decide to extend credit you should consider two questions:

1. *Do I have enough capital?* An additional capital investment equal to roughly one and a half months' credit sales is needed if selling terms are 30 days. For example, if a store is doing $12,000 a month in cash sales, and this is shifted to credit terms of 30 days, $18,000 additional capital is needed to maintain a comfortable

operation. Even if collections are made reasonably promptly, about $17,000 or $18,000 will appear as a new accounts receivable asset in your statement.

2. *Do I know how to collect?* Credit granting and collecting demand skill. Judgment is needed when opening the credit account, and persistence in getting the money is a must. Some people do not have the skill.

Unless the answer is "yes" to both questions, you are better off not to extend credit. If you find that you have no choice but to extend credit, you may be better off to do it through a national credit card and assume that cost. While bank credit cards are costly—typically 2 to 6 percent of the sales transaction—they have relieved the credit problem for most small retailing businesses.

Taking Too Much Out for Yourself

A stumbling block for some business owners is "living too high on the business." When you open a business, you must be prepared to lower your standard of living and make personal sacrifices until the business begins to prosper. However, whenever profits decline, personal expenses should also decline. Here is one business owner's experience:

> Within a very short period of time after I started the business, I found I was taking more out than I was taking in. I had to make a choice of either sinking slowly or finding some way of getting by with less money. My choice, though obvious, was a difficult one to make. It was to work a double shift, 16 hours daily, and on occasion work outside the business in order to operate for the second year without taking any money out.

An established business owner who is caught in a money bind must be willing to put the survival of the business above his or her desire for a continuous high income.

Unplanned Expansion

Expansion of the firm can be from within—a steady, gradual growth in sales or profits while capital and experience grow. Expansion can also come with more rapid acquisition of new units. One unit is going well—why not get a second and do twice as well?

Business growth by addition or acquisition must be carefully planned. Generally, additional capital is needed, but, more important, the ability to manage people is required. As one retailer describes:

> Things ran very smoothly until I expanded, putting in a new store across town. Then I found that my managers could not grasp my method of operation. I couldn't teach them. Therefore, I had to be in both stores at the same time in order to obtain the maximum business. I made a little from the store where I wasn't until my wife took sick and couldn't help out there. Then my latest manager offered to buy me out and I sold. Now I only have the new store and things are running smoothly again.

Recognizing one's limitations is important to running a successful business. Every business, small or large, finds itself limited to certain areas or to certain products.

Having the Wrong Attitude

Having the wrong attitude is yet another pitfall. One business owner writes, "There are troubles, sure, but when you get down to it, I guess it's a problem of attitude and attention. When you look at your business the right way, you get along. If you don't have the attitude, don't start on your own."

Having the right attitude means recognizing plain hard work. The feeling that "I'm the boss now and I can take off any time I want," may be the undoing of a good concern.

It also requires knowing the extent to which one should get involved in things outside the business. It outside interests are not part of the operation, sound management raises the question: "How much time and energy can I take from my business and still have it remain healthy?"

In light of the numerous challenges facing small business, it is not surprising that small business failure rates are very high. Failure rates, as well as their causes, should be studied in order to learn from mistakes made by others and thus increase one's own probability of success.

SMALL BUSINESS PERFORMANCE

The rewards of owning and operating a small business are often measured by the desire for independence, recognition, privacy, the chance to do the type of work one really wants to do, and the opportunity to live in a community of one's choice. These are important nonfinancial rewards for going into business, yet one cannot remain in business unless there is also a financial reward. Prospective business owners should be aware of the profitability of different lines of business, the rate of business dissolutions, and the primary causes underlying business failures.

Financial Performance

Current financial performance information for different lines of business can be obtained from several sources, including annual statement studies reported by Robert Morris Associates and financial profiles reported by Dun and Bradstreet. Both organizations provide historical performance data that allow for comparative analysis, which is critical to an accurate financial appraisal. In addition, many trade associations publish detailed operating results for their respective industries on an annual basis.

Robert Morris Associates, the national association of bank loan and credit officers, publishes annual *Statement Studies.* The *Statement Studies* contain composite financial data on manufacturing, wholesaling, retailing, service, and contracting lines of business. Financial statements on each industry are shown and are accompanied by widely used ratios. Income data (net sales, gross profit, operating expenses, operating profit, all other expenses, and profits before taxes) is provided for most industries.

Dun and Bradstreet publishes *Dun's Financial Profiles,* which include a financial profile report and an industry norm report. The financial profile report is a detailed spreadsheet of up to three years' financial data, with item-by-item comparisons of trend and industry position, plus commonly used ratios measuring solvency, efficiency, and profitability. **Solvency,** or liquidity, measurements are significant in evaluating a company's ability to meet short- and long-term obligations. **Efficiency** ratios indicate how effectively a company uses and controls its assets. **Profitability** ratios show how successfully a business is earning a return to its owners.

A common factor of all businesses, large and small, is that each business has something to sell. One cannot overemphasize the importance of sales to the financial health and profitability of a business. The cost of sales (cost of doing business)—such as the purchase of goods, space rental, employee wages and benefits, and taxes—also plays an important role in determining a business's financial health. However, without sales there are no profits and without profits there is no business.

Small businesses show greater performance variations than large firms from year to year and during the ups and downs of business cycles. Empirical studies have shown that small firms are especially sensitive to changes in the business cycle. They often have less diverse product lines and are less able to take advantage of economies of large-scale production, marketing, and finance, making them more vulnerable to downturns in economic activity. Consequently, their change in operations during the upturn usually is more pronounced than for large firms, and their recovery from the lower base of operations is usually sharper.

Exhibit 2–1 shows the performance variations of wage-and-salary and proprietorship income from 1981 to 1987. Small businesses did well throughout the five-year expansion period following the end of the 1981–1982 recession. At no point during the expansion did small business earnings grow at a rate of less than 9.7 percent per year.[10]

EXHIBIT 2–1 ***Change in Wage-and-Salary and Proprietorship Income, 1981–1987***

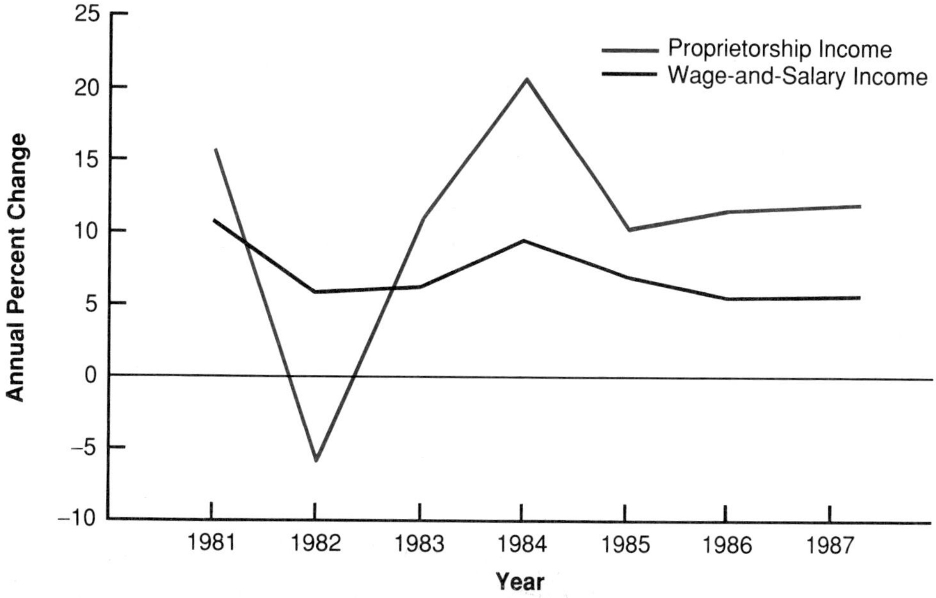

Source: U.S. Department of Commerce, Bureau of Economic Analysis, *Business Conditions Digest*, various issues.

Business Dissolutions

A business may dissolve for a variety of reasons, including merger, retirement of the owner, failure with no loss to a creditor, or failure with a loss to a creditor (bankruptcy). The vast majority of **business dissolutions** in the United States are failures with no reportable loss to a creditor. Exhibit 2–2 presents a preliminary report of business failure rates for 1988.

The probability of surviving can be related to the age of a business. Exhibit 2–3, based on preliminary findings from 1988, shows that 9.5 percent of all firms failed within one year; 33.4 percent failed during the first three years; and 51.8 percent failed during the first five years.

Although the total business failures in the economy can be a useful general economic indicator, that number tends to mask the strengths and weaknesses in the economy that can be observed only at an industry level. The business failure rates are higher in the retail trade and services sector of the economy than in construction, manufacturing, and wholesale trade.

The rate of failure for selected types of retail firms and service firms is presented in Exhibits 2–4 and 2–5. As these exhibits illustrate, failure rates vary considerably by industry and line of business.

Causes of Business Failures

Knowing and understanding the primary causes of business failures and the pitfalls of management discussed earlier should help entrepreneurs lessen their chances of failure.

According to Dun and Bradstreet,[11] the single most common cause of business failures, accounting for 71.7 percent of all failures, is economic in nature. *Economic factors* include insufficient profits, high interest rates, loss of market, no consumer spending, and no future.

EXHIBIT 2–2 ***Business Failures per 10,000 Firms, 1988****

Industry	Failures per 10,000 Firms
Business Services	379
Personal services	40
Manufacturing	98
Wholesale trade	88
Retail trade	79

Note: Business failures do not represent total business closings, which consist of both business failures and business discontinuances. As defined in Dun and Bradstreet's statistics, business failures consist of businesses involved in court proceedings or voluntary actions involving losses to creditors. In contrast, businesses that discontinue operations for reasons such as loss of capital, inadequate profits, ill health, retirement, and so on, are not recorded as failures by Dun and Bradstreet if creditors are paid in full.

*1988 figures are preliminary.

Source: Adapted from Dun and Bradstreet, *Business Failure Record* (New York: The Dun and Bradstreet Corp., 1989), 6–9.

EXHIBIT 2–3 ***Age and Life Expectancy of Business Firms, 1988****

Age of Firm	Percent of Total Business Failures*
One year or less	9.5
Two years	12.4
Three years	11.5
Total three years or less	**33.4**
Four years	10.1
Five years	8.3
Total five years or less	**51.8**
Six years	6.5
Seven years	5.4
Eight years	4.6
Nine years	3.9
Ten years	3.5
Total six to ten years	**23.9**
Eleven years and over	24.3
Total over ten years	**24.3**
TOTAL	**100.0 percent**

*1988 figures are preliminary.

Source: Adapted from Dun and Bradstreet, *Business Failure Record* (New York: The Dun and Bradstreet Corp., 1989), 17.

EXHIBIT 2–4 ***Retail Trade Business Failures per 10,000 Firms, 1988****

Retail Trade	Failures per 10,000 Firms
Apparel and accessory stores	144
Stationery stores	111
Furniture and home furnishing stores	104
Eating and drinking places	89
Sporting goods	89
Nonstore retailers	83
Hobby, toy and game shops	77
Building materials and garden supplies	76
Gift, novelty and souvenir shops	71
General merchandise stores	69
Jewelry stores	69
Book stores	61
Luggage and leather goods stores	57
Food stores	55
Automotive dealers and service stations	51
Sewing, needlework and piece goods	45

➤

EXHIBIT 2–4

Retail Trade Business Failures per 10,000 Firms, 1988* *(continued)*

Retail Trade	Failures per 10,000 Firms
Liquor stores	38
Used merchandise stores	37
Drug and proprietary stores	35
Fuel and ice dealers	20
Other retail stores	95
Total Retail Trade	**79**

*1988 figures are preliminary.

Source: Adapted from Dun and Bradstreet, *Business Failure Record* (New York: The Dun and Bradstreet Corp., 1989), 8.

EXHIBIT 2–5

Service Business Failures per 10,000 Firms, 1988*

	Failures per 10,000 Firms
Business Services	
Advertising	117
Services to buildings	114
Consumer credit reporting and collection	98
Computer and data processing services	91
Mail, reproduction and steno services	68
Personnel supply services	65
News syndicates	0
Miscellaneous business services	661
Total Business Services	**379**
Personal Services	
Photographic portrait studios	46
Laundry, cleaning and garment services	43
Shoe repair and hat cleaning shops	35
Beauty shops	34
Barber shops	16
Funeral services and crematories	15
Miscellaneous personal services	118
Total Personal Services	**40**

*1988 figures are preliminary.

Source: Adapted from Dun and Bradstreet, *Business Failure Record* (New York: Dun and Bradstreet Corp., 1989), 9.

The second most frequent cause of business failures, accounting for 20.3 percent of all failures, is *lack of experience,* which includes incompetence, lack of line experience, lack of managerial experience, and unbalanced experience.

Other causes of business failures include the following factors:

- *Lack of sales*(11.1%)—competitive weaknesses, economic decline, inadequate sales, inventory difficulties, and poor location.
- *Expenses*(8.1%)—burdensome institutional debt and heavy operating expenses.
- *Neglect*(1.6%)—bad habits, business conflicts, family problems, lack of interest, marital problems, occupational conflicts, and poor health.
- *Customers*(0.4%)—receivable difficulties and too few customers.
- *Disaster*(0.4%)—Act of God, burglary, employee fraud, fire, death of owner, and strike.
- *Lack of capital*(0.5%)—burdensome contracts, excessive withdrawals, and inadequate start capacity.
- *Assets*(0.2%)—excessive fixed assets and overexpansion.
- *Fraud*(0.3%)—embezzlement, false agreements, false statements, irregular disposal of assets, misleading name, and premeditated overbuy.
- (Due to the fact that some failures are attributed to a combination of causes, the total of the major categories exceeds 100 percent.)

Although economic causes are the primary reason for business failures, it should be noted that management inexperience and incompetence is a key reason why roughly 40 percent of all businesses fail during the first three years. Weak management can result in neglect, fraud, sales decline, excessive expenses, receivable difficulties, inventory problems, and excessive fixed assets. Without question, therefore, balanced management experience is a critical factor in business success.

SUMMARY

1. An overwhelming majority of new businesses succeed: They are still going concerns after three years.
2. The six most common characteristics among successful new businesses are owner's self-confidence, size as measured in capital and employees, emphasis on service rather than price, working hard but knowing when to stop, devoting full time to the business, and having product knowledge.
3. There are several areas in which small business entrepreneurs enjoy distinct advantages, including their personal approach with customers and employees, their detailed knowledge of markets, their close ties to the local community, their flexibility in management, and government procurement preference.
4. Personalized customer service provided by small business owners is the single major advantage of a small business.
5. The major disadvantages of being small include lack of management expertise, capital shortages, high interest rates, inability to absorb losses, product liability, personnel recruiting difficulties, rural locations, government regulations and paperwork, and psychological conflicts in the case of some women entrepreneurs.
6. Nine pitfalls of managing a small business are: lack of experience, lack of money, being in the wrong location, inventory mismanagement, too much capital going into fixed assets, poor credit-granting practices, taking too much out of the business for personal needs, unplanned expansion, and having the wrong attitude.

7. To be successful, business owners need to have balanced and varied experience.
8. The rewards of owning and operating a small business are often measured in nonmonetary terms, such as the desire to "be your own boss." However, one cannot remain in business if there is no financial return on the investment.
9. Current business financial performance is reported by Robert Morris Associates, Dun and Bradstreet, and trade associations.
10. Financial performance is measured in terms of solvency, efficiency, and profitability.
11. Small firms typically show greater performance fluctuations from year to year than large businesses.
12. Business dissolutions are due to mergers, retirement of the owner, and failure which may or may not result in a loss to creditors.
13. Approximately 13 percent of all firms fail within the first year; 39 percent fail within three years; and 55 percent fail within five years.
14. The major causes of business failure include economic factors, lack of experience, lack of sales, high expenses, neglect, lack of customers, disaster, lack of capital, excessive assets, and fraud.
15. Approximately 70 percent of all business failures are due to economic reasons, with management inexperience and incompetence being a major contributing factor.

KEY TERMS AND CONCEPTS

Personalized customer service
Strict liability
Balanced experience
Solvency
Efficiency
Profitability
Business dissolutions

QUESTIONS FOR DISCUSSION

1. Why is the personal approach with customers and employees an advantage in the small business?
2. What is meant by flexibility in management?
3. Why is lack of management experience a major disadvantage for small business?
4. Do small businesses and large firms have the same access to capital? Why or why not?
5. Why are small businesses less able to absorb unexpected losses than large businesses?
6. What special handicap can face women who start their own businesses?
7. In broad categories, do rural areas fail to provide an environment conducive to the success of a business?
8. What is meant by balanced management experience?
9. What is meant by the cost of location?
10. Where can one obtain current performance information on specific industries?
11. Why must growth by addition or acquisition be carefully planned?
12. What are the major causes of business failure?
13. What is the relationship between business failure and the age of the business?
14. What should be included in measuring the financial performance of a business?
15. Do business dissolutions generally result in losses to creditors? If not, why not?

SELF-TEST REVIEW

Multiple Choice Questions

1. Which of the following is an advantage of small business?

b. Detailed knowledge of customers.

a. Close contact with customers.

   c. Close contact with employees.
   d. All of the above.
2. Which of the following is a characteristic of flexibility in small business management?
   a. Inability to make decisions quickly.
   b. Ease of entering a business.
   c. Inability to implement a decision quickly.
   d. None of the above.
3. Which of the following is a major cause of the small firm's inability to absorb losses?
   a. Lack of diversification.
   b. Too much diversification.
   c. Lack of initiative.
   d. None of the above.
4. Which of the following is a characteristic of small business performance?
   a. No fluctuations.
   b. Small fluctuations.
   c. Large fluctuations.
   d. None of the above.
5. Which of the following ratios indicates how effectively a company uses and controls its assets?
   a. Efficiency ratio.
   b. Profitability.
   c. Solvency.
   d. All of the above.

True/False Statements

1. Personalized service is often cited as a main reason for patronizing a small business.
2. Small businesses frequently specialize on the basis of products carried and customers served.
3. One common disadvantage of small business is the inability to absorb unexpected losses.
4. In recent years, product liability insurance costs for small businesses have decreased.
5. One of the problems of small businesses is complying with all government rules and regulations and completing the necessary paperwork.
6. The small business owner should always choose the location that costs the least.
7. Costly bank credit cards have relieved the credit problems for most small business retailers.
8. Business dissolutions almost always result in losses to creditors.
9. When evaluating small business failures by age of business, it is evident that if a firm can survive the first three years, the probability of continued survival increases substantially.
10. Small business owners cannot remain in operation for long without receiving a financial return on their investment.

MARIE'S FITNESS CENTER

Throughout her college years, Marie Mackey was a participant in various programs of weight reduction, body building, stretching, contouring, and dieting. Keeping trim and healthy was more important to her than graduating with a degree in communications. Upon graduation, she spent six frustrating months trying to get her first job. However, none of her search efforts resulted in a firm job offer.

Dejected and at a loss for what to do, Mackey sought out a career counselor who recommended that she should pursue the field of greatest interest to her, namely the fitness industry. This was precisely the advice she was looking for, and she immediately began to study the industry in earnest.

Mackey noted that a number of fitness centers were located in her community, but that none catered specifically to women. There appeared to be a need for a fitness center that did not claim to turn every woman into a Jane Fonda. Furthermore, she discovered that many of her friends shared her interest in fitness and had not been able to find the kind of program where women could exercise to attain only the level of physical fitness they wanted. Her friends wanted an environment to exercise in that was supportive and not based primarily on weight loss. The local health clubs that catered both to men and women were too male-oriented in their equipment and program set-up. Accordingly, Mackey decided to open a women's fitness center, which she called Marie's Fitness Center.

The Fitness Center opened its doors in a neighborhood shopping center last August. Start-up capital of $15,000 for fixtures, a six-month lease, insurance, advertising, and equipment was provided by her parents, who expected the loan to be paid off within one year. Mackey calculated that she would reach a breakeven point if she had 400 members signed up with six-month memberships. With a six-month membership costing $97, the total revenue would be $38,800.

During the first three months of operation, Marie's Fitness Center grew to 250 members. At that point, Mackey decided to expand into the vacant space next door. This additional space was to be devoted to a juice and yogurt bar and exercise equipment. She was confident that many more women would be interested in a salon that provided these additional amenities.

The women who signed up during the first quarter of operation had memberships from a minimum of three months up to a maximum of 24 months. Different membership programs cost different prices. The memberships were paid in full upon sign-up. For the purpose of projecting the first year's income, Mackey worked out the following figures:

Month	*Membership*	*Income*
August	100	$ 1,500
September	200	3,000
October	250	3,750
November–July	350	37,500

The projection for the year surpassed Marie Fitness Center's breakeven point of $38,800 by $6,950. Marie felt confident that she could sign up enough members to generate the necessary revenues and make a small profit.

QUESTIONS

1. How well is Marie Mackey suited to be the owner/manager of Marie's Fitness Center?
2. What are the strengths and weaknesses of Marie's Fitness Center?
3. What are the major pitfalls Mackey needs to recognize and confront to make the Salon successful?

NOTES

1. Based on Marguaret Peterson, "Success in a New Business," *The Sacramento Bee,* October 11, 1989, E1.
2. Based on Cable News Network's "Pinnacle," February 27, 1988. Guest: Safford Sweatt, Lenox China and Crystal.
3. "Home, Not-So-Sweet Home Business," *The Wall Street Journal,* November 3, 1989, B1.
4. Based on Roger Ricklefs, "Traumas of a New Entrepreneur," *The Wall Street Journal,* May 10, 1989, B1.
5. "Is There a Substitute for Experience?" *The Wall Street Journal,* February 14, 1989, B1.
6. Sanford L. Jacobs, "Women Business Owners List Causes of Their Worst Problems," *The Wall Street Journal,* July 7, 1980, 13.
7. Based on Cable News Network's "Pinnacle," November 14, 1987. Guest: Mark Stevens, Häagen-Dazs.
8. Roger Ricklefs, "Despite Big Rise in Sales, Venture Ends in Failure," *The Wall Street Journal,* June 12, 1989, B1.
9. W. H. Kuehn, *The Pitfalls in Managing a Small Business,* (New York: Dun and Bradstreet, 1976), 6.
10. *The State of Small Business: A Report of the President* (Washington, D.C.: U.S. Government Printing Office, 1988), 18.
11. The discussion of business failure causes is based on Dun and Bradstreet, *Business Failure Record* (New York: Dun and Bradstreet Corp., 1987), 18.

Chapter Three

Small Business and Industry

Chapter Outline

CLASSIFYING TYPES OF BUSINESS FIRMS
RETAIL TRADE
- The Nature of Retailing
- Scope of Retail Trade
- Competitive Position of Small Retailers
- Managerial Considerations Retailers Face
- The Retail Owner-Manager

THE SERVICE SECTOR
WHOLESALE TRADE
- Scope of Wholesale Trade
- Services Provided by Wholesalers

SMALL BUSINESS IN MANUFACTURING
- Recent Changes in Manufacturing

SUMMARY

Learning Objectives *The objectives of this chapter are to assist you in understanding:*

1. The Standard Industrial Classification (SIC) system.
2. The nature and scope of retail trade.
3. The growing importance of the service sector in the economy.
4. The nature and scope of wholesale trade.
5. The role of small business in manufacturing today.

Entrepreneurial activity is found in all industries in the U.S. economy. Thousands of small businesses are started each year in retail trade, services, manufacturing, wholesale trade, construction, transportation, finance, insurance, and real estate. Small firms have demonstrated capabilities for innovation in each of these sectors of the economy.

Overall, retail trade and services continue to account for the majority of all new business starts in the United States. In 1987, 65,381 firms were started in retail trade and 54,788 were started in services.[1] Together, these accounted for 51.5 percent of total U.S. business starts. The vast majority of firms in both of these industries are small, independently owned and operated businesses. One important recent trend in small business, however, has been the growth of small manufacturing firms.

CLASSIFYING TYPES OF BUSINESS FIRMS

Statistical data about different types of business firms can be obtained from studying the U.S. Census Bureau reports. These are compiled on a regular basis and are available for

EXHIBIT 3–1 ***Standard Industrial Classification (SIC) Codes***

SIC Code—Manufacturing (Major Groups)

20 Food and kindred products
21 Tobacco manufacturers
22 Textile mill products
23 Apparel and other textile products
24 Lumber and wood products
25 Furniture and fixtures
26 Paper and allied products
27 Printing and publishing
28 Chemicals and allied products
29 Petroleum and coal products
30 Rubber and miscellaneous plastic products
31 Leather and leather products
32 Stone, clay, and glass products
33 Primary metal industries
34 Fabricated metal products
35 Machinery, except electrical
36 Electric and electronic equipment
37 Transportation equipment
38 Instruments and related products
39 Miscellaneous manufacturing industries

SIC Code—Wholesale Trade (Major Groups and Subgroups)

50 Wholesale trade—durable goods
501 Motor vehicles and automotive equipment
502 Furniture and home furnishings
503 Lumber and construction materials
504 Sporting goods, toys, and hobby games
505 Metals and minerals, except petroleum
506 Electrical goods
507 Hardware, plumbing and heating equipment
508 Machinery, equipment, and supplies
509 Miscellaneous durable goods
51 Wholesale trade—nondurable goods
511 Paper and paper products
512 Drugs, proprietaries, and sundries
513 Apparel, piece goods, and notions
514 Groceries and related products
515 Farm-product raw materials
516 Chemicals and allied products
517 Petroleum and petroleum products
518 Beer, wine, and distilled beverages
519 Miscellaneous nondurable goods

reference at many libraries. The Census of Business, published by the Bureau of the Census, is taken every five years and published in years ending in the numbers 2 and 7 (for example, 1982 and 1987). It contains statistics on the distribution industries (retail and wholesale trade) and service industries in the United States. A detailed census of manufacturers is also published. From these data, one can obtain information on the relative importance of distribution, services, and manufacturing industries in the economy.

To make it possible to compare statistics describing the various facets of the economy, the **Standard Industrial Classification** (SIC) system has been developed. The SIC system subdivides all U.S. businesses into more detailed product industries or market segments.

Exhibit 3–1 lists the SIC codes for major retail, wholesale, service, and manufacturing groups. This exhibit is a useful guide for research purposes. An example of major food store groups and subgroups illustrates the detailed classifications found in the *Standard Industrial Classification Manual,* available in many libraries.

The SIC coding system first divides the nation's overall economy into ten basic industries, each of which is given a range of two-digit classification codes. For example,

EXHIBIT 3–1 ***SIC Codes*** *(continued)*

SIC Code—Retail Trade (Major Groups)

Code	Group	Code	Group
52	Building materials, hardware, and farm equipment dealers	56	Apparel and accessory stores
53	General merchandise group stores	57	Furniture and home furnishings
54	Food stores	58	Eating and drinking places
55	Automotive dealers and service stations	59	Miscellaneous retail stores

SIC Code—Food Stores

Code	Group	Code	Group
54	Food stores	5441	Candy, nut, and confectionery stores
541	Grocery stores	545	Dairy products stores
5411	Grocery stores	5451	Dairy products stores
542	Meat markets and freezer provisioners	546	Retail bakeries
5422	Freezer and locker meat provisioners	5462	Retail bakeries–baking and selling
5423	Meat and fish (seafood) markets	5463	Retail bakeries–selling only
543	Fruit stores and vegetable markets	549	Miscellaneous food stores
5431	Fruit stores and vegetable markets	5499	Miscellaneous food stores
544	Candy, nut, and confectionery stores		

SIC Code—Services (Major Groups)

Code	Group	Code	Group
70	Hotels and other lodging places	81	Legal services
72	Personal services	82	Educational services
73	Business services	83	Social services
75	Auto repair, services, and garages	84	Museums, botanical, zoological gardens
76	Miscellaneous repair services	86	Membership organizations
78	Motion pictures	88	Private households
79	Amusement and recreation services	89	Miscellaneous services
80	Health services		

Source: Executive Office of the President, Office of Management and Budget, *Standard Industrial Classification Manual,* 1987.

retailing has eight two-digit codes (52 to 59), each representing a major group, such as food stores (SIC 54). These, in turn, are subdivided into three-digit industry groups, such as retail bakeries (SIC 546). At the next level of detail, they are subdivided into four-digit specific industries, such as retail bakeries engaged in baking and selling (SIC 5462) and retail bakeries engaged in selling only (SIC 5463).

Data on the number of establishments, their sales volume, and the number of employees is published for each SIC code industry. Developed initially for the government for statistical purposes, the SIC is now widely used by individual business firms, market research firms, and trade and professional associations.

RETAIL TRADE

Consider for a moment the different types of retail outlets where you and your friends shopped during the past month. In all likelihood, the list is lengthy. It might include such giant department stores as Sears or J.C. Penney, discounters such as K Mart or Target, and chains such as Radio Shack or The Limited. Smaller retailers might include your college bookstore, a fast-food restaurant, a video rental outlet, a movie theater, a service station, a hairstyling salon, or perhaps one of Mortimer Levitt's custom shops.

Back in 1937, with no experience but an extraordinary aptitude for clothes, Mortimer Levitt opened up his first Custom Shop.[2] He says he capitalized on the concept of custom made clothing, priced the same as ready mades of comparable quality, and more than 51 years later, he owns 82 stores nationwide, selling more than $50 million worth of custom-made shirts and suits. While Levitt indicates that he was not equipped to go into business (he had no experience at all), his idea was so sound that he just could not fail. At the age of 75, he acted on a long suppressed desire to write. He is now the author of four books, two of which are Book-of-the-Month selections. His books include *The Executive Look* (1981), *Class,* (1984), and *How to Start Your Own Business Without Losing Your Shirt* (1988).

Ranging from the small "mom and pop" retailers to the large corporate-owned chains, retailers are the dominant type of business in the United States. They must regularly satisfy the needs of over 250 million people. If a customer has a need for almost any product, chances are that several businesses are competing to satisfy such a need. Gift selling, for example, involves thousands of diverse and competitive retail enterprises. In stores that range in size from 100-square-foot stalls to 25,000-square-foot mini-department

Mortimer Levitt, capitalizing on the concept of custom made clothing, launched his lifelong career in the retail trade by opening the Custom Shop over 50 years ago. He now runs eighty-one stores across the country that still rely on the custom made shirt as the best way to improve the customers' self image. (Photograph courtesy of The Custom Shop, Shirtmakers)

stores, the nation's gift retailers sell everything from mass-produced trinkets to expensive, unique handcrafts and antiques.

In the gift industry as a whole, 3,410 new shops were started in 1987. These stores can be classified into four general types according to location, clientele, and merchandise: souvenirs, decorative items, tabletop (china, glassware, flatware), and specialty items stores. Each gift store expresses the style and personality of the owner. While huge discount stores and department stores are the independent gift store's major competitors, they have their limitations. Discount stores offer mainly low-priced merchandise that most gift store sellers avoid. Department stores compete directly with retailers selling china, glassware, and flatware, but because of their size, they are unable to match the personal attention available to shoppers at the independent stores.

The Nature of Retailing

Retailing includes all activities involved in the sale of goods and/or services directly to the final consumer for personal nonbusiness use. While any establishment—manufacturer, wholesaler, or retailer—can engage in retailing, goods are typically sold through retail outlets, including those that sell through the mail or via telephone.

The Census Bureau defines **retail trade** as places of business primarily engaged in selling merchandise for personal or household consumption (over one half of the annual sales volume). Manufacturers and wholesalers that sell directly to consumers are not retailers because their primary function is to sell to other businesses and private and public nonprofit organizations.

Scope of Retail Trade

Retailing is predominantly characterized by smallness, in terms of both number of establishments and annual sales per establishment. Results of the 1987 Census of Retail Trade, illustrated in Exhibit 3–2, show that of approximately 1.3 million retail establishments with payrolls that operated for the entire year, only 20 percent had sales of $1 million or more in 1987; 63.9 percent had sales from $100,000 to $999,999; and 16.1 percent had sales of less than $100,000.

The significance of retail store sales by kind of business is illustrated in Exhibit 3–3. The data reveal that in 1987, sales made by automotive dealers amounted to approximately $325 billion and exceeded sales of all other types of retail stores, including food stores.

The most popular retail operations are eating and drinking places, apparel and accessory stores, and furniture and home furnishings stores. Exhibit 3–4 shows that these three types of businesses accounted for almost one half (47.6 percent) of all business starts in 1987.

Competitive Position of Small Retailers

The relative competitive position of small retailers in today's economy, noted for its large-scale retailing, is due to a number of developments. One such development has been the expansion of franchising operations. Franchises allow small-scale business operators to run their own businesses under the name and management guidance of a large

EXHIBIT 3–2 **Retail Trade: Number of Establishments and Sales Size, 1987***

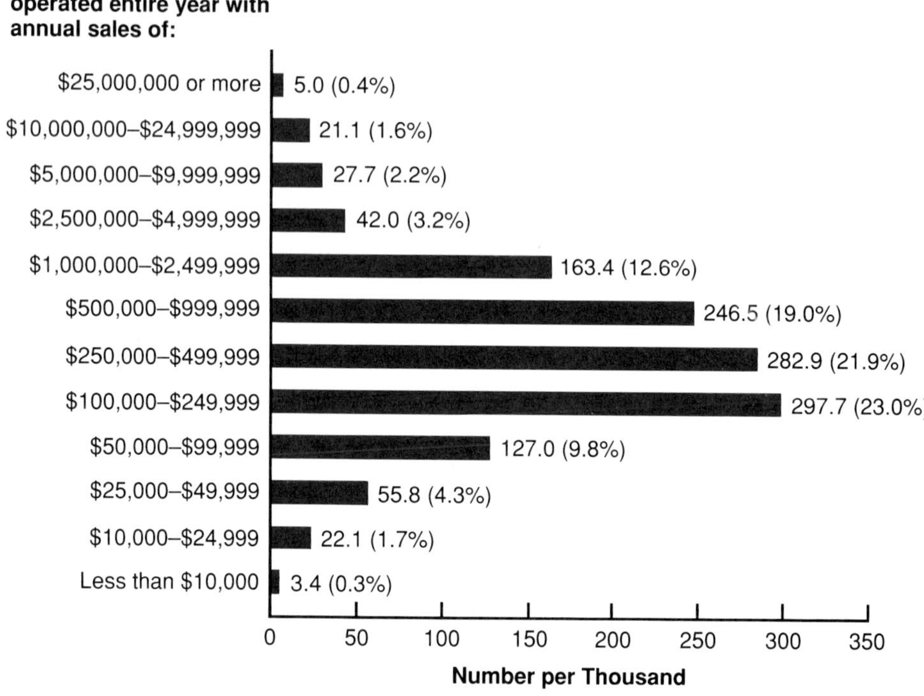

Source: U.S. Bureau of the Census, 1987, *Census of Retail Trade: Establishment and Firm Size* (Washington, D.C.: U.S. Government Printing Office), January 1990, 1–3.

company, giving small entrepreneurs many of the same competitive advantages of large retailers.

Change in the consumer market is another development that works to the advantage of the small retailer. Boutiques and other specialty stores are growing rapidly and doing well in response to consumer buying preferences. Small retailers are flexible and can adapt products and services quickly to their markets. Compared with large retail chains, a small store can more easily establish an individual personality for itself through means of a distinctive atmosphere and friendly service.

One of the retail trade businesses that illustrates the competitive position of small retailers is the food service industry. All kinds of separate eating places are in operation in the United States. There are, in fact, well over 100 basic types of restaurants, each developed from an idea conceived by an entrepreneur striving to win customers in a highly competitive industry. Choices available to the dining public include fast-food outlets, cafeterias, coffee shops, *haute cuisine* restaurants, ethnic restaurants, self-service lunchrooms, "mom and pop" family restaurants, dinner houses, caterers, and others.

EXHIBIT 3–3

Retail Store Sales by Kind of Business, 1985 to 1987

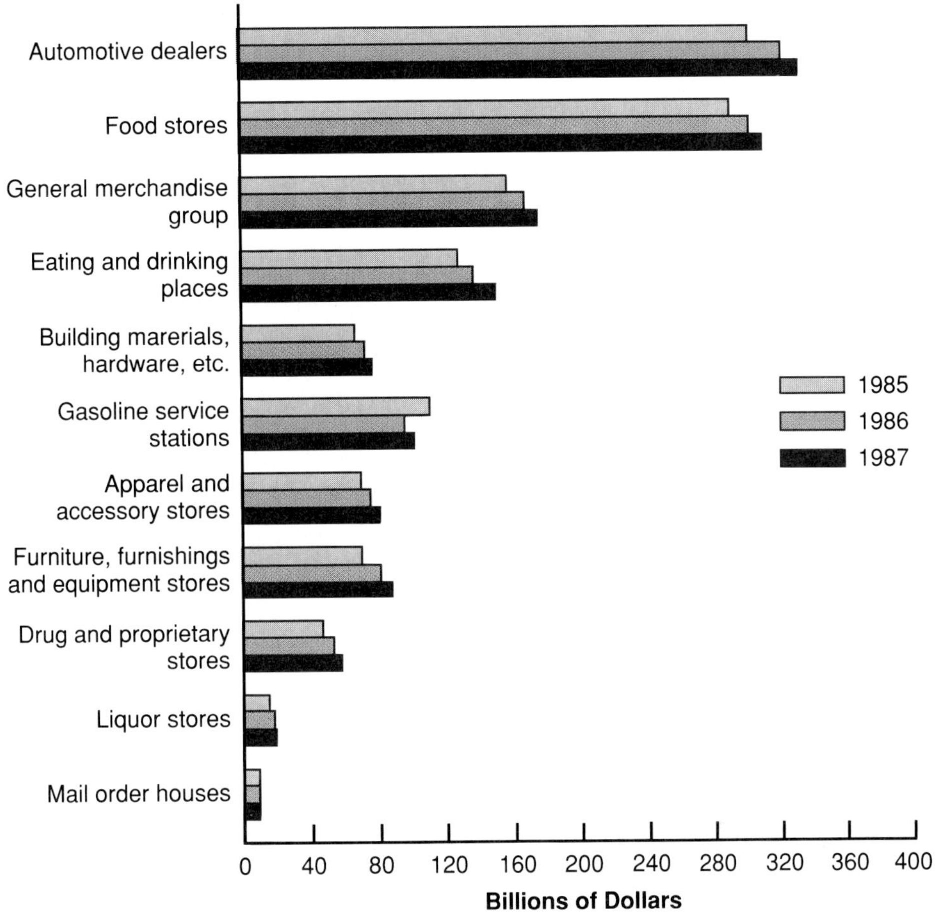

Automotive dealers
Food stores
General merchandise group
Eating and drinking places
Building marerials, hardware, etc.
Gasoline service stations
Apparel and accessory stores
Furniture, furnishings and equipment stores
Drug and proprietary stores
Liquor stores
Mail order houses

1985
1986
1987

0 40 80 120 160 200 240 280 320 360 400

Billions of Dollars

Source: U.S. Department of Commerce, Bureau of the Census, *Statistical Abstract of the United States,* 1988, 750.

Joseph Baum's respect for talented people, his commitment to high standards, and his delight in fine foods have made him an entrepreneurial maestro in the restaurant business.[3] His appetite for life stretches across the Manhattan skyline, where he opened up a host of extraordinary restaurants. Over the past 30 years, his collection of luxury eateries has included Windows on the World on the one hundred seventh floor of the World Trade Center; the world famous Four Seasons, his own Aurora Restaurant; and, most recently, the restored Rainbow Room atop Rockefeller Plaza. The restaurant business is in Joe Baum's blood. He grew up in the business at his parents' hotel, where he remembers learning the importance of delivering both quality and creativity in the dining experience. To this day, dining remains an adventure for Baum. He is a sixty-nine-year-old entrepreneur whose curiosity and dedication to detail never cease.

EXHIBIT 3–4 **Business Starts by Retail Trade, 1987**

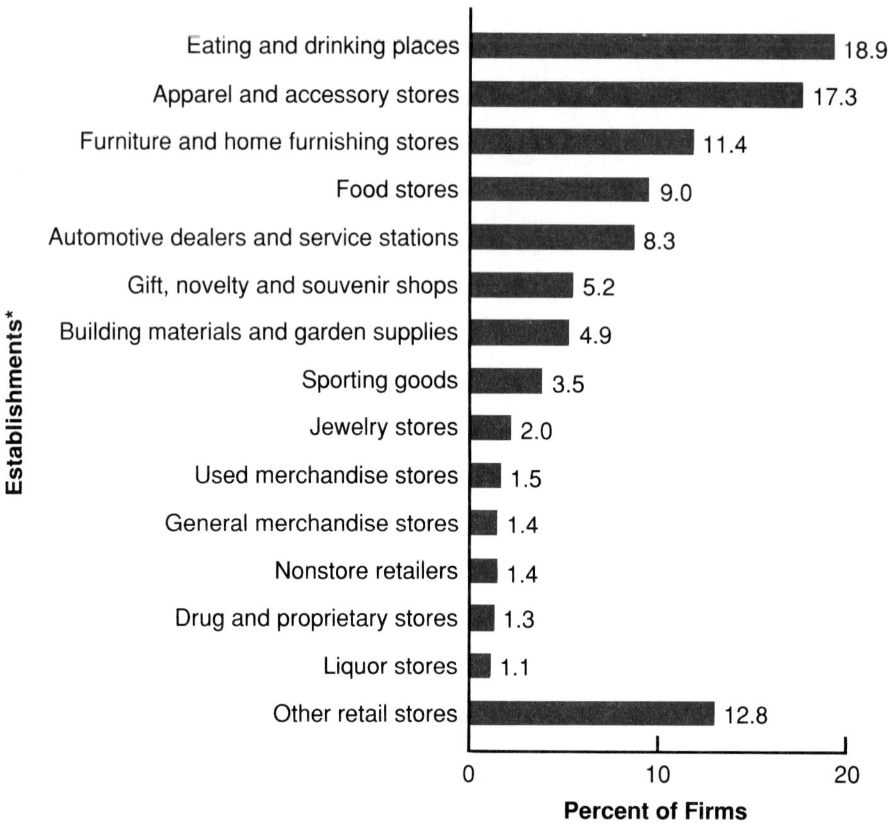

*An establishment is a single physical location at which business is conducted.

Source: Adapted from Dun and Bradstreet, *Business Starts Record,* 1986–1987 (New York: The Dun and Bradstreet Corp., 1988), 8.

It is apparent that the choice to operate a restaurant appeals to many people. In 1987, restaurant openings again outpaced all other retail business starts as 12,361 establishments (Exhibit 3–4) entered the competition for discriminating patrons. Some of these restaurants may operate in such locations as hotels, stores, or office buildings, where they are incidental to the larger business. The vast majority, however, are what the industry calls *separate eating places*—independently operated restaurants.

Whatever atmosphere or image they choose to develop for their establishments, prospective restaurant operators should not lose sight of the traditional essentials for success in this competitive field: good service, good food, and sharp management. Management must develop the ability to monitor changing consumer tastes and the flexibility to adapt to such changes.

Although prospects for certain kinds of restaurants may be excellent, the statistics that underlie the overall outlook for restaurants are grim. For example, 80 to 90 percent of all independents fail in the first two years of operation. Market research studies suggest that first-time operators can increase their chances for success by opening restaurants that offer a limited menu, provide an interesting or unusual atmosphere, achieve high volume, and cut wage costs by requiring some self-service.

Managerial Considerations Retailers Face

Small retailers are involved in many key decision areas, from deciding where to locate the store to deciding what merchandise to stock, how to price and promote products, what customer services to offer, and how to build and maintain a desired image.

Retailer and Purchasing Agent for the Customer

When a retail store opens, it should adopt the philosophy that it will serve the customer; the retailer should be the purchasing agent for the customer rather than the distributing agent for the manufacturer. This means that from the outset merchandise offered should be what customers want rather than what the manufacturer or distributor wants the store to carry. By acting as the purchasing agent for customers, the retailer assures a greater probability of success.

The Retail Owner-Manager

The store owner-manager should like people. People are customers, and they represent *stock in trade.* As a representative of customers in the market, the retailer should purchase merchandise that customers will buy. He or she should associate with manufacturers, wholesalers, manufacturers' representatives, and other intermediaries who are responsible and who will stand behind their merchandise.

Retailing is vitally concerned with motivating customers and learning why they will purchase one product rather than another of equal price and quality. Customers today are more sophisticated than ever before. Dealing with them effectively requires salespeople who are trained and articulate.

Another important consideration in today's retailing environment is the mobility of customers. Approximately 20 percent of customers move each year. If the retailer fails to replace this 20 percent with new customers, there may be an inadequate customer base, which can cause business failure.

Planning for the New Store

When a decision has been made to open a retail store, the prospective retailer should have experience in the particular line of merchandise to be sold. Too many entrepreneurs believe that because they sold a certain type of merchandise for another retailer, they are qualified to go into business for themselves. As pointed out in Chapter 2, this notion is a frequent cause of business failure. There is much more to becoming a successful retailer than previous sales experience. When buying merchandise for resale, the retailer should be able to judge what the customer will pay for the item. The fact that another retailer's customers will pay a higher price for an item is not a logical basis for making a pricing decision.

Opening a new store involves numerous other dimensions, including selection of a retail location and specific site (discussed in Chapter 10), and planning the store layout and design. In choosing the retail location, one must become sophisticated in the use of demographics and analyze the area from which customers will be drawn. After selecting the retail location, one must consider the specific site best suited for the store. The basic types are freestanding, central business district, and shopping center. Planning the store layout and design projects its image and is often what gives it a competitive edge. Combined with advertising and promotional techniques, a unique visual image will help to identify the store with the goods it sells.

THE SERVICE SECTOR

The **service sector** of the economy has been growing since the turn of the century and has enjoyed rapid expansion in recent years. This growth is largely due to the increased affluence of consumers, more leisure time, and shifts in spending behavior. As shown in Exhibit 3–5, services account for the fastest-growing segment of the U.S. economy. Over 70 percent of available jobs are in the service sector and over two thirds of the gross national product is derived from services. In the past 20 years, 9 out of 10 new jobs have been in services. Of the more than 22 million women added to the work force during this time, 33 out of 34 found a job in services.[4]

A **service** is defined as any activity, benefit, or satisfaction that is offered for sale. It is essentially intangible and does not result in the ownership of anything. Its production may or may not be tied to a tangible product. For example, legal services are not tied to physical products, but automotive services are. This essential difference between goods businesses and service businesses is critical because it directly affects the design and implementation of marketing strategies in service organizations. However, this fact does

EXHIBIT 3–5 **GNP Originating in Domestic Trade and Services in Constant (1982) Dollars, 1970–1986**

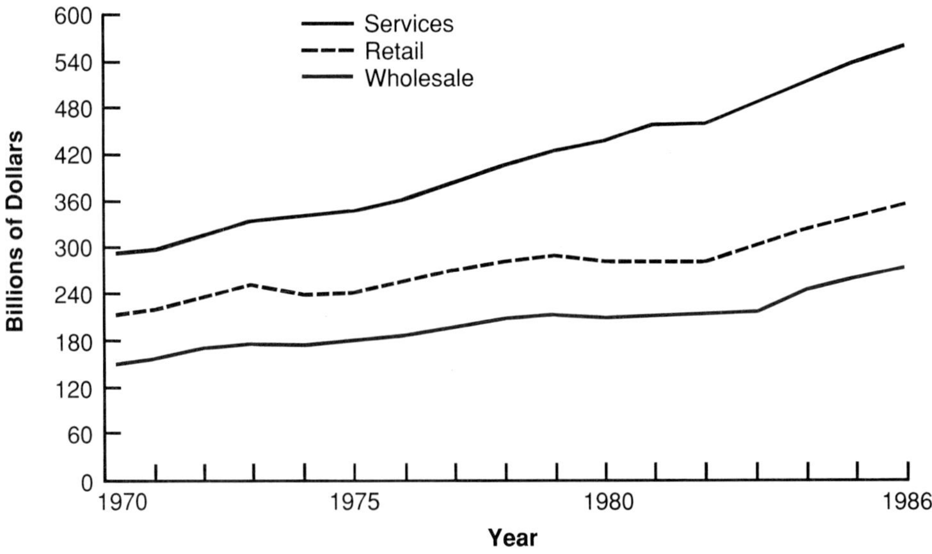

Source: U.S. Department of Commerce, Bureau of the Census, *Statistical Abstract of the United States,* 1988, 733.

Louis Krouse, founder of National Payments Network, fills a gap for about thirty million American households without checking accounts, by collecting their utility bills and providing them with financial services. The utilities traditionally contract with banks, who would rather not use expensive-to-provide teller services to collect bills from utility customers who are not buying anything that the banks sell. The idea came to Krouse while he was working for NYNEX in New York. NYNEX encouraged him to check it out and even funded an experimental demonstration project, but declined to develop it. "You do it," they told Krouse who went home and started National Payments Network. Now it looks as if he started more than a company—maybe a whole new industry—financial services for the poor. (Source: *Inc.*, Jan. 1990, p. 59; photograph courtesy of Louis Krouse)

not imply that services and goods marketing are basically different. Marketing of both goods and services shares many of the same practices, principles, and concepts that are discussed in later chapters of this book.

The difference between goods and services marketing is that the managerial problems—such as maintaining consistent service quality and meeting unanticipated demand (since services are intangible, they cannot be stored)—facing entrepreneurs in the service sector are indeed different than those facing manufacturers and distributors of goods. As a result, creative thinking and unique approaches are required to solve such problems.

One of the notable developments in services marketing is the trend toward standardization. Standardization connotes a sameness, an identical approach to individuals regardless of their separate needs. Illustrations of leading standardized consumer services range from quick auto service providers, such as oil-change, muffler, and tune-up shops, to cleaning services and specialized medical services. Among the benefits to the user of such standardized services are:[5]

- Relatively predictable quality of the services perceived and rendered regardless of where these services are performed,
- Time and/or money savings,
- Increased options and greater freedom of choice, and
- Such services can be backed by warranty, guarantee, and/or other assurances of satisfaction.

The growth of standardized services assures greater consumer confidence that what is promised will be delivered, and without concern as to who delivers it. This reduces unpredictability of the quality of the services provided.

The gross national product's growth in service industries between 1980 and 1986 was 87.2 percent. This tremendous increase reflects the greater role that services, such as those listed in Exhibit 3–6, are playing in the economy. Today, out of every dollar that consumers spend, about 50 cents goes for services, and this figure is expected to increase. While major services such as health care and utilities account for a large portion of the consumer's dollar, spending on other services is growing fast. Among those consumer services that are experiencing fast growth are video rentals, lotteries, investment services, cable TV, vocational schools, employment agencies, child day-care centers, and elder-care centers.

Opportunities abound for entrepreneurs who can provide services to individuals and/or business firms. The demand for such business services as computer and data processing;

EXHIBIT 3–6 **Selected Service Industries**

	Employees per Establishment
Rooming houses, camps, and other lodging places	
Rooming and boarding houses	5
Camps and recreational vehicle parks	5
Personal services	
Laundry, cleaning, and garment services	8
Photographic and portrait studios	5
Beauty and barber shops	5
Tax return preparation services	11
Business services	
Advertising agencies	11
Photocopying and duplicating services	8
Secretarial and court reporting	4
Commercial photography, art, and graphics	5
Disinfecting and pest control	7
Window cleaning	5
Equipment rental and leasing	7
Computer rental and maintenance services	10
Sign-painting shops	4
Interior designing	4
Telephone answering services	11
Automotive repair, services, and parking	
Automotive parking	5
Automotive repair shops	4
Carwashes	8
Amusement and recreation services	
Video tape rental	5
Dance studios, schools, halls	11
Physical fitness facilities	11
Health services	9
Legal services	6
Child care services	7

Source: Adapted from U.S. Department of Commerce, Bureau of the Census, *1987 Census of Service Industries* (Washington, D.C.: U.S. Government Printing Office, November 1989), 14–17.

mail, reproduction and stenography services; advertising and personnel supply services is growing rapidly.

The ever-increasing emphasis on the service sector of the economy favors small business, and in fact, the large majority of all business starts in the service sector are small businesses. The nature of services, particularly personal service, tends to make the industry structure one of many small businesses.

WHOLESALE TRADE

Wholesaling is one of the oldest forms of economic activity and represents an important component of the small business sector in the economy. The U.S. Bureau of the Census defines **wholesaling** as "the activities of those persons or establishments which sell to retailers and other merchants and/or industrial, institutional, and commercial users, but who do not sell in significant amounts to ultimate consumers." The term *wholesaler* applies only to those wholesaling establishments that take title (that is, ownership) to the goods they handle.

Scope of Wholesale Trade

In the United States there are approximately 416,000 establishments in **wholesale trade,** including manufacturers having wholesale operations, with sales above $2.5 trillion. The number and types of wholesalers and percentage of total sales of each, as reported in the 1987 Census of Wholesale Trade, are shown in Exhibit 3–7.

Merchant wholesalers, accounting for 83.3 percent of all wholesale establishments and 58.6 percent of sales, take title to the goods they sell. Included here are such types of establishments as wholesale merchants or jobbers, industrial distributors, voluntary group wholesalers, importers, exporters, and cash-and-carry wholesalers.

Manufacturers' sales branches and offices make up only 7.7 percent of the total number of wholesale establishments, but are responsible for 31 percent of total sales. These establishments are maintained by manufacturing, refining, and mining companies, away from their plants or mines, for marketing their products at wholesale.

Agents, brokers, and commission merchants account for 9 percent of all wholesale establishments and 10.4 percent of total sales. These establishments are in business for themselves and are primarily engaged in selling or buying goods for others.

Services Provided by Wholesalers

Wholesalers perform various services for their customers. Some wholesalers provide only those services facilitating sales, while others offer a broad range of services, including:

- *Buying goods*—the wholesaler anticipates customers' needs and buys accordingly.
- *Selling goods*—the wholesaler provides a sales force for producers to reach retailers and industrial users.

EXHIBIT 3–7 ***Wholesale Trade by Type of Operation, 1987***

Type of Operation	Number of Establishments	Percent of Total Establishments	Sales in Billions of Dollars	Percent of Total Sales
Merchant wholesalers	390,982	83.3	1,478	58.6
Manufacturers' sales branches and offices	36,310	7.7	783	31.0
Agents, brokers, and commission merchants	42,247	9.0	263	10.4
TOTAL	469,539	100.0	2,524	100.0

Source: U.S. Bureau of the Census, *1987 Census of Wholesale Trade: Establishment and Firm Size* (Washington, D.C.: U.S. Government Printing Office, February 1990), 1–3.

- *Dividing goods*—the wholesaler buys in carload and truckload lots and then resells in case lots or less to provide the assortment desired by customers at the lowest possible price.
- *Delivering goods*—the wholesaler provides frequent and prompt delivery to customers.
- *Storing goods*—the wholesaler provides a service to both customers and suppliers by reducing their inventory carrying costs.
- *Financing goods*—the wholesaler grants credit to customers, sometimes for extended periods of time, thus reducing their capital requirements.
- *Assuming risks*—the wholesaler reduces a producer's risks by taking title to the products. Losses due to spoilage or obsolescence are then carried by the wholesaler.
- *Providing market information*—the wholesaler supplies information regarding new products, competitors' sales activities, special sales by producers, prices, and technical information.
- *Providing management services*—the wholesaler offers managerial services and advice. Increasingly, wholesalers aid in training retail sales personnel, help with store layout, provide systems for accounting and inventory control, and offer assistance in merchandising.

Small wholesalers are increasingly few. The volume of sales necessary for profitable operations demands high volume and high capacity utilization. To compete with large wholesalers, they must carefully consider their strategic alternatives, that is: concentrate on limited product lines, establish long-term contracts with clients in concentrated geographic markets, and become a valued and profitable client for their suppliers.

SMALL BUSINESS IN MANUFACTURING

Manufacturers engage in the production of goods for individual and business use. They produce items ranging from common household goods such as ice cream, light bulbs, shoes, and clothing, to sophisticated electronic computers, airplanes, and earth-moving machinery. Although the success stories of manufacturers are many, so are the failures. Indeed, bankruptcies are as frequent in manufacturing as in other types of businesses.

Small business is an important part of **manufacturing** in the United States. Small business employment in manufacturing (8.5 million) is about the same magnitude as in retail trade (10.4 million) and about two thirds that in services (13.2 million).[6]

Small manufacturers account for over 90 percent of all manufacturers in the United States. As illustrated in Exhibit 3–8, 66.1 percent of all manufacturing establishments have under 20 employees and 90.2 percent employed under 100 workers.

Recent Changes in Manufacturing

Since 1976, the United States has experienced two recessions, the longest period of economic expansion in the postwar period, years of double-digit inflation, a massive swing in the trade balance, and other shocks to the economy. Amid these changes, there has been a shift toward small firms in the manufacturing sector.[7]

Small manufacturers have expanded relative to large manufacturers for a number of reasons. These include the emergence of new technologies, the relative costs of the factors of production, deregulation, the emergence of new markets for business services,

EXHIBIT 3–8 **Manufacturers by Employee Size Class**

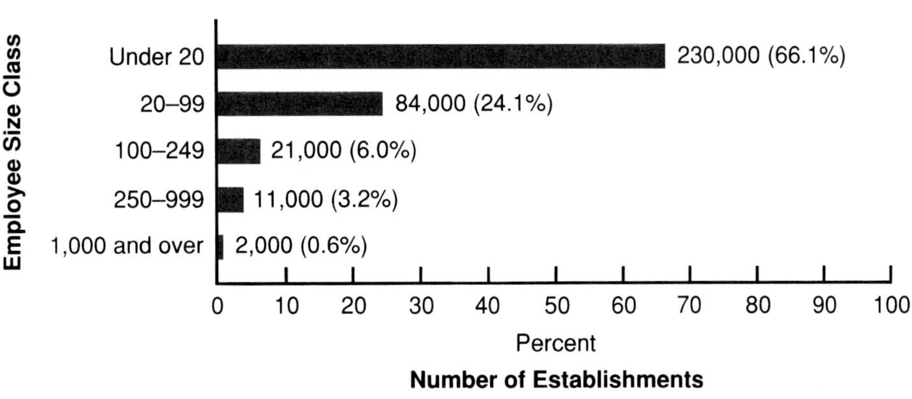

Source: U.S. Department of Commerce, Bureau of the Census, *Statistical Abstract of the United States, 1989,* 719.

the growth of procurement by large firms from small firms, changes in financial markets, improved management techniques, and the relative efficiency of small firms.

New Technologies

In a market economy, technology is at the heart of the industrial structure. The technological possibilities—how labor, capital, and other resources can be combined to produce goods and services—set the boundaries within which firms choose to operate. The greater the ability to substitute among the factors of production—for example, to use unskilled labor in place of skilled labor—the larger the advantage accruing to smaller, adaptive, flexible businesses.

Häagen-Dazs

The Häagen-Dazs plant in Wood-Ridge, New Jersey, is considered a state-of-the-art operation, with 600 employees working around the clock, making most of the Häagen-Dazs ice cream sold in America.[8] Quality control in manufacturing is uppermost in importance for Häagen-Dazs. It buys the most expensive ingredients from the finest suppliers and uses the latest manufacturing technology. Some of this technology is European, and so the company manufactures almost as though it were in Europe. They believe this is part of the very special way they do things. It is not necessarily the fastest way to make ice cream, but the people at Häagen-Dazs believe it is the best way to make ice cream.

New information-based technologies are transforming the nature of manufacturing products, processes, companies and industries. These technologies will be especially beneficial to small manufacturers because they lower entry and set-up costs and reduce the minimum efficient size of production runs.

Computers, data recognition equipment, and new communications technologies allow small manufacturers to profit by exploiting opportunities to make customized products and to serve narrower niches in the marketplace. Computer-controlled machines can be faster, more accurate, and more flexible than their mechanically controlled predecessors. This provides an opportunity for small firms to achieve lower costs and greater product differentiation.

Relative Factor Costs

The relative costs of labor, capital, and other resources have changed to favor small firms. Small manufacturing firms use relatively more labor and less capital than large firms. Since 1978, the real cost of capital has risen relative to the price of labor. This trend favors small manufacturing businesses.

The decrease in the cost of labor relative to the cost of capital means that production costs for small manufacturers declined relative to those of large firms. Given comparable demand conditions, profit margins of small firms would be expected to rise and the small firm market share would be expected to expand.

Deregulation

Deregulation by federal and state authorities has helped small companies. In the drug industry, for example, opening the market to generic drugs and expanding the market for over-the-counter drugs has allowed new firms to enter the industry and existing small firms to grow rapidly.

Availability of Business Services

The rapid growth of independent business services firms also helps small manufacturing firms compete more effectively. Historically, large manufacturing enterprises gained competitive benefits from internalizing all of their administrative and support service activities. Computer services, personnel, advertising and public relations, legal services, and market and management research and development were carried on inside large firms as *overhead.* Recently, large firms, to reduce costs, have been contracting out these functions. Small manufacturing firms now have greater access to these services and purchase them from other, typically small, independent businesses that are broadening their base of customers.

Large Firm Procurement from Small Firms

Not only are large manufacturers turning to outside firms to provide business services, they are also *out-sourcing* the manufacture of components. To meet the rigors of international competition, and to exploit new product designs and process technologies more quickly, small independent manufacturers are finding a growing market among previously fully integrated companies. These small firms provide the large manufacturer access to the latest changes in technology, provide lower cost and higher quality components, and are able to meet just-in-time inventory requirements (discussed in Chapter 20), helping the larger firm reduce its costs.

More Diversified Financial Markets

Changes in financial markets have provided better access to capital for small manufacturers. Small firms now have a wider field of options because of innovations in equipment leasing, the development of the venture capital industry, the growth of informal investor networks, increased foreign investment, and the availability of specialized, asset-based lenders. Innovative sources of capital are allowing more small firms to start up and expand.

Improved Management Techniques

Paralleling the development of computer-based manufacturing processes has been small firms' growing use of modern management techniques. Once the province of specialized administrative departments in large firms, computer-based management methods have become accessible to smaller businesses through the diffusion of small companies. Management information systems linking engineering, production, sales, accounting, and finance now provide accurate and timely information to all types of businesses. Specialized software readily available to small companies now performs such tasks as production control, scheduling, sales forecasting, payroll, managerial accounting, and financial analysis. These systems help to diminish the advantage that size once conferred on large manufacturers.

The Efficiency of Small Firms

Small businesses compete differently than large firms in the same industry. By following different strategies, they can exploit their comparative strengths and prosper. Small firms appear to be more flexible in their ability to respond to changes in product demand, more sensitive to local market conditions, more likely to utilize large amounts of excess capital and equipment, and more innovative in appropriating new products and processes.

Small firms differ from large firms in other ways. They are less burdened with layers of internal bureaucracy, so that information can flow more easily and decisions can be made more rapidly. Their managers are more likely to be owners and have fewer conflicts concerning company policy. Their utilization of labor is characterized by more intense monitoring, greater training, less rigid work rules, and more active employee participation in company decisions.

All of these factors have combined to increase the economic efficiency of small manufacturing firms, whose increased role in the manufacturing sector is witness to their growing competitive strength.

Regional breweries such as Harpoon Ale have grown up around the country. Small brewing companies are able to compete with the larger firms because they can be more sensitive to local market conditions. (Photograph © David Dempster)

SUMMARY

1. Small firms have demonstrated capabilities for innovation in every sector of the U.S. economy.
2. The Standard Industrial Classification (SIC) system divides the entire economy into industry segments and each segment into groups and subgroups for statistical and comparative purposes.
3. Retailing is the dominant type of business in the United States. It is characterized by smallness, in terms of both number of establishments and annual sales per establishment.
4. Retailers are merchants whose primary business is selling directly to final consumers.
5. Small retailers are very competitive due to franchising, offering personalized service, and developing distinctive personalities for their stores.
6. Small retailers are involved in many key decision areas, including purchasing, store location, pricing, promotion, and customer service.
7. The service sector of the economy has enjoyed rapid growth and is dominated by small business.
8. Opportunities abound for entrepreneurs who provide services to consumers and/or business firms.
9. Wholesalers sell to intermediate customers and are generally classified as merchant wholesalers, agents and brokers, and manufacturers' sales branches and offices.
10. Merchant wholesalers buy and sell merchandise on their own account, carry inventory, make deliveries, extend credit, supply market information, and service customers.
11. Agents and brokers are engaged primarily in selling or buying goods for others. They do not take title to the goods they handle.
12. Small manufacturers account for over 90 percent of all manufacturers in the United States.
13. Small manufacturers have expanded relative to large manufacturers in recent years due to these reasons: application of new technologies, low factor of production costs, deregulation, greater access to business services, procurement preferences by large firms, more diversified financial markets, improved management techniques, and efficiencies in operation.

KEY TERMS AND CONCEPTS

Standard Industrial Classification (SIC)
Retailing
Retail trade
Service sector
Service
Wholesaling
Wholesale trade
Manufacturing

QUESTIONS FOR DISCUSSION

1. What is the purpose of the Standard Industrial Classification (SIC) system?
2. Why is the SIC a potentially useful tool for the small business manager?
3. What are some of the advantages small retailers have vis-à-vis large retailers?
4. Discuss the basic characteristics of retail trade as revealed in the 1987 Census of Retail Trade.
5. What types of experience would be especially valuable to an entrepreneur opening a retail store?
6. In what way is franchising advantageous for a would-be entrepreneur?
7. What are the reasons for the continuing growth of the service sector of the economy?
8. Why does the increased emphasis on the service sector favor small business?
9. What fundamental characteristics distinguish wholesaling?
10. Differentiate among merchant wholesalers, agents, and brokers.

11. List the types of services provided by merchant wholesalers to their customers.
12. What is the role of small business in manufacturing?
13. Why have small manufacturers assumed a greater role relative to large manufacturers in recent years?
14. What new technologies are especially beneficial to small manufacturers? Why?
15. Why have more diversified financial markets benefited small business?

SELF-TEST REVIEW

Multiple Choice Questions

1. The basic system for classifying businesses into detailed product industries is the SIC system. The letters "SIC" stand for:
   a. Standard Industrial Code.
   b. Standard Industrial Classification.
   c. Standard Industry Code.
   d. Stratified Industrial Classification.
2. Approximately __ percent of all retail establishments have annual sales of less than $100,000.
   a. 25 percent.
   b. 40 percent.
   c. 75 percent.
   d. 90 percent.
3. Consumer services that are experiencing fast growth include:
   a. Investment services.
   b. Cable television.
   c. Child care.
   d. All of the above.
4. Which of the following is the predominant type of wholesaler?
   a. Merchandise agents and brokers.
   b. Merchant wholesalers.
   c. Manufacturers' sales offices.
   d. Manufacturers' branches.
5. Which of the following does not represent a recent change in manufacturing?
   a. The application of new technologies.
   b. Large firm procurement from small firms.
   c. Increased efficiency of small firms.
   d. Growth of large manufacturers vis-à-vis small manufacturers.

True/False Statements

1. Small firms have demonstrated capabilities for innovation only in the manufacturing sector of the economy.
2. A business primarily engaged in selling merchandise for nonpersonal use is called a retail establishment.
3. Approximately 20 percent of customers move each year and must therefore be replaced with new customers.
4. The basis for distinguishing between retailing and wholesaling is the purpose of the purchase.
5. Service firms provide services for individuals but not for business or government agencies.
6. Small retailers are flexible and can adapt products and services quickly to their market.
7. Services are intangible and do not result in ownership of anything.
8. Agents and brokers provide more services than merchant wholesalers.
9. Bankruptcies are less frequent in manufacturing than in either retail or service businesses.
10. Deregulation has provided few new opportunities for small manufacturers.

HAPPY HOOKER BAIT

Happy Hooker Bait is a wholesaler of various types of fishing bait. The firm was started two years ago and has yet to show a profit. During the first year of operation, the business showed a $3,555 loss, and during the first six months of the second year, losses totaled $2,768. Leo Kelp, sole owner of Happy Hooker Bait, needs to build additional sales volume just to break even.

The market served is within a 75-mile radius of Happy Hooker Bait's location. The region is virtually a fisherman's paradise, with countless lakes, reservoirs, and inland waterways. Combined with a high population density, the market area contains an unusually large number of active fishermen.

There are no statistics available on the quantity of bait used in the market area served by Happy Hooker Bait. A survey conducted by Kelp indicated that 174 shops serving the region carry bait on a regular basis. Sporting goods stores, some grocery stores, liquor stores, and quick-stop markets stock various types of bait throughout the year. Kelp wants to serve each of these stores. After 18 months, Happy Hooker Bait has 42 steady accounts and 51 retailers who purchase bait from various wholesalers, including Happy Hooker on an occasional basis, usually once a month or less.

Happy Hooker Bait handles the following types of bait: sardines (frozen), anchovies (frozen), squid (fresh and frozen), bullheads (fresh and frozen), crawdads (frozen), minnows (live), red worms (live), night crawlers (live), grubs (live), mealworms (live), bloodworms (live), pile worms (live), and lugworms (live). The bait assortment is the most complete line available from any wholesaler serving the market area.

Kelp recognizes that strong loyalties exist between retailers and their suppliers. At the same time, retailers tell Leo that they have mixed feelings about the services their wholesalers provide. Several wholesalers are characterized as seasonal or "here today, gone tomorrow." Only two long-established wholesalers are consistently given high praise as reliable sources of quality bait. Several retailers indicate that they need three or more suppliers to obtain all the bait they need.

Evaluating his sales results to date, Kelp realizes that while he carries the most complete line of live, frozen, and fresh baits, he frequently runs out of stock. Furthermore, his two part-time salespeople have such a large territory that only 65 percent of the steady accounts are visited on a weekly basis. This is especially troublesome when customers run out of bait. Special deliveries are then made, resulting in average losses per delivery of approximately $9.25. During the past six months alone, 168 special deliveries had to be made.

Kelp knows that something has to be done to bring about a profitable turnaround in his business. He realizes that he cannot continue working three to four days a week as a fishing guide in order to pay his mounting debts. During a discussion of his frustrations, a client asked, "Have you tried to get some help through the Small Business Institute at the University?"

Kelp learned that the Small Business Institute offers free business counseling to small firms in the community. On the following day, Kelp decided to make an appointment with a counselor.

QUESTIONS

1. As a counselor from the Small Business Institute, what advice would you give Leo Kelp?
2. As one of several wholesalers serving the region, how can Kelp stand out from his competitors in terms of services provided, and still realize a profit?
3. Should Kelp devote all of his efforts to Happy Hooker Bait and phase out of his guiding activities?

NOTES

1. Dun and Bradstreet, *Business Record* (New York: Dun and Bradstreet Corp., 1988), 2.
2. Based on Cable News Network's "Pinnacle," June 11, 1988. Guest: Mortimer Levitt, The Custom Shop.
3. Based on Cable News Network's "Pinnacle," March 19, 1988. Guest: Joseph Baum, Restaurateur.
4. James L. Heskett, "Thank Heaven for the Service Sector," *Business Week*, January 26, 1987, 22.
5. " 'Standardized' Services Run Gamut From Mufflers to Wills," *Marketing News* (April 10, 1987), 17.
6. Small Business Administration, *Small Business in the American Economy* (Washington, D.C.: U.S. Government Printing Office, 1988), 48.
7. Excerpted from *Small Business in the American Economy*, 49–59.
8. Based on Cable News Network's "Pinnacle," November 17, 1987. Guest: Mark Stevens, Häagen-Dazs.

CHAPTER FOUR

The Personal Decision-Making Process

CHAPTER OUTLINE

OBJECTIVES OF GOING INTO BUSINESS
- Profit and Wealth
- Personal Satisfaction
- Family Involvement
- Independence and Power
- Social Status

REASONS FOR NOT GOING INTO BUSINESS
- Financial Loss
- Lack of Job Security
- Uncontrollable Environment
- Work and Time Demands
- Impact on the Family

SKILLS NEEDED FOR SUCCESS
- Ability to Mesh Personal and Business Goals
- Ability to Conceptualize and Plan
- Ability to Manage Others
- Ability to Manage Time and to Learn
- Ability to Adapt to Change

APPRAISING READINESS TO BECOME AN ENTREPRENEUR
- Personal Considerations
- Financial Considerations
- Marketing Considerations
- General Management Considerations

SUMMARY

LEARNING OBJECTIVES *The objectives of this chapter are to assist you in understanding:*

1. The motivations of prospective entrepreneurs.
2. The reasons why some people do not go into business for themselves.
3. The ways in which business and personal objectives must mesh if a venture is to succeed.
4. The personal characteristics that are essential for business success.
5. How to make an appraisal to determine personal readiness to go into business.

Going into business can be an exciting and, at times, a depressing experience. Opportunities and challenges associated with entrepreneurship make it exciting, but the risk of loss and fear of the unknown will be troublesome. Because this is such an important step, the decision to start a business should be made in a deliberate and objective manner. The emotional aspects of fulfilling a life-long dream of ownership should not supercede a realistic assessment of one's entrepreneurial skills and what is needed to be successful.

Many people have dreams of being entrepreneurs and suddenly going from rags to riches. The achievements of people like Steven Jobs (Apple Computer), Ray Kroc (McDonald's), and Nolan Bushnell (Atari) illustrate that it is possible to do well as an entrepreneur. However, small business ownership is not for everyone.

After careful thought, some prospective owners will not want to put in the time and effort necessary to build profitable ventures; others will not like the challenges and uncertainties that go with ownership; still others will find that they do not possess the appropriate skills to be successful entrepreneurs; and a few will remember that success can be fleeting. After great achievements in founding Atari, Nolan Bushnell moved on to create Pizza Time Theatre with its robot characters entertaining patrons. He reportedly lost $100 million on that business, and failed in six of the 14 ventures he started.[1]

Before making a decision to start a small business, the prospective owner needs to:

1. Have clear objectives for what is to be gained by being an owner,
2. Examine the possible drawbacks to ownership, and
3. Assess personal skills and abilities to become a successful owner both now and in the future.

Making this a formal process provides an opportunity to fully understand what it takes to be successful and to determine whether entrepreneurship is as rewarding as it may initially appear to be. After making objective evaluations of the advantages and disadvantages of entrepreneurship and the skills needed, some prospective owners will decide that their objectives cannot be met by starting businesses (see Exhibit 4–1).

EXHIBIT 4–1 **The Entrepreneurial Decision Process**

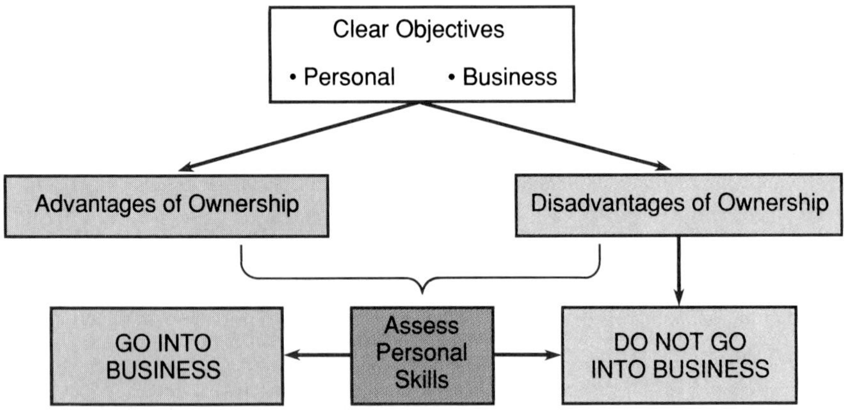

Clear Objectives
• Personal • Business
Advantages of Ownership
Disadvantages of Ownership
GO INTO BUSINESS
Assess Personal Skills
DO NOT GO INTO BUSINESS

OBJECTIVES OF GOING INTO BUSINESS

The most important issue facing the prospective owner is what will be achieved by going into business for oneself. This will have a significant impact on the eventual decision to become an entrepreneur. The goals will provide the basis for future management decisions and the standard upon which to evaluate the venture's performance. As shown in Exhibit 4.2, among the many objectives individuals have for going into business are profit and wealth, personal satisfaction, family involvement, independence and power, and social status.

Profit and Wealth

One of the main reasons for going into business is the potential for **profits** and the accumulation of **wealth.** Many prospective entrepreneurs believe the adage that "you never get rich by working for someone else." Faced with the prospect of remaining an employee who receives wage increases that are only commensurate with inflation, many individuals understandably view ownership as one of the few ways to acquire wealth.

The well-publicized success stories of Henry Ford (Ford Motor Company), Frank Perdue (Perdue chickens), R. David Thomas (Wendy's Old Fashioned Hamburgers), Mitchell D. Kapor (Lotus Development Corporation), and Deborah Fields (Mrs. Fields' Cookies) illustrate that it is possible to become rich by starting one's own business. Even though millionaires are the exception rather than the rule in small business tales, ownership can offer reasonable levels of profits. Exhibit 4–3 shows average profits for several types of smaller firms. While most owners in these industries might not become extremely wealthy, they can earn returns on their investments that provide enjoyable lifestyles.

EXHIBIT 4–2 ***Reasons for Going into Business***

Profit and Wealth
Dollar profits
Return on investment
Accumulation of wealth

Personal Satisfaction
Create something new
Make a success story
Interesting job
Changes in work over time

Family Involvement
Mutual goals
Gain assistance
Gain expertise
Give members jobs

Independence/Power
Freedom to come and go
Make management decisions
Run the business

Social Contacts
Community contacts
Civic involvement
Opportunities for business

EXHIBIT 4–3 Examples of Higher Returns

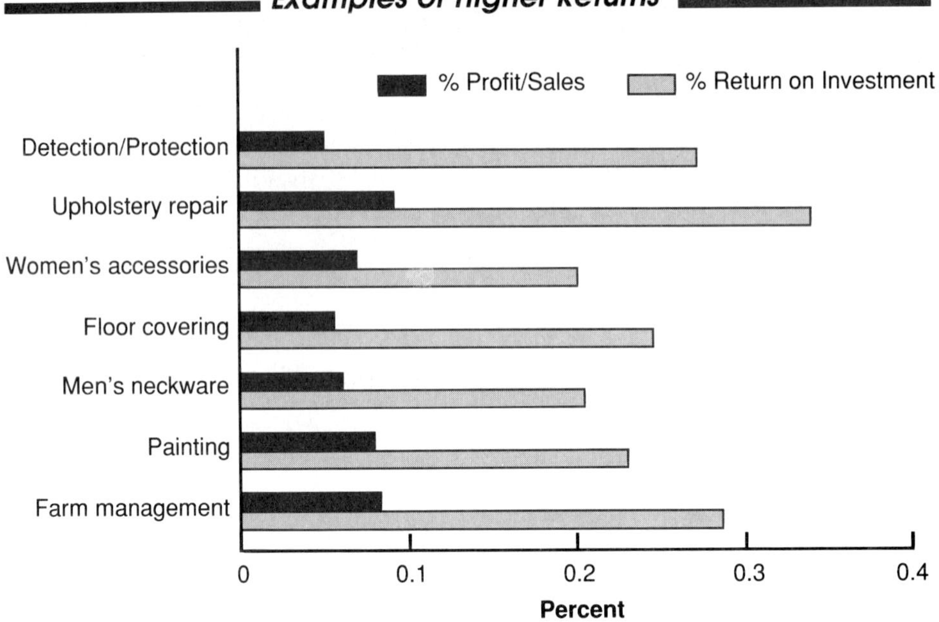

Source: Adapted from Robert Morris Associates, "Business Ratios," 1989 and Dun and Bradstreet, "Key Business Ratios," 1989.

A key issue for the prospective entrepreneur, therefore, is what level of profit is needed to make a venture personally worthwhile. There is a big difference between a comfortable living and the life of luxury. Determining how much profit the entrepreneur needs will influence whether to start a business and nearly all future management decisions, since higher returns are usually associated with greater risks.

Consequently, profit must be evaluated in relation to the amount of risk that is acceptable and the time frame desired to achieve the profit goal. There tends to be a close link between dollar profit expectations, the speed with which those profits are obtained, and the amount of risk incurred. Generally, greater and more rapid profits require higher levels of risk and increased likelihood that the business will fail. The prospective entrepreneur has to balance the profit objective with other aspects of ownership. As one article in *Fortune* reported: "The easiest way to make a small fortune? Start with a large one."[2]

Personal Satisfaction

Building a business from scratch, or taking over an obscure venture and turning it into a success, is a great **personal satisfaction.** For many prospective owners, this desire to be the key element in the development and growth of a business is an exciting prospect and powerful motivator. It provides a sense of accomplishment that is difficult to achieve as an employee.

An example of this achievement was Robert Tezak's International Games. Not

This interior designer gets great personal satisfaction from working with clients to help them create an attractive living space. (Photograph © Ann M. Mason)

enthusiastic about the family funeral business, Tezak found something more to his liking while visiting relatives and playing a card game called Uno. The game was invented by a Cincinnati barber who had been selling it from the trunk of his car. Tezak found the inventor, bought the copyright and inventory for $87,000, and set up operations with his brother-in-law in the back of the family florist shop next to the funeral home. They changed some of the rules of the game, repackaged the deck of 108 multicolored cards, and began marketing Uno. Sales grew from 5 thousand to one million units within five years, and to 14 million units four years later.[3]

An added benefit to the entrepreneur is that the business activity is likely to be personally interesting. Given the fact that close to 25 percent of an average individual's life span is consumed earning a living (assuming an eight-hour work day), most people would like to be doing something they enjoy. Starting a business provides an opportunity to create the perfect job—one you enjoy.

As Ronald Rule, chairman of U.S. Playing Card (the world's largest manufacturer of playing cards), says, "Business should be fun. To me, if business isn't fun, you shouldn't be in it. And I guess that means excitement. I have found . . . that you have to get some good people and let them do their thing, and if you do, I think you can reap some excellent results." This followed from his having spent much of his youth and college years on the Southern California beaches. However, in reflecting on his career, Rule indicated that he had not spent as much time as he would have liked with his family. "You know, sometimes you look at that in hindsight and . . . I traveled more than I wish I had because they [the years] go by in a hurry."[4]

Of course, the perfect job may change over time, depending on how successful the venture becomes. The initial role of being both manager and worker will evolve into more manager and less worker as the business grows. However, most entrepreneurs find that their interests change as well. A job that was once exciting from the viewpoint of a worker tends to become dull and secondary to that of a manager making financial, production, and personnel decisions. In any event, the choice of which role to perform will be up to, and designed by, the owner's interests and business needs at the time.

Family Involvement

Closely related to the personal satisfaction an individual receives from owning a business is the fact that it offers opportunities for **family involvement.** Sharing the ups and downs of a business venture can do much to strengthen the family unit. This is especially important since the trend toward households with both the male and female employed has continued into the 1990s. Having separate careers, and the pressures that

The members of this family work together to ensure the success of the family business while providing an opportunity for the family members to mature and gain valuable business experience. (Photograph © Ann M. Mason)

creates, can disrupt family relationships, while owning a business can focus on mutually defined goals and work patterns.

In many small business ventures, the spouse provides much-needed part- or full-time assistance. Traditionally, the wife has served in this supporting role to answer the telephone, keep company records, and assist in other areas as needed. However, as more women have work experience to bring to the venture, their role is changing; the wife often becomes a key manager. In 1950, for example, women comprised only 28.9 percent of the labor force. Just over 25 years later, they comprised 43.2 percent, and 45.2 percent of those between the ages of 25 and 44.[5] In many instances, too, the roles are reversed—husbands often provide the supplemental support functions.

Irrespective of whether the husband or wife is the real entrepreneur, efforts of the spouse can contribute to overall family life and the future success of the business. The spouse can provide added expertise, which reduces expenses and maintains the funds for business operations. Employing children of the family not only provides them with jobs, but more importantly gives them opportunities to mature and gain valuable business experience. However, it is estimated that only one in three businesses is passed on to children.[6]

A small retail apparel store, for example, contains many types of jobs that can bring a family together. One member of the family may be especially adept at selecting merchandise that is in fashion and displaying it within the store in a manner that will attract attention. Another family member may keep the financial records and manage receipts and disbursements. Others may be involved in sales, delivery, alterations, store maintenance, and so on.[7]

While family involvement can be desirable, it seldom is a main reason for going into business. Bringing family members into a new business usually is done to minimize labor costs rather than create jobs for them. But doing this also carries some potentially significant disadvantages to the family unit, as will be described later in this chapter.

Independence and Power

Being one's own boss can be an especially appealing aspect of going into business. In large companies, the ability to come and go as one pleases, make important decisions, and not report to a superior is limited to the relatively few who achieve upper-level management positions. By starting or taking over a small business venture, the entrepreneur instantly turns some of these possibilities into realities, gaining **independence and power.**

An owner of a small manufacturing plant, for example, will have the ultimate responsibility for deciding what to produce, how to finance the operations, whom to buy from, how to organize the business with respect to management positions, how many people and whom to hire, what prices to charge for output, and so on. Few of these decisions can be made by mid- or upper-level managers in large organizations without approval from superiors or committees. Entrepreneurship provides opportunities to make a variety of critical decisions.

Unfortunately, some of these desires prove to be unattainable in the short term. Even though the owner can decide to go to the office at noon rather than 8:00 A.M., the likelihood of success is closely tied to the amount of time and energy committed to the venture. Owners who spend little time at the business site tend to fail quickly.

Nevertheless, there is psychological value in the fact that the owner *can* decide what to do and when to do it. Even though in reality there are few options available to entrepreneurs who want to succeed, the choices still are theirs.

Social Status

On becoming a small business owner, an individual opens up a whole new realm of social contacts. The movement from working for somebody else to being the owner-manager typically generates community contacts and respect from businesspeople in both large and small companies. Many civic functions are based on support from the business community, and with the **social status** of an owner, the entrepreneur gains access to a variety of events and organizations.

For many entrepreneurs who enjoy and are comfortable in social settings, the new-found status is an important ingredient in business success. Membership in such community groups as the chamber of commerce, Rotary Club, and others are excellent vehicles for developing name recognition for oneself and the business. Contacts with key business and civic leaders create opportunities to promote the business and establish a name for oneself that is not possible as an employee in less than a top management position.

REASONS FOR NOT GOING INTO BUSINESS

Going into business for oneself carries with it drawbacks, which at times outweigh the advantages (see Exhibit 4–4). It has been said, and probably correctly, that entrepreneurship is not for the faint of heart. An individual who enjoys an orderly and scheduled environment, for example, may find the daily crises of owning a small business to be intolerable. Accordingly, the prospective owner must evaluate the benefits of having a business against possible financial loss, lack of job security and control over the environment, work and time demands, and impact on the family.

Financial Loss

Any business venture, large or small, carries the risk of **financial loss.** While some firms are highly profitable, many are either operating at a loss or just breaking even. A study commissioned by American Express Small Business Services in 1989 found that 77 percent of the nearly 3,000 businesses surveyed were still in existence after five years.[8]

EXHIBIT 4–4 **Reasons for Not Going into Business**

Financial Loss
Dollar losses
Loss of personal wealth
Loss of retirement funds

Lack of Job Security
Uncertain future business
Uncertain income stream
Lost free time

Uncontrollable Environment
Economy
Social/Cultural
Regulatory
Technology
Foreign

Work and Time Demands
Varied jobs
Diversity of skills
Time demands
Long working hours

Impact on the Family
Financial pressures
Time pressures
Link of personal/business life

It is estimated, however, that as many as 50 percent of all smaller businesses are only breaking even or are losing money. This is especially common among firms that are in their first year or two of operation. Even potentially profitable businesses tend not to make money at the start, forcing the entrepreneur to use private funds or debt to meet operating and personal living expenses. Examples of firms in selected industries that are not generating much in the way of profits are shown in Exhibit 4–5.

Financial loss also includes risks to the entrepreneur's personal wealth. Malcolm McLean, for example, developed the concept of container shipping, and just over a decade later sold his company, Sea–Land Corporation, for a reported $157 million profit. His later venture, McLean Industries, was involved in shipping oil, and ended up with a $1.3 billion loss.[9]

If the business is formed as a proprietorship or partnership, creditors can seek payment from the individual's personal assets. Corporate forms of ownership provide protection from such creditor claims. However, most entrepreneurs who seek financing for their new corporations either have to invest considerable personal sums into the company or secure the debt with personal guarantees. Thus, this risk seldom is avoided.

Even owning a franchise can prove to be expensive and a drain on a prospective owner's financial reserves. While a Jazzercise franchise can be started with as little as $2,200 to $8,400, a Wendy's Old-Fashioned Hamburgers franchise requires between $645,000 and $1,346,000, including the cost of land, equipment, and inventory.

An entrepreneur must be prepared financially and emotionally to cope with business loss at least in the short term, and possibly for quite some time. As Nolan Bushnell

EXHIBIT 4–5 **Examples of Lower Returns**

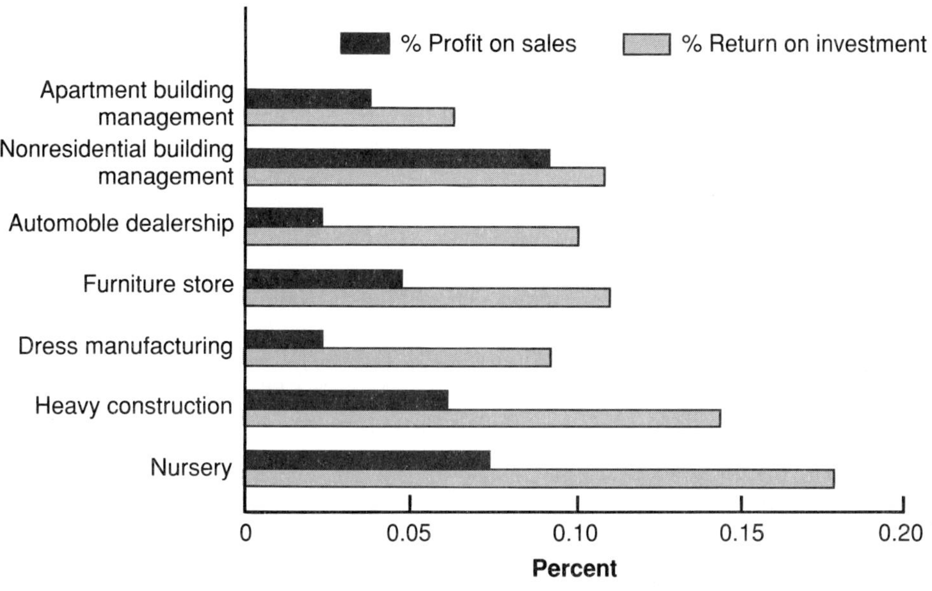

Source: Dun and Bradstreet, "Key Business Ratios," 1989; Robert Morris Associates, "Business Ratios," 1989.

stated, "I always knew, even when I was at the bottom, that I would pick myself up and make it all back again."[10] Many prospective owners either are unwilling or unable to make these financial commitments.

The risks involved in starting and managing a business have effects even into retirement. Many nest eggs have been lost because of unsuccessful ventures. A good pension plan may be given up when an employee makes the transition to entrepreneurship. The new owner often must use some of the money previously set aside for retirement just to get the business going.

It takes considerable courage to risk forfeiting financial security in retirement years to decide to go into business for oneself. Being employed allows a person to predetermine the approximate amount of money that will be available in later years and to plan for additional savings.

With small business ownership, funds available for future retirement are much more difficult to predict. Initial profits during the firm's infancy usually are put back into the operations, and later profits may be used to expand. Many entrepreneurs mistakenly believe that they can sell their businesses and use that money to enjoy the good life. As a practical matter, however, many smaller firms are not easy to sell. Finding a buyer who has adequate cash takes time, and most entrepreneurs are reluctant to carry loans on the business and allow new owners to take over. Furthermore, many owners experience serious emotional problems when it comes time to sell—it's like losing a member of the family.[11]

Many individuals try to operate a business on a part-time basis while maintaining the security of a salaried position. While this approach to entrepreneurship might have the advantages of minimizing risk taking, it is not conducive to either testing whether the business can realize its full potential or testing the entrepreneurial skills of the owner.

Not making a full commitment to the business may prove to be a distraction to both the new venture and the individual's current job. It could reduce opportunities for advancement and job enrichment at the current place of employment. The part-time entrepreneur may want to return to the decision-making process outlined in Exhibit 4–1.

Lack of Job Security

There is much to be said for the job and income security that go with working for a large corporation or government agency. Although even large firms such as Chrysler and Bank of America have had their problems, employment is relatively constant: work hours are well-defined; income is dependable; vacations can be planned; and the employee can be away for extended periods.

Relatively few entrepreneurs would dare leave their businesses for more than several days or a week. Few owners of restaurants, clothing stores, pharmacies, or auto repair shops, for example, have individuals they can rely on to manage their businesses for two or more weeks. Even within this relatively short period of time, irreparable damage could be done to a small business's fragile financial and market position.

The entrepreneur must be ready to substitute at least some of the pleasures of stable employment for the business-related satisfaction described earlier in this chapter. Possibilities of business downturns or failure have to be accepted as threats to self-employment and income. Business crises also can disrupt time available for family and friends. Thus, the entrepreneur **lacks the security** of working and having leisure time.

Despite the stigma often attached to wanting security, it is a comfortable feeling that allows the employee to plan and make the best use of time. Thus, the normalized nature of being employed offers many advantages to people who derive much of their satisfaction from activities other than work.

Uncontrollable Environment

The prospective entrepreneur must be aware of the external environment and the factors that could affect the business. It is quite possible for a business to fail due to factors beyond the control of the owner. Economic recession, for example, has dealt death blows to many firms, while economic prosperity has kept marginal firms alive. For example, high interest rates and a very sluggish economy had a devastating impact on the lumber and housing industries in the early 1980s. Environmental protection laws restricting the harvesting of forests that had been subject to fires and disease (even though much of the lumber was salvageable) also slowed the growth of the lumber industry and forced many mills out of business in the late 1980s.

Social, cultural, legal, and regulatory forces can make or break smaller businesses. For example, despite federal deregulation of the airline industry in 1978, commuter airlines have had difficulties filling the gaps left in service to smaller cities that major carriers abandoned. Even though improvements have been made in safety, accident rates are as much as three times higher in commuter airlines than they are for large carriers. Because of their safety records and cramped physical space, these airlines are still feared by many travelers. As one airport aviation director commented, "When the first small commuter plane showed up for boarding at one of the gates, most of the 13 waiting passengers turned around and headed for their cars."[12] Overcoming these forces is very difficult even for large companies with greater resources. Smaller firms have even less chance of changing buyer attitudes.

Technological change and foreign competition can significantly affect small business. Innovations made by smaller firms can quickly propel them into the forefront of their industries. In the late 1980s, computer-related companies seemed to offer the greatest chances for high growth and profits. Eighteen small companies in this industry were listed among the top 100 fastest growing smaller firms in the United States. Technological advances created many new markets for retail and industrial firms alike. Aldus Corp., for example, focuses on computer software for desktop publishing, and experienced a three-year growth rate of 322.2 percent in profits.[13]

Similarly, innovation can render an existing firm's products obsolete. Many smaller businesses do not have the financial resources or expertise to keep abreast of change. Manufacturing plants, for example, may not have the latest equipment that allows them to produce goods of quality and cost comparable to those produced by their larger or foreign competitors. Furthermore, often locked into a single product or service, the small firm may be unable to adapt to the changing marketplace created by rapidly advancing technology.

During the past decade, foreign competitors entered many markets with relatively low-cost products that still carried credible brand names. Differences in costs of labor and other production factors hurt large and small manufacturers alike. Foreign-made stereo systems, televisions, and computers, for example, have made significant inroads into domestic markets. This, in turn, affects the many smaller businesses that either compete in this market or supply larger domestic producers of comparable products.

Many prospective entrepreneurs have difficulty coping with the fact that the success or failure of their ventures may be determined by an **uncontrollable environment** of economic, socio-cultural, legal-regulatory, technological, and/or foreign forces. In some respects, this directly conflicts with the entrepreneurial desire to have greater influence over one's destiny. Being at the mercy of environmental forces can tarnish the attractiveness of ownership.

Work and Time Demands

One of the distinguishing characteristics of small business ownership is the varying nature of the tasks to be performed by the owner-manager (see Exhibit 4–6). During the early years, and when cash and profit margins are low, the owner will have to do many of the managerial and nonmanagerial jobs in order to control expenditures. **Work and time demands** are significant.

In discussing the attributes that made him successful, Pat Taylor, founder of Taylor Energy Company (one of the last independent oil producers in Texas) had some definite views. Having worked in all areas of his business, from oil field roughneck to engineer to owner and to chief executive officer, Taylor stated, "More than anything it's hard

EXHIBIT 4–6 **Job Changes Over Time**

Owner Tasks	Importance of Management Task*		
	Early Years	Middle Years	Later Years
Accounting	Primary	Primary	Primary
Administrative	Primary	Secondary	Secondary
Clerical	Secondary	Secondary	Secondary
Financial	Secondary	Primary	Primary
Personnel Management	Secondary	Secondary	Primary
Production	Primary	Secondary	Secondary
Sales and Marketing	Primary	Primary	Primary

**Primary:* Of major importance as a management task.
Secondary: Of somewhat less importance as a management task.

work and integrity and guts. I'm not a self-made man, there's been too many key individuals . . . [who] were there to either give me a helping hand or just allowed me to do something . . ."[14]

While this is attractive to those who like new challenges, being continually confronted with new and different tasks can make the work physically and mentally taxing. Little time is available to become comfortable with all of the unique problems and opportunities that arise. The owner of a restaurant, for example, may have to assume several roles. They include deciding on menu items and daily specials, purchasing food items and supplies, acting as maître d' or just greeting patrons, being chef or assisting in the kitchen, scheduling personnel, and so on. Similar broad ranges of tasks face nearly all owner-managers of retail and industrial businesses.

In many respects, being employed often means less demanding work. As an employee in a larger business or government agency, one's job usually is well-defined and routine. Specialization of labor is one of the strengths of large companies, even though repetition also has its drawbacks.

Some prospective owners, of course, would thrive on the newness of each work day, while others would find it too demanding. Many people are uncomfortable with the combination of possible financial loss and the diversity of tasks to be performed. They would prefer to have the opportunity to become highly skilled in a narrower range of tasks.

Time pressures placed on entrepreneurs also are a drawback to going into business. An owner's time is demanded by many audiences: Customers want to talk to the boss, suppliers want to deal directly with those who have the authority to purchase goods and services, employees want access to their superiors, and family members would like personal time. The entrepreneur who believes that going into business will mean days off from work and time on the golf course is in for a rude awakening.

Being employed for eight hours a day, five days a week, can be very attractive. Home, leisure, and vacation time are all well defined. Some larger companies like Hewlett–Packard, Control Data Corporation, and Mutual of New York have experimented successfully with flexible working hours that allow employees to partially determine when they come to work and when they leave. This gives employees opportunities to have some degree of control over their work schedules.

Successful small business ownership means long hours and little vacation time, especially in the venture's early life. What work is not finished at the end of the day must be taken home. It will not be completed by somebody else, nor will there be time for it the next day. And it simply may cost too much to hire others to perform the tasks the owner does not want or have time to do.

Impact on the Family

The risks of financial loss, lack of job security, and work and time demands also take their toll on the entrepreneur's personal life, and have a serious **impact on the family.** While small business ownership brings a family closer together because of the commonality of purpose, the pressures can serve to tear it apart. Periods when the business is losing money, or is beset with cash shortages, or has just lost a key employee, create pressures on the family. Personal budgets may have to be trimmed, time with the family sacrificed, and so on.

As already described, an employee's income stream and work schedule are better defined. Earning a living tends not to place the same types of strains on family life, and there are fewer crises with which to deal.

Later, handing the business down to the children can be difficult. In one study, small business owners expressed serious concerns: 31 percent about being fair to all children, 22 percent about the reactions of nonfamily employees, and 20 percent about possible family conflicts. Even more important is ensuring that the children are capable of managing the business. Children often want to start at or near the top, but do not have the experience to do the job. Family feuds are quite common in these situations, as heirs see their inheritances being lost.[15]

To be successful, the entrepreneur must have the support of the family. It is nearly impossible to separate the business from personal life, so a prospective owner needs the commitment of the family before proceeding to start a venture.

One example of the problems of a family-owned business was described by Robert Mondavi, founder of Robert Mondavi Winery in Napa, California. With respect to his children, he noted, "At first we had differences because one child wanted to dominate the other. Now they've gotten to the point where they both realize that they can work together in harmony and achieve the goal. . . . We know that this is going to be passed on to the next generation."[16]

SKILLS NEEDED FOR SUCCESS

One of the common errors made by prospective owners is to decide to go into business solely because they think they have good ideas for products or services. While this is essential, it is not the only factor needed for success. How the entrepreneur manages the firm will be equally important. A good idea coupled with poor management will lead to failure just as will a bad idea and good management.

According to Dun and Bradstreet, approximately 95 percent of all business failures are the result of poor management.[17] Many prospective entrepreneurs mistakenly believe that being a good worker or technician is the main requirement for being a manager. While the owner needs to be well versed in the technical aspects of operations, this alone is not sufficient. There are several other skills that must be present.

Häagen-Dazs

How well suited an individual is to become a small business owner is a critical issue. There is no standard set of personal characteristics. With respect to what it takes to be successful, Mark Stevens, the chief executive officer of Häagen-Dazs, commented about his own talents upon receiving his MBA from the Wharton School, "I was unbelievable. If I would have had the opportunity, I would have fired me. . . . I was cocky, egocentric, remarkably self-indulgent. . . . I'm still a poor listener. I'm not as rotten as I once was, and I'd like to change that."[18]

Successful entrepreneurs come in all sex, age, income, and ethnic categories. They have varying levels of formal education and occupational experience. However, there are some skills that many successful owners have in common, including abilities to mesh their personal and business goals, conceptualize and plan all facets of the business, manage others, manage time, and adapt to change.

Ability to Mesh Personal and Business Goals

In large corporations, the objectives for survival and growth tend to be somewhat divorced from the personal goals of lower-level employees. Some companies, of course, try to hire people who have personal goals that are compatible with those of the company. One of the classic examples of this was the Ford Motor Co. during the reign of its founder, Henry Ford. Having a dislike for alcoholic beverages, smoking, and marital cheating, Henry Ford, through his "Sociology Department," made periodic visits to employees' homes to check on their personal habits. Those who did not conform or could not be reformed reportedly were replaced.

In modern times, efforts to match personal and business goals are focused primarily on those in mid- and upper-level management positions. Preemployment testing, extensive interviewing, and so on, all serve to better identify how well suited individuals are for the corporate way of life. It is not uncommon, for example, to find corporate policies dictating that males in management positions wear specific styles of suits and colors of shirts, or that women wear dresses or suits.

In a small business, the personal goals of the owner are the dominant forces in determining the firm's goals. If the owner is willing to take great risks in order to grow, or prefers not to deal with certain types of suppliers, so too will the firm. If the owner prefers a casual dress code and informal working environment, that will be the policy of the firm. In essence, the goals and likes and dislikes of the owner will be reflected in the direction and style of the firm.

Unfortunately, however, personal goals and company goals are not always compatible. This is shown in Exhibit 4–7. For example, if the owner is using the business as a vehicle for drawing a high salary and enjoying the finer things in life, it may drain the company financially and affect its ability to survive and grow. Similarly, if the owner wants to be overly paternalistic and a financial benefactor to employees, this could deplete the firm's capital resources.

An illustration of this is a relatively small electronics firm that was having problems paying its bills—to the point of deliberately writing bad checks to suppliers. On close examination, it was found that the owner had policies that included providing coffee, doughnuts, and beer during work breaks; taking employees on fishing trips twice a year; paying employees' gasoline expenses to and from work; and even making alimony payments for one worker. Over a three-month period, these expenses were greater than the

EXHIBIT 4–7 **Merging of Personal and Professional Goals**

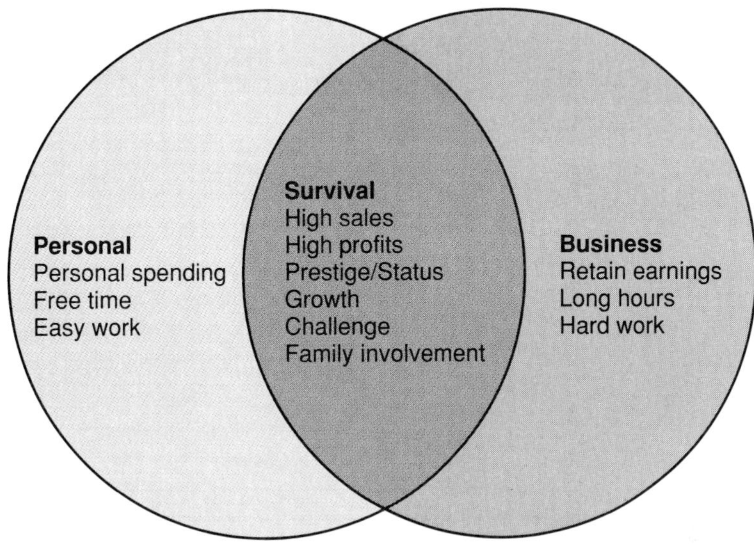

costs of the supplies that were paid for with bogus checks. The owner, trying to be good to employees, endangered the very survival of the business and thereby the employment of the workers.

As is described more fully in Chapter 8, the goals of the firm must be related to survival, profit, and growth. The entrepreneur must recognize that these goals take priority, and that they must be satisfied if personal goals are to be achieved.

Other areas in which there must be a **meshing of personal and business goals** include the types of markets being served (for example, upper or lower income, specific ethnic group); quality of products and/or services produced (for example, high, low); and extent of community leadership and involvement (for example, sponsorship of a Little League team, contribution to the United Way). Neither the firm nor the owner can be all things to all people. Compromises must be made, and the successful entrepreneur can merge personal objectives into company objectives of survival, profit, and growth.

Ability to Conceptualize and Plan

One of the keys to a successful venture is the ability of the owner to **conceptualize and plan** business operations (see Exhibit 4–8). Can the owner view the firm in its entirety and understand how it relates to the external environment? Or does the owner only look at the technical aspects of production or sales?

A good manager is able to understand how all facets of the firm operate as an interrelated unit, and can create plans to ensure that these facets work in a coordinated manner. For example, what impact does a sale have on the operations of a retail clothing store? Offering products at reduced prices may draw more customers and increase the total revenues. But if the store accepts credit cards or offers its own credit program, some

EXHIBIT 4–8 **Conceptualizing and Planning**

Goals	• Personal • Business
Resources	• Financial • Personnel • Material • Market image
Activity	• Production • Administration • Sales • Personnel management
Result	• Survival • Profit • Growth

of these people may charge their purchases. The store receives a discounted amount from credit card companies, and in-store credit programs invariably mean delayed payments and higher bad debts. As a result, the store may face cash shortages because the revenues were discounted by credit card companies or because a portion of the sales was not in cash. Increased customer traffic also may require more personnel to provide an appropriate level of service, resulting in greater labor costs. Additionally, if rent is computed as a percentage of sales, these costs would rise. The result of the promotion, therefore, may be to decrease rather than increase profits.

The entrepreneur must recognize and be able to evaluate the implications of these types of interactions not only on short-term operations, but for the long term as well. Decisions about lines of merchandise to produce or sell, prices to charge, types of expertise to hire, and so on, can impact the firm over several years. Planning major decisions from a long-term perspective is a mark of a good owner-manager.

Michael Dell is chairman and CEO of Dell Computer Corporation, a company which designs, develops, manufactures, and sells personal computers directly to customers without the use of an intermediary. Dell Computer provides products, service, and support at a low price. Dell's key to success is his ability to look at the complete picture, bringing together the disparate disciplines of marketing and technology. While Dell employs a sizeable research staff, he has considerable understanding and ability in the computer field himself. At the same time, Dell knows how to sell the fruits of his design teams. (*Source:* " 'Mail Dominance' Pays Off," *PCs Limited,* Mark Henricks; photograph courtesy of Michael Dell)

Ability to Manage Others

In addition to being a managerial prophet, the owner must be able to **manage others,** whether there be two or 200 employees. As many entrepreneurs soon recognize, being a good employee is not the same as being a good employer. As a business grows, the owner must rely more heavily on employees to carry out production, sales, and other tasks. Increasing amounts of the owner's time will be devoted to planning and budgeting the firm's resources.

An entrepreneur, therefore, needs to develop the ability to organize work groups who will strive to achieve the firm's goals. This is an ability to work with and through others in both the short and long term. Keeping people motivated and productive is a challenging task, and good business owners develop strong leadership and communication skills.

One example of this was a small business owner who was highly competent in selling window blinds and shutters manufactured by her firm. The increasing amounts of time she devoted to selling meant that she was away from the plant for extended periods. Unfortunately, when she left the plant, her work force went on break. Nobody was in charge, and the production process stopped. As a result, there were severe backlogs on orders, and some were cancelled due to the excessive delays.

Making the transition from employee to owner-manager-worker can be awkward. Without prior experience in managing people, many new entrepreneurs have difficulty identifying competent and honest employees, delegating work to them, and then rewarding their efforts in a manner that develops long-term business relationships. Over time, however, the entrepreneur needs these skills if the firm is to grow to its potential.

Ability to Manage Time and to Learn

As was described earlier in this chapter, the time demands on a small business owner can be stifling. Since the entrepreneur initially must be a jack-of-all-trades, the ability to "work smarter, not harder" becomes especially important. Effective and efficient **time management** is essential if all facets of the firm's operations are to receive the attention they deserve (see Exhibit 4–9).

The entrepreneur also must allocate **time to learn** new skills in preparation for changing times. As a business grows, the entrepreneur will have to learn more about investing profits, hiring specialized personnel (for example, account, personnel director,

This entrepreneur has learned that he must allocate time for each of his business operations—accounting, finance, personnel, administration, marketing, and production—if the firm is to grow to its potential.
(Photograph © Ann M. Mason)

EXHIBIT 4–9 **Business Operations Needing Time and Attention**

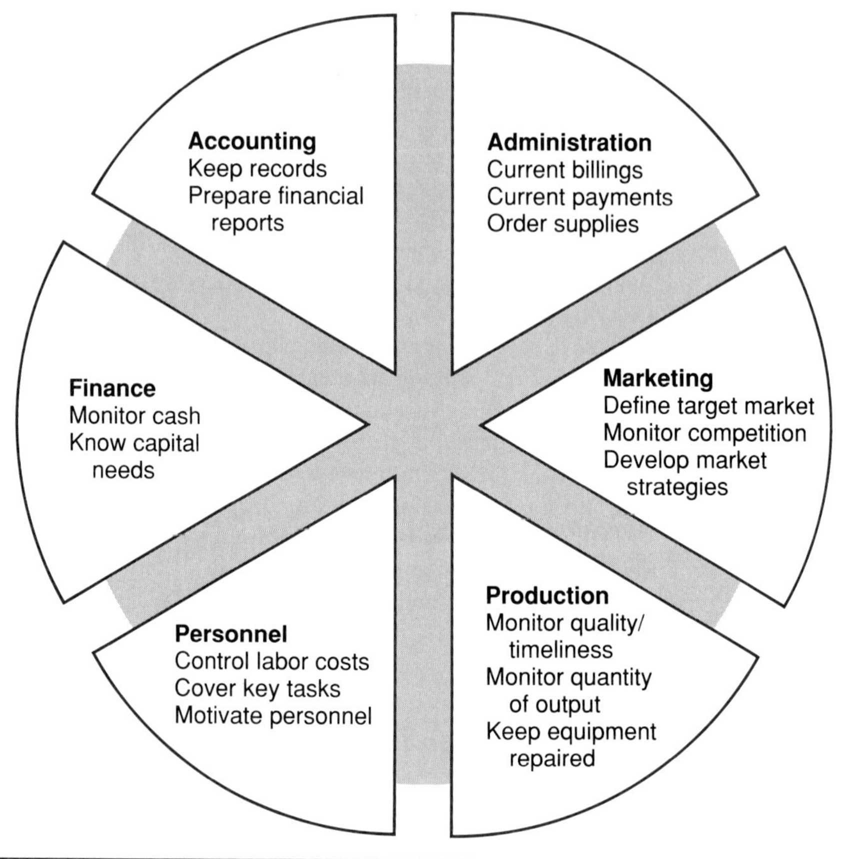

sales manager), and evaluating business opportunities. The skills that served the new owner well in the beginning will not be adequate as the firm expands its sales and numbers of employees. Successful entrepreneurs develop the talents needed to run their firms under the different internal and environmental conditions they face from time to time.

Workshops and college courses can supplement on-the-job education. These include basic courses in small business management and specialized courses in accounting, finance, marketing, and human relations management.

Ability to Adapt to Change

The entrepreneur who is unwilling to grow personally and professionally, at least at the same rate as the business, will soon be in trouble. The ability to **adapt to change** includes not only learning new skills, but also changing management roles.

As any business grows, the owner must be willing to become separated from many of the day-to-day operations. Eventually, the entrepreneur shifts roles from that of technician to planner and administrator. The job becomes one of overseeing internal activities and examining the environment within which the firm operates to identify new opportunities.

APPRAISING READINESS TO BECOME AN ENTREPRENEUR

Although entrepreneurs are the principal source of their firms' management expertise and labor, relatively few have all of the necessary skills when starting into business. They tend to learn them over time on an as-needed basis.

While this is to be expected, prospective owners should nevertheless try to determine how well prepared they are, and assess what talents they need immediately and which ones they can develop in the future. Generally, a self-assessment focuses on **personal, financial, marketing, and managerial readiness.**

Personal Considerations

The skills and personality of the owner play an important role in a small business. The successful entrepreneur is one who:

- Has clear goals that are reasonable given the resources available,
- Has the personal abilities described earlier in this chapter,
- Has some management experience and/or training,
- Is willing to work long and nontraditional hours,
- Has the ability to work hard without adversely affecting one's physical and mental health,
- Is self-confident, but understands one's own weaknesses,
- Can make decisions, can do so quickly when necessary, and is right most of the time,
- Is a self-starter and likes to take initiative,
- Is willing to perform every job within the business, from the highest-level management decisions to cleaning the toilet,
- Likes people and feels comfortable in dealing with them as customers, employees, and so on,
- Enjoys learning to do new things even though they take time,
- Is willing to alter one's lifestyle to meet the needs of the business,
- Has the ability to keep business and professional problems from overly affecting one's personal and family life,
- Has the support of one's family, and
- Does not get discouraged easily, yet is realistic about one's future options.

A prospective small business owner should begin such a pursuit with energy and optimism. Nevertheless, the reality of entrepreneurship must be faced—it requires total personal and family commitment, and even then it can result in failure. The individual who has a personality that can cope with these facts of business life is much better prepared for ownership than one who naïvely takes the plunge.

Financial Considerations

A small business owner must be able to determine the financial position of the firm and understand the financial implications of alternative business decisions. How much capital is needed to start and run the business? What expenses will be incurred? How much profit is needed to sustain the owner's lifestyle and provide for business growth? What will happen to sales and profits if investments are made in new machinery or a promotional campaign? Such questions continually are addressed by entrepreneurs.

In addition to evaluating decisions based on the financial issues, the owner-manager must be able to convert theoretical business plans to dollars in the form of budgets. It has been said that money is the language of business, and that is true for much of the management process. Since businesses need profits to survive, most of the firm's operations eventually have to be translated into dollar terms.

With respect to financial attributes, an entrepreneur should be one who:

- Has extra funds available so that not all financial resources are being used to open or buy the business,
- Can project revenues, expenses, and profits with reasonable accuracy,
- Can do all of the bookkeeping, and can prepare financial statements and use them in making management decisions,
- Can prepare budgets and adhere to them,
- Has estimated all the costs of going into business and the extra expenses that will be incurred during the first few months of operations,
- Knows how to prepare a loan package to meet initial, growth, or emergency capital requirements,
- Understands the differences between using personal funds and debt to finance the business, and
- Knows how much money is needed to maintain an acceptable lifestyle, and what expenses can be trimmed if necessary.

Although they recognize the importance of the financial aspects of owning and operating a business, many entrepreneurs do not like dealing with budgets, bookkeeping, and financial statements. This is unfortunate because few ventures succeed unless the owner-manager has an understanding of and control over this critical component of the firm.

Marketing Considerations

A firm's marketing efforts are its direct link with the buying public. Through its product, price, distribution, and promotion efforts, the firm attracts customers and sells them merchandise and/or services to satisfy their needs. Being able to evaluate the marketplace and the existing and potential competition is a key element to survival.

It is unusual to find a firm enjoying any measurable degree of success if it offers nothing distinctly different from its competitors. Customers do not seek out new ventures—they must be told that the business exists, what it offers to satisfy customer needs, and why customers should patronize it rather than one of its competitors. Too often, entrepreneurs open their doors and expect to be besieged by buyers. The high failure rate among small businesses attests to the fact that it just does not happen that way.

In terms of marketing attributes, the successful entrepreneur is one who:

- Knows how to evaluate the marketplace and identify the needs of different groups of potential customers,

- Can identify the major competitors, define their relative strengths and weaknesses, determine who their customers are, and isolate the marketing strategies they are using,
- Appreciates the importance of product, price, distribution, and promotion strategies, and how they interrelate,
- Understands what motivates buyers to purchase goods and services, and their reasons for patronizing one company as opposed to another,
- Is always looking for new strategies to reach potential customers and better satisfy their needs,
- Understands customer perceptions of the relationship between price and value of a product or service,
- For retail stores, appreciates how to attractively exhibit merchandise, and
- Knows how to conduct simple marketing research to better define possible markets and needs for products and services.

General Management Considerations

Managerial skills in planning and dealing with people will be developed as the business grows. However, the entrepreneur should possess at least some talent for organizing and operating the various facets of the firm before going into business.

Generally, the management skills needed are defined in terms of planning operations; organizing the firm's financial, personnel, and material resources; staffing the firm; directing the labor to achieve the firm's goals; and controlling operations to ensure that the goals are achieved. Because these are rather broad areas, they tend to overlap with some of the attributes described as personal considerations. In terms of general managerial attributes, a successful entrepreneur is one who:

- Has an ability to develop policies for the firm's operations, and can design procedures to ensure that they conform to those policies,
- Understands the various specialized skills needed to effectively manage a business through periods of growth and decline,
- Knows how to delegate authority to make decisions, and can be comfortable in letting others make decisions even though there might be occasional mistakes,
- Can develop methods of making employees feel that they participate in the success of the firm,
- Understands how to select competent personnel, and gives them jobs commensurate with their skills and personal objectives,
- Knows how to motivate people to achieve the firm's short- and long-term goals, and
- Can develop means for evaluating both personnel and the overall performance of the firm.

SUMMARY

1. Before making the decision to start a business, the prospective entrepreneur needs to have clear goals, examine the disadvantages of ownership, and assess personal skills and abilities to become successful in business.
2. The reasons for starting a business are varied,

but often relate to profit and wealth, personal satisfaction, family involvement, independence and power, and social status.

3. Going into business carries with it disadvantages such as possible financial loss, lack of job security and control over the environment, work and time demands, and impact on the family.
4. The costs and benefits of starting a business must be weighed carefully—entrepreneurship is not for everyone.
5. In a small firm, it is especially important that the goals of the owner and the firm be compatible.
6. To achieve success, the entrepreneur needs to develop strong managerial skills, because most business failures have been attributed to lack of good management.
7. The owner of a small firm must be able to conceptualize and plan business operations.
8. The ability to manage others, to organize work groups, and to work through others is important to a firm's long-term development.
9. The entrepreneur must make effective and efficient use of time, and develop a learning-while-doing style.
10. The owner must be willing to grow to meet the challenges of a growing firm and a changing environment.
11. In assessing entrepreneurial readiness, several factors must be taken into account: personal, financial, marketing, and general management considerations.

KEY TERMS AND CONCEPTS

Profit and wealth
Personal satisfaction
Family involvement
Independence and power
Social status
Financial loss
Lack of security
Uncontrollable environment
Work and time demands
Impact on the family
Meshing personal and business goals
Conceptualize and plan
Manage others
Time management
Time to learn
Adapt to change
Personal readiness to become an entrepreneur
Financial readiness to become an entrepreneur
Marketing readiness to become an entrepreneur
General management readiness to become an entrepreneur

QUESTIONS FOR DISCUSSION

1. What does a prospective small business owner need to have before making a decision about entrepreneurship?
2. What are some of the attractions of starting a small business?
3. What are some of the disadvantages of going into business for oneself?
4. Describe the uncontrollable forces with which the entrepreneur must deal in managing a business.
5. What resources must the entrepreneur manage when striving to make a business successful?
6. In what ways do the entrepreneur's personal goals and business objectives have an impact on management decisions?
7. What is the cause of most business failures?
8. What are the essential personal skills of a successful entrepreneur?
9. Describe the personal attributes of a successful entrepreneur.
10. What are the characteristics of a good small business owner with respect to financial matters?
11. List the marketing issues with which an entrepreneur should be able to deal.
12. What are the general management attributes of a successful entrepreneur?

SELF-TEST REVIEW

Multiple Choice Questions

1. Which of the following advantages of small business ownership is mostly an illusion in the short term?
   a. Interesting work.
   b. Social status.
   c. Independence and power.
   d. Ego satisfaction.
2. Which of the following is not a major consideration when setting profit objectives for the business?
   a. Level of wealth desired.
   b. Amount of risk that is acceptable.
   c. Amount of time in which to achieve the profit goal.
   d. All of the above are major considerations.
3. A disadvantage of business ownership is:
   a. Lack of family involvement.
   b. Lack of power.
   c. Lack of social status.
   d. Lack of job security.
4. Which of the following is not a skill needed for success?
   a. Ability to mesh personal and business goals.
   b. Ability to remain the same over time.
   c. Ability to manage time.
   d. Ability to manage others.
5. Which of the following is not a personal attribute of a successful entrepreneur?
   a. Willingness to perform every job within the firm.
   b. Has some managerial experience or training.
   c. Makes all decisions slowly and carefully.
   d. Can work hard without having it adversely affect one's health.

True/False Statements

1. Business ownership provides an opportunity to create a perfect job for oneself right from the beginning of the venture.
2. Spouses and other family members tend to be of little help to entrepreneurs; in fact, they are a major obstacle to success.
3. Greater and more speedy profit expectations often mean higher levels of risk.
4. One common disadvantage to small business ownership is the lack of job stability and security.
5. Compared with employees of large corporations or government agencies, entrepreneurs in general face fewer work and time demands.
6. In small businesses, the goals of the entrepreneur most often are separated from those of the business.
7. The entrepreneur must be able to conceptualize and plan if the business is to have a real chance of success.
8. An individual who was a good employee will also be a good employer.
9. As a business grows, its owner must be ready and willing to step away from day-to-day operations.
10. An understanding of bookkeeping is not an important characteristic of a successful entrepreneur since there are specialists available to do this work.

G & J's FOOD GALLERY

After working for a large supermarket chain in the Midwest for nearly 15 years, Glenn Schaffer and Jack Grange decided to quit and open their own specialty food store. During the four years that it has been open, sales have nearly tripled, while profits have increased by about 50 percent.

G & J's Food Gallery is a 9,000-square-foot market that primarily caters to upper-income groups with tastes for gourmet meats, produce, and specialty packaged foods. There are two other similar stores in the town, which sell comparable products at about the same prices. However, G & J's is the only store that will special order nearly any food item a customer wants, and at least one owner is in the store from the time it opens (7 A.M.) until it closes (10 P.M.), six days a week.

Both Schaffer and Grange work more than 60 hours per week in the store, spending much of that time running the cash registers (30 percent), stocking shelves (30 percent), and just walking around and talking to shoppers (40 percent). They have hired a larger number of employees than other stores its size to ensure that attentive customer service is maintained. These policies of having the owners

TABLE 1 **Data on Expanded Lines, G & J's Food Gallery**

Specialty Item	Initial Cost	Mark-Up	Expected Sales	Additional Expenses*
Natural products in bulk	$3,500	25%	$84,000	$17,000
Deli items	$4,000	80%	$60,000	$40,000
Natural juices	$1,000	60%	$25,000	$10,000

*Includes labor, spoilage, lost profits on items being taken out to make space, and so on. This does not include cost of goods.

available to shoppers and plenty of support personnel to provide fast service are thought to be the primary factors in their success to date. With labor costs of $15 per hour, however, they are trying to keep control over expenses.

In reviewing their operations over the past four years, the owners feel they have to make some decisions that will significantly affect their future. First, Schaffer is getting tired of working so many hours and having little time for his family. He wants to reduce his time in the store to 45 hours per week. Grange is not married, and does not seem to mind the long hours. These differences have caused some friction to develop between them in the last year.

Second, quite a few of the better customers have asked that the store carry some new lines of food items. The requests center mostly on a wider selection of natural food items in bulk and an expanded deli section with natural juices. With the limited space available and the added costs of expanding, the owners know that they have to be careful about adding lines. Schaffer has collected some information on expected sales and expenses for each. These are shown in Table 1. Schaffer is concerned that if they do not make these additions, they might lose some of their customers.

Third, the owner of one relatively small specialty store located on the other side of town is preparing to retire, and has asked Schaffer and Grange if they are interested in buying him out. Although they have not discussed price, it appears to the owners that a reasonable agreement can be reached. Of greater importance is whether they want to expand their operations. This other store is about half the size of G & J's, and focuses much more heavily on meats and produce than on packaged items. Its hours are 9 A.M. to 7 P.M., but the current owner feels that he has to be there most of the time to watch over the meat section because of the high cost of goods and labor.

At this time, the owners are beginning to evaluate each of these three issues. Although they do not want to make hasty decisions, they feel that they must take some action on these matters soon.

QUESTIONS

1. How should the owners go about evaluating each of these issues?
2. How can the owners resolve their differences with respect to working hours?

NOTES

1. "Great Fortunes Lost," *Fortune*, July 18, 1988, 75–77, 80–81, 84.
2. *Ibid.*
3. Frederick C. Klein, "Uno Owners Have Made It Big by Playing Their Cards Right," *The Wall Street Journal*, November 1, 1982, 27.
4. Based on Cable News Network's "Pinnacle," March 11, 1989. Guest: Ronald Rule, U.S. Playing Card.
5. *Statistical Abstracts of the United States*, U.S. Government Printing Office, 1986, 394.
6. John Emshwiller, "Handing Down the Business," *The Wall Street Journal*, June 19, 1989, B1.

7. Bank of America, "Steps to Starting a Business," *Small Business Reporter,* 1983, 1.
8. Marguaret Peterson, "Success in a New Business," *Sacramento Bee,* October 11, 1989, E1.
9. "Great Fortunes Lost," *Fortune,* July 18, 1988, 75.
10. "So You Want to Get Rich?" *The Wall Street Journal,* May 15, 1987, 15D.
11. Roger Ricklefs and Udayan Gupta, "Traumas of a New Entrepreneur," *The Wall Street Journal,* May 10, 1989, B1.
12. Harlan S. Byrne, "Fast-Growing Commuter Airlines Finding Survival, Success Difficult," *The Wall Stree Journal,* August 23, 1982, 19.
13. "The Hot 100 Growth Companies," *Time,* May 23, 1988, 120–138.
14. Based on Cable News Network's "Pinnacle," March 7, 1987. Guest: Patrick Taylor, Taylor Energy Company.
15. Cecile Sorra, "Reviving Firm by Being Tough with the Family," *The Wall Street Journal,* August 14, 1989, B1.
16. Based on Cable News Network's "Pinnacle," November 21, 1987. Guest: Robert Mondavi, Mondavi Winery.
17. Dun and Bradstreet, *Business Failure Record,* (New York: Dun and Bradstreet Corp., 1988), 15.
18. Based on Cable News Network's "Pinnacle," November 14, 1987. Guest: Mark Stevens, Häagen-Dazs.

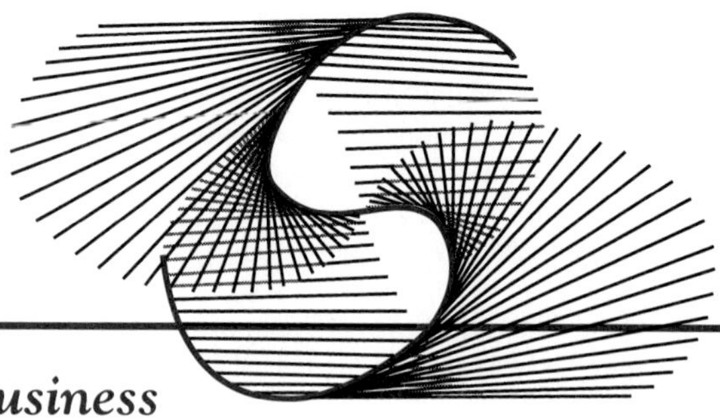

Chapter Five

Starting or Buying a Business

Chapter Outline

Learning Objectives *The objectives of this chapter are to assist you in understanding:*

1. The reasons why entrepreneurs start ventures from scratch.
2. The steps that must be taken in starting a business.
3. The advantages and disadvantages of buying a business.
4. The factors to consider in evaluating a business that is for sale.
5. The factors to consider in pricing a business that is for sale.

One of the most important questions that a person interested in owning and operating a small business must answer is this: Which is better, to buy an existing firm or to start a new one? The answer to this question depends on many factors and circumstances. While hundreds of small businesses change hands every day, thousands more are started every year by new entrepreneurs. Indeed, about 80 percent of business owners start their own firm, rather than acquiring a business that is already in existence, including family businesses. Consultants estimate that fewer than one in three family businesses is passed down to the next generation.[1] Exhibit 5–1 illustrates that only 12.5 percent of women-owned businesses and 14.6 percent of men-owned businesses were acquired by purchase in 1982.

When an entrepreneur decides to buy or sell a small business, he or she must be aware of the complexity of the transaction and the many factors involved in the process. If the business owner is the seller, these factors include preparing the business for sale and finding buyers. If it is a family business, the biggest concerns entrepreneurs have in passing the business on to their children are, in order of importance: treating all children fairly, reaction of nonfamily employees, family communication conflict, and estate taxes.[2] For the buyer, they include determining why the business is for sale, pricing the business, and financing the purchase.

A prospective business owner may want to buy a franchise instead of an independent business. This alternative, discussed in Chapter 6, appeals to more and more entrepreneurs because it is generally less risky than starting from the beginning.

STARTING A NEW VENTURE

Starting a new business venture from scratch is the most common method of getting into business. As is the case when evaluating an established business, a great deal of

EXHIBIT 5–1 ***Distribution of Men- and Women-Owned Businesses by Manner of Business Acquisition, 1982***

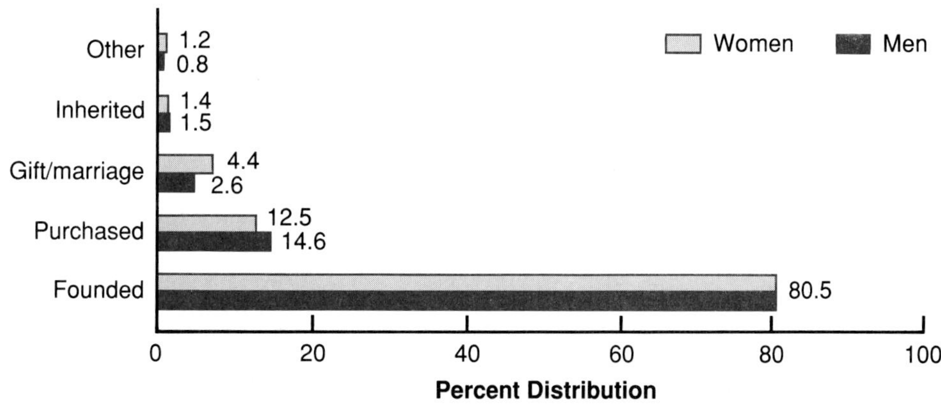

Source: Faith Ando and Associates, Inc., *Minorities, Women, Veterans and the 1982 Characteristics of Business Owners Survey: A Preliminary Analysis* (Washington, D.C.: research in progress for the U.S. Small Business Administration, Office of Advocacy, under award no. SBA-3026-OA-88, 1988).

When Earl Graves started Black Enterprise *magazine in 1970, his mission was to inspire other black entrepreneurs to prosper in business by reporting on successful, black-owned businesses. Over the years, the magazine has established itself as the premiere source of business information for the upwardly mobile black in America.* (Photograph courtesy of BLACK ENTERPRISE MAGAZINE)

investigation and analysis is required to increase the new venture's probability of success. It may be prudent to incur some expense to obtain help in areas where one lacks experience and/or knowledge in starting a new business. As stressed in previous chapters, a major pitfall of starting a new business is lack of experience.

For various reasons, many entrepreneurs prefer starting their own business over buying an existing one. For example, according to Earl Graves, founder and publisher of *Black Enterprise* magazine, the purpose of starting a magazine is to have the challenge of being in business.[3] Since its founding, *Black Enterprise* has established itself as a premier source for upwardly mobile blacks in America. Graves' success has been recognized in numerous ways, including the First Annual Chivas Regal Young Entrepreneur Award.

One of the greatest success stories of American entrepreneurs is one of the newest, Compaq Computer. Founded in 1982, it is now the world's largest producer of portable computers and the second-biggest maker of personal computers for business use. According to Rod Canion, cofounder, president, and chief executive of Compaq Computer, there is nothing quite like starting a company and having it grow rapidly.[4]

Starting a business allows the individual greater freedom in selecting the location, physical facilities, equipment, suppliers, products, and services. Furthermore, the entrepreneur is not bound to the established policies and practices of a going concern, or hampered by existing legal commitments. In addition, possible ill will from customers, suppliers, employees, and creditors is not inherited.

One of the strongest arguments for starting a new business venture from the beginning is that it allows the entrepreneur to be truly innovative. Jerry Della Femina, for example, is an unconventional advertising man who thrives on risk, excitement, and creativity.[5] His firm, Della Femina, McNamee, Inc., bills $750 million a year, and over the past 23 years the agency has developed a sterling reputation as a creative boutique with a string of ingenious commercials, including the Joe Isuzu campaign. In 1967, Della Femina decided to leave the Ted Bates advertising agency and go out on his own. He wanted to run an agency that was not like any agency he had ever worked for. To realize his dream, to run an agency where he would always have fun, meant starting his own business.

Innovative methods of operation should be tried when existing businesses do not adequately satisfy market needs and wants. As a case in point, Michael Cahlin sells chocolate by the byte. In 1984, while working as a public relations consultant, Cahlin created chocolate floppy disks as a promotional item to help sell a software cookbook. Retailers loved the chocolate but hated the cookbook. So Cahlin decided to sell just the chocolate instead. In the first three years the Chocolate Software Co., of Los Angeles, sold 50,000 pieces at about $10 each. Most of the chocolate is sold to retailers and computer companies, who send them to customers.[6]

Customers may be dissatisfied with the availability, distribution, and/or prices of products and services. On the other hand, rapid market expansion, changing customer needs, and new government regulations may have created new opportunities that established firms have not already exploited.

A field that is turning out to be a boon to many small businesses, for example, is the nation's hazardous waste problem. Federally mandated efforts to clean up contaminated sites and reduce pollution are spurring the creation of hundreds of companies that provide such services. Many are consulting and engineering firms that identify problem sites and design solutions. Others perform actual clean-ups, while still others offer ancillary services such as laboratory analysis, well-drilling, transportation, and training in toxic waste management. Small businesses are especially well suited to the industry because they can provide the specialization it requires.

The Market Assessment

Whether starting a new venture or buying an existing firm, a prospective business owner must carefully assess the market potential (possible total sales) of a chosen trade area. It does not matter how good a product or service appears to the entrepreneur or how efficiently the firm is operated if people do not need the product or service. Although this seems quite obvious, far too many new businesses are started because the entrepreneur is convinced that his or her intuition about a better mousetrap will be shared and translated into future sales by potential customers. While such feelings may be shared by friends and family members, one should be wary of relying solely on their judgments. A proper assessment of the market potential helps to substitute objectivity for emotions and wishful thinking.

In assessing the market potential, one needs to consider several market opportunity factors, including:

- The changing demographic characteristics of potential customers,
- The economic features of the trade area, such as income and growth projections,
- The strengths and weaknesses of competitors,
- The social and cultural dimensions of the market, and
- The buying characteristics and preferences of potential customers.

Entrepreneurs need to be sensitive to these factors, noting how they affect their current business operations and what new business opportunities they create.

Among the entrepreneurs who have recently recognized specialized market opportunities and acted on them are:

- Mamie Waters, who opened McCoy's Cake and Pie Shop in Milwaukee. Until Waters opened her shop, Milwaukeeans with roots in the South could not find a sweet potato pie, a caramel cake, or an egg custard pie in any local store. Like a true market-driven entrepreneur, Waters says she opened her shop "because I felt there was a need for it." Her shop was an immediate success.[7]
- Donna M. Squilla, who started an errand-running service called Do Me A Favor. After several years of commuting to her job in Manhattan, she was well acquainted

with the problem of keeping up with chores and losing every weekend to errands. Tired of the rat race, she quit her job to start her errand-running service. Each morning she parks her car at the train station, where commuters give her items for the cleaner, the tailor, and the shoe repair shop. Commuters pick up the items at the station when they return in the afternoon.[8]

- Mark Wilson, who started selling pieces of Alaskan glaciers to Japanese liquor stores, restaurants, and hotels. Workers at his five-year-old Anchorage company collect the lighter-colored ice that crashes into the sea from the upper portions of glaciers. That ice is filled with tiny pockets of air, and as it warms in a drink the air expands and cracks the ice, giving off a distinct popping sound. The ice is graded and cut into cubes, then put on freighters bound for Japan. A two-pound bag of ice cubes sells for about $6. The initial reaction was so favorable in Japan, where Alaskan ice has the image of purity, that the business took off. In addition to the overseas business, inroads are being made on the West Coast, where a seven-pound bag sells for about $2.50.[9]
- Carolyn Parrs and her husband Irv Weinberg, who opened a company called Poochi Canine Couture. The entrepreneurs recognized that pet owners' love for their animals can know no bounds. As a result, they create and sell designer apparel and accessories for pooches. Their company sells a line of matching sweaters for dogs and owners, along with collars and leashes in leopard, zebra, and red python leather prints. The goods are sold in department stores, pet and gift shops, and pet catalogs.[10]

Steps in Starting a New Venture

In the complicated process of starting a business, certain steps must be taken, the order of which will depend on the type of business. For practically every business the following steps need to be taken:

- Planning the business,
- Choosing the legal form of business,
- Obtaining financing,
- Selecting a location,
- Obtaining licenses,
- Setting up records,
- Insuring the business,
- Promoting the business, and
- Managing the business.

Advice and assistance are available for each of these steps. Small business owners starting a new venture can obtain advice from numerous sources. Among the most important are accountants, bankers, other business owners, suppliers, family and friends, and lawyers (see Exhibit 5–2).

Planning the Business

Regardless of the nature of the proposed business, the prospective business owner needs a comprehensive plan in order to transform an idea into a successful business operation. The business plan should describe, in writing, the proposed business and its

EXHIBIT 5–2 **Importance of Information Sources Used in Forming a Business**

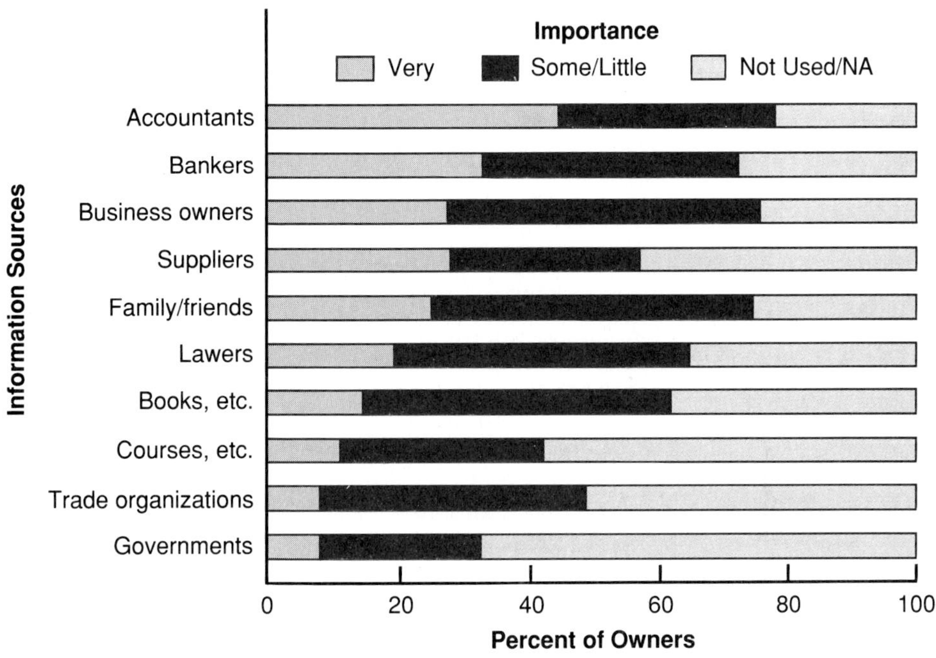

Source: Data developed and provided by The NFIB Foundation and sponsored by the American Express Travel Related Services Company, Inc.

products, services, or manufacturing processes. It should include an assessment of the market, a marketing strategy, an organizational plan, and measurable financial objectives.

Choosing the Legal Form of Business

A prospective entrepreneur should consult an attorney to clarify technical aspects of the different forms of business organization. The major legal forms of business are the sole proprietorship, the general partnership, the limited partnership, and the corporation.

Obtaining Financing

Most entrepreneurs lack the necessary financial resources to launch a new business. In addition to using their own savings, they must secure funds from other sources, such as family members, bank loans guaranteed by the Small Business Administration, and venture capital firms.

Selecting a Location

The location decision involves selection of the trade area and selection of a site from which the business is conducted. Specific site requirements will depend on the type of products or services to be sold and the market served.

Obtaining Licenses

The owner of a new business must obtain licenses and comply with federal, state, and local regulations. Federal regulations generally apply to businesses that engage in interstate commerce, while individual states license and regulate occupations. At the local level, zoning laws; building codes; and standards set by health, fire, and police departments must be observed.

Setting Up Records

Every business should have up-to-date records that provide:

1. Accurate and thorough statements of sales and operating results, fixed and variable costs, profit or loss, inventory levels, and credit and collection totals,
2. Comparisons of current data with prior years' operating results and budgeted goals,
3. Financial statements suitable for use by management or submission to prospective creditors,
4. Tax returns and reports to regulatory agencies, and
5. A method for uncovering material waste and record-keeping errors.

Insuring the Business

An insurance agent or broker should be consulted before one opens a business. A comprehensive insurance plan should be designed, which might include fire insurance, liability insurance, crime coverage, automobile insurance, workers' compensation insurance, business interruption insurance, employee health insurance, and key person insurance.

Promoting the Business

A new business owner must be prepared to inform potential customers. Few establishments can count on word of mouth alone to bring in customers. Advertising is needed to inform, persuade, and remind people about the business.

Managing the Business

As the prime initiator of the business firm, the new owner must be involved with planning, staffing, directing, and controlling the entire operation. The business must be firmly managed and operated in order to succeed.

BUYING AN ESTABLISHED BUSINESS

Buying a business can be one of the most treacherous experiences in an entrepreneur's career. Buyers of small businesses are more vulnerable to making costly mistakes because they frequently lack sophistication and do no know where to seek advice. Many believe they do not need it. Others get so caught up in the aura of a business's success that they will believe anything the seller tells them without checking it out. They rush ahead, willing to risk their life's savings while often doing less research than they would if they were buying a house.

One entrepreneur, who bought a name-plating company a few years ago, made the mistake of taking the seller at his word. He says he should have known the seller was

When Victor Kiam, owner of Remington Products, was shopping for a football team, he was not looking for just another financial investment. He was looking forward to the challenge of turning the club into an athletic and fiscal success. In order to do that, he needed the power of being a majority owner. What had started out as a far-fetched fantasy became a reality for him when the sale of the New England Patriots to Victor Kiam was complete. (*Source:* *Going for It,* Victor Kiam. New York: William Morrow and Company, 1986; photograph courtesy of Victor Kiam)

not disclosing everything when the seller's wife refused to part with the firm's record of payables. Disregarding his instincts as an accountant, the entrepreneur signed the deal anyway. "I guess I was naïve," he reflects. "The seller was presented as a religious and honest person, and I couldn't put two and two together when the person was so nice." As a result, terrible surprises followed: $2,500 in court claims from unpaid suppliers, overdue tax bills of $6,600, and $15,000 in bills from other suppliers the seller had promised to pay.[11]

Another entrepreneur, a twenty-four-year-old business student, says he discovered hidden environmental hazards after he bought a commercial lot and found underground storage tanks that had been left when a gas station closed years ago. With federal and state laws requiring property owners to remove unused tanks and clean up any damage they have caused, his cleanup bill could run from $25,000 to $500,000.[12]

When considering buying (or selling) a business, it is prudent to obtain professional advice. Whatever type of business one plans to buy, one should not try to handle all the details alone in any business purchase. Failure to seek professional advice could be very costly.

The Role of Advisors

A variety of resources is available for those buyers and sellers who want to obtain professional advice.[13] These include business owners in the industry, Small Business Administration (SBA) counselors, industry consultants, business valuation experts, intermediaries (wholesale and retail distributors), accountants, and attorneys. Each of these resources can be of assistance and each has its limitations.

Business owners, SBA counselors, consultants, and intermediaries are the best sources of industry information and operating suggestions. SBA counselors provide their services free of charge and can be reached through local SBA offices. Business owners may be able to give free advice, and they are often the best source of information. No one knows more about an industry than someone who is successfully running a business in that industry.

Business valuation experts can independently appraise a business's value. It should be remembered, however, that they rely on the representations of the seller. They render a conditional opinion based on the assumption that the financial statements are accurate and complete. They will attempt to independently verify only certain information.

Accountants are best used to perform an audit, if one is needed; help interpret financial statements; or provide advice in structuring the transaction to minimize unfavorable tax consequences for the buyer and seller.

Probably the most frequently consulted advisor in the purchase or sale of a business is an attorney. Attorneys are asked to do everything from assessing the viability of a business and appraising its value, to negotiating the purchase price and preparing the necessary documents. The primary function of an attorney is to prepare the purchase and sale documents as negotiated by the parties.

Attorneys cannot assess the viability of a business undertaking—that is something only the buyer and seller can do. Also, attorneys generally cannot assess a dollar value on a business, but they can occasionally help negotiate a price between buyer and seller. The involvement of an attorney (or any individual other than the principals) can, however, strain the lines of communication between buyer and seller, so they should be allowed into the negotiation process only after careful consideration.

Experience and reputation are important criteria when selecting an attorney. The attorney chosen should have experience handling similar transactions. It may make sense to choose one attorney to represent both buyer and seller. This avoids the adversarial relationship that opposing attorneys often adopt and improves the odds of successfully completing the transaction. It also eliminates some of the emotion in the negotiation process, improves the lines of communication between the parties, expedites completion of the deal, and is less expensive.

Advantages of Buying an Established Business

There are a number of possible advantages to buying an established business. These should be thoroughly evaluated before a decision is made to start a new venture from scratch.

- Buying a business will save the time, cost, and effort of finding a location. A major difficulty in starting a new business is finding the right place to locate. An existing business has already demonstrated the value of its location.
- An established firm can be evaluated to determine its ability to attract customers. In buying an existing business, one normally acquires customers who are accustomed to trading with the establishment.

- Uncertainties regarding physical facilities, inventory requirements, and personnel needs are reduced. The current owner can also share the benefit of his or her experience in the business and in the community.
- An existing business may be available at a bargain price. For personal reasons, an owner may be willing to make a quick sale and offer favorable terms.

In short, a business that is already established and operating has a track record that can be evaluated and compared with others in the industry.

Disadvantages of Buying an Established Business

A number of factors might rule against the purchase of an existing business. Indeed, on close examination the advantages just cited can turn out to be disadvantages.

- The business location may no longer be convenient to customers. Parking problems, deterioration of the neighborhood, and shifts of pedestrian and traffic flows plague many existing establishments.

- The current owner and/or business may have a poor reputation and image. A new entrepreneur would be faced, at least initially, with the prejudices and skepticism of customers and perhaps of suppliers.
- The physical facilities may be outmoded, in need of repair, and/or inefficient. Fixtures, equipment, and additional space can be costly to acquire.
- Too much of the inventory on hand may be obsolete, poorly selected, or slow-moving. Yesterday's breadwinners may be tomorrow's dead stock.
- The price of the business may be too high because of the former owner's misrepresentation or the buyer's inaccurate appraisal.

All of these factors are potentially serious disadvantages to buying an existing business. A careful and timely evaluation of the business is essential.

Reasons for Selling

Sellers offer many reasons for getting out of business. The most common include retirement, illness, family pressures, and employment or management opportunities elsewhere. The real reasons for selling may be quite different, however. There is always the danger that the reasons cited by the seller are not the real ones.

Questioning competitors, customers, suppliers, employees, previous owners, and local banks may reveal that the business is having difficulty being competitive; is experiencing high labor turnover rates; has a poor credit rating; has ill will in the community; or has legal problems stemming from business operations. There may be other hidden reasons for selling, such as cancellation of an exclusive sales franchise, a planned shopping center development with several competing stores, or impending new regulatory and/or environmental requirements. Knowing the true reasons for selling will enable the buyer to evaluate the business more realistically. A checklist of possible reasons for selling, ranging from more to less attractive, appears in Exhibit 5–3.

To avoid the less obvious business problems that may be causing the sale, buyers should study the business and research its markets very carefully. The prospective new business owner should determine whether sales are increasing or declining in the business area. The current business owner should provide evidence of the customer base and the size of the territory the business serves.

The prospective new business owner should also determine if there is growth potential for the business. Small business experts advise buyers to be careful when considering a business that reflects a temporary trend in demand. They contend that you risk enough buying a more traditional business without assuming the risk of a fad business that may soon disappear.[14]

Evaluating the Business

The first step a buyer must take in evaluating a business for sale is to review its history and the way it operates.[15] It is important to learn how the business was started, how its mission may have changed since its inception, and what past events have occurred to shape its current form. A buyer should understand the business's method of acquiring and serving its customers and how the functions of sales, marketing, finance, and operations interrelate. General information about the industry can be obtained from trade associations.

EXHIBIT 5–3 **Some Reasons That Prompt Company Owners to Sell**

Reasons owners would be more likely to volunteer

1. Owner wants to retire
2. Owner wants to collect his winnings and enjoy them
3. Owner wants to live somewhere else
4. Illness pressuring owner to leave the business
5. Need to cope with estate and inheritance problems
6. Owner discontent with line of business he or she is in
7. Dispute between co-owners

Reasons less likely to be volunteered by owners

8. Family pressures
9. Marital problems
10. Owner sees a better business opportunity
11. Owner tired of coping with unions, regulations, taxes, consumer groups, stockholders, inflation, or insurance costs
12. Company needs more financing than owner can raise
13. Currently depressed market for what company offers
14. Company losing money for reasons owner cannot diagnose

Reasons still less likely to be volunteered by owners

15. Bigger companies squeezing ones like this out
16. New zoning laws too restrictive
17. Competitors moving in with more effective products or methods
18. Union settlements cutting into profits
19. Owner wants to start a competitive firm with greater potential
20. Plant has become worn out or obsolete
21. New government regulations too expensive to comply with
22. Supply sources have become restricted or eliminated
23. Location becoming obsolete
24. Product or service company offers becoming obsolete
25. Franchise being canceled
26. Company needs more cash than operations can justify
27. Key employees leaving (maybe as competitors)
28. Impending threat of major lawsuit
29. Major customer returns likely from previous sales
30. Company committed to backlog with major built-in losses

Source: Karl H. Vesper, *New Venture Strategies,* © 1980, 259. Reprinted by permission of Prentice–Hall, Englewood Cliffs, N.J.

Earning Power of the Business

The true **earning power** of a business is the profit it can generate under the most competent management. It is not, as is commonly assumed, profit under ideal conditions, because ideal conditions seldom exist. A prospective buyer is really buying the expectations of future profits and return on investment.

In evaluating the business itself, the best place to start is to analyze the profit and loss statements for at least the last five years. If the seller will not provide or does not have audited profit and loss statements, the buyer should be cautious. Other documents to investigate include balance sheets, income tax returns, and, if available, cash flow statements. If the buyer is not qualified to prepare projected financial statements, an independent accountant should be consulted. This will involve some expense, but the cost will be small compared to the loss that might result if one invests in a business with a doubtful future.

If the analysis discloses that the business is not profitable, the buyer must determine whether new management can improve the profit generation of the business. If the buyer's skills are no better than those of the present owner, there will be no real chance of improvement unless other factors come into play, such as expanded local population or growth trends.

Although there is no handy formula that will neatly calculate a business's value, an old-fashioned way to gauge a private concern's worth is to look at the price–earnings ratio of comparable companies. For a wide range of businesses and prices, one can consult the quarterly edition of *Mergers & Acquisitions* magazine.

Evaluating an Income Statement

The potential earning power of the business should be analyzed by reviewing profit and loss statements for the past five years. It is important to substantiate financial information by reviewing the business's federal and state tax returns. The business's earning power is a function of more than bottom line profits or losses. The owner's salary and fringe benefits, noncash expenses, and nonrecurring expenses should also be calculated.

PRICING THE BUSINESS

Determining the value of a business is the part of the buy–sell transaction most fraught with potential for differences of opinion.[16] Buyers and sellers usually do not share the same perspective. Each has a distinct rationale, and that rationale may be based on logic or on emotion.

The buyer may believe that the purchase will create economies of scale because of the way the business will be operated under new ownership. The buyer may also see the business as an especially good lifestyle fit. These factors are likely to increase the amount of money a buyer is willing to pay for a business. The seller may have a greater than normal desire to sell due to financial difficulties or the death or illness of the owner or a member of the owner's family. For the transaction to come to conclusion, both parties must be satisfied with the price and be able to understand how it was determined.

Factors That Determine Value

As noted previously, the process of determining the value of a business takes into account many variables and requires that a number of assumptions be made. Six of the most important factors are:

1. Recent profit history,
2. General condition of the company, for example, condition of facilities, completeness and accuracy of books and records, morale, and so on,
3. Market demand for the particular type of business,
4. Economic conditions,

5. Ability to transfer goodwill or other intangible values to a new owner, and
6. Future profit potential.[17]

These six factors can determine the fair market value. However, businesses seldom change hands at fair market value. The reason is that other factors come into play when the principals arrive at an agreed-upon price. Other factors include:

- Special circumstances of the particular buyer and seller,
- Tradeoffs between cash and financing terms, and
- Relative tax consequences for the buyer and seller, which depend on how the transaction is structured.

The definition of **fair market value** is the price at which property would change hands between a willing buyer and a willing seller, both being adequately informed of all material facts and neither being compelled to buy or to sell. In the marketplace, buyer and seller are nearly always acting under different levels of compulsion.

Rule-of-Thumb Formulas

The best advice about using **rule-of-thumb formulas** for pricing a business is not to use them. The problem with rule-of-thumb formulas is that they address few of the factors that impact a business's value. They rely on a "one size fits all" approach when, in fact, no two businesses are identical.

Rule-of-thumb formulas do, however, provide a quick means of establishing whether a price for a certain business is "in the ballpark." Formulas exist for many businesses. They are normally calculated as a percentage of either sales or asset values, or a combination of both.

Balance Sheet Method of Valuation

The **balance sheet method of valuation** approach calls for the assets of the business to be valued. It is most often used when the business being valued generates earnings primarily from its assets rather than from the contributions of its employees. It is also used when the cost of starting a business and getting revenues past the breakeven point does not greatly exceed the value of the business's assets.

There are a number of balance sheet methods of valuation including book value, adjusted book value, and liquidation value. Each has its proper application.

The most useful balance sheet method is the **adjusted book value method.** This method calls for the adjustment of each asset's book value to equal the cost of replacing that asset in its current condition. The total of the adjusted asset values is then offset against the sum of the liabilities to arrive at the adjusted book value.

Adjustments are frequently made to the book values of the following items:

- *Accounts receivable*—often adjusted down to reflect the uncollectability of some receivables.
- *Inventory*—usually adjusted down since it may be difficult to sell off all the inventory at cost.
- *Real estate*—frequently adjusted up since it will often have appreciated in value since it was placed in service.

- *Furniture, fixtures, and equipment*—adjusted up if those items in service have been depreciated below their market value, or adjusted down if the items have become obsolete.

Income Statement Method of Valuation

Although a balance sheet formula is sometimes the most accurate means to value a business, it is more common to use an **income statement method of valuation.** This method is most concerned with the profits or cash flow produced by the business's assets. One of the more frequently used methods is the discounted future cash flow method. This method calls for calculation of the future cash flows of the business.

Valuation of Intangible Assets

Intangible assets are those economic resources owned by a firm that have an impalpable value. Such assets have no physical existence but have value because of the rights they confer on the owner. They might include:

1. A lease,
2. A franchise,
3. Customer lists,
4. Trained personnel,
5. Trademarks, copyrights, and patents,
6. Creditor and supplier relations,
7. Goodwill.

These intangible assets are discussed below.

1. *Lease*—will the lease be transferable to the buyer and included in the contract, or will it be a sublease? What are the duration and the terms? A title insurance policy will protect the buyer and ensure that the lessor will be able to keep commitments in any lease contract.
2. *Franchise*—will an exclusive right to sell a product be transferable? Must the franchisor be contacted? What are the terms, length, and expiration of the franchise? Did the seller have to pay a fee, and will the buyer have to pay a transfer fee? These items must be considered in determining whether the franchise has a value, and the pertinent points above must be put into the contract of sale if the franchise is to be transferred.
3. *Customer lists, mailing lists, credit and business lists*—well-developed and maintained lists can be valuable and should be included in the contract of sale.
4. *Trained personnel*—are the employees, particularly key employees, considered assets or liabilities, and will they stay with new ownership?
5. *Trade and service marks, copyrights and patents, business name*—if these are essential to the success of the business, they should be included in the contract of sale. However, valuation should include whether their value may diminish in the future.
6. *Creditor and supplier relations*—what is the state of these relationships, and will they continue if ownership changes? Unless tied by firm contracts, should the

prospective owner consider other sources? What deliveries are expected, and should they be reduced, increased, or canceled?

7. *Goodwill*—often the area of goodwill is a stumbling block between buyer and seller because its valuation is the most difficult to determine. What is the value of the reputation of the business in the community and among its customers? Will customers trade with a new owner, or is their current business the result of a personal attachment to the seller? Does the business have contracts with key customers? If so, are they for a fixed period, open-ended, or cancelable? Will the seller agree not to reenter the business in competition, and for what period? Valuation of goodwill must take all these things into consideration.

Determining Goodwill

Goodwill value is the amount the owner is asking for the favorable public attitude toward the business. It arises from the seller's successful operations in the past—its reputation for excellent customer service, its friendly and capable employees, its reputation for high-quality products and fair prices, and its convenient location. It is not to be confused with net worth, which is the difference between the dollar value of the assets and liabilities of the business. Rather, it is the ability of the business to realize a higher-than-ordinary rate of return on the investment.

No fixed formula can substitute for good judgment in determining the value of goodwill. Since it is payment for favorable public attitude, one should make some effort to determine this attitude by questioning customers, suppliers, bankers, and others who should have unbiased opinions. Then one must consider who will have the goodwill after the business changes hands. Does it belong to the business, or is it personally attached to the seller?

One method of determining the value of goodwill is to calculate it as a percent of net income before the owner's salary and taxes. One business broker, with 25 years of experience, judged that a reasonable sum to be paid for the goodwill of a business would vary from 0 to 150 percent of net income, as shown in Exhibit 5–4.

A test of the amount asked is to compare it with past profits of the business. How many months or years will it take before the price of the goodwill can be paid for out of profits? Another way of judging the value of goodwill is to estimate how much more income will be earned through buying the established business than by starting a new one. The price the buyer should be willing to pay for goodwill is one that is fairly related to the earning power of the business.

Arriving at a Selling Price

Once the business has been evaluated with positive results, the buyer must have an idea of a realistic price for the business. Valuation of a business for sale is a complicated process that varies with each type of business. The services of an experienced business appraiser can be invaluable if the buyer can afford it. An independent accountant familiar with the particular type of business can sometimes be a substitute for an appraiser. The values determined by the business broker must be carefully evaluated by the buyer, because the broker is the seller's agent, and the size of the broker's fee is determined by the sale

EXHIBIT 5–4 **Goodwill Value of Selected Small Businesses**

Type of Business	Goodwill as a Percentage of Net Income
Arts and craft shops	15%
Auto parts	25
Beer distributorship	150
Cameras (specialty shops)	10–15
Clothing stores	10–20
Computer service bureaus	125
Grocery stores and meat markets	0
Hardware and appliance stores	20
Hobby shops	20
Music stores	33
Paint stores	10
Pet shops	35
Photo studios	50
Restaurants and lounges (the "good" ones only)	100

Source: Abstracted from James M. Hansen, *Guide to Buying or Selling a Business* (Mercer Island, Wash.: Grenadier Press).

price. As a final check, the prospective buyer can consult books on the subject. Caution should be exercised, however, since every formula for arriving at a selling price contains subjective decisions that the inexperienced can misapply.

MAKING AND EVALUATING THE OFFER

The purchase of a business can be profitable if one knows what factors should be considered in making the offer and how to evaluate it correctly. It involves great risk if one is inexperienced or has not carefully prepared for the purchase.

Making the Offer

Before making an offer, a buyer will typically investigate a number of businesses.[18] At some point in the investigation process, it may be necessary to sign a confidentiality agreement and show the seller a personal financial statement. A confidentiality agreement pledges that the prospective buyer will not divulge any information about the business to anyone other than immediate advisors.

A buyer should determine a range of value for the business. An appraisal of the business as is can be used to establish a pricing floor. A pricing ceiling can be established by using an appraisal that capitalizes projected future cash flows under new management.

A buyer should have access to all records needed to prepare an offer. If some information is lacking, the buyer must make a decision to either discontinue the transaction or make an offer contingent on receiving and approving the withheld information. The nature and amount of withheld information determines which course of action to take.

An offer may take the form of a purchase and sale agreement or a letter of intent. Purchase and sale agreements are usually binding on the parties, while a letter of intent is often nonbinding. The latter is more often used with larger businesses.

Regardless of which form of the agreement is used, it should contain the following:

1. Total price to be offered.
2. Components of the price (amount of security deposit and down payment, amount of bank debt, amount of seller-financed debt).
3. A list of all liabilities and assets that are being purchased. The minimum amount of accounts receivable to be collected and the maximum amount of accounts payable to be assumed may be specified.
4. The operating condition of equipment at settlement.
5. The right to offset the purchase price in the amount of any undisclosed liabilities that come due after settlement, and in the amount of any variance in inventory from that stated in the agreement.
6. A provision that the business will be able to pass all necessary inspections.
7. A provision calling for compliance with the Bulk Transfer provisions of the Uniform Commercial Code.
8. Warranties of clear and marketable title, validity and assumability of existing contracts if any, tax liability limitations, legal liability limitations, and other appropriate warranties.
9. A provision (where appropriate) to make the sale conditional on lease assignment, verification of financial statements, transfer of licenses, obtaining financing, or other provisions.
10. A provision for any appropriate prorations such as rent, utilities, wages, and prepaid expenses.
11. A noncompetition covenant. This document is sometimes part of the purchase and sale agreement and is sometimes a separate exhibit to the purchase and sale agreement. (Because of noncompete agreements, entrepreneurs often cannot start a company in the same field for several years, a period in which the market may become crowded, and they usually cannot hire trusted former employees).
12. Allocation of the purchase price.
13. Restrictions on how the business is to be operated until settlement.
14. A date for settlement.

The purchase and sale agreement is a complex document and it is a good idea to get professional help in drafting it.

Evaluating the Offer

The types of offers a seller is likely to receive depend in some measure on the size of the business. A seller should ask for a résumé and financial statement from an individual buyer and an annual report if the buyer is another company. One has to find out what the buyer brings. Sometimes, a buyer with a commitment to the work ethic is all that is needed. In other cases, successful related work experience may be important. If the acquirer is another company, one has to look for the logic behind the acquisition. Perhaps some kind of synergy or an economy of scale is created. A buyer should prepare and show the seller a postacquisition business plan.

As a final note, one should carefully study offers to determine what assets and liabilities are being purchased. An offer for the assets of a business may be worth considerably less than an offer for its stock, even though the price offered for the assets is higher.

CLOSING THE TRANSACTION

There are several legal aspects to consider when closing the transaction. The prospective buyer must obtain complete information about all legal aspects concerning the closing, because failure to do so can invalidate the transaction.

Meeting Conditions of Sale

After buyer and seller have entered into a binding contract, there may be several conditions to be met before the sale can be closed.[19] These conditions often address such issues as assignment of the lease, verification of financial statements, transfer of licenses, or obtaining financing. There is usually a date set for meeting the conditions of sale. If a condition is not met within the specified time frame, the agreement is invalidated.

Types of Settlements

Business settlements or closings, as they are called, are usually done in one of two ways.

In the first case, an attorney performs the settlement. In this procedure, the attorney for the buyer, or an independent attorney acting on behalf of both buyer and seller, draws up the necessary documents for settlement. Buyer and seller meet with the settlement attorney at a predetermined time (after all conditions of sale have been met). At the meeting, documents are signed by buyer and seller.

A good settlement attorney is also a good problem solver. He or she can help find creative ways to resolve differences of opinion. The settlement attorney holds money in escrow and disburses it when all the appropriate documents are signed.

In the second case, an **escrow settlement,** the money to be deposited, bill of sale, and other documents, are placed in the hands of a neutral third party or escrow agent. The escrow agent is usually an escrow company or the escrow department of a financial institution. Buyer and seller sign escrow instructions that name the conditions to be met before completion of the sale. Once all conditions are met, the escrow agent distributes previously executed documents and disburses funds. There usually is no formal final meeting at which the signing of the documents takes place. Buyer and seller usually sign them independently of one another.

Regardless of whether escrow or a settlement attorney is used, requirements of the **Bulk Sales Act** must be met if the assets of the business are being sold. This law calls for the business's suppliers to be notified of the impending sale. The supplier must respond within the allowed time frame if money is owed by the seller. A lien search is also performed by the attorney or escrow agent. This determines if any liens against the business's assets have been filed in the records of the local courthouse.

Documents

A number of documents are required to close a transaction. The purchase and sale agreements used to close the transaction are created. The documents most often used in closing a transaction are described below. Other documents not described below might also be needed, depending on the particulars of the transaction.

The **settlement sheet** shows, as of the date of settlement, the various costs and adjustments to be paid by or credited to each party. It is signed by buyer and seller.

The **escrow agreement** is used only for escrow settlements. It is a set of instructions signed by buyer and seller in advance of settlement which sets forth the conditions of escrow, the responsibilities of the escrow agent, and the requirements to be met for the release of escrowed funds and documents.

The **bill of sale** describes the physical assets being transferred and identifies the amount of consideration paid for those assets. It must always be signed by the seller and is often also signed by the buyer.

The **promissory note,** used only in an installment sale, shows the principal amount and terms of repayment of the debt by the buyer to the seller. It specifies remedies for the seller in the event of default by the buyer. It is signed by the buyer, and the buyer often must personally guarantee the debt.

The **security agreement** creates the security interest in the assets pledged by the buyer to secure the promissory note and underlying debt. It also sets forth the terms under which the buyer agrees to operate those assets which constitute collateral. It is used only in an installment sale. It is signed by both parties.

The **financing statement** creates a public record of the security interest in the collateral and therefore notifies third parties that certain assets are encumbered by a lien to secure the existing debt. The cost to record the financing statement varies by jurisdiction. It is used only in installment sales. It is signed by buyer and seller.

The **covenant not to compete** protects the buyer and his investment from immediate competition by the seller in his market area for a limited amount of time. The scope of this document must be reasonable in order for it to be legally enforceable. The covenant not to compete is sometimes included as a part of the purchase and sales agreement and is sometimes written as a separate document. It is signed by both parties. It is not required in every transaction.

The **employment agreement** specifies the nature of services to be performed by the seller, the amount of compensation, the amount of time per week or per month the services are to be performed, the duration of the agreement, and often a method for discontinuing the agreement before its completion. Employment agreements are not required in all transactions, but they are used with great frequency. It is not uncommon for the seller to remain involved with the business for periods of as little as a week or as much as several years. The length of time depends on the complexity of the business and the experience of the buyer. For periods of more than two to four weeks, the seller is often compensated for his or her services. It is signed by both the buyer and the seller.

Contingent Liabilities

Contingent liabilities must be taken into account and provided for when a business is sold. They most often occur because of pending tax payments, unresolved lawsuits, or anticipated but uncertain costs of meeting regulatory requirements. Contingent liabilities can be handled by escrowing a portion of the funds earmarked for disbursement to the seller. The sum escrowed can then be used to pay off the liability as it comes due. Any remaining money can then be disbursed to the seller.

SUMMARY

1. The alternatives for entering a business are to start a new one from scratch or to buy an established business. Each has advantages and disadvantages.
2. Starting a business from scratch is the most common method of getting into business.
3. In starting a new business, the following steps need to be taken: planning the business, choosing the legal form of business, obtaining financing, selecting a location, obtaining licenses, setting up records, insuring the business, promoting the business, and managing the business.
4. Professional advice should be obtained when buying an established business. Advisers to consult include accountants, attorneys, business valuation experts, SBA counselors, and business owners.
5. A buyer should always attempt to determine the real reasons why a particular business is for sale.
6. In evaluating a business that is for sale, one needs to determine the earning power of the business.
7. Factors that determine the price of a business include the business's recent profit history, economic conditions, ability to transfer goodwill, and future profit potential of the business.
8. Methods that can be used to determine the price of a business include rule-of-thumb formulas, balance sheet method of valuation, and income method of valuation.
9. Intangible assets, including goodwill, are difficult to value, but they cannot be ignored.
10. Purchase and sales agreements are complex documents that should be drafted with the help of professionals.
11. Business settlements or closings can be performed by attorneys or in an escrow settlement.
12. Documents required in closing a business sale often include a settlement sheet, an escrow agreement, a bill of sale, a promissory note, a security agreement, a financing statement, a covenant not to compete, and an employment agreement.

KEY TERMS AND CONCEPTS

Earning power
Fair market value
Rule-of-thumb formulas
Balance sheet method of valuation
Adjusted book value method
Income statement method of valuation
Intangible assets
Goodwill
Escrow settlement
Bulk Sales Act
Settlement sheet
Bill of sale
Promissory note
Security agreement
Financing statement
Covenant not to compete
Employment agreement

QUESTIONS FOR DISCUSSION

1. What are the arguments for starting a new business from scratch?
2. What factors should be considered in a market assessment?
3. What steps need to be addressed when starting a new venture?
4. What are the advantages of buying a small business?
5. What are the disadvantages of buying a small business, and how might they cause problems?
6. Why is it important for the buyer to carefully investigate the owner's reasons for selling a business?
7. What is the meaning of "true earning power" of a business? How is it determined?
8. What factors determine the value (price) of a business?
9. Differentiate between tangible and intangible assets and give examples of each.
10. Why is it so difficult to determine the true value of good will?
11. In addition to determining the value of a business, what other questions should be considered in deciding whether to buy an existing business?
12. Why is it advisable to obtain professional assistance when buying or selling a business?
13. What should be included in a purchase and sales agreement?
14. How are settlements or closings usually done?
15. What documents are typically required in closing a business sales transaction?

SELF-TEST REVIEW

Multiple Choice Questions

1. Which of the following is (are) often an advantage to buying an established business?
   a. Easier to innovate.
   b. Established customer goodwill.
   c. On-hand inventory.
   d. All of the above.
2. Which of the following may be a disadvantage to buying an established business?
   a. Inefficient facilities.
   b. Bad customer relations.
   c. Obsolete inventory.
   d. All of the above.
3. The first step in starting a new business should be:
   a. Obtaining licenses.
   b. Preparing a written plan of action.
   c. Obtaining financing.
   d. Selecting a location.
4. When a business owner tells the prospective buyer the reason for selling, the buyer should:
   a. Accept the explanation.
   b. Reject the explanation.
   c. Attempt to find out if it is the real reason.
   d. Forget all about it.
5. In evaluating an established business, it is best to begin by analyzing:
   a. Profit-and-loss statements.
   b. Balance sheets.
   c. Cash flow statements.
   d. Income tax returns.

True/False Statements

1. One advantage of starting a new business is that it allows the entrepreneur to be innovative.
2. A person buying or starting a business should depend on instincts about the proposed venture even though these feelings are not shared by potential customers.
3. A person buying or starting a business can ignore competition in the market assessment if he or she plans to be more efficient than the competition.
4. One advantage of buying an established business is that it has a location with a demonstrated value.
5. Customer attitude toward an established firm is always an advantage when buying a business.
6. The owner of a business will always tell you true reasons for selling the firm.
7. The earning power of a business is the profit it can generate under ideal conditions.
8. Tangible assets usually include inventory, equipment, building fixtures and furniture, and the reputation of the business.
9. Goodwill is an example of an intangible asset.
10. Before purchasing an established business, an attorney should be consulted to check all aspects of the transaction.

BOB'S BICYCLE BARN

Ron Sterling has been a successful salesperson in a sporting goods store for the past ten years. Now he wants to go out on his own and pursue his dream—to own and manage a bicycle shop.

During the ten years that Sterling has worked for the Big Ten Sporting Goods Store, his primary responsibility has been the bicycle department. He has become well acquainted with the various suppliers of bicycles during these years, including those who carry Raleigh, Sekai, Ron Cooper, and Univega. Furthermore, he has acquired intimate knowledge of exercise bicycles, which have represented 15 to 25 percent of sales during recent years.

Sterling wants to locate in the growing town of Salem, only 15 miles from his current residence. He feels comfortable with the small-town atmosphere and the growth prospects of the community. There are presently only two bicycle stores in town, although one mass merchant and two toy stores also carry a limited line of family bicycles. According to the National Bicycle Dealers Association, a market the size of Salem can support another bicycle shop.

Of the two bicycle shops in Salem, Bob's Bicycle Barn is the oldest, with 15 years in the same location. The store enjoys a solid reputation for quality service and repair, performed largely by Bob Franklin and his son Michael. But Michael Franklin is about to move to a neighboring state to start his own shop. His father had wanted to turn over the business to Michael, but there are hard feelings between father and son.

Bob's Bicycle Barn is on the eastern edge of town, an area that is not in the growth pattern and population movement of the past three years. Nevertheless, customers are willing to drive to Bob's. Unfortunately, though, the physical facilities are old and the store's fixtures and equipment need costly repairs. Franklin wants to retire and does not want to invest about $15,000 in the store to make it more modern. So he has approached Ron Sterling, whom he has known for several years, during which time they have frequently hunted together. He has offered his business to Sterling for $72,500, based on the following calculations:

1. Adjusted value of tangible net worth (assets less liabilities)	$65,000
2. Earning power at 10 percent of an amount equal to the adjusted tangible net worth if invested in a comparable-risk business, security, and so on	6,500
3. Reasonable salary for owner-operator	25,000
4. Net earnings of the business over past two years	34,000
5. Extra earning power of the business (number 4 minus numbers 2 and 3)	2,500
6. Value of goodwill (3 times number 5)	7,500
7. Final price (number 1 and 6)	72,500

The valuation of goodwill is simply a fair estimate, according to Franklin. An income statement for this year and last year is as follows:

Income Statement

	This Year	Last Year	Two Year Average
Net sales	$291,666	$264,514	$278,090
Cost of sales	180,833	166,644	173,738
Gross profit	110,833	97,870	104,352
Expenses	75,833	64,870	70,352
Net income	35,000	33,000	34,000

Sterling is excited about Franklin's offer. He knows that to start a new bicycle shop in Salem would require lots of hard work, which he can avoid if he takes over Bob's Bicycle Barn. Otherwise, Sterling knows he would have to find a suitable location; obtain necessary licenses; invest in inventory, including bicycles, parts, and accessories; purchase repair equipment; and make the store known on opening. Various other headaches would surely occur. Furthermore, Sterling knows that Franklin will help out during the first several months of operation and will be available for repair work, about which Sterling knows relatively little.

Sterling faces a major decision. He knows that he can be in business for himself almost immediately if he buys Bob's Bicycle Barn. On the other hand, waiting a while will make it possible to look into a new location for the business. Sterling also does not know whether the asking price is too high. He is bothered by the $7,500 asked for goodwill and by some of the inventory on hand, which consists of three-speed and single-speed bicycles. These bicycles represent less than 15 percent of sales in the sporting goods store where Sterling is now working.

QUESTIONS

1. Should Sterling buy Bob's Bicycle Barn, or should he start his own shop?
2. Is the asking price for the Bicycle Barn realistic?

NOTES

1. John R. Emshmiller, "Handing Down the Business," *The Wall Street Journal,* May 20, 1989, B1.
2. *Ibid.*
3. Based on Cable News Network's "Pinnacle," May 23, 1987. Guest: Earl Graves, *Black Enterprise* magazine.
4. Based on Cable News Network's "Pinnacle," October 4, 1987. Guest: Rod Canion, Compaq Computer.
5. Based on Cable News Network's "Pinnacle," May 7, 1988. Guest: Jerry Della Femina, Della Femina, Travisano and Partners.
6. "Chocolate Chips by the Bits," *Venture,* April, 1988, 12.
7. Steven P. Galante, "Urban Entrepreneurs Tutored in How to Read Market Cues," *The Wall Street Journal,* August 10, 1987, 25.
8. "Doing Commuters Favors," *Venture,* November, 1987, 14.
9. "Alaska's Glacier Ice Finds Ready Market," *The Sacramento Bee,* December, 1987, 10.
10. "Fashions for Fido," *Venture,* September, 1988, 7.
11. Barbara Marsh, "It's So Easy to Get Burned when Buying a Small Firm," *The Wall Street Journal,* September 21, 1989, B1.
12. *Ibid.*
13. This section is excerpted from the Small Business Administration, *How to Buy or Sell a Small Business,* Management Aids No. 2.029, 8.
14. Bank of America, "How to Buy and Sell a Business or Franchise," *Small Business Reporter,* 1987, 2.
15. *How to Buy or Sell a Small Business,* 2–3.
16. *Ibid.,* 5–7.
17. Shannon Pratt, *Small Businesses and Professional Practices* (Homewood, IL: Dow–Jones Irwin, 1986).
18. Excerpted from *How to Buy or Sell a Small Business,* 10–11.
19. *Ibid.,* 11–12.

Chapter Six

Franchising

Chapter Outline

Learning Objectives *The objectives of this chapter are to assist you in understanding:*

1. The nature, meaning, and different types of franchising.
2. The major advantages and disadvantages of franchising.
3. The scope of franchising in the U.S. economy.
4. The factors to consider in investing in a franchise.
5. The trends and outlook for franchising in the 1990s.

Re/Max, the second largest U.S. residential real estate franchise network, offers its franchisees a support system that includes custom-designed office computer software and national advertising. In return Re/Max agents pay a monthly franchise fee; but unlike traditional companies that split commissions on a 50/50 basis, Re/Max agents keep 100 percent of their commissions. (Photograph by Ed Dosien, courtesy of Re/Max International. Inc.)

THE NATURE OF FRANCHISING

More than 800,000 people own and operate franchise establishments in the United States and Canada.[1] Rather than starting a business from scratch, this alternative appeals to many entrepreneurs because of its relative safety, instant product recognition, and the management assistance that one can expect to receive from the franchising company.

Franchising represents the small entrepreneur's best chance to compete with the giant companies that dominate the marketplace. Without franchising, thousands of businesspeople would never have had the opportunity to own their own businesses and would never have felt the immense satisfaction of being a part of the free enterprise system.

Indications are that by the end of this century, franchising will be the primary method of conducting business. According to the U.S. Department of Commerce, sales of goods and services of the more than 509,000 franchised outlets reached $553 billion in 1988, or 34% of total retail sales (see Exhibit 6–1).[2] These outlets employ more than 7.3 million workers.

Movement by U.S. franchisors to foreign markets continues to grow at a rapid rate, and in 1986 there were 354 U.S. franchisors with over 31,600 outlets located in most countries of the world (see Exhibit 6–2). With the 1992 unification of the European Economic Community, Europe holds tremendous potential for growth. For example, an American owner of 100 Dairy Queen stores has formed a joint venture with an Italian investor to expand into Italy, Spain, and Portugal. Steamatic, a carpet cleaning business, is actively scouting for European franchisees.[3]

Franchising continues its steady growth in sales, employment units, and international expansion, offering tremendous opportunities to individuals seeking their own businesses and to companies looking for wider distribution for their products, systems, and services. Franchising has become so powerful partly because economic factors have made growth through company-owned units difficult for many businesses. In addition, franchisees are enjoying a competitive edge over other small business entrepreneurs through the use of trade names, marketing expertise, acquisition of a distinctive business appearance, standardization of products and services, training, and advertising support from the parent organization.[4]

Although few franchises have managed to match the strides of proven winners like McDonald's, Domino's, or Subway Sandwiches, new franchises are on a roll. Among

EXHIBIT 6–1 Franchising Encompassed 34 Percent of Retail Sales in 1988

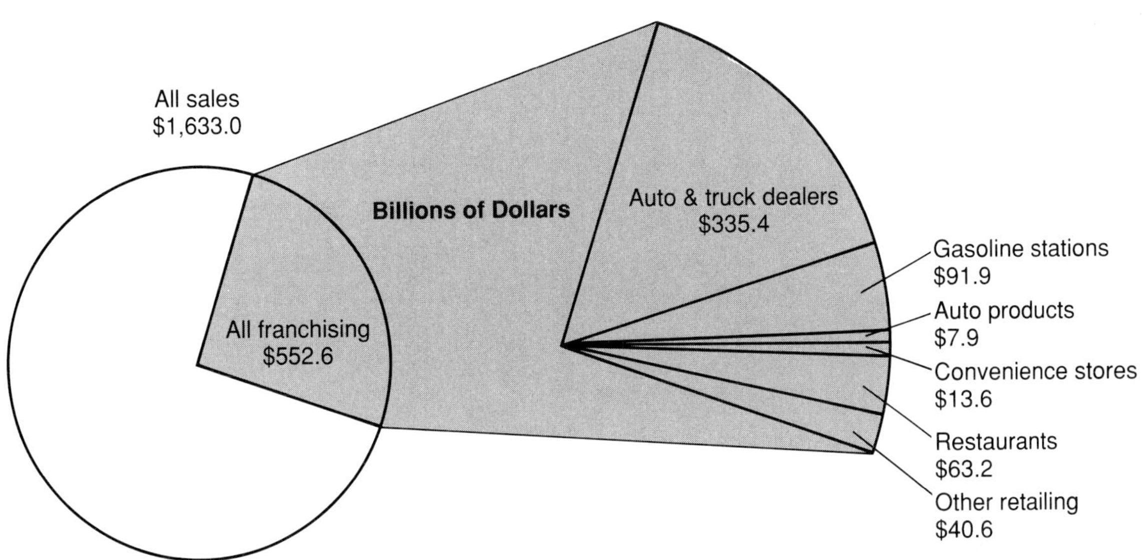

Source: U.S. Department of Commerce, *Franchising in the Economy, 1986–1988* (Washington, D.C.: U.S. Government Printing Office, February 1988), 15.

those that grew fast in recent years are T.J. Cinnamons Bakeries, Novus Windshield Repair, The Box Shoppe, American Mobile Power Wash, Penguin's Place Frozen Yogurt, Hampton Inn, Dial-a-Gift, Stork News, Zack's, and Chem-Dry.[5] With the continued growth of franchises that sell fast food, cleaning services, quick-stop groceries, and home decorating, it is clear that giving people what they want in a hurry is good business.

Dreaming up ideas for intriguing new franchises comes easy. Survival and growth, especially for an entrepreneur with a new twist on an old industry, do not present insurmountable problems either. People are eager to get in on new franchises. For example, franchises standing out from the crowd of newcomers include:[6]

AutoSpa Auto Malls franchises stores and services devoted exclusively to auto care.

CelluLand franchises retail stores specializing in cellular telephones and portable communication products, such as laptop computers and facsimile machines.

Papyrus Franchise Corp. franchises upscale Papyrus greeting card stores catering to sophisticated tastes.

The Sour Exchange franchises restaurants featuring a 20-item buffet-style salad bar, four homemade soups, and homemade corn muffins, plus fresh-baked chocolate chip cookies distributed free on the hour.

Valvoline Instant Oil Change franchises quick lube centers.

Imposters franchises stores selling excellent imitations of the kind of jewelry found at Tiffany and Cartier.

EXHIBIT 6–2 International Franchising, 1986

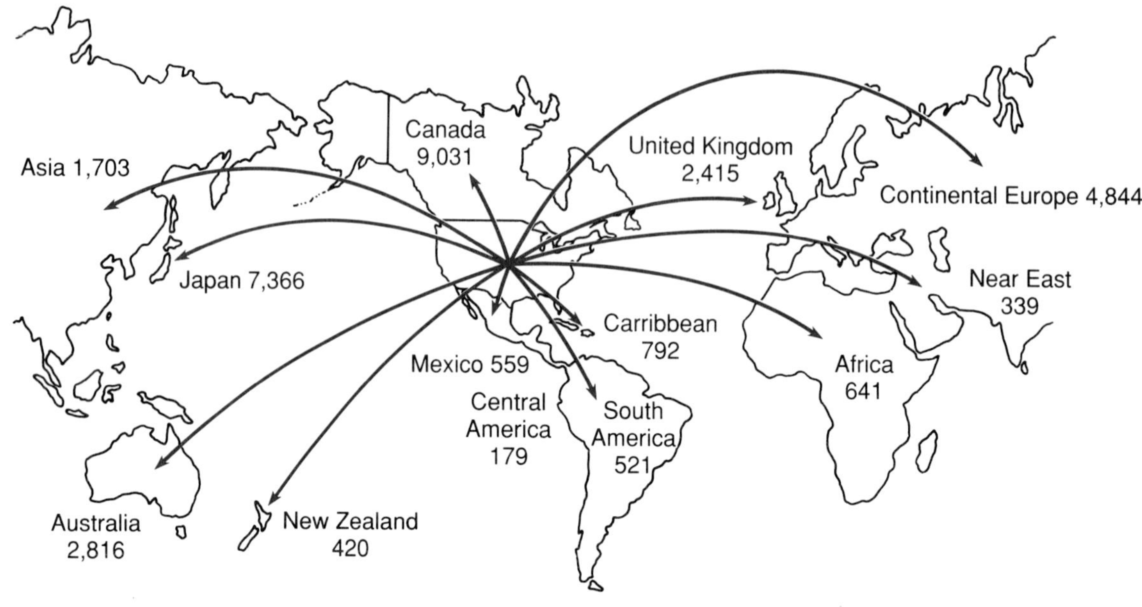

Note: In 1986, 354 U.S. business format franchisors operated 31,626 outlets covering most countries of the world.
Source: U.S. Department of Commerce, *Franchising in the Economy, 1986–1988* (Washington, D.C.: U.S. Government Printing Office, February 1988), 8.

The International Connoisseur franchises stores that sell gift packages of wines and champagnes, crystal gift sets, and gourmet gifts of wines, cheeses, meats, nuts, and pastas.

Nine Spice Tandoori Kabob franchises restaurants specializing in Indian food dishes such as Hurry Curry and Golden Triangles.

ProForma franchises stores selling business products such as business forms, commercial printing, office supplies, and computer supplies.

Whether or not these newcomers to franchising will endure cannot be predicted. Entrepreneurs choosing to enter into franchise agreements with these or any other franchisors have to recognize that—not unlike starting a business from scratch—in the long run the most important ingredient to success is hard work.

Franchising Defined

Franchising may be defined as "a business opportunity by which the owner (producer or distributor) of a service or a trademark product grants exclusive rights to an individual for the local distribution and/or sale of the service or product, and in return receives a payment or royalty and conformance to quality standards."[7] The word **franchise** means a right or privilege. The individual, group, or company that sells franchises to others is called the **franchisor.** The individual, group, or company that purchases a franchise is called the **franchisee.** The **franchise agreement** is a written contract detailing the mutual responsibilities of the franchisor and franchisee.

The International Franchise Association, a nonprofit trade association representing more than 550 franchising companies in the United States and around the world, provides a broader definition of franchising: "A continuing relationship in which the franchisor provides a licensed privilege to do business plus assistance in organizing, training, merchandising, and management in return for a consideration from the franchisee." Franchising has also been described as a convenient and economic means for the fulfillment of a drive or desire for independence with a minimum of risk and investment and maximum opportunities for success through the utilization of a proven product or service and marketing method.

However, the owner of a franchised business must give up some independence of action in business decisions that would be open to the owner of a nonfranchised business. In a way, the franchisee is not his or her own boss. The franchisor, in order to maintain the distinctiveness and uniformity of the product or service and to ensure that the operations of each outlet will reflect favorably on the organization as a whole—to protect and build its goodwill—usually exercises some degree of continuing control over the operations of franchises and requires them to meet certain standards. The extent of such control varies. In some cases, franchisees are required to conduct every step of their operations in strict conformity with a manual furnished by the franchisor, and this may be desirable. In return, the individual franchisee can share in the goodwill built up by other outlets that bear the same name.

A company that depends on the successful operation of franchise outlets needs individuals who are willing to learn the business and who have the energy to put forth a considerable amount of effort; it can supply the other essentials for successful operation of the outlet. Many a successful entrepreneur resists becoming a franchisor due to concerns about the willingness and ability of potential franchisees to truly learn the business.

GOLDEN DOOR®

RANCHO LA PUERTA®

For example, Deborah Szekely, founder of the model spa Golden Door has resisted numerous offers to franchise. The recent explosion of spas across the country does not concern her. She has her own way of dealing with the competition.[8]

Types of Franchising

In the United States, there are two major types of franchising: product and trade name franchising, and business format franchising.

Product and Trade Name Franchising

Product and trade name franchising consists primarily of product distribution arrangements in which the franchisee agrees to sell certain products or product lines. In this relationship, the dealer (franchisee) acquires the trade name, trademark, and/or product from the supplier (franchisor) and is thus identified with the supplier through the product line. Typical of this type of franchising are automobile and truck dealers, gasoline service stations, and soft drink bottlers. Together they dominate the franchise field, accounting for an estimated 70 percent of all franchise sales for 1988.[9]

Business Format Franchising

Business format franchising is typical of the newer types of franchising that range from restaurants and nonfood retailing to lodging, personal and business services, and real estate services. This type of franchising is characterized by an ongoing business relationship between franchisor and franchisee that includes not only the product, service, and trademark, but the entire business concept itself—a marketing strategy and plan, operating manuals and standards, quality control, and a continuing process of assistance and guidance.

The volume of sales and the number of units owned or franchised by business format franchisors have been responsible for much of the growth of franchising in the United States. In contrast to product and trade name franchises, which had approximately 141,000 establishments in 1988, the number of business format franchising establishments totaled approximately 368,000 in 1988,[10] although these franchises were responsible for only about 30 percent of total franchise sales.

FRANCHISING: ADVANTAGES AND DISADVANTAGES

Most franchising agreements are mutually beneficial to both the franchisor and the franchisee. The advantages to be gained from a successful franchising agreement are many. However, there are also some disadvantages to the franchisee.

Advantages of Franchising

The principal advantages of franchises are that a business can be started with a well-established product or service, limited experience, a relatively small amount of operating capital, a well-established product or service name, optimum operating efficiency, and access to management assistance and services.

Established Product or Service

The major advantage of franchising is that the franchisee enters a business that has the benefit of a proven and well-known product or service. The franchise has instant recognition in the market because the name and reputation of the product or service are already known to customers. This advantage is assured to the franchisee because franchisors spend large sums of money every year promoting their products or services.

Limited Experience

The franchisee takes advantage of the franchisor's experience, which might otherwise have to be obtained through risky trial and error. Franchisors use their experience in site selection, management, marketing, product research and development, and so on to enable franchisees to start and operate outlets with minimum friction. Indeed, the greatest difference between starting a franchised business and opening a business from scratch lies in the extensive training and preparation provided to the franchisee prior to the opening of an outlet. A franchisee is taught everything that is required to open, operate, and control the business.[11]

Relatively Small Amount of Operating Capital

In many cases a franchisee can open a franchise with less cash than if he or she were to open a business independently. Often a franchisee can start up with considerably less operating capital. A franchise may not require as much inventory as a comparable nonfranchised business, because the knowledge and experience of the franchisor concerning how much inventory is needed and when to reorder can dramatically reduce the potential for aging inventory, waste or spoilage of perishables, and unprofitable storage of low-demand items.[12]

Optimum Operating Efficiency

The utilization of automated equipment and sophisticated marketing techniques made available by the franchisor can reduce personnel needs and result in productivity gains. Examples include the introduction of computerized records for inventory control among retailing establishments and chain-wide reservation systems in franchised hotels and motels. In fast-food operations, technological standardization and central purchasing and advertising have reduced personnel requirements and permitted the extension of the limited-menu technique to chefless restaurants.

Management Assistance and Services

Under the franchising system, franchisors offer management assistance and various types of services on an ongoing basis. Among the services commonly offered are:

- Location analysis and counsel,
- Store development aid, including lease negotiation,
- Store design and equipment purchasing,
- Employee and management training, and continuing management counseling,
- Advertising and merchandising counsel and assistance,
- Standardized procedures and operations,
- Centralized purchasing and consequent savings,
- Financial assistance in the establishment of the business,
- Current marketing research findings.

It should be noted, however, that some franchisors have a bad reputation for service to franchisees. Anyone considering a franchise should be aware of this and should talk to other franchise owners to see how things really are.

Disadvantages of Franchising

Franchising does have some drawbacks that should be considered by potential franchisees. Contrary to what people may think, franchising is not a get-rich-quick deal that involves little effort in personal time and sacrifice.

Loss of Personal Identity and Control

A major disadvantage of franchising is the loss of personal identity and control to the parent company. Contrary to the "be your own boss" lures in franchise advertisements, the franchisee is not his or her own boss. In the first place, the personal identity of the franchisee is subjugated to the name of the franchisor. Second, the franchisor exercises control over policies and procedures of the franchisee. The franchising contract can contain restrictions or requirements that an independent businessperson would not have to worry about. This means that the franchisee loses the freedom to make decisions—to be his or her own boss.

Sharing Profits

The franchisor normally charges a royalty or a percentage of gross sales. This royalty fee must ultimately come out of the profits of the franchise, or be paid whether the franchise makes a profit or not. At times such fees are exorbitant—way out of proportion to the profit.

Strict Control over Standardized Operations

In order to maintain the distinctiveness and uniformity of the operation, the franchisor usually exercises some degree of continuing control over the operations of franchisees and requires them to meet stipulated operating standards. The extent of such control varies. In some cases franchisees are required to conduct every step of their operations in strict conformity with a manual furnished by the franchisor. In such cases it may be impossible to adjust operations to unique local market conditions. The franchisor may also require the franchisee to handle specific products or provide certain services that may not be profitable, to remain open during specified hours and days, and to follow other policies that are profitable to some but not all franchisees.

Duration of Franchise Relationship

The duration, renewal, termination, and transfer of a franchise agreement can present major disadvantages to franchisees. Virtually every franchise agreement contains provisions concerning these issues, and the relationship can be changed by the franchisor if the franchisee fails to abide by all the provisions of the franchising agreement.

In 1986, 73 percent of the currently operating business format franchising companies issued franchise agreements of lengths varying all the way from one year to perpetuity.[13] In all companies, these agreements provided an opportunity for the franchisee to enter into a new agreement at the end of the original term.

Of the 12,999 franchise agreements that came up for renewal in 1986, 93 percent were renewed. Of those not renewed, 21 percent were not renewed because of objections by the franchisor, 39 percent because the franchisee did not want to renew, and 40 percent by mutual agreement.[14]

There were 7,361 terminations (as opposed to nonrenewals) of franchise agreements in 1986, of which 3,075 (42 percent) were terminated by franchisors: 54 percent for nonpayment of royalties or other financial obligations, 7 percent for the franchisee's failure to comply with quality control standards, and 39 percent for other reasons not identified. Franchisees were responsible for terminating 3,914 (53 percent) franchise agreements, while an additional 372 (5 percent) were terminated by mutual consent.[15]

A total of 4,202 franchisees in 1986 asked permission from their franchisors to sell their franchises to other businesspeople; all but 94 (2 percent) transfers were approved.

THE SCOPE OF FRANCHISING

Retailing is the prime area of growth for the business format approach to franchising. Much of this growth has taken place in the restaurant business, convenience store operations, nonfood merchandising, auto products and services, the leisure and travel business, and business and personal services.

Retailing Dominates Franchising

Retailing dominates franchising, accounting for 87 percent of all franchising receipts in 1987.[16] The retail sales of all firms associated with franchising reached about $522 billion in 1987, or 34 percent of all U.S. retail sales, which are estimated at $1.5 trillion.

The marketplace will continue to diversify, with specialty retail stores offering more services and providing an increasing array of new products. Apparel stores, especially stores that sell women's ready-to-wear clothing, should show considerable gains.

Restaurants (All Types)

Franchise restaurants are faced with growing competition from within the industry and to a limited extent from supermarkets and specialty food stores that prepare take-out orders. Other competitors include department stores, which offer various options, ranging from fast-food outlets to expensive restaurants. Hotels also compete in this market through service in dining rooms and as caterers.

Restaurant franchisors are reacting to intensified competition in a variety of ways. They are redefining their objectives and returning to their original concepts, concentrating on food sales, broadening their menus, and maintaining good customer relations.

More and more franchisors are initiating home delivery service to satisfy growing consumer demand for this type of service. Home delivery is particularly successful in fast-food sales but is also spreading to gourmet-type restaurants making specialty dishes.

To compete with other restaurant chains, many franchise operators have become more customer-oriented and are offering such amenities as waiter/waitress service, self-service, and/or drive-in/drive-through service. Most restaurants offer one type or another; 20 franchisors offer two types of services, although one type clearly dominates.

Convenience Stores

Convenience food stores are an important factor in food retailing. Because of changing demographics and lifestyles, they have expanded rapidly, evolving into a large and sophisticated segment of food retailing. Many resemble scaled-down modern supermarkets and offer on-premises food service facilities and self-service gasoline.

Currently, food services (that is, restaurant-style foods and beverages prepared in the store for consumption elsewhere) is becoming more important. Almost all convenience stores offer some type of food service, at least hot beverages and fresh pastries. Many stores offer a wide variety of food service items: cold sandwiches, hot sandwiches, pizza, and hot dogs. Many stores have installed bulk soft drink (post-mix) dispensers because of higher profit margins compared with bottled or canned beverages.

Food Retailing Other than Convenience Stores

The retailing of food by specialty food shops, ice cream stores, coffee services, doughnut shops, bakeries, cookie shops, candy stores, nut stores, and others continues to grow. Two of the better known groups in this category are doughnut shops and ice cream and yogurt stores.

Nonfood Merchandising

Changing economic and demographic factors have created a large, sophisticated, and dynamic group of consumers. Retailing of nonfood general merchandise items is now a more competitive category because of improved buying and selling systems, new and better products, and new management techniques developed in recent years. To satisfy this growing trend, retailers are turning in large numbers to franchising.

This category includes a wide assortment of general merchandise retailing, such as catalogue stores, home appliances, drugs and cosmetics, gift shops, furniture, shoes and apparel, sporting goods, hardware, paints, consumer electronics, computers, and others.

Auto Products and Services

Retail outlets of tire manufacturers lead the auto product and service field. In addition to selling tires, radio and television sets, and other household appliances, most of these outlets perform a full range of auto services.

Other franchises in this category include small and specialized car washes, muffler shops, brake and diagnostic shops, lube and oil change centers, transmission shops, and general car-care centers—all growing in sales and number. With the closing of over 111,000 gasoline stations since 1972,[17] there is a rising demand for services in the huge automotive service and repair market. One of the fastest-growing categories in this group is quick lube and oil change shops.

Leisure and Travel Business

Americans are increasing their weekend and vacation travel, which, although affected periodically by changes in the economy, has grown steadily in recent years. Factors that have fostered this growth include expanded leisure time, rising disposable personal income, lower gasoline prices, and the mounting number of single-member households.

Hotels, Motels, and Campgrounds

The economy's rate of growth, shifting demographic patterns, the use of new technology, government policies, and the availability of qualified personnel will influence the size and direction of the lodging industry over the next five years. The trend toward diversification in the accommodations offered by hotel chains is expected to continue, although at a somewhat slower pace. The greatest growth is expected to occur in all-suite properties and the other end of the spectrum, inexpensive hotels with small rooms. Older citizens constitute a fast-growing segment of the population, and hotels are expected to launch more programs aimed at them.

Recreation, Entertainment, and Travel

Rising personal income, stable prices, and high levels of consumer optimism were expected to generate increased leisure and travel time. The downward shift in the strength of the U.S. dollar against many foreign currencies has helped to increase domestic travel. The number of Americans expected to take a vacation trip will grow, and their trips will get longer in both distance and duration. As a result, franchising firms engaged in the recreation, entertainment, and travel businesses are expanding rapidly.

The power of the press.

We handle it all–brochures, bulletins, business forms, flyers, labels, manuals, newsletters, reports, catalogs, stationery, press releases and menus, just to name a few. Come in today and let us put the power in your hands!

- **Graphic design & layout**
- **Color printing & copying**
- **Typesetting**
- **High-volume copying/duplicating**
- **Custom binding & finishing**
- **FAX approvals & communications**
- **Professional consultation**

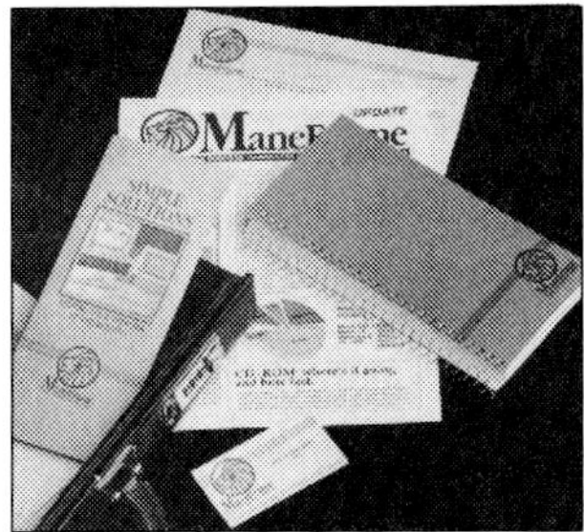

WE PRINT SUCCESS STORIES.®

(ADDRESS AND PHONE)

Printing and copying services is one of the industries that is relying more and more upon franchising as a means of doing business. Note space for insertion of the address and phone number of the individual franchisee. (Photograph and advertisement courtesy of Postal Instant Press (PIP) Printing)

Business and Personal Services

The rising demand for a variety of business and personal services, reflecting changing business service needs and shifting consumer spending patterns, is creating numerous opportunities for the franchise entrepreneur. An ever-widening array of business firms now rely on franchised establishments for such basic requirements as automobile and truck rentals, printing and copying services, tax preparation, accounting, educational services, and other business aids and services.

Business Aids and Services

Franchised businesses in this group include tax preparation, accounting, general business systems, employment services, printing and copying services, real estate, and a miscellaneous business sector that covers such diverse fields as business brokers, advertising, consulting services, marketing research, computer systems, fund raising, installation of security systems, and others.

Auto and Truck Rental Services

In a move to increase revenues, rental companies are stressing increased services, more movement into leasing, and new marketing procedures. Nearly all are offering flat fees with unlimited mileage. Some are stressing express booths at airports to speed up the rental process, and are aggressively selling to business executives and corporate accounts.

Construction, Home Improvements, and Cleaning Services

Franchising is a leading force in the growth of on-location cleaning of carpeting and upholstery in homes, mothproofing, soil and flame retarding treatments, static removal, and minor carpet repairing. Some firms furnish complete professional cleaning services that include the cleaning of walls, floors, and fixtures, while others specialize in sewer- and drain-cleaning services. Lawn and garden franchise services range from automated lawn care to consultation and analysis of lawn problems. Franchising has also pressed ahead in home remodeling construction, while other maintenance and improvement franchising businesses specialize in a variety of services such as water conditioning and porcelain and furniture refurbishing and repair. A rapidly growing category in this sector is franchisors providing cleaning or maid services.

Laundry and Drycleaning Services

The impact of new textile developments and improved home laundering equipment continues to lower consumer demand for professional laundry and drycleaning services. Many franchised laundry and drycleaning establishments have broadened their services to include drapery processing, rental of rug shampooers, and alteration work.

Educational Services

Businesses engaged in franchising educational services tend to be extremely specialized. For instance, increased leisure time has created a growing market for diet and exercise training centers that have been successfully promoted by many franchised systems. Franchisors have also entered the growing field of early childhood education with the establishment of day-care centers with modern learning and play equipment. The dominant type of franchisor operating in this category—in number of units and in sales—is weight reduction/diet control firms.

INVESTING IN A FRANCHISE

Anyone planning to invest in a franchise business should first make a thorough investigation. This should include an evaluation of his or her own skills and attitude toward the type of activity under consideration. It should also include a careful review of the terms and conditions of the franchise contract. No one should enter a contract without thoroughly understanding the terms of the agreement and the obligations it places on both parties. Review of a proposed contract or franchise agreement by a competent attorney is essential to the protection of a franchise.

The competition for a franchise from such well-known franchisors as McDonald's is fierce. Well over 2,000 people apply to become McDonald's franchisees in the United

The increased leisure time of many Americans has helped create a niche for many small businesses such as this health club. (Photograph © David Dempster)

States each year, but only about 150 applicants succeed.[18] It requires someone who is thrifty, clean, hard-working, and so forth. The company wants only owner-operators committed to working 12–to–18–hour days, seven days a week, personally managing their own stores. In general, applicants aged between thirty-five and forty and with at least 10 years business experience make the most likely candidates.[19] It also requires at least $66,000 in cash up front. Some successful applicants also say it helps to have something else—pull—although McDonald's officials deny that personal connections are needed to become one of their franchisees.

Small companies looking to expand through franchising indicate that there is a shortage of desirable people who want to buy franchises. They say that the competition to attract good candidates is impossibly tough in the face of established franchisers. Wallis Arnold, for example, who started International Sun Shade in 1988, thought he would have at least 25 franchises by 1989. Instead, he only had nine franchises.[20] Another franchisor, Hooper's, found only one qualified potential franchisee during three years of searching.[21]

An entrepreneur looking for franchising opportunities should consult the latest edition of the U.S. Department of Commerce *Franchise Opportunities Handbook.* This publication identifies franchisors who do not discriminate on the basis of race, color, or national origin in the availability, terms, or conditions of their franchises. The listing of equal-opportunity franchisors provides a brief summary of the terms, requirements, and conditions under which the franchises are available. The information included in each listing is provided primarily by the franchisor. Examples showing the type of information provided appear in Exhibit 6–3.

EXHIBIT 6–3 *Franchise Company Data of Selected Franchisors*

McDONALD'S CORPORATION
1 McDonald's Plaza
Oak Brook, IL 60521
Licensing Department

Description of Operation: McDonald's Corporation operates and directs a successful nationwide chain of fast-food restaurants serving a moderately priced menu. Emphasis is on quick, efficient service, high quality food, and cleanliness. The standard menu consists of hamburgers, cheeseburgers, fish sandwiches, French fries, apple pie, shakes, breakfast menu, and assorted beverages.

Number of Franchisees: Over 1,800 in the United States

In Business Since: 1955

Equity Capital Needed:

Conventional Franchise: $160,000 minimum from nonborrowed funds and ability to acquire outside financing for an additional $218,000 to $293,000.

Business Facilities Lease: $66,000 from nonborrowed funds.

Financial Assistance Available: None

Training Provided: Prospective franchisees are required to complete a structured training program which includes approximately 12–18 months of in-store training (on a part-time basis) and 5 weeks of classroom training. ➤

EXHIBIT 6–3 Franchise Company Data of Selected Franchisors *(continued)*

Managerial Assistance Available: Operations, training, maintenance, accounting, and equipment manuals provided. Company makes available promotional advertising material plus field representative consultation and assistance.

Information Submitted: May 1987

DOMINO'S PIZZA, INC.
3001 Earhart Rd.
P.O. Box 997
Ann Arbor, MI 48105
Deborah S. Sargent, National Director of Franchise Services

Description of Operation: Pizza carry-out and delivery service.

Number of Franchisees: Approximately 683 in the United States, Canada, West Germany, Australia, Hong Kong, Japan, and the United Kingdom.

In Business Since: 1960

Equity Capital Needed: $84,700 to $135,500.

Financial Assistance Available: Domino's Pizza does not directly provide financing but can refer to lending institutions who will consider providing financing to qualified franchisees.

Training Provided: Potential franchisees must complete the company's current training program which shall consist of both in-store training and classroom instruction.

Managerial Assistance Available: Domino's Pizza only franchises to internal people, and the kinds and duration of managerial and technical assistance provided by the company is set forth in the franchise agreement.

Information Submitted: May 1987

T. J. CINNAMONS, LTD.
555 Plaza Center Building
800 West 47th St.
Kansas City, MO 64112
Avery Murray, Vice President/Franchise Sales & Marketing

Description of Operation: T. J. Cinnamons operates and franchises retail bakery operations. These bakeries specialize in cinnamon-related bakery products. Bakeries range from 700 square feet to 1,200 square feet and are located in major shopping malls and strip centers. Units are open 7 days per week, approximately 12–14 hours per day.

Number of Franchisees: 106 in 30 States and Canada

In Business Since: 1985

Equity Capital Needed: Varies by territory, but a minimum of $100,000–$150,000.

Financial Assistance Available: None.

Training Provided: Intensive 12-day mandatory training course is required for each person who will be responsible for the overall day-to-day management of a bakery. This course is held in Kansas City and is tuition-free. A T. J. Cinnamons' trainer goes to help open the first two bakeries opening in each territory for a four-day period at each bakery.

Managerial Assistance Available: Assistance includes ongoing managerial, operations, and bakery consultation. Our Vice President/real estate assists with real estate contracts, lease

EXHIBIT 6–3 Franchise Company Data of Selected Franchisors (continued)

consultation, etc. Complete manuals and specifications for opening and operating a bakery are provided as is assistance in using this material. Advertising and marketing guidance is provided. T. J. Cinnamons also conducts ongoing market research into new products and monitors quality standards of the franchise operations.

Information Submitted: May 1987

THE SOUTHLAND CORPORATION
2828 North Haskell Ave.
Box 719
Dallas, TX 75204-0719
Wayne Beeder, Manager Franchise Affairs

Description of Operation: Convenience grocery stores (7–Eleven).

Number of Franchisees: 3,177 in 20 states plus District of Columbia.

In Business Since: 1927, franchised operations since 1964.

Equity Capital Needed: Total Investment Required: The cost of a Store's inventory and cash register fund average $38,806 and $773 respectively. The cost of all necessary business licenses, permits, and bonds is approximately $500. The franchise fee is computed for each store as follows: The initial franchise fee for a store that has not been continuously operated for the preceding 12 calendar months is an amount equal to 15% of the previous calendar year's annualized average per store month Gross profit (excluding Gross Profit from gasoline) for all stores located within the District in which the franchised store is or is to be located. If the store has been continuously operated for at least the preceding 12 calendar months, the franchise fee is an amount equal to 15% of that store's Gross Profit (excluding Gross Profit from gasoline) for the immediately preceding 12 calendar months.

Minimum Initial Investment: The minimum initial investment required includes the franchise fee, the amount of the cash register fund, and a portion of the cost of the initial inventory and of business licenses, permits, and bonds. Except where a franchisee transfers from one 7–Eleven Store to another, the franchisee is required to provide, in cash, as a portion of the cost of the inventory, a down payment of the greater of $12,500 or an amount equal to the average weekly sales of the Store for the prior 12 month period or such shorter time as the Store has been open.

Financial Assistance Available: The remainder of the investment in the inventory and of the cost of business licenses and permits may be financed with Southland, as well as the franchisee's continuing purchases and operating expenses.

Training Provided: 2 weeks in local training store and 1 week in a regional training center are provided.

Managerial Assistance Available: Continuing advisory assistance is provided by Field Consultants and other 7–Eleven personnel. 7–Eleven has been a member of The International Franchise Association (IFA) since beginning franchised operations.

Information Submitted: May 1987

FLOWERAMA OF AMERICA, INC.
3165 West Airline Highway
Waterloo, IA 50703
Chuck Nygren, Vice President

Description of Operation: Flowerama of America, Inc., franchise offers a unique and innovative approach to the retail floral business. Two types of stores (kiosk—450 square feet and in-line—

➤

EXHIBIT 6–3 **Franchise Company Data of Selected Franchisors** *(continued)*

1,000 square feet) located in prime locations in enclosed mall shopping centers only, offer fresh cut flowers, floral arrangements, potted plants, and other horticultural related products plus related floral accessories and gifts, to the consumer public at popular prices. Flowerama provides a service, from site selection to store design and construction under long-term leases to its franchisees.

Number of Franchisees: 86 in 23 States plus 12 company-owned shops.

In Business Since: 1966

Equity Capital Needed: $20,000 to $40,000 cash requirement.

Financial Assistance Available: Assists franchisee in obtaining financing from local bank. Supplies merchandise for resale on 30-day account basis.

Training Provided: 5 days at home office, 5 days on-the-job training and 10 days to 2 weeks at shop location.

Managerial Assistance Available: Flowerama provides continual management service for the life of the franchise in such areas as bookkeeping, advertising, store operations, inventory control. Complete manuals of operations, forms, and directions are provided. Field representatives and staff personnel are continually available to provide franchise owners with assistance in the operation of their retail floral shop.

Information Submitted: May 1987

H & R BLOCK INC.
4410 Main St.
Kansas City, MO 64111
Christopher Meck, Director, Franchise Operations

Description of Operation: The function of an H & R Block franchisee is to prepare individual income tax returns. The franchise is operated as a sole proprietorship or partnership. The only warranty made by the franchisee is to respect and uphold a specific code of ethics and to abide by the policy and procedures of the company.

Number of Franchisees: Over 8,800 offices throughout the United States, Canada and 17 foreign countries. Over 4,000 offices are franchised with the balance operated by the parent company.

In Business Since: 1946

Equity Capital Needed: $2,000–$3,000

Financial Assistance Available:

Training Provided: Each year a training program is held for all new owners. Prior to tax season each year, a training program for all employees is conducted in major centers. Each fall a meeting is held for all owners for 2–3 days to discuss all phases of the operation and new developments and ideas.

Managerial Assistance Available: We work very closely with our franchisees through a network of Satellite franchise directors and provide any and all assistance required or needed.

Information Submitted: May 1987

Source: U.S. Department of Commerce, International Trade Administration and Minority Business Development Agency, *Franchise Opportunities Handbook* (Washington, D.C.: U.S. Government Printing Office, January, 1988), 32, 110, 137, 151, 227.

Also important is an investigation of franchise outlets. Visits to outlets in other areas and discussions with the owners can reveal facts not otherwise available. In this process, assistance may be obtained from commercial firms such as Dun and Bradstreet, from local bankers or other local businesspeople, from the Council of Better Business Bureaus, and from the International Franchise Association.

In the long run, the best protection is to know one's legal rights, candidly evaluate one's own abilities, and thoroughly investigate a franchise before making a commitment to invest. This will take some time and effort at the outset, but one may save a great deal of time and money later on. A list of questions that are helpful in evaluating a franchise opportunity appears in Exhibit 6–4.

EXHIBIT 6–4 Checklist for Evaluating a Franchise

The Franchise

1. Did your lawyer approve the franchise contract you are considering after he or she studied it paragraph by paragraph?
2. Does the franchise call upon you to take any steps which are, according to your lawyer, unwise or illegal in your state, county, or city?
3. Does the franchise give you an exclusive territory for the length of the franchise, or can the franchisor sell a second or third franchise in your territory?
4. Is the franchisor connected in any way with any other franchise company handling similar merchandise or services?
5. If the answer to the last question is "yes," what is your protection against this second franchisor organization?
6. Under what circumstances can you terminate the franchise contract and at what cost to you, if you decide for any reason at all that you wish to cancel?
7. If you sell your franchise, will you be compensated for your goodwill, or will the goodwill you have built into the business be lost by you?

The Franchisor

1. How many years has the firm offering you a franchise been in operation?
2. Has it a reputation for honesty and fair dealing among the local firms holding its franchise?
3. Has the franchisor shown you any certified figures indicating exact net profits of one or more going firms which you personally checked yourself with the franchisee?
4. Will the firm assist you with:
   - A management training program?
   - An employee training program?
   - A public relations program?
   - Capital?
   - Credit?
   - Merchandising ideas?
5. Will the firm help you find a good location for your new business?
6. Is the franchising firm adequately financed so that it can carry out its stated plan of financial assistance and expansion?
7. Is the franchisor a one-man company or a corporation with an experienced management trained in depth so that there would always be an experienced man (or woman) at its head?
8. Exactly what can the franchisor do for you which you cannot do for yourself? ➤

EXHIBIT 6–4 **Checklist for Evaluating a Franchise** *(continued)*

9. Has the franchisor investigated you carefully enough to assure itself that you can successfully operate one of their franchises at a profit both to them and to you?
10. Does your state have a law regulating the sale of franchises and has the franchisor complied with that law?

The Franchisee

1. How much equity capital will you need to purchase the franchise and operate it until your income equals your expenses? Where are you going to get it?
2. Are you prepared to give up some independence of action to secure the advantages offered by the franchise?
3. Do YOU really believe you have the innate ability, training, and experience to work smoothly and profitably with franchisor, your employees, and your customers?
4. Are you ready to spend much or all of the remainder of your business life with this franchisor, offering his or her product or service to your public?

The Market

1. Have you made any study to determine whether the product or service which you propose to sell under franchise has a market in your territory at the prices you will have to charge?
2. Will the population in the territory given you increase, remain static, or decrease over the next five years?
3. Will the product or service you are considering be in greater demand, about the same, or less demand five years from now than today?
4. What competition exists in your territory already for the product or service you contemplate selling? Nonfranchise firms? Franchise firms?

Source: U.S. Department of Commerce, *Franchise Opportunities Handbook* (Washington, D.C.: U.S. Government Printing Office, 1988), xxxiii–xxxiv.

International Franchise Association

The **International Franchise Association (IFA)** is a nonprofit trade association representing more than 550 franchising companies in the United States and around the world.[22] It is recognized as the speaker for responsible franchising.

The IFA historically has supported the principle of full disclosure of all pertinent information to potential franchisees. It annually distributes thousands of copies of its booklet, "Investigate Before Investing," which provides guidance for potential franchisees. Its Code of Ethics and Ethical Advertising Code are widely respected. The Small Business Administration, in its booklet, "Franchising Index/Profile," reprints the codes and the IFA's membership requirements and suggests: "It is worth a letter to the IFA requesting a copy of the International Association Membership Directory to determine whether or not the franchise you are interested in is a member. The codes themselves are reassuring."[23]

Self-Evaluation

There are some important steps one can take to help reduce the risk before making a commitment to buy a franchise.[24]

The first step, and often the most difficult, is to take a hard look at oneself. One should ask whether or not one is really willing to make the personal sacrifices—long hours at the franchise, hard work, financial uncertainty—that are often necessary for a successful business. Does one enjoy working with others? Is one a good supervisor? Is one an organized person? Or is one simply attracted by the potential profits?

Some franchisors will help one take this careful look at oneself. A reputable franchisor, after all, is investing in a franchisee because the franchisor will profit from one's continued success. Others may only check to be sure that one has the necessary money or credit to invest. In that case, one should still ask the right questions for the self-evaluation. Family and friends can make an important contribution to one's self-evaluation, and their answers will probably be more objective than the answers of a franchise salesperson.

The second step is to investigate the franchisor and the franchise business as thoroughly as possible. The best way to proceed is to do what most people do when they buy a new car or a new home. One should do some comparison shopping, looking at more than one franchise, just as one would look at more than one car or house before deciding to buy.

Disclosure Statements

If the initial information received from a franchisor does not include a **disclosure statement** (sometimes called an *offering circular* or *prospectus)*, one should be sure to ask for one. It will be a great help in comparing one franchise with another, understanding the risks involved, and learning what to expect and what not to expect from the franchise in which one has decided to invest. One should study the disclosure statement carefully before making an investment decision.

A trade regulation rule—Federal Trade Commission (FTC) Rule 436.1—requires the nationwide use of disclosure statements. This document must contain comments that either positively or negatively respond to each disclosure subject required to be answered under the FTC Rule. Franchisors are also required by state law in 15 states to provide disclosure statements to protect prospective franchisees. The states requiring disclosure statements are: California, Connecticut, Illinois, Indiana, Maryland, Michigan, Minnesota, Nebraska, New York, North Dakota, Rhode Island, South Dakota, Virginia, Washington, and Wisconsin. The regulations vary, but in most of these states, franchisors must register with a government authority, such as the attorney general or securities division, before offering franchises for sale.

The disclosure statement required by the FTC will contain detailed information on some 20 different subjects that may influence one's decision to invest or not to invest:[25]

1. Information identifying the franchisor and its affiliates, and describing their business experience,
2. Information identifying and describing the business experience of each of the franchisor's officers, directors, and management personnel responsible for franchise services, training, and other aspects of the franchise program,
3. A description of the lawsuits in which the franchisor and its officers, directors, and management personnel have been involved,
4. Information about any previous bankruptcies in which the franchisor and its officers, directors, and management personnel have been involved,

5. Information about the initial franchise fee and other initial payments that are required to obtain the franchise,
6. A description of the continuing payments franchisees are required to make after the franchise opens,
7. Information about any restrictions on the quality of goods and services used in the franchise and where they may be purchased, including restrictions requiring purchases from the franchisor or its affiliates,
8. A description of any assistance available from the franchisor or its affiliates in financing the purchase of the franchise,
9. A description of restrictions on the goods or services franchisees are permitted to sell,
10. A description of any restrictions on the customers with whom franchisees may deal,
11. A description of any territorial protection that will be granted to the franchisee,
12. A description of the conditions under which the franchise may be repurchased or refused renewal by the franchisor, transferred to a third party by the franchisee, and terminated or modified by either party,
13. A description of the training programs provided to franchisees,
14. A description of the involvement of any celebrities or public figures in the franchise,
15. A description of any assistance in selecting a site for the franchise that will be provided by the franchisor,
16. Statistical information about the present number of franchises, the number of franchises projected for the future, the number of franchises terminated, the number the franchisor has decided not to renew, and the number repurchased in the past,
17. The financial statements of the franchisors,
18. A description of the extent to which franchisees must personally participate in the operation of the franchise,
19. A complete statement of the basis for any earnings claims made to the franchisee, including the percentage of existing franchises that have actually achieved the results that are claimed, and
20. A list of the names and addresses of other franchisees.

After having read the disclosure statement carefully, and having compared it to other disclosure statements, one should check the accuracy of the information disclosed. A good way to start is to contact several of the franchisees listed in the disclosure statement and ask them about their experience in the business. They can indicate whether the information provided, and any other claims that are made by the franchisor, accurately reflect their experience in the business.

One should talk to more than one franchisee. No single franchisee can ever be a very adequate representative of a franchise program. He or she is likely to be either better than the average franchisee or below average. If the franchise is worth considering at all, it should be worth one's time to talk to three or more franchisees. While one may want to talk to franchisees recommended by the franchisor, one should also make a point of talking to franchisees who have not been recommended.

One should look at franchisees who have been in the business for at least a year. If none have been in business that long because the franchise is a new one, the risks one will run by investing in the franchise will obviously be higher than those one would face if one invested, instead, in a well-established franchise with a track record.

One should also talk to franchisees who have been in business for only a few years. They are the ones who will be able to provide the best advice about what to expect during the first year of operation. That is important because the first year is often the period during which the success or failure of a new franchise is determined.

Earnings Claims

If the franchisor or its representative makes any claims about the sales, income, or profits one can expect from the franchise, one should examine these earnings claims carefully, and demand written substantiation for them.[26] One should remember that earnings claims are only estimates and there is absolutely no assurance that one will do as well.

Franchisors are now required by law in the 15 states identified earlier to provide detailed substantiation to prospective franchisees of any earnings claims they make. A trade regulation rule issued by the FTC extends that protection to prospective franchisees in every state.

This documentation of earnings claims, which will appear in either the disclosure statement or a separate document, is required whenever an earnings claim is made—whether it is presented orally, in writing, or in advertising or other promotional materials. It is required regardless of whether the earnings claim is based on actual or projected results, or on average figures for all franchisees as opposed to figures met by a small number of franchisees.

One should examine the documentation carefully and be certain that one understands the basis for the earnings claim and the assumptions that were made in preparing it. One should ask what would happen if an assumption proved to be wrong. For example: What if the wages one must pay employees turn out to be higher than predicted? What if one must pay a higher than usual rate of interest for any financing one needs in order to obtain the franchise?

If one does nothing else, one should note what percentage of the franchisor's present franchisees have actually had sales, profits, or income that equalled or exceeded the amount claimed. Then one should find out how many franchisees did that well during their first year of operation, when their operating results may not have been as good. One's own first-year operating results are more likely to be like those of other first-year franchisees than those of franchisees who have been in business for several years.

Franchise Agreements (Contracts)

A copy of the franchisor's standard franchise agreement must be given to the prospective franchisee when the Basic Disclosure Document is furnished. When properly constructed, the franchising agreement takes into account the interests of both franchisor and franchisee.

Typical elements commonly found in franchise agreements are as follows:[27]

- Franchising fee,
- Term and renewal,
- Franchisor–franchisee relationships,

- Site selection/location requirements,
- Franchisor approval to lease,
- Exclusive territory,
- Products and/or services available,
- Equipment and facilities,
- Business hours,
- Personnel (appearance and training),
- Advertising by franchisor and franchisee,
- Royalties,
- Maintenance and cleanliness,
- Standards of operation,
- Noncompetition,
- Reporting and bookkeeping, and
- Approval of sale by franchisor.

This list does not include the specific elements found in all franchise agreements, nor does it list all elements that might be included. Rather, this list indicates what is typically included in franchise agreements.

Legal Rights

The trade regulation rule issued by the Federal Trade Commission provides prospective franchisees a number of important legal rights under federal law:[28]

1. The right to receive a disclosure statement at the first personal meeting with a representative of the franchisor to discuss the purchase of a franchise,
2. The right to receive documentation stating the basis and assumptions for any earnings claims that are made at the time the claims are made,
3. The right to receive sample copies of the franchisor's standard franchise and related agreements at the same time as one receives the disclosure statement, and the right to receive final agreements one is to sign at least five business days before signing them,
4. The right to receive any refunds promised by the franchisor, subject to any conditions or limitations on that right that have been disclosed by the franchisor,
5. The right not to be misled by oral or written representations made by the franchisor or its representatives that are inconsistent with the disclosures made in the disclosure statement.

Additional rights are available under state law if one is a resident of a state with a franchise disclosure law, or if the franchise is to be located in such a state.

One final word of caution is important. One should not make the mistake of thinking that an investment in a franchise is risk-free, or virtually risk-free, just because federal or state law may provide some protection. That protection is subject to limitation, and may not be able to remedy every case.

As a result, investing in a franchise will always involve a certain degree of risk, which one can ignore only at one's own peril. It is always better to do everything possible to protect oneself than to be forced to rely on legal rights and potential remedies.

Obtaining Professional Advice

One would be well advised to obtain independent professional assistance in reviewing and evaluating any franchise that might be considered.[29] Such assistance is particularly important in reviewing the financial statements of the franchise and the franchise agreement to be signed.

The reason state and federal law requires franchisors to include their financial statements in the disclosure statement is to permit one to determine whether the franchisor has adequate financial resources to fulfill its commitments to the franchisees. The financial statements will reveal to a professional accountant, banker, or other experienced business advisor whether a franchisor's financial condition is sound, or whether there is a risk that it will not be able to meet its financial and other obligations.

Unless one has considerable business experience, one may need professional assistance in reviewing the franchisor's financial statements to determine whether special precautions should be taken to insure that one receives the services and assistance that have been promised in return for the investment. The costs of securing this advice before investing will be a small price to pay if it saves one from getting involved with a franchisor that cannot meet its obligations.

The advice of a lawyer is unquestionably the most important professional assistance to obtain before investing in a franchise. One should not make the mistake of assuming that the disclosure statement tells all that one needs to know about the consequences of signing a franchise agreement and related contracts. The disclosure statement is not designed to serve that purpose.

A lawyer can advise fully about one's legal rights if one enters a franchise agreement, and the obligations that will be legally binding on the franchisee as a result. In addition, a lawyer may be able to suggest important changes in the contracts one is asked to sign so that they will provide better protection for one's interests.

A lawyer will be able to offer advice about any requirements of state and local law that will affect the franchised business, and to assist with the taxation and personal liability questions that must be considered in establishing any new business.

The cost of obtaining legal advice will be relatively small in comparison to the total investment for a franchise. Moreover, the cost of legal advice at the outset is invariably less than the cost of later representation to solve legal problems that could have been avoided in the first place.

At the very least, one should be certain that every promise one considers to be important made by the franchisor and its representative is stated clearly and in writing in the franchise agreement. If such promises do not clearly appear in the contracts signed, one may be legally required to comply with one's own continuing obligations under the franchise agreement.

FRANCHISING TRENDS AND OUTLOOK

Franchising, still in a relative state of infancy compared to the life span of other marketing methods, has played an important role in the evolution of the service sector of the American economy.[30] All trends indicate that franchising will continue to expand rapidly, creating great opportunities for existing and new businesses, developing new entrepreneurs, new jobs, new products, new services, and providing new export opportunities for firms engaged in franchising.

Rising personal income, stable prices, high levels of consumer optimism, and increased competition for market share are causing many companies, both small and large, to turn to franchising. More than 500 companies became franchisors in the two-year period ending in 1987; this growth trend is expected to continue for the next few years. Franchising can enable these new franchisors to saturate existing markets or penetrate new markets at minimal cost.

Education will play an important role in the evolution of franchising, as programs related to franchising are increasingly being taught in courses in small business management, entrepreneurship, and marketing. In colleges and universities throughout the United States, the study of franchising is becoming recognized as a new and important part of business studies.

Changing patterns in U.S. household formation, coupled with the new status of working women in our society, are influencing the entry of women into franchising in larger numbers than ever before. Franchising is offering new opportunities for women who are entering the professional and management ranks and want to be part of the business world or to invest in a business career. Starting their own businesses through franchising lessens the risk factors for women with little or no business experience. A study of 124 franchisors ranging from fast food to day-care centers taken by a Boston-based company, Women in Franchising, indicated that 11 percent of current franchisee-owned outlets are run solely by women. Additionally, 18 percent of franchisee-owned outlets are run by female–male partners.

Furthermore, a slowly growing U.S. population, shifting demographic patterns, and the use of new technology have intensified competition among franchising companies. These factors have increased the number of mergers and acquisitions in the franchising system, and it is expected that this will persist during the next few years.

Some specific franchise areas that bear scrutiny in the 1990s are quick lube and oil change centers, diet services, beauty salons, maid services, temporary help services, carry-out restaurant services, and expansion by U.S. franchisors to foreign markets throughout the world.

In summary, major changes are in progress in the economy as a whole. As we move into the 1990s, creativity and imagination in the treatment of goods and services will be richly rewarded. Education, computer usage, and the ability to work with and manage people will be profitably utilized by new emerging businesses. All these developments suggest that franchising will be the leading method of doing business in the 1990s.

SUMMARY

1. Franchising represents the entrepreneur's best chance to compete with giant companies that dominate the marketplace.
2. Franchising is a business opportunity in which the owner (franchisor) of a service or a trademark product grants exclusive rights to an individual (franchisee) for the local distribution and/or sale of the service or product.
3. The two types of franchising are product and trade name franchising, and business format franchising.
4. The principal advantages of franchising include public recognition of the franchisor's product or service, optimum operating efficiency, relatively small amount of operating capital required, and various management services provided to the franchisee on an ongoing basis.
5. Some drawbacks of franchising are the loss of

personal identity and control, sharing of profits, and potential problems with the duration, termination, and transfer of a franchise agreement.

6. Total retail sales of all firms associated with franchising accounts for slightly more than one third of total retail sales in the economy.
7. Numerous franchising opportunities are found in all types of restaurants; convenience stores; nonfood merchandising; auto parts and services; leisure and travel businesses; hotels, motels, and campgrounds; recreation and entertainment; and business and personal services.
8. When considering franchise opportunities, one should make a thorough investigation of the franchisor, the product or service, the franchise agreement, disclosure statements, and earnings claims.
9. One of the most important steps to take before making a commitment to buy a franchise is a critical self-evaluation.
10. The International Franchise Association supports the principle of full disclosure of all pertinent information to potential franchisees.
11. The Federal Trade Commission requires that detailed information be provided in the disclosure statement on some 20 different subjects. In addition, 15 states require disclosure statements to protect prospective franchisees.
12. One is well advised to obtain independent professional assistance from accountants, bankers, and lawyers when reviewing and evaluating any franchise. This pertains especially to financial statements in the disclosure statement.
13. The advice of a lawyer is unquestionably the most important professional assistance to obtain before investing in a franchise.
14. All trends indicate that franchising will continue to expand rapidly in the 1990s.

KEY TERMS AND CONCEPTS

Franchising
Franchise
Franchisor
Franchisee
Franchise agreement
Product and trade name franchising
Business format franchising
Disclosure statement

QUESTIONS FOR DISCUSSION

1. What is the definition of franchising? Franchisor? Franchisee?
2. What is the difference between product and trade name franchising and business format franchising?
3. What are the major advantages of franchising?
4. What are the major disadvantages of franchising?
5. In relation to total retail sales in the economy, where does franchising fit in?
6. In what sectors of retailing is franchising especially popular?
7. What services are increasingly being franchised?
8. Why should franchise opportunities be thoroughly investigated?
9. Where can a potential franchisee obtain information about franchise opportunities?
10. What role does the International Franchise Association serve in franchising?
11. What type of information is provided in the disclosure statement?
12. What are typical elements commonly found in franchise agreements?
13. What are the important legal franchise rights under federal law?
14. From what sources can independent professional assistance be obtained?
15. What is the outlook for franchising in the 1990s?

SELF-TEST REVIEW

Multiple Choice Questions

1. The company that licenses another business to sell its products or services in a specific geographical area is:
   a. The franchisee.
   b. The franchisor.
   c. The retailer.
   d. None of the above.
2. Which of the following is a disadvantage of franchising?
   a. Large amount of operating capital required.
   b. Large amount of control required.
   c. Large amount of experience required.
   d. All of the above.
3. Under Federal Trade Commission rules, franchisors must provide:
   a. The Basic Disclosure Statement.
   b. The Earnings Claim document if any claims are made about actual or potential earnings.
   c. Copies of the proposed franchise agreement.
   d. All of the above.
4. Which of the following factors needs to be investigated by anyone planning a franchise agreement?
   a. The franchise contract.
   b. The demand for products and services.
   c. The experience of existing franchisees.
   d. All of the above.
5. Which of the following is not a legal right under federal law?
   a. The right to receive a disclosure statement.
   b. The right to earn profits.
   c. The right to receive refunds promised by the franchisor.
   d. The right to receive documentations stating the basis and assumptions for any earnings claims made.

True/False Statements

1. Business format franchising dates from before the turn of the century.
2. Franchisees do not have to give up any of their independence regarding business decisions.
3. One of the advantages of franchising is that the franchisee is guaranteed an adequate income.
4. Franchisors provide both management and financial assistance to franchisees.
5. Franchisors may not require franchisees to remain open 24 hours a day.
6. The greatest dollar volume of sales in franchising is from fast-food restaurants.
7. The Federal Trade Commission encourages, but does not require, the nationwide use of disclosure statements.
8. Franchise agreements should take into account the interests of both franchisor and franchisee.
9. The advice of an accountant is unquestionably the most important professional advice to obtain before investing in a franchise.
10. Indications are that franchising will be the leading method of doing business in the 1990s.

MANFRED'S FLOWER BASKET

David Lindley, age twenty-three, has recently graduated from a state college with a major in floriculture. Now he wants to enter the florist industry by opening his own store. A trend that one of his professors had discussed at length during Lindley's last semester is the growth of franchised flower shops nationwide. Lindley remembers that being a franchisee has several distinct advantages, and having had little experience in the industry, he is considering contacting Manfred's Flower Basket, one of the fastest-growing franchised chains.

Manfred's, the franchisor, offers a six-week training course at the home store for any prospective franchisee who has little or no experience. Upon completion of the course, the participant is given the opportunity to purchase an exclusive franchise for a specified geographic region. The required investment of $35,000 includes the fee and the cost of site selection, as well as the necessary fixtures, such as refrigerators and display cases. It does not include the deliverv vehicle, a requirement for every franchise. Royalties are 6 percent of gross sales and an additional 6 percent for advertising. Although advertising has been limited, Manfred's promises that a region-wide promotion campaign is about to begin.

In addition to the $35,000 investment, Lindley can count on spending $25,000 more for the necessary inventory of plants, fresh flowers, dried flowers, terrariums, and various supplies. The minimum capital required to start the franchise is therefore $60,000. Manfred's does not offer any assistance in financing the business.

Essentially, Manfred's provides a business format franchising for flower shops. Existing franchisees, a total of seven, receive a fully integrated relationship that includes the name Manfred's Flower Basket, a proven marketing strategy, operations manuals and standards to which each franchisee is exposed during the six-week training course, and the opportunity to purchase any needed inventory on a low-cost cooperative basis among all franchisees.

Lindley certainly has the drive and enthusiasm to open a flower shop. Although he lacks the needed capital, he believes that sufficient money could be raised from relatives, friends, the Small Business Administration, and possibly the sale of his $22,000 sailboat. He also feels a strong urge to be his own boss and to have the freedom to run the business with little outside interference. For example, he wants to offer an innovative plant care and maintenance program based on his frequent observations of sickly looking plants in public places. Manfred's Flower Baskets are strictly retail outlets providing flowers and arrangements for every occasion. Plant rentals and maintenance programs are not part of the format provided.

Two important florist industry trends are the location of florist shops in shopping centers and the growth of retail florist chains. In addition, a large portion of the floral market is being taken by nonflorists, including food stores, drugstores, and discount stores. Fortunately, Manfred's site selections are always in shopping centers. Manfred's experience and past success with shopping center developers is the envy of many in the industry. Lindley has no idea what might be involved in securing rental space in a shopping center and what to be aware of.

Manfred's Flower Baskets average $150,000 in annual sales. Total operating expenses average 42 percent, or $63,000 annually. The cost of merchandise for this size of operation runs about 40 percent or $60,000 annually, leaving a net profit after taxes of 18 percent, or $27,000.

Lindley has to make a decision about whether to start a flower shop from scratch or enter into a franchise agreement with Manfred's Flower Basket. He feels somewhat uncomfortable with Manfred's disclosure document, which fails to mention anything about restrictions of sales; termination, cancellation, and renewal of the franchise; guarantees of any kind; and franchisee participation in the advertising program that was designed to help all franchisees. The loss of personal identity and control should he open a Manfred's Flower Basket also bothers Lindley somewhat. In spite of these concerns, Lindley keeps remembering what his professor told his class about the advantages of franchising.

QUESTIONS

1. What can Lindley do to lessen his worries about some of the unknown aspects of Manfred's Flower Basket operation?
2. Does the franchising route appear to be the best choice for Lindley? Why or why not?

NOTES

1. Dennis L. Foster, *The Rating Guide to Franchises* (New York: Facts on File Publication, 1988), front flap.
2. U.S. Department of Commerce, *Franchising in the Economy, 1986–1988* (Washington, D.C.: U.S. Government Printing Office, February 1988), 1.
3. "Overseeing Overseas: Franchisors Go Abroad," *The Wall Street Journal*, November 2, 1989, B1.

4. Excerpted from *Franchising in the Economy, 1986–1988,* 1.
5. David M. Roth, "The Secret? Easy Does It," *Venture,* November, 1987, 38.
6. Echo M. Garrett, "Ten Franchises on a Fast Track," *Venture,* March, 1989, 21–28.
7. Robert Justis and Richard Judd, *Franchising* (Cincinnati: South-Western Publishing Co., 1989), 6.
8. Based on Cable News Network's "Pinnacle," April 22, 1989. Guest: Deborah Szekely, Golden Door.
9. *Franchising in the Economy, 1986–1989,* 1.
10. *Ibid.*, 4.
11. Justis and Judd, 35.
12. *Ibid.*, 38.
13. *Franchising in the Economy, 1986–1989,* 13.
14. *Ibid.*, 14.
15. *Ibid.*
16. This section is excerpted from *Franchising in the Economy, 1986–1989,* 14–25.
17. *Ibid.*, 20.
18. Barbara Marsh, "Going For The Golden Arches," *The Wall Street Journal,* May 1, 1989, B1.
19. *Ibid.*
20. Jeffrey A. Tannenbaum, "Small Companies Lament a Lack of Willing Franchisees," *The Wall Street Journal,* November 14, 1989, B1.
21. *Ibid.*
22. Excerpted from U.S. Department of Commerce, *Franchising Opportunities Handbook* (Washington, D.C.: U.S. Government Printing Office, January, 1988), xli.
23. *Ibid.*, xli.
24. *Ibid.*, xxx.
25. *Ibid.*
26. *Ibid.*
27. Adopted from Edward L. Dixon, Jr., Editor, *The 1988 Franchising Annual* (New York: Info Press, 1988), H52.
28. Excerpted from *Franchising Opportunities Handbook,* xxxii.
29. *Ibid.*, xxxi.
30. Excerpted from *Franchising in the Economy, 1986–1988,* 5–6.

CHAPTER SEVEN

Legal Forms of Ownership

CHAPTER OUTLINE

LEARNING OBJECTIVES *The objectives of this chapter are to assist you in understanding:*

1. What constitutes a sole proprietorship, and its advantages and disadvantages.
2. What constitutes a partnership, and its advantages and disadvantages.
3. What constitutes a corporation, and its advantages and disadvantages.
4. What is involved in incorporating a small business.
5. Why the role of a lawyer is crucial in deciding on the legal form of ownership.

Prospective or current owners of small businesses need to consider several factors in deciding which form of ownership to adopt. Among the most important of these considerations are:

- Federal and state income tax laws,
- Need for additional capital,
- Need for certain managerial expertise,
- Need to limit liability for business debts, and
- Desire for business continuity.

Ownership of a business may take several different legal forms, each of which carries certain rights and responsibilities. Each form has distinct rules regarding taxation, management, liabilities of the owner, and division of profits. Furthermore, each form of business organization has advantages and disadvantages. It is therefore not surprising that there is no single best legal form of ownership. Legal advice is necessary to determine which form is most appropriate for any one particular business establishment.

KINDS OF BUSINESS OWNERSHIP

The three principal forms of business structure are the sole proprietorship, the partnership, and the corporation. These legal forms of organization are usually defined as follows:

A **sole proprietorship** is a business that is the legal extension of its owner. It is owned and operated by one person.

A **partnership** is a business with more than one owner, legally organized to remove the owners from personal liability for business operations while taxing the owners as individuals. It is a voluntary association of two or more persons to carry on as co-owners a business for profit under the Uniform Partnership Act.

A **corporation** is a business that is chartered by the state and legally operates as an entity separate from its owners. It is an artificial being, invisible, intangible, and existing only in contemplation of the laws.

The major characteristics of sole proprietorships, partnerships, and corporations are listed in Exhibit 7–1. Exhibit 7–2 presents an overview of situations that are more or less favorable to each of the principal forms of organization.

Business Firms by Legal Form of Organization

Almost all small businesses, including those operated as part-time ventures, are sole proprietorships. Corporations, the second-most common form of business, are the most common form of business structure for large firms. The least common form of business structure is the partnership, and most of those are relatively small businesses.

Exhibit 7–3 shows that in 1985 some 70.5 percent of all business firms in the United States were sole proprietorships. The corporate form of organization represented 19.4 percent of all firms in 1985, while partnerships accounted for 10.1 percent.

EXHIBIT 7–1 Comparison of Major Characteristics of Business Organizations

Characteristics	Type of Organization			
	Sole Proprietorships	*General Partnerships*	*Limited Partnerships*	*Corporations*
Costs, procedures in starting	Easiest to get started. Costs are low. Usually only a license is needed.	Also easy. An oral or written agreement is acceptable.	More difficult to set up. File with the state. Written contract.	More complicated. Follow strict state procedures.
Liability	Personally liable for all debts—to extent of personal property.	Responsible for the debts of the partnership.	Only the capital that they have invested.	Only to the limit of assets of the corporation.
Continuity	No time limit by law. Are not usually perpetual.	Usually terminated by a death or withdrawal.	Same as general partnership.	Most permanent of all.
Legal restriction	None between states. State is required to acknowledge, even if not based in that state. Are liable to each state's laws.	Same as for sole proprietorship.	Same as for sole proprietorship.	No other state is required to recognize the corporation. Must comply with special regulations.
Attraction of capital	By borrowing, buying on credit, or investing own capital.	Easier, as more people to invest own money. Also easier to borrow.	Same as for general partnership.	Usually in the best position. Sell stocks or securities.
Management authority	Policy and operation rests in one individual. Sometimes delegated to others, but main responsibility on owner.	Each partner has an equal role. Can lead to policy disagreements.	May not engage in management functions. Can otherwise become liable financially.	Centralized in a small group of executives.

Although sole proprietorships are the dominant legal form of ownership, they accounted for only 5.8 percent of total business receipts in 1985, whereas corporations accounted for 90.2 percent of receipts, and partnerships for 4.0 percent. On the other hand, proprietorships accounted for 24.8 percent of net income in 1985, while corporations realized 75.2 percent of total net income. Partnerships reported a net loss.

EXHIBIT 7–2 Principal Forms of Business Organization Compared*

Qualities	Sole Proprietorship	Partnership		Corporation		
		General	Limited	Small Single Owner	Small Several Owners	Large Publicly Held
Ease of starting	1	2	3	4	4	5
Cost of organizing	1	2	3	4	4	5
Credit rating (without personal cosigning)	4	2	3	5	5	1
Credit rating (with personal cosigning)	4	2	3	2	2	—
Access to risk capital	5	4	3	2	2	1
Flexibility	1	3	2	1	3	4
Ease of expansion	6	4	3	5	2	1
Access to skilled professional management	4	2	3	3	2	1
Government regulation of firm	1	2	3	4	5	6
Ease of offsetting firm losses (e.g., interest, depreciation)	1	1	1	2	2	2
Ease of transferability of ownership equity	6	5	2	4	3	1
Continuity ("perpetual life")	4	3	3	3	2	1
Ease of termination (when desired)	1	2	3	4	4	5
Liability of firm owners for debts of the firm ("unlimited liability")	2	3	1	1	1	1

*A "1" indicates most favorable situations; higher numbers are less favorable

Note: Individual circumstances may cause deviation from the ratings

SOLE PROPRIETORSHIP

The sole proprietorship form of ownership is ideal for the small enterprise, especially when it is just starting. At the formative stages of operation, this is the simplest form of business organization.

As a sole proprietor, this owner of a small restaurant is in direct control of his business. All the profits go directly to him, his start-up costs were relatively low, and he is not liable for double taxation that corporations must pay. (Photograph © Ann M. Mason)

EXHIBIT 7–3

Business Firms by Legal Form of Organization: Number of Firms, Receipts, and Net Income—1985

Item	Unit	1985
Number		
Proprietorships	1,000	$11,929 (70.5%)
Partnerships	1,000	1,714 (10.1%)
Corporations	1,000	3,277 (19.4%)
Receipts		
Proprietorships	Bil. $	540 (5.8%)
Partnerships	Bil. $	368 (4.0%)
Corporations	Bil. $	8,398 (90.2%)
*Net Income (less deficit)**		
Proprietorships	Bil. $	79 (24.8%)
Partnerships†	Bil. $	−9 (0.0%)
Corporations	Bil. $	240 (75.2%)

*Net income (less deficit) is defined differently by form of organization, basically as follows: (a) Proprietorships: Total taxable receipts less total deductions, including cost of sales and operations; investment and other income are excluded. (b) Partnerships: Total taxable receipts less total deductions, including cost of sales and operations; investment and other income, except capital gains, are included. (c) Corporations: Total taxable receipts less total deductions, including cost of sales and operations; investment and other income, such as capital gains and income from foreign corporations considered received for tax purposes only, are included; net income is before income tax.

†Net losses in partnerships are not included in the totals.

Source: U.S. Department of Commerce, *Statistical Abstract of the United States,* 1989 (Washington, D.C.: U.S. Government Printing Office, 1987), 516.

In the sole proprietorship, individuals engage in business on their own account. The business has no existence apart from the owner. Therefore there is no legal distinction between the business and the owner's (proprietor's) private affairs. The liabilities of the business are the personal liabilities of the proprietor, and the owner's proprietary interest terminates at the owner's death. The proprietor undertakes the risks of business to the extent of all assets, whether used in the business or personally owned.

A small business owner might well select the sole proprietorship to begin with. Later, if the owner succeeds and feels the need, he or she can form a partnership or corporation.

Management Advantages of Sole Proprietorships

The sole proprietorship form of business ownership has several advantages that help explain its widespread use:

1. *Ease and low cost of starting*—a major advantage of the sole proprietorship is the ability to start a business with few legal complications and low start-up costs. It needs little or no government approval and is usually less expensive than a partnership or a corporation.
2. *All profits to the owner*—the sole proprietorship allows the owner to receive all profits earned in the business.

3. *Owner is in direct control*—the owner has freedom to manage and operate the business without consulting other parties. Being one's own boss is a major attraction of the sole proprietorship.
4. *Tax savings are realized*—special taxes levied against the corporate form of ownership are not applicable. The owner is taxed, not the business.
5. *Minimum legal restrictions*—sole proprietorships enjoy the greatest freedom from regulations.
6. *Freedom to terminate the business*—termination of the business is accomplished easily because no legal procedures are necessary.

Management Disadvantages of Sole Proprietorships

Some major disadvantages of the sole proprietorship include the following:

1. *Owners have unlimited liability*—the individual owner is legally liable for all debts of the business. This means that the owner's personal property, such as house and car, may be attached by creditors.
2. *Lack of continuity*—the life of the business is limited to the life of the owner. This means that the business is dissolved on permanent illness, death, or bankruptcy of the individual or owner.
3. *Difficulty in raising capital*—owners of sole proprietorships must rely on their own ability to borrow money in order to start the business and finance the operation. Consequently, earning potential is limited.
4. *Limited opportunities for employees*—basically, employees of the firm will always remain employees. The owner may thus be unable to attract and/or keep highly qualified people who seek opportunities to manage, operate, and share in the profits of the business.

PARTNERSHIP

The Uniform Partnership Act, adopted by many states, defines a partnership as "an association of two or more persons to carry on as co-owners of a business for profit." Though not specifically required by the Act, written Articles of Partnership are strongly recommended and customarily executed. These articles outline the contribution by the partners to the business (whether financial, material, or managerial) and generally delineate the roles of the partners in the business relationship.

There are two types of partnerships—the general partnership and the limited partnership. In a **general partnership** all participants are required to have at least one *general partner* who must carry the burden of financial liabilities of the entire enterprise. It is the least popular form of organization. A **limited partnership** is a partnership of one or more general partners who manage the business and are personally responsible for partnership debts, and one or more limited partners who contribute capital, share in profits, but take no part in running the business and incur no liability for partnership obligations beyond their contribution. As long as the *limited partner* does not participate in the management and control of the enterprise or in the conduct of its business, the limited partner is generally not subject to the same liabilities as a general partner.

Peter Peterson (left) and Stephen Schwartzman (right), former colleagues at Lehman Brothers, formed a private investment firm, The Blackstone Group. As general partners they slowly built up their business of advising multinational clients on multibillion dollar deals to 100 employees. (Photographs courtesy of The Blackstone Group)

The general partnership can be a very effective form of organization provided the partners are right for each other. According to Peter Peterson, chairman of The Blackstone Group (a small merchant bank Peterson started with former Lehman Brothers colleague Stephen Schwartzman), a good partnership has two ingredients.[1] One is a very good personal chemistry and the other is complementarity. Schwartzman and Peterson had a very happy and successful relationship at Lehman, which they continue to use to good advantage as partners of The Blackstone Group.

Joseph Baum, maestro in the restaurant business, also attributes much of his firm's success to his longtime partners, Michael Whiteman and Dennis Sweeney.[2] Now that their Rainbow Room atop Rockefeller Plaza is complete, they are working on another major project, not in the Big Apple, but in Taiwan. The partnership's success is testimony to what the right partners can accomplish.

Partnerships can easily dissolve, however, when the partners disagree over business strategy. This is illustrated by the experiences of two entrepreneurs, former students at the University of Cincinnati and later partners in the manufacture and sale of radar detectors. Early prosperity enjoyed by the partners brought disagreements over strategy. Eventually, the partnership was terminated. Although both partners came away with a great deal of money, they also came away with extremely hard feelings. According to one of the partners, "I think if the company had plodded along and we were making reasonable salaries, we'd still be good friends."[3]

Some characteristics that distinguish a partnership from other forms of business organization are the limited life of a partnership, the unlimited liability of at least one partner, co-ownership of the assets, the sharing of management, and the sharing of partnership profits.

Types of Partners

Partners' rights and responsibilities may differ with respect to the management of the enterprise and sharing in its profits and the extent of its liabilities. The major types of partners include:

1. **General Partner.** A general partner has unlimited liability for the firm's debts. General partners may therefore have to furnish money, in addition to the initial investment in the business, from their own personal assets to pay the debts of the partnership. The general partner(s) can enter into contracts in the name of the partnership and usually take an active part in its operation.
2. **Limited Partner.** A limited partner's liability in the partnership is limited to his or her financial investment in the firm. The partner knows in advance the extent of possible losses. The contributions of a limited partner may be cash or other

property, but not services. As such, a limited partner is like a shareholder in a corporation, that is, primarily an investor. A limited partner can take no part in the management or operation of the business, nor is the limited partner an agent for the partnership.
3. **Silent Partner.** A silent partner is a limited partner who does not participate actively in managing the firm and whose role in the partnership is not disclosed to the public.
4. **Secret Partner.** A secret partner is a limited partner who actively participates in managing the firm but whose role as a partner is not disclosed to the public.
5. **Dormant Partner.** A dormant partner is a limited partner who does not actively participate in managing the firm and whose role in the partnership is not disclosed to the public.
6. **Nominal Partner.** A nominal partner is not an actual partner (owner) of the firm, but allows his or her name to be identified with the business. Promotional benefits are realized from using a well-known name, such as a celebrity's, for which the person is usually paid a fee.

Articles of Partnership

The agreement to form a partnership, sometimes known as the Copartnership Articles, is actually a written agreement containing the articles on which the partners have agreed. Articles of partnership typically cover the following points:

1. Name and location of the firm,
2. Names of partnership owners,
3. Date the partnership is formed,
4. Nature and scope of the business,
5. Duration of the partnership agreement,
6. Amount of each partner's financial contribution,
7. Distribution of profits or losses,
8. Provisions for salaries of partners,
9. Each partner's duties and responsibilities,
10. Provision for accounting systems and their accessibility to partners,
11. Procedures for arbitration of disputes,
12. Terms of withdrawal of any partner,
13. Procedures for dissolving the partnership, and
14. Distribution of net assets if dissolved.

Uniform Limited Partnership Act

The **Uniform Limited Partnership Act** provides for formation of a limited partnership. It requires that two or more persons desiring to form such a partnership shall sign and swear to a certificate that contains the following information:

1. Name of the partnership,
2. Character of the business,

3. Location of the principal place of business,
4. Name and place of residence of each member,
5. Designation of general and limited partners,
6. Amount of cash and any other property contributed by each limited partner,
7. Additional contributions, if any, to be made by each limited partner and the times at which they shall be made,
8. Times, if agreed on, when the contribution of each limited partner is to be returned,
9. Share of profits or other compensation by way of income, which each limited partner is entitled to receive.

Management Advantages of Partnerships

The advantages of partnerships include:

1. *Ease of formation*—all that is essentially needed in a partnership is an agreement between the partners. The copartnership articles are usually prepared in writing, but an oral contract is acceptable.
2. *Additional sources of capital*—since partnerships have two or more owners, more sources of funds may be available than in the case of the sole proprietorship. Banks may also be willing to loan more money when two or more owners are responsible for repayment of the debt.
3. *Broader management base*—each partner may have expertise and responsibility in different functions of the firm, such as production, advertising, selling, or financing. The firm can therefore draw on a greater internal pool of talent.
4. *Possible tax advantages*—as with the sole proprietorship, partners are taxed as individuals, and no specific tax is levied against the partnership.
5. *Employee incentives*—a loyal and highly competent employee can be made a partner of the firm, providing an incentive for remaining with the business.

Management Disadvantages of Partnerships

The major disadvantages of a partnership include:

1. *Unlimited liability*—general partners have unlimited liability. If the assets of the partnership are insufficient to meet its obligations, creditors may sue any of the general partners to settle the debt. An individual partner may thus be obligated to repay the debts of the partnership from his or her personal assets.
2. *Divided authority*—since the partnership consists of two or more owners, authority is divided and decisions may be difficult to reach. If the partners cannot compromise, the only recourse may be to dissolve the partnership.
3. *Lack of continuity*—a partnership has a limited and uncertain life. It can be terminated by the partners themselves at any time or in the event of death of any partner.
4. *Frozen investment*—it is often difficult for a partner to withdraw his or her investment. Buying out a partner can be difficult, unless specifically arranged for in the written agreement.

5. *Capital limitations*—a partnership has relative difficulty in obtaining large sums of capital.

THE CORPORATION

The corporate form of ownership is used in a variety of business situations, and represents an organizational structure entirely different from the sole proprietorship or partnership. A corporation is a legal entity separate and distinct from its owners (stockholders), employees, and officers. In 1819, the U.S. Supreme Court defined the corporation as "an artificial being, invisible, intangible, and existing only in contemplation of the laws," and more recently, as "an association of individuals united for some common purpose, and permitted by law to use a common name, and to change its members without dissolution of the association." This means that a corporation is recognized by the courts as a legal person and a business entity that can sue and be sued, manage its own affairs, and own and sell property.

Countless entrepreneurs dream of building their businesses to the point that they can go public, that is, sell stock to public investors. Based on the experience of some entrepreneurs, however, this dream may be vastly overrated. When the principal owner of a marine hardware company took the company public, the money spent on attorneys, accountants, and general public relations was "difficult to swallow. That's when the fun stopped," according to the founder of the company. "Suddenly the rules of the game are changed and everything's driven by the bottom line."[4]

Advantages of the Corporation

The corporate form of organization has the following advantages:

1. *Limited liability*—the corporate legal structure provides the owners (stockholders) and officers the greatest possible legal protection against financial risk. Unlike the owners of the sole proprietorship and the general partnership, who are subject to unlimited liability, stockholders and officers of a corporation are not exposed to any personal financial liability beyond their investment in the stock of the corporation. If the corporation is unable to meet its debt, bankruptcy may be forced on the corporate entity, but the owner's (stockholders') personal property may not be attached.

   While limited liability is true in law, for many small businesses, particularly for those that are new, the owner(s) must personally sign for loans, lease agreements, and so on. This has the effect of negating the so-called *limited liability* concept.
2. *Specialized management*—depending on its size and scope of operations, a corporation can more easily justify hiring management specialists.
3. *Transferability of ownership*—ownership in a corporation can be transferred with relative ease. Stockholders may dispose of all or some of their shares of stock by any legal means at any time. In small corporations, however, transfer of ownership may be difficult, due to a lack of prospective stockholders.
4. *Continuous existence*—the legal existence of the corporation is not affected by the death of a stockholder. A corporation can be dissolved only by court order,

as in the case of bankruptcy; by the approval of a majority of stockholders (owners); or by the expiration of the corporate charter.

5. *Greater ease of raising capital*—from the standpoint of capital formation, the corporation has less difficulty attracting capital than do the sole proprietorship or the partnership. Through the sale of stock, the corporation has an opportunity to obtain well-dispersed ownership in the company.

   Although corporations generally find it easier to raise capital, a new or small corporation may not find it easier to get capital than a sole proprietorship or partnership. In fact, in some cases restrictions are placed on the number and type of persons to whom stock can be sold.

6. *Possible tax advantages*—no income tax is imposed on the stockholder until a distribution of earnings in the form of cash, dividends, or other property is received. Depending on the tax bracket of the corporate stockholder, significant tax advantages may thus be enjoyed through participation in a corporation rather than a partnership.

Disadvantages of the Corporation

On the undesirable side, the corporate form of organization has the following features:

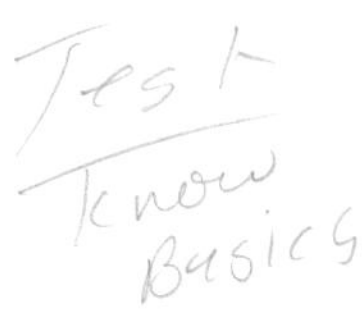

1. *Complicated to organize*—forming a corporation is costly, complicated, and time-consuming. Legal requirements vary from state to state, and it may be months before a firm is formally recognized. Once recognized, it has no legal status outside the state where it was formed.
2. *Government controls*—corporations are saddled with more government rules and regulations than are sole proprietorships or partnerships.
3. *Charter restrictions*—the charter permits the corporation to engage in only those activities that are specified or implied in the document.
4. *Double taxation*—the corporation is a taxable entity for state and federal income tax purposes. Earnings distributed to stockholders (owners) in the form of cash or dividends are taxed again as income to stockholders.
5. *Impersonality and lack of secrecy*—unlike the sole proprietorship and partnership, the corporation has a dispersed ownership, which leads to impersonality and consequent avoidance of personal interest and responsibility. The required publication of financial reports allows others to obtain potentially useful competitive information. Confidentiality in various aspects of the operation may be impossible to maintain.

INCORPORATING A SMALL BUSINESS

One should always seek professional legal guidance when incorporating a small business.[5] There is no substitute for professional advice. Legal guidance will ensure that the articles of incorporation and the bylaws are tailored to the needs of the particular business enterprise; that the tax obligations involved are understood; and that the corporation will be in compliance with state, local, and federal laws.

Laws governing the procedure for obtaining a corporate charter vary from state to state. The requirements of a particular state can be obtained from the designated state official who grants charters.

Where to Incorporate

The majority of small- and medium-sized businesses, especially those whose trade is local in nature, find it advisable to obtain their charter from the state in which the greatest part of their business is conducted.

Out-of-state, or *foreign,* incorporation often results in the additional payments of taxes and fees in another jurisdiction. Moreover, under the laws of many states the property of a foreign corporation is subject to less favorable treatment, especially in the area of attachment of corporate assets. This legal difference could prove especially hazardous to a small business.

On the other hand, one should look into possible benefits to be gained from incorporation in another state. Such factors as state taxes, restrictions on corporate powers and lines of business in which a company may engage, capital requirements, restrictions on foreign corporations in a state, and so forth should be taken into consideration in selecting the state of incorporation. For example, one should be aware that some states require a foreign corporation to obtain a certificate to do business in their state. Without such certification the corporation may be deprived of the right to sue in those states. The fee or organization tax charged for incorporation varies greatly from state to state.

Certificate of Incorporation

Generally, the first step in the required procedure is preparation, by the incorporators, of a **certificate of incorporation.** Most states once required that the certificate be prepared by three or more legally qualified persons, but the modern trend is to require only one incorporator. An incorporator may, but not necessarily must, be an individual who will ultimately own stock in the corporation.

For purposes of expediting the filing of articles, *dummy incorporators* are often employed. These dummy incorporators are usually associated with a company that performs this service or with an attorney for the organizers. They typically elect their successors and resign at the meeting of the incorporators.

Many states have a standard certificate of incorporation form that may be used by small businesses. Copies of this form can be obtained from the designated state official who grants charters and, in some states, from local stationers as well.

The following information is usually required in a certificate of incorporation:

1. *The corporate name of the company*—legal requirements generally are that the name chosen must not be so similar to the name of any other corporation authorized to do business in the State, and that the name chosen must not be deceptive, so as to mislead the public. One company that recently was forced to change the name of its product because it referred to the state in which it is incorporated is Mad River Traders. The company, based in Vermont, named its new drink Vermont All Natural Soda. The drink is made with New Jersey tap water (the main ingredient) and bottled in Trenton, New Jersey. The only thing Vermontish about Mad River's product is that the company—all two employees—is situated and incorporated in Vermont. The labeling implied there was a use of Vermont natural water, and that is not the case. As a result, the

start-up company had to stop labeling its product Vermont All Natural Soda and delete other references to the Green Mountain State.[6]

In order to be sure that the name selected is suitable, one should investigate the availability of the name through the designated state official in each state in which one intends to do business before drawing up a certificate of incorporation. This check can be made through a service company. In some states, there is a procedure for reserving a name.

2. *Purposes for which the corporation is formed*—several states permit very broad language, such as "the purpose of the corporation is to engage in any lawful act or activity for which corporations may be organized." However, most states require more specific language in setting forth the purposes of the corporation. Even where state law does not require it, the better practice is to employ a **specific object clause,** which spells out in broad descriptive terms the projected business enterprise. At the same time, one should take care to allow for the possibility of territorial, market, or product expansion. In other words, the language should be broad enough to allow for expansion and yet specific enough to convey a clear idea of the projected enterprise.

   The use of a specific object clause, even where not required by state law, is advisable for several reasons. It will convey to financial institutions a clearer picture of the corporate enterprise and will prevent problems in qualifying the corporation to do business in other jurisdictions. Reference books or certificates of existing corporations can provide examples of such clauses.
3. *Length of time for which the corporation is being formed*—this may be a period of years or may be perpetual.
4. *Names and addresses of incorporators*—in certain states one or more of the incorporators is required to be a resident of the state within which the corporation is being organized.
5. *Location of the registered office of the corporation in the state of incorporation*—if one decides to obtain the charter from another state, one will be required to have an office there. However, instead of establishing an office, one may appoint an agent in that state to act on the incorporator's behalf. The agent will be required only to represent the corporation, to maintain a duplicate list of stockholders, and to receive or reply to suits brought against the corporation in the state of incorporation.
6. *Maximum amount and type of capital stock that the corporation wants authorization to issue*—the proposed capital structure of the corporation should be set forth, including the number and classification of shares and the rights, preferences, and limitations of each class of stock.
7. *Capital required at time of incorporation*—some states require that a specified percentage of the par value of the capital stock be paid in cash and banked to the credit of the corporation before the certificate of incorporation is submitted to the designated state official for approval.
8. *Stockholder rights and restrictions*—provisions for preemptive rights, if any, to be granted to the stockholders and restrictions, if any, on the transfer of shares, must be listed.
9. *Internal affairs*—provisions for regulation of the internal affairs of the corporation must be delineated.

10. *Directors*—names and addresses of persons who will serve as directors until the first meeting of stockholders, or until their successors are elected and qualify, must appear on the certificate.
11. *The right to amend, alter, or repeal any provisions contained in the certificate of incorporation*—this right is generally statutory, reserved to a majority or two thirds of the stockholders. Still, it is customary to make it clear in the certificate.

If the designated state official determines that the name of the proposed corporation is satisfactory, that the certificate contains the necessary information and has been properly executed, and that there is nothing in the certificate or the corporation's proposed activities that violates state law or public policy, the charter will be issued.

Officers and Stockholders

Next, the stockholders must meet to complete the incorporation process. This meeting is extremely important. It is usually conducted by an attorney or someone familiar with corporate organizational procedure.

In the meeting the corporate bylaws are adopted and a board of directors is elected. This board of directors in turn will elect the officers who actually will have charge of the operations of the corporation—for example, the president, secretary, and treasurer. In small corporations, members of the board of directors frequently are elected as officers of the corporation.

Bylaws

The **bylaws** of the corporation may repeat some of the provisions of the charter and state statute but usually cover such items as the following:

1. Location of the principal office and other offices of the corporation,
2. Time, place, and required notice of annual and special meetings of stockholders, and the necessary quorum and voting privileges of the stockholders,
3. Number of directors, their compensation, their term of office, the method of electing them, and the method of creating or filling vacancies on the board of directors,
4. Time and place of the regular and special directors' meetings, as well as the notice and quorum requirements,
5. Method of selecting officers, their titles, duties, terms of office, and salaries,
6. Issuance and form of stock certificates, their transfers and their control in the company books,
7. Dividends, when and by whom they may be declared,
8. The fiscal year, the corporate seal, the authority to sign checks, and the preparation of the annual statement, and
9. Procedure for amending the bylaws.

Special Tax Laws

At the time of the first meeting of the corporate board of directors, and prior to issuance of any shares, one might consider adoption of a plan under a section of the

Internal Revenue Code (IRC 1244) that grants ordinary rather than capital treatment of losses on certain small business stock. Among the requirements for qualification as *section 1244 stock* are

1. The stock must be common stock,
2. The stock must be issued by the corporation for money or other property pursuant to a written plan containing several limitations,
3. The amount of contribution received for the stock and equity capital of the corporation must not exceed maximum dollar limits.

One should also be aware of the possibility of electing **subchapter S** status. The purpose of subchapter S is to permit a small business corporation to elect to have its income taxed to the shareholders as if the corporation were a partnership. One objective is to overcome the double-tax feature of the present system of taxation of corporate income. Another purpose is to permit the shareholders to have the benefit of offsetting business losses by the corporation against their income.

Among the qualifying requirements for electing and maintaining subchapter S eligibility are that the corporation have no more than 10 shareholders, all of whom are individuals or estates; that there be no nonresident alien shareholders; that there be only one class of outstanding stock; that all shareholders consent to the election; and that a specified portion of the corporation's receipts be derived from actual business activity rather than passive investments. No limit is placed on the size of the corporation's income and assets.

Other Considerations

If the business is at present a sole proprietorship or partnership, one will need to secure a new taxpayer identification number and an unemployment insurance account. One should find out in advance whether present licenses and leases will be transferable to the new corporate entity.

Additional considerations when incorporating are illustrated by The Timberland Company and Lillian Vernon Corporation. According to Sidney Swartz, chairman, chief executive officer, and president of Timberland, there was good news and bad news when

In 1987, when Lillian Vernon decided to go public and sell stock in her company at $15 per share, she was faced with new kinds of pressures; she now had to consider the stock holders' interests in every business decision. (Photograph courtesy of Lillian Vernon Corporation)

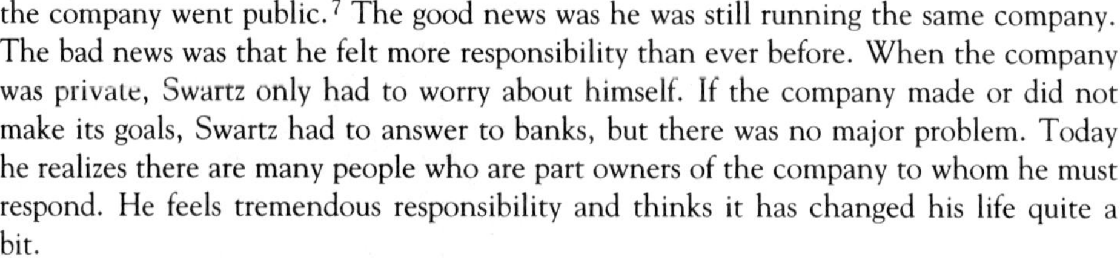

the company went public.[7] The good news was he was still running the same company. The bad news was that he felt more responsibility than ever before. When the company was private, Swartz only had to worry about himself. If the company made or did not make its goals, Swartz had to answer to banks, but there was no major problem. Today he realizes there are many people who are part owners of the company to whom he must respond. He feels tremendous responsibility and thinks it has changed his life quite a bit.

LILLIAN VERNON®

The mail order firm Lillian Vernon Corp. experienced new kinds of pressures when it decided to go public in 1987 at $15 a share. After the October 1987 stock market crash, Lillian Vernon's stock lost more than half its value.[8] The firm's principal underwriter continues to recommend the stock, however, believing the company can continue growing at 10 to 15 percent a year.

ROLE OF THE LAWYER

The complexity of laws in general, and those pertaining to legal forms of business ownership in particular, make it impossible for small business owners to know all their opportunities and rights under the law. It is therefore necessary to consult a lawyer who will be available for advice on routine as well as major decisions.

Many business owners consult lawyers only when their firms are involved in lawsuits. They fail to realize that legal troubles can be reduced or avoided by a continuing program of consultation. The day-to-day advice and recommendations of a lawyer help prevent costly and time-consuming problems.

Legal services are a necessity when the choice of organization requires contracts, partnership agreements, or the filing of a certificate of incorporation. Many municipal and state law requirements are attached to beginning a new business. Full legal compliance can be best assured with advice from a lawyer.

Legal advice also should be sought when making plans for continuing the business in event of the owner's death. Such long-range plans for transferring ownership of the firm should be made early in the firm's existence, because it may be difficult if not impossible at a later date.

Tax Advice

In many instances, the advice of an attorney with tax experience is essential. Among the tax planning factors that may require legal advice are

1. The fiscal year to use,
2. The legal aspects of adopting a profit-sharing or pension plan,
3. The means and methods of capitalizing the business to minimize taxation,
4. The availability of stock-option plans to the owners, if the business is a corporation,
5. The legal implications of insurance programs that the firm can adopt, and
6. The election of the form of taxation available to the owner.

Legal advice and assistance on such matters can be helpful not only when the business is showing profits but also when it has losses. For example, the effects of a loss when a newly established firm is trying to reach its breakeven point may sometimes be lessened by using the loss in relation to other income.

After the business is established, regular checks should be made as the business grows. For example, a sole proprietorship may have been desirable in the first years of operation when losses were incurred and could be used to offset other income of the owner. When a firm grows and prospers, however, the owner-manager might want to incorporate in order to obtain a tax advantage and at the same time reduce personal liability for any losses of the business. As management responsibilities increase, the owner might want to form a partnership to help carry the load. Or the owner might want to take advantage of the increasing value of the business by incorporating and selling shares in the business to the public.

SUMMARY

1. The three most common legal forms of ownership are the sole proprietorship, the partnership, and the corporation.
2. The sole proprietorship is the most common form of ownership among firms in the United States.
3. A lawyer and a tax adviser should always be consulted for advice regarding legal forms of ownership, taxation, and other major decisions.
4. A sole proprietorship is a legal form of ownership that has no existence apart from the owner; that is, there is no legal distinction between the business and the owner's private affairs.
5. Major advantages of a sole proprietorship include ease of starting the business with few legal complications; all profits earned go to the proprietor; total control of the business rests with the proprietor; and freedom to terminate the business at any time.
6. Major disadvantages of a sole proprietorship are unlimited liabilities of the individual owner; lack of continuity of the business due to owner's permanent illness or death; difficulty in raising capital; and limited opportunities for employees.
7. A partnership is an association of two or more people to carry on as co-owners of a business for profit.
8. There are two types of partnership. In the general partnership all participants are required to have at least one general partner who must assume the liabilities of the business. In a limited partnership there is at least one general partner and one or more limited partners who have limited liability.
9. Among the primary advantages of partnerships are the number of sources of funds and the amount of management expertise that may be available. Disadvantages include the unlimited liability of general partners and not being one's own boss.
10. A corporation is a legal entity separate and distinct from its owners, employees, and officers.
11. Advantages of the corporate form of organization include its limited liability, specialized management, transferability of ownership, continuous existence, and relative ease of raising capital. Disadvantages are the number and complexity of regulations, double taxation, and the impersonality of a corporation.
12. Laws governing the procedure for obtaining a corporate charter vary among states.
13. Incorporating a business requires preparation of a certificate of incorporation.
14. The groups that make up the corporate structure include stockholders (owners), the board of directors, and the officers.
15. Determining the best legal form of ownership for tax purposes continues to trouble owners and advisors alike.
16. Subchapter S was added to the Internal Revenue Code to permit small corporations that are essentially partnerships to enjoy the advantages of the corporate form of organization without the possible tax disadvantages of the corporation.
17. Legal advice is essential when deciding on the legal form of organization and in complying with state and federal tax laws.

KEY TERMS AND CONCEPTS

Sole proprietorship
Partnership
Corporation
General partnership
Limited partnership
General partner
Limited partner
Silent partner
Secret partner
Dormant partner
Nominal partner
Uniform Limited Partnership Act
Certificate of incorporation
Specific object clause
Bylaws
Subchapter S

QUESTIONS FOR DISCUSSION

1. What is the meaning of the following form of ownership: Sole proprietorship? Partnership? Corporation?
2. Why is the most popular legal form of organization the sole proprietorship?
3. What are the management advantages of the sole proprietorship form of ownership?
4. What are the disadvantages of the sole proprietorship form of ownership?
5. What are the advantages and disadvantages of a partnership?
6. What is the difference between general and limited partners?
7. What are some of the more specialized forms of partnerships?
8. How does the Uniform Limited Partnership agreement differ from the Articles of Partnership?
9. What is meant by a corporation's being a legal entity?
10. What are the major advantages and disadvantages of a corporation?
11. Why should legal advice be sought when incorporating a small business?
12. Why do most small- and medium-sized businesses find it advisable to obtain a charter from the state in which the greatest part of their business is conducted?
13. What information is usually required in the certificate of incorporation?
14. What is the purpose of electing subchapter 5 status?
15. What are some of the factors in tax planning about which legal advice should be sought?

SELF-TEST REVIEW

Multiple Choice Questions

1. The form of ownership that is the most popular in the United States is the:
   a. Sole proprietorship.
   b. Partnership.
   c. Corporation.
   d. Subchapter S.
2. Which of the following is an advantage of the sole proprietorship?
   a. Employee incentives.
   b. Total authority.
   c. Limited liability.
   d. All of the above.
3. The type of partner that has unlimited liability is the:
   a. Silent partner.
   b. General partner.
   c. Dormant partner.
   d. Secret partner.
4. Which of the following is not a member of the corporate structure?
   a. Stockholders.
   b. Board of directors.
   c. Officers.
   d. Employees.
5. Subchapter S gives certain tax advantages to the:
   a. Sole proprietorship.
   b. Small corporation.
   c. Large corporation.
   d. None of the above.

True/False Statements

1. One advantage of the sole proprietorship is that it is relatively easy to establish.
2. The life of the sole proprietorship is limited to the life of the owner.

3. In a limited partnership, there are only limited partners.
4. In forming a partnership, an agreement called the Copartnership Articles must be completed.
5. One disadvantage of the partnership is that it is subject to authority disputes among the partners.
6. The corporation is a legal entity that can sue and be sued, manage its own affairs, and own and sell property.
7. One of the disadvantages of the corporation is that its owners have limited liability.
8. Many special legal restrictions on corporations do not exist for sole proprietorships and partnerships.
9. In small corporations, members of the board of directors are frequently elected as officers.
10. There are no special qualifying requirements for subchapter S eligibility; any small corporation is eligible.

SPORTS UNLIMITED

Sports Unlimited is a successful sporting goods store specializing in hunting supplies and accessories. Among the guns carried are Colt, Ithaca, Marlin, Mossberg, Remington, Savage, and Winchester. Sports Unlimited also provides complete gunsmithing services and stocks five kinds of reloading equipment. Harvey Becker, the sole proprietor of Sports Unlimited, has been working at least ten hours a day, six days a week, and never seems to catch up on all the work. Furthermore, he faces constant cash-flow problems and cannot take advantage of quantity discounts offered by suppliers. To deal with the pressures of running and owning the business, Becker is considering bringing a partner into the business.

For several years Joe Bostnick, his longtime hunting and fishing companion, has been interested in running a sporting shop. Now that Bostnick is retired, he wants to start a new venture. Bostnick is only fifty-five-years old, has lifelong experienced in selling, and loves fishing and hunting above all else. During a hunting trip, Bostnick suggested to Becker that Sports Unlimited could be enlarged to carry a complete line of fishing equipment for which Bostnick could have full responsibility. Bostnick also proposed that he become a general partner. He said he would be willing to provide the capital to enlarge the store's inventory. Together they could better meet the competition, which tends to carry both hunting supplies and fishing tackle.

Becker is giving serious consideration to this opportune offer. He knows something must be done about those long hours, and he recognizes that his competitive position in the market is weak. He cannot compete on a price basis with larger stores, which purchase in great volume to take advantage of quantity discounts. The thought of having a partner who would not only bring in needed capital but also broaden the management base is appealing.

Becker is also thinking about his annual hunting trip to the Yukon in September, remembering that Bostnick takes the same time every year to fish in Alaska. And he is bothered by the prospect of having unlimited liability as one of the partners. Yet he knows the time has come to make a decision on whether to continue running a store that is barely providing a satisfactory return on investment. Unfortunately, Becker is too young to retire. Bostnick is a good friend, and the prospect of having him as a partner appears to be just what is needed.

QUESTIONS

1. Do the advantages of bringing Bostnick in as a general partner outweigh possible disadvantages?
2. Would the problems facing Becker really be solved by forming a general partnership?

NOTES

1. Based on Cable News Network's "Pinnacle," May 13, 1989. Guest: Peter Peterson, The Blackstone Group.
2. Based on Cable News Network's "Pinnacle," March 19, 1988. Guest: Joseph Baum, Restaurateur.

3. Barry Stavro, "A License to Speed," *Forbes*, September 10, 1984, 94–102.
4. Eugene Carlson, "Going Public, Warns Entrepreneur, Can Be the End of the Good Times," *The Wall Street Journal*, January 8, 1990, B1.
5. This section is excerpted from Small Business Administration, *Incorporating a Small Business*, Management Aid Number 6.003 (1985).
6. Diane Tracy, "It's True That 'Cool Refreshment' Isn't What Trenton Brings to Mind," *The Wall Street Journal*, April 17, 1989, B1.
7. Based on Cable News Network's "Pinnacle," August 30, 1987. Guest: Sidney Swartz, The Timberland Company.
8. Based on Cable News Network's "Pinnacle," December 18, 1988. Guest: Lillian Vernon, Lillian Vernon Corporation.

CHAPTER EIGHT

Developing Business Plans and Policies

CHAPTER OUTLINE

LEARNING OBJECTIVES

The objectives of this chapter are to assist you in understanding:

1. The importance of objectives, plans, and policies and procedures to successful business operations.
2. The types of goals a firm might have.
3. The steps in the strategic planning process.
4. The major obstacles to planning.
5. When and on what basis reviews of goals, plans, and policies and procedures should be undertaken.

Small business statistics show that 95 percent of the 400,000 annual small business failures can be attributed to poor management.[1] Individuals who know only the technical aspects of producing products are likely to lead their firms to the small business graveyard. To be successful, entrepreneurs must not only have good products and services, but they must also be able to plan their ventures' future courses of action and develop **policies** and **procedures** for moving them toward their predetermined goals. This is illustrated in Exhibit 8–1.

IMPORTANCE OF OBJECTIVES, PLANS, POLICIES AND PROCEDURES

Successful small business management begins with an identification of **goals** and a recognition of the need to develop plans for their achievement.[2] An entrepreneur enters the business arena for a variety of reasons, and it is important that these reasons provide the direction for the firm regarding what products to produce, what services to offer, what prices to charge, how to grow, and so on.

Strategic plans may contain a variety of different issues. For example, Southeast Banking Corporation in Florida has a strategic plan that focuses much of its attention on its market area. In commenting on the bank's strategic plan, Charles Zwick, its chief executive officer, stated: "We have a strategic plan that says we will target selected markets. We are the dominant bank in South Florida. We are going to maintain that position."[3]

Some small business owners, of course, have become successful without utilizing sound planning processes—everybody gets lucky now and then. The idea of entrepreneurship, however, is to become successful *because* rather than *in spite of* one's efforts. Humana, for example, was started by six people who contributed $1,000 each to start a nursing home in 1961. By 1966, they owned three such facilities, and began to realize that what they had learned about nursing homes could be applied to hospital management.

EXHIBIT 8–1 ***The Process of Planning***

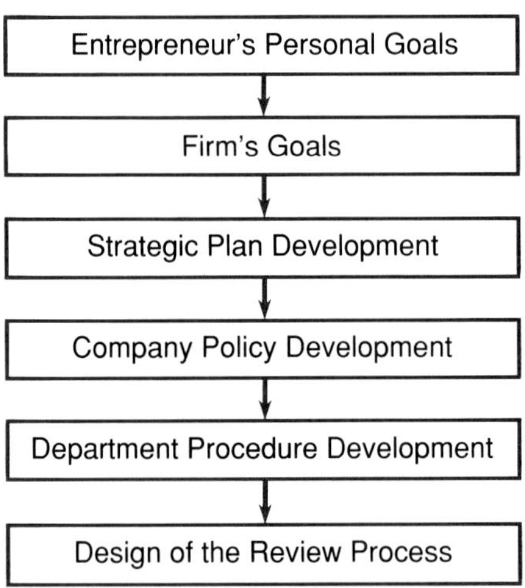

Charles Zwick of S.E. Banking Corporation believes that being big is not necessary these days in order to be successful. A small business that knows its customers, targets marketing activities, keeps costs low, and does a better job than its competition can be successful in the marketplace. (Photograph courtesy of Southeast Banking, N.A.)

They planned their business strategies, and by 1988 Humana had become the second-largest company in the medical care business, with sales in excess of $3.4 billion.[4]

Those who sit down with a road map to plot the best route for a vacation without first deciding where they want to go quickly realize the folly of their efforts. It is impossible to decide the best route until a destination has been decided upon. The same holds true for the entrepreneur. Decisions must first be made about where the firm is headed, and then a business plan can be prepared.

Lotus Development

Every company needs to have direction and strategic plans. The company should decide what products it wants to produce and what markets it wants to serve. It then sets out to accomplish defined objectives in a systematic fashion. Lotus Development is an example of a company that knows where it is headed. According to its chief executive officer, Jim Manzi, "Our strategic areas for the company are spreadsheet, data base and graphics. . . ." Lotus Development has plans to introduce its new products in a sequential manner.[5]

A strategic plan helps the entrepreneur:

1. Focus on and take advantage of the firm's strengths,
2. Eliminate or reduce the firm's weaknesses,
3. Capitalize on opportunities and emerging trends in the marketplace, and take defensive steps to reduce potential threats to the firm's existence,
4. Bring together all of the firm's resources and direct them toward specific goals in such areas as sales, profitability, and growth, and
5. Prioritize and document all of the entrepreneur's objectives over the next one to three years, and assign responsibilities and timetables to ensure that they are accomplished.

Business Goals

Business goals can take many forms, but they tend to fall within three broad categories: survival, profit, and growth. The synthesis of these three categories into a single set of goals for the firm establishes the basis for future planning. For example, if the entrepreneur's objectives lean heavily toward survival, extreme caution will prevail in creating business strategies, and risks will be minimized. On the other hand, if the objective is high profits or high rates of growth, more speculative strategies may be necessary.

Goals are set for both the short and long term. Short-term goals are for periods of one year or less, while long-term goals range for periods of one to five years. The entrepreneur should begin by setting objectives for the longer term and then create a series of short-term goals that, when accomplished, will lead to achievement of the long-term goals.

Survival

The primary objective of most small businesses is to survive. Indeed, in the infancy stage, this may well be the only goal. Although some ventures are set up for a limited life span, all entrepreneurs must confront the question, "What actions will be necessary just to keep the business going for the desired amount of time?" To some extent, the **survival objective** may conflict with other goals such as profits or growth. Given the general rule that greater profits and/or more rapid rates of growth require greater risks, the entrepreneur must make trade-offs between this survival goal and other objectives (See Exhibit 8–2).

EXHIBIT 8–2 ***Business Goals and Their Interactions***

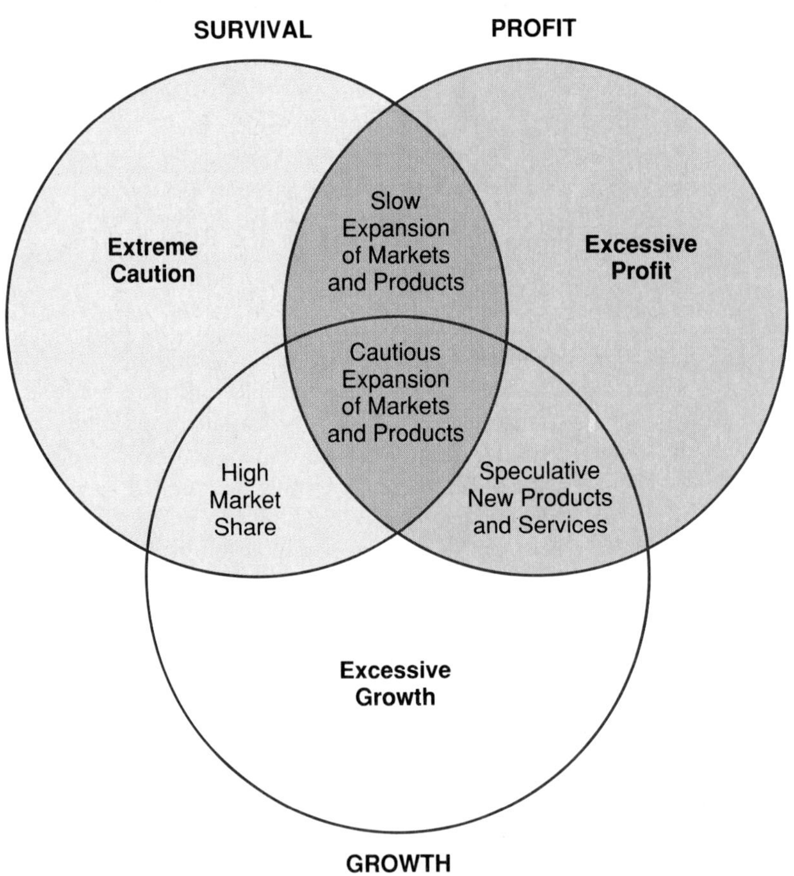

Profit

Certainly one of the reasons most commonly cited for going into business is the hope for wealth through highly profitable business activities. Examples of profitability levels achieved in various industries are shown in Exhibit 8–3.

Establishing a goal "to make money" is not sufficient when it comes to planning the firm's operations. If, for example, the firm generates $1 in profit at the end of its fiscal year, has the profit objective been obtained? Does a profit of $50,000 or $500,000 satisfy the entrepreneur's desire "to make money," and how much risk to the survival of the firm must be incurred to achieve those dollar levels? As should be evident, **profit objectives** must be stated in quantitative terms. A goal of earning $50,000 for the fiscal year provides greater direction than does a goal of "making money." Each business decision can be made in terms of how it will help the firm earn $50,000.

Profit goals also must be realistic in the sense that they should be achieved without incurring unacceptable levels of risk to the firm. Wanting to achieve a $500,000 profit when the total potential for all firms within the industry is $750,000 does not give the entrepreneur a good perspective in planning, since the goal is nearly impossible to achieve.

Entrepreneurs can establish quantitative goals on the basis of *net sales, net profits, market share,* and/or *return on investment.* Net sales and net profits are defined in absolute dollar terms, such as sales of $1 million or net profits before or after taxes of $75,000. Market share is measured in percentage terms based on the firm's sales in relation to those of its competitors. For example, a 25 percent market share for wide-screen televisions means that the firm's sales are 25 percent of those for all firms selling wide-screen televisions within the market area.

Although these first three goals are widely used, a better one is return on investment (ROI). This is measured by dividing the net profit of the firm, typically before taxes,

EXHIBIT 8–3 **Comparative Profitability by Type of Business: Determining Where the Business Should Be**

	Average Annual Sales	Net Profit	Return on Investment
Services			
Farm management	$739,058	$62,820	28.9%
Plumbing, heating, air conditioning	$600,000	$34,800	19.4%
Electrical	$592,148	$37,305	18.3%
Manufacturing			
Men's and boy's nightwear	$1,566,411	$75,188	16.1%
Fabric, dress, and glove	$212,566	$53,102	9.3%
Children's outerwear	$2,587,286	$82,793	10.5%
Retail			
Furniture stores	$514,464	$24,694	11.1%
Drugstores	$575,000	$24,150	17.7%
Liquor stores	$574,581	$17,237	16.2%

Source: The Dun & Bradstreet Corporation, "Key Business Ratios," 1987–88.

by its net worth (total assets minus total liabilities). The attraction of ROI is that it examines profits in relation to how much the entrepreneur has invested to generate those profits. For example, if two firms, A and B, each were to earn $50,000 in profits, would they be equally profitable? The answer is "no" if the owner of firm A invested $500,000 and the owner of B invested $1 million. The ROIs would be 10 percent (that is, $50,000 divided by $500,000) and 5 percent (that is, $50,000 divided by $1 million) respectively.

Over the long term, the ROI should be greater than what could be earned by placing the money in a savings account at a commercial financial institution. For example, if the interest rate on a five-year account at a bank was 8 percent, the owner of firm A would be better off with the earnings of the business while the owner of B would make more money by taking the $1 million and placing it in the savings account. In the short term, the owner of B might accept lower returns if the expected profits in future years grew more attractive.

Growth

One of the more important goals for a business is growth. Too often, the entrepreneur focuses only on survival and profits, and neglects the fact that most successful ventures need to grow over time. A key to the **growth objective** is to define rate and consistency. Every effort should be made to ensure that the venture grows in a stable fashion, rather than haphazardly. Only in this way can the entrepreneur plan and utilize the firm's resources to maximum advantage.

For example, it would be difficult to plan for the type of growth shown in Exhibit 8–4(A) than it would be for the pattern shown in Exhibit 8–4(B). When sales or profits rise and fall radically, it is difficult to know when to buy more inventory and equipment, hire more personnel, build larger facilities, and so on. It is a tremendous challenge for companies like Aldus Corporation (maker of software for desktop publishing), whose

EXHIBIT 8–4 **Differences in Growth Patterns**

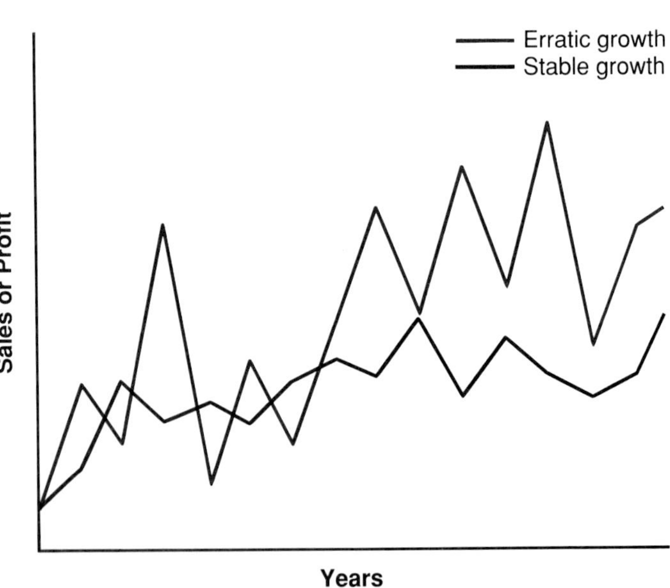

average sales growth from 1985 to 1987 was 320.7 percent, to manage that increase productively, even though its profits rose by a similar amount.[6]

Growth goals must be quantified and realistic, and they typically focus on increases or stability in the profit goals. Generally, the goals are defined in percentage terms over some specified time period. For example, the entrepreneur may want a 5 percent average growth in sales, a 2 percent increase in market share, or a 1 percent rise in return on investment over a one-year period.

McArthur/Glen Group, a real estate development company, specializes in creating shopping malls that house discount designer clothing outlets. From a start in 1988, the company had built five such malls by the end of 1989, and planned eight more to be completed by 1993. Despite its success, the company has had to temper its growth plans. In making an assessment of its opportunities, McArthur/Glen Group executives realized that clothing manufacturers do not want to anger traditional outlets by supplying discounters who locate nearby. Accordingly, the company had to limit its new malls to areas geographically separated from existing major department stores.[7]

Strategic Planning within Small Businesses

Strategic planning is a process by which the entrepreneur and other key people within the firm:

1. Define the firm's mission,
2. Assess its current situation,
3. Decide what the firm is to look like in one to three years, and
4. Design a course to bring the firm from where it is now to where it should be, recognizing its strengths and weaknesses, and the opportunities and threats confronting it.

When designed properly, a strategic plan is a means of combining separate marketing, financial, production, human resource, and other plans. In this way, the entrepreneur can better integrate and utilize the resources available to achieve a predetermined set of objectives.

In very small businesses with only an owner and a few employees, plans often are developed by the entrepreneur and then passed on to employees. However, in somewhat larger companies, where there are middle managers, the planning process should be undertaken throughout the firm. Most plans, of course, ultimately are decided upon by

For the past sixteen years Leslie Otten has run the Sunday River Ski Resort in Newry, Maine. When he saw that the owner wasn't likely to do anything with Sunday River, he started talking about what he'd do "if this were my place." In the fall of 1980 he bought it the only way he could—with virtually no money down. Otten's course of action to turn around Sunday River was simple: He would concentrate on the steak, not the sizzle. In the ski business that means providing the best possible snow conditions and enough uphill transportation to get people to it without worrying about the peripheral amenities. Otten couldn't guarantee outstanding ski conditions, but he wanted to convince the market that on any given day, he would have as good as, if not better, skiing than any place in the region. (*Source: Inc.*, January 1990, p. 53, 56; photograph courtesy of Leslie B. Otten, Sunday River Ski Way Corp.)

the entrepreneur and key managers. The top level of management needs to establish broad long-range goals and the necessary framework for policies and procedures. This sets the guidelines for the total venture and focuses on the need to mesh all activities into a coordinated whole.

Lower levels of the organization will develop specific policies and procedures oriented to what is to be done and how it is to be accomplished. The emphasis will be on the shorter-term perspectives necessary to support and blend with the long-range plans. Particular concern must be given to ensuring that all of the production, marketing, and financial activities are included in the plan.

Plans also must be made according to the same time lines for the goals they are to achieve. **Short-term plans** are for one year or less, while **long-term plans** typically cover periods from one to five years.

Some entrepreneurs start with short-term plans and build up longer-term plans accordingly. After deciding what is to transpire in one year, the owner can then identify what is to be achieved over a two-to-five-year period. L.A. Gear, for example, is a manufacturer of fashionable sports apparel primarily for women and children. The founder originally started with the idea of creating a name that could be licensed by an apparel manufacturer. He did not plan to be the producer himself. However, the initial success modified that plan, and sales over a recent three-year period rose 109.6 percent, and profits grew 335 percent—yielding a return on investment of 44.8 percent.[8]

For many companies, however, this approach has serious pitfalls. Most importantly, the result of this effort is that the entrepreneur often focuses on what *can* rather than what *should* be accomplished over the long term. In addition, in the long term the firm evolves from a disjointed series of decisions rather than from a conscious effort to model the firm into something specific.

A preferred approach is one in which long-term objectives and plans are established and used as guidelines for shorter-term ones. Sometimes known as the *breakdown method,* this technique forces the entrepreneur to identify where the firm should be over time and then implement the necessary short-term policies and procedures to ensure achievement of those goals. Each decision, then, is viewed from this perspective and provides a better way for the entrepreneur to identify and plan for the firm's future.

THE STRATEGIC PLANNING PROCESS

The planning process is one of the many responsibilities that rest ultimately with the small business owner. Given its importance and the need for the firm's plans to mesh with the personal goals of the entrepreneur, this vital function cannot be passed on to others. The process itself can be both challenging and time-consuming, depending on how well defined the goals are, what is to be accomplished, the complexity and size of the firm's operations, and the state of the environment (for example, number of competitors, economic conditions, potential for technological advances). Standard business plans usually are about ten pages long and can take six to eight months to develop.

Generally, for entrepreneurs who know what they want for their firms, and who have some degree of management expertise, planning the course of their firms' operations can be enlightening experiences. In the case of new ventures, the planning process usually takes a form similar to what is contained in a loan package (see Chapter 11). For established companies, the planning process should follow the steps described below.

Steps in Strategic Planning

Actual planning involves working through a series of questions designed to learn about the business and make decisions about future courses of action. By addressing six major questions that form the planning process, the entrepreneur should be able to develop a set of strategies to guide the firm's future activities.

What is the Current Status of the Firm?

It is impossible for the small business owner to develop a set of plans and strategies for the future without assessing the firm's present situation. The entrepreneur must analyze the present status of the firm with respect to its goals, financial position, operating capabilities, management and labor expertise, and market position and marketing capabilities. This is shown in Exhibit 8–5.

Complementing this evaluation of the present should be an examination of *why* and *how* the firm came into its present position. Experiences of the past can assist in future planning. A retrospective look at past decisions will often provide a sound basis for plotting future operations.

Wataru Ohashi, for example, is the founder of Footwork, a Japanese company that caters specifically to the needs of affluent people. With the experience he gained in his parcel-delivery service, he quickly expanded into having his route people sell a variety of food and other products to people who are receiving parcels. Sales in 1988 reached $115 million.[9]

However, past actions are not always indicative of the future. Given changes in individual and firm goals and the highly volatile business environment, what was good or bad in the past may not be so in the future. Consequently, the entrepreneur also should evaluate how well the past coincides with the present and what can be expected over the next year.

The techniques that are used to make this analysis vary by the nature and size of the firm. In very small businesses, the entrepreneur will use a format similar to that described below. Owners of somewhat larger firms often request the same types of assessments by key managers of specific operations (for example, sales manager, production manager, bookkeeper).

One cannot overemphasize the importance of this first step of the planning process. Not only does it establish the initial framework for business planning, but such an analysis can also prove to be an excellent learning experience for the entrepreneur.

Where Should The Firm Be at Present?

Realistic assessments of the present status also demand that consideration be given to where the entrepreneur and the firm *should* be. Of particular concern are the firm's financial, management, and marketing positions. What should be the sales level of the firm? How much profit should it generate? How many employees should the firm have? These and other questions provide a basis for determining the difference between where the entrepreneur and firm are, and where they should be.

Creating business plans right from the start is a critical element of success. John Rollwagen, chief executive officer of Cray Research, a manufacturer of supercomputers, described the process used by the company: "When we started, our first product was delivered in 1976. We calculated very carefully what our market potential was. We knew

EXHIBIT 8–5 **Analyzing the Business's Current Situation**

Factor	Strength	Weakness
Financial Resources:		
Cash	______	______
Accounts receivable	______	______
Inventory	______	______
Fixtures	______	______
Equipment	______	______
Current liabilities	______	______
Long-term liabilities	______	______
Net worth	______	______
Profitability:		
Dollar profits	______	______
Profits as a percent of sales	______	______
Return on investment	______	______
Marketing:		
Percent market recognition	______	______
Percent market share	______	______
Competitive advantages of products	______	______
Competitive advantages of services	______	______
Competitive advantages in pricing	______	______
Dollars available for promotion	______	______
Human Resources:		
Number of employees	______	______
Average years of service	______	______
Special skills of employees	______	______
Percent employees are utilized	______	______
Number of positions open	______	______
Production Resources:		
Percent utilization of production capacity	______	______
Specialized production capacity	______	______
Quality of equipment	______	______
Efficiency of equipment	______	______
Other:		
______________________	______	______
______________________	______	______
______________________	______	______
______________________	______	______
______________________	______	______

that there were 86 potential customers in the whole world for supercomputers. We figured that the market could support about 12 machines a year and it's said that our company could be at best about $100 million."[10]

To make this assessment, the entrepreneur can compare performance to past periods and to industry averages as reported by such companies as Robert Morris Associates and Dun and Bradstreet. Examples of this are shown in Exhibit 8–3.

EXHIBIT 8–6 Sample Mission Statements and Objectives

Sample Mission Statements:

"The ABC Company of Iowa is dedicated to maintaining its position as a leader in providing quality products and services to businesses and individuals through a staff of highly trained people who share a tradition of integrity and service to its clients."

"DEF Travel provides economical vacation travel and related services to customers in the greater metropolitan area, who expect efficient, trouble-free travel arrangements at low cost."

"GHI Nurseries' goal is to provide a full range of high-quality wholesale and retail nursery products to professional landscapers and discriminating homeowners."

"JKL Market's goal is to be the lowest-cost provider of quality foods and groceries in the suburban area of town."

Sample Objectives:

"Produce and market one new product every six months."

"Achieve a sales volume of $1,500,000 by December 31, 1995."

"Achieve a return on investment of 28% by December 31, 1995."

"Hold employee salaries to 14% of sales for the next five years."

"Achieve a positive cash flow by the end of the next fiscal quarter."

Source: Adapted from Michael L. Policastro, Small Business Administration, *Developing a Strategic Business Plan,* Management Aid Number 2.035.

Of particular concern is how well the firm is progressing toward its overall mission and specific objectives. The mission statement describes the purpose of the company, the philosophy of the firm, and the reasons the entrepreneur is in business. By reviewing the mission statement (see Exhibit 8–6) and objectives, the entrepreneur can compare where the firm is now and where it should be.

The small business owner must take into consideration the market and environmental conditions to make these evaluations of the firm's position. Changes in economic conditions, number and quality of competitors, and other factors have a bearing on where the firm should be relative to its goals at any point in time. Variables outside the entrepreneur's control can be examined when evaluating how close the firm should be to its stated goals (see Exhibit 8–7). However, market and environmental conditions cannot be used as excuses for poor performance—the entrepreneur must cope with and make the best of the conditions within which the firm operates.

What Will Happen to the Firm if No Changes Are Instituted?

Change for its own sake is at best useless, and at worst a practice detrimental to the stability of the small business. Since changes in business practices tend to create uncertainty and disrupt previously standard procedures, they should be made only when they are warranted in order to achieve the entrepreneur's and the firm's goals.

EXHIBIT 8–7 **Controllable and Uncontrollable Marketplace Variables**

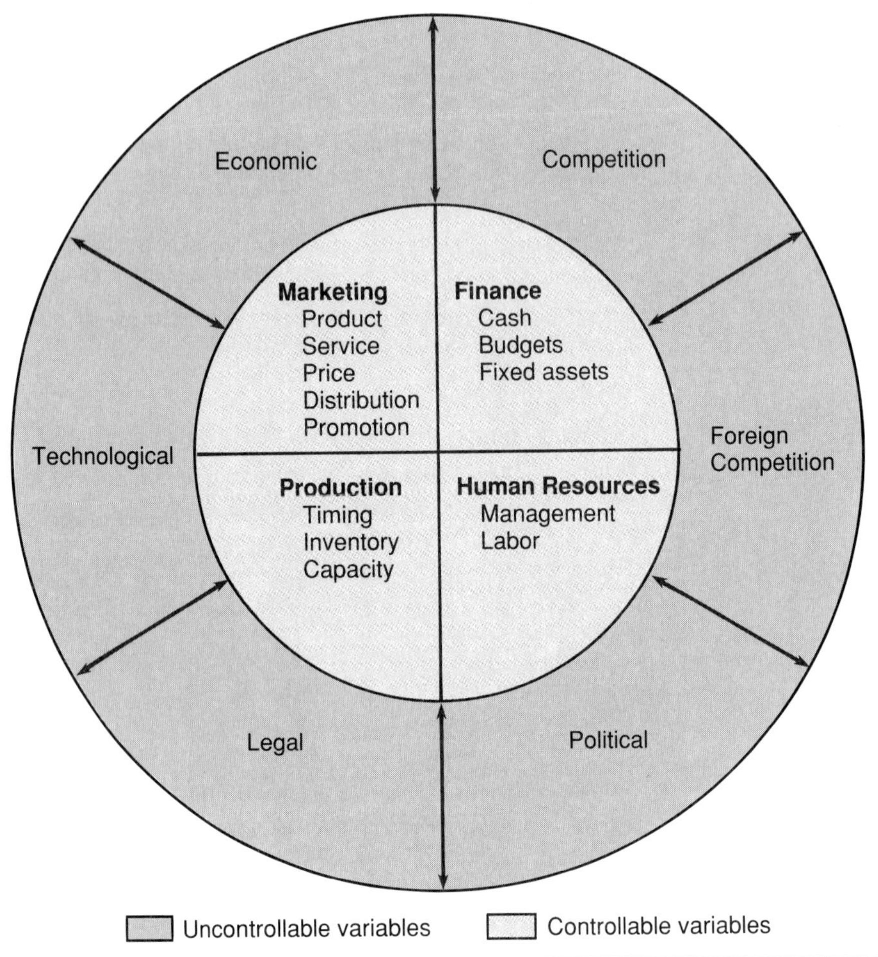

Consequently, the small business owner should carefully consider what the result will be if the firm keeps its present plans and courses of action. Are the strategies accomplishing what they are supposed to? Are there other strategies that would be better suited to the current environmental conditions? Answers to these and other questions will help the entrepreneur evaluate the wisdom of continuing the firm's present course.

If desired goals can be attained with little or no change, then the status quo should be maintained. Only when the expected outcome does not meet the objectives should changes in activities be planned and implemented.

If changes are necessary, the entrepreneur must not only prepare for them but also assess their impact on the firm. Will they create confusion and inefficiency? Will there be employee unrest? Can the changes be effectuated easily and quickly? In essence, will the changes create more harm that good?

Although this is not the typical situation, the entrepreneur may be confronted with a no-win decision. For example, if needed changes are not made, the firm will surely not achieve its goals. On the other hand, changes that are implemented could so disrupt the normal operations that goal achievement also will be difficult. For example, the entrepreneur is faced with laying off some employees in order to reduce costs. Profits will suffer if they are not released, but human relations problems almost certainly will occur among those not discharged—after all, they could be next.

In practice, change is frequently necessary and serves a definite purpose. Firms that remain static, whether oblivious to change or fearing it, often become stagnant and out of tune with reality. One of the classic cases of a company that avoided change was the Elgin Watch Company in the late 1960s. Keeping its grand tradition of manufacturing high-quality, expensive timepieces, this company lost sight of the inroads being made by Timex and others satisfying the more current demands for low-priced watches being purchased at discount stores. Had Elgin not reassessed its position and begun selling to more price-conscious buyers, the existence of the company could have been in jeopardy. Change can be advantageous if properly nurtured. Firms should maintain reasonable degrees of flexibility and adaptability to varying conditions.

In General, What Should the Firm Do?

After assessing the firm's present situation, the next step is to determine how the firm should proceed. This requires developing an overall game plan that will serve later as the framework for more detailed plans (see Exhibit 8–8).

Not all facets of the firm's operations will need revision. General plans should be developed for those that do. General guidelines should be established for each activity that requires modification—whether it be marketing, finance, production, or personnel. From these, specific strategies can be developed to insure a cohesive and coordinated effort. In many dentists' offices there is a placard that reads: "You don't need to use dental floss on all of your teeth—just the ones you want to keep!" In many respects, strategic planning is the same. Entrepreneurs need to plan only for those facets of their businesses they want to be profitable.

What Specific Policies and Procedures Need to be Developed and Implemented?

To be effective, every plan must be specified in detail. Policies are statements that in general terms describe how the goals are to be achieved. Procedures are the specific steps that the entrepreneur and employees of the firm take to ensure that the policies are carried out and the goals of the firm are achieved (see Exhibit 8–9).

One example of a unique strategy for success is One Price Clothing Stores, founded in 1984. The founder developed methods for locating unsold apparel from manufacturers, brokers, and others, purchasing the garments for very low prices—sometimes below the manufacturers' costs—and offering them to the public at a single price of $6.00. Over three years, sales grew 140.7 percent and profits rose 115.9 percent. Success relies on well-defined strategies for finding garments and getting them to market quickly—within two days of reaching the firm's distribution center.[11]

Unless the details are attended to, implementation of any course of action is likely to be disjointed. In cases where programs are to be changed, it is essential that the necessary new policies and procedures be formulated and that existing ones be reviewed

EXHIBIT 8–8 **Sample Business Plan Outline**

I. Summary (one to three pages)
  A. Description of the business
    1. Firm name
    2. Address
    3. Telephone number
    4. General type of business
    5. Products/services sold
    6. Market area and competitive position
  B. Goals of the firm
    1. Long-term goals
    2. Short-term goals
  C. Summary of financial position
    1. Cash situation
    2. Accounts receivable situation
    3. Sales and profit patterns
    4. Funding needs for future growth
II. Market Analysis
  A. Description of the market area
    1. Geographic characteristics
    2. Demographic characteristics
    3. Operating characteristics
  B. Nature of the industry
    1. General situation
    2. Trends from the past
    3. Expectations for the future
  C. Economic conditions
    1. Income
    2. Employment
    3. Disposable spending
    4. Overall prosperity
  D. Technology
    1. Areas of development
    2. Long-term prospects for change
  E. Political and legal situation
    1. Political climate
    2. Applicable laws
III. Competitive Analysis
  A. Number of competitors
  B. Competitors' strengths
  C. Competitors' weaknesses
  D. Competitors' target markets
IV. Target Market and Competitive Advantages
  A. Target market
    1. Characteristics
    2. Sales and profit potential
  B. Competitive advantages
    1. Tangible advantages
    2. Intangible advantages
V. Products and Services
  A. Product/service mix
    1. Number
    2. Consistency between types
    3. New offerings
  B. Characteristics
    1. Physical characteristics
    2. Benefits provided
    3. Advantages over those offered by competitors
VI. Marketing Strategies
  A. Product/service strategies
  B. Distribution strategies
  C. Price strategies
  D. Promotion strategies
VII. Management Strategies
  A. Business organization chart
  B. Number of employees, by areas of expertise
  C. Description of management team
  D. Primary duties and responsibilities of individual managers
VIII. Financial Strategies
  A. Evaluation of financial condition
  B. Income statements
  C. Balance sheets
  D. Cash flow statements
  E. Capital budgets

for possible modification. Frequently, this latter activity is overlooked and new policies and procedures are stacked on top of others. Over time, this will present a cumbersome problem for the entrepreneur who wants a more streamlined and efficient operation. Conflicting or overlapping programs do little to strengthen the firm.

What Controls Should Be Built into the Plan?

It often is thought that sound management includes a yearly review of plans to determine whether the goals have been achieved. While such reviews are useful for

EXHIBIT 8–9 **Sample Planning Matrix**

Goal: Increase net profits by 5%

Time Frame: One year

Plan for Goal Achievement:
Increase product line by two items.
Raise prices by 1.5%.
Promote to new market: 65 years and older.
Increase personal selling effort.

Policies to Be Followed:
Sell only high-quality merchandise.
Offer full personal service.
Provide adequate warranties.
Train sales staff in selling techniques.

Procedures to Be Followed:
Buy goods only from companies on the approved list.
Hire two new sales people during rush hours.
Guarantee items purchased for six months.
Have sales staff complete five hours of training per month.
Purchaser of product will be contacted within one week to ensure satisfaction.

Responsibility for Completion:
Each department manager will achieve 5% increase in profits.

future planning, they are insufficient because at that point it is too late to take corrective action. An evaluation at the end of a fiscal year provides no vehicle to assure goal achievement.

Consequently, checkpoints need to be established within the plan itself. When these are examined periodically, problems can be identified and remedied before they hinder the achievement of the firm's goals. Examples of these checkpoints include:

- Quality control checks on a production line,
- Quarterly market share calculations for all product lines, and
- Quarterly profitability tests through such ratios as return on investment and percent profits on sales.

In sum, policies and procedures should be developed to include the types of controls, how and when they are to be implemented, and who is to be responsible. As part of the established strategic plan, they will serve to keep the firm on a proper course and minimize differences between expected and attained results.

Obstacles to Strategic Planning

The planning effort essentially allows the small business owner to decide in definitive terms what the firm should accomplish in the future. Given the great importance of planning business operations, however, it is difficult to understand why so few entrepreneurs do so, despite the fact that there are some **obstacles to planning.**

The inexact nature of planning is the most common excuse. Many entrepreneurs think that planning is a waste of time because the future is so uncertain. Since plans must deal with the unknown, the possibility of errors in definitive plans is a problem. Nevertheless, planning provides the entrepreneur with opportunities to study these ambiguities and develop contingency plans to prepare for various possibilities. The successful entrepreneur recognizes that plans are not set in concrete and can and should be revised. Flexible plans are a must—they need to be adaptable to uncontrollable environmental and market changes.

Some entrepreneurs couple the inexactness of planning with the fact that the business world is in a constant state of flux. While there is considerable variability in the business environment, this too is a poor excuse. To the extent possible, the entrepreneur should change the environment through the firm's operations, rather than simply react to changes. By focusing on major areas of uncertainty, and developing contingency plans, the entrepreneur can be in a better position to make things happen and use change to the best advantage.

Many entrepreneurs do not know how to plan and fail to allocate enough time to the process. Planning is more time-consuming than it is difficult, and primarily requires the small business owner to run the firm rather than being run by it.

Finally, some small business owners have no clear goals for their firms. They enter into business for ill-defined reasons and have no particular concerns about what their firms will be in the future. Their perspectives are myopic and focused only on the immediate issues of the day. This approach to management is commonly found among small business failures.

Häagen-Dazs

The value of a strategic plan lies partly in its development. Häagen-Dazs, for example, has a corporate constitution, and according to Mark Stevens, its chief executive officer, "In some ways the document itself is less remarkable than the group of people who put it together. You have several alternative ways to go about trying to write such a thing and we elected to try to do it by pooling a cross-section of all our employees. We had management, we had hourly workers, we had union employees. We had secretaries, all kinds of people from all over the company . . . They talked about the fact that we serve, we exist to serve the public and an unflinching commitment to people and to people who are committed to perfection."[12]

REVIEW OF FIRM'S GOALS AND ITS STRATEGIC PLAN

Setting goals and developing strategic plans are not once-in-a-lifetime projects. They are processes that must be reviewed and modified as conditions warrant over the entire life of the firm. As goals, individuals, technology, and the business environment change, so too must the firm's internal objectives, plans, and policies and procedures. But how often do these need to be reviewed? The answer to this depends on the size of the firm, its age, and the type of industry within which it is competing.

When to Evaluate Goals and Strategic Plans

Periodic reviews of key aspects of the firm's operations must be made frequently to ensure that goals are achieved. In cases such as quality control, this may be hourly or daily. Assessing the firm's financial position may take place monthly, and evaluations of its marketing efforts may be undertaken quarterly. Under most circumstances, key

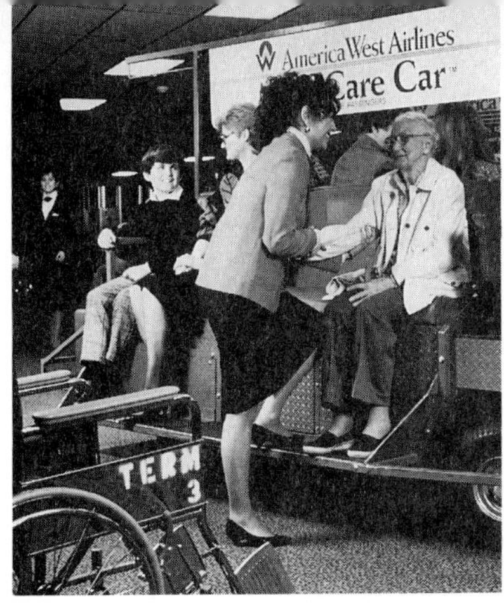

Periodic review of key aspects of the firm's operations must be made frequently to ensure that goals are achieved. America West Airlines' strategic plan for success is to create an airline with an emphasis on people—both customers and employees. For customers, they offer competitive fares and quality service with extra amenities such as this "More Care" car. For employees, America West provides a comprehensive benefit and compensation package and an "Employee Assistance Program" which is designed to provide confidential services to employees in such areas as financial, family, or personal problems. (Photograph courtesy of America West Airlines, Inc.)

issues must be reviewed at least quarterly to provide the small business owner with sufficient opportunities to take corrective action if warranted.

Even though changes in policies may at times be minor, the review process itself serves a useful function. It forces the entrepreneur to regain a perspective on the firm as a whole. Because many entrepreneurs do much of the actual day-to-day work, it is easy for them to lose sight of all facets of the business while concentrating on a few problems or opportunity areas. Quarterly reviews serve to reeducate the entrepreneur and ensure that the firm does not get out of touch with reality.

Recognizing that there are costs involved in policy evaluation, the entrepreneur should attempt to standardize this procedure to the greatest extent possible. The essential points of goal, plan, and policy evaluation include not only the timing of the review, but also making the review process effective and efficient.

Which Factors to Evaluate

In any firm, certain problems or opportunity areas will demand more attention than others. Consequently, review processes are apt to become molded around the peculiarities of the firm. While this is to be expected, it also can be dangerous if any facets of the business are continually slighted by the entrepreneur. Some of the more common problems are highlighted in Exhibit 8–10.

EXHIBIT 8–10 **Common Business Problems for Which Plans Are Needed**

A. Loss of Working Capital
   1. Signs of trouble
      a. Inadequate cash supply
      b. Inability to take advantage of supplier deals and discounts
      c. Build-up in accounts payable
      d. Inability to meet loan payments
   2. Possible causes of trouble
      a. Undercapitalization of firm
      b. Continual or large business losses
      c. Large nonrecurring expenses or losses
      d. Higher-than-anticipated operating costs
      e. Large investment of cash in fixed assets (such as fixtures or equipment)

EXHIBIT 8–10

Common Business Problems for Which Plans Are Needed *(continued)*

B. Low Sales
   1. Signs of trouble
      a. Cash flow problems
      b. Sales below forecasted levels
      c. Customer complaints
      d. Loss of market share
      e. Inventory turnover declines (cost of goods sold ÷ average inventory)
   2. Possible causes of trouble
      a. Increased number of competitors
      b. More aggressive marketing efforts by competitors
      c. Poor location
      d. Poor salesmanship
      e. Change in consumer demographics or their buying processes
      f. Failure to keep up with consumers' current product or service needs

C. Low Profits
   1. Signs of trouble
      a. Higher-than-anticipated costs
      b. Lower-than-expected sales
      c. Loss of working capital
      d. Increases in debt
   2. Possible causes of trouble
      a. Slow collection of receivables
      b. Excessive inventory
      c. Improper pricing
      d. Poor marketing program
      e. Internal and/or external theft
      f. Poor control over operating costs

D. High Levels of Debt
   1. Signs of trouble
      a. High interest payments
      b. Loss of working capital
      c. Inability to borrow additional funds
   2. Possible causes of trouble
      a. Overinvestment in fixed assets
      b. Overinvestment in inventory
      c. Inability to convert receivables into cash
      d. Borrowing on bad terms
      e. Lack of operating cost control
      f. Slow sales
      g. Undercapitalization

Plans and the resulting policies and procedures alone will not solve or prevent business problems. They must be solved by the *people* who own and manage the firm. However, general policies serve to identify and formalize basic processes, with the intent of providing standard approaches to business opportunities and problems. While unique problems cannot be covered by preestablished policies and procedures, those that are recurring can be resolved expediently. This frees entrepreneurial time for more pressing issues for which policies and procedures have not been prepared.

SUMMARY

1. One of the primary causes of business failure is the entrepreneur's inability or unwillingness to develop goals and strategic plans, which take the place of separate plans for individual facets of the firm's operations.
2. The goals of a firm can be broadly categorized as survival, profit, and growth.
3. Objectives provide the overall direction of the firm; policies give general guidelines for their accomplishment; procedures are specific statements that describe how the policies are to be carried out to achieve the goals.
4. Developing goals, plans, and policies and procedures requires planning at all levels within the firm and for a predetermined period of time.
5. One major obstacle to planning in smaller businesses is the entrepreneur's inability to set personal goals and goals for the firm.
6. Other obstacles to planning include inexactness, variability, and lack of time.
7. Actual planning involves working through a series of questions focusing on the business's current situation and where it is headed in the future.
8. Six major questions form the planning process:
   - What is the current status of the firm?
   - Where should the firm be at the present time?
   - What will happen to the firm if no changes are instituted?
   - In general, what should the firm do?
   - What specific policies and procedures need to be developed and implemented?
   - What controls should be built into the plans?
9. General planning is an ongoing process of integrating the changing goals, individuals, technology, and environment of the firm.
10. Because small firms are more affected than large firms by minor fluctuations in the business environment, objectives, plans, and policies and procedures should be evaluated at least quarterly.

KEY TERMS AND CONCEPTS

Policies
Procedures
Goals
Strategic plans
Survival objectives
Profit objectives
Growth objectives
Short-term plans
Long-term plans
Obstacles to planning

QUESTIONS FOR DISCUSSION

1. What are the three categories by which goals can be classified?
2. In which ways do the goals of a firm sometimes conflict?
3. Why is return on investment a preferred method for establishing profit objectives?
4. What is the difference between short- and long-term goals, and how do they fit together?
5. Why should goals be realistic and be quantified?
6. At what levels of the organization should goals be set and plans established?
7. Why is a strategic plan better than a series of separate plans for individual facets of a firm's operations?
8. What are the six steps in strategic planning?
9. What are the main obstacles to successful planning?
10. How often should goals, plans, and policies and procedures be reviewed?

SELF-TEST REVIEW

Multiple Choice Questions

1. Which of the following goals is the primary objective of most small businesses?
   a. Profit.
   b. Growth.
   c. Survival.
   d. Market share.
2. Which of the following is the preferred measure of firm profits?
   a. Dollar profits.
   b. Dollar sales.
   c. Market share.
   d. Return on investment.
3. For most firms, the bulk of planning undertaken at the lower levels of the organization consists of:
   a. Developing broad long-range plans dealing with the establishment of goals.
   b. Developing short-range plans focusing on policies and procedures for goal achievement.
   c. Developing techniques for reviewing goals, plans, and policies and procedures.
   d. No planning should be done at lower levels.
4. Which of the following is the most common obstacle to planning?
   a. Fear of planning.
   b. Inexact nature of planning.
   c. Lack of knowledge about planning.
   d. Insufficient time to develop plans.
5. The first step in the strategic planning process is to:
   a. Establish check points for plan review.
   b. Evaluate the firm's current position.
   c. Set goals for the firm.
   d. Decide where the firm should be if no changes are taken in the current management processes.

True/False Statements

1. A key to successful small business management is the identification of goals and a recognition of the need for strategic planning.
2. Goals of net sales and market share are defined in absolute dollar terms.
3. Stable growth leads to the most effective business planning.
4. Entrepreneurs should start by setting short-term goals and then make longer-term ones.
5. Plans should be flexible enough to be acceptable to uncontrollable environmental changes.
6. The planning process is more time-consuming than it is difficult.
7. Procedures should always be set in general rather than specific terms.
8. Small businesses do not need to make internal assessments of their current situations before undertaking the strategic planning process.
9. Goal and plan reviews need not be undertaken more than once each year.
10. Policies and procedures serve to resolve many of the routine problems that can consume considerable entrepreneurial time.

LOCKHARDT'S COFFEE SHOP

When Mark Kilgore purchased Lockhardt's Coffee Shop nearly six months ago, he did not realize how poorly it had been run. Although Lockhardt's is the most popular coffee shop in town, Kilgore has found that internal operations are in disarray. Customers are not being served promptly, and the quality of food is inconsistent. For the first few months, Kilgore has tried to learn the business and not make any radical changes. Now that six months have passed and sales are down nearly 15 percent, he believes that some actions are necessary before his investment is lost.

Located in a midwestern town of approximately 70,000 people, Lockhardt's is the oldest of the five independent and three franchised coffee shops in the area. Over the years, Lockhardt's has remained popular because of the personality of the owner, low prices, and spacious premises. Unlike the other coffee shops in town, Lockhardt's is large enough to seat 150 to 200 people at a time. It has become a meeting place for residents, a place where they can relax and visit as well as eat. With his outgoing personality, the original owner, Fred Lockhardt, had cultivated this atmosphere by taking time to chat with the patrons as they entered and dined. Even the 10 waiters and waitresses, who have worked an average of nearly nine years at Lockhardt's, have been encouraged to mingle with customers and to provide relaxed, slow service.

During the 25 years that Lockhardt owned and managed the coffee shop, he became quite wealthy. Over the last five years, he has begun lowering prices and raising employee wages as a means of showing his appreciation for the loyalty his customers and employees have shown him. As a result, business has grown even more. A year ago, however, Lockhardt decided to retire, and he sold the coffee shop to Kilgore, a relatively new resident in town who previously worked as an assistant manager of a local department store.

Kilgore has indicated that he wants to maintain the same image and atmosphere that Lockhardt had so successfully created. But he cannot ignore the casual approach to operations. Most surprising to Kilgore is that employees set their own work schedules, have no predetermined tables to wait on, and do not have job descriptions detailing what they are supposed to do. In addition, waitresses sit and visit with customers, make them special items, and at times give them discounts.

Kilgore's training in department store management leads him to believe that a more structured operation is necessary for long-term success. This perspective has caused two waitresses to threaten to take jobs with a competitor. They complain that Kilgore says he wants to maintain the same type of business, but that he frequently criticizes them for not serving customers more rapidly, and for spending too much time with other customers. These waitresses also are receiving some complaints from customers that prices are rising and that the coffee shop does not have its traditional warm, friendly atmosphere.

QUESTIONS

1. Evaluate the approach Kilgore has taken to managing Lockhardt's since buying the coffee shop.
2. What actions does Kilgore need to take if he is to build Lockhardt's into a successful business?

NOTES

1. Dun and Bradstreet, *Business Failure Record,* (New York: Dun and Bradstreet Corp., 1988), 20.
2. "Planning . . . The Most Important Ingredient," *Focus on the Facts,* U.S. Small Business Administration and Apple Computer, 1988, 1.
3. Based on Cable News Network's "Pinnacle," September 11, 1988. Guest: Charles Zwick, Southeast Banking Corporation.
4. "Humana—83 Hospitals Strong, and an Early SBA Lift," *Network,* March–April 1989, U.S. Government Printing Office, 3, 9.
5. Based on Cable News Network's "Pinnacle," June 18, 1989. Guest: Jim Manzi, Lotus Development.
6. "The Best Small Companies," *Business Week,* May 23, 1988, 127.
7. "Cherly McArthur: Discount Outlets for Mall Mavens," *Business Week,* November 6, 1989, 117.
8. "The Hot 100 Growth Companies," *Business Week,* May 23, 1988, 121.
9. "Deliverymen Who Always Ring Twice," *Business Week,* May 23, 1988, 135.
10. Based on Cable News Network's "Pinnacle," June 14, 1987. Guest: John Rollwagen, Cray Research.
11. "One Word for One Price: Success," *Business Week,* May 23, 1988, 123.
12. Based on Cable News Network's "Pinnacle," November 14, 1987. Guest: Mark Stevens, Häagen-Dazs.

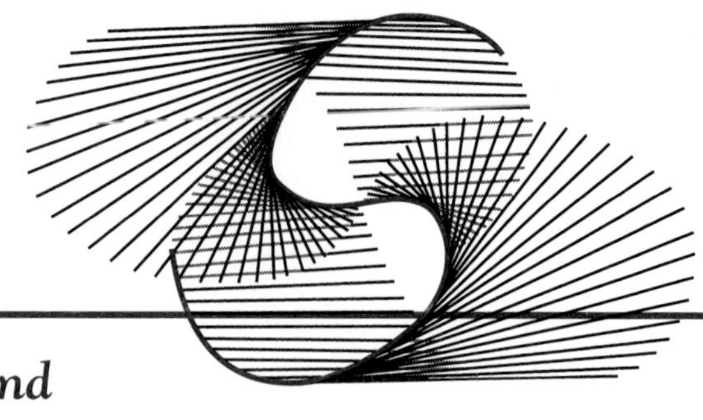

Chapter Nine

Marketing Research and Market Assessment

Chapter Outline

THE NATURE OF MARKETING RESEARCH
- Why Do It?
- Conducting Research with Limited Budgets

THE MARKETING RESEARCH PROCESS
- Defining the Problem
- Assessing Available Information
- Gathering Additional Information
- Going Outside for Marketing Research Data

COLLECTING SECONDARY DATA

COLLECTING PRIMARY DATA
- Observation Method
- Survey Method
- Experimentation Method

DEVELOPING THE QUESTIONNAIRE
- Question Design
- Question Sequencing
- Questionnaire Design

SAMPLING PLANS

INTERPRETING THE DATA

MARKET ANALYSIS
- Demographic Characteristics
- Population and Income Trends
- Competition
- Estimating Market Potential

SALES FORECASTING
- Forecasting Methods
- Seasonality of Sales
- Short-Term Sales Forecasting
- Distribution of Sales by Month
- Cumulative Percents
- Accuracy of Sales Forecasts

SUMMARY

Learning Objectives

The objectives of this chapter are to assist you in understanding:

1. The steps involved in the marketing research process.
2. How to obtain secondary and primary data.
3. Factors to consider in developing a questionnaire.
4. Factors to consider in conducting a market analysis.
5. How to forecast sales.

Successful planning of business strategies and programs requires information—about customers, competitors, and market characteristics. It is the job of marketing research to help gather and analyze the information needed. Without sound marketing information, managers operate on the basis of hunches. In a dynamic and competitive environment, such an approach is likely to result in failure.

No business can afford to make many errors, or proceed very far with inadequate information. Consider, for example, the number of stores that fail because something was overlooked in site selection. Consider the slow-moving, unprofitable merchandise occupying shelf and storage space in many stores. And consider the consumers who cannot find the goods or services that they want. All of these situations can be improved when management does not neglect marketing research.

To direct a business, managers must be future-oriented. They must recognize changes in the market and anticipate tomorrow's developments so that they can adjust business operations accordingly. In short, management needs to assess the market and the environment on a continuing basis to discover new business opportunities. To do this, one must gather information, analyze it, and put it to good use. Examples of entrepreneurs who have recently done this include Mark Swislow, Paul Hait, Bob Ronstadt, John Marsden, and Edward Harrigan.

- Mark Swislow was a salesman by day and an MBA student by night when he was assigned to research a new business opportunity for his marketing class. On the advice of a distributor friend after he participated in a computer show, he developed computer dustcovers. Today his Computer Coverup employs 50 people and has several million dollars in sales.[1]
- Paul Hait is an inventory–entrepreneur who turned a backyard hobby of smoking meat into Pyromid grills. When he experienced problems with rain dousing his campfire, he tried building his fire under a pyramid of stones. The structure's shape not only kept out the rain but made cooking more efficient. Seeing an opportunity, he developed a successful line of cookers around the concept of heat reflectivity. After a number of false starts, Pyromid is approaching $1 million in sales.[2]
- Bob Ronstadt, who taught, wrote, and gave advice about entrepreneurship as a professor, left his tenured university position to become an entrepreneur. He did so after determining that students had difficulty generating the financial statements that investors want. As a result of this observation, he created a new software package called Ronstadt's Financials. The software takes the user's assumptions and turns them into a set of financial statements, while allowing comparisons of various scenarios. An industry newsletter said the program "has the kind of intuitive feel and power that we've come to associate with perfectly designed tools. We suspect that a lot of small-business spreadsheet users will very quickly start switching to Ronstadt's Financials."[3]
- John Marsden and Edward Harrigan came up with a great solution to the problem of not having suntan lotion in a convenient container while at the beach. They realized that many sunbathers left their big clumsy bottles of suntan lotion at home and were left frying to a crisp. They decanted one ounce of coconut-scented waterproof suntan lotion into a hollow plastic bracelet and sold it for $4.99 in over 200 stores in Southern California, Florida, and Cape Cod.[4]

THE NATURE OF MARKETING RESEARCH

To be successful, a small business must have useful information for marketing decision-making, regardless of the number of years that it has been in business or its present profitability. To be useful, information must be available when needed and it must be relevant, that is, it must fit the decision-making requirements. **Marketing research**—the systematic gathering, recording, and analyzing of data about the problems relating to the marketing of products and services—must be conducted to accomplish this.

Marketing research is an organized way of finding objective answers to questions every business must answer to succeed. Every small business owner must ask:[5]

- Who are my customers and potential customers?
- What kind of people are they?
- Where do they live?
- Can and will they buy?
- Am I offering the kinds of goods and services they want—at the best place, at the best time, and in the right amount?
- Are my prices consistent with what buyers view as the products' values?
- Are my promotional programs working?
- What do customers think of my business?
- How does my business compare with my competitors'?

Marketing research is not a perfect science. It deals with people and their constantly changing likes and dislikes, which can be affected by hundreds of influences, many of which simply cannot be identified. Marketing research does, however, try to learn about markets scientifically. That, simply, is to gather facts in an orderly, objective way; to find out how things are, not how the business owner thinks they are or would like them to be; what people want to buy, not just what the business wants to sell them.[6]

Why Do It?

Marketing research may involve substantial effort and cost, depending on the information required. Yet a lack of research or even insufficient research may be far more costly to the business when decisions are made based on incomplete facts or mere hunches. Some experts believe that small companies actually have greater need for research than

The entrepreneur conducting this interview hopes to draw conclusions about the shopping habits of these customers by analyzing the information they give about themselves in the survey. (Photograph © Ann M. Mason)

do large companies because of their smaller resources and reduced ability to change course and try again.[7] Unfortunately, small business owners talk a lot about marketing research but do not often use it. It is too easy to take a shortcut in reaching a decision—to talk to a few customers, friends, or people at a cocktail party, and then make a decision. This is not sound marketing research.

Conducting Research with Limited Budgets

In large companies, marketing research is usually the responsibility of a staff of in-house research specialists operating with relatively large budgets. For most small business firms, in-house marketing research specialists are not practical, because this requires talent the firm cannot afford to employ on a full-time basis. There are, however, a number of ways for small firms to conduct marketing research with limited budgets.

Initially, small business owners should investigate available information, including reports of trade organizations, government studies, and research findings reported in local business publications. Considerable information can also be gained through observation—as was demonstrated by the entrepreneurs profiled earlier in this chapter—and through close contacts with customers.

Small business owners often have a feel for their customers that comes from years of experience. Experience can be a two-edged sword, though, since it comprises a tremendous mass of facts acquired at random over a number of years. Information about markets gained from long experience might no longer be timely enough to base selling decisions on. In addition, some "facts" may be vague, misleading impressions or folk tales of the "everybody knows that . . ." variety.[8]

Trash and Peanuts

Some marketing research material is nothing but garbage.[9] Marketing research can be done for peanuts—even without peanuts. Shocking statements? Perhaps, but both of them are literally true.

Take garbage, for instance. Inspection of outgoing waste has been a practice of many small restaurants. Initially, many people may order the flounder à la marzipan because of the novelty of the dish, but if a restaurateur finds most of it leaving the tables uneaten, it had better come off the menu, because it will not be in demand much longer.

One can use trash positively, too, to find out what people like. It may not be very dignified to check trash cans for cartons and containers, but they are direct indications of what consumers are buying. One could also find out what competitors are selling (or at least ordering) by checking their trash as well.

The point here is not to turn one into a scavenger, but to suggest that marketing research is not done only by sophisticated staffs of statistical technicians working with powerful computers and grinding up figures from elegant surveys. Marketing research does not have to be fancy and expensive.

It can be done with peanuts, as one creative discount merchandiser discovered. During a three-day promotion the merchant gave away free to customers "all the roasted peanuts you can eat while shopping our store." By the end of the promotion the merchant had litter trails that provided information on the traffic pattern within the store. Trampled peanut hulls littered the most heavily traveled aisles, and were even heaped up in front of displays of merchandise of special interest to customers. In short, the merchant learned how people acted in the store and what they wanted, and observed their behavior.

Convincing Skeptics

Small business owners may have to be shown how and why research can be a powerful marketing tool, as illustrated in the following two cases.

Case 1. A small company was directing the major part of its advertising dollars toward its heavy users—a common and often effective practice. But evaluation of the market indicated that the heavy-user group did not offer growth potential. The company had reached a high degree of saturation in the heavy-user market. Thus, its growth would have to come from light users and/or nonusers.

Research pointed out that advertising that had been effective in attracting heavy users was not motivating light users and nonusers. In fact, it was turning them off! Once this was realized, the heavy-user advertising was altered, both in appearance and media approach, with the appeal directed toward the light and nonuser groups. The strategy worked.

Perhaps logic, experience, or intuition could have identified and solved this problem. But they did not. Research did, and the research investment was small.[10]

Case 2. A small consumer products company discovered that current customers agreed on one of its product's strong selling points. The customers felt the benefit was real and important in differentiating the product from competitors.

It was obvious that the benefit could be the key for a new advertising campaign that was being developed. However, research uncovered the fact that potential customers did not find the benefit believable, even though it was real.

As a result of the research, the benefit was used in the advertising campaign. But the advertisements emphasized and dramatized the believability of the claim, rather than the importance of the claim. The creative techniques used in the campaign, suggested by the research, succeeded in changing the target audience's perception of the benefit.[11]

In both cases, research helped solve a problem faced by the respective businesses. These examples suggest that the decision to use and trust marketing research is a difficult one for many small business owners.

Regardless of who actually conducts marketing research, the value of such efforts can be best realized if the person using the results understands the basic step-by-step approach to solving marketing problems. Small business owners should ask themselves these questions when considering marketing research:

- What am I trying to find out?
- Why do I want to know?
- What can I do with the answer?
- What will the answer mean?
- Will the research provide the facts needed?

THE MARKETING RESEARCH PROCESS

The **marketing research process** is a step-by-step approach that guides the research effort and provides a framework for conducting the research.[12] An orderly procedure helps

EXHIBIT 9–1

The Marketing Research Process

I. Define the Problem (Limit and state clearly)
II. Assess Available Information
III. Assess Additional Information, if Required
   1. Review internal records and files
   2. Interview employees
   3. Consult secondary sources of information
   4. Interview customers and suppliers
   5. Collect primary data
IV. Organize and Interpret Data
V. Make Decision
VI. Watch the Results of the Decision

Source: Small Business Administration, *Researching Your Market,* Management Aid Number 4.019 (1988), 2.

clarify what needs to be done, and will greatly improve the ability to plan marketing research projects and solve the right problems. Exhibit 9-1 shows the steps in the marketing research process.

Defining the Problem

This, the first step of the research process, is so obvious that it is often overlooked. Yet it is the most important step of the process.

One must be able to see beyond the symptoms of a problem to get at the cause. Seeing the problem as a "sales decline" is not defining a cause, it is listing a symptom.

In defining a problem one should list every possible influence that could have caused it. Has there been a change in the areas customers traditionally come from? Have their tastes changed? All possible causes should be listed. Those causes that cannot be measured should be set aside, since one will not be able to take any action on them.

One must establish an idea of the problem with causes that can be objectively measured and tested. Ideas of the causes should be put in writing. These should be reread frequently while gathering facts to keep on track, but they should not get in the way of the facts either.

Assessing Available Information

Once the problem has been formally defined, one should assess one's ability to solve it immediately. One may already have all the information needed to determine if one's hypothesis is correct, and solutions to the problem may have become obvious in the process of defining it. At this point one should stop. One will only be wasting time and money if one does further marketing research.

What if one is not sure whether or not additional information is needed at this point? What if one would feel more comfortable with additional data? Here, one must make a subjective judgment to weigh the cost of more information against its usefulness.

One faces a dilemma similar to guessing in advance the return on dollars spent on advertising. One does not know what return one will get, or even if any return will be obtained. The best one can do is to ask oneself how much making a wrong decision will cost and to balance that against the cost of gathering more data to make a better-informed decision.

Gathering Additional Information

One should think cheap and stay as close to home as possible. Before considering anything fancy like surveys or field experiments, one should examine internal records and files. One should look at sales records, complaints, receipts, or any other records that can show where customers live or work or how and why they buy.

One small business owner found that addresses on cash receipts allowed the pinpointing of customers in his market. With this kind of information he could cross-reference his customers' addresses and the products they purchased. From this information he was able to check the effectiveness of his advertising placement.

Customers' addresses alone can reveal a lot about them. One can pretty closely guess customers' lifestyles by knowing what the neighborhoods they live in are like. Knowing how they live can provide solid hints on what they can be expected to buy.

Credit records are an excellent source of information about markets, too. In addition to the always valuable addresses of real customers, they give information about customers' jobs, income levels, and marital status. Granting credit, so that this information can be seen, is a multifaceted marketing tool—though one with well-known costs and risks.

Once finished checking internal records, one can go to that other valuable internal source of customer information: employees. Employees may be the best source of information about customer likes and dislikes. They hear customers' minor gripes about the store or service—the ones the customers do not think are important enough to take to the owner-manager. They are also aware of the items customers request that should be stocked. Employees can probably also provide pretty good seat-of-the-pants customer profiles from their day-to-day contacts.

Going Outside for Marketing Research Data

Once the best sources for information about the market have been exhausted, where does one go? The next steps in the process are to do primary and secondary research on the outside. Primary research involves gathering primary data. **Primary data** are data collected by the researcher from the original source for the particular purpose of the study. Secondary research involves obtaining secondary data. **Secondary data** are data that have already been collected for some other purpose.

Secondary Research First

Secondary research should be done before any primary research is undertaken. Secondary research simply involves going to already published surveys, books, magazines, and the like and applying or rearranging the information in them to bear on one's particular problem or potential opportunity.

For example, suppose the business sells tires. One might reasonably guess that sales of new cars three years ago would have a strong effect on present retail sales of tires. To test this idea, one might compare new car sales of six years ago with the replacement tire sales from three years ago.

Suppose one finds that new tire sales three years ago were 10 percent of the new car sales three years previous to that. Repeating this exercise with car sales five years ago and tire sales for two years ago and so on, one might find that in each case tire sales were about 10 percent of the new car sales made three years before. One could then logically conclude that the total market for replacement tire sales in the local area this year ought to be about 10 percent of the new car sales in the locality three years ago.

Naturally, the more localized the figures one can find, the better. While, for instance, there may be a decline nationally in new housing starts, if one sells new appliances in an area where new housing is booming, one obviously would want to base the estimate of market potential on local conditions. Newspapers and local radio and television stations may be able to help find this information.

There are many sources of such secondary research material, as pointed out later in this chapter. One can find it in libraries, universities and colleges, trade and general business publications, and newspapers. Trade associations and government agencies are especially rich sources of information.

Primary Research, the Last Step

Primary research on the outside can be as simple as asking customers or suppliers how they feel about one's business, or as complex as the surveys done by the sophisticated professional marketing research firms. It includes among its tools direct mail questionnaires, telephone or on-the-street surveys, experiments, panel studies, test-marketing, behavior observation, and the like.

Primary research is often divided into *reactive* and *nonreactive* research. The peanut shell study discussed earlier in this chapter is an example of nonreactive primary research: it was a way of seeing how real people behaved in a real market situation (in this case how they moved through the store and which displays attracted their attention) without influencing that behavior even accidentally.

Reactive research (surveys, interviews, questionnaires) is probably what most people think of when they hear the words "marketing research." It is the kind that may, at times, best be left to experts, unless one knows the right questions to ask. There is also the danger that either people will not want to hurt one's feelings when asked their opinions about the business, or they will answer questions the way they think they are expected to answer, rather than the way they really feel. If one cannot afford professional marketing research services, one can ask nearby colleges or university business schools for help, or seek out books on do-it-yourself marketing research.

COLLECTING SECONDARY DATA

As indicated previously, no research project should be undertaken without a thorough search of secondary sources. This search should be done early in the problem-definition stage and prior to collecting data by means of observations, surveys, or experiments for several reasons:

- Secondary data may solve a problem without the need to collect primary data.
- The cost of collecting secondary data is substantially lower than that of collecting primary data.
- Obtaining secondary data is quicker than gathering primary data.

External secondary data sources are varied and numerous. While it is not feasible to make use of all possible sources of market data, some of the readily available sources of information should be familiar to every small business owner-manager. Secondary research materials can be found in public and government libraries, colleges and universities, trade associations and government agencies, newspapers and magazines.

Periodicals

Managers interested in current articles on entrepreneurship and various small business management subjects can consult a number of periodicals. The following periodicals are especially noted for their focus on small business operations:

- *American Journal of Small Business,*
- *INC.,*
- *Journal of Small Business Management,*
- *Nation's Business,* and
- *Venture.*

Periodicals such as these are valuable sources on the subjects of entrepreneurship, small business start-ups, small business management, venture capital, innovation and technology, laws and regulations, marketing for small business, counseling small business, franchising, and small business trends.

Trade Associations

Almost every industry has a trade association that publishes industry-related data in a journal, newsletter, or some other format. These provide excellent data on market trends and developments, surveys, and forecasts. In addition, advertisements in trade publications are excellent sources of information about new product developments and competitors.

Most libraries have reference books that list trade associations by industry groups. These books should be consulted to determine associations from which appropriate information can be requested.

Directories

Names and information about companies in a particular market, industry, state, or region are generally available from hundreds of directories published annually. These directories provide information from which prospective customers for given products can be identified, plants located, and new sources of supply discovered.

Detailed information on research organizations and consultants is also available in a number of directories. The information provided generally includes breakdowns by location, area of specialization, size of staff, and other important data.

Predicasts F&S Index

Predicasts F&S Index United States covers company, product, and industry information from over 750 financial publications, business-oriented newspapers, trade magazines, and special reports. Indexes contain information on corporate acquisitions and mergers, new products, technological developments, and social and political factors affecting business.

Each entry in *Predicasts F&S Index United States* contains a brief description of the contents of the article, a standardized abbreviation for the publication from which the entry was abstracted, and the date and page on which the article appears. Information on availability and cost of publications indexed is found in the Source Pages.

The Industries & Products section of *Predicasts F&S United States* reports on new products, new capacities, product demand, end uses, and sales. Also included in this section are general economic factors such as population, wages, consumer spending, business investment, construction outlays, and government regulation and spending.

The Companies section of *Predicasts F&S Index United States* is arranged by company name. This section contains merger and acquisition data, joint venture information, sales and profits, analyses of companies by securities firms, and other corporate and financial data.

U.S. Government Publications

Local, state, and federal governments are rich sources of information for specific industries and economic conditions. Government-published information is generally available in most libraries or can be obtained from the appropriate publishing agency. The primary government business information sources are the Small Business Administration (SBA), the U.S. Department of Commerce, and the Bureau of the Census.

U.S. Small Business Administration

The U.S. Small Business Administration issues a wide range of management and technical publications designed to help owner-managers of small business. In 1986, the SBA distributed over 6.2 million business publications to entrepreneurs. All SBA business publications are easy to read and provide basic information about starting, running, or expanding a successful small business. The practical guidance found in these publications provides knowledge about successful small business management. For general information about the SBA and its policies and assistance programs, one should contact the nearest SBA office.

A listing of currently available publications can be obtained free from U.S. Small Business Administration, P.O. Box 15434, Fort Worth, TX 76119. Publications in the form of Business Development Pamphlets cover the following broad topics:

- Financial management and analysis,
- General management and planning,
- Marketing,
- Personnel management, and
- New products/ideas/inventions.

A series of Management Aids pamphlets is also published. These pamphlets are organized by a broad range of management principles. Each pamphlet in the series discusses a specific management practice to help the owner-manager of a small firm with management problems and business operations. A section on marketing covers a wide variety of topics from advertising guidelines to marketing research to pricing.

COLLECTING PRIMARY DATA

The major methods of gathering primary data include observations, surveys, and experiments.

Observation Method

The **observation method** is used by actually viewing, either by personal observation or through mechanical means such as hidden cameras, the overt actions of the respondent. Although other methods of collecting data have become highly sophisticated, there is still much merit in simple personal observation of the market to get a feel for the situation. Examples of direct observation include counting the number of people (or cars) passing by a store window, the number of people handling and purchasing a special display item, or the frequency of sales during specific days and at particular times when a store is open for business.

Automobile license plate analysis can yield important information about where a car's owner lives. One can generally get information from state agencies on how to extract this information from license numbers. By taking down the numbers of cars parked in a particular location one can estimate the trading area of the businesses situated at such location. Knowing where customers live helps focus advertising efforts.

Much can be learned about customers just by looking at them. How are they dressed? What is their gender? How old do they appear to be? Do they have children with them? This technique is rather obvious and most owner-managers get a feel for their clientele in just this way. But how about running a tally sheet for a week, keeping track of what one is able to tell about customers from simple outward clues? It might only confirm what appears obvious, but it might also be instructive.

Data gathered through observation can be biased if respondents realize they are being studied. Because of this, the observer may be concealed to assure that respondents act naturally. To help assure that observation studies are accurate, one may want to rely on tape recorders and/or cameras to record behavior.

Survey Method

The **survey method** is the most common method of gathering primary data. This method relies on individuals to answer questions for the purpose of drawing conclusions. It is an effective means of obtaining feedback from past, current, and prospective customers. By developing a short customer questionnaire—such as those illustrated in Exhibit 9-2 for a restaurant and in Exhibit 9-3 for an apparel store—and making it readily available to customers, one can collect feedback information and analyze it for better decision making.

The three basic survey techniques are personal interviews, mail surveys, and telephone interviews. Each of these techniques has advantages and disadvantages, as pointed out in Exhibit 9-4.

Personal Interviews

Personal interviews are the most flexible and informative type of survey method, although they tend to be relatively costly and require much planning and supervision. Interviewers need to be selected, trained, supervised, and provided with enough financial incentive to prevent temptations to shortcut the interviewing process or fake some interviews.

The danger of bias can be significant. A good rapport between interviewer and interviewee can lead the subject to answer questions the way the interviewer wants. Or the interviewer might ask questions in a way that leads to an anticipated response.

EXHIBIT 9–2 Customer Opinion Survey for a Restaurant

To Our Guests:

At ________, we are dedicated to maintaining our commitment to quality food, good service, cleanliness, and outstanding value.

We know that you, our customer, expect to eat in clean surroundings and like to be treated with genuine courtesy and friendliness. Therefore, we continually monitor our restaurant to insure that you receive the service and quality of food desired. We would appreciate it if you would help by answering the questions below. Then simply hand this questionnaire to the cashier or mail it to our personal attention.

Thank you for your cooperation.

Sincerely,

________, Owner

How did you first hear about this restaurant? (Check One)

Friend ___ Just stopped by ___ Mailing Advertisement ___ Newspaper ___
Radio ___ Yellow Pages ___ Other ________________

Please indicate below how you would rate your eating experience at ________ by circling the number that corresponds to your rating.

	Excellent	Good	Average	Poor	Not Able To Rate
Service					
1. Friendliness/courtesy	1	2	3	4	5
2. Prompt service	1	2	3	4	5
3. Employee appearance	1	2	3	4	5
4. Employee friendliness	1	2	3	4	5
Food					
5. Hot foods (hot?)	1	2	3	4	5
6. Taste	1	2	3	4	5
7. Food variety	1	2	3	4	5
8. Beverage variety	1	2	3	4	5
9. Value for the money	1	2	3	4	5
Restaurant Appearance					
10. Dining room	1	2	3	4	5
11. Waiting room	1	2	3	4	5
12. Restrooms	1	2	3	4	5

Please indicate any other comments or suggestions you may have regarding ________:

____

____

Thank you.

EXHIBIT 9–3

Customer Opinion Survey for an Apparel Store

Dear Customer:

At ________, we value you as our customer and want to continue providing you with a quality shopping experience. Our business has grown through the years because of you, our customer. We do not want to ever lose sight of that fact.

Please take a moment to fill out this questionnaire, so we may improve where needed, and carry on where you feel we have done a good job. When finished, simply hand this questionnaire to the cashier or mail it to our personal attention. Thank you for your time and opinions.

Sincerely,

________, Owner.

How did you first hear about this store? (Check One)

Friend ____ Just stopped by ____ Mailing Advertisement ____ Newspaper ____

Radio ____ Yellow Pages ____ Other ________________________________

Please indicate below how you feel about each of the following areas of the store by circling the number that corresponds to each item.

	Excellent	Good	Fair	Poor	Not Able To Rate
Merchandise					
1. Selection of styles, colors, and fashion	1	2	3	4	5
2. Selection in my size	1	2	3	4	5
3. Quality of merchandise	1	2	3	4	5
4. Availability of merchandise	1	2	3	4	5
Customer Service					
5. Received prompt attention	1	2	3	4	5
6. Sales people were knowledgeable	1	2	3	4	5
7. Sales people were friendly	1	2	3	4	5
8. Returns and/or exchanges were handled courteously	1	2	3	4	5
9. Credit authorizations were prompt	1	2	3	4	5
Store Appearance					
10. Merchandise displays attractive and eye-catching	1	2	3	4	5
11. Selling areas neat and clean	1	2	3	4	5
12. Fitting rooms neat and clean	1	2	3	4	5
13. Restrooms clean	1	2	3	4	5

Please indicate any other comments or suggestions you may have regarding ________:

____

Thank you.

EXHIBIT 9–4 **Comparison of the Three Basic Survey Methods**

Characteristics	Personal Survey	Mail Survey	Telephone Survey
Flexibility	Excellent	Poor	Good
Speed of data collection	Good	Poor	Excellent
Control of sample	Fair	Fair	Excellent
Quantity of data that can be collected	Significant	Varies*	Moderate
Respondent cooperation	Excellent	Moderate	Good
Interviewer bias	High	None	Moderate
Cost	Highest	Lowest	Low to moderate

*Depends on incentive

Mail Questionnaires

Mail questionnaires cost less than personal or telephone interviewing. In addition, there is no problem of interviewer bias, which often results from personal distraction in face-to-face or telephone interviews.

Problems associated with mail questionnaires are the difficulties of compiling a mailing list—although they can be purchased—and obtaining a good return rate in a reasonable period of time. Frequently it is necessary to offer an incentive for the respondents to return the completed questionnaire, and to send one or more requests to encourage a greater return. Because most people do not respond to mail questionnaires, a low return can lead to a distorted sample of the population being studied.

Telephone Interviews

Telephone interviews can usually be conducted more rapidly and at a lower cost than personal interviews. In addition, the response rate is generally higher than for mail questionnaires.

Telephone interviewing does have several drawbacks. The telephone is usually not a very good contact method if the interviewer is trying to get confidential personal information—such as details of household income and ethnicity. Respondents are not certain who is calling or how such personal information might be used. Furthermore, many consumers view telephone interviews with skepticism and even anger due to the increased solicitation of business conducted via telephone under the guise of marketing research. Interviewer bias may also be introduced by the way interviewers talk. Small differences in how they ask questions may affect respondents' answers.

Experimentation Methods

Experimentation is an effort to measure cause-and-effect relationships under controlled conditions. This method consists of establishing a control group in which all factors remain constant, and one or more test groups in which one factor is changed. A business may be trying to determine whether to change its price policies. In Store A, products are sold for the traditional price, while in Store B products are sold at a different price. All other factors are kept constant. Thus by measuring the sales in Stores A and B over a period of time, the business hopes to determine the effect of the new price.

Experimental methods can be used to determine the effect of alternative courses of action of various operational aspects of the business. Their use in marketing is widespread, especially in test-marketing new products. The greatest problems encountered in testing marketing variables are selecting the control and test markets, and controlling the variables. It is difficult to carry out an experiment that determines the effect of one marketing variable, such as price or advertising, while all variables are interacting at once.

DEVELOPING THE QUESTIONNAIRE

There are many different types of questionnaires. Initially, the researcher must decide whether to use one that is structured or unstructured. If a personal or telephone interview is used, the most common is the **structured questionnaire,** in which every question is worded and sequenced, and the interviewer does not depart from it at all. No other questions can be asked, nor can different sequences be used. An advantage to this questionnaire is that it minimizes possible interviewer discretion resulting in bias.

An **unstructured questionnaire** contains a limited number of questions, allowing the interviewer some freedom to vary the wording after the sequence, or probe for more data based on the respondent's answers. For example, the interviewer may ask, "What do you like or dislike about coffee?" Depending on the response, the interviewer may proceed to another subject, or continue on with, "Is there anything else you like or dislike?" or, "What about instant coffee?" The advantage of the unstructured questionnaire is that some valuable data can be obtained by the additional questions. The main disadvantages, however, are that the interviewer must be highly skilled in using this method, and unstructured interviews tend to be more time-consuming and expensive.

Question Design

In designing questions, one must carefully prepare each question, whether it is in a structured or an unstructured questionnaire. Most importantly, questions must be appropriately formed and worded for the specific data being sought. The researcher can use open-ended, dichotomous choice, or multiple choice questions. Open-ended questions allow the respondent to answer in his or her own words so that exact data can be collected. Dichotomous choice questions limit respondents to two choices—yes or no, hot or cold, and so on. Multiple choice questions force respondents to select one of several preestablished answers.

Question Sequencing

The questionnaire is not simply an assortment of questions that happen to be grouped together. If the questions are improperly ordered, respondents may not answer any of them, or they may not answer them accurately. The questions are interrelated, but must be sequenced logically so that they flow together, assisting the respondent to answer correctly and truthfully. In general, questions should be ordered:

- From easy to difficult,
- From general to specific,

- From insensitive to sensitive (or confidential),
- In groups by topical area, and
- With demographic questions toward the end.

Questionnaire Design

A questionnaire consists of four parts: the introduction, the set of instructions to the interviewer and respondent, the set of questions, and the closing. The wording and arrangement of these parts affect the quality of data they generate and the ease with which the data can be taken from the questionnaire and analyzed.

The introduction is especially important because it helps the interviewer gain rapport with the respondent. It also gives the respondent some general information on what the study is about, and why it is being conducted. Basically, it provides a brief orientation without revealing the specifics of the study until the questions are asked.

Instructions are often ignored by inexperienced researchers. Interviewers and respondents need to know how the interview will proceed and how responses are recorded on the questionnaire.

After the questions, a courteous closing is called for, in deference to the respondent's cooperation. In mail surveys, the closing is a way of inducing the respondent to return the questionnaire.

Physical layout is a final consideration in questionnaire design. Proper use of white space (blank space on a page), quality printing, and paper are all important, especially for mail questionnaires. Location and spaces for responses to the questions are also concerns, and they should be arranged to simplify transferring the data to tally sheets or computers.

SAMPLING PLANS

It is generally unnecessary to survey every person of a population in order to make inferences about the characteristics of the population. If a business owner-manager needs information about customers' attitudes toward the business, it is not necessary to interview every customer. Instead, a representative sample of all customers can be chosen. The attitudes of this sample should correspond to the views of all customers. The fundamental idea of **sampling** is that if a small number of units (called a *sample)* is chosen at random from a large number of units (called a *population* or *universe),* the sample will tend to have the same characteristics as the population.

One of the key questions in sampling is deciding how large the sample should be. This depends on the accuracy required. The sample should be large enough to satisfy the researcher that the answers are a true reflection of the population. It is difficult to predict how much will be enough, but one will be able to tell whether answers received become repetitive or form a pattern or trend.

Various sampling techniques may be used in marketing research. The most commonly used techniques are random sampling, stratified sampling, and area sampling.

Random sampling is used when the researcher wants to ensure that all units in a population have an equal chance of appearing in the sample. Random sampling is costly because it requires defining with absolute precision the population from which the sample is taken.

Stratified sampling involves dividing sample units into strata, or smaller populations, according to common characteristics, such as age, sex, and marital status. It is often used when there is reason to believe that there are differences among various types of respondents in the total population.

Area sampling is a variation of a simple random sample. It is used when it is not economically feasible to use a random sample of the population, or when a complete list of the population is not available. An example of an area sample would be to list all blocks in a city and then select the sample randomly from these blocks.

To gain a deeper understanding of sampling plans, the reader is encouraged to consult a marketing research or statistics book in his or her college library. A very practical, easy-to-understand book is George Edward Breen and A.B. Blankenship's *Do-It-Yourself Marketing Research* (New York: McGraw–Hill Book Company, 1982).

INTERPRETING THE DATA

Data by themselves generally do not provide a solution to the marketing research problem. They must be tabulated and interpreted before conclusions can be drawn. Statistical analysis, personal judgment, and intuition must be applied to the tabulated data in order to analyze and interpret research findings.

Today's availability of simple-to-use software enables a researcher to tabulate, analyze, and interpret masses of data quickly and at relatively low cost. Internal company sales data, for example, automatically tabulated and analyzed by electronic cash registers, help identify and solve problems relating to profitability of individual items or product lines, bad debts, inventory turnover, and salesforce productivity.

The final step in the marketing research process is the researcher's conclusions and recommendations. These should be supported by any necessary analysis and made available in a written report.

Far too many business owner-managers undertake formal research studies, reach conclusions and recommendations, and then file the report without taking any action. The value (and cost) of the research study is thereby lost. This is why researchers should follow up their studies to determine whether their recommendations are being implemented. If they are not implemented, the business and the researcher should make an effort to determine why. A review of each step of the marketing research process would be advisable.

MARKET ANALYSIS

Marketing research is essential in assessing market characteristics. The primary objective of such an analysis is to arrive at a realistic projection of sales. This requires a critical assessment of a firm's target market. Generally, a **market** is defined as people or organizations who have needs to satisfy and the ability (money) and willingness to pay. A **target market** is a particular market segment or group of customers that a business proposes to serve, or whose needs it proposes to satisfy.

The importance of analyzing markets and market trends is illustrated by Philip Knight, founder of Nike and the company's president. He sees growth coming in the future not from the company's traditional target market, but from what he calls "performance footwear," geared to generic or even specific athletic activity and, more im-

Pamela Kelley, owner of Rue de France—a manufacturer and distributor of French lace curtains through mail order, knows that she must study the market in order to find her potential customers. (Photograph courtesy of Pamela F. Kelley, president and founder of Rue de France)

portant, fashionable. He thinks that the fashion side of the business is an area from which Nike can get increased sales. He becomes very uncomfortable, however, at the thought of structuring Nike so that it is a fashion shoe company.[13]

Market segmentation is the process of taking the total market for a product or service and dividing it into several segments or submarkets that have similar characteristics. The restaurant market, for instance, can be segmented into the following types: haute cuisine, traditional table service, ethnic restaurant, specialty restaurant, coffee shop, cafeteria, drive-in, buffet/smorgasbord, and fast food. Each of these types of restaurants caters to the wants of a specific market segment. No single restaurant can satisfy everyone in the market.

Demographic Characteristics

Sound business decisions can only be made if, as a first step, the market that the entrepreneur wishes to serve has been thoroughly studied. Potential markets should be evaluated in terms of their changing demographic characteristics. Prospective entrepreneurs can then determine the viability of specific market segments.

LILLIAN VERNON®

Demographic characteristics, such as age, sex, family size, income, expenditures, occupation, marital status, education, religion, race, ethnic origin, and employment are used to describe the size, composition, and distribution of the population. These characteristics can be readily identified, obtained, measured and analyzed. For example, Lillian Vernon, chief executive officer of the mail order firm Lillian Vernon Corp., knows the demographics of her customers. They are thirty-nine years old, are more likely to be married than single, and have more children than the national average. They live in households with annual incomes of over $44,500. Over 65 percent work outside the home.[14]

Demographic data can be obtained from the Census of Population published by the U.S. Department of Commerce. These data are available for states and counties, and for every city, town, or village. For cities with a population of at least 50,000 (a metropolitan statistical area) data are tabulated by census tracts, small areas with an average population of 4,000 or 5,000. Summary data are available for each metropolitan statistical area in the United States in which such a city is located, as well as for individual blocks within the city.

Changes in demographics can have dramatic impact on marketing strategy. Changing wants may be anticipated and opportunities for new enterprises, products, and services discovered by careful analysis of census data. For example, the shift to an older population—the aging of the baby boom generation (those born between 1946 and 1964)—provides new opportunities for health care, travel, entertainment, and restaurants. The increasing number of affluent consumers represents lucrative markets for vacation homes, luxury autos, pleasure boats, haute cuisine restaurants, and financial services. The increase in the number of women in the labor force offers new opportunities for time-saving goods and services, such as prepared foods, prewrapped goods, day-care centers, nail care, and home-care services.

Small manufacturers, wholesalers, and retailers should keep track of the changing demographic factors in their respective markets. One way to help accomplish this is to review the local newspapers, trade journals, and magazines that publish annual market profiles for their trading area.

Population and Income Trends

Before selecting a particular community or location within a community to locate in, the owner-manager should become knowledgeable about the characteristics of the market or trading area. Because few markets remain stable for long, it is important to monitor the changes and trends of the market, notably population and income trends.

Among the questions to consider in analyzing population are these:

- What has been the change in total population in a specified market over the past five years?
- What has been the change in the average family size?
- What is the population distribution by age group?
- What percent of the population can be classified as urban, suburban, rural?
- What percent of the total population are potential customers?

These and similar population-related questions help owner-managers make decisions on what kinds of products or services to offer and where to locate. The most promising opportunities, of course, are in growing communities. Relatively few opportunities are found in communities with static populations or those showing long-term declining trends.

A study of income in the market area is an additional factor to consider in assessing the attractiveness of a market. Changes in income are important because they reflect changes in spending patterns for goods and services.

Competition

Few businesses operate free of competition. All firms compete with one another, either directly or indirectly, for the buying power of consumers. From a practical stand-

These entrepreneurs are looking for a growing community in which to locate their new business. They hope to find one with enough willing customers with needs that can be met by their product. (Photograph © Ann M. Mason)

point, however, a business usually views as competition those firms that sell identical or very similar products and services in the same trading area. A small gift store, for example, views all independent gift stores and gift departments of large stores in the trading area as competitors. Similarly, a small manufacturer of designer jeans faces competition from all other manufacturers of jeans.

Häagen-Dazs

Häagen-Dazs realizes the importance of keeping track of competition. A few years ago, they were the only people making premium ice cream in this country. Today there are many other competitors challenging Häagen-Dazs, such as Ben & Jerry's and Frusen Gladje. According to Mark Stevens, Häagen-Dazs's chief executive officer, competition is very healthy. It makes Häagen-Dazs a better company and it keeps it on its toes. The company was forced to keep raising its standards to become better than its competitors.[15]

To be successful, each competitor must differentiate itself from all others competing in the same market, as illustrated in the following example.

Gaining a foothold in the volatile designer jeans market requires a bit of luck and certainly a canny understanding of jean buyers' behavior. Makers of Jordache, Murjani, Sergio Valente, and others secured a niche in the designer jean market during the early days of the boom. One small company, makers of Tale Lord jeans, had to fashion a survival strategy to stay alive in the highly competitive jeans market. (Who ever heard of Tale Lord?)

Like many small companies, the Tale Lord Manufacturing Co. had been around for some time, but was unprepared for the sudden appearance of tough new competition in the jeans market. As a result, the company was feeling the effects of imported jeans from Hong Kong, and both sales and profits suffered accordingly. Therefore, Theodore Boshnack, thirty-one, owner of Tale Lord Manufacturing Co., decided to fly to Hong Kong to study the jeans business from thread to final product. He reasoned that if he could produce jeans of equal quality in the United States and move faster than imports on fashions, he could gain a toehold in the designer jeans market.

Boshnack's strategy consisted of using a computerized embroidery machine to create any stitched design for which the computer was programmed. Most back pockets of designer jeans show the maker's logo and distinctive stitching. Tale Lord pockets show full scenes, such as a motorcyclist cruising through the mountains or a tiger stalking prey under palm trees. The idea of sporting full scenes on back pockets was the result of a thorough market assessment. The strategy helped boost company sales and profits.[16]

While many entrepreneurs are discovering the value of competitor intelligence (the gathering of data and information about all aspects of a competitor's marketing and business activities for the purpose of formulating plans and strategies and making decisions), others are realizing how expensive it is not to track the competition. A few years ago, Maria Iriti, owner of Serpentino Glass, put out a bid to repair stained glass windows in a church. Without checking competitors' prices, Iriti bid $18,000. The next lowest bid, she later discovered, came in at $76,000. "We were shocked," she recalled.[17]

In assessing competition, attention should be given first to competitors of about the same type and size as the business in question, since they are on a more realistic level of competition. A small clothing store would be wise to concern itself with other small clothing stores rather than with a high-volume department or discount store. In time, a small operation might grow to the point of competing successfully with major firms, but the immediate pull of competition will come from other businesses of about the same size and description.

It is important for a business to know everything there is to know about competitors. Both the number and location of competitors and their aggressiveness and methods of operations should be analyzed. This can be done in various ways. For example, the yellow pages of the telephone book list the number and location of competitors. A telephone survey of these competitors will determine their basic marketing policies, including products carried, prices and credit terms, delivery services, and hours of operation. By visiting competitors' outlets, one can observe merchandising methods used, customers attracted to the business, quality of merchandise offered, adequacy of available parking, and so on. By conducting a mail survey or personal interviews, one can determine how customers feel about competitors, what they consider to be competitors' major strengths and weaknesses, and their image.

Questions to consider in analyzing competition include:

- How many competitive businesses are there within the trading area of the business? Where are they located?
- What can be found out about competitors? From whom?
- How many competitive businesses have closed or moved out of the market within the past year?
- How many competitive businesses have opened in the market area within the past year?
- What is the total known or estimated volume of competitive business within the trading area?
- What sort of sales effort does the competition make?
- What is the general physical appearance of competitive establishments?
- What competitive businesses are known to be for sale within the trading area?
- Can the competition be rated, taking all factors into account, from the strongest or most dominant to the weakest?
- How influential has the competition been in enlarging the overall market?
- Is there evidence of cooperative effort on the part of the competition to increase the total market?

Questions such as these should be addressed periodically, preferably every year. This helps spot competitors' strengths and weaknesses. Competitors' strengths need to be evaluated to determine if there is any way to offset them. Competitors' weaknesses should be exploited. For the small business owner who cannot afford consulting fees to keep abreast of competitors, there are newsletters, guides, workshops, and many how-to books on competitive intelligence.

Estimating Market Potential

Timberland®

The **market potential** for a product or service is the expected combined sales volume for all sellers of that product or service during a specified period of time in a given market. In attempting to assess the market potential for its products, The Timberland Company believes that it has just scratched the surface in the market it is already in, rugged outdoor boots and shoes. Whether it is a boat shoe or a boot or a casual outdoor shoe, the company thinks there is absolutely no limit to where it can go.[18]

Entrepreneurs sometimes estimate market potential based on hunch, as was the case with Wally Amos. He started making cookies at home in 1970, just as a hobby, because

When Wally Amos decided to give up his show business career to sell chocolate chip cookies, he had the plan all mapped out. His proposal indicated what he was going to do, how and why he would do it, and what it would cost to open his first store. (Photograph and logo© courtesy of The Famous Amos Chocolate Chip Cookie Corporation)

Famous Amos

he loved chocolate chip cookies. Then he started sharing them. He would go into meetings and break out cookies, and people would always say, "Hey, man, you ought to sell those, you ought to open up a store." But Amos was in show business, and who ever heard of somebody quitting show business to sell cookies? But when Amos could no longer stand the heat of the Hollywood scene, he got into the kitchen, turned entrepreneur, and whipped up a business out of his old hobby, ignoring those who had said he had bitten off more than he could chew. Intuitively, Amos came to the right conclusion that there was ample market potential for his cookies.[19]

In the case of Compaq Computer, a different approach is used to estimate market potential. The company estimates that it has only about 20 percent penetration in the white collar workforce of America. There are roughly 55 or 60 million white collar workers across the United States, and so at 20 percent penetration, Compaq Computer estimates that roughly 10 million of those workers now use business computers.[20]

One of the best-known sources of market potential data for consumer goods is provided by *Sales and Marketing Management* magazine. This magazine publishes an annual survey of buying power, with data and estimates on population, households, income, and certain categories of retail sales for cities, counties, and metropolitan areas. This survey is quite useful for comparative purposes. For example, buying power indexes for a particular year can be used to compare the buying power of one area with that of another area.

Owner-managers can use the buying power index to assess the overall sales opportunities in various trade areas. In order to determine the market for a specific product or service, one can evaluate the trade areas in terms of customer buying characteristics, social and political conditions, the competitive environment, ease of access, and regulatory requirements.

SALES FORECASTING

LILLIAN VERNON®

When market characteristics, competitors, and the market potential of a trade area have been analyzed, the potential sales volume of the business can be forecast. The **sales forecast** is an estimate of the sales, in dollars or physical units, for a certain time period. A short-term forecast covers a few months, seldom more than a year. Intermediate forecasts should be limited to one or two years. Whatever the duration of the forecast, difficulties are usually encountered, as illustrated by Lillian Vernon Corporation. In anticipating Christmas season demand for her catalog sales in 1988, Lillian Vernon thought it would be a sensational season, even with the election, the Olympics, the conventions, and all the distractions that go with an election year. She felt it would be a very strong Christmas for her company and hoped it would be true for the industry. In other words, the forecast was based on events whose combined impact could only be guessed. (Unfortunately, it turned out to be a bad season.)[21]

Sales forecasting is necessary for planning, implementing, and controlling business strategies. Indeed, the sales forecast is the basis for budgeting and operations of the firm. Yet most small business owners find that forecasting as a basis for major decisions is difficult for them, usually for one of the following reasons:

1. The likelihood of product or technological changes,
2. Inherently unpredictable markets or business conditions,
3. The reluctance of owner-managers to commit themselves into the future,
4. The tendency to be overly optimistic.

This explains why many firms hire consultants to help prepare forecasts, while others use an intuitive approach. Many small businesses are dominated by one person whose intuition provides its only guidelines.

In the majority of markets, demand is not stable from one year to the next, and good forecasting becomes a key factor in company success. Poor forecasting can lead to overly large inventories and costly price reductions, or lost sales from being out of stock. The more the demand fluctuates, the more important it is to forecast. Owner-managers should be familiar, therefore, with the major forecasting methods and understand the advantages and disadvantages of each.

Forecasting Methods

Sales forecasts require a blending of observations about what has happened in the past and judgments about what is likely to happen in the future. Therefore, few firms rely on only one forecasting method. Most combine several methods that have been effective for their particular circumstances. The principal methods of forecasting sales are summarized in Exhibit 9-5.

Salesforce estimates are frequently used for sales forecasts, especially in industrial markets. This approach takes advantage of the salesperson's familiarity with customer expectations and competitors' plans. Each salesperson's estimates are combined to establish a composite forecast. Although salespeople can be biased in their estimates and not knowledgeable about the impact of various market forces on future sales, they are closest to the customers and therefore more familiar with expected customer purchases.

Executive or expert opinion is similar to the salesforce method except that the opinions come from executives. Typically, key executives from marketing, procurement, finance, and production render their own sales forecasts based on opinion, previous experience, and available data. An average of the estimates is then used to serve as the sales forecast. This method has the advantage of being inexpensive, quick, and based on different points of view. A main drawback is that executive opinion may be too subjective and not based on hard data.

Customer surveys can also be used for sales forecasting. If one can be reasonably sure that customers know their future buying intentions and are willing to reveal them, the firm has a strong basis for accurate forecasting. Unfortunately, these conditions are seldom found in the real world. If the firm serves only a few customers, however, such as specialized industrial accounts, this method may be the best one.

Trend extension or extrapolation of historical data is simply a projection of past sales behavior into the future. Sales data from five previous years may indicate that annual sales growth has been 10 percent. From this it is extrapolated that next year's sales will

EXHIBIT 9–5 Sales Forecasting Methods

Sales Forecasting Methods	Advantages	Disadvantages
1. *Sales Force Estimates*—Obtains combined views of the salesforce as to the sales outlook. To ensure that estimates are realistic, they are likely to be reviewed at successive management levels.	1. Salesforce's familiarity with customers. 2. Salesforce's knowledge about competitors. 3. Participation may motivate salesforce.	1. Forecast may be tailored to own advantage. 2. Lack of familiarity with broad economic events. 3. Lack of knowledge about company plans.
2. *Executive or Expert Opinion*—Combines views of key executives or experts to obtain a sounder sales forecast than might be made by a single estimator.	1. Can be done quickly and inexpensively. 2. Takes advantage of different points of view. 3. May be only alternative if basic data are lacking.	1. May rely simply on intuition or guesswork. 2. May rely excessively on past sales. 3. Responsibility is dispersed.
3. *Customer Surveys*—Involves asking product users about the quantities they expect to buy in the forecast period. By combining customer responses, the interviewer can estimate total demand for the product (or service) and then determine the portion of that demand the company expects to fill.	1. Appropriate when there are few customers. 2. Appropriate when the cost of reaching customers is low. 3. Appropriate when customers have clear intentions. 4. Appropriate when customers disclose their intentions. 5. Appropriate when customers carry out their intentions.	1. Selecting the sample of potential buyers. 2. Customer's lack of knowledge about future intentions. 3. High cost and large amount of time required.
4. *Trend Extension*—Relies on statistical analysis of past sales data as a basis for forward projections (e.g., determining long-term growth patterns, cyclical fluctuations, seasonal variations, and irregular movements, and estimating their future effects).	1. Can be done quickly. 2. Inexpensive and easy to apply.	1. Evaluating the impact of trend, seasonal, and cyclical fluctuations. 2. Validity of assumptions made about past.
5. *Mathematical Models*—Makes use of mathematical techniques that seek to relate the pattern of an industry's or a company's sales to other factors believed to have some causal influence on them. In this method, such a relationship is expressed in one or more mathematical equations, constituting a mathematical model of the relationship.	1. Establishes direct relationships between sales and independent variables.	1. Complicated to use. 2. Difficult to isolate important independent variables. 3. Statistical sophistication required.

be 10 percent greater than sales for the current year. For example, past sales might reveal the following data:

Year	Sales	Sales growth as a percent of previous year's sales
1986	$55,000	—
1987	61,000	10.0
1988	66,000	9.0
1989	74,000	11.3
1990	81,200	9.7

Average annual sales growth for the years 1986–1990 is 10 percent. Sales for 1991 are therefore forecast to be $89,320. It is naïve, however, to expect that what has happened in the past with respect to trend, seasonal, and cyclical fluctuations will continue in the future. Therefore, one should never rely completely on this simplistic method of forecasting sales.

Mathematical models, such as correlation analysis, are concerned with discovering direct relationships between sales (dependent variable) and certain demand factors (independent variables). A statistical relationship may be found to exist between sales and disposable personal income, for example, or any number of other factors, including economic indicators (rate of unemployment, cost of living index, and so on) and demographic factors. Once the independent variables influencing sales are identified, an equation can be constructed that expresses the relationship between the independent variables and sales. One should consult marketing research texts to gain additional insights into the use of mathematical models.

Seasonality of Sales

Seasonality of sales is one of the most significant factors in small business failures, because it directly affects numerous decision areas, notably inventory, employment, promotion, and cash flow. Yet this aspect of sales forecasting is often the least understood, especially by new entrepreneurs.

To plan and anticipate for seasonal sales fluctuations, a small business owner-manager must be aware of the typical range of sales fluctuations for the particular industry. Published seasonal indexes (of past sales records) should be consulted to obtain an overview of the monthly percentage of a year's total sales. Local newspapers and chambers of commerce sometimes provide such seasonal indexes.

Short-Term Sales Forecasting

For a short-term forecast, which usually covers a few months and seldom more than a year, it is usually enough to know the sales for the past few weeks or months in comparison with the corresponding period of the year before. If sales for the past four weeks were 8 percent more than the corresponding four weeks of the preceding year, sales for the next few weeks can reasonably be expected to be 8 percent ahead of the corresponding period a year ago.

Adjustments must be made for any known or predicted conditions that will change this rate of increase, such as unusual weather, short-lived labor disputes, or changes in the dates of events, such as major holidays.

Distribution of Sales by Months

A longer-term method of forecasting is based on the distribution of sales by months. This method works best if the monthly variations over a period of years have been small.

Suppose that a short-term forecast is being made in June. For the past several years, sales in July have been between 11 and 13 percent of annual sales, with an average of 12.5 percent. During the same period, May sales have averaged 10 percent of annual sales. Sales during the May just past were $8,000. Then $8,000 divided by .10 equals $80,000, the estimated annual sales. Projected sales for July will be 12.5 percent of $80,000, or $10,000. Sales for other months can be forecast in the same way.

Cumulative Percents

Another method of short-term forecasting is the cumulative-percent method. The percent of total sales is figured for each week during the past year and added to the percent for preceding weeks, as shown in this example:

Weeks	*Weekly Percent*	*Cumulative Percent*
1	0.9	0.9
2	1.1	2.0
3	1.4	3.4
4	1.7	5.1
5	1.9	7.0
6	2.4	9.4
7	2.6	12.0
8	2.9	14.9
9	3.1	18.0

If sales during the first four weeks amount to $4,000, the annual total will be estimated at $4,000 divided by .051, or $78,430. To forecast sales for the next four weeks, add the percentages for those weeks and multiply the annual estimate by the result ($78,430 times .098 equals $7,686). This method works best for goods or services that are not subject to wide variations in sales volume or large price fluctuations.

Accuracy of Sales Forecasts

The accuracy of sales forecasts can vary substantially, regardless of the methods used. Indeed, it is rare when a forecast turns out to be completely accurate. Too many market variables are unpredictable, too many underlying assumptions are educated guesses, and too many data are subjective in nature. Industry forecasts can vary 10 percent or more, and sales estimates for firms can vary by an even wider margin.

When start-up entrepreneurs search for financing, prospective investors usually require a business plan with detailed sales projections, although such forecasts can be poor indicators of actual sales. Most entrepreneurs are simply too optimistic in their forecasts. One straightforward way to determine the accuracy of an entrepreneur's sales forecast is to ask how much he or she cares about its accuracy. Those who believe it is important to have an estimate that approximates actual sales tend to generate significantly better estimates than those who are not as concerned.[22]

The reliability of a forecast is thus always uncertain. Past performance is no guarantee of the future. The basic value in making a forecast is that it forces a business to look at the future objectively. A forecast does not eliminate the need for value judgments, but it does require the forecaster to identify elements that might influence the future.

SUMMARY

1. Marketing research is the systematic gathering, recording, and analyzing of data about market characteristics.
2. Marketing research fulfills one of the most important needs of owner-managers of small businesses by providing relevant information for improved decision making.
3. The cost of conducting marketing research can be high, but decisions based on no research or insufficient research may be more costly to the business.
4. Small business owner-managers may have to be shown how and why marketing research is a powerful tool.
5. Marketing research can be performed with limited budgets.
6. Marketing research should be based on a step-by-step approach that includes defining the problem, assessing available information, and gathering and analyzing additional information.
7. A research project should include a thorough investigation of secondary research sources before primary research is conducted.
8. Secondary data sources are varied and numerous. Among the more readily available sources are trade associations, periodicals, the *Predicasts F&S Index,* business directories, directories of research organizations, market studies, and governmental agencies, notably the Small Business Administration.
9. The major methods of collecting primary data are observations, surveys, and experiments.
10. The observation method is used by actually viewing, by personal observation or mechanical means such as hidden cameras, the overt actions of the subject.
11. The survey method relies on individuals to answer questions for the purpose of drawing conclusions. Typical techniques are mail and telephone questionnaires and personal interviews.
12. Experimentation is an attempt to measure cause-and-effect relationships under controlled conditions.
13. The two types of questionnaires that are used for research purposes are structured questionnaires and unstructured questionnaires.
14. When developing a questionnaire, one must pay attention to the question design, question sequencing, and the overall questionnaire design.
15. The survey method involves choosing a sample that is representative of the population under study. The various sampling techniques used include random sampling, stratified sampling, and area sampling.
16. Markets are defined as people who have needs to satisfy and the ability and willingness to buy.
17. Market segmentation is the process of subdividing the total market into submarkets that have similar characteristics.
18. Demographic characteristics, such as age, sex, occupation, and race, suggest ways to segment a market.
19. Three fundamental factors to consider in a market analysis are population trends, income trends, and competition.
20. The sales forecast forms a basis for much of the

planning, budgeting, and general operations of the firm.
21. There are several methods for making a sales forecast, and most firms use a combination of these methods to determine an overall forecast.
22. The accuracy of sales forecasts may vary, but the value of forecasting lies in forcing the entrepreneur to look at the future objectively.

KEY TERMS AND CONCEPTS

Marketing research
Marketing research process
Primary data
Secondary data
Observation method
Survey method
Experimentation
Structured questionnaire
Unstructured questionnaire
Sampling
Market
Target market
Market segmentation
Market potential
Sales forecast

QUESTIONS FOR DISCUSSION

1. Why is the need for marketing research especially great in small businesses?
2. What are the steps involved in the marketing research process?
3. Why should secondary research be conducted prior to initiating a primary research study?
4. What is the difference between primary and secondary data?
5. What problems can arise when using the observation method for primary data collection?
6. What are the advantages and disadvantages of mail questionnaires, telephone interviews, and personal interviews?
7. What factors must be considered in designing a questionnaire?
8. What is the basic idea underlying sampling?
9. Why might the cost of a research study be wasted after the study is completed?
10. Why might a small business firm compete more effectively in only one or two market segments?
11. How can knowledge about population and income trends help the entrepreneur?
12. In assessing competition, why should a firm focus its attention on firms of the same type and size?
13. What are the reasons underlying sales forecasting difficulties?
14. What are the principal methods of sales forecasting, and what are the drawbacks of each?
15. What business decisions are governed by seasonality of sales?

SELF-TEST REVIEW

Multiple Choice Questions

1. Marketing research includes which one of the following?
   a. Gathering data.
   b. Recording data.
   c. Analyzing data.
   d. All of the above.
2. Which of the following represents an acceptable alternative for the small businessperson in marketing research?
   a. In-house specialists.
   b. Large marketing research budgets.
   c. Assistance from local colleges.
   d. All of the above.
3. Data gathered specifically to solve a marketing problem are:
   a. Primary data.
   b. Secondary data.
   c. Published data.
   d. None of the above.
4. Which of the following is a source of secondary data?
   a. Internal business records.
   b. Trade journals.
   c. Government publications.
   d. All of the above.

5. The process of taking the total market for a product and dividing it into several submarkets is:
   a. Market allocation.
   b. Market segmentation.
   c. Market management.
   d. None of the above.

True/False Statements

1. In their formative years, small businesses should not consider marketing research, because they have limited time and money.
2. The first step in the marketing research process is to gather primary and secondary data.
3. The most difficult step in the marketing research process may be defining the problem.
4. Primary data are data that have already been gathered and published.
5. The survey method relies on individuals to answer questions for the purpose of drawing conclusions.
6. When preparing a questionnaire, one's first step is to formulate the questions.
7. Market researchers should follow up their studies to determine whether recommendations are being followed.
8. Small business firms will compete most effectively in a large number of market segments.
9. In assessing competition, the small firm should give first attention to larger competitors in the same line of business.
10. The sales forecast is the basis for budgeting and operations of a business.

TINY TOTS PRESCHOOL

Tiny Tots Preschool opened in August 1989 in a house that the owner, Mrs. Kellogg, had renovated to serve as a day nursery. Within 6 weeks she had 25 children enrolled, and early in 1990 Tiny Tots had reached capacity enrollment of 33. As owner-manager of Tiny Tots, Kellogg has found that it is difficult to meet the needs of both the two-to-five-year-olds and the school-age children in a single facility, so she has decided to look into building an addition on the site and increasing capacity to 80 children.

The major asset of Tiny Tots is the experience and skill of Kellogg and her three assistants. The children relate to all four staff members in an unstructured family-like program. The teachers seem to enjoy what they are doing, and the children appear to be happy, busy, and content.

As of May 1990, Tiny Tots is one of 17 licensed day-care centers in the town of Arlington, which has a total licensed capacity of 740. Included among the day-care centers in Arlington are five church-sponsored facilities (capacity 100) and the arts-oriented Inverness Day School (capacity 20), which follow a specialized emphasis or philosophy. Not included are two school-district sponsored nursery schools that require parent participation in the program as well as attendance at parent education classes; both offer only morning or afternoon preschool programs, not full-day care.

Nine of the other preschools offer generally the same type of service that Tiny Tots offers, although some have a more structured program. Many of the nine, including Tiny Tots, are members of the Private Nursery Schools Association and are mutually supportive. None of the competitors (except the Montessori schools) is a chain or franchise organization.

In considering whether to build additional facilities, Kellogg must decide exactly what age groups she will be serving and how she will utilize the present building. She is faced with three options:

1. To expand her program, including building additional facilities to include caring for infants,
2. To use the present building but expand her program to include caring for infants,
3. To expand the two-to-five year age range, with the two-year-olds remaining in the present homelike facility and the others being placed in a new facility.

The second option is especially appealing because there is currently no licensed infant care center in Arlington.

QUESTIONS

1. Define the problem facing Kellogg and suggest what she should do in her initial investigation to get a better feel for the situation.
2. What information is needed to make the choice among the three alternatives, and how can such information be obtained?

NOTES

1. "Making The Grade," *Inc.*, January 1989, 20.
2. "Fire Starter," *Inc.*, February 1989, 22.
3. "Up From Academe," *Inc.*, November 1988, 15.
4. "The Sunny Side Is Up," *Inc.*, January 1987, 10.
5. J. Ford Laumer, Jr., James R. Harris, Hugh J. Guffey, Jr., and Robert C. Erffmeyer, Small Business Administration, *Researching Your Market*, Management Aid Number 4.019 (1988), 1.
6. *Ibid.*
7. Arthur S. Katz, "Marketing Research Can 'Work' for Small Business, If They Ask the Right Questions," *Marketing News*, September 17, 1982, Section 1, 6.
8. Excerpted from "Researching Your Market," 1.
9. Arthur S. Katz, 6.
10. *Ibid.*
11. This section is largely excerpted from *Researching Your Market*, 2–3.
12. *Researching Your Market.*
13. Based on Cable News Network's "Pinnacle," March 22, 1987. Guest: Philip Knight, Nike.
14. Based on Cable News Network's "Pinnacle," December 18, 1988. Guest: Lillian Vernon, Lillian Vernon Corporation.
15. Based on Cable News Network's "Pinnacle," November 14, 1987. Guest: Mark Stevens, Häagen-Dazs.
16. This example is based on Gail Bronson, "How Old-Line Jeans Producer Fashioned Survival Strategy," *The Wall Street Journal*, May 4, 1981, 25.
17. Mark Robichaux, " 'Competitor Intelligence': A New Grapevine," *The Wall Street Journal*, April 12, 1989, B2.
18. Based on Cable News Network's "Pinnacle," August 30, 1987. Guest: Sidney Swartz, The Timberland Company.
19. Based on Cable News Network's "Pinnacle," September 24, 1988. Guest: Wally Amos, Entrepreneur.
20. Based on Cable News Network's "Pinnacle," October 4, 1987. Guest: Rod Canion, Compaq Computer.
21. Based on Cable News Network's "Pinnacle," December 18, 1988. Guest: Lillian Vernon, Lillian Vernon Corporation.
22. "Sales Projections: Facts or Wishful Thinking?" *The Wall Street Journal*, July 7, 1989, B1.

Chapter Ten

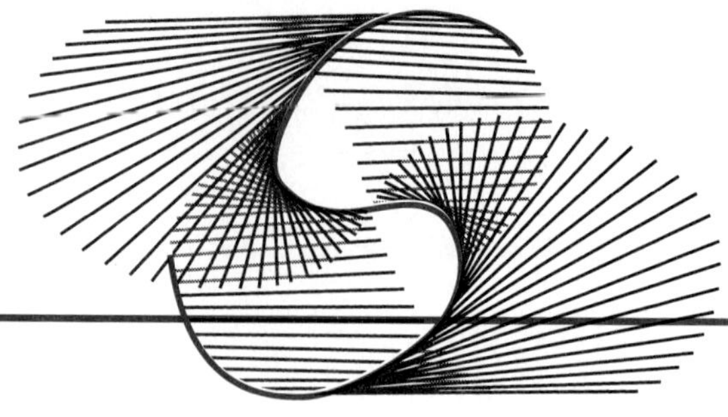

Selecting a Location

Chapter Outline

FACTORS TO CONSIDER IN CHOOSING A RETAIL OR SERVICE LOCATION
- Trading Area Analysis
- Selecting the Community
- Choosing a Location within a Community
- Selecting the Site
- How to Make a Traffic Count

TYPES OF PLANNED SHOPPING CENTERS
- Neighborhood Shopping Center
- Community Shopping Center
- Regional Shopping Center

FACTORS TO CONSIDER IN A SHOPPING CENTER CHOICE
- Retail Compatibility
- Rental and Lease Arrangements
- Equipment Leasing

LOCATING OR RELOCATING A MANUFACTURING PLANT
- The Market
- The Labor Force
- Transportation
- Raw Materials
- Suitable Site
- Community Interest
- Using a Score Sheet

SUMMARY

Learning Objectives *The objectives of this chapter are to assist you in understanding:*

1. The importance of a good business location.
2. What factors to consider in choosing a retail or service location.
3. How to make a traffic count in retail site selection.
4. What factors to consider when locating in a shopping center.
5. What factors to consider when locating or relocating a manufacturing plant.

One of the most crucial decisions an entrepreneur makes involves the selection of a business location. For retail and service firms, a good location allows ready access and attracts large numbers of customers. Furthermore, the proliferation of retail and service outlets with nearly identical product or service offerings means that even slight differences in location can have a significant impact on sales and profitability. While location is critical for retailers and service firms, it also plays an important role in manufacturing and wholesaling.

The relatively lasting effects of location decisions make them so important. Because the location decision represents a long-term fixed investment, the disadvantages of a poor location can be difficult to overcome. Once the business is established, it is costly and perhaps impractical to move. If the initial choice of location is especially poor, the business may never be able to get off the ground, irrespective of what other advantages the business might offer vis-à-vis competitors.

Sometimes businesses suffer because they are just outside the flow of traffic, not quite visible from the street, or "one block away from success." On the other hand, location is often less of a problem than it might seem. In Dun and Bradstreet's 1987 *Business Failure Record,* poor location is cited as a reason for only 0.08 percent of business failures. Even for retailers, the figure is only 2.5 percent. For service firms it is 0.4 percent, for wholesale trade 0.5 percent, and for manufacturers 0.2 percent.[1]

GOLDEN DOOR®

RANCHO LA PUERTA®

The importance of a good location was recognized by Deborah Szekely when she founded the model health spa, Rancho Lapuerta. Szekely settled under the slopes of Mount Kuchima more than 50 years ago. She chose this location because it was the most appropriate for her business. Mount Kuchima is legendary as a place where ancient wisdom meets the modern age and the mind and body find harmony. Later came the sister spa, the celebrated Golden Door, nestled in the mountains of Southern California. It is an upscale boot camp for the famous and successful living nearby.

FACTORS TO CONSIDER IN CHOOSING A RETAIL OR SERVICE LOCATION

A prime location is one of the strongest competitive edges a retail or service firm can have. Among the most important factors determining a prime location are heavy customer traffic and minimum competition. Finding a prime location, however, is no small task. Chain store organizations spend thousands of dollars on market surveys before entering a market area. Independent small business owners should imitate them insofar as careful community and site evaluations are concerned.

Deborah Szekely knew when she selected the location for this health spa, The Gold Door, the lovely setting nestled in the mountains was an essential element in her business's success. (Photograph courtesy of The Golden Door, photograph by John Durant)

Underestimating the importance of a carefully selected location can be the first and final mistake for the fledgling entrepreneur. The prospect of low rents and attractive leaseholds can lure the uninitiated into an unrewarding trap, squelching what might become a profitable business. "Every business venture is a risk," advises one industry spokesperson, "but with a poor location you are challenging fate."

Several sources of information are available for an accurate and complete evaluation of a prospective location. Helpful data can be obtained from the following references:

- Chambers of commerce provide a general overview of an area, with economic profiles and residential characteristics. They usually have up-to-date information on population growth, property taxes and sales taxes, data on the labor market, wage rates, housing, community facilities, and major industries.
- Bankers are well-established sources of general business information, and will propose plans for financing the prospective business.
- Real estate brokers are able to give advice on relative land values as well as information on sites available for rent or purchase.
- Professional consultants who have had experience with particular types of businesses can provide valuable information.

Trading Area Analysis

A **trading area** is a geographic area containing the customers of a particular firm for specific goods or services. A trading area can be divided into three zones of influence:

1. The **primary trading area** encompasses roughly 55 to 70 percent of a store's customers. It is the area closest to the business and possesses the highest density of customers to population and per capita sales.
2. The **secondary trading area** contains an additional 15 to 25 percent of a store's customers. It is located outside the primary trading area, and customers are widely dispersed.
3. The **tertiary (fringe) trading area** includes all the remaining customers, and they are more widely dispersed. It consists of customers who patronize the business for reasons not related to proximity to residence.[3]

Locating a business involves finding the answers to three major questions regarding the trading area:

1. What community has the greatest opportunity for the particular type of business under consideration?
2. What area within a community indicates strong potential for growth?
3. What specific site within the area of the community meets the requirements of the particular business?

Selecting the Community

In selecting the community that will be the trading area, one should remember that the majority of customers will be drawn from within a relatively short distance of the business. Key factors in choosing the community include:

- Population characteristics,
- Competitive characteristics,
- Labor characteristics,
- Transportation characteristics,
- Economic characteristics,
- Materials and services,
- Government and taxes,
- Financing,
- Location characteristics, and
- Media characteristics.

These factors are highlighted in Exhibit 10-1. They must be analyzed with a preselected target market in mind.

EXHIBIT 10–1

Factors to Consider in Evaluating a Community

Population Characteristics
- Total size
- Growth trends
- Age distribution
- Income distribution
- Occupation trends

Competitive Characteristics
- Number of competitors
- Size distribution of competitors
- Location of competitors
- Competitive growth trends

Labor Characteristics
- Labor force inventory
- Wages and hours
- Unions
- Personnel policies in area
- Vocational training
- Labor legislation
- Commuting patterns

Transportation Characteristics
- Highway transportation
- Trucking service
- Other motor transportation
- Rail transportation
- Commercial air service

Economic Characteristics
- Number and types of industries
- Dominant industries
- Growth projections

Materials and Services
- Raw material availability
- Storage facilities
- Routine supplies
- Technical services

Government and Taxes
- Local government and financial condition
- Local planning, zoning, and ordinances
- Local and state licensing
- Local and state taxes
- Future tax prospects
- Environmental regulations

Financing
- Requirements
- Sources of funds
- Credit factors
- Special inducements

Location Characteristics
- Number and type of locations
- Accessibility to customers
- Accessibility to transportation
- Owning/leasing options

Media Characteristics
- Type of media coverage
- Media costs

Choosing a Location within a Community

Where to locate within a community—whether in a central business district, a solo location, or a shopping center—is determined by the type of goods sold, the class of customers desired, accessibility and convenience for customers, the adjacent stores, and the neighborhood. In short, different stores have different location requirements.

Downtown Business District

A central or downtown business district is common to every community. In large communities, the central business district might contain hundreds of retail outlets and office buildings. Although declining in relative importance for most retailers and service firms, the downtowns of large cities have become increasingly important as centers for administrative, financial, and professional services. Other attractions of many downtown areas include the location of hotels, convention facilities, and cultural events. Downtown stores cater largely to downtown workers, downtown apartment house occupants, regional shoppers, tourists, and other occasional visitors.

Solo Location

Some retailers and service firms may want to locate in a solo or free-standing location. Free-standing locations on heavily traveled streets have several advantages, including:

- The lack of close competition,
- Lower rent,
- More space for parking and expansion, and
- Greater flexibility in store hours.

The most successful stores in such locations are those with strong customer loyalty.

Shopping Centers

A **shopping center** is a geographic cluster of retail stores. These stores collectively offer a variety of goods and services designed to serve the needs of customers within the trading area of the center. Shopping centers, notably malls, provide a convenient location, free parking facilities, uniform operating hours, and special events to create an overall retailing environment to attract shoppers. For many small businesses, however, the terms of lease contracts and uniform operating hours are distinct disadvantages.

This fish market's solo location ensures plenty of space for customer parking and no nearby competition. (Photograph © Ann M. Mason)

Selecting the Site

The selection of the actual business site is especially important. When choosing a specific site, one should consider the following factors:

- Potential of the trading area,
- Customer accessibility to the location,
- Assessment of the competition,
- Potential to attract new business, and
- Cost of the location.

Exhibit 10-2 lists a number of questions to consider when gathering information about these factors. Some of these factors may be determined by a pedestrian and/or automobile traffic count, which will indicate whether the specific site has the potential to draw enough customers.

Once the specific site has been selected, there must be a decision whether to build, buy, or lease the business facilities. The first two choices involve a considerable outlay of funds and raise problems with respect to future relocation. Major considerations are the following:

1. *Zoning*—can the business be operated without an exemption, or will a delay be involved? How many permits are required?
2. *Remodeling*—will a use permit be required?
3. *Rental expense*—how is the rent determined: flat rate, percentage of gross sales? What about sublet rights?
4. *Lease terms*—what are the options to renew or cancel the lease?

EXHIBIT 10–2

Site Analysis

The questions that follow should prove useful in gathering information about a location. Such information will enable the entrepreneur to compare available locations by developing a location profile of the potential trading area, accessibility, competition, and cost.

Potential of the Trading Area

1. How big is the trading area? _____ square miles.
2. What is the customer potential within five miles? _____ customers. Within 30 minutes travel time? _____ customers.
3. What is the density of population? _____ people per square mile.
4. Is there adequate transportation? _____ Yes. _____ No.
5. What is the income level of the trading area? $_____ per capita.
6. Is the local employment pattern good? _____% people unemployed.
7. What is the general makeup of the community? _____ Residential. _____ Old. _____ Growing.
8. What are the trends in population and income? _____ Up. _____ Down.
9. Is new construction on the increase? _____ Yes. _____ No.
10. Are school enrollments up? _____ Yes. _____ No.
11. Are retail sales on the increase? _____ Yes. _____ No.

➤

EXHIBIT 10–2

Site Analysis (continued)

12. Have average business improvements been made recently? _____ Yes. _____ No.
13. Is there a high vacancy rate for business property? _____ Yes. _____ No.
14. Have shopping patterns changed drastically in recent years? _____ Yes. _____ No.
15. Are customers moving to or away from the potential location? _____ Yes. _____ No.
16. What are the present zoning restrictions? _____________________________

Can Customers Get to the Location?

1. Is the area served by adequate public transportation? _____ Yes. _____ No.
2. How broad an area does the transportation service encompass? _____ square miles.
3. Is the area generally attractive to shoppers? _____ Yes. _____ No.
4. Can it be easily reached by automobile? _____ Yes. _____ No.
5. Is public parking adequate and relatively inexpensive? _____ Yes. _____ No.
6. How many spaces in the available, nearby parking area are taken up by all-day parkers? _____ Many. _____ Few.
7. If located on a highway, is the location easily accessible from the main traffic flow? _____ Yes. _____ No.
8. What are restrictions on signs and store identification?
   ____
9. If on a limited-access road, how close is the nearest interchange? _____ miles.
10. Is the location accessible to delivery trucks? _____ Yes. _____ No.
11. Is the traffic speed too fast to encourage entrance by automobile? _____ Yes. _____ No.
12. Are the customers who drive past the location on their way to work or on shopping trips? _____ On their way to work. _____ On shopping trip.
13. Will nearby stores help you? Are the other stores in the shopping center, neighborhood, or highway location of a nature that will attract customers who will also become patrons of your store? _____ Yes. _____ No.
14. What are the prospects for changes in traffic flow in the near future? _____ Slight. _____ Likely.
15. Will anticipated changes improve or damage the location? _____ Improve. _____ Damage.
16. Are zoning changes planned that would affect accessibility of the location? _____ Yes. _____ No.

Judging the Competition

1. Are there other competing businesses, and if so, how many, between the prospective location and the most highly populated area? _____ stores.
2. Is this spot the most convenient store location in the area? _____ Yes. _____ No.
3. How many other competing stores are in this trading area? _____ stores.
4. How many of them will compete for the same customers? _____ stores.
5. Do they have better parking facilities? _____ Yes. _____ No.

EXHIBIT 10–2 **Site Analysis** *(continued)*

6. Do they offer the same type of merchandise? _____ Yes. _____ No.
7. Are they more aggressive or less aggressive than the planned store? _____ More. _____ Less.
8. What other competing stores are planned in the future? _____
9. Are other potential sites that are closer to the majority of customers likely to be developed in the near future? _____ Yes. _____ No.
10. Are major competitors well-known, well-advertised stores? _____ Yes. _____ No.
11. Is there actually a need for another store of this kind in the area? _____ Yes. _____ No.
12. How well are the demands being met? _____ Well. _____ Fairly. _____ Poorly.
13. If there are empty stores or vacant lots near the location, what is planned for them? _______________

Can the Location Attract New Business?

1. Is the location in an attractive business district? _____ Yes. _____ No.
2. Are there numerous stores that will draw potential customers into the area? _____ Yes. _____ No.
3. Is the location near well-known and well-advertised stores? _____ Yes. _____ No.
4. Is the location the most attractive one in the area? _____ Yes. _____ No.
5. Is the location on the side of the street with the biggest customer traffic? _____ Yes. _____ No.
6. Is the potential location nearer to the general parking area than locations of competing firms? _____ Yes. _____ No.
7. Is the location in the center of or in the fringe area of the shopping district? _____ Center. _____ Fringe.
8. Is it near common meeting places for people, such as prospective customers? _____ Yes. _____ No.
9. Are most of the people passing the store prospective customers? _____ Yes. _____ No.
10. Are the people who pass usually in a hurry or are they taking time to shop? _____ In a hurry. _____ Out shopping.

Cost of the Location

1. What will the rent be? $_____ per month.
2. Who will pay the utility costs? _____ You. _____ Others.
3. Who pays additional costs such as taxes, public services, and costs of improvements? _____ You. _____ Others.
4. What are the possibilities for eventual expansion? _____ Good. _____ Poor.
5. Are good employees available? _____ Yes. _____ No.
6. Will potential income justify the costs? _____ Yes. _____ No.

Source: Small Business Administration, *Starting and Managing a Small Retail Hardware Store,* Starting and Managing Series, vol. 10 (Washington, D.C.: Small Business Administration), 17–20.

5. *Additional costs*—what is the condition of the facility? How much remodeling will be necessary? Does it need additional lighting, air conditioning, heating, plumbing, or other installations?
6. *Lot and building size*—can expansion be accommodated? If leased, will the lessor erect additional facilities? If lessee remodels or makes additions, who owns such improvements?
7. *Storage capacity*—is there enough to meet the needs of the business?
8. *Parking space*—is adequate parking space available?
9. *Exterior facilities*—is exterior lighting in the area adequate to attract evening shoppers and make them feel safe? Does the store have awnings or decks to provide shelter during bad weather?
10. *Insurance*—what insurance does the lessor carry? Must the lessee purchase additional coverage?

How to Make a Traffic Count

The first consideration is to determine whether or not a traffic count is necessary.[4] Although knowledge of the volume and character of passing traffic is always useful, in certain cases a traffic survey may not really make any difference. Other selection factors involved may be so significant that the outcome of a traffic study will have relatively little bearing on the site decision. When other selection factors, such as parking, operating costs, or location of competitors, become less important and data on traffic flow becomes dominant, then a count is indicated.

Once it is determined that a traffic count is really needed, the general objective is to count the passing traffic—both pedestrian and vehicular—that would constitute potential customers who would probably be attracted into the type of store under consideration. To evaluate the traffic available to competitors, one may want to conduct traffic counts at their sites, too.

Data from a traffic count should not only show how many people pass by, but also generally indicate what kinds of people they are. Analysis of the characteristics of the passing traffic often reveals patterns and variations not readily apparent from casual observation.

For counting purposes, the passing traffic is divided into different classifications according to the characteristics of the customers who would patronize the particular type of business. Whereas a drugstore is interested in the total volume of passing traffic, a men's clothing store is obviously most concerned with the amount of male traffic.

It is also important to classify passing traffic by its reasons for passing. A woman on the way to a beauty salon is probably a poor prospect for a paint store, but she may be a good prospect for a drugstore. The hours at which an individual goes by are often an indication of his or her purpose. In the late afternoon, a person is usually going home from work. When one chain organization estimates the number of potential women customers, it considers women passing a site between 10 A.M. and 5 P.M. to be the serious shoppers.

Evaluation of the financial bracket of passersby is also significant. Out of 100 women passing a prospective location for an exclusive dress shop, only 10 may appear to have the income to patronize the shop. Of course, the greater one's experience in a particular retail trade, the more accurately one can estimate the number of potential customers.

To determine what proportion of the passing traffic represents potential shoppers, one should interview some of the pedestrians about the origins of their trips, their destinations, and the stores in which they plan to shop. This sort of information can provide a better estimate of the number of potential customers.

In summary, the qualitative information gathered about the passing traffic should include counting the individuals who seem to possess the characteristics appropriate to the desired clientele, judging their reasons for using that route, and calculating their ability to buy.

Pedestrian Traffic Count

In making a pedestrian count one must decide who is to be counted, where the count should take place, and when the count should be made. In considering who is to be counted, one must determine what types of people should be included. For example, the study might count all men presumed to be between the ages of sixteen and twenty-five. The directions should be completely clear as to the individuals to be counted so that the counters will be consistent and the total figure will reflect the traffic flow.

Traffic Related to Types of Consumer Goods

Pedestrian traffic is closely related to the types of goods bought by consumers. Goods can be grouped into three major categories:

- **Convenience goods**—usually means low unit price, purchased frequently, little selling effort, bought by habit, and sold in numerous outlets. Examples are candy bars, cigarettes, and milk.
- **Shopping goods**—usually means high unit price, purchased infrequently, more intensive selling effort required on the part of the salespeople, price and features compared, and sold in selective outlets. Examples are men's suits, furniture, and automobiles.
- **Specialty goods**—usually means high unit price (although price is not a major purchase consideration), bought infrequently, requires a special effort on the part of the customer to make the purchase, no substitutes considered, and sold in exclusive outlets. Examples are designer jewelry, exclusive apparel, and certain imported goods.

For stores handling convenience goods, the quantity of pedestrian traffic is most important. The corner of an intersection that offers two distinct traffic streams and a large window display area is usually a better site than the middle of the block. Downtown convenience goods stores, such as low-priced ready-to-wear stores and drugstores, have a limited ability to generate their own traffic. In merchandising convenience goods, it is easier to build the store within the traffic than the traffic within the store. Convenience goods are often purchased on impulse in easily accessible stores.

For stores handling shopping goods, the quality of the traffic is more important. While convenience goods are purchased by nearly everyone, certain kinds of shopping goods are purchased only by certain segments of shoppers. Moreover, it is sometimes the character of the retail establishment rather than its type of goods that governs the selection of a site. For example, a conventional menswear store should be close to a traffic generator like a department store. On the other hand, the owner of a discount store handling menswear would prefer an accessible highway location.

The number and type of shopper attracted by the Fifth Avenue address will help to ensure the success of The Timberland Company's New York City Showroom. (Photograph courtesy of The Timberland Store)

Specialty goods are frequently sought by consumers who are already sold on the product, brand, or both. Stores catering to this type of consumer can use relatively isolated locations because they generate their own consumer traffic.

Automobile Traffic Count

A growing number of retail firms depend on drive-in traffic for their sales. Both the quantity and quality of automotive traffic can be analyzed in the same way as pedestrian traffic. For the major streets in urban areas, data on traffic flows can be provided by the city engineer, the planning commission, the state highway department, or an outdoor advertising company. However, one may need to modify the information to suit special needs. For example, one should supplement data relating to total count of vehicles passing the site with actual observation in order to evaluate such influences on traffic as commercial vehicles, changing of shifts at nearby factories or offices, highway-bound traffic, and increased flow caused by special events or activities.[5]

In general, the greater the automobile traffic, the greater the sales of convenience goods catering to drive-in traffic. For the drive-in store selling low-priced convenience goods, the volume of traffic passing the site is a very important factor in making a site decision. Consumers purchase these goods frequently. They want them to be readily available, and they are reminded when passing a convenience goods store, such as a 7-Eleven outlet, that they need a particular item.

If consumers must make a special trip to purchase such convenience staple goods as food and drug items, they want the store to be close to home. One study of food store purchases in a central city area revealed that nearly 70 percent of the women patronized stores within one to five blocks of their homes. Another study of food stores indicated that for suburban locations, the majority of customers lived within three miles of the stores, while the maximum trading area was five miles. For rural locations, the majority of customers lived within a 10-minute drive to the store, with the maximum trading area within a 20-minute drive. A West Coast supermarket chain wants a minimum of 3,500 homes within a mile-and-a-half radius of a shopping center before considering it for location. Research indicates that 80 percent of the customers of pizza carryouts live within a mile of the establishments.[6]

Retailers selling shopping goods or specialty goods draw from a much wider trading area than stores selling convenience goods. Without a heavily trafficked location, but with the help of adequate promotion, these retailers can generate their own traffic. In this case, a location with low traffic density but easy accessibility from a residential area is a satisfactory site. Consumers buy shopping and specialty goods relatively infrequently. They deliberately plan their purchases. And they are willing to travel some distance to find the particular products or brands they favor.

TYPES OF PLANNED SHOPPING CENTERS

There are three common types of shopping centers, distinguished by size and type of stores: the neighborhood shopping center, the community shopping center, and the regional shopping center.

Neighborhood Shopping Center

The **neighborhood shopping center** typically consists of 5 to 15 stores with an emphasis on convenience goods and a trading area of about five minutes' driving time from the center. It is designated to serve fewer than 20,000 people. The major store—and the prime traffic generator in the center—is typically a supermarket. The other stores in the center, which may include a drugstore, a hardware store, a bakery, and a beauty shop, offer convenience goods and services. The most common form of neighborhood shopping center is the unplanned *strip center.*

Community Shopping Center

A **community shopping center** usually consists of 15 to 50 stores with an emphasis on both convenience and shopping goods, and a trading area of about 10 to 20 minutes' driving time from the center. The dominant store is generally a junior department store, such as J.C. Penney or Montgomery Ward, or a large variety store.

Community shopping centers serve between 20,000 and 100,000 people. Unlike the neighborhood center, a community shopping center is carefully planned and coordinated. It is likely to have several major annual events in order to generate publicity and to attract shoppers.

Regional Shopping Center

A **regional shopping center** is designed to serve from 100,000 to 1,000,000 or more customers who can be expected to drive thirty minutes or more to reach it. A regional complex often has three or more major department stores in addition to over 100 stores

The stores in the neighborhood shopping center consist of between 5 and 15 stores and generally offer convenience goods and services. The major store and prime traffic generator is typically a supermarket. (Photograph © Ann M. Mason)

The shoppers at this regional mall may have driven for thirty minutes or more in order to shop here. (Photograph © Ann M. Mason)

carrying shopping and specialty goods. However, a number of stores also carry convenience goods.

New regional centers are almost exclusively closed malls with walkways. They are managed as a unit and sponsor numerous special events to attract shoppers. Today they account for more than 40 percent of total retail sales, providing people not only with goods and services, but also eating facilities, night life, and a place to socialize.

FACTORS TO CONSIDER IN A SHOPPING CENTER CHOICE

Whether or not a small retailer can get into a particular shopping center depends on the market and the management. A small shopping center may need only one children's shoe store, for example, while a regional center may expect enough business for several. The management aspect is simple to state: Developers and owners of shopping centers look for successful retailers.[7]

In finding tenants whose line of goods will meet the needs of the desired market, the developer-owner first signs on a prestigious merchant as the lead tenant. Then, the developer selects other types of stores that will complement each other. In this way, the *tenant mix* offers a varied array of merchandise. Thus, the center's competitive strength is bolstered against other centers, as well as supplying the market area's needs.

To finance a center, the developer needs major leases from companies with strong credit ratings. The developer's own lenders favor those tenant rosters that include the triple-A ratings of national chains. However, local merchants with good business records and proven understanding of the local markets have a good chance of being considered by a shopping center developer.

Retail Compatibility

For a small retail store in its first year of operation, with limited funds for advertising and promotion, retail compatibility can be the most important factor in the survival of the store. Will the store be located next to businesses that will generate traffic? Or will it be located near businesses that might clash?

For example, if a store offers shopping goods, the best location is near other stores carrying shopping goods. Conversely, locating a shopping goods store in a convenience goods area or center is not recommended.

With the advent of the *super mall* and regional shopping center, shopping goods and convenience goods outlets may be found coexisting easily under the same roof. In this situation, it is still important for a store to be located in a section of the shopping complex that will not clash with what it is selling, and will in fact be conducive to sales. For example, a pet store should not be located immediately adjacent to a restaurant, dress shop, or salon. A gift shop should be near places like department stores, theaters, restaurants—in short, any place where lines of patrons may form, giving potential customers several minutes to look in the gift shop's display windows.

According to Mathias DeVito, president of Rouse Co., even very good shopping centers could be helped tremendously by merchandising, promotion, and redesign. He feels that Rouse Co. has become one of the leaders in its business by bringing into the project the hottest, newest, best tenants in the region or the nation, keeping the tenant mix very exciting. Some projects need to be physically renovated and need to have a state-of-the-art style—plants, lighting, new floors—to bring them into this century. DeVito believes that there are many projects in good markets, in good locations, that really could be terrifically energized by good management.[8]

The kinds of tenants that would help to make a shopping center more of a success include Banana Republic, The Sharper Image, and The Limited. The department store has become less important than it used to be. Today, specialty merchants are very important, although Rouse Co. would think many times about developing a shopping center in the suburbs without a department store. They still advertise a lot, they bring a lot of name recognition to a center, and they bring loyalty in terms of customers.

Rental and Lease Arrangements

Most shopping center leases are negotiated. Rental payments are usually arranged in one or two ways: either a flat monthly rate or a percentage-of-sales sum involving a base amount and/or a percentage of gross monthly sales. Flat monthly rents stay the same from month to month, allowing owners to project operating budgets more easily. Frequently a flat rental lease contains an escalator clause, which adjusts the rent upward over a period of time.

Under a percentage-of-sales agreement, which is typically between 5 and 7 percent of gross sales, rent is generally based on the square footage of the store and its sales volume. The percentage payments depend primarily on the sales volume expected and what the landlord will provide in the way of physical facilities.

Percentage-of-sales agreements are normal for stores located within a shopping center. It is also common for these payments to be made in addition to a regular flat monthly fee. In signing such agreements, the operator might request an *exclusivity clause* to prevent other shops in the center from selling the same type of merchandise. Increasingly, however, such clauses have been ruled to be in violation of antitrust laws.

Before an owner-operator signs a lease arrangement, an attorney should review the contract. This is essential for anyone who wants a clear understanding of lease clauses covering nonrent charges, escalation clauses, subleasing, and renewal options. Nonrent charges, for instance, are normally made in planned shopping centers where all tenants share costs for services, such as maintenance and security guards.

Other experts should also be consulted to check the condition of heating, plumbing, and air-conditioning equipment. An insurance agent should be asked to determine the amount of insurance needed to cover both liability and property damage claims if the lease agreement does not provide for them.

Equipment Leasing

Leasing equipment, rather than purchasing or renting, has become an attractive alternative for many firms. A firm considering leasing usually has at least one of these characteristics:

- Satisfactory credit, but little or no cash on hand,
- Low or nonexistent tax obligations (for example, the firm may be a good credit risk but have no tax obligations because of tax shelters created by other capital expenditures),
- Rapid expansion and need for working capital to increase inventories, expand plant facilities, or meet a growing payroll,
- High capital requirements for needed but costly equipment, and
- Need for frequent replacement of equipment (in a fast-growing industry, such as electronics, expensive and technologically complex equipment must be replaced frequently).

Today lease transactions include all types of equipment, including cash registers, computers, automobiles, restaurant fixtures, and air-pollution control devices. One California company recently leased a herd of cows to a farm co-op; other firms have leased tennis courts, golf carts, and even winery storage tanks.[9]

LOCATING OR RELOCATING A MANUFACTURING PLANT

Many location decisions are based on the personal preferences of the owner of the plant.[10] Such preferences can mean anything from locating the business within walking distance of one's home to buying a building from a friend merely because that friend wants to sell. In choosing a location, the first consideration should be to eliminate personal preferences that are emotional rather than rational.

During the initial stages of manufacturing, it is not uncommon for an entrepreneur to locate in a garage or home basement. These location decisions are made because of the low overhead costs. When the business grows, it becomes necessary to find a larger location site because the garage or basement is not suitable for expansion.

The general procedure for plant location or relocation consists of an organized development and assessment of the following factors: the market, the labor force, transportation, raw materials, suitable site, and community interest.

The Market

Perhaps the most important consideration in any location is being able to satisfy the target market. One must study the market and determine who is interested in buying the product. The plant must be located with convenient access to all customers, present and potential. A good method for evaluating this factor is to mark the locations of customers with pins on a large map. It might also be desirable to indicate the locations of major competitors. By examining the map, one can usually determine the center of the market area and the location that will best serve customers.

The Labor Force

The next consideration is where the labor force will come from. Although labor is more mobile today than it was 15 years ago, some areas do not always have an adequate group of people to draw on. One rule of thumb is that the ideal site is in an area that can provide 10 people for consideration for each one to be hired. Furthermore, prevailing wage rates in the area must be in line with competitors in other areas. Small towns generally have lower wage rates than large cities.

A number of firms considering relocating to another city have tested the labor market by advertising for prospective help in the local paper to determine the number of respondents. These people are interviewed, and many ideas can result from the interviews. Firms have found in many cases that the labor supply was different from what the population and employment figures had indicated.

The importance of attracting the right labor force is illustrated by The Timberland Company, which started in New Hampshire. Unemployment in New Hampshire became so low that the company was in trouble. Timberland could not even get people to run the switchboard or to be secretaries. To get a skilled shoe worker was nearly impossible. As a result, the company opened plants in Tennessee, Puerto Rico, and the Dominican Republic.[11]

Transportation

Transportation is another factor in locating or relocating a plant. Radical changes in the past 10 years have increased flexibility when locating or relocating a factory. The growth of air shipping makes sites near airports more attractive. Interstate highways have increased the popularity of trucks as a method of moving goods. More pipeline facilities are available. Railroads are indispensable for certain products.

Raw Materials

The sources of raw materials should be marked with pins on a large map. If they all come from one area, one should consider what advantages a competitor located adjacent to the source has over a more remote facility. It may be more important to be closer to raw materials than to customers, or vice versa. For example, vegetable canneries are located near farms, and lumber mills are located near forests. On the other hand, bottling companies and bakeries are located near markets.

Suitable Site

Is a suitable site available in the general area in which one wants to locate or relocate the plant? One has to consider whether or not the terrain is suitable and the foundations are adequate. Is needed rail or highway transportation available in the area? Can any needed zoning changes be obtained? Is adequate water and sewer service available?

In recent years, problems in securing proper zoning have been more intense. Delays have become unbelievably long and, in more than a few instances, zone changes have never been granted. As a result, most firms will no longer even consider a site that is not ready to build on.

Community Interest

Whether or not the community or area that one is considering wants the business is also important. Some areas aggressively seek development. They welcome new industry and therefore eliminate many of the small problems that arise. Other communities' attitudes toward development range from passivity to open hostility. Obviously, one should avoid the city or region that does not want industry.

Using a Score Sheet

In considering the factors relevant to a plant location or relocation decision, it is advisable to have some type of score sheet, such as the one illustrated in Exhibit 10-3, which can be used to evaluate sites. Such a rating sheet, when completed for each site that is considered, will help one to see the strengths and weaknesses of each. It also helps one to eliminate the factors that may be equal in all the sites.

In tallying the sheet, some factors may be more important to one type of business than to another. For example, if the entrepreneur is in the apparel business, the availability of qualified labor may be far more important than any other factor. It would be wise to assign some weight to those factors that are unusually important because of the nature of the business.

EXHIBIT 10–3 ***Rating Sheet on Manufacturing Sites***

Grade each factor: 1 (lowest) to 10 (highest)
Weigh each factor: 1 (least important) to 5 (most important)

Factors	Grade (1–10)	Weight (1–5)
1. Centrally located to reach markets	____	____
2. Raw materials readily available	____	____
3. Quantity of available labor	____	____
4. Transportation availability and rates	____	____
5. Labor rates of pay/estimated productivity	____	____
6. Adequacy of utilities	____	____
7. Local business climate	____	____
8. Provision for future expansion	____	____
9. Tax burden	____	____
10. Topography of the site (slope and foundation)	____	____
11. Quality of police and fire protection	____	____
12. Housing availability for workers and managers	____	____
13. Environmental factors (schools, cultural, community atmosphere)	____	____
14. Estimate of quality of this site in future years	____	____
15. Estimate of this site in relation to major competitors	____	____

Source: Fred I. Weber, Jr., Small Business Administration, *Locating or Relocating Your Business,* Management Aid Number 2.002 (1988), 6.

An owner-manager must reassess the situation regularly to determine if the present site is an advantage or a disadvantage. A location that suited the business needs even three years ago might not be a prudent one today.

SUMMARY

1. A good location is one of the most important factors for business success, partly due to its relatively lasting effect.
2. Major factors to consider in choosing a retail or service location include the community, the location within the community, and the specific site.
3. Sources of information about locations include chambers of commerce, bankers, real estate brokers, and professional consultants.
4. A trading area consists of customers for a particular business.
5. Key factors to consider in selecting a community include characteristics pertaining to population, competition, labor, transportation, economics, materials availability, government, financing, location, and media.
6. Choosing a location within a community involves the choice of locating in a downtown business district, in a solo location, or in a shopping center.
7. Major considerations in selecting a specific site include the potential of the trading area, customer accessibility, competition, potential to attract new business, and cost factors.
8. A pedestrian or automobile traffic count may be desirable in deciding on a specific site.
9. The amount of pedestrian traffic is closely related to whether the goods are convenience goods, shopping goods, or specialty goods.
10. There are three types of planned shopping centers: neighborhood centers, community centers, and regional centers.
11. The right tenant mix in a shopping center is essential to the individual retailer's and center's success.
12. Retail compatibility can be the most important factor in the survival of stores in a shopping center.
13. Shopping center rental and lease agreements should be reviewed with the advice of experts.
14. There are usually two ways in which rental or lease payments are arranged: flat monthly rent or a percentage-of-sales agreement.
15. Leasing has become a popular alternative to buying. Firms that consider leasing usually have several characteristics in common, most of which are related to the availability of capital.
16. Locating or relocating a manufacturing plant involves assessment of the market, labor force, transportation, raw material availability, suitable sites, and community interest.
17. It is advisable to use a score sheet in evaluating alternative sites.

KEY TERMS AND CONCEPTS

Trading area
Primary trading area
Secondary trading area
Tertiary trading area
Shopping center
Convenience goods
Shopping goods
Specialty goods
Neighborhood shopping center
Community shopping center
Regional shopping center

QUESTIONS FOR DISCUSSION

1. Why is location one of the most important decisions facing an entrepreneur?
2. What sources of information are available for assessing alternative locations for a business?

3. What are the main questions that need to be answered regarding a business's trading area?
4. What are the key factors to consider in choosing a community in which to locate a business?
5. What are the alternative location choices within a community?
6. What decisions must be made once a specific site within a community has been selected?
7. How do traffic counts contribute to the selection of a retail or service outlet?
8. What is the relationship between traffic counts and types of consumer goods?
9. What are the advantages and disadvantages of a planned shopping center?
10. What are the characteristics of the three major types of shopping centers?
11. Why is the proper tenant mix crucial to the success of a shopping center?
12. What is the meaning of "retail compatibility?"
13. How are rents and leases arranged in a shopping center?
14. What are the primary factors that must be assessed in locating or relocating a manufacturing plant?
15. How can a score sheet be used when evaluating alternative sites?

SELF-TEST REVIEW

Multiple Choice Questions

1. The first step in the choosing of a retail or service location should be:
   a. Selection of the community.
   b. Selection of the area within the community.
   c. Selection of the specific site.
   d. None of the above.
2. A primary trading area contains:
   a. 15 to 25 percent of a business's customers.
   b. All customers that are loyal to the business.
   c. 55 to 75 percent of a business's customers.
   d. Customers who are widely dispersed.
3. A geographic cluster of retail stores in which each kind of store is designed to serve the specific needs of a particular market is a:
   a. Secondary shopping area.
   b. Planned shopping center.
   c. Downtown business district.
   d. All of the above.
4. Rental and lease agreements in shopping centers are usually negotiated on the following basis:
   a. A flat monthly fee.
   b. A percentage-of-sales agreement.
   c. Either a or b.
   d. None of the above.
5. Which of the following factors is an important consideration in location analysis for manufacturers?
   a. Location of raw materials.
   b. Location of markets.
   c. Availability of transportation.
   d. All of the above.

True/False Statements

1. A poor location is the major reason for business failures.
2. A prime location is one of the strongest competitive edges a small business can have.
3. The major area from which a business draws its customers is called the tertiary trading area.
4. In selecting the community, the small business owner should remember that most customers will come from within a five-mile radius.
5. In selecting a specific site, the small business owner should consider the type of goods sold.
6. Stores handling shopping goods have a much wider trading area than do stores handling convenience goods.
7. Planned shopping centers are usually classified according to their size or the number of customers they serve.
8. In planned shopping centers, rental payments are always made on a flat monthly basis.
9. The selection of a plant site generally involves fewer location factors than the selection of a store site.
10. Once a good location has been selected, a business should always remain at that location.

THE BOOKWORM

The Bookworm is an old bookstore that has been owned and operated by Jim Michaels for over 15 years. It is located in the downtown area of a city dominated by a state university. Michaels does most of the work himself, hiring minimum outside help; buys and controls inventory wisely; and manages all other costs closely. Long store hours and courteous personal attention to individual customer needs generate between $75,000 and $100,000 in annual sales volume. This volume has tended to be closer to the $75,000 mark in the past three years, and Michaels wonders what can be done to increase sales volume and profits. His average gross profit margin is 35 percent of sales.

According to the American Booksellers Association, a potential total sales volume of $100,000 to $150,000 per year is essential for an independent bookstore to be successful. One critical factor in a bookstore's success is location. Desirable sites include premises in downtown business districts and shopping areas with high pedestrian traffic and ample parking. The Bookworm's location is in the older, rundown part of the downtown district, where there is almost no pedestrian traffic after dark. But the store does attract curious customers who respond to the Yellow Pages' ad that has the headline, "If It's Legal, We Sell It."

Items commonly stocked by the Bookworm include hardback fiction and nonfiction (30 percent of sales), mass market and trade paperbacks (31 percent of sales), magazines (10 percent of sales), diaries (0.5 percent of sales), soft-core porn paperbacks (23.5 percent of sales), and a small collection of college textbooks (5 percent of sales). College books are stocked only when the publisher agrees to buy back any unsold copies and when a sufficient number of students request them.

Students at the state university purchase almost all their class needs at the campus bookstore. While many students are unhappy about the high prices at the campus bookstore, they have little choice but to patronize the store. Whenever the Bookworm carries titles that are also carried by the campus bookstore, Michaels lowers the price by 10 percent. He sees sales of these books as a means of generating store traffic, and does not expect to make the same 35 percent gross margin realized on other book sales.

In January, a customer had told Michaels that a 2,000-square-foot store in a small shopping strip located next to the university was available for rent. The customer had suggested in jest that Michaels relocate the business (two miles away from the existing store) and compete with the campus bookstore. Michaels has heard students in his store constantly complaining about the bookstore on campus, so he is intrigued by the possibility of relocating. Perhaps this is the answer to his low sales volume. After all, he knows that the student population has grown steadily over the past decade.

Michaels is looking into moving to the new location. He has discovered that the zoning would not cause any problems, that there is ample parking space, that the exterior facilities are attractive, and that the shopping area is safe after dark. But the rent would be $750 a month, compared to $450 in his current location, and a two-year lease is required, with an option to renew or cancel after each two-year period. Storage capacity is also limited, although additional storage space is available at low cost nearby. The most appealing aspect of the location is the high student pedestrian traffic during nine months of the year. Student enrollment varies between 19,500 and 22,570, but during the summer session, student enrollment at the university is less than 20 percent of the population during the regular term. Why no other bookstore has ever located in this apparently prime location is a mystery to Michaels.

QUESTIONS

1. What factors should Michaels investigate before making a decision to relocate the Bookworm?
2. If Michaels decides to move to the new location, should he continue using the slogan, "If It's Legal, We Sell It"?

NOTES

1. Dun and Bradstreet, *Business Failure Record* (New York: Dun and Bradstreet Corp., 1988), 19.
2. Based on Cable News Network's "Pinnacle," April 22, 1989. Guest: Deborah Szekely, Golden Door.
3. Barry Berman and Joel Evans, *Retail Management,* 3rd ed. (New York: Macmillan, 1986), 192.
4. Excerpted and adapted from Small Business Administration, *Choosing a Retail Location,* Management Aid Number 2.021, 1988, 8.
5. *Ibid.*, 9.
6. *Ibid.*, 3.
7. *Ibid.*, 6.
8. Based on Cable News Network's "Pinnacle," July 5, 1987. Guest: Mathias DeVito, Rouse Company.
9. Bank of America, "Equipment Leasing," *Small Business Reporter,* 1978, 1.
10. Excerpted and adapted from Small Business Administration, *Locating or Relocating Your Business,* Management Aid Number 2.002, 1988, 1–4.
11. Based on Cable News Network's "Pinnacle," August 30, 1987. Guest: Sidney Swartz, The Timberland Company.

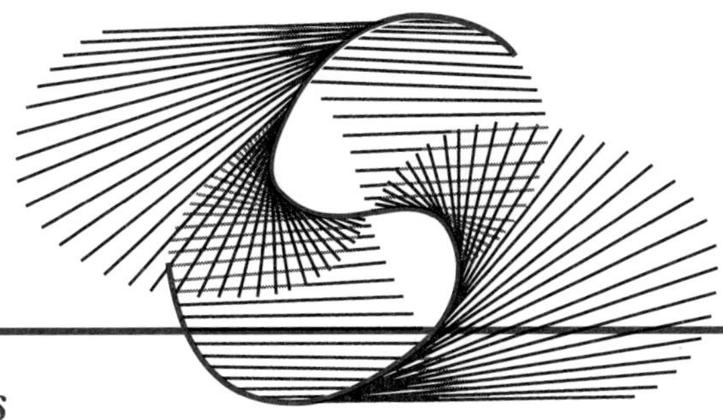

CHAPTER ELEVEN

Financing the Business

CHAPTER OUTLINE

DETERMINING FINANCIAL NEEDS
- Nature of Capital Needs
- Determining Owner Needs for Financial Assistance
- Projecting Future Capital Requirements

TYPES OF CAPITAL
- Debt Financing
- Equity Financing

SOURCES OF FINANCING
- Sources of Debt Financing
- Sources of Equity Financing

THE FUNDING PROCESS
- Selecting a Funding Source
- Preparing the Financing Package
- Presenting the Request for Funds

SUMMARY

LEARNING OBJECTIVES *The objectives of this chapter are to assist you in understanding:*

1. The needs for capital for business set-up, start-up, and operating capital.
2. How capital requirements can be estimated.
3. The types and sources of debt financing.
4. The types and sources of equity financing.
5. How the entrepreneur should seek funding for the firm.

Planning and developing a viable business rests not only on capable management and an available market, but also on a solid financial foundation. It is often said that it takes money to make money, and this certainly applies to small businesses. Though skillful entrepreneurship and pure luck can keep a business alive for a short period, there is no substitute for a good financial base if the firm is to survive and grow over the long term.

LILLIAN VERNON®

Basically, it takes money to go into business, and proper management of that money to ensure that the venture reaches its fullest potential. Money to start a business can come from a variety of sources. Lillian Vernon, for example, founded the Lillian Vernon Corp. (1989 sales of $150 million) with money she received as wedding gifts: "My seed money was wedding gift money. You put it away, you don't spend it, and that's what I used. I only had $2,000 and I put it into the business."[1]

Similarly, Mortimer Levitt, founder of The Custom Shop, a maker of custom-made shirts priced the same as ready mades, got his money in a different way: "I had this idea. A man had a business on the lower East Side (of New York City) . . . he was charging $1.25—cut, make and trim for a shirt, using the customer's fabric. I figured it must cost him seventy-five cents, so it would cost me seventy-five cents . . . I didn't know how he made it, but whatever he did I knew I could do it better because he lacked my sense of style . . . I had $1,000 and I borrowed $1,000 on my life insurance . . ."[2]

All too often, an individual will go into business with a few dollars saved, only to find that it is not enough. Unfortunately, this recognition comes by way of a financial crisis—suppliers want payment on delivery, the landlord wants payment of the rent, and sales are below expectations. Some owners already in business see opportunities for growth, and begin an expansion without carefully examining its financial requirements. The same types of financial crises can occur.

Even the best financial planning will not prepare the entrepreneur to meet all monetary problems. However, having a well-developed evaluation of financial needs before starting the venture or making changes in existing operations will reduce the odds of confronting insurmountable financial problems and immediate business failure.

Consequently, the entrepreneur must face up to these key financial questions:

- How much money is needed to start the venture or fund the desired operations of an ongoing business?
- Where will the money come from?
- How will the funds be used?
- How long will it take before the use of those funds yields profits?
- How can additional funds be obtained in case of an emergency?
- How will the money be paid back to lenders, or adequate returns provided to investors?

After answering these questions, the entrepreneur will be in a better position to obtain the funding needed, and to use it effectively.

DETERMINING FINANCIAL NEEDS

Determining the monetary requirements of a proposed business or an existing firm lays the cornerstone for effective financial management. By identifying the costs of operating, and assessing the personal financial commitment to be made, the entrepreneur can make

EXHIBIT 11–1 ***Small Business Needs for Capital***

Set-Up Capital	Start-Up Capital	Operating Capital
Beginning inventory Equipment Fixtures Insurance Lease deposit Legal and accounting services Prepaid expenses Professional expenses Renovation/remodeling	Decorative fixtures Office supplies Promotion Special inventory Special labor	Cash shortages Expansion Major purchases Seasonal needs

many difficult decisions and deal with important issues before they become crises. In doing this, the small business owner must define the aspects of the business that will need funding, determine how much outside financial assistance will be needed, and project the longer-term capital requirements of the business.

Nature of Capital Needs

The financial requirements of a business revolve around three interrelated needs: **set-up capital, start-up capital,** and **operating capital.**[3] The first two focus on the periods before operations begin, while operating capital can be needed at any point during the firm's life (see Exhibit 11-1).

Capital Needs for Set-Up

Depending on the nature of the business, considerable costs can be incurred due to its size or location, just to prepare for it to begin operating. Capital is needed to set up the venture, including payments for licenses and permits, deposits on facilities and equipment, legal expenses, and so on. Starting a business involves a great deal of preparation that can be expensive. An example of the possible magnitude of set-up costs is shown in Exhibit 11-2.

EXHIBIT 11–2 ***Sample Estimated Set-Up Capital Requirements***

	Yogurt Shops	Restaurants	Gift Stores
Beginning inventory	\$10,000–\$25,000	\$30,000–\$75,000	\$10,000–\$35,000
Fixtures and equipment	\$5,000–\$15,000	\$50,000–\$100,000	\$2,500–\$15,000
Insurance	\$1,500–\$5,000	\$1,000–\$5,000	\$1,500–\$5,000
Lease deposit	\$1,000–\$5,000	\$5,000–\$15,000	\$1,000–\$5,000
Leasehold improvements	\$15,000–\$45,000	\$100,000–\$250,000	\$35,000–\$100,000
Professional fees	\$1,000–\$5,000	\$2,500–\$10,000	\$1,000–\$5,000

The owner of this retail store has calculated and planned for the expenses incurred in this major renovation project in order to conform to the requirements of the business. (Photograph © Ann M. Mason)

One of the largest initial capital expenditures will be for the lease deposit and renovation or remodeling of the store or plant to make it conform to the requirements of the business. While a facility should be sought that closely fits expected needs, it is common for none to be available in a good location or at a reasonable price. As a result, the entrepreneur must analyze the costs of renting a building and remodeling it into an appropriate structure. Irrespective of how suitable a facility is, however, the entrepreneur will want to make at least minor changes so that it will conform to personal desires and expectations. These costs can be sizable, and must be estimated and planned for, because they are incurred before any revenue is generated.

The second major initial capital requirement is for the equipment and fixtures needed to run the business. Such items as cash registers, computers, minor office equipment (file cabinets, desks, tables, chairs), specialized machinery, and transportation equipment can represent significant expenditures depending on the nature of the business. Even seemingly inexpensive items, such as minor office equipment, can be substantial when considered collectively.

A third capital requirement will be for the firm's beginning inventory. Materials and/or merchandise will have to be acquired before operations can begin. While some suppliers provide needed inventory on credit or consignment, most will want payment from a new venture on delivery. Uncertainties about the possible success or failure of the business, coupled with the owner's lack of a track record in paying bills, often preclude using credit to obtain initial inventory.

A fourth major capital need is one that is often neglected by prospective owners: licenses and permits, professional fees, and prepaid expenses. Business licenses and required permits, and prepayments on various operating expenses (for example, insurance, utilities) can be significant. Even more expensive, however, are the legal and accounting services often needed to set up the venture. Fees for establishing corporations, obtaining copyrights and/or patents, and so on, will vary with the type of ownership and the owner's expertise in these areas. Even for entrepreneurs who have some background in business law and accounting, these expenses will be sufficiently high to include when planning capital requirements.

Capital Needs for Start-Up

In addition to the funds needed to set up the business, there will be capital requirements for getting the business started (see Exhibit 11-3). Labor, promotion, office supplies, decorative fixtures, and a variety of other items will have to be purchased. Start-up expenses are those that are incurred immediately prior to opening and during the first few weeks or months of operation. The distinguishing feature of start-up costs is that they tend to be unique to starting the business, and do not recur in later years.

EXHIBIT 11–3 ***Sample Estimated Start-Up Capital Requirements***

	Yogurt Shops	Restaurants	Gift Stores
Cash	$1,000–$5,000	$5,000–$1,500	$1,000–$5,000
Office supplies	$1,000–$2,500	$1,500–$4,000	$1,500–$3,000
Interior decorations	$1,000–$2,500	$5,000–$15,000	$1,500–$4,000
Exterior signs	$500–$2,500	$1,000–$25,000	$1,000–$3,000
Introductory promotion	$500–$2,500	$2,500–$25,000	$1,000–$3,500
Wages and fringe benefits	$3,000–$10,000	$3,500–$15,000	$3,000–$10,000

During this time, for example, there may be an introductory promotional program, design of signs, design of business cards and brochures, purchase of office supplies, specialized labor (for example, plumbers, electricians), and other expenses that are not incurred on a regular basis. As in the case of some set-up expenses, these might not be especially high when considered individually, however, collectively they can consume a large portion of the entrepreneur's initial capital.

The importance of start-up costs is magnified even more by the fact that both revenues and total expenses tend to fluctuate widely during this initial time in the life of the firm. The nature and extent of demand for the firm's products and services, the timing of sales, and the appropriate level of expense necessary to generate those sales all take time to stabilize and project with a reasonable degree of accuracy. During this trial-and-error period, it is likely that expenses will exceed revenues and cash flow will be a problem. Accordingly, start-up capital may be needed to cover these costs and help the firm get through its first three to six months.

Operating Capital Needs

Over the life of the business, there will be occasional needs for funding, as shown in Exhibit 11-4. The entrepreneur might need to stabilize cash inflows and outflows, expand operations, or help the firm get through difficult times. While the entrepreneur will pass through the set-up and start-up stages rather quickly, operating capital needs can occur throughout the firm's life.

The most common uses for operating capital are to overcome cash flow problems, to survive downturns in business, and to finance expansion. Nearly every firm, large or

EXHIBIT 11–4 ***Operating Capital Needs for a Small Business***

Early Years	Middle Years	Later Years
Cash shortages Seasonal needs	Purchase of new equipment Hiring administrative staff Debt restructuring Renovations Expansion	Lease of new equipment Debt restructuring

small, successful or unsuccessful, will experience cash flow problems at some time. Sooner or later, cash inflows will be insufficient to cover cash outflows, and the firm will have to rely on cash reserves or outside financing to balance the flow. If this becomes a recurrent problem, it may be necessary to revamp the firm's capital structure—the balance of debt and owner investment in the firm.

A common need for operating capital is to overcome business downturns. Economic recession, loss of one or more major clients, and so on, can have a serious effect on the firm's operations. Funds may be required just to continue operations, or to reposition the firm in the marketplace.

Finally, most firms that attempt to grow and expand their spheres of operation need more funds than they can generate and retain internally. Expansion often requires outlays for added facilities, equipment, inventory, labor, and promotion. In many respects, planning capital needs for this type of activity is similar to starting a new business—except that the entrepreneur's earlier success means there may be more to lose.

Financing the business is a never-ending issue. For example, The Timberland Company, the maker of rugged outdoor boots, shoes, apparel and accessories, made a public issue of stock in order to repay some of its debt and provide funds for capital. The company added to its capacity so that it could expand its sales.[4]

Determining Owner Needs for Financial Assistance

Once the owner has assessed the capital needs for set-up, start-up, or operating capital, an *equity position* can be determined. This is the money the owner is willing and able to commit to the business versus the amount supplied by creditors and other investors. While some prospective entrepreneurs have sufficient capital personally available, most must borrow money or find other people to invest in the business. Recognizing the need for outside capital is critical—being undercapitalized is a common trait of small businesses and a major cause of failure.

One of the most significant sources of capital funding for a new venture is personal monetary resources. If these are insufficient, the entrepreneur may have to borrow from family, friends, lending institutions, and/or suppliers. The borrowing process marks a significant milestone, as these liabilities must be repaid with either the firm's assets or those of the owner personally—including home, car, lamps, and carpet.

If the entrepreneur does not want to borrow, outside investors may be sought. While these funds do not have to be repaid if the business is not profitable, another set of milestones is reached. The owner is giving up some authority and may not be able to control the firm's destiny.

Sidney Swartz, after a successful initial public offering of Timberland stock, obtained the needed capital to enable the company to increase the firm's manufacturing capacity so that it could expand sales. Timberland has since opened a Boston specialty store in 1988 and a Sausalito, California store in 1989. (Photograph courtesy of The Timberland Company)

EXHIBIT 11–5

Worksheet for Computing Set-up Capital Needs

	Minimum	Probable	Maximum
Beginning inventory	$ ______	$ ______	$ ______
Equipment	$ ______	$ ______	$ ______
Fixtures	$ ______	$ ______	$ ______
Insurance	$ ______	$ ______	$ ______
Lease Deposit	$ ______	$ ______	$ ______
Leasehold improvement	$ ______	$ ______	$ ______
Licenses and tax deposit	$ ______	$ ______	$ ______
Professional fees	$ ______	$ ______	$ ______
Security system	$ ______	$ ______	$ ______
Other:			
______________	$ ______	$ ______	$ ______
______________	$ ______	$ ______	$ ______
______________	$ ______	$ ______	$ ______
______________	$ ______	$ ______	$ ______

Ideally, of course, the entrepreneur will try to raise only the amount of capital that is needed to finance the business. Obtaining too much can be costly in terms of paying interest on borrowed funds or yielding too much control of the firm to others. Obtaining too little financing, however, means not being able to do all that needs to be done to make the venture successful.

As a result, financing must be planned very carefully. Attaining a desirable mix of personal equity and debt that will cover capital needs cannot be left to chance. One of the best ways to determine financing needs for set-up, start-up, and operating capital is to project them using the worksheets shown in Exhibits 11-5, 11-6, and 11-7.[5]

Essentially, what is involved in these three worksheets is projection of the revenues and expenses of the firm over the relevant time periods. For business set-up costs,

EXHIBIT 11–6

Worksheet for Computing Start-up Capital Needs

	Minimum	Probable	Maximum
Cabinets	$ ______	$ ______	$ ______
Cash requirements	$ ______	$ ______	$ ______
Decorative fixtures	$ ______	$ ______	$ ______
Desk	$ ______	$ ______	$ ______
Exterior sign	$ ______	$ ______	$ ______
Office supplies	$ ______	$ ______	$ ______
Promotion	$ ______	$ ______	$ ______
Wages and fringe benefits	$ ______	$ ______	$ ______
Other:			
______________	$ ______	$ ______	$ ______
______________	$ ______	$ ______	$ ______
______________	$ ______	$ ______	$ ______
______________	$ ______	$ ______	$ ______

EXHIBIT 11–7

Worksheet for Computing Operating Capital Needs

	Minimum	Probable	Maximum
Administrative staff addition	$ ______	$ ______	$ ______
Business downturns	$ ______	$ ______	$ ______
Cash shortages	$ ______	$ ______	$ ______
Equipment purchases	$ ______	$ ______	$ ______
Expansion—geographic	$ ______	$ ______	$ ______
Expansion—products	$ ______	$ ______	$ ______
Expansion—services	$ ______	$ ______	$ ______
Renovations	$ ______	$ ______	$ ______
Seasonal fluctuations	$ ______	$ ______	$ ______
Other:			
______________	$ ______	$ ______	$ ______
______________	$ ______	$ ______	$ ______
______________	$ ______	$ ______	$ ______
______________	$ ______	$ ______	$ ______

estimating capital requirements is basically a matter of researching the probable costs from suppliers, government agencies, and others. For some types of businesses, professional or trade associations compile information on capital requirements. However, generally it is best to research the likely costs rather than to rely on statistics that might be outdated or might apply to different geographical areas. Since no revenues will be generated during this stage of the firm's development, all expected expenditures should be included in the worksheet provided in Exhibit 11-5.

Estimating start-up and operating capital needs is somewhat different, since some revenues can offset the expenditures. Consequently, the process is more than just a matter of researching costs. Forecasting sales for a new venture or expansion into a different area of business is difficult at best, since no past records are available. Usually, the entrepreneur will estimate revenues after analyzing the market potential and estimating the sales volume of competitors. Ways to do this were described in Chapter 9.

Once the entrepreneur has a sales projection, the firm's expenses can be estimated in several different ways. Certainly the best approach is to research the probable expenses in much the same way as was done for set-up costs. The value of this approach is that it forces the entrepreneur to make some critical decisions about the nature of the business. For example, how much insurance is to be carried? What type of telephone system and how many lines will be needed? How many employees will be hired, at what wages, and with what benefits? The quality of the estimate of capital needs improves greatly when the entrepreneur can make these and other decisions, and gather information about probable costs.

Another common approach to forecasting expenses is to use industry averages. These are usually given in dollar amounts and as percentages of sales. Average percentages can be applied to the owner's projected sales to arrive at estimates of costs of goods and other operating expenses. Additionally, averages often are provided in terms of dollars held in inventory, accounts receivable, equipment and other fixed assets, and short- and long-term liabilities. Industry averages can be obtained from published sources like Robert Morris Associates, Dun and Bradstreet, and Valueline. The entrepreneur also may be able to obtain this information from industry sources, such as professional or trade associations, manufacturers, or consulting firms. The advantage of using industry averages is that it is relatively easy to do.

The key to successfully estimating capital needs is to have reasonable expectations of revenues and costs. It is quite common, however, for entrepreneurs to be so enthusiastic about their businesses that they become overly optimistic about sales, and underestimate the costs of doing business. Generally, it is best to take a conservative approach in projecting sales and a liberal approach to estimating expenses. By doing this, the entrepreneur prepares for the worst-case scenario for capital needs.

After making projections of the amount of capital that will be needed, the entrepreneur can determine how much, if any, outside financing will be required. A worksheet for making this evaluation is provided in Exhibit 11-8.

EXHIBIT 11–8 ***Worksheet for Estimating Outside Capital Needs***

	Minimum	Probable	Maximum
Costs of Living	$ ______	$ ______	$ ______
Fixed monthly expenses	$ ______	$ ______	$ ______
Variable monthly expenses	$ ______	$ ______	$ ______
Taxes	$ ______	$ ______	$ ______
Total	$ ______	$ ______	$ ______
Business Costs	$ ______	$ ______	$ ______
Set-up	$ ______	$ ______	$ ______
Start-up	$ ______	$ ______	$ ______
Operating	$ ______	$ ______	$ ______
Total	$ ______	$ ______	$ ______
Other:			
______________	$ ______	$ ______	$ ______
______________	$ ______	$ ______	$ ______
______________	$ ______	$ ______	$ ______
______________	$ ______	$ ______	$ ______
Total	$ ______	$ ______	$ ______
Total Capital Needs	$ ______	$ ______	$ ______
Capital Available			
Personal savings	$ ______	$ ______	$ ______
Personal checking	$ ______	$ ______	$ ______
Personal stocks	$ ______	$ ______	$ ______
Personal loans	$ ______	$ ______	$ ______
Business loans	$ ______	$ ______	$ ______
Business investors	$ ______	$ ______	$ ______
Other:			
______________	$ ______	$ ______	$ ______
______________	$ ______	$ ______	$ ______
______________	$ ______	$ ______	$ ______
______________	$ ______	$ ______	$ ______
Total Capital Available	$ ______	$ ______	$ ______
Total Excess/Deficit	$ ______	$ ______	$ ______

Projecting Future Capital Requirements

Needs for capital are not unique to the start of business operations. As the firm grows, requirements for more capital can exceed cash reserves. Consequently, even a successful firm must borrow money to buy more equipment, land, inventory, labor, and so on. While it is difficult to predict when additional capital will be needed, the entrepreneur should be aware of these possibilities.

The capital requirements for the next two to four years should be estimated and planned for. Forecasting future levels of business activity is the first step in this process. Once the firm has been operating for a year or two, a thorough review of the financial records will provide signs of future capital needs. This review process is described in Chapter 15. Most importantly, the entrepreneur must effectively prepare the firm for future capital requirements, whether to overcome difficult times or to expand operations.

TYPES OF CAPITAL

Once the capital requirements have been decided upon, the entrepreneur must identify potential sources of funding. Even in the unlikely event that the owner personally has adequate funds, it is important to have alternative sources delineated so that comparisons can be made of the benefits of using owner-supplied funds versus using debt financing.

Assuming the personal capital contribution is insufficient to cover all needs for capital, the entrepreneur should begin to identify different sources. Some provide almost all the capital needed, while others will provide money only for particular segments of the business's activities. Some sources provide cash, while others only grant lines of credit. Accordingly, sound financial planning demands that the entrepreneur identify both the sources of funds and the types of capital available. A summary of sources and principal uses of capital is presented in Exhibit 11-9.

Many entrepreneurs believe that all they have to do to finance a business is go to a bank, tell a loan officer all about their great ideas, and walk out with sacks of money. It seldom happens that way.

Financing can be difficult to obtain, and distinctly different types of capital are available depending on the nature of the business, one's current financial situation, the amount of funding needed, and many other variables. Importantly, too, each type of capital offers unique costs and benefits that may or may not be appropriate for a particular business. Understanding the various sources of funds and their implications for the business is a key to successful capital generation and financial management. The two main types of funding are debt financing and equity financing.

Debt Financing

The most common means of funding a small business is **debt financing.** Borrowing capital from outside sources does not infringe on the ownership of the firm. Instead, loans are based on the assets of the firm and/or those of the entrepreneur. The advantages of debt financing focus on the earnings and management of the firm. Since ownership is not diluted, profits are reserved for the entrepreneur. Additionally, the entrepreneur retains greater control over the actual management, although with some forms of debt, restrictions are placed on certain activities.

EXHIBIT 11–9 **Small Business Financing Guide**

Use of Funds	Type of Money	Source	Financing Vehicle
Business Start-up	Equity	Nonprofessional investor	Partnership formation Stock issue
		Venture capitalist SBIC-MESBIC	Stock issue Convertible debentures Debt with warrants
	Long-term debt	Bank Savings institution	Term loan (limited) Unsecured term loan Equipment loan Equipment leasing Real estate loan
		Commercial finance company	Equipment loan Equipment leasing Real estate loan
		Life insurance company	Policy loan Real estate loan
		Leasing company	Equipment leasing
		Consumer finance company	Personal property term loan
		Small Business Administration	Term loan guarantee Direct term loan (limited)
		SBIC-MESBIC	Term loan (limited) Unsecured term loan Equipment loan Equipment leasing
		Certified or local development company	Facilities/equipment financing
		Farmers Home Administration Economic Development Administration	Term loan guarantee
Working Capital	Long-term debt	Bank Savings institution	Unsecured term loan Equipment loan Real estate loan
		Commercial finance company	Equipment loan Real estate loan
		Life insurance company	Policy loan Real estate loan Unsecured term loan (limited)
		Consumer finance company	Personal property loan
		Small Business Administration SBIC-MESBIC	Term loan guarantee
		Farmers Home Administration Economic Development Administration	Term loan guarantee

➤

EXHIBIT 11–9 Small Business Financing Guide *(continued)*

Use of Funds	Type of Money	Source	Financing Vehicle
Seasonal Peak	Short-term debt and line of credit	Supplier	Trade credit
		Bank Savings institution	Commercial loan Accounts receivable financing Inventory financing Flooring Indirect collection financing Unsecured line of credit
		Commercial finance company	Accounts receivable financing Inventory financing Factoring
		Factor	Factoring
		Life insurance company	Policy loan
		Consumer finance company	Personal property loan
		Small Business Administration	Line of credit guarantee (limited)
Equipment or Facilities Acquisition	Long-term debt	SBIC-MESBIC	Term loan
		Bank Commercial finance company Savings institution	Equipment loan Equipment leasing Real estate loan
		Life insurance company	Policy loan Unsecured loan (limited) Real estate loan
		Consumer finance company	Personal property term loan
		Leasing company	Equipment leasing
		Small Business Administration	Term loan guarantee Direct term loan (limited)
		Certified or local development company	Facilities/equipment financing
		Farmers Home Administration Economic Development Administration	Term loan guarantee
Sharp, Sustained Growth	Equity	Nonprofessional investor	Partnership formation Stock issue
		Venture capitalist SBIC-MESBIC	Stock issue Convertible debentures Debt with warrants
	Long-term debt	SBIC-MESBIC	Term loan
		Bank Savings institution	Unsecured term loan Equipment loan Equipment leasing Real estate loan

Reprinted with permission of Bank of America NT&SA, "Business Financing," *Small Business Reporter®*, copyright September 1988.

EXHIBIT 11–9 **Small Business Financing Guide** *(continued)*

Use of Funds	Type of Money	Source	Financing Vehicle
		Commercial finance company	Equipment leasing Real estate loan
		Life insurance company	Unsecured term loan Policy loan Real estate loan
		Consumer finance company	Personal property loan
		Leasing company	Equipment leasing
		Small Business Administration	Term loan guarantee Direct term loan (limited)
		Certified or local development company	Facilities/equipment financing
		Farmers Home Administration Economic Development Administration	Term loan guarantee
	Line of credit	Supplier	Trade credit
		Bank Savings institution	Unsecured line of credit Accounts receivable financing Inventory financing Flooring Indirect collection financing
		Commercial finance company	Accounts receivable financing Inventory financing Factoring
		Factor	Factoring
		Small Business Administration	Line of credit guarantee (limited $ amount) *No revolving line is presently available*

Reprinted with permission of Bank of America NT&SA, "Business Financing," *Small Business Reporter*®, copyright September 1988.

The main disadvantages of debt financing are that loans must be repaid, and that they must be repaid on a defined time schedule. Furthermore, the amount of debt that can be incurred is limited by the value of the assets and the firm's earnings record or potential.

Generally, debt financing sources can be grouped on the basis of the lengths of the loans. Different types of lending carry various time frames for paying back borrowed money. **Short-term financing** involves loans that must be repaid within one year, while **long-term financing** is paid back over a period of time greater than one year.

Short-Term Financing

This includes loans for working capital derived from trade credit, short-term borrowing from financial institutions, financing accounts receivable, and financing inventories. Some of the common types of short term financing are:[6]

1. **Commercial loans**—a very popular type of loan for three to six months. Usually, a single *balloon payment* is made at the end of the defined period. These loans may be unsecured, or secured with the assets of the firm. For larger commercial loans, usually over $100,000, *compensating balances* may be required. This means that the entrepreneur must leave a portion of the loan on deposit with the lender even though interest is being paid on the entire amount. For example, if an entrepreneur borrows $100,000 and must keep 10 percent in a compensating balance, only $90,000 is available for use. The entrepreneur pays interest on the full $100,000 and earns bank interest on the $10,000 held on deposit. Effectively, what this does is increase the cost of borrowing, since the interest rate on the loan will be higher than what is paid on the deposit. Additionally, the lender is more secure, since it will require $100,000 in collateral for an effective loan of $90,000.
2. **Accounts receivable financing**—a specialized type of loan that is secured by the receivables of the firm. Normally, financial institutions will lend up to 65 to 80 percent of the face value of receivables that are less than 60 to 90 days old. When receivables are paid off, the firm will repay the lender with interest. This approach is used relatively often by firms that experience seasonal fluctuations in sales.
3. **Inventory financing**—a specialized type of loan that is secured by the inventory of the firm. Financial institutions typically only lend up to 50 percent of the value of the inventory. A lower percentage is loaned on inventory than on receivables because the latter are more readily salable than inventory.
4. **Discounting installment contracts**—these are similar to accounts receivable financing, and are used to finance high-cost merchandise. The lender will either advance the firm a part (usually 70 to 80 percent) of the installment contract, or buy the contract outright, often at face value. Repayment is made as the customer pays off the installment. If the firm sells the contract, it still will be held liable if the customer defaults on payments. This is an especially valuable source of funds for firms that deal in expensive products for which customers commonly want to pay on time.
5. **Flooring**—a specialized version of a discounted installment contract. Under a flooring plan, the lender finances specific merchandise until it is sold. The firm pays interest only on the loan, but must repay the loan in full upon sale of the merchandise, or discount the resulting installment contract. As with discounting installment contracts, flooring helps the entrepreneur avoid tying up needed cash.
6. **Line of credit**—one of the best methods of financing for intermittent capital needs. Lending institutions commonly establish credit limits, and the firm can borrow up to a defined limit at any time. The firm pays a fee to establish the line of credit, and pays interest on any funds borrowed. The entrepreneur can continue to borrow and repay on the line as long as the total at any one time does not exceed the limit.

There are advantages to using short-term borrowing effectively. It represents a ready source of funds to help the business meet pressing obligations or take advantage of opportunities that arise suddenly. Unexpected expenses, slow sales, and so on, often create financial problems for small businesses. Short-term borrowing serves to cover these contingencies, and to help the firm act quickly to minimize potential disruptions to its operations.

There are, however, some disadvantages to short-term borrowing. As a ready and tempting source of funds, it can be used too quickly and too often. It cannot be viewed as a substitute for sound financial management. Because the payback period is relatively brief, the entrepreneur must consider the revenues and expenses of the firm over this period and be sure that enough money will be generated to pay off the loan. If, for example, the entrepreneur borrows $10,000 and must pay back both the $10,000 and the interest within six months, there must be a reasonable expectation that sales will exceed other expenses by at least that amount.

Long-Term Financing

Longer-term financing includes both intermediate and long-term borrowing. Intermediate financing usually is for periods ranging from two to five years, while longer term loans may go for five or more years. Generally, these types of loans are used to finance the acquisition of land, buildings and fixtures, and machinery and equipment. As is described later in this chapter, the sources of such funding are varied.

Typically included in long-term financing are mortgages, bonds, stock offerings, and long-term loans from various private and public institutions. Some of the more common types of these loans are:[7]

- *Unsecured term loans*—usually reserved for firms that have established track records and can demonstrate abilities to repay loans. For new ventures, financial institutions often require the entrepreneur to contribute at least half of the funds needed for start-up. In many instances, the lender will place certain restrictions on the operations of the firm, including how much additional debt the firm can incur, how much can be paid for executive salaries, and so on. In some cases, too, the entrepreneur may be asked to secure the loan for personal assets or those of the firm.
- *Equipment loans*—special long-term loans specifically designed to finance the purchase of equipment. These usually are limited to between 60 and 80 percent of the cost of the equipment and must be repaid during its useful life.
- *Real estate financing*—a special long-term loan oriented to the purchase of real estate. Funds normally are provided for up to 75 percent of the value of the property, and may be repaid over an extended period of time.
- *Equipment leasing*—a highly specialized financing program in which the lending institution purchases the equipment and then leases it to the firm. This type of loan allows the firm to retain its financial resources and make payments over a long period.

The principal advantage of long-term financing is that it provides an extended period of time before which the full loan must be repaid. This gives the entrepreneur a greater opportunity to develop a profit base from which repayment is made. Although definite provisions must be made for repayment, this type of borrowing is not as subject as short-term financing to minor fluctuations in business activity. By using various types of long-term funding, the entrepreneur can exercise considerable flexibility in the payback schedule. If, for example, loans are staggered so that repayment times are three to six months apart, the firm may be better able to prepare for the payback. Similarly, the small business owner can establish repayment schedules based on seasonality and other factors.

Used effectively, long-term borrowing can provide added profit potential for the entrepreneur who uses leverage wisely. Leverage is the use of borrowed funds to grow. The entrepreneur who can earn a 25 percent profit on a $10,000 loan with an interest rate of 15 percent realizes a net profit on the leverage of 10 percent, or $1,000. It is not always advisable to do this, however, if it means borrowing the maximum possible. The entrepreneur should keep some long-term debt capacity available for emergencies and opportunities that must be taken advantage of immediately.

There are several disadvantages to long-term borrowing. First, the risk of loss to the lender is higher because the longer time period is more difficult to predict. Accordingly, interest rates for long-term loans tend to be higher than for short-term loans. Second, the debt is fixed and must be repaid. If the firm runs into a long period of slow sales, it might not be able to repay. Third, very high levels of long-term debt may on occasion mean a dilution of the effective ownership and management of the firm. For example, lenders may require the firm to file special reports, not borrow additional funds from other sources, limit management salaries and/or bonuses, or subordinate the interests of the entrepreneur to those of the lending institution.

Equity Financing

The other type of capital that can be obtained by the entrepreneur is **equity financing.** This involves selling part of the ownership in the firm to others. Financing in this manner can only be accomplished if the firm is a partnership or corporation, or when a proprietorship is converted to either a partnership or a corporation.

In the case of partnerships, the original owners can add new owners as general and/or limited partners. *General partners* share in the actual management of the firm and its profits, but also are liable for its debts. *Limited partners* cannot be involved in the actual management, but their risks are limited to the amount of capital they invest. Income from the partnership will be distributed to limited partners in some manner agreed upon at the time the limited partners are added. Technically, adding partners means that the firm becomes a new company, and a new partnership agreement will have to be prepared.

For a corporation, or by incorporating a proprietorship or partnership, the entrepreneur can attempt to obtain equity financing by selling common stock, preferred stock, convertible debentures (a form of long-term debt that partially or totally is convertible to common stock instead of being repaid), and debt with warrants (a form of long-term debt that allows the lender to purchase within a specified period of time a certain amount of stock at a set price even after the debt has been repaid). As was described in Chapter 7, a corporate form of ownership limits the liabilities of investors to the amount of money they have contributed. Repayment, however, is made through the appreciation in the value of the stock and/or dividends.

Although it is possible for the venture to go public as a corporation, it is rare that it will be traded on the New York or American stock exchanges, or even in a national over-the-counter market (for example, NASDAQ). Even if it were possible, most small business owners would find the reporting forms and filing requirements cumbersome at best.

With corporations, it is most common for shares to be sold to private investors, larger businesses, and/or government-subsidized businesses that specialize in providing equity capital to small firms. These sources were briefly described in Chapter 7, and are treated in more detail later in this chapter.

The advantages of equity financing center on the fact that it can reduce the amount of debt that must be repaid at a particular point in time. Holders of common or preferred stock, for example, may not have to be paid dividends on their investments if the firm experiences little or no profit. Therefore, the distribution of the corporation's funds can be deferred until the firm is in a more favorable position.

Even though equity financing may appear to be advantageous, there are drawbacks. First, few small businesses can expect to derive much funding in this manner. Most potential investors shy away from new small businesses because of their high failure rates and the likelihood of sparse profits during the early years. Second, the ownership of the firm is partially passed from the entrepreneur to others, thereby reducing the entrepreneur's decision-making control—a main reason for going into business in the first place. Third, dividends are paid out in after-tax dollars, so the corporation gains no tax advantages, as it would when writing off interest on short- and long-term debt. Finally, as in the case of debt financing, there is a limit on how many investors the firm can realistically expect to attract. As the number increases, the earnings of the venture will have to be portioned out, possibly to the point that it will be worthless to all concerned.

SOURCES OF FINANCING

Two of the most critical decisions in seeking outside financing involve how much money to obtain and from what source(s). Earlier in this chapter, consideration was given to how much funding would be required. These issues, of course, are highly interrelated, since there is only so much financing available from debt and from equity sources. Perhaps more importantly, the choice of source of financing should be made carefully. Although many entrepreneurs may not have many options available, the approach of "I'll take it from whoever will give it to me" can be especially dangerous. The entrepreneur needs lenders and/or investors who understand the unique nature of small business and are realistic in their expectations of the firm's possible performance.

Sources of Debt Financing

Entrepreneurs often discover that obtaining adequate sources of financing is one of their most difficult problems. Many banks cater to the needs of larger businesses and make it more difficult for small businesses to meet established lending criteria. Furthermore, entrepreneurs frequently do not have the experience they need with respect to preparing loan requests and their accompanying documentation. Credit ratings and financial statements for small businesses may show poor past performance, thus bringing into question the firm's potential for success and making it a high risk for the bank.

Loans, nevertheless, are available to smaller firms. While large banks tend to make the majority of their loans to large companies, medium-sized banks commonly have been more receptive to small business requests for financing. This is a market niche that many of these institutions have been trying to capture.

Banks, however, are not the only sources of debt financing. Others include commercial and consumer finance companies, the federal government, and some specialized lenders.[8] In relatively rare instances, financing can be obtained from large companies. For example, Kathy Taggares formed K.T.'s Kitchens to sell Bob's Big Boy Salad Dressing. She bought the rights from the Marriott Corporation for $6 million—$5 million of which was financed by Marriott over 20 years at 10 percent interest.[9] Ordinarily, however, financing comes from more traditional sources, which are described below.

Commercial Banking Institutions

Commercial banks and savings and loans are the sources one thinks of first when seeking debt financing. Although under certain circumstances commercial banking institutions will make long-term loans, they typically lend on short-term bases for start-up rather than set-up, and require the signature of the owner to secure the loan with personal assets. As a source of working capital, commercial banking institutions offer several types of lending programs. The most common types of loans made by these institutions are commercial loans, accounts receivable financing, inventory financing, discount installment contracts, flooring, and lines of credit. These were described earlier in this chapter.

Commercial Finance Companies

While commercial banking institutions tend to be quite conservative in their lending practices, commercial finance companies often are willing to loan funds to more risky prospects. It is common for entrepreneurs to be refused loans by commercial banks and savings and loans, but to be granted them by commercial finance companies. The loan programs offered by these sources are similar to those of commercial banking institutions. The most common types of lending are on accounts receivable, outright purchase of receivables (called *factoring*), inventory loans, and equipment leasing programs.

The main differences between these two types of lending sources center on the availability, terms, and costs of the loans. The types of loans available from commercial finance companies tend not to be as uniform as they are among commercial banking institutions. For example, some commercial finance companies do not make real estate loans, while others actively encourage them.

Another difference is that commercial finance companies generally require the loans to be secured with all or part of the firm's or the entrepreneur's assets as collateral. While commercial banking institutions take a hard look at a firm's track record and prospects, commercial finance companies often look mostly at the collateral offered. In addition, since finance companies may loan to more risky prospects, they tend to charge higher interest rates than commercial banking institutions do.

Commercial finance companies provide an important source of funding, especially to entrepreneurs who have difficulty obtaining debt capital. This source is also attractive to firms that can provide assets as collateral for their loans even though they do not have good track records in sales and profits.

Consumer Finance Companies

Consumer finance companies do not make direct loans to businesses. Instead, they make personal short- and long-term loans to business owners. These funds, generally up to $25,000, can be used as set-up, start-up, or operating capital. Typically, these loans must be secured by the personal assets of the borrower, although some also offer *signature* or unsecured loans. Collateral for these loans usually includes personal items (for example, cars, boats) for loans under $10,000, and second mortgages on borrowers' homes when over $10,000.

The advantage of this type of borrowing is that the funds can be used for any purpose. Other sources of financing often restrict how the funds can be used. The disadvantage is that these loans tend to have relatively high interest rates when compared to loans from commercial banking institutions and commercial finance companies. Nevertheless, this can be an important source of financing when the venture is just getting started or is experiencing very difficult times.

Small Business Administration

The Small Business Administration (SBA) was established as a federal agency to promote small business development and growth. In addition to a variety of other forms of assistance, the SBA has several types of loan programs, which are summarized in Chapter 22. A general description of the SBA lending process is described in Exhibit 11-10.

To qualify for an SBA loan, the firm must first meet the definition of a small business as described in Chapter 1. Additionally, it must satisfy all of the following criteria in that the firm cannot:[10]

- Get money on reasonable terms from other sources, such as financial institutions, personal credit, or the sale of assets,

EXHIBIT 11–10 **Sample Loan Package Outline**

I. Introduction/Cover Letter
A brief cover letter outlining amount of capital requested, use of the funds, purpose of request, suggested repayment date and source(s) of repayment.

II. Summary
- **A. Nature of business**
- **B. Amount and purpose of loan**
- **C. Repayment terms**
- **D. Equity share of borrower** (debt/equity ratio after loan)
- **E. Security or collateral**
  - List with market value estimates and quotes on cost of equipment to be purchased with the loan proceeds.

III. Personal Information
- **A. Background** For all corporate officers, directors, and any individuals owning 20 percent or more of the business, provide key information.
  - Provide a résumé for each business associate, which details education and work experience and emphasizes experience in the particular business or industry.
  - Give credit references.
  - Provide income tax returns (last three years).
  - Provide financial statements (balance sheet and income and expense statements) not more than 60 days old.

Reprinted with permission of Bank of America NT&SA, "Business Financing," *Small Business Reporter*®, copyright September 1988.

EXHIBIT 11–10 **Sample Loan Package Outline** *(continued)*

IV. **Firm Information**

A. **New Business**
- Provide business plan.
- List life and casualty insurance coverage.
- Describe lease agreement.
- Provide partnership, corporation, or franchise papers, if applicable.

B. **Business Acquisition (buyout)**
- Provide information on acquisition:
  1. Business history (include seller's name, reasons for sale).
  2. Current balance sheet (not more than 60 days old).
  3. Current profit and loss statements (preferably less than 60 days old).
  4. Business's federal income tax returns (past three to five years).
  5. Cash flow statements for last year.
  6. Copy of sales agreement with a breakdown of inventory, fixtures, equipment, licenses, goodwill, and other costs.
  7. Description and dates of permits already acquired.
  8. Lease agreement.
- Include business plan.
- List life and casualty insurance.
- Provide partnership, corporation, or franchise papers, if applicable.

C. **Expansion of Existing Business**
- Provide information on existing business:
  1. Business history.
  2. Current balance sheet (not more than 60 days old).
  3. Current profit and loss statements (not more than 60 days old).
  4. Cash flow statements for past year.
  5. Federal income tax returns for past three to five years.
  6. Lease agreement and permit data.
- Include business plan.
- List life and casualty insurance.
- Provide partnership, corporation, or franchise papers, if applicable.

V. **Projections**

A. **Profit and loss projection** Provide monthly projections for one year or term of loan and an explanation of projections. Forecast your business expenses and revenues.

B. **Cash flow projections** Provide monthly projections for one year or term of loan and explanation of projections. Forecast the actual cash surplus or deficit.

C. **Projected balance sheet and explanation of projections** Show in this forecast the impact of loan proceeds on assets and liabilities for a given time (one year, two years, term of loan).

Reprinted with permission of Bank of America NT&SA, "Business Financing," *Small Business Reporter®*, copyright September 1988.

- Use the funds, directly or indirectly, to pay off creditors, pay the owner(s) of the business, or replenish working capital that had been used to pay the owner(s) of the business,
- Use the funds to change the ownership of the business,

- Use the funds for speculative purposes, or to finance the purchase of assets that are primarily held for sale,
- Use the funds to create a monopoly, for business activities oriented to gambling, or for purposes that do not benefit the public good.

The most common type of financing by the SBA is the guarantee of loans made by other financial institutions. Direct loans are made very infrequently.

Programs similar to the loan guarantee program include Operation Business Mainstream (OBM) and the Economic Opportunity Loan (EOL). Both provide loan guarantees and are available only to economically or socially disadvantaged minorities, or other disadvantaged or physically handicapped individuals. Information on the differences in loan qualifications and the amount of funding available is provided by SBA field offices.[11]

Specialized Sources of Debt Financing

In addition to the general sources of debt financing previously described, some institutions provide specialized types of funding. At times, these can be attractive, depending on the particular needs of the entrepreneur.

- **Factors**—financial concerns that provide funding by purchasing accounts receivable are called factors. In a strict sense, this approach to financing is not a loan. Rather, the business can sell its accounts receivable at a discount, usually 60 to 80 percent of their face value. The factor, as owner of the receivables, assumes responsibility for collection, and the risk in case of default. Although the high discount rate can make this an expensive source of funds, it does offer the entrepreneur an opportunity to gain immediate cash rather than waiting for normal payment.
- **Trade Credit**—one important source of both short- and long-term funding for the purchase of materials and equipment is suppliers. Trade credit, the lending of money by suppliers to their customers, can be valuable to the new and/or growing small business. In an effort to gain a new customer, a vendor or equipment manufacturer often will provide external credit or carry the loan itself. Whether the cost of such financing is favorable or not depends on the supplier's policies, its general financial situation, and how much it wants to make the sale.

Sources of Equity Financing

Debt financing has been the predominant means of generating capital other than that initially supplied by the entrepreneur. However, as was described earlier in this chapter, there are times when it is best to seek equity capital. Unfortunately, smaller businesses have had difficulties finding investors to provide needed capital for starting up, overcoming hard times, or expanding. Consequently, entrepreneurs have resorted to using more of their personal funds or to seeking debt financing.

Part of the problem in equity financing is the risky nature of many smaller firms. However, an even more significant part of the difficulties of equity financing stems from the lack of established sources of equity capital. Where does the small business owner go to find investors? The three main sources are private investors, private venture capitalists, and government-supported venture capitalists.

Private Investors

One source of equity funding is **private investors,** who become general or limited partners, or shareholders in a corporate form of business. Most commonly, investments are made through friends and relatives. Knowing the owner and something about the firm often is a key issue in investing, and friends and family tend to be in the best position to assess the owner's ambitions, integrity, and personal and managerial strengths and weaknesses.

Private Venture Capitalists

Some individuals and private companies are in the business of providing capital to entrepreneurs. They seek out new or growing businesses that look promising but are considered too risky for commercial lenders. Hoping for large capital gains on their investments, these **private venture capitalists** may loan significant sums of money to help small businesses get off the ground or expand their operations.

Private venture capital firms often are family-owned firms or offshoots of large corporations such as oil, insurance, or manufacturing enterprises. Both groups can provide sizeable amounts of start-up money or funds for operating capital needs.

In a different twist to stock investing, some investment firms have developed partnerships with private investors who buy units of the partnership for $1,000 to $5,000 each. Money raised in such partnerships is invested in a variety of smaller firms, thereby spreading the risks of loss to investors.

Venture capitalists represent an important source of funding and often are not overly interested in direct participation in the management of the small business. Nevertheless, they are owners, and have the potential to involve themselves actively in the daily operations if they chose to do so. Advice from Rod Canion, cofounder of Compaq Computer, in seeking venture capital: "Do your homework and make sure you have a well-thought-out plan and then select your venture capital company very carefully. You get a lot more from a venture capital company than just money."[12]

Government-Supported Venture Capitalists

Historically, private venture capitalists have been unable to meet the needs of small businesses for equity financing. In 1958, Small Business Investment Companies (SBICs) came into existence. These **government-supported venture capitalists** are privately owned, but capable of making investments in small businesses by obtaining SBA loans. Licensed and regulated by the federal government, SBICs receive loans or loan guarantees from the SBA and either invest in or make long-term loans to small businesses. Investments typically are made through the purchase of common or preferred stock, income-generating debentures, or debts with warrants. While funding may be large, it tends to be less than that of private venture capitalists, partly due to regulations on how much of their capital they can invest in any one venture. The maximum is 20 percent, and they are prohibited from obtaining controlling interests in ventures.

In 1969, Minority Enterprise Small Business Investment Companies (MESBICs) were created to aid only minority groups. These also are part of the SBA's lending program, and operate in a fashion similar to SBICs.

On a more local basis, many states have developed State Business and Industrial Development Corporations (SBIDCs). Rather than being state-regulated and -funded, the SBIDCs are only state-condoned. Funding for these typically comes from consortia of large corporations and financial institutions. Although restrictions vary on who qualifies and how much can be loaned, funding tends to be equity investments and/or long-term loans.

Finally, in many communities Local Development Companies (LDCs) have been formed by individuals and funded by the SBA. They must meet SBA lending requirements as described earlier in this chapter, and the funds must be used to foster business and economic development by and for local citizens.

THE FUNDING PROCESS

The actual process of obtaining funds only begins by identifying the amount and type of capital needed. Unfortunately, many entrepreneurs believe the rest of the effort is routine. An old marketing axiom, "Nothing happens until a sale is made," applies here. Proper selection of a source of capital, development of a well-prepared funding proposal, and the quality of the formal request for funds will have an impact not only on whether the funds are provided, but also on the terms and conditions of the financing.

Selecting a Funding Source

Nearly anybody can obtain money, and for almost any reason. "Loan sharks" specialize in making funds available. The question is not so much whether money can be obtained, but whether the entrepreneur is willing to give—in the Shakespearean sense—a pound of flesh for nonpayment, or pay outrageously high interest rates, or meet other requirements that are obviously unfavorable.

The most desirable situation is one in which a reputable financing source is impressed with the proposed venture or current operation, and is willing to help make it a success. Finding the ideal source is a difficult task. Nevertheless, the entrepreneur should discuss financing possibilities with a number of potential sources. In this way, the owner will better understand the range of possibilities and find a satisfactory source of capital. In making this search, the entrepreneur should try to obtain answers to the following questions:

1. How experienced is the source in providing funds to small businesses? Is the source familiar with the unique problems confronting entrepreneurs? Minor fluctuations in business activity can have a great effect on small firms. Additionally, few small businesses maintain a specialized staff of experts in accounting, finance, marketing, personnel, and so on. Consequently, dealing effectively with smaller firms tends to take more time, patience, and confidence. Does the source have this capacity?
2. How reputable is the source, and how compatible is the source with the small business owner? While the common perception of a lender or investor is of someone who is strictly business, there can be little doubt that financing also is a personal business. Often, the success of the small business will hinge on the quality of the working relationship between the funding source and the entrepreneur. There simply is no substitute for finding a lender or investor with a reputation for honesty and fairness, and a desire to work with the entrepreneur.
3. What sort of management assistance can the funding source offer? Can the lender or investor act as a business counselor? One of the greatest advantages of the

SBA loan program is that the SBA makes several types of management assistance programs available to its clients. This can be especially valuable for entrepreneurs who are not well versed in all areas of business and who need specialized expertise. Some commercial banking institutions offer counseling to their clients, although not on the scale that is offered by the SBA.

4. What other services does the source provide? In some cases, sources of funds make available free or low-cost services, such as compiling income statements and balance sheets, and analyzing financial positions. Depending on the source, ancillary services can provide valuable assistance and save the firm considerable sums of money.

Preparing the Financing Package

Making the rounds to identify possible sources of financing should involve asking questions about the type and substance of the **financing package** (known as a *loan package* for debt financing) required by the lender or investor. Although the requirements of the package will vary, several points are common to all (see Exhibit 11-11):

EXHIBIT 11–11 **General Guidelines of SBA Lending**

Maximum Amount, Repayment, Collateral

Guarantee(s) totaling a maximum of $750,000
More than one loan is possible
A 90% guarantee for loans under $155,000
An 85% guarantee for loans over $155,000
Monthly installments of principal and interest
No balloons; no penalty for prepayment
May delay first payment up to six months
Take all collateral available; may include personal property

What the S.B.A. Looks For

Management ability
Experience in the field
Adequate investment (approximately 30%–50% equity) by the owner in new business starts
Ability to repay the loan from the projected cash flow and profits

What Borrower Needs to Take to the Lender

Statement of what the loan will be used for
History of the business
Financial statements for three years (balance sheet and income statements) for existing businesses
Schedule of term debts (for existing businesses)
Aging of accounts receivable and payable (for existing businesses)
Lease details (if available)
Amount of investment in the business by owner
Projections of income, expenses, and cash flow
Signed personal financial statements
Personal résumés

EXHIBIT 11–11 **General Guidelines of SBA Lending** *(continued)*

A Longer Term

Usually 5–7 years for working capital
Up to 25 years for real estate

Interest Rate

Both fixed and variable rates
Rate pegged to the lowest prime rate as listed in *The Wall Street Journal*
Pegged at $2\frac{1}{4}$% over the lowest prime rate for loans of 7 years or less
Pegged at $2\frac{3}{4}$% over the lowest prime rate for loans over 7 years

Who Qualifies

Independently owned and operated businesses not dominant in their fields
Businesses unable to obtain private financing on reasonable terms, but with a good chance of succeeding

Maximum Size Standards

Manufacturing—varies by industry from 500–1500 employees
Wholesaling—up to 100 employees
Services—varies by industry from $2.5 million to $14.5 million in annual receipts
Retailing—from $3.5 to $13.5 million
Construction—from $7.0 to $17 million

Loan Purposes

To expand or modernize facilities
To purchase machinery, equipment, fixtures, and leasehold improvements
To finance increased receivables and augment working capital
To refinance existing debt provided the lender is not in a position to take a loss
To provide seasonal lines of credit
To construct new commercial building
To purchase existing land and/or buildings

How It Works

SBA guarantees up to 90% of a loan made by lender
Lender checks with SBA prior to formal application for "ballpark" feasibility of project
Lender submits letter of intent to SBA if interim financing is to be supplied prior to formal financing of the project
Lender forwards application and deals directly with SBA officers
Completed applications are processed by SBA in ten working days

Source: Small Business Administration, *Lending the S.B.A. Way* (Washington, D.C.: U.S. Government Printing Office).

- The net earning power of the firm,
- The capability of the firm's management,
- The long-range prospects of the firm in terms of sales, market share, and profits, and
- The long-range prospects of the industry.

Typical questions a lending officer or investor will ask include:

1. How much money is needed?
2. How will the funds be used?
3. What are the primary sources of repayment?
4. For loans, what kind of collateral is available to support the request for funds?
5. Does the firm have the services of an accountant and an attorney?
6. Does the entrepreneur have a life insurance policy that is held by the firm?
7. Does the business have fire, liability, and other appropriate insurance?
8. How much does the entrepreneur know about owning and managing a business of this sort?
9. How much money has the entrepreneur contributed to the business—money that is at risk if the business fails?
10. How much competition does the firm face?

Whether all of these issues are considered in a formal loan package will depend on the needs of the financing source and its familiarity with the entrepreneur and the firm. Nevertheless, the entrepreneur should be prepared to discuss these issues knowledgeably. Nothing is worse than presenting a poorly prepared request for funding, and then not having the answers ready for questions asked by the lender or investor.

Presented in Exhibit 11-11 is a guide for preparing a financing package for potential lenders or investors. Much information is required, which means that the entrepreneur must know a great deal about the business venture. The entrepreneur must be able to demonstrate a business plan, including projections of profits or losses, cash flows, and asset utilization.

Although this process is tedious, it can significantly enhance the probabilities of successful small business ownership. All too often, individuals jump into business or expansion programs without adequate planning. Developing a financing package forces the owner to recognize and deal with problem areas before they become crises that threaten the venture's existence.

Wally Amos, founder of Wally "Famous" Amos Chocolate Chip Cookies, received $25,000 from a group of people, including Jeff Wall, Artie Mogul, Helen Reddy, and Marvin Gaye. When asked if he knew what he would do, Amos responded:

> I had the whole thing planned out. I did what I called a proposal. I later discovered that it was a business plan but I didn't know business. But I showed what I was going to do, how I was going to do it, and why, and I had my budget planned out for what it was going to cost me to open a store, and all my materials, and whatnot.[13]

Presenting the Request for Funds

Proper development of an attractive package will significantly affect the decision to grant financing. However, a business is not run by a plan alone—it is run by people. Loan officers and investors, therefore, will judge not only the formal package, but also the entrepreneur and the management team.

How well the entrepreneur presents the package will affect the decision. Since much of the future success or failure of a small business depends on the owner, the lender's decision will be based partly on personal interaction with the entrepreneur at the time the funds are requested. The owner's personality, vitality, and ability will be thoroughly scrutinized. Answers to the following questions will weigh heavily on financing decisions:

1. Is the entrepreneur organized? If no organization for this important matter is apparent now, how can the financing source expect the firm to operate in an organized manner later? Being or appearing to be poorly organized is the quickest way to be refused financing.
2. Is the entrepreneur realistic? Does the individual have a solid grasp of the realities of going into business—the risks involved, the time it will take, the wide range of expertise called for, and the amount of funds needed? The owner's dreams and ambitions must be based on a comprehension of the realities of business life.
3. Does the entrepreneur appear competent? Does the owner have a good understanding of accounting, financing, marketing, and other aspects of management? If not, has the entrepreneur obtained a source of expertise that can be utilized until individual competence is achieved?
4. How good a salesperson is the entrepreneur? If the small business owner cannot sell the venture to the financing source, how can the individual sell the firm's goods and services? The ambitiousness and manner of the entrepreneur will be studied closely in this regard.
5. Does the entrepreneur appear to be honest? Will the entrepreneur admit errors, or attempt to duck or hide from tough issues? If the financing source perceives any dishonesty, financing will not be made available.

The entrepreneur must be prepared for personal contact with the loan officer or investor, and have a general sense of what the financing source will want to know. A succinct and well-presented request for financing not only increases the likelihood of being granted funds, but also builds a solid base for productive long-term relationships.

SUMMARY

1. A solid financial foundation is necessary to the development of a viable concern. In planning, this involves such key issues as: Where will funding come from? How can it be obtained? Where can additional funds be found in an emergency?
2. A firm's capital needs revolve around three interrelated areas: capital to set up the venture, capital to start up the business once it has been set up, and operating capital for supporting activity throughout the firm's life.
3. After an assessment of capital needs is made, an equity position can be developed—how much money the owner will put into the business versus the contributions of creditors and lenders.
4. One method for estimating capital requirements utilizes projected sales and then determines associated costs. These estimates should be made for a two-to-four-year period.
5. Once the needs of the firm have been identified, the next step is to identify potential sources of short- and long-term funds.
6. There are advantages and disadvantages to both short- and long-term financing, and the firm may use a combination of these types if debt financing is to be sought.
7. Equity financing is an alternative to debt financing, and may be advantageous in some instances, since it reduces the amount of debt the firm will have. However, it often is difficult to find investors, and when equity financing is used, some element of ownership passes to others.
8. Sources of debt financing available to small firms

include commercial banking institutions, commercial finance companies, consumer finance companies, and Small Business Administration loans. There also are some specialized sources of financing that can be used in selected instances.

9. Sources of equity financing include private investors, private venture capital firms, and government-supported venture capitalists on federal, state, and local levels.
10. After making decisions regarding financing, the entrepreneur must begin the process of obtaining the needed funds. This process includes selecting the lender or investor, developing a financing package, and formally requesting funds.
11. Choosing a lender or investor involves discussions with various possible sources to determine what services they offer.
12. The entrepreneur should be well prepared to answer all questions relating to the firm, how the funds will be used, and how repayment to lenders will be made or profits to investors will be distributed.

KEY TERMS AND CONCEPTS

Set-up capital
Start-up capital
Operating capital
Debt financing
Equity financing
Short-term financing
Long-term financing
Commercial loan
Accounts receivable financing
Inventory financing
Discounting installment contract
Flooring
Line of credit
Factors
Trade credit
Private investors
Venture capitalist
Government-supported venture capitalist
Financing package

QUESTIONS FOR DISCUSSION

1. List the key financial issues a prospective small business owner must consider before starting a venture.
2. What capital expenditures are needed for setting up a business?
3. What capital expenditures are needed for starting the business?
4. When and for what reasons would the firm need operating capital?
5. What is the difference between short-term and long-term financing?
6. List the sources of funds that may be available to an entrepreneur.
7. What factors must an entrepreneur consider in deciding whether to use debt or equity financing?
8. List possible sources of debt financing.
9. List possible sources of equity financing.
10. What must a small business owner take into consideration when seeking a lender or investor?
11. List the issues that are commonly covered in a financing package.
12. What questions are entrepreneurs likely to be asked by potential lenders or investors?

SELF-TEST REVIEW

Multiple Choice Questions

1. An advantage of long-term debt in comparison to short-term debt is that:
   a. It has lower interest rates.
   b. It has a longer repayment period.
   c. It is easier to obtain because of the low risk.
   d. All of the above are advantages of long-term debt.
2. The most common method of financing is:
   a. Debt financing.
   b. Equity financing.

   c. Stock sales.
   d. Partnership investments.
3. Which of the following is an advantage of equity financing?
   a. It allows the owner to retain control over the business.
   b. Payments to investors are tax-deductible.
   c. It is the easiest source of funds for the owner to obtain.
   d. Payments to investors may not be made on a fixed schedule, as is the case with debt financing.
4. Which of the following typically are covered in a financing package?
   a. Net earnings power of the firm.
   b. Capability of the firm's management.
   c. The long-range prospects for the industry within which the firm operates.
   d. All of the above typically are covered in a financing package.
5. Which of the following is the quickest way to be refused financing?
   a. The entrepreneur is not organized.
   b. The entrepreneur is not realistic.
   c. The entrepreneur does not appear to be competent.
   d. The entrepreneur is not a good salesperson.

True/False Statements

1. All of the capital needs of a venture occur just before and/or immediately after the business is started.
2. A conservative estimate of sales and a liberal projection of expenses will result in being undercapitalized.
3. Typically, short-term financing is considered to be debt that must be paid back within one year.
4. Debt financing involves selling part of the ownership to others.
5. Commercial banking institutions are primarily sources of short-term capital.
6. The most common type of financing used by the SBA is the direct loan program.
7. Factors purchase accounts receivable from businesses at their full face value.
8. In an effort to gain new customers, suppliers sometimes will provide credit or carry a loan.
9. Small Business Investment Companies receive loans from the SBA and invest those funds in small businesses.
10. Typically, a financing package does not ask for a great deal of detail.

GARVEY AUTO REPAIR

A mechanic for nearly 10 years at a major automobile dealership located in the Northeast, Terry Garvey has decided to open a business of his own. Unlike many of the other general repair shops, however, Garvey's will cater primarily to domestic and foreign sports and prestige cars, such as Cadillacs, Lincolns, Mercedeses, and BMWs. Although he has been considering such a venture for some time, he has never fully planned it out, especially in terms of how much money would be needed and where the funds would come from.

Garvey does not have any formal training as a mechanic, but he has an extensive background in the business. Because his father was a master craftsman in both automobile repair and body and fender work, he has continually been exposed to the various aspects of the business. In addition, many years ago his father helped him get a job with a major automobile dealer, and his skills have led him to become service manager in charge of all repair work for the most successful dealership in this city of nearly 300,000 people (see Table 1). Loyalty to the dealer, coupled with the security of employment, have kept him from making this career move earlier.

He has made many customer contacts in his four years as service manager. Garvey believes this will help him make Garvey Auto Repairs a success. Owners of several automobile rental agencies have expressed an interest in contracting with him should he open his own business, and the owner of one rental agency wants to enter into a partnership with Garvey by supplying some of the capital. Additionally, owners of a few garages that specialize in different types of automobile repair want to establish a system of referring customers to each other for work they cannot handle themselves.

In planning for the opening of Garvey Auto Repairs, Garvey has assembled as much of the pertinent cost information as he can find in the time available. This is shown in Table 2. He believes a very im-

TABLE 1
Selected Market Data

City Population: 300,000

Number of Households by Income	
Under $15,000	22,800
$15,000 to $25,000	33,500
$25,001 to $40,000	24,200
$40,001 to $50,000	18,500
$50,001 to $75,000	13,800
Over $75,000	2,600
Number of Automobiles by Type	
Subcompacts	77,100
Compacts	41,200
Standard	56,500
Sports	13,900
Prestige	7,500
Automobile Repair Shops	
Automobile dealerships	12
Foreign service only	17
Domestic only	29
Foreign and domestic	62
Other specialty	17
Service stations	Unknown

TABLE 2
Selected Financial Data

Projected Set-Up Costs	
Equipment, fixtures, automobile	$95,000
Inventory	47,000
Lease deposit	6,000
Utilities and telephone	1,000
Licenses and taxes	1,000
Insurance	1,500
Projected Start-Up Costs (first month)	
Rent	$ 3,000
Advertising	4,000
Utilities	900
Supplies	2,500
Employee wages	7,000
Transportation	1,000
Owner's draw	2,000
Miscellaneous	4,500

Projected Average Repair Bill: $165.45

portant factor in a successful start is the location of the facility. It must be convenient, inexpensive, and big enough for all the necessary equipment and materials. Garvey plans to initially employ an office manager and three mechanics.

Garvey is confident that he can create a high-quality repair service. What concerns him most is the financial side of the business. Over the last five years, he has managed to save nearly $30,000. He realizes this will not be enough money to do everything necessary, but he is not sure whether he should postpone his planned opening until he has all the money needed, scale back his plans to what he can afford, take the rental agency owner's offer of a partnership for 50 percent of the business with a capital investment of $25,000, or borrow the necessary funds if he can.

QUESTIONS

1. How much money does Garvey need to get started as planned?
2. Evaluate each of the alternatives to obtaining the capital Garvey needs to go into business. Which options should he select?
3. If Garvey was to borrow funds, what other information would he need to acquire in order to prepare a financing package?

NOTES

1. Based on Cable News Network's "Pinnacle," December 18, 1988. Guest: Lillian Vernon, Lillian Vernon Corporation.
2. Based on Cable News Network's "Pinnacle," June 11, 1988. Guest: Mortimer Levitt, The Custom Shop.
3. Small Business Administration, A *Handbook of Small*

Business Finance, (Washington, D.C.: U.S. Government Printing Office).

4. Based on Cable News Network's "Pinnacle," August 30, 1987. Guest: Sidney Swartz, The Timberland Company.
5. Small Business Administration, *Retailers* (Washington, D.C.: U.S. Government Printing Office).
6. Bank of America, "Financing Small Business," *Small Business Reporter,* 1983.
7. *Ibid.*
8. Small Business Administration, *The ABCs of Borrowing,* (Washington, D.C.: U.S. Government Printing Office).
9. "Kathy Taggares: Her Fast Foods Are Really Cooking," *Business Week,* December 4, 1989, 69.
10. Small Business Administration, *Business Loans from the SBA,* (Washington, D.C.: U.S. Government Printing Office).
11. Small Business Administration, *Lending the SBA Way,* (Washington, D.C.: U.S. Government Printing Office).
12. Based on Cable News Network's "Pinnacle," October 4, 1987. Guest: Rod Canion, Compaq Computer.
13. Based on Cable News Network's "Pinnacle," September 24, 1988. Guest: Wally Amos, Entrepreneur.

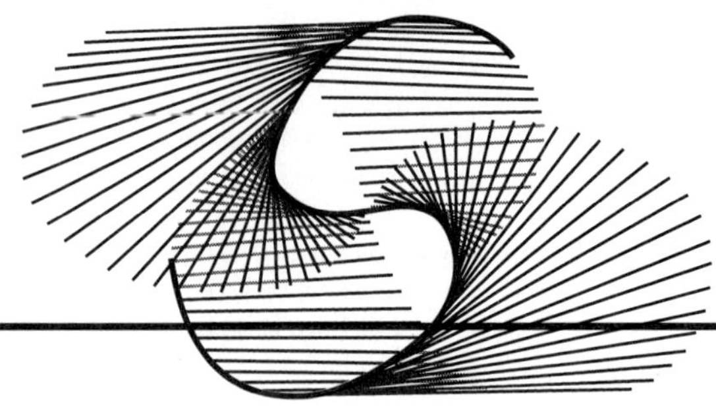

CHAPTER TWELVE

Risk and Insurance Management

CHAPTER OUTLINE

LEARNING OBJECTIVES *The objectives of this chapter are to assist you in understanding:*

1. The types of noncriminal business risks faced by small businesses.
2. The types of criminal business risks small businesses face.
3. Methods of reducing the risks of criminal losses.
4. The insurance needs of a small business.
5. How to decide on the type of insurance coverage and insurance company.

An inherent part of any business activity is risk. It takes many shapes and forms and seems to follow Murphy's Law, which states that anything that can go wrong will go wrong—and usually at the worst time. While business losses or failure often are the result of poor management, they also can be due to conditions beyond the control of the entrepreneur. Even though risk affects large and small businesses alike, the latter are particularly susceptible to business downturns and losses. Lacking a diversified base and sufficient capital and insurance, small businesses tend to be in highly vulnerable positions.

One unique way companies have found worthwhile for managing risk associated with expansion is to use separate companies to take the chances. If the expansion fails, it might not have as detrimental an effect on the parent company as it would have otherwise. If it succeeds, the separate company can be folded back into the parent. Compaq Computer did this in 1984. Exploring some areas involving telecommunications that the company considered to be of high risk, it created a subsidiary to separate the new venture from Compaq's existing channels. Later, it evolved into a research and development division of the parent company.[1]

Examples of this abound. Companies that are the victims of fires, earthquakes, tornadoes, and so on, often do not have adequate insurance to cover their losses. If the owner of the firm becomes ill and cannot manage the business, the firm can suffer irreparable damage. Importantly, therefore, factors well beyond personal control can have a significant impact on the survival and success of the small business.

SMALL BUSINESS RISK AND ITS CONTROL

Entrepreneurs must plan and prepare for risks within and beyond their personal control. In most cases, business risk cannot be eliminated completely. Some risks are unavoidable, and others would be too costly to fully protect against.

Risk management, therefore, does not mean risk avoidance. Rather, it implies that risk will be assessed, measured, and reduced to the extent that is economically feasible. Perhaps the key to this process is making sure that unexpected or uncontrollable circumstances cannot unilaterally destroy the venture.

Compaq Computer Corporation, the world's largest producer of portable computers, explored back in 1984 the possibility of a telecommunications division. Rod Canion realized that this experiment involved a great deal of financial risk, so he channelled that operation into a separate subsidiary in order to protect the existing business. The subsidiary sold many telecommunications products, but it has since evolved into a research and development division to support the telecommunication aspects of personal computers. (Photograph reprinted with permission of Compaq Computer Corporation. All Rights Reserved)

Noncrime-Related Business Risks

The more common types of **noncrime-related business risks** (see Exhibit 12–1) that can be guarded against include:

- Fire,
- Natural disasters,
- Personal liabilities,
- Economic downturns,
- Business interruptions, and
- Loss of key personnel.

Fire

Threat of fire is probably the first fear that comes to the mind of a small business owner. Many entrepreneurs seek to allay this fear solely through the purchase of fire insurance. They mistakenly assume that such protection will fully cover their losses.

While fire insurance can cover most of the monetary costs, it cannot completely protect against lost customers, records, and so on. Consequently, fire insurance should be viewed as a fail-safe mechanism, supplemental to a sound fire safety program. The goals here are to reduce both the threat of fire and the losses if fire should occur.

A program of fire protection essentially is a set of procedures for making sure that the physical premises, employees, and customer practices do not create unnecessary fire hazards. Facilities used for business should be inspected periodically for faulty construction or wiring. Use of fire-resistant materials and insulation also serves to reduce the likelihood of fire. In addition, employee and customer activities should be closely scrutinized.

EXHIBIT 12–1 The Different Types of Noncrime-Related Risks

Cigarette or cigar smoking, smoldering ashes, or haphazard placement of combustible materials frequently are causes of fire. Smoking sections and appropriate disposal and storage mechanisms clearly identified and placed add considerable protection.

Natural Disasters

High winds, floods, earthquakes, tornadoes, and hurricanes are other calamities that can affect business activities. Usually unpredictable, they can quickly destroy or damage business establishments. In the 1920s, for example, George Merrick began developing Coral Gables, Florida as a community to which the wealthy can retire. By 1925, Merrick was worth an estimated $80 million as he capitalized on the popularity of Florida. On September 17, 1926, much of Miami Beach was destroyed by a hurricane, and people decided this was not the place to retire. However, Merrick struggled to keep his venture alive—and it remained so until another hurricane hit in 1928, taking his fortune with it.[2]

Depending on the geographic area, the entrepreneur must identify which disasters are most likely. For example, California is prone to earthquakes, parts of Texas have a considerable number of tornadoes, and the southeastern seaboard occasionally is hit by hurricanes. Purchasing insurance frequently is a good hedge against some risks, and may be the only protection available.

Personal Liabilities

Entrepreneurs, whether manufacturers, wholesalers, or retailers, incur risks from injury to third parties caused in the course of business activities. If a customer is injured in the store or is injured while using the firm's product, damage suits can result. Similarly, if the company car becomes involved in an accident, the firm may be liable.

SIX FLAGS

For some companies the greatest risks are possible injury to their customers. For example, Six Flags, a theme park in New Jersey, had a fire in its Haunted Castle, which killed eight teenagers. Spending over $8 million annually on safety precautions illustrates the priority placed on customer and employee safety. According to Larry Cochran, chief executive officer, "We never let the financial aspect of this company control safety." The 1984 fire hurt Six Flags due to the negative publicity, and the resulting decline in admissions had a major impact on profitability.[3]

Even though most businesses carry insurance to protect against major lawsuits, they still need to safeguard their products and premises. In the area of product safety, companies must be alert to product defects, and adhere to reasonably stringent quality control standards. In addition, how products are to be stored and used must be clearly specified so that customers do not become injured through misuse. The extent to which firms need to delineate the dos and don'ts of product usage, however, has remained unclear. No court has answered the question of how far the firm must go to protect consumers from their own stupidity.

More clearly established are safety issues from injury at the firm's place of business or by a company-owned vehicle. Elimination of hazardous conditions and safety programs for employees are essential to reducing the risks of liability.

Economic Downturn

Changes in the business economy loom as a significant risk, but are largely beyond the control of the small business. Inflation, recession, or high unemployment rates threaten the survival and stability of the firm.

While these create problems for all businesses, they are particularly troublesome for small firms that are struggling between success and failure. Even sudden upturns in economic activity can hurt small firms that cannot keep pace with increasing demand for their products and services. Customers might seek other suppliers rather than wait for production to catch up.

Shifts in social and cultural patterns also cause changes in selected industries. For example, the leather-trimmed tennis shoe craze that began in the mid-1980s reflected the desire among people in nearly all age groups for a casual, informal look. While it has been a boon for such companies as Reebok, it has created serious problems for shoe manufacturers that were oriented to more formal attire as well as for those that produced canvas tennis shoes.

Business risks also exist in terms of innovation. For example, George Hatsopoulos, founder of Thermo Electron Corp., spent thirty years searching for a way to convert heat directly into electricity, by heating up metals that emit electrons that can be captured to produce electricity. The process, known as thermionics, was not practical in 1989, but the company continued to develop the idea with the belief that it would become a major source of power in the future.[4]

Economic changes cannot be controlled, but they can be anticipated to some extent. Building financial reserves during prosperous times will enhance the stability of the firm during economic downturns. Increasing the owner's equity and working capital positions through increased current assets can act as a buffer for business fluctuations.

Social and cultural changes can be prepared for if the entrepreneur maintains a reasonable degree of flexibility and does not become tradition-bound. The ability to adapt quickly to changing market conditions can give small businesses competitive advantages over larger ones. Big companies tend to get caught up in bureaucratic structures that slow their reactions during highly volatile times.

One of the greatest areas of business risk centers on keeping abreast of technological change. Research costs are very high, especially for smaller firms with limited capital. One of the reasons that Cray Research has grown is that it spends 15 percent of its revenues each year on research and development. A percentage this large may not be necessary in order to avoid becoming obsolete within some industries, but in others even higher allocations of revenues may be needed.[5]

Business Interruptions

The entrepreneur must be concerned with disruptions in business due to labor actions, building renovations, street work, and other factors that can limit potential business (see

Cray Research's mission is to develop and market the most powerful computer systems available. For more than a decade, Cray Research has been the industry leader in large-scale computer systems. John Rollwagen, Chairman and CEO, believes that channeling fifteen percent of the firm's revenues into research and development has given Cray the resources needed to develop the technology necessary for acceptance in diverse governmental and industrial environments. (Photo by Paul Shambroom, courtesy of Cray Research, Inc.)

EXHIBIT 12–2 *Types of Business Interruptions*

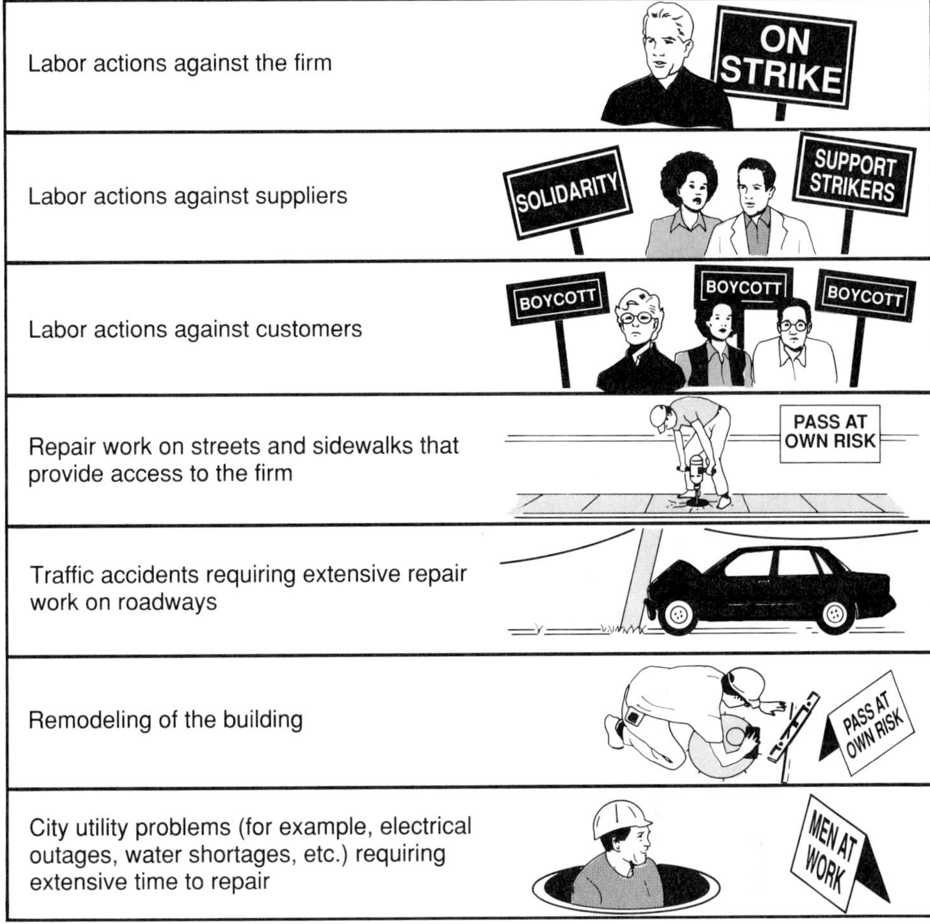

Exhibit 12–2). Labor strikes can severely disrupt business activity. Furthermore, many consumers are reluctant to cross picket lines, and resent being placed in the situation of having to make that decision. Some sources of business interruption stem from renovations to the building or street. Both can inhibit customer access to the firm's offices, or make the entrance more difficult to find.

In many cases, little can be done to avoid these types of problems. However, foresight and a strong financial position can do a great deal to help the firm survive. With prior warning, the entrepreneur can take steps to improve the firm's working capital position through more prudent buying, expense control, and debt restructuring that allows more time to pay.

Loss of Key Personnel

Human resources in small businesses are especially critical because these firms tend to have less depth of quality personnel than do large companies. The success of a small firm often hinges on the abilities of one or a few individuals. A top-notch salesperson or technician may be the key to the small business's prosperity. Loss of this person through death, incapacitation, or pirating by another company, especially if sudden, can pose a serious threat to the firm's existence.

A common example of this is in fine restaurants, where the loss of the chef can be devastating. Many patrons follow their favorite chef, and a restaurant can lose a significant part of its business literally overnight if the chef leaves.

Two precautions can be taken to protect the firm from loss of key personnel. First, a sound training program can prepare other employees to replace key individuals. There is no substitute for having some depth of quality personnel. Second, the entrepreneur can buy **key-person insurance.** While this will not be a substitute for the individual, it will provide funds to help the company survive while management looks for a replacement.

Crime-Related Business Risks

The costs of crime have become an increasingly important factor in operating a business. Taking steps to protect against criminal activity, and absorbing the losses that still can occur, can be significant. The most common types of **crime-related business risks** (see Exhibit 12–3) include:

Test

- Burglary,
- Robbery,
- Shoplifting,
- Credit card fraud and bad checks, and
- Employee theft.

EXHIBIT 12–3 ***The Different Types of Crime-Related Risks***

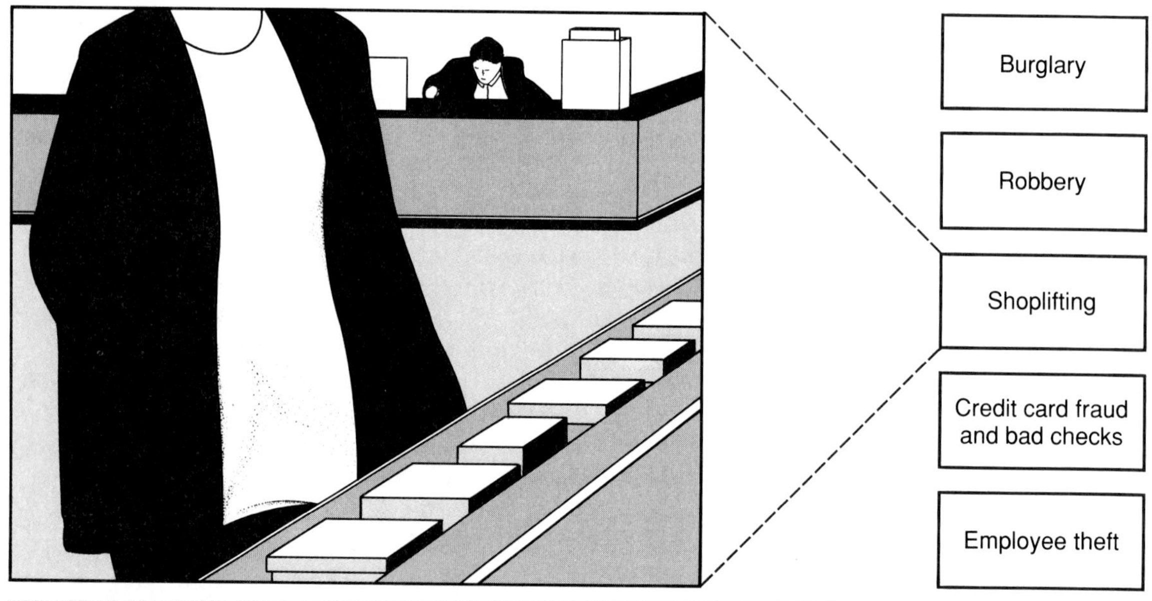

Burglary

At every place of business there are valuables that might attract burglars. Whether these items are inventories, fixtures, or even office equipment, all companies must be considered likely targets. Consequently, protective measures against **burglary** (breaking into any building to commit theft) are a necessity. Typically, the entrepreneur will purchase insurance and then neglect some simple methods of protection. Installation of sturdy deadbolt locks on doors and making windows jimmy-proof are low-cost means of protection. In addition, well-lighted premises, trimmed shrubbery, and screens and bars provide safeguards.

While these should be standard precautions, some entrepreneurs go to extra efforts, such as employing guards, security patrols, or watchdogs that can be purchased or leased. Purchasing safes and buying or leasing alarm systems also are common approaches to deterring would-be intruders. The key to this process is to make entry difficult and noisy—most burglars will shy away from those situations and opt for firms and residential units that are not well protected.

Robbery

Although less common than burglary, **robbery** (feloniously taking another's property from his person or in his immediate presence by the use of violence or intimidation) is more serious since it can pose a threat to the lives of the owner, employees, and customers. Businesses that are open at night, such as drug and convenience stores, are especially likely targets.

Deterrents to robbery include alarm systems, ample lighting, uncluttered windows that keep the robber in view from the outside, and surveillance cameras. The best protection, however, is to keep as little cash and other valuables on the premises as possible, and to publicize that fact.

Shoplifting

One of the most common criminal risks faced by the small business owner is that of **shoplifting** by professionals and by everyday customers. Professional shoplifters are a major concern because they are difficult to identify and apprehend. Additionally, they tend to target on products that are valuable and quickly marketable.

Aside from the professionals are the new and loyal customers. Children take merchandise without realizing they are committing crimes, teenagers do it on a dare, and

Losses from criminal acts will disrupt normal operations and may cause a firm to go out of business. (AP/Wide World Photos)

others steal out of anger and frustration over a delay at checkout registers or as an impulse. The point is that every person who enters the premises has the capacity to steal merchandise, no matter how serious or harmless the intent. According to the Small Business Administration, there is a retail theft every five seconds in the United States—costing each American in excess of $150 per year.

One of the best deterrents to shoplifting is an alert group of employees (see Exhibit 12–4). Customers who act nervous and circle one particular area, as well as those with bags, boxes, or briefcases, should be watched closely.[6]

One of the more novel security devices to monitor customers and employees as well is a store mannequin, Anne Droid. This device has a camera in her eye and a microphone in her nose, allowing the retailer to watch and listen. The particular value of the listening device is to monitor customer reactions to products and various displays in order to provide market information to the retailer. In the early part of 1989, Anne Droid sold for nearly $2,000.[7]

Trained salespeople are alert to shoplifters' early warning signals.[8] Employees should be on the lookout for customers carrying concealment devices, such as bulky coats and large shopping bags or purses. Salespeople can watch groups of shoppers who enter the store together, then break up and go in different directions. A customer who attempts to monopolize a salesperson's time may be covering for a companion who is stealing elsewhere in the store.

Ordinary customers want attention, but shoplifters do not. When busy with one customer, the salesperson should acknowledge others who are in the store. This will make legitimate customers happy and shoplifters uneasy.

Customers who handle considerable amounts of merchandise but take unusually long periods of time to make decisions may be viewed with suspicion. Shoplifters often linger in one area, loiter near stockrooms or other restricted areas, or wander aimlessly through the store.

EXHIBIT 12–4

Protection from Shoplifters

Business Policy

- Prosecute shoplifters
- Have the store "shopped" by a professional security firm periodically

Employees

- Acknowledge customers when they enter the store
- Be alert for unusual customer dress
- Monitor customers' movements in the store
- Watch groups of customers who disperse after entering store

Store Layout

- Keep low end displays
- Use low shelving
- Have mirrors for hard-to-watch areas
- Provide ample lighting in all areas of the store
- Use surveillance cameras
- Keep expensive merchandise in locked cases
- Use electronic tags on expensive apparel

Aside from the efforts of employees, the general layout of the premises can be designed to minimize opportunities for shoplifting. A key to preventing shoplifting is to maintain adequate lighting in all areas. By keeping protruding "wings" and end displays low, not more than three feet high, one can enhance visibility. Additionally, small items of high value often are kept behind counters, or locked in special cases.

Finally, protective devices such as one-way mirrors, closed-circuit television, and convex wall mirrors can be utilized. Ticket-switching on merchandise can be discouraged through the use of tamper-proof tags. Electronic tags can be attached to soft articles such as apparel, and will trigger an alarm if the shoplifter attempts to carry the articles from the store. This has become an especially popular protective device in large department stores for higher-cost merchandise such as leather coats and furs.

Credit Card Fraud and Bad Checks

Losses to business through the use of stolen or fake credit cards and bogus checks pose a continuous risk to entrepreneurs. In many cases, however, these risks can be reduced significantly through proper controls and common sense (see Exhibit 12–5).

Credit card problems typically occur when a business accepts expired cards, stolen or otherwise invalid cards, and cards for purchases above the maximum established by the issuer. Simple care in observing expiration dates usually eliminates the first problem. Many retailers require clerks to circle the expiration dates on sales slips to ensure that they have been noticed.

Stolen or otherwise invalid cards often are listed on an issuer's "hot sheet," which is sent to businesses accepting its cards. Clerks can then check each credit card number against the sheet. While this will provide some protection, it does not guard against very recent thefts. Close examination of signatures to ensure that the one on the card is similar to the one on the receipt, and inspections of other forms of identification, will serve to reduce the more flagrant abuses.

Finally, many entrepreneurs pay little attention to maximum limits on purchases established by issuers. By simply charging the purchase or by split-ticketing the purchase

EXHIBIT 12–5

Protection from Credit Card Fraud and Bad Checks

Business Policy

Seek collection of all bad checks
Establish policies concerning which checks and credit cards to accept
Establish limits for check cashing and credit card acceptance by employees without manager's approval
Do not allow split-ticketing for credit cards

Employees

Train employees to examine checks and credit cards
Require at least two pieces of identification that have pictures and signatures
Watch for inconsistencies between customer appearance and type of merchandise purchased
Keep records on the number of bad checks and fraudulent credit cards employees accept, and include this information as part of their evaluations

(placing part of the cost on one charge receipt and the rest on a second), businesspeople often invite credit card misuse. Most credit card issuers ask merchants to call a special number for approval of purchases over a designated level. By following this procedure, business owners can control losses due to overdrawn and delinquent accounts.

Modern electronic credit card verification and insurance systems are a relatively quick way to protect against **credit card fraud.** While they must be paid for, these systems can ensure that the firm does not sustain large losses.

Acceptance of bad checks, like credit card fraud, often is the result of poor business practices by the entrepreneur.[9] Winning the battle of wits against criminal check-passers is a matter of knowledge and vigilance. A business is apt to receive six different types of checks as well as money orders:

1. *Personal check*—written and signed by the individual offering it, the check is made out to the firm.
2. *Two-party check*—issued by the maker to a second person, who endorses it so that it may be cashed by a third party, this type of check is most susceptible to fraud because the maker can stop payment before it is cashed by the third person.
3. *Payroll check*—issued to employees for services performed, the check usually contains the printed name of the employer, an imprinted identification number from a check-writing machine, and a signature. The employee's name is either typed in or printed on the check by the machine. Generally, it is risky to accept checks that are hand printed, rubber stamped, or typewritten as payroll checks.
4. *Government check*—issued by a local, state, or federal agency, they often are stolen and have forged endorsements. In some areas, this is such a problem that banks refuse to cash welfare, relief, or tax refund checks unless they know the customer or the customer has an account with the bank.
5. *Blank check*—sometimes known as a universal check, this is no longer acceptable to most banks due to Federal Reserve Board regulations prohibiting standard processing without the encoded characters. This type of check can be used, but it requires special and more expensive processing. Entrepreneurs should be very cautious about accepting blank checks.
6. *Traveler's check*—a check with a preprinted amount (usually in denominations of $10, $20, $50, and $100); these are sold to travelers who do not want to carry large amounts of cash. The traveler signs the check at the time of purchase and countersigns it in the presence of the person cashing it. In vacation and resort areas, travelers' checks are common forms of payment for retail purchases.
7. *Money order*—a "check" that can be purchased for a specified amount and sent to another party; these are typically bought to send in the mail by people who do not have checking accounts. Most retailers do not accept them for payment in face-to-face transactions, and firms that sell money orders should never accept personal checks for payment—there is little need for money orders if the person has a checking account.

A check carries several key items that should be examined before being accepted. To identify a worthless check, the entrepreneur should look for:

- *Nonlocal banks*—require extra identification, and if the check is sufficiently large, contact the bank to verify that the person has an account. List the customer's local and out-of-town addresses and telephone numbers on the back of the check.

- *Date*—examine the date for accuracy. A check should not be accepted if it is dated in the future, or if it is more than two to five days old.
- *Location*—the check should show the name, branch, town, and state where the bank is located.
- *Amount*—the numerical amount must agree with the written amount.
- *Legibility*—a check that is not written in a legible manner should not be accepted. It should be signed in ink and contain no erasures.
- *Payee*—the customer should make the check payable to the firm. It should not be left blank unless the store's stamp is used immediately to identify the payee.
- *Checks over a preestablished limit*—the entrepreneur should preestablish a limit on the value of checks that are accepted. Only in special cases, and where the customer is well-known to the entrepreneur, should this policy be violated.
- *Low sequence numbers*—historically, there has been a higher incidence of bad checks among those with sequence numbers below 300. Extra care in obtaining forms of identification may be warranted in those instances.
- *Amount of check*—most bad-check passers write checks in the $25 to $50 range, on the assumption that the retailer will be less cautious with these than with larger ones.
- *Types of merchandise purchased*—salespeople should be alert for the purchase of random sizes and selections, and apparent lack of concern about prices.

Bad-check artists can fool all but the best detection available, and as such find small businesses relatively easy prey. While some protective measures are possible, they do add to the cost and complexity of completing a transaction. Use of check verification services, photographic equipment, and other devices often wards off those who prefer easier victims.

Of equal importance is guarding against forgers. Careful examination of the check can identify poorly forged or altered checks. Additionally, properly signed identification cards should be requested to provide more protection.

The entrepreneur should develop specific policies regarding two-party checks, out-of-state checks, checks for amounts above the purchase, and so on, and discuss them with all sales employees. These policies ensure that employees know what should and should not be accepted, and keeps them on notice that this is a critical concern.

Employee Theft and Embezzlement

Most entrepreneurs take some precautions to guard against external factors such as robbery, burglary, and fraud. Unfortunately, they tend to neglect protection from internal theft.

Employee theft and embezzlement are two of the greatest risks faced by all business owners.[10] According to some experts, small firms are more vulnerable. They tend to have relaxed accounting systems, preferring to sacrifice some control for the cost savings. Additionally, with relatively few employees there is not as much segregation of duties. One employee may do several jobs which in larger firms would be separated for security purposes.

Employee crime can be costly. A few examples reported over the years include a bookkeeper who deposited $750,000 in bill payments to her own bank account, and a trusted employee of 28 years who was an expert at filling orders for himself and never reporting the shipments to the billing department. Losses were estimated to have run into the hundreds of thousands of dollars.

The Department of Commerce estimates that 8 to 10 percent of all employees are hard-core pilferers and that 15 to 80 percent of all retail shortages are caused by employee theft.[11] The ready availability of cash and merchandise can tempt even the honest employee. Consequently, the small business owner must take steps to minimize this type of risk.

The process of reducing internal theft must begin with a careful assessment of where opportunities for theft are the greatest.[12] Storage rooms, cash registers, and open desks where payment invoices and blank checks are kept are especially vulnerable. A simple tour of the premises with the idea of trying to steal something will help the entrepreneur pinpoint trouble spots (see Exhibit 12–6).

Although specific safeguards will depend on the areas most likely to be vulnerable to internal theft, some standard precautions include:

- Segregate duties related to payments, receipts, purchasing, inventory control, inventory receiving, and so on. When employees are allowed to handle two or more of these functions, the opportunities for theft and embezzlement increase greatly.
- Maintain good records and review them both periodically and at random times. This makes it more difficult for employees to steal and makes it easier to track down any shortages.

EXHIBIT 12–6

Protection Against Employee Theft and Embezzlement

Preventing Employee Theft

Prosecute all employees caught stealing
Segregate duties that allow funds to come into and go out of the firm
Keep good records that create proper trails of revenues and expenses, and review them periodically
Use outside auditors/accountants to review the books at least once per year
Minimize access to cash, company checks, and purchase and receipts documents
Keep valuable inventory under special security
Inspect incoming and outgoing shipments, employee lunch boxes, and automobiles on a periodic basis insofar as there is compliance with all local, state, and federal laws
Rotate security guards periodically to ensure that they do not become overly friendly with other employees

Clues to Embezzlement

Unusually high levels of sales returns
Unusually high bad-debts write-offs
Reductions in cash sales that appear unexplainable
Cash register shortages or overages
Inventory shortages of items that are easily marketable
Increases in expenses that are not explainable
Employees who appear to be living beyond their means
Imbalances between cash receipts and cash deposits
Checks being issued to unknown or unusual suppliers

- Make sure that the paperwork ties in with the bookkeeping. For example, payments should be made only when all the paperwork has been completed and everything tallies correctly.
- Special safeguards such as locked cabinets and screened-in areas should be used for protecting valuable inventory. Expensive merchandise and equipment should be watched closely.
- Pay employees fairly. Poorly paid employees tend to feel more justified in stealing than people who believe they are being paid appropriately.
- Be especially careful of the most trusted employees. These are the people who receive less attention and are provided with more opportunities to commit crimes against the firm.
- Prosecute employees who are caught stealing—settling for restitution and an apology is inviting theft to continue.
- Do not assign two or more members of the same family to work in the same area.
- Do not allow any truck to approach a loading platform until it is ready to load or unload. This makes it more difficult for unauthorized vehicles to approach the business for purposes of theft.
- At random times, check incoming materials to ensure that there is no collusive activity between drivers and employees who are in charge of receiving inventory.

What distinguishes **embezzlement** from pilferage and other internal theft is that it is "the fraudulent appropriation of property by a person to whom it has been entrusted." The embezzler typically is a trusted employee, and therefore is not viewed with suspicion until extensive theft is evident.

Common clues to embezzlement include:[13]

- An increase in overall sales returns, which might represent concealment of accounts receivable payments. For example, an employee who was stealing payments on credit sales could issue a fake sales return slip to reduce the amount the customer owed by the amount of the payment. The only discrepancy would be in inventory, which could have shrunk from pilferage, and would be hard to trace back to the employee.
- A decline or unusually small increase in cash or credit sales that might mean some sales are not being recorded.
- Inventory shortages can be caused by fictitious purchases, unrecorded sales, or employee pilferage.
- Profit declines and/or increases in expenses can be a sign that cash is being siphoned off illegitimately.
- Slow collections can be caused by an employee trying to hide attempts to collect on fictitious accounts. For example, an employee may "purchase" goods on credit, setting up a fake buyer name. The employee will have the merchandise, and the company will have a debt from a nonentity. This would only become evident during the collection process.

There are many ways to reduce the possibility of losses through embezzlement. The entrepreneur should check the background on all prospective employees. This may involve making telephone calls or writing letters, or turning the matter over to a credit bureau or similar agency that can conduct background checks. A key concern with this, however, is to protect the rights of individuals furnishing information as well as those of the prospective employee. If the firm has a payroll department, no new employees should be added to the payroll without the personal approval of the entrepreneur or designated manager.

A small business owner also should attempt to get to know employees well enough to recognize signs of financial or other personal problems that could make it more likely that the individual would need money in a hurry. Many entrepreneurs prefer to have a post office box for receiving mail to ensure that checks and cash that do come in can be picked up by a designated person. When mail comes into the company directly, more people have access to letters and envelopes.

Other safeguards to protect against embezzlement include:

- Prepare daily cash deposits with a record of the cash and checks received.
- Arrange for bank statements and other correspondence from banks to go to a post office box. The entrepreneur should reconcile the statements personally, or have an outside accountant do them to ensure the propriety of all transactions.
- Examine canceled checks of the firm for any that appear unusual, or where too many are written to a particular person.
- Employees who are in positions to misappropriate funds should be bonded as a matter of policy.
- The entrepreneur should personally approve unusual discounts, bad-debt write-offs, and credit limits for customers.
- The entrepreneur should personally sign all checks and approve all cash disbursements to the extent possible. Periodically, the owner should examine invoices and supporting data before signing checks. Special attention can be directed to possible fictitious purchases from unknown companies.

INSURANCE NEEDS FOR SMALL BUSINESS

While some risk is inherent in any business situation, it can be controlled or reduced with a little extra care. One means of reducing the threat of significant loss is by purchasing insurance. Used as a hedge against major losses that could endanger the survival of the firm, insurance is a means of reducing uncertain losses for relatively certain costs. As such, insurance allows the entrepreneur to direct more attention and resources to other facets of the firm's operations.

Unfortunately, many small business owners believe that insurance provides them with a risk-free environment. The statement, "I'm not worried, I have insurance," often is used by the unknowing owner. Policies typically are written with deductible clauses and limitations on coverage. Full (no deductible) and comprehensive insurance is very expensive and usually not warranted except in extraordinary situations. Consequently, most entrepreneurs use insurance as a fail-safe program to augment standard risk-reduction precautions.

Risk Coverage

The most common types of insurance include:

- Fire and natural disaster,
- General liability and casualty,

- Workers' compensation and liability,
- Fidelity and surety bonds,
- Business interruptions, and
- Life and key person insurance.

Whether any or all of these areas need coverage and the extent to which they should be insured are complex issues. Insurance should not be taken out for trivial risks—it makes little sense, for example, to safeguard a $50 asset. Similarly, the entrepreneur should not spend inordinate sums for premiums whose total coverage is unnecessary. In most instances, it would be foolish to have a $50 deductible policy when a $200 deductible is available at reasonable savings in premiums. The extra $150 is not likely to have a major impact on the survival of the firm.

The entrepreneur must carefully weigh the costs of the policy with the potential amount of loss and its probability of occurring. Threats to the firm's survival take on special importance, and often make some insurance justified even though the likelihood of its being needed is remote.[14]

Fire and Natural Disaster

Fire insurance is the most common type of policy purchased by entrepreneurs. This covers all or part of the losses resulting from fire and lightning. Additional coverage also may be purchased to protect the business against hail, wind storms, riot, explosion, smoke, and auto and aircraft damage. In some cases, these types of protection may be quite necessary. For example, if the business is located near an airport, the danger of crashes is greater than when the site is many miles off normal air traffic patterns.

General Liability and Casualty

General liability and casualty insurance policies basically cover automobiles, crime, and injury to others. While these policies are expensive to maintain, they should be considered a normal cost of doing business. This is especially true for automobiles used in the course of business, and general protection from injury to others. Automobile accidents and injury to customers often turn into lawsuits, which can result in very expensive attorney fees and judgments against the business.

Crime insurance to protect the business against burglary, robbery, and theft also is warranted in many cases. This depends heavily on the location and nature of the business. For the entrepreneur who opens a pharmacy or jewelry store situated in a high-crime area, this insurance becomes a must. On the other hand, for the owner of a magazine shop located in an office building within a low-crime area, the need for crime insurance is reduced considerably.

Unfortunately, insurance in high-crime areas is very expensive, if it can be obtained at all. Some states have Fair Access to Insurance Regulations (FAIR) plans in which the federal and state governments work in cooperation with insurance companies to make crime insurance available to businesses operating in selected locations.

Workers' Compensation and Employer Liability

Business owners are required by common law to provide a safe working environment for employees and to warn them of any unavoidable hazards. Even if the entrepreneur fully conforms to Occupational Safety and Health Act (OSHA) regulations, accidents can occur and employees can sue the business. Despite the best employer–employee relationships, this risk is too great to leave uncovered, because court judgments can be high.

The type and extent of **workers' compensation** coverage varies on a state-by-state basis, since the benefits to be paid are determined by the individual states. Generally, these benefits will include payments for medical care, death, disability, and income payments to the disabled or surviving dependents.

Fidelity and Surety Bonds

Fidelity and surety bonds are specialized forms of insurance designed to protect the business and its customers from dishonest employees and those unable to fulfill contracts. **Fidelity bonds** typically are purchased to protect the firm from internal theft. Employees who are in contact with considerable sums or very expensive merchandise can be covered in this way. Such insurance should be considered in terms of its costs versus potential losses through theft, embezzlement, and other internal crimes.

Surety bonds are used to assure the firm's customers that it will meet its contractual obligations. In some industries, such as construction, bonding may be necessary if the firm is to generate any business whatsoever.

Business Interruption

Losses resulting from the disruption of business due to fire or other disasters can be protected against by business interruption insurance. This reduces the risks of a prolonged downtime when no revenues are being generated and some fixed costs are still being incurred. Normally, these policies cover loss of profits as well as the firm's fixed expenses.

While losses from a disaster itself may be high, it is possible that disruption to the business will be even costlier. Over an extended period of time, the interruption could threaten the survival of the firm. For this reason, many small business owners add this coverage to their policies to tide them over until they can build a new clientele base.

Life and Key-Person Insurance

What would happen to the business if one or more key persons died? In the case of a sole proprietorship, the death of the owner can seriously reduce the value of the business for the heirs. For partnerships and some closely held corporations, the death of one partner can so disrupt business that it may cease.

Consequently, many partnerships have life insurance on each partner to provide the surviving partner with funds to buy out that portion of the deceased's estate. The Small Business Administration has developed a list of suggestions on life insurance for various types of business ownership. These are listed below.[15]

Business Life Insurance for the Sole Proprietor Life insurance protection provides an owner-manager's dependents or heirs with cash representing the sound valuation of the business at death. Such insurance also can ensure business continuity. The policy should meet the conditions of a will or trust agreement if selling or liquidating the business is desired. In addition, thought should be given to selecting an appropriate beneficiary and determining who is to pay the insurance premiums.

A most important consideration is who takes custody of the business in case of death. If the family is continuing the business and nobody in the family has the necessary experience, someone will probably have to be hired to manage the firm. The business will need working capital, at least for a period of readjustment. If employees take over the business, they will need funds to purchase the business.

Business Life Insurance for the Partnership Unless the partners have provided otherwise, a partnership dissolves when one partner dies. For practical purposes, the business is finished. The surviving partners become *liquidating trustees.* The only business allowed is that of winding up affairs of the partnership. If the business is continued, the surviving partners become personally liable for any losses incurred should assets not cover losses.

One way to avoid these difficulties is an adequately financed buy-and-sell agreement. Such an agreement provides for the purchase at a prearranged valuation of the deceased partner's interest. An attorney can prepare the necessary papers carrying out the wishes of the partners. If a buy-and-sell agreement is decided on, the next step is to fund the arrangement. This can be done through a life insurance policy that enables surviving partners to reorganize at once and continue in business. Such insurance liquidates the interest of a deceased partner without loss. It also enables the beneficiaries of a deceased partner to secure full, fair value for the interest in the firm if the policy is kept up to date and commensurate with the increasing value of the firm.

There are various ways of establishing a partnership insurance plan, each with advantages for particular requirements. One plan involves the purchase by each partner of a policy on the life of the other partners. Each partner pays the premiums. Another plan, when there are three or more partners, is to have the firm buy a policy on the life of each. The questions of how much each partner should pay, the amount of insurance needed, the beneficiary arrangements, the tax effects, and the policy assignments necessary comprise only a few of the questions involved.

The valuation of the partnership is a vital problem to be met in setting up a partnership insurance. A formula must be set up under which full value is to be paid the deceased partner's heirs at some future time. The formula must be equitable and must satisfy all partners, or it could become the basis of lengthy controversy and litigation.

Corporate Business Life Insurance Because the success of a corporation depends largely on the skills and talents of those who run it, the death of any one executive can lead to financial loss for the corporation. Life insurance can protect the corporation against the loss of the services of its executives. It also can provide funds for their replacement.

Death of the principal stockholder in a close corporation (one with a few stockholders, all of whom usually are actively engaged in the management of the business) can lead to management or personnel clashes that might seriously affect the business. It can result in credit impairment, direct loss of business, or damage to employee morale. Unless otherwise provided, the deceased stockholder's stock becomes a part of the estate and passes into the hands of the administrator of the estate during the period of settlement. The administrator can vote the stock, and if it is a controlling interest, the administrator could even name a new board of directors and take full control.

Many hazards can be eliminated through a stock purchase and sale agreement with life insurance written into it to guarantee the funds for carrying it out. Such an agreement determines in advance just what will be done upon the death of a major stockholder. It also makes funds immediately available for accomplishing the objectives of the plan.

There are many benefits to using insurance. Continuity of management without interruption is guaranteed. No outsiders can come into the business unless agreed to in advance. The cash needed to carry out the purchase of the stock is automatically provided on a basis previously agreed to as fair. The common causes of friction between heirs and surviving stockholders are removed. Finally, spouses or heirs are not burdened by business responsibilities or worries. Having a guaranteed price, they are protected against shrinkage of stock values.

In addition to life insurance on the owner, key-person insurance should also be considered. The death of a highly valuable employee might seriously disrupt the ability of the firm to continue, and must be protected against. In industries in which highly technical employees are difficult to find, the time to locate a replacement for an employee can be costly in terms of lost revenues.

Group Life and Health Insurance A final area of consideration should be group life and health insurance. Making these provisions for employees often is worth the cost, since it can improve employee morale and loyalty. Such decisions, however, need careful planning and cost-benefit evaluations. This topic is further discussed in Chapter 18.

Selecting the Insurance Company

Because insurance is important and can be a relatively high-cost item, sound insurance management is essential. Selection of an insurance company, economical purchase of insurance, and a plan for managing the insurance must all be considered.

Even though there are many types of insurance companies, the small business owner most likely will buy from either a mutual or a stock company. While both are chartered by the states, the former is a nonprofit organization owned by the policyholders, and the latter is a profit-seeking enterprise. There is no inherent advantage to either. Each prospective company should be evaluated on the basis of the types of insurance offered, the company's financial stability, its ability to adapt policy coverage to the entrepreneur's needs, the premium costs, and the company's willingness to pay benefits.

Since many insurance companies specialize in specific types of coverage, some may not be appropriate for the entrepreneur's needs. Similarly, companies differ in the flexibility of the programs they offer. Some tailor policies to the entrepreneur's specific needs, while others are not able or willing to do this. The small business owner, of course, will want to have and pay for only the needed coverage.

Insurers differ greatly in their financial stability. A relatively simple check of Best's Insurance Reports will provide an assessment of the financial positions of various companies. A financially weak insurer may not be able to help if and when the need arises, and such weakness may be indicative of forthcoming increases in policy costs.

Of equal importance as the stature of the company is the skill and reputation of the agent. Since the entrepreneur typically deals exclusively with the insurer's representative rather than with the company itself, the small business owner must select an agent who is fair and will work with the policyholder.

Purchasing Insurance Economically

Choosing the most economical insurance for a business involves a number of elements:

1. Decide which kind of risk protection will work best and most economically. Commercial insurance is only one way of handling risk. Investigate the other methods—such as loss prevention, self-insurance, no insurance, risk transfer—to see if they offer better coverage for the firm's specific needs.
2. Cover the largest loss exposure first, and then the less severe ones as the firm's budget permits. Use the premium dollar where the protection need is greatest. Some firms insure their automobiles against collision loss, but do not purchase adequate insurance on their liability coverage. Collision losses seldom bankrupt a firm, but liability judgments often do.
3. Make proper use of deductibles. Full coverage can be uneconomical because of the high cost of covering the first dollar of loss. Make the deductible an affordable amount.
4. Review the firm's insurance periodically. Automatically renewing policies increases the likelihood that the firm will fail to increase limits of liability where indicated, or that possible rate reductions are not taken.
5. Check the market occasionally to see that the firm is getting insurance for a reasonable price. Do not switch insurers each time a lower price is quoted, but keep aware of average costs for the amount and types of coverage required.
6. Analyze insurance terms and provisions. When a small business owner attempts to save money by purchasing a cheaper policy, it sometimes is discovered that the specific hazard it wanted to insure is not adequately covered because of a technicality.
7. Insure the correct exposure. One firm purchased coverage against equipment breakdown but later found that defective design was the real cause of the trouble. Correcting the design removed the exposure. Another business bonded its employees who handled cash but did not bond those who handled materials.
8. Investigate whether certain administrative duties required by the policies can be assumed. Usually, the amount saved in premiums will more than offset the expense of performing the service. For example, the firm may have to report changes in inventories for a commercial property policy.
9. Buy insurance in as large a unit as possible. Take advantage of the savings most insurers allow for large-unit policies, particularly for life insurance and many types of property insurance. Usually, the more property included in a single policy, the cheaper it is for the insurer to handle.

SUMMARY

1. Risk management does not mean risk avoidance. It implies that risk is assessed, measured, and reduced to the extent that is economically feasible.
2. The more common types of noncriminal business risks include fire, natural disasters, personal liabilities, economic downturns, business interruptions, and loss of key personnel.

3. Insurance for fire, natural disasters, or personal liability is often a good hedge against the risks involved, but programs designed to prevent hazards and problems from occurring are essential to minimizing these risks.
4. The entrepreneur can be prepared for economic downturns, business interruptions, and the loss of key personnel by keeping alert to changes in the firm and its environment.
5. The main types of criminal risks are burglary, robbery, shoplifting, credit card fraud, bad checks, and employee theft.
6. Protection against internal theft by employees often is neglected. The entrepreneur must be aware of opportunities for theft and control such areas, and must carefully evaluate individuals before hiring them.
7. Most of the risks described in this chapter are insurable, and coverage should be considered for each.
8. The most common types of insurance are fire and natural disaster, general liability and casualty, workers' compensation and liability, fidelity and surety bonds, business interruptions, and life and key-person insurance.
9. Insurance should not be taken for trivial risk areas or for expensive total coverage that is unnecessary.
10. In determining the amounts and types of insurance to buy, the entrepreneur should place special importance on areas that threaten the firm's survival and the particular areas, whether geographical or occupational, that are peculiar to the firm.
11. In choosing an insurance company, the following should be evaluated about the company: types of insurance offered, financial stability, ability to adapt coverage to the entrepreneur's needs, premium costs, and willingness to pay benefits.
12. Of equal importance as the stature of the insurance company is an agent who is fair, capable, and will work with the policyholder.

KEY TERMS AND CONCEPTS

Noncrime-related business risks
Key-person insurance
Crime-related business risks
Burglary
Robbery
Shoplifting
Credit card fraud
Embezzlement
General liability and casualty insurance
Workers' compensation
Fidelity bonds
Surety bonds

QUESTIONS FOR DISCUSSION

1. What are the noncriminal business risks?
2. Describe precautions that can be taken to protect the firm from loss of key personnel.
3. List the criminal business risks.
4. What measures can be taken to prevent burglary losses?
5. What is the most common risk taken by the small business owner, and how can it be best deterred?
6. List some standard precautions against internal theft.
7. What are the common clues to embezzlement?
8. Name some common types of business insurance.
9. What is the difference between a mutual and a stock company?
10. What must be taken into account when selecting an insurance company?

SELF-TEST REVIEW

Multiple Choice Questions

1. Which of the following is a noncriminal business risk?
   a. Business interruptions.
   b. Credit card fraud.
   c. Shoplifting.
   d. Employee theft.
2. The *best* deterrent to robbery is to have:
   a. Uncluttered windows.
   b. Little cash on hand.
   c. Ample lighting.
   d. Surveillance cameras.
3. Key-person insurance is especially important in industries requiring:
   a. Unskilled employees.
   b. Highly technical employees.
   c. Highly paid employees.
   d. Limited amounts of labor.
4. Which of the following is the most common criminal risk faced by the small business owner?
   a. Shoplifting.
   b. Burglary.
   c. Robbery.
   d. Employee theft.
5. Which of the following is a nonprofit insurance company owned by policyholders?
   a. Mutual company.
   b. Stock company.
   c. Consolidated company.
   d. Conglomerated actuarial company.

True/False Statements

1. The key to risk reduction is making sure that some unexpected or uncontrollable circumstances cannot unilaterally destroy the business.
2. Fire insurance will fully cover losses due to fire.
3. Burglary is a less common risk than robbery in most small businesses.
4. Purchasing insurance is one of the best hedges against natural disasters.
5. Fewer than 2 percent of all employees are hardcore pilferers.
6. The key to protection against burglary is to make entry difficult and noisy.
7. Losses stemming from credit card fraud and bad checks often are the result of poor business practices by the entrepreneur.
8. Theft is the fraudulent appropriation of property by a person to whom it has been entrusted.
9. Surety bonds are used to protect a business from losses due to external theft.
10. Life insurance is important to individuals, but of little importance to small firms.

CUSTOM HAIR CARE

Because business has been burglarized three times in seven weeks, Jon Anderson has decided it is time to reassess his risks and review insurance needs for his hair salon, Custom Hair Care. The last year has been a bad one for Anderson. The shop has been burglarized five times, he has been subject to one armed robbery, and he has caught an employee not ringing up a $70 payment for a haircut and permanent.

Custom Hair Care is a hair salon catering to both men and women. When Anderson opened the salon nearly five years ago, he knew that the site he selected was not in the best part of town, but the rent on his eight-year lease is relatively low and the landlord agreed to some leasehold improvements on a shared-cost basis. Believing that the deal was too good to pass up, Anderson has accepted the fact that he faces greater risks than he would if he had located in another part of this southeastern town of 200,000 people.

Still, he never believed that a hair salon would be the target of much crime. The equipment and inventory are not especially valuable, except for his stereo system. And, as part of his leasehold improvements, he has installed a silent alarm system on the doors and the windows.

While the burglaries were more nuisances than costly losses, the recent armed robbery was another matter. Entering the salon late in the afternoon, one robber held three customers at gunpoint while another took their wallets, jewelry, and the salon's cash receipts and new stereo—the old stereo had been stolen two weeks earlier.

Also of concern to Anderson is the incident of an employee not recording a payment. Although the monetary loss is not critical, he is wondering if this is the only time it has happened, especially since he leaves the salon on several occasions each week. Ever since he employed four other hair stylists, there always seems to be new personnel. While he believes that he treats his employees fairly, a degree of transience in the business creates some risk.

Given the history of problems in this location, Anderson is reluctant to buy more insurance. He is paying nearly $6,000 annually due to the claims he has submitted, and additional coverage would cost another $2,500, which would come directly from salon profits. He does not like the idea of protecting windows with bars, since that would create a negative image for the salon. Furthermore, to protect against robbery, he thinks he might have to keep the door locked at all times and let in only those customers he or other stylists recognize.

Similarly, Anderson does not know how to protect himself from the employee problems he has experienced. He cannot be in the salon every minute, and he wants to make employees feel he trusts them.

Considering the business risks and insurance needs, Anderson wants to balance the probable losses with the costs of protection. Even though most of the losses have been small, he realizes that they add up to a considerable sum—too much for him to continue to absorb for the remaining three years of his lease.

QUESTIONS

1. Evaluate Anderson's philosophy concerning business risk and insurance.
2. How can Anderson determine the right balance between the risks of loss and the costs of insurance?
3. How should Anderson solve the problem of employees not accounting for all of their receipts?

NOTES

1. Based on Cable News Network's "Pinnacle," October 4, 1987. Guest: Rod Canion, Compaq Computer.
2. "Great Fortunes Lost," *Fortune,* July 18, 1988, 74–84.
3. Based on Cable News Network's "Pinnacle," July 22, 1989. Guest: Larry Cochran, Six Flags.
4. Based on Cable News Network's "Pinnacle," December 6, 1987. Guest: George Hatsopoulos, Thermo Electron Corporation.
5. Based on Cable News Network's "Pinnacle," June 14, 1987. Guest: John Rollwagen, Cray Research.
6. Addison H. Verrill, Small Business Administration, *Reducing Shoplifting Losses,* Management Aid No. 3.006, 2.
7. "A Security Mannequin to Spy for Stores," *Insight,* March 27, 1989, 45.
8. Adapted from Addison H. Verrill, Small Business Administration, *Reducing Shoplifting Losses,* Management Aid No. 3.006.
9. Adapted from Small Business Administration, *Outwitting Bad Check Passers,* Management Aid No. 3.008, 2–3.
10. Bank of America, "Crime Prevention for Small Business," *Small Business Reporter,* vol. 13, no. 1 (1977), 14.
11. Small Business Administration, *Preventing Embezzlement,* Marketer's Aid No. 151, 2.
12. *Ibid.*
13. *Ibid.*
14. Adapted from Small Business Administration, *Insurance and Risk Management,* Series No. 30, 63–65.
15. Adapted from Small Business Administration, *Business Life Insurance,* Management Aid No. 222, 4–6.

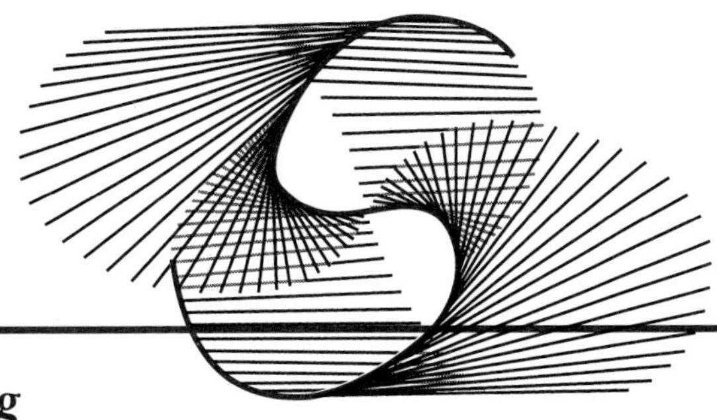

Chapter Thirteen

Organizing and Staffing the Firm

Chapter Outline

Learning Objectives *The objectives of this chapter are to assist you in understanding:*

1. The various organizational principles.
2. The different forms of organization and methods for organizing a small business.
3. How to develop and plan work force requirements and develop job descriptions.
4. The process used to recruit personnel.
5. The process for selecting an applicant to work for the firm.

No matter how large or small the firm, it must be organized in some manner. Whether organization is formal or informal, activities and employees should be defined in terms of what is to be done and who is to do each task.

THE NEED FOR ORGANIZATION

Many sole proprietors view organizing as a waste of time. A typical comment is: "Why should I develop an organizational chart? There are only three people here—myself and two employees. We all know what we are supposed to do, and I'm the boss." There is some merit to this perspective—at least until an important task is left undone and creates a crisis for the firm.[1]

Overly complex organizations, however, can stifle the entrepreneur. John Rollwagen, chief executive officer of Cray Research, reflected on the life of Seymour Cray, founder of the company:

> He helped start Univac [now part of Unisys]. . . . He was a founder of Control Data. . . . In his . . . prior experiences, there came a time when the company experienced so much success based on his technology that he could no longer continue his work, that a bureaucracy grew up around him of guidelines, procedures, policies, and so on that it began to confound him. . . . It started to confine him.

The solution for Seymour Cray was to hold no title with the company, but to become an independent contractor who is paid for his work and contributions.[2]

The Nature and Importance of Organization

The term *organization* often is misused. It frequently is used as though it were synonymous with the firm itself: "Our organization makes good products." Properly defined, however, **organization** refers to the designated structure of the activities, processes, and people who make up the business. Even in the smallest venture many marketing, finance, accounting, and personnel activities must be defined and assigned to one or more individuals. While the entrepreneur may recognize all the management functions, although this is unlikely, some will surely be forgotten or bypassed in the hustle and bustle of daily activity. As a result, bills may not be paid, supplies may not be ordered with sufficient lead time, and collections may not be made from customers. Accordingly, the entrepreneur will spend increasing amounts of time fighting unnecessary fires. Having a good organization will help reduce these types of problems.[3]

All employees need to know specifically what they are supposed to do, what they are responsible for, whom they are to report to, and who is to report to them. An ambiguous work environment will result in unperformed tasks and will breed frustration and uncertainty about the future. In a small business, where each employee can have a marked impact on the firm's survival and success, this is of paramount importance.

Organizational structure is important, yet it can insulate top management from lower-level employees. To avoid this, Ronald Rule, chairman of U.S. Playing Card, had a solution:

> We have formal staff meetings, of course, once a week, but I like to have more informal meetings . . . just sitting down and doing some blue skying. . . . I think the other area is that we work very much with all employees. I do something that's called "pop with the pres" and I do it about once a week with . . . workers out in the plant, and we talk about what's going on with the company . . . and . . . what's on their mind[s].

Even in small firms, this type of contact can be critical to keeping attuned to all facets of operations and maintaining employee morale.[4]

Organizational Principles and Practices

Just as there is no one right way to manage, so too is there no one right way to organize. Each business is unique, and will reflect the interests and personality of the entrepreneur and the type of industry and environmental setting in which it is involved. However, there are some general principles of organization that can be applied to most businesses.[5]

Division of Work

Except in the case of the entrepreneur who owns and operates the business alone, work efforts must be divided among employees in some logical manner. Early concepts of work division implied a narrowly defined job for each employee.

Modern views, however, suggest that while the work should be divided, it should not be so specialized that the employee cannot see the end result of the work effort. Consequently, many firms are moving to job enrichment in an attempt to expand the job vertically and make the task large enough so the worker can see the value of his or her labor. In a cabinet shop, fitting a hinge on a door may seem inconsequential to a worker, but assembling the entire cabinet would appear to be a more significant contribution to the completed product.

Parity of Authority and Responsibility

Employees should have authority to ensure the proper completion of activities they are asked to perform. Workers who are given authority over some functions also should be held responsible for them.

Unity of Command

Within any firm that has more than one employee, a chain of command must be established, and every worker needs to be supervised by one and only one superior. Many growing small businesses have lines of authority that are unclear, and employees receive orders from several people at once—orders that may be conflicting.

Unity of Direction

Each employee should have a clear understanding of, and a willingness to work for, the goals of the business. Without this unified effort, the firm is likely to become fragmented and to work in several directions at once. A classic example of this is the case of Esprit, a highly successful maker of designer apparel for women. The owners, a husband and wife, had conflicting views about their target markets. This led to considerable turmoil within the firm, as each tried to design the company's product lines for different groups.

Scalar Chain

In any organizational structure, ultimate authority rests at the top and flows downward. Scopes of and limits to authority and responsibility must be well delineated on paper as well as in the minds and actions of managers and employees.

Span of Control

The principle of **span of control** states that there are only so many employees a manager can effectively supervise.[6] A general rule of thumb is that at lower levels managers can oversee between eight and twenty employees, while at upper levels the number is reduced to between four and eight. The reason for the lesser number at higher levels is that there is a greater amount of communication needed to operate the firm.

Key factors affecting the span are:

- Employee training,
- Employee communications,
- Extent of planning, and
- Use of assistants.

If the entrepreneur wants to relinquish some decision-making authority, it is necessary to prepare a comprehensive training program and develop an effective line of communications among personnel at all levels and between management and nonmanagement employees.

Delegation of Authority

While responsibility for decisions cannot be passed on, authority to make them can be vested with others. **Delegation of authority,** however, often is not accomplished within smaller firms. Owners, having gone into business to become bosses, and after developing and nurturing their firms, tend to be unwilling to share control with many others. Even in those companies where delegation has occurred, owners frequently centralize authority during times of crisis or when they do not feel that their employees are performing as they should.

In terms of the formal organization, lack of delegation is typified by a flat pyramid as opposed to a tall one (see Exhibit 13–1). Entrepreneurs tend to use more decentralized organizations when they feel comfortable that employees want to make and are capable of making decisions, and when the nature of the environment is such that it is better for decisions to be made close to the scene.

FORMALIZING THE ORGANIZATIONAL STRUCTURE

Developing the proper structure involves a two-step process. First, the small business owner identifies a relatively standard organizational design that most closely fits the firm's needs. Then this design is molded to coincide with the unique desires of the entrepreneur.

EXHIBIT 13–1 ***Flat and Tall Organizational Structures***

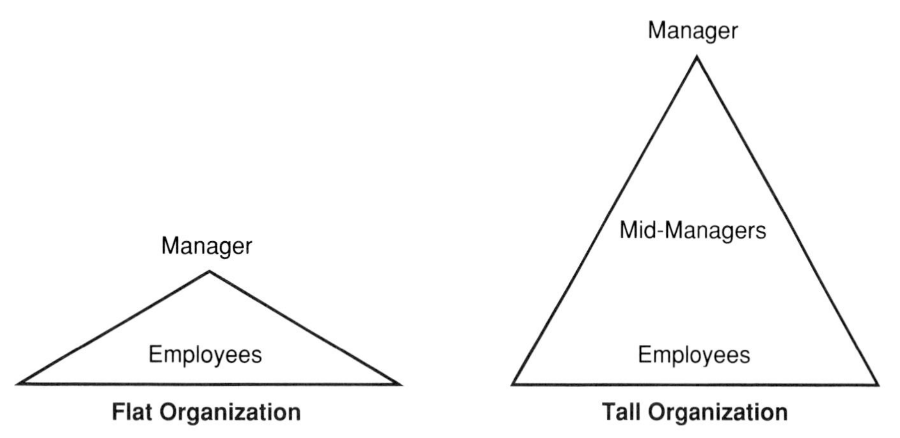

Formal Organizational Structures

Several preestablished organizational models are available to the entrepreneur. While somewhat standardized, they serve as a basis for customizing a structure to meet the preferences of the owner and the goals of the firm.

One example of this was a small computer software company based in Cincinnati. After the firm experienced severe cash problems and stagnating growth, a new chief executive came in and designed the company's first organizational chart and set of performance goals for various operating units. This helped structure the company and gave it direction. In two years, sales nearly doubled and profits more than tripled.[7]

Line Organization

The most common method for organizing an enterprise is on the basis of line authority. Under this concept, all employees are involved in the manufacture or sale of the firm's output, and managers have the right to demand compliance from their subordinates.

A **line organization** approach, as illustrated in Exhibit 13–2(A), is found mostly in small firms that employ relatively few people—typically eight to fifteen. This method is the most effective and efficient in a small firm. As the firm grows and becomes involved in more complex and specialized matters (for example, tax and legal issues, centralized purchasing) this structure does not allow for inflow of the expertise needed to deal with these considerations.

Line-and-Staff Organization

To compensate for the lack of needed specialists within a line organization, a line-and-staff structure evolved. This form of organization, illustrated in Exhibit 13–2(B), is the most common for small businesses that have experienced a degree of success and growth. The key benefit to this approach is that line management still is held responsible

EXHIBIT 13–2 *Line and Line-and-Staff Organizations*

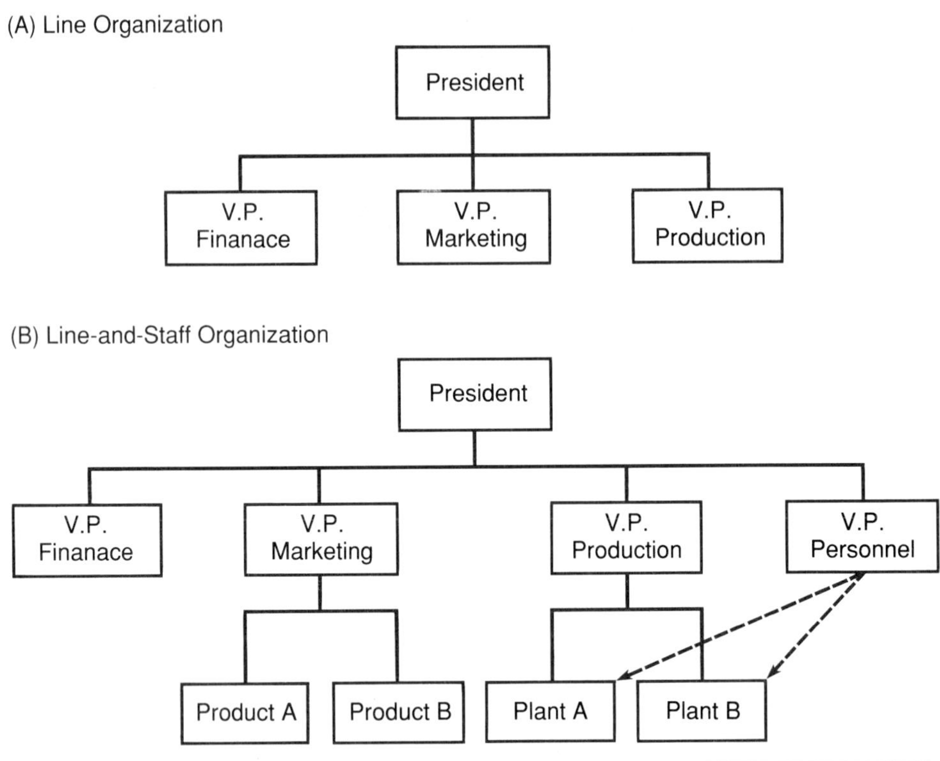

for the operation of the business, but now they are assisted by technical specialists who have expertise in some of the finer points of business.

Problems with this form of organization center on violations of the principle of unity of command. Nonmanagement employees often find themselves being given direction by both line and staff personnel.

A common example of this is between production supervisors and quality control experts. If the quality control staff is given authority to stop manufacturing lines when production is not within tolerance levels, this conflicts directly with the production manager's responsibility for output. The most effective way to control this problem is to give line managers absolute authority, and use staff members as advisors to line management only.

The Informal Organization

Despite almost every attempt to the contrary, an **informal organization** will develop within even very small companies. Since organizations are made up of people, natural and spontaneous human interaction can drastically influence the effectiveness of formal structures. Consequently, informal leader–follower relationships develop, which will not necessarily conform to those prescribed or desired by the entrepreneur.

A firm's informal organization can strengthen the cohesiveness within the firm and also increase the chance of goal achievement. (Photograph © Ann M. Mason)

The leader position often is the result of a nonjob-related skill. The strongest physically, best bowler, consumer of the most alcoholic beverages, most personable, or best-looking, and so on, may be the informal leader.

Informal organizations can strengthen cohesiveness within the company and increase the chances of goal achievement for all. The only time severe action should be taken against the informal organization is when its goals become counterproductive to those of the entrepreneur and the firm. In most instances, however, the informal group will neither help nor hinder the company's operations to any significant extent.

Methods of Organizing the Small Business

Workers and their work need to be grouped in some manner. Then a manager should be assigned to oversee their functioning. The basic process of organizing follows a series of seven steps:

1. Define the goals of the firm.
2. Identify and define each task to be completed.
3. Group related tasks into jobs that can be assigned to an employee or group of employees.
4. Group the jobs in units that are related in some manner (for example, skills needed, facet of the firm's operations).
5. Assign a manager to each unit and provide the manager with the necessary authority and responsibility to complete the jobs within the unit.
6. Arrange these units relative to one another, both horizontally and vertically (for example, who reports to whom).
7. Establish a control system for measuring the progress and achievements of each group.

One of the most common difficulties found among small business owners with respect to organizing is their uncertainty about how to group jobs and their collective units. On what bases should job activities be joined? There is no one right answer. It depends on the type of business, the industry, and the personal preferences of the entrepreneur.

Organization by Time

One of the easiest methods for organizing a homogeneous group of employees is on the basis of their working hours. If, as shown in Exhibit 13–3(A), the firm operates day and night shifts, workers and managers can be assigned to each shift. This logical and convenient approach often is overlooked because of its simplicity. A danger of this method lies in trying to establish too many organizational units and increasing the costs

EXHIBIT 13–3 **Methods of Organizing the Small Business**

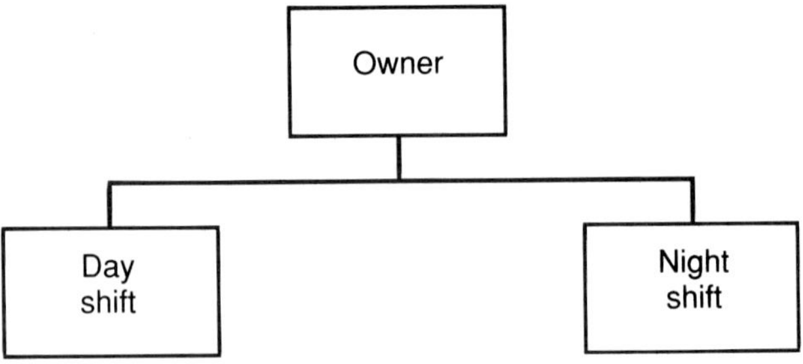

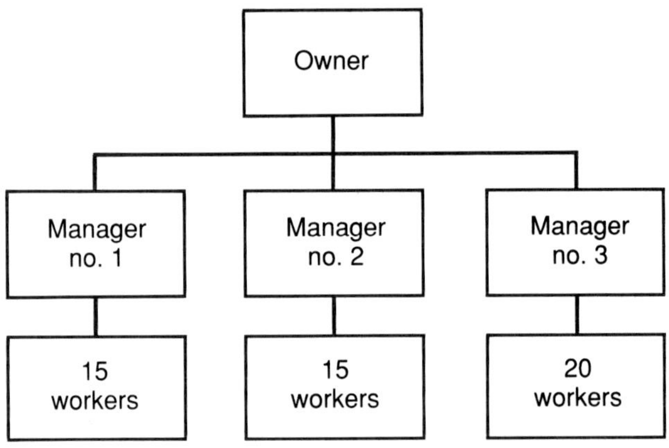

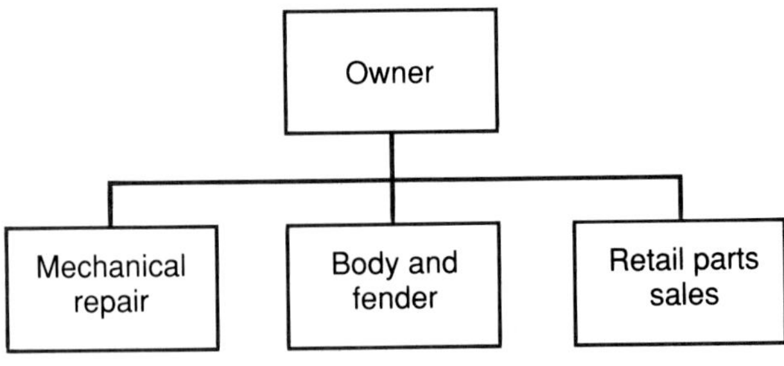

EXHIBIT 13–3 Methods of Organizing the Small Business *(continued)*

(D) Organization by Product

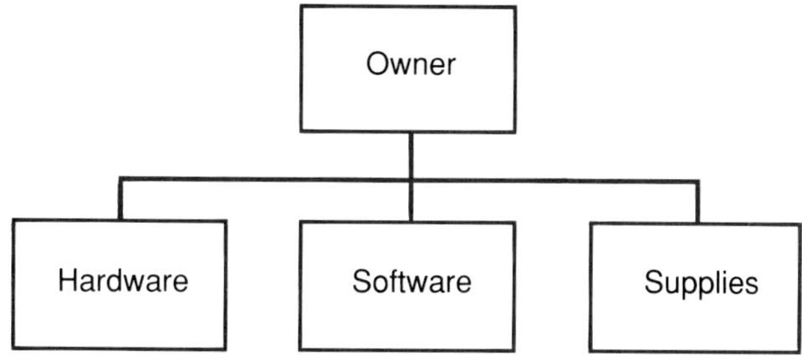

(E) Organization by Territory

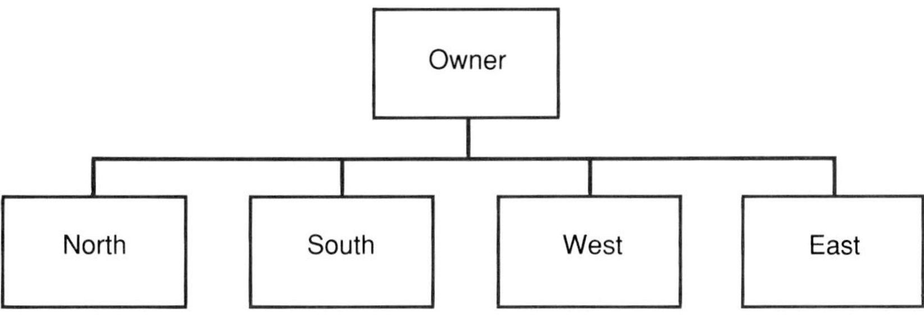

(F) Organization by Customer

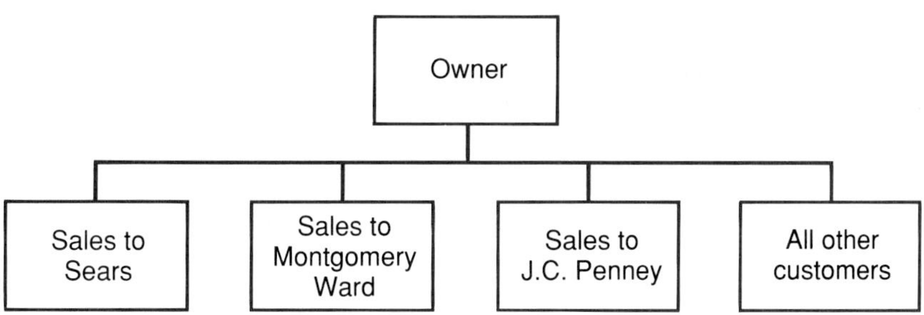

(G) Organization by Project

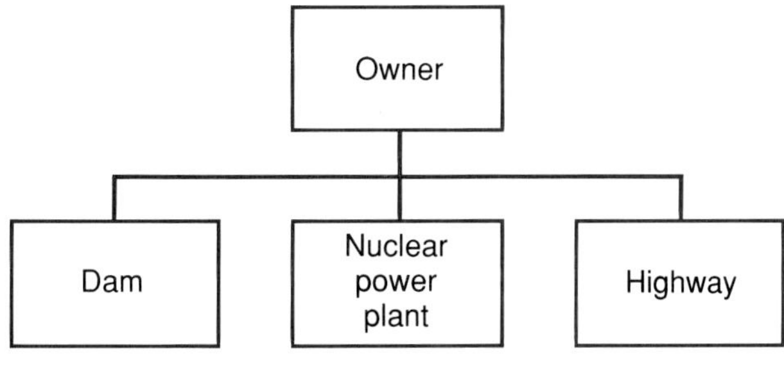

of managing. For example, stores that are open from 10 A.M. to 7 P.M. might not need to have more than one organizational unit.

Organization by Number

A homogeneous group of employees too large to be effectively supervised by one individual can be grouped on the basis of numbers. As illustrated in Exhibit 13–3(B), the management of 50 workers was separated into three groups of nearly equal size. A disadvantage of this approach is that employees can become isolated from each other and not share information on improving their skills and so on.

Organization by Function

Organization by function applies to situations in which there is considerable diversity in jobs and the skills required to perform them satisfactorily. As shown in the example of an automobile repair shop in Exhibit 13–3(C), the specialists can be divided and a manager placed in charge of each unit. The commonality of tasks not only is a logical method of division, but also serves to strengthen the work group and provide a means for sharing expertise. The danger of this approach is that the work units may become too specialized, and employees may not be able to see the contributions they make to the final product.

Organization by Product

In some cases, the entrepreneur may find it expedient to organize on the basis of different products manufactured or sold, as illustrated in Exhibit 13–3(D). This is especially beneficial when dealing with highly complex products that require great amounts of technical knowledge, such as office machinery and computer systems. The key advantage of this approach is that the firm can be organized along **profit centers,** in which each product is held accountable for the costs it incurs and the revenue and profits it generates. The disadvantage lies in ensuring that all of the organizational units are coordinated to work together for the good of the firm.

Organization by Territory

For entrepreneurs who have customers scattered over broad geographic areas, it sometimes is best to organize by territory. As shown in Exhibit 13–3(E), each territory can be a separate, autonomous unit that will respond to the specific needs of the market area being served. From a logistics perspective, considerable time and money can be saved by having managers and employees working within designated territories. The primary drawback to this is that coordinated efforts between geographic areas in terms of dealing with customers and sharing ideas tend to be more difficult to maintain.

Organization by Customer

Structuring by customer is advantageous to industrial firms that sell to other businesses. The *80–20 principle* applies to most large and small firms, in which 80 percent of the firm's revenues come from about 20 percent of its customers. By selecting the larger accounts and organizing on that basis, the main customers get the recognition they deserve. For example, a small clothing manufacturer may find an organizational structure like that shown in Exhibit 13–3(F) to be quite advantageous. The main danger in this approach is that adequate attention might not be given to customers who are growing and who could become members of the 20 percent in the future.

EXHIBIT 13–4

Combination of Methods of Organizing the Small Business

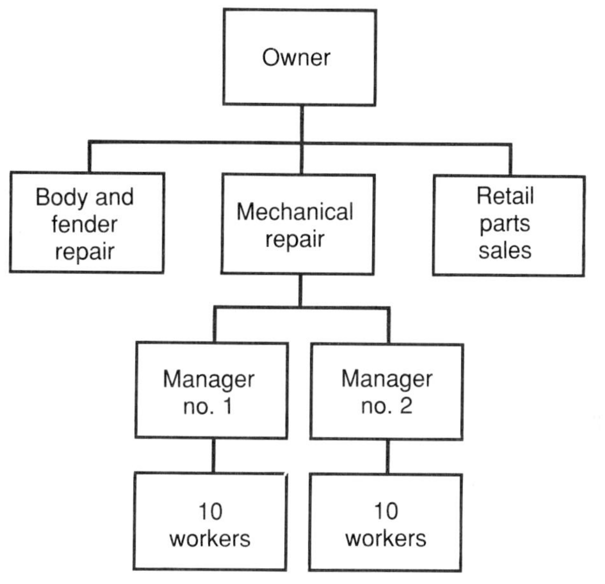

Organization by Project

For small contracting firms, organizing by project provides a ready mechanism for control, as seen in Exhibit 13–3(G). In this way each business effort can be kept separate to ensure its profitability and completion. This method is quite appropriate for construction projects, contracts with governmental agencies, and other organizations in which large jobs are well defined. Organizing by project is not as effective for firms that have a large number of small jobs. The costs of having several managers, maintaining separate records, and so on, usually are too high to warrant this approach.

Organization by a Combination of Methods

Because each firm's organizational structure will be unique, none of the methods described may prove satisfactory. Instead, it may be best to organize using a combination of methods. This is illustrated in Exhibit 13–4. While the structure should be kept as simple as possible, in some instances several organizational approaches may be needed to meet the needs of the firm.

EVALUATING THE ORGANIZATIONAL STRUCTURE

Just as goals and plans must be continually monitored and adjusted to changing internal and environmental conditions, so too should the organizational structure. One of the primary advantages of smaller firms is their flexibility to adapt to changing environmental conditions. Does it still suit the owner's needs and desires? Is it still appropriate for the

Lotus Development Corporation opened in 1982 with $1 million in venture capital and eight employees. In 1984, when Jim Manzi was named president and chief operating officer, Lotus had 741 employees and $157 million in revenues. The year 1989 ended with 2,700 employees and $556 million dollars in revenues. Over the years, this growth has kept the company in an environment of constant change with a continuous need to evaluate and re-evaluate organizational strategies to keep Lotus moving forward as a finely managed company. (Photograph courtesy of Lotus Development Corporation)

environmental conditions within which the firm operates? How well do employees and their capabilities match the structure?

Lotus Development

Organizational changes are a necessary part of business life for firms that are growing and reacting to market conditions. In 1989, Jim Manzi, chief executive officer of Lotus Development, reflected on change:

> Lotus didn't exist seven years ago. In our first year we did 53 million dollars, going to 157 million, going to 225 million, and so on . . . we are approaching half a billion dollars or 600 million dollars in business this year. That is going to change and stress all sorts of things. The organization, the strategy, the people, and so on . . . if there isn't change, if there isn't that kind of dynamism . . . we won't grow as a company.[8]

When to Evaluate the Structure

Evaluation of the organizational structure should be a continuous process, especially for companies experiencing rapid growth or decline, and those in highly volatile industries. The entrepreneur must be alert to organizational units that are not operating effectively, since their performances may be due to antiquated structures. However, care also should be taken to keep changes to a minimum to avoid creating unnecessary disturbances to operations.

For most small businesses, a yearly in-depth organizational appraisal is sufficient. An evaluation can be made along with the normal appraisal of sales and expenses, profitability, and market share. When conducted in this manner, the proper role of the structure can be maintained with the perspective, "Can these areas be improved by reorganizing the company?"

How to Evaluate the Structure

Most evaluations of company organizations are made on crisis bases. When operations start going poorly, many entrepreneurs look to the structure as a vehicle for turning the firm around. While a "troubled times" approach is not the most desirable, it often is perceived to be the easiest solution.

There are tell-tale signs of faulty organization. Employee conflict often is a clue that authority relationships are improperly defined. Unresolved problems with customers or personnel might indicate that nobody has been placed in charge. Ballooning departments in terms of expenses and/or personnel may be indicative of empire-building by one or more lower-level managers. Confusion as to what should be done next can be a symptom of a poor communication system from the top to the bottom of the organization.

THE STAFFING PROCESS

Once the firm has been organized into operating units, staffing becomes a critical issue. The company cannot afford to hire or retain bad employees or those who do not fit with what the firm is attempting to accomplish. Because employees do the work, and are a major expense, the entrepreneur must carefully staff the organization.

The Staffing Process Defined

The basic staffing process can be synthesized into a series of eleven steps, many of which can be undertaken simultaneously:

Step One. Based on company objectives and level of business activity, forecast future personnel needs in terms of both numbers and types of positions.

Step Two. Based on the entrepreneur's personal goals, determine how many management positions will open in the future and in what technical areas.

Step Three. Specify each type of job identified in Steps One and Two in terms of job descriptions.

Step Four. Assess the internal aspects of employment in terms of working conditions, company policies, and other factors that may affect future employees' satisfaction with their jobs. Make sure, too, that the work environment conforms to federal, state, and local regulations.

Step Five. Based on the positions open and their job descriptions, determine where the right kinds of potential employees might be found.

Step Six. Actively recruit good employees by promoting job opportunities, paying commissions to employment agencies for top quality or hard-to-hire personnel, or utilizing other means of attracting applicants.

Step Seven. Select individuals for employment on the basis of a formalized screening process. This process must be nondiscriminatory, and conform to various employment laws (see Exhibit 13–5).

Gail and Dave Liniger founded Re/Max International, an international real estate firm, on the principal that the key to solving the basic problems faced by any business is to bring out the best in the best people one can hire. The people who feel like winners act like winners, become winners, and attract other winners to the company. (Photograph by Ed Dosien, courtesy of Re/Max International, Inc.)

EXHIBIT 13–5 Government Employment Regulations

Listed below are some regulations affecting personnel working in small businesses. There are exemptions available to some employers based on the nature and size of the business, the number of employees, and other variables. Because specific statutes vary by state, and may change rapidly, the employer should determine which regulations are applicable. For more information, business owners should contact state and local authorities or consult their attorneys and/or accountants.

Hiring and Regulations

1. *Civil Rights Act*

   This act has been amended several times, but the key provision is Title VII which applies to employers who have at least a specified number of employees. Essential aspects of this act are that employers are prohibited from discriminating on the basis of gender, race, religion, age, national origin, etc. This law applies to employment practices related to hiring, wages and benefits, seniority accumulation, promotions, firing, and retirement. Employers who are regulated by this act also are required to maintain records of hiring on the basis of specific criteria. Firms that violate this law may be required to take remedial action to rectify past discriminations in employment.

2. *Age Discrimination in Employment Act*

   This 1967 federal law made it illegal to discriminate against people between the ages of 40 and 65 years due to their age. More recent legislation has increased the upper age limit. There are some exemptions to this requirement at both federal and state levels. Additionally, some differences exist between state and federal statutes as they pertain to age discrimination, but most prohibit any advertising for personnel that states or implies that older workers will not be considered for employment.

3. *Comprehensive Employment and Training Act*

   There are many different work programs, some of which are grants under the Comprehensive Employment and Training Act and the Job Training Partnership Act. Under certain circumstances, employers can obtain financial incentives for hiring individuals who are determined to be hard-to-employ. In conjunction with state and local Employment and Training Agencies, employers can have portions of employee wages paid by the government, and receive credits while handicapped or economically disadvantaged personnel undergo training. Local agencies also assist employers who want to participate in this program to find employees who will qualify for these credits.

4. *Veterans Acts*

   Employers who have federal contracts or subcontracts may be required to take steps to hire disabled, Vietnam, or other veterans. Many aspects of the Veterans Assistance Act of 1974 have lapsed, but businesses who contract with state or federal governmental agencies should determine if there are any affirmative action mandates still in effect.

EXHIBIT 13–5

Government Employment Regulations (continued)

Working Environment Regulations

5. *Occupational Safety and Health Act (OSHA)*

   This law requires employers to provide employees with a safe and healthy work environment. Standards are established by the Occupational Safety and Health Administration (OSHA) and its state counterparts in a wide range of areas, including protective garments, wash rooms, first aid services, heating and lighting, and so on. Additionally, OSHA provides for periodic government inspection of work places. Considerable recordkeeping and reporting requirements are established for illnesses and accidents.

6. *Labor Relations*

   There are a variety of laws that affect employer–employee relations, unionization, and so on. These statutes include the Taft-Hartley Act, Landrum-Griffin Act, National Labor Relations Act, and so on. However, not all employers are subject to such statutes.

Wage and Hour Laws

7. *Wage and Hour Laws*

   A variety of wage and hour laws apply to employers with specified numbers of employees and/or gross sales exceeding a designated amount. Minimum hourly wages have been established, with some provisions to pay lesser amounts to those in training programs or within certain age categories (for example, minors). The Fair Labor Standards Act requires employers to pay employees at a rate of one-and-one-half times regular wages for work in excess of 40 hours per week. Because wage and hour laws vary between states, the employer must determine the applicable regulations.

8. *Equal Pay Act*

   This federal law essentially requires employees to pay equivalent salaries for "substantially equal" work. Its particular concern is to prevent discriminatory pay for women or others who might be paid less than others for comparable work.

9. *Employee Retirement Income Security Act (ERISA)*

   Nearly all employers who offer benefit and pension plans will be affected by the Employee Retirement Income Security Act (ERISA). Regulations established by the federal government pertain to funding, accrual of benefits, vesting of benefits, and management of benefit and pension funds. Employers must also comply with certain governmental reporting requirements, and adequately inform their employees of the benefits available to them. ERISA does not require employers to provide pension plans and certain benefits to all employees. For example, relatively new and part-time employees may be excluded.

➤

EXHIBIT 13–5

Government Employment Regulations
(continued)

Taxation of Employers and Employees

10. *Federal Income Taxes*

Nearly all employers who pay wages or salaries to employees, or have employees who receive tips, will have to comply with federal income tax withholding. The company will have to obtain an employer identification number from an Internal Revenue Service (IRS) office, furnish employees with a withholding exemption certificate (W-4), and withhold money from employee wages at rates established by the IRS. Deductions will be taken from each paycheck during the course of the year. Employers will deposit these employee withholdings in approved banks or a Federal Reserve Bank, and then remit the money to the IRS at designated times. At the end of the year, the employer must provide the employee with a wage and earnings statement (W-2) showing the amount of wages earned and the amount of federal taxes withheld.

11. *Federal Insurance Compensation Act (FICA)*

Social security taxes (FICA) are applicable to all employers who pay wages or salaries that are taxable under federal law. Employers will have to withhold a specified percentage of an employee's wages for this tax, deposit it in an approved bank or a Federal Reserve Bank, and then remit the money at designated intervals to the IRS. There are limits to the amount that have to be contributed during the course of a year, and the employer will deduct the employee's share from each paycheck until that limit is reached. The amount held for FICA will be shown on the wages and earnings statement (W-2) at year end. Employers are required to match the contributions made by employees.

12. *Federal Unemployment Insurance (FUTA)*

Employers who hire people for a minimum specified number of weeks, or pay at least a set amount in wages per year, are subject to FUTA taxes. They are required to contribute a predetermined percentage of employees' wages for unemployment. These funds are paid into an authorized bank or Federal Reserve Bank on a quarterly basis. Unemployment insurance is administered by the state in conjunction with the federal government. The employer must file Form 940 for this tax.

13. *State Unemployment Insurance (SUI)*

Some states mandate that employers pay a payroll tax (SUI) equal to a set percentage of gross wages paid per employee. This money is paid to the state which administers unemployment benefits. The money is then placed into a fund for payment to those who have rightful claims for unemployment. The rate paid by the employer will be based on the amount drawn out of the fund by exemployees.

14. *State Workers Compensation Insurance*

Employers are required to contribute to a workmens' compensation insurance plan to cover their employees in the event of injuries on the job or suffering from job-related

EXHIBIT 13–5

Government Employment Regulations (continued)

illnesses. While this type of insurance is mandatory, it may be funded either through the state or by an approved private insurance plan. The rates charged to the employer are based on the number of employees and the relative riskiness of the jobs they perform.

15. *State Disability Insurance*

    Some states require employees to pay disability insurance from their wages. This is withheld in specific amounts from each paycheck. The program is administered by the state. Employees who suffer from nonwork related illnesses or injuries not covered by ERISA can receive benefits.

Step Eight. Actively orient employees to their new positions and to the company. Making individuals feel that they fit in as soon as possible is critical to long-term employee–employer relationships.

Step Nine. Train employees to do their jobs, and develop them for any planned advancements. Without an effective training program, none of the previous eight steps will be of much consequence.

Step Ten. Develop wage and benefit programs that are fair to the employees and affordable to the company. Wages should be competitive and commensurate with the tasks to be performed.

Step Eleven. Motivate employees and evaluate their activities. Being sensitive to their problems and complaints, and stimulating their productive efforts, is important to an effective and efficient operation. To the extent possible, try to make the personal objectives of employees attainable through helping the firm to achieve its goals.

Planning Work Force Requirements

Entrepreneurs should consider staffing to be one of their most important management functions. Since most employees are hired for the long term, building a competent work force whose objectives are compatible with those of the entrepreneur is a major determinant of the firm's ultimate success or failure.

As organizations grow, the structures and management skills needed change. Philip Knight, chairman of Nike, addressed these issues by saying: "I think that the management skills required at a company of a different size, at 10 million, 100 million . . . they're different, and to the extent that we grow this company . . . I think the skills will continue to be different. . . . We've tried to address that by bringing in different types of management skills at these different periods. . . ."[9]

The Role of Entrepreneurial Goals

The goals of the small business owner play a significant part in the staffing process. How big will the firm become? How many of the management activities will in time be passed to nonowners? Over which management processes will the owner want to keep personal control? These are issues only the entrepreneur can decide.

One exemplar of this is Judi Sheppard Missett. In 1969 she noticed that women in her jazz classes were not finding enjoyable ways to keep fit. Accordingly, she started offering a combination of jazz and exercise. After teaching every class by herself for five years, she began training others and ultimately franchised her business—Jazzercise.[10]

As the firm grows in size over time, the number of workers and managers must also increase, and authority must be delegated to others. Therefore, the entrepreneur needs to consider what types of jobs to create and what types of people to employ over both the short and long term.

Whittle communications

Changes occur in all facets of business. According to Christopher Whittle, chairman of Whittle Communications: "Businesses grow because people grow, and at the moment the business leader stops growing, the business stops growing." Whittle has plenty of experience with this—his publishing company has doubled in size every two years for the past 20 years.[11]

Personnel Policies

Of critical importance to the staffing process is establishing employment policies. With these, both the small business owner and prospective employees will understand what employment with the firm means. Some of the more important policy areas are:[12]

- *Hours*—a major issue is the number of hours to be worked per week, the number of days per week, evening and holiday work, and the time and method of payment for both regular and overtime work.
- *Compensation*—the bulk of a person's earnings come from a base salary or wage and incentives like commissions or bonuses. Competitive wages must be paid to attract and retain competent personnel. However, some balance must be maintained between what the firm has to pay and what it can afford to pay.
- *Fringe benefits*—health insurance, discounts on merchandise, pension plans, and other benefits can play a major role in staffing. They also can add between 20 percent and 40 percent to wages—making them extremely costly to the entrepreneur. A major problem in setting policies regarding fringe benefits occurs in firms in which there are wide disparities in income among employees. Minimim wage employees want immediate income to cover living expenses, while higher-paid managers prefer benefits that are tax-free. The high cost of health care benefits, in fact, has caused major shifts in who pays for fringe benefits and how much of the firm's budget can be devoted to them.[13]
- *Vacations*—how long will vacations be? When can they be taken? While it is important for employees to have vacation time, such scheduling cannot be allowed to disrupt the operation of the business.
- *Time off*—to what extent will employees be allowed time off for personal needs, emergencies, holidays, birthdays, and so on? As in the case of vacations, these are important, but can be disruptive to company operations.
- *Training*—each employee should be given adequate training for the job. In a small firm, responsibility for training often is vested in the owner, who may or may not be a good teacher.

- *Grievances*—conflicts with employees will occur. The best course of action is to plan for them and establish a procedure for handling grievances in an expeditious manner.
- *Promotion*—a major consideration in the staffing process is whether higher-level positions can be filled from within the firm. Promoting an insider as opposed to hiring an outsider is a sensitive matter, and one that impacts the firm's ability to retain good employees.
- *Personnel review*—will there be periodic reviews of employee performance? What factors will be included in such a review? How will the reviews be used? Evaluations are a sensitive matter, and must be conducted properly in order to minimize employee grievances and violations of employment laws.
- *Termination*—sooner or later, an employee will have to be discharged. To make the termination as clean as possible from both an operational and a legal standpoint, clear written policies must be developed. The entrepreneur should prepare policies concerning such matters as conditions warranting summary discharge, layoffs, seniority rights, and severance pay.

Developing Job Descriptions

Anyone who has ever had a job can probably remember the first day of work. Individuals are unsure of exactly what their jobs will be, whether they can handle the duties, what the working conditions will be like, and how they will be treated by fellow employees and the boss. For many, this is a terrifying experience.

Perhaps it also should be so for the entrepreneur. After all, any person being hired can significantly affect the immediate and future success or failure of the firm. A dishonest or incompetent employee can be very damaging. A top-notch one, on the other hand, can improve the firm's operations and profitability.

To reduce some of the trauma for the prospective employee, and to increase the chances of hiring the right individual, a job description should be developed for each position within the company. This will be beneficial in the hiring process and help to keep job functions from changing unintentionally over time.[14]

A **job description** is a statement that identifies what the job consists of and what qualifications are needed to perform the task satisfactorily. Specifically, it answers the following questions:

- What is the employee to do? What activities are part of the job? How much authority and responsibility are included? Where does this job fit within the organizational structure? (For example, who reports to the jobholder, to whom does the jobholder report.)
- What qualifications are needed for this job? Are any special skills involved? Is any experience needed? What personal characteristics, if any, are required—physical, mental, or emotional?

A sample job description is provided in Exhibit 13–6. Not only does a description serve as an initial screening process for would-be applicants, it also better defines each activity within the firm itself. Most important, it tells the applicant what the job consists

EXHIBIT 13–6 **Sample Job Description**

Position: Office Manager

Reports To: General Manager

Supervises: Secretarial and clerical personnel, bookkeeper and/or accountants

Primary Function: The office manager is responsible for maintaining accurate and current records to be used for internal management decision-making and outside reporting as required by law. He or she processes purchase orders and creditor claims and performs normal clerical and recordkeeping duties.

Principal Duties: The duties of the office manager, with whom authority and responsibility are vested, are to:

1. Secure the department in such a manner so as to reduce the risks of robbery, theft, disaster, and accidents,
2. In coordination with the general manager, develop operating objectives and budgets for the department,
3. Provide financial records to the general manager relative to budget expenditures and revenues,
4. Maintain all financial records pertaining to the pharmacy's operations, including the basic books of record:
   - general journal,
   - purchases journal,
   - cash disbursements journal,
   - sales journal,
   - cash receipts journal.

of, and what will be expected of the employee who fills the position. Similarly, it tells the entrepreneur what kind of individual to look for.

Working Conditions and OSHA

The conditions under which any employee—temporary or permanent—will be expected to carry out an assignment should be clearly delineated, especially in instances in which conditions are dangerous, dirty, or difficult. Nobody likes those kinds of surprises.

The Work Environment

Providing an environment conducive to good work should be of prime concern to the small business owner. Work areas that are properly lighted, free from disruptive noises, neither too hot nor too cold, and equipped with proper rest facilities serve to improve employee morale and productivity. The physical layout should be planned to follow standard work flows, as described in Chapter 21.

Safety also must be considered. Cluttered rooms or walkways, poor lighting, faulty wiring, machinery without safety guards, and so on, increase the likelihood of accidents. Lost employees often mean decreased productivity, and the costs can be high. In addition, most states require employers to carry workers' compensation insurance, and as accident rates climb, so do the insurance premiums.

Occupational Safety and Health Act

The Occupational Safety and Health Act is a federal statute enacted in 1970 "to assure so far as possible every working man and woman in the nation safe and healthy working conditions and to preserve our human resources." To maintain this protection, the **Occupational Safety and Health Administration (OSHA)** was created within the Department of Labor and applies to any employer "engaged in a business affecting commerce who has employees."

In addition to establishing standards, OSHA sends inspectors to business establishments to determine whether work conditions could cause employee death or physical harm. This can only be done, however, with the owner's permission or a search warrant. In the past, emphasis was given to safety standards, but recent focus has been on the realm of employee health. In addition to making unannounced visits, OSHA requires businesses to keep records on all injuries or illnesses that result in:

- Death,
- One or more lost workdays,
- Restriction of work or motion,
- Loss of consciousness,
- Transfer to another job,
- Medical treatment other than first aid, and
- Illnesses caused by exposure to environmental factors associated with acute and chronic diseases.

RECRUITING AND SELECTING EMPLOYEES

Recruitment and selection of employees have become some of the more complex elements of the staffing process in most small businesses. Errors made in hiring can have a significant impact on the firm's ability to survive—it cannot afford to hire a few bad employees before finding "Mr. or Ms. Right."

Recruiting Applicants

A common misconception among some small business owners is that it is easy to find qualified employees. This is considered especially true during times of high unemployment when workers supposedly are readily available.

Unfortunately, most well-qualified people are already working for others. It is not likely that a host of top-notch applicants will come running as soon as a "help wanted" sign is placed in the company's window, or an advertisement is placed in the local newspaper. Some excellent employees are hired as a result of these approaches, but generally they are ineffective for finding highly talented people.

Modern staffing requires serious consideration of where good prospects are likely to be, and development of an active **employee recruitment** effort. Some of the most common sources of potential employees are described below.

Company Employees

One of the most readily available sources of applicants is the firm's labor force. If the job opening represents an advancement in terms of added responsibility and prestige, more money, and/or better working conditions, one of the present employees may want to take the job.

This approach can serve as an incentive to capable employees, and it takes some of the guesswork out of the hiring process because many of the applicant's strengths and weaknesses are already known. The disadvantage of this method is that a new employee must be hired to fill the position vacated by the advancing employee.

Referrals

Once an entrepreneur lets it be known to friends, business associates, employees, and acquaintances that a position is open, names of potential prospects may be offered. Employees, friends, relatives, and others may know of people who are qualified and seeking employment. Such referrals often turn out to be good prospects. Most people will not recommend individuals they know to be inept, and they usually are willing to pass on more information about the individual than could be obtained through normal letters of reference.

There are dangers to this approach, however. An individual who recommends a friend may intentionally or unintentionally make the candidate look better than he or she really is. Most people see only certain aspects of other individuals, and as such are not qualified to give a full professional appraisal of the candidate. Accepting a recommendation from a relative or friend may create problems if the applicant is not qualified, or is hired and must be dismissed soon thereafter. Hiring a friend of another employee can create an internal clique that in time might be difficult to deal with. In a small business with few employees, two close friends can have a monumental impact on the firm's operations.

Employees of Other Companies

Recruiting employees from other companies has long been a method of staffing, although it raises ethical considerations the owner must personally reconcile. Nevertheless, hiring an employee from a competitor has some advantages: it brings a well-qualified person who knows the business and the competition, and it hurts the competitor.

It is also common to recruit people from noncompeting firms. Since the entrepreneur deals directly with many other companies in the daily course of business, it is possible to identify excellent prospects who are working for suppliers, customers, and so on. Over time, the entrepreneur may develop a reasonably good assessment of an individual's qualifications and keep these in mind for future personnel needs. Of course, taking a good employee away from a customer may not be ethical, and almost certainly it is not good business.

Employment Agencies

There are two types of employment agencies, public and private. Public agencies are operated by each state, typically have geographically dispersed offices, and maintain lists of individuals seeking employment and their respective qualifications. Positions ranging from unskilled to professional often can be filled through public agencies. A prime benefit of this approach is that it is free to both the firm and the applicant.

Private employment agencies also maintain lists of individuals looking for jobs. Many applicants go to private agencies because they feel, correctly or not, that they will get more personalized service and better jobs than they would through public employment agencies. In any event, these private services screen applicants and send to the firm only people they feel are qualified. These agencies charge a fee for their services, which is typically either a flat rate or a percentage of the applicant's income. Depending on the circumstances, either the firm or the new employee will pay the fee.

Educational Institutions

High schools, vocational and trade schools, and colleges and universities can be sources of potential employees. When an owner-manager is seeking unskilled labor needing little in the way of specialized education or experience, high school placement offices can be of assistance. Vocational or trade schools are sources of employees trained in some particular skill. They specialize in trades such as electronics, computer programming, engineering, automobile repair, photography, and dog grooming.

For the more highly skilled positions, colleges and universities maintain free placement offices and facilities to help employers find qualified individuals. Many small business owners have found that college students trying to work their way through school are a source of excellent part-time assistance.

Labor Unions

In some cases, the entrepreneur may seek the aid of labor unions in finding qualified employees. Many unions maintain lists of members who are seeking jobs, and will readily assist the small business owner in finding an applicant who fits the need. This approach ordinarily is used only when the entrepreneur's employees are or will be members of a union.

Advertising

Advertising that a position is open is one way of reaching the full spectrum of possible applicants. The extent and placement of the advertisement depend on the type of individual desired. While most people tend to think of local newspapers, this is an alternative that is best suited for less-skilled labor. Advertising in trade journals and other periodicals can be an effective method of recruiting applicants for high-level and/or highly technical positions.

Although advertising is used frequently, some small business owners have not been especially pleased with the results. Often, people apply who do not have the appropriate skills, or they are more interested in short-term employment.

Drop-Ins

A "help wanted" sign in a firm's window is a specialized form of advertising. On rare occasions this is worthwhile, especially when one is looking for unskilled or part-time labor. Generally, however, the approach of waiting for the right person to come in is inefficient and ineffective. It takes too long and often results in hiring less-than-optimal people.

Selecting an Employee

The entrepreneur must have a procedure for screening applicants—a means of sorting out the qualified from the unqualified. An established procedure ensures that all relevant questions are asked and important information is obtained. Perhaps even more importantly, it ensures that the entrepreneur or a manager will not ask questions that are discriminatory, and thereby put the firm at risk for a lawsuit (see Exhibit 13–7).

A well-prepared process for selecting an employee also makes the entrepreneur and the firm look good. The owner does not want to scare off promising applicants by appearing disorganized or being an inept businessperson. Since most applicants come with the hope and expectation of a long-term relationship, they will be assessing the firm and the entrepreneur—just as the entrepreneur will be appraising the applicant.

The selection procedure need not be overly complicated, but it should be standardized to the extent possible. The basic procedure consists of six steps, some of which can be undertaken simultaneously:

Step One. Provide the applicant with an application form.
Step Two. Review the completed application form and conduct a personal interview.
Step Three. Check the references provided by the more promising applicants.
Step Four. Administer a battery of skill and/or personality tests to the more promising applicants.
Step Five. Have the most promising applicant(s) take a physical examination.
Step Six. Decide which, if any, of the applicants to hire.

EXHIBIT 13–7 **Employment Questions That Cannot Be Asked**

Maiden name
Own or rent a home
Age, date of birth, dates attended school
Birthplace, whether has citizenship
Nationality, ancestry, national origin
Sex
Marital status
Family status, number of children, ages of children
Pregnancy, child bearing, birth control
Height, weight
General medical condition
Religion
Military service record
Arrest record
Membership in nonjob-related organizations
Current or past assets, liabilities, credit rating

The Application Form

In most instances, the entrepreneur will not know anything about the people who apply for a job. Thus, the entrepreneur needs a mechanism to provide at least a basic sketch of the individual and his or her background and qualifications. The easiest method for doing this is to have the applicant complete an **application for employment** form. Although there is some variation among application forms, nearly all contain questions about personal information, references, educational background, work history, and space for the employer/interviewer's comments.

Personal information typically requested from the applicant includes name, address, telephone number, Social Security number, and physical characteristics that are important to performing the job. Importantly, the application cannot ask questions pertaining to sex, age, race, and other matters that may be deemed discriminatory.

Most application forms request the names, addresses, and telephone numbers of people who will supply additional information on the applicant, or vouch for the individual's moral character and/or qualifications. While these should be checked, they cannot be given too much weight unless the references are of known stature. Since most individuals will list only people who will provide good recommendations, these cannot be taken as definitive measures.

A listing of the applicant's educational background is useful for two reasons. First, it is a measure of the individual's professional qualifications. The second reason for asking for educational background is to be able to trace the individual's movements since high school. This helps create a total perspective on the applicant. Frequent changes in colleges, for example, may be indicative of a wandering nature, immaturity, or a less-than-brilliant mind. Employment laws preclude asking for dates of attendance or the year in which the individual graduated.

For reasons similar to those of educational background, the applicant's work history should be traced. How far back it should be traced depends on the desires of the owner. Some entrepreneurs want a listing of every full- and part-time job ever held. Others want only the last two or three positions. The types of positions held and the reasons for leaving are important to the screening process.

A personal interview with each person, who appears to be qualified based on the application form, is essential. This allows an interchange of questions between employer and applicant. (Photograph © Ann M. Mason)

On receiving the completed application form, the small business owner should examine the information and note any pertinent data. Questions for future interviews also should be noted.

Conducting Personal Interviews

For applicants who appear to be qualified based on the application form, a personal interview with each is essential. This allows the entrepreneur to ask more questions, clarify existing ones noted on the application form, and simply gain a more complete general impression of the individual. In addition, it provides an opportunity for the applicant to ask questions and decide whether he or she wants to work for the company.

Since interviews are hardly conducive to a relaxing and casual chat, the entrepreneur must try to make applicants feel at ease so they can speak freely. Based on the applicant's answers and questions, the small business owner should be in a better position to appraise the individual's qualifications. Sample questions to include in the interview are shown in Exhibit 13–8.

Checking the Applicant's Past

Verifying the applicant's statements on the application form as well as from the personal interview is critical. Any serious errors or omissions may indicate that the

EXHIBIT 13–8 **Information to Obtain about Potential Employees**

Questions to Ask Applicants

1. Why are you applying here?
2. Why should this company hire you?
3. With respect to employment, what do you want to be doing five years from now?
4. What do you know about this company? This industry?
5. What are your greatest strengths? Weaknesses?
6. Why are you leaving your present job?
7. With respect to your employment, what accomplishment are you most proud of?

What to Watch for

1. Several jobs in a short period of time.
2. Formal education and grades received.
3. Career and personal goals.
4. Health problems that could restrict ability to perform job.
5. Reasons for leaving present job.
6. Ability to get along with people with diverse personalities.
7. Communication skills.
8. Knowledge of the industry and the job.
9. Energy level.
10. Appearance.
11. Willingness to perform menial tasks.
12. Priorities between work and play.
13. Maturity.

individual is undesirable. This includes a check on personal references and previous schools and employers.

The value of personal references has been called into question by many entrepreneurs, since court rulings in the 1980s made written reference checks available to the applicant, opening up the possibility of lawsuits in the instance of unfavorable comments. Because of this, many people will not provide written statements. In such cases, personal telephone calls or visits are preferable. The entrepreneur should be on the lookout for vague recommendations and anything else that is less than a glowing endorsement.

Administering Employment Tests

There are essentially two types of tests that can be used in the screening process. One is a job proficiency examination, in which the applicant is given an opportunity to demonstrate occupational skills. Typing tests, bookkeeping questions, demonstrations of ability to operate machinery, and so on, are frequently used.

The second type of test includes a series of psychologically related examinations. These include aptitude, personality, and vocational interest tests. They can be administered by the entrepreneur, but are most often handled by a paid professional who will both administer and interpret the test. Because of the complexity of interpretation and the costs, small business owners tend to use psychological tests only for top managers in especially critical positions.

Requiring a Physical Examination

Although most small businesses do not employ physicians, it is wise on occasion to make arrangements with a local physician to examine an applicant before hiring. A medical history may be required for employee medical insurance or workers' compensation. To some extent, too, the entrepreneur then is protected from being charged for injuries that occurred before the employee came to work for the firm. Because the employer usually must pay for the physical, it should be provided only for the individual likely to be hired.

Making a Selection

Selection of an applicant should be the culmination of an intensive search and screening process, and based on the objective data collected and the entrepreneur's intuitive judgment. Throughout this procedure, the small business owner must be using a process of elimination (that is, each step in the process should result in fewer and fewer applications still under consideration), and trying to sell the applicants on the benefits of coming to work for the company.

Eventually, some decision must be made. If one applicant is selected, procedures should be established to inform the others and present the firm in the best light while maintaining the dignity of those not selected. Names of applicants who were not hired may be retained in a file for future consideration.

Importantly, too, the small business owner may decide that none of the applicants suits the company's needs. Selecting the best of a group of undesirable applicants is rarely a good decision. Instead, the process of searching and screening should be reviewed and repeated if no procedural flaws are discovered. Temporary help can be used as an interim measure.

Using Temporary Help

Another aspect of work force planning, and an important concern in the overall staffing process, is the possible use of **temporary help.** In some instances, it may be preferable to use part- or full-time people on a very short-term basis.[15] This commonly occurs when the business is highly seasonal—Christmas season for department stores and the summer for food processors—or when regular employees quit or are fired, ill, or on vacation. From time to time, most entrepreneurs find themselves with too few employees but are unsure whether to hire additional ones on a regular basis.

One company that specializes in providing executives and middle management is the Corporate Staff, based in San Francisco. With a pool of over 2,000 managers with at least ten years of experience in their fields, the company provides skilled personnel at rates ranging from $30 to $90 per hour in 1989, and the employer usually does not have to pay fringe benefits. Many of the personnel are consultants, early retirees, and women with families who want project-oriented assignments rather than full-time work.[16]

The use of temporary personnel might not be desirable if it becomes a regular part of the business. It may hamper efforts to attract good permanent employees, and the time spent orienting new people for short-time employment tends to be excessive for the benefits received.

Nevertheless, temporary help does offer the entrepreneur flexibility in coordinating short- and long-term work force needs. As an interim or emergency approach, it can be very valuable.

The financial aspects of hiring short-term personnel are also important. On the surface, it may appear that using temporary personnel costs more than hiring additional employees. However, this might not be the case, since such mandatory costs as Social Security, unemployment insurance, and workers' compensation can amount to between 10 and 15 percent of the basic wage. Payment for time not worked, including vacations, holidays, and sick days, amounts to another 10 to 12 percent of wages. Then there are company-paid benefits such as health insurance, pension plans, discounts, recordkeeping, payroll, and other paperwork, which can add another 5 to 10 percent to wages. Total hidden costs, therefore, may run between 25 and 40 percent. Therefore, a $10 per hour wage could cost the company $12.50 to $14.00—or $100 to $160 extra per week.

People supplied by a temporary help service ordinarily are readily available. Usually they can start the day after the request has been made, and in some cases can even be available the same day. If they are experienced and well qualified, they might be able to walk in and function right away. Some agencies specialize in specific occupational categories, such as legal secretaries or medical personnel. Others offer a wider selection, including office workers (for example, stenographers, secretaries, bookkeepers), industrial labor (for example, work crews, truck drivers), marketing (for example, demonstration personnel, interviewers for research projects), and technical (for example, accounting, drafting, engineering) personnel.

SUMMARY

1. A proper organizational structure will help a firm survive by ensuring that tasks are completed and a foundation is laid for future growth.
2. Line and line-and-staff structures are forms of organization based on authority relationships. Line management involves generalists, while

line-and-staff involves both generalists and specialists.

3. Due to human nature, informal organizations develop within the firm despite attempts to the contrary. An attempt should be made to blend this informal structure into the formal structure of the firm.
4. The basic process of organizing involves clearly defining goals, identifying and defining jobs, grouping tasks into units, assigning managers with the necessary authority and responsibility to those units, arranging groups relative to each other, and establishing control measures over those groups.
5. The grouping of jobs depends on the business and industry as well as the personal preferences of the entrepreneur. The most common methods of grouping are time, number, function, product, territory, customer, project, or a combination of methods.
6. Job descriptions are beneficial to the hiring process and help keep job functions from changing unintentionally over time.
7. The Occupational Safety and Health Act (OSHA) was enacted to protect the working population from unhealthy and dangerous working conditions.
8. The employee selection process starts with finding prospective employees. Several sources include company employees, referrals, employees of other companies, employment agencies, educational institutions, labor unions, advertising, and drop-ins.
9. In selecting possible employees, the entrepreneur must be organized and follow an established procedure that ensures that all relevant information is obtained, and no employment laws are violated.
10. Most applications for employment contain five sections: personal information, references, educational background, work history, and employer comments.
11. After receiving and reviewing the applications, the entrepreneur should conduct personal interviews, verify the applicant's past, administer any employment tests desired, and request that the applicant have a physical examination.
12. The use of temporary help provides the entrepreneur with flexibility in coordinating short- and long-term work force needs.

KEY TERMS AND CONCEPTS

Organization
Parity of authority and responsibility
Unity of command
Unity of direction
Scalar chain
Span of control
Delegation of authority
Line organization
Line-and-staff organization
Informal organization
Profit centers
Job description
Occupational Safety and Health Act (OSHA)
Employee recruitment
Application for employment
Employment tests
Temporary help

QUESTIONS FOR DISCUSSION

1. Discuss the importance of an organizational structure for a small firm.
2. What relationship exists between authority and responsibility?
3. What problems can occur when an established chain of command is violated?
4. What is the significance of the key factors in determining span of control?
5. Compare and contrast the merits of line-and-staff organization and line organization for the small business.
6. What are the important considerations in the basic process of organizing?
7. How often should a firm evaluate its organizational structure?
8. What steps are involved in the basic staffing process?

9. Name some common sources for potential employees.
10. What steps should be considered when selecting the most qualified applicant for the job?
11. What are the functions and benefits of a formal job description?
12. What is OSHA and what is its purpose?
13. Name the sections contained on an application form, and briefly discuss their relevance.
14. Explain the factors the entrepreneur should consider in making the final selection of an employee.
15. Name two ways of acquiring temporary help.

SELF-TEST REVIEW

Multiple Choice Questions

1. Which of the following is a true statement?
   a. Each employee should be given responsibility to perform a task even if not given commensurate authority.
   b. Each employee should always report to only one superior.
   c. Each job should be narrowly defined and highly specialized.
   d. The number of people a manager can effectively control increases at higher levels within the organization.
2. Which of the following is the most common structure in small businesses that have experienced a reasonable degree of success and growth?
   a. Functional.
   b. Line.
   c. Line and staff.
   d. None of the above is more common.
3. For most small businesses, an in-depth organizational appraisal should be made:
   a. Once a year.
   b. Once every two years.
   c. Only in times when performance is poor.
   d. Only in times of change or crisis.
4. Which of the following is not true about the staffing process?
   a. It is closely intertwined with company objectives.
   b. It is typically a short-term process.
   c. It can usually be accomplished quickly and easily.
   d. All of the above are true.
5. Employment tests designed to measure an applicant's occupational skills are:
   a. Aptitude tests.
   b. Job proficiency tests.
   c. Personality tests.
   d. Vocational interest tests.

True/False Statements

1. Organization refers to the defined structure of the activities, processes, and people who make up a business.
2. As an entrepreneur decreases the number of managers, he or she also decreases the span of control.
3. If recognized and contended with in a positive manner, informal groups can be valuable resources to the business.
4. Organizing by number is an effective method of dealing with heterogeneous groups of employees.
5. A common error in planning organizational structure is to give employees diverse areas of responsibility.
6. Job descriptions should be developed only for non-management positions in the small firm.
7. It is easy to find top-quality staff during periods of high unemployment.
8. Waiting for the right person to drop in is an efficient and effective approach to finding most employees.
9. Psychologically related employment tests are costly, but commonly used by small business owners.
10. Public employment agencies typically charge high fees for their services.

DOWNS ELECTRONICS

David Platz, executive vice president of Downs Electronics, has just been put in charge of a task force to review the company's organizational structure. The company has experienced rapid growth for the last two years, and Larry Downs, president of Downs Electronics, feels that such a reassessment is needed.

Despite a 72 percent increase in sales, profits have risen only 9 percent and the company's administrative expenses have nearly doubled. Both Platz and Downs believe that the sudden growth has created a variety of operating inefficiencies. Accordingly, Platz and the office manager and plan manager have been asked to make recommendations on how to improve the company's organization, as a first step in an intensive review of every facet of Downs Electronics' operations.

Downs Electronics is a small, relatively new manufacturer of specialized circuit boards. Located in the western United States, the company produces circuit boards under government contracts directly and as a subcontractor for larger electronics firms situated in the West and South exclusively. Recognized as a high-quality producer, Downs Electronics has found itself in the position of being able to sell all it can manufacture. Downs and Platz therefore have embarked on an expansion program through the purchase of more advanced machinery and the hiring of 75 more people, 17 of whom are electronics professionals. This has increased the company's physical production capabilities by 90 percent.

Along with the increased production capabilities, Downs and Platz have planned for the time when demand for the company's products will level off. Not wanting to be left with larger capacity and higher overhead costs, they have created a small research and development department to explore new areas for production, and have added the manufacture of plastic casing for electronic products to their product line. They have also enlarged the salesforce by six people to sell their new capabilities and cultivate future goodwill.

Both Downs and Platz consider this buildup to be an investment in the company's future, and they anticipate some growing pains as a result. They feel that it is best to take these steps now, while the company has a good inflow of revenues. Nevertheless, they also want to minimize inefficiencies and lost profits.

As Platz and other members of the task force begin to examine the organization of the company, they realize that the original structure, shown in Exhibit A, is no longer being utilized. Accordingly, they are attempting to define the actual organization of Downs Electronics at this point in time. To the

EXHIBIT A

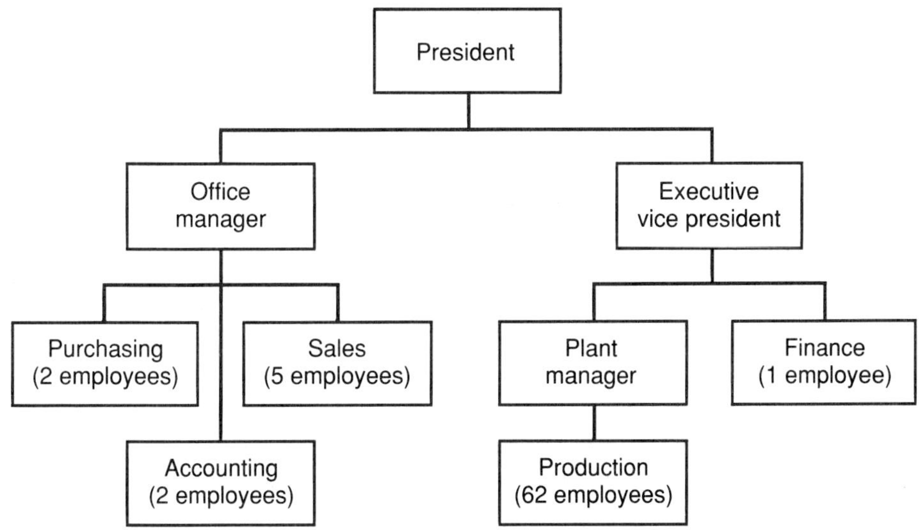

EXHIBIT B

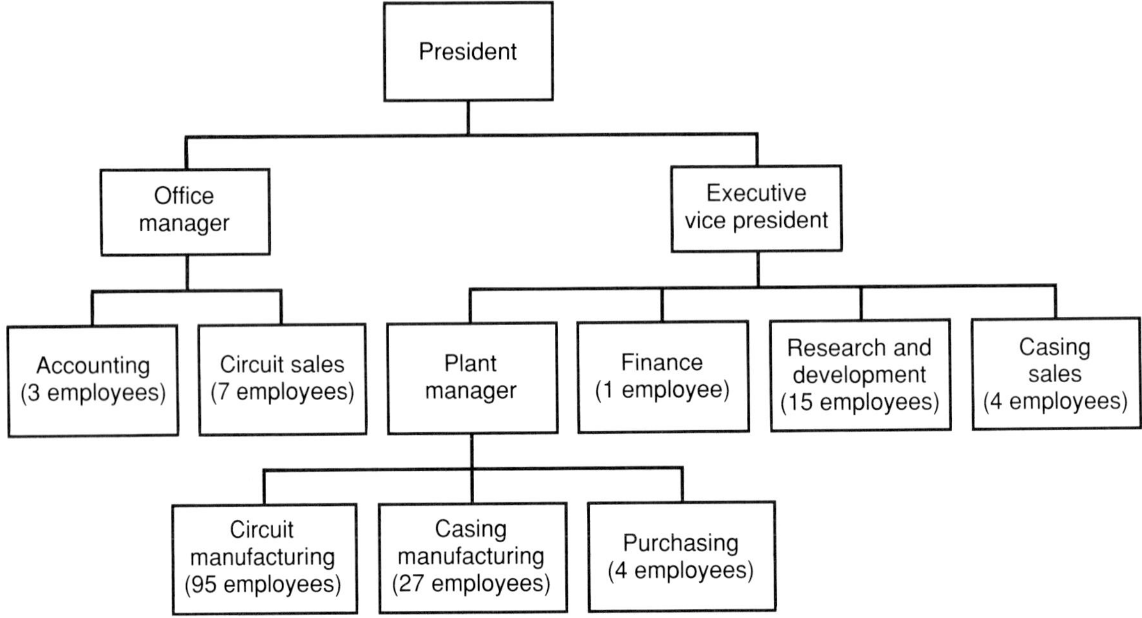

best of their knowledge, a more realistic depiction of the operations of the company is shown in Exhibit B. No one is quite sure how the new structure evolved, but everyone agrees that it happened more by chance than by conscious decision.

With this framework in mind, the members of the task force have decided to evaluate the new organizational structure to see if it is more suitable for the company than the one established years earlier. They also agree that changes can be made in the existing structure as necessary.

QUESTIONS

1. What problems, if any, exist in the original organizational structure of Downs Electronics (Exhibit A)?
2. What changes should be made in the company's present organizational structure (Exhibit B)? What should the new organizational chart look like?

NOTES

1. "Traumas of a New Entrepreneur," *The Wall Street Journal,* May 10, 1989, B1.
2. Based on Cable News Network's "Pinnacle," June 14, 1987. Guest: John Rollwagen, Cray Research.
3. "An Expansionary Tale," *The Wall Street Journal,* May 15, 1987, 5D, 8D.
4. Based on Cable News Network's "Pinnacle," March 11, 1989. Guest: Ronald Rule, U.S. Playing Card.
5. Harold Koontz, Cyril O'Donnell, Heinz Weihrich, *Essentials of Management* (New York: McGraw–Hill, 1982).
6. "Is Your Company Too Big?" *Business Week,* March 27, 1989, 84–94.
7. Peter Pae, "Big-Company Tactics Spur Turnaround at Small Firm," *The Wall Street Journal,* August 15, 1989, B1.
8. Based on Cable News Network's "Pinnacle," June 18, 1989. Guest: Jim Manzi, Lotus Development.
9. Based on Cable News Network's "Pinnacle," March 22, 1987. Guest: Philip Knight, Nike.
10. "Companies To Watch—Jazzercise," *Fortune,* April 10, 1989, 90.

11. Based on Cable News Network's "Pinnacle," March 4, 1989. Guest: Christopher Whittle, Whittle Communications.
12. Walter E. Green, Small Business Administration, *Staffing Your Store,* Management Aid No. 5.007.
13. "Patient Data May Reshape Health Care," *The Wall Street Journal,* April 17, 1989, B1.
14. Bank of America, "Personnel Guidelines," *Small Business Reporter,* 1985.
15. William Olsten, Small Business Administration, *Pointers on Using Temporary Help Services,* Management Aid No. 5.004.
16. "For Rent: Experienced Executives," *Insight,* March 20, 1989, 42.

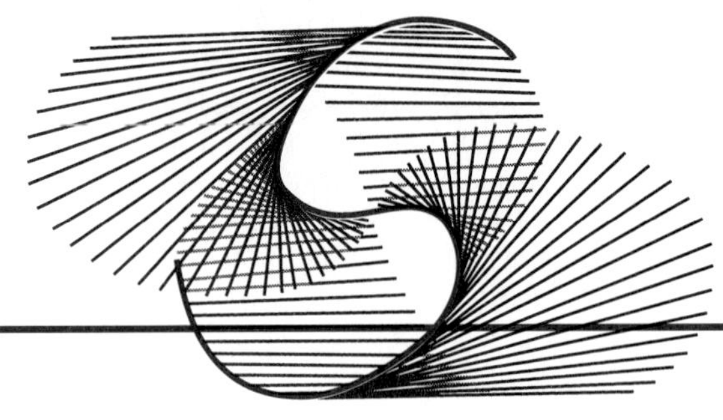

CHAPTER FOURTEEN

Accounting and Financial Records

CHAPTER OUTLINE

WHY KEEP RECORDS?
- Records for Internal Purposes
- Records for External Purposes

FINANCIAL RECORDS
- Necessary Attributes of an Accounting System
- Basic Books for Recordkeeping
- Financial Statements

HOW TO KEEP RECORDS
- Recording Information
- Maintaining the Books

SUMMARY

LEARNING OBJECTIVES *The objectives of this chapter are to assist you in understanding:*

1. Why records are kept for a small business.
2. What the basic books for recordkeeping are.
3. What financial statements must be prepared and what they consist of.
4. How financial records are kept.
5. How financial records are maintained.

There is an old saying in business, "If you sell your products below cost, you can't make it up on volume." Entrepreneurs often look only at the sales level of their firms for indications of success or failure. "We had a good month" generally refers to how fast and at what volume the merchandise or service was sold. What these small business owners do not realize is that the key issue is how much profit they made. It may be, for example, that it cost the business more to operate, more to promote, and more payroll dollars than the added sales volume provided. Good financial records can resolve this and other issues associated with developing profitable businesses.

Entrepreneurs must come to grips with the concept that profit is a function of revenues minus costs, and that costs need to be monitored just as sales do. Many small business owners do not know their costs of doing business, or whether they are making profits or incurring losses. They often have no way of developing exact reports on costs, revenues, and profits or losses.

It is not uncommon to find "checkbook businesses"—businesses whose financial transactions are contained in the entrepreneur's personal checkbook. Business transactions conducted in this manner may become almost impossible to separate from personal transactions. A typical dilemma is: "Was that $25.95 check to K Mart for office supplies or for a wading pool for the kids?"

SIX FLAGS

The importance of having a financial background was described by Larry Cochran, chief executive officer of Six Flags theme park, "I never in college or high school had an accounting course. . . . Everything I know financially is self-taught . . . if I had my life to live over and my college career and high school I would have taken more financial courses."[1]

WHY KEEP RECORDS?

Many entrepreneurs wonder why the lack of records is bad and why a personal checkbook cannot be used for business transactions. Since they own the business, who cares if expenses are all mixed together? For one, the Internal Revenue Service (IRS) cares. Declaring a $25.95 wading pool as a business expense violates tax laws. IRS agents will want clearly detailed accounts of the activities of the business. Creditors and potential lenders also care about the state of the firm's records. They want to see how profitable the company is—without wading pools, underwear, and groceries. Finally, the entrepreneur should care if the business is run properly. Records provide a visual and permanent basis for observing the operation of the company, and are a management tool for sound decision making.

GOLDEN DOOR®

RANCHO LA PUERTA®

Some very successful entrepreneurs, of course, have difficulty with the financial aspects of their companies. For example, Deborah Szekely, founder of the Golden Door health resort, commented, "Look at the bottom line? My CPA used to say I just couldn't focus. My husband called me a disaster with figures. Thank God my son isn't. You know, I'll add [some things] . . . and not subtract anything and that upsets CPAs. . . . I have been comfortable in my ignorance."[2]

Good records are needed for both internal and external purposes.[3] The types of books needed for internal management, however, might be different from those called for by outside creditors. It is not uncommon to find entrepreneurs who maintain two sets of books. One highlights management decision areas, and another is for outside sources. While often thought to be indicative of unscrupulous business practices, the use of two systems may instead signify sound management.

One example of this is the use of different approaches to valuing inventory. For tax purposes, it may be best to use a LIFO (last in, first out) method, in which the value is based on the most recent acquisition costs of the merchandise. For internal use, however, the firm may use a FIFO (first in, first out) method—using the actual acquisition costs at the time the merchandise was purchased. The key point is that the types of records needed by the IRS, lending institutions, and others may not be suitable for management decision making.

Records for Internal Purposes

Sound business management relies not only on good executive judgment, but also on high-quality and timely data with which judgments can be made. Internal records for these purposes typically center on keeping track of revenues and expenses.

Records on the generation of revenue by the business may include information on who made purchases, how much was purchased in both quantity and monetary terms, and when the purchases occurred. For a small business, this information can be used to identify more important customers and their buying patterns. For example, some buyers may purchase in large quantities during certain months, while others may buy in small quantities on a more frequent basis. Knowing that a customer purchased large amounts in June will help the entrepreneur schedule sales calls, production, labor, purchases of materials, and so on.

With the following basic records, an accounting system can be created:[4]

- *Cash receipts journal*—used to record the cash that comes into the business,
- *Cash disbursements journal*—used to record the business' expenditures,
- *Sales journal*—used to record and summarize monthly revenues,
- *Purchases journal*—used to record purchases of merchandise bought for processing or resale,
- *Payroll*—used to record employee wages and deductions, such as those for income and Social Security taxes,
- *Equipment*—a record of the firm's capital assets, such as equipment, office furniture, and motor vehicles,
- *Inventory*—a record of the firm's investment in merchandise and parts, which is needed for arriving at a true profit on financial statements and for income tax purposes,
- *Accounts receivable ledger*—used to record the balances that customers owe the firm,
- *Accounts payable ledger*—used to record what the firm owes its suppliers and other creditors.

The mainstay of a sound internal recordkeeping system is the company budget, which is described in Chapter 15. Since the budget essentially is a quantified planning and controlling device, it must be kept current and evaluated often. Is the sales volume where it should be? Is too much or too little being spent on inventory for the level of sales being generated? Are office expenses too high for the sales volume?

These and other questions need to be answered if the entrepreneur and the firm are to achieve their goals. In addition, any "yes" answer to one or more of these questions must be followed up with "why?" and "what is the impact?" Answers to the latter two questions may not be contained in the financial records of the company. Nevertheless, finding that something is amiss requires sound recordkeeping. From that point, the entrepreneur can take the necessary steps to correct the situation.

Records for External Purposes

Records must be maintained to satisfy local, state, and federal agencies, as well as customers and creditors. Depending on the type of business and its location, the amount of data required will vary. If for no other purpose, detailed records on revenues and expenses need to be maintained for the IRS and the state tax agency.

In addition to government requirements, creditors may well demand periodic reports on the financial position of the company. Some commercial lending institutions, for example, want from their borrowers quarterly, semiannual, or annual reports of income and assets and liabilities. For the small business that requests a loan, these statements are mandatory not only for the current period, but most likely for previous years. It is rare for a commercial lender to provide funds without these reports.

Businesses that are incorporated will have to file a number of statements for tax and other purposes at both the federal and state levels. Complete financial disclosure will be needed if the firm's stock is traded nationally.

Recognition of what data is necessary and useful in this regard is important. Although in some instances the records needed for external purposes may differ substantially from those wanted for internal management, in most cases they can be blended to serve both purposes simultaneously. This eases the recordkeeping burden and expense.

FINANCIAL RECORDS

Many small business owners do not keep their own books. Instead, they hire a certified public accountant (CPA) or bookkeeping service to record and prepare their statements. Even if the entrepreneur does not physically undertake the accounting functions, it is critical that he or she understand the meaning of the reports that are generated.

Necessary Attributes of an Accounting System

Developing a set of financial records is the entrepreneur's responsibility. Only in this way is there any guarantee that the books will be understood and used in the process of managing the firm. Therefore, the financial recordkeeping system must be geared, within limits, to the needs of the owner and other managers who use financial information.

While certain conventions in recordkeeping must be adhered to, the system itself can be fairly closely tailored to the individual entrepreneur and to the company in general. Most of the material presented in this chapter deals with standard approaches to bookkeeping systems.

A good recordkeeping process should serve the entrepreneur by being:

- Simple to understand,
- Flexible and adaptable to the changing needs of the entrepreneur and the firm,
- Inexpensive to operate,
- Not excessively time-consuming to maintain,
- Handy and convenient to use for internal and external purposes.

For a bookkeeping system to be valuable, it should be as simple as possible. Otherwise, its value will be impaired and it will fade into obscurity. Sophisticated terminology can be replaced with more pedestrian language. *Owner's equity*, for instance, may be changed to *owner's investment in the firm*. Similarly, buzz words can take the place of more conventional terms if they aid in clarity and are defined. Generalized entries also can be broken down into their component parts so that the entrepreneur can readily see what each entry contains. *Prepaid expenses*, for example, can be itemized out on the balance sheet to show advance payments for insurance, advertising, and other expenses, if this helps simplify the process and makes the reports more understandable and usable.

A second attribute of a good bookkeeping system is its flexibility and adaptability to change. As a small business grows, the types of entries in the financial records may have to be altered. This usually is handled by adding categories to account for new or different types of customers and/or goods and services produced and sold. Space should be left for such additions. When setting up the system, one should give consideration to the categories established and their capacities for expanding with new facets of business. Some companies, for example, use a *miscellaneous investments* category on the balance sheet to house activities that are not a direct part of the businesses, but are considered part of its asset structure. Ownership of land or buildings not used by the business per se fits well in this category.

A third attribute is that the system should be relatively inexpensive to operate. Elaborate processes can cost more than good financial controls can save. It makes little sense to spend $1,000 to keep track of an expense category that only amounts to $700 annually. For most small businesses, one bookkeeper is sufficient, and the need for a computerized system varies greatly by the size and nature of the firm.

Related to this is the fact that maintaining the records must not demand inordinate amounts of time, especially for the entrepreneur. The system should work for the owner—the owner should not be working for the recordkeeping system. As the process begins to consume more and more management time, maintaining and using the financial records becomes burdensome and is more likely to be neglected.

Finally, the financial records must be readily available to the entrepreneur for everyday use. They should be kept up to date on a monthly basis and stored in a place convenient for the entrepreneur and other managers. However, access to the records must be limited to only those who need the information to perform their duties.

Basic Books for Recordkeeping

When referring to financial records, most entrepreneurs think in terms of income statements and balance sheets. These are important for internal and external purposes, yet it is often erroneously assumed that these can be prepared easily from even the most rudimentary records—such as loose receipts and canceled checks.

Journals

Maintaining a modest set of books is a prerequisite for preparing useful statements for management purposes. The first step in establishing a sound recordkeeping system is to develop the necessary journals that will be used to record business transactions. From these, financial information can be transferred to appropriate ledgers that serve as a means of classifying each transaction into specified groups. Note that in **double entry bookkeeping** there must be offsetting entries for all transactions. Thus, for every debit amount there must be a corresponding credit amount. This serves to create a check-and-balance system and reduce the likelihood of error. As shown in the exhibits that follow, the total of debits (DR) made in a transaction equals the total credits (CR).

The **general journal** essentially is a book within which some or all of the business activities can be recorded. Typically, this is done by the date, type of transaction, and the amount of money involved. An example of a general journal is presented in Exhibit 14–1.

In some instances, this journal can be the only one used by the firm. Normally, however, it serves as a catch-all for transactions that are not appropriate for one of the other journals. The main reason for not using it alone is that it is more tedious and difficult to sort out the larger number of entries at later points. Since the entry must be made anyway, why not do the sorting at the same time? A number of specialized journals can be used to record and sort the transactions concurrently.

The **purchases journal** is used by the entrepreneur to record credit purchases for the business. Because cash payments for supplies will be recorded in a different journal, these credit transactions serve to identify the supplier, the merchandise bought, the amount owed, and when payment is due (see Exhibit 14–2). At any time, the small business owner can tally the amount of money owed suppliers and array the payment dates.

EXHIBIT 14–1 Sample General Journal

Cash		Date					Sundry	
Debit	Credit	Mo.	Day	Yr.	Description	Post	Debit	Credit

EXHIBIT 14–2 Sample Purchases Journal

Date	Supplier	Type of Merchandise (DR)	Quantity	Amount Due (CR)	Payment Due	General Ledger Items (DR) (CR)
March 10	Acme Shoes	Women's Sandals (Stock No. 108)	20 pr.	$126.00	Mar. 31	

Source: "Financial Recordkeeping for Small Stores," Small Business Administration Management Series No. 32, 30.

A **sales journal** is critical for companies that sell goods and services on credit. These journal entries essentially become the accounts receivable of the firm, and keeping track of those who owe the company is of obvious importance. The sales journal records to whom the sale was made, the date, the merchandise involved, and the amount due (see Exhibit 14–3). A comparison of this and the purchases journal will provide the entrepreneur with a quick means of analyzing the differences between some of the anticipated cash inflows and outflows. Gross disparities will signify potential periods when cash will be plentiful and when it will be in short supply.

Payments to suppliers on a cash basis or payments on credits previously entered in the purchases journal are recorded in the **cash disbursements journal.** Other cash outlays also will be entered in this journal. Each transaction will be recorded in terms of to whom the payment was made, the amount owed, the date, any discounts taken, and the actual amount paid (see Exhibit 14–4).

This journal is especially important in that all outflows of money from the firm will pass through here. In many cases, the petty cash held in the company cash register to handle the nickel-and-dime transactions is accounted for only as a total in the cash disbursements journal. As long as petty cash expenditures do not become excessive, they usually are not worth the effort for individual entry in the journal.

All cash sales and payments from credit customers previously entered in the sales journal are recorded in the **cash receipts journal.** Included here is information telling from whom the cash was received, the date, any discounts taken by the buyer, and whether it was to repay on the account from the sales journal or an outright purchase previously unentered (see Exhibit 14–5).

This journal is highly important because it identifies strictly cash customers and how much they buy. Comparisons of this journal to the sales journal also will reveal which customers pay their bills promptly and which do not. In addition, an examination of this journal together with the cash disbursements journal will reasonably reflect the overall cash inflows and outflows of the firm. As is described in Chapter 15, control of cash flow is critical to the survival of most small businesses.

EXHIBIT 14–3 Sample Sales and Cash Receipts Journal

Date 19—		Description and/or Account	PR	Total Sales	Charges to Customers	Collections on Account	Miscellaneous Income	Miscellaneous Expense	General Ledger Items		Total Cash Deposit
				(CR)	(DR)	(CR)	(DR)	(CR)	(DR)	(CR)	(DR)
Mar	23	Daily Summary		660 00	225 00	100 00					544 00
		Refund on merchandise						15 00			
		Cash short					6 00				
Mar	23	Daily Summary		660 00	225 00	100 00					562 00
		Refund on merchandise						15 00			
		Cash short					6 00				
		Exchange								18 00	

Source: "Financial Recordkeeping for Small Stores," Small Business Administration Management Series No. 32, 18.

EXHIBIT 14–4 Sample Cash Disbursements, Purchases, and Expense Journal

Date 19—		Payee and/or Account	Ch. No.	Amount of Check	Merchandise Purchases	Gross Salaries	Payroll Deductions: Income Tax	Payroll Deductions: Soc. Sec.	Miscellaneous Income	Miscellaneous Expense	General Ledger Items	
				(CR)	(DR)	(DR)	(CR)	(CR)	(DR)	(CR)	(DR)	(CR)
		Miscellaneous entries—rent, merchandise purchase, asset purchase, spoiled check, payroll										
Jul	1	John Smith—Rent	92	200 00					200 00			
	14	ABC Company	93	115 00	115 00							
	19	Z Company—Furn. & Fix.	94	30 00							30 00	
		VOID	95									
	20	Payroll	96	50 85		58 50	5 90	1 75				

Source: "Financial Recordkeeping for Small Stores," Small Business Administration Management Series No. 32, 26, 7.

EXHIBIT 14–5 ***Sample Sales and Cash Receipts Journal Showing Taxable Sales and Sales Tax***

Date 19—	Description and/or Account	PR	Total Sales	Taxable Sales	Charges to Customers	Collections on Account	Sales Tax	Miscellaneous Income	Miscellaneous Expense	General Ledger Items	General Ledger Items	Total Cash Deposit
			(CR)	(Memo)	(DR)	(CR)	(CR)	(DR)	(CR)	(DR)	(CR)	(DR)
May 23	Daily Summary		651 00	300 00	225 00	100 00	9 00					544 00
	Refund on merchandise								15 00			
	Cash short							6 00				

Source: "Financial Recordkeeping for Small Stores," Small Business Administration Management Series No. 32, 120.

Ledgers

Once the transactions are recorded in the appropriate journals, they need to be posted to the ledger accounts. Ledgers provide a convenient way to systematize the financial activities and prepare them for use in the income statement and balance sheet. This is the function of the **general ledger**—to provide a handy mechanism for scrutinizing the financial position of the company. The **accounts receivable** and **accounts payable ledgers** are used to keep track of payments due and owed.

The accounts within the general ledger should roughly correspond to the accounts within the income statement, balance sheet, and other statements described later in this chapter. Entries made from the specified journals are recorded in debit and credit fashion and provide an easy way to total individual accounts and keep track of each aspect of the company's financial activities (see Exhibit 14–6). From this ledger, most closing or final statements for internal and external purposes are derived.

Although sometimes contained within the general ledger, two accounts are often broken up for extra analysis and control. If the firm buys from many suppliers and sells to many customers, it is too cumbersome to keep all these within the general ledger. Consequently, accounts receivable and accounts payable ledgers (see Exhibits 14–7 and

EXHIBIT 14–6 **Journal and Ledger Posting**

Posting from the Sales and Cash Receipts Journal

The Total Sales column and the summary of the Miscellaneous Income and Expense Items column in the *Cash Receipts Journal* have already been posted to the Profit and Loss Statement. The remaining column totals are posted to the *General Ledger* as follows:

The Charges to Customers column is posted in the debit column of the Accounts Receivable account.

The Collections on Account total is posted in the credit column of the Accounts Receivable account.

The General Ledger columns have already been summarized by accounts. Each net total, debit or credit, is posted in the proper column of the corresponding account in the *General Ledger.*

The Total Cash Deposit column is posted in the debit column of the Cash in Bank account.

Posting from the Cash Disbursements Journal

The columns headed "Merchandise Purchases," "Gross Salaries," and "Miscellaneous Income and Expense Items" in the *Cash Disbursements Journal* have already been posted to the Profit and Loss Statement. The other column totals are posted to the *General Ledger* as follows:

The Amount of Check column is entered in the credit column of the Cash in Bank account.

Payroll Deductions are entered in the credit columns of the corresponding accounts.

The General Ledger items, as in the *Cash Receipts Journal,* have already been summarized by accounts. Each net total, debit or credit, is posted to the corresponding *General Ledger* account.

Finishing Touches in the Journals and Ledger

As in posting to the Profit and Loss Statement, when each total is posted from the journals, a checkmark (√) should be made beside the column total in the journal to show

►

EXHIBIT 14–6 Journal and Ledger Posting *(continued)*

that it has been posted. Entries in the *General Ledger* should be dated as of the end of the month to which they apply. The posting reference in the *General Ledger* (column headed "PR" or "Ref.") should be "CR" for the *Cash Receipts Journal* or "CD" for the *Cash Disbursements Journal,* followed by the number of the journal page from which the item was posted.

General Ledger Sheet

ACCOUNT: NO.

Date		Description	PR	Items posted				Balance			
				Debit		*Credit*		*Debit*		*Credit*	

Source: "Financial Recordkeeping for Small Stores," Small Business Administration Management Series No. 32, 63–64.

EXHIBIT 14–7 Sample Accounts Receivable Ledgers

Accounts Receivable Ledger: Customer's Account

JOHN DOE
345 Sixth Street

Date		Item	Debit		Credit		Balance	
Sep	1	Balance					47	62
	8	Sales check #195	4	50			52	12
	10	Received on account			47	62	4	50
	19	Sales check #231	42	50			47	00
	20	Sales check #243, return sale	35	00			12	00

Accounts Receivable Ledger: Control Sheet

Accounts Receivable Control Sheet

Date		Item	Debit		Credit		Balance	
Nov	1	Balance brought forward					2395	00
	1		80	00			2475	00
	2		230	00	195	00	2510	00

Source: "Financial Recordkeeping for Small Stores," Small Business Administration Management Series No. 32, 76, 78.

14–8, respectively) are used partly for convenience and partly for control purposes. These ledgers help the entrepreneur to examine how much is owed, and who owes and is owed. If the firm establishes credit limits for its customers, or if credit limits are established by the firm's suppliers, these can be noted in the ledgers so that when the limits are approached, the entrepreneur will be notified.

Financial Statements

While many types of statements could be constructed from journal and ledger entries, the three most important statements for internal and external use are the balance sheet, the income statement, and the cash flow statement. The use of these reports for management purposes provides an excellent picture of the firm 's business activities in terms of asset and debt position, profits or losses, and how efficiently cash is being used.

The Balance Sheet

The **balance sheet** is a statement of the firm's financial condition at a given point in time. Composed of three basic parts, the balance sheet keeps track of what the firm

EXHIBIT 14–8 ***Sample Accounts Payable Ledgers***

Accounts Payable Ledger: Customer's Account

ACME SHOE COMPANY
910 W. Elm Street
Central City, USA

Date		Item	Debit		Credit		Balance	
June	1	Balance					90	50
	1	Purchase Order #1086			110	00	200	50
	2	Paid on account	90	50			110	00
	19	Purchase Order #1087			135	50	245	50
	20	Credit P.O. #1087, Returned	135	50			110	00

Accounts Payable Ledger: Control Sheet

Accounts Payable Control Sheet

Date		Item	Debit		Credit		Balance	
June	1	Balance brought forward					1750	00
	1				110	00	1860	00
	2		90	50			1769	50

Source: "Financial Recordkeeping for Small Stores," Small Business Administration Management Series No. 32, 80, 81.

owns, what it owes, and what the owner has invested in the company (see Exhibit 14–9).

Entries and evaluations of balance sheet accounts are based on the conventional accounting equation:

$$\text{Assets} = \text{Liabilities} + \text{Net Worth}$$

What this says is that anything owned by the company (assets) is either owed to creditors (liabilities) or to the owner (net worth).

The assets of the company can be divided into three conventional categories: current, fixed, and intangible. This is shown in the sample balance sheet presented in Exhibit 14–9. Assets are the income-producing agents of the firm. They are obtained or purchased and then used in the manufacture and/or sale of outputs to generate income.

Some of the assets of the firm are more *liquid* than others, meaning that they can more quickly be turned into cash. These are called *current assets,* and generally are convertible into cash within one year. They typically include cash, accounts receivable, office supplies, inventory, and short-term investments (for example, stocks, bonds). If the firm has any long-term debt due to it within a one-year period, this will be transferred from fixed assets to current assets. Similarly, any prepaid expenses that will be used up within the year should be part of the current assets. An insurance premium that is paid in advance is an example of a prepaid expense.

Fixed assets are assets that are not so liquid and will not be used up within a one-year period. Shop and/or store equipment, machinery, automobiles and trucks, office equipment, buildings, and land are the most common types of fixed assets found in a small business. If the firm holds any notes from borrowers that are not due within one year, they too are considered fixed assets. For fixed assets that are used up over the course of some time period in excess of a year, depreciation should be taken and deducted from the value of the asset. Most equipment, machinery, and automobiles and trucks need to be reduced in value (that is, depreciated) to show a truer value of the asset based on its being used up or worn out.

In some cases, the entrepreneur will want to place a value on some aspects of the firm that are not tangible. Goodwill, copyrights, and patents are examples of these *intangible assets.* If the firm was purchased by the present owner at a cost higher than the asset value, this difference can be listed as goodwill. Similarly, the income-generating potential of copyrights and patents can be estimated and shown as intangible assets. While this is an acceptable practice, it is somewhat misleading to value intangibles like patents and copyrights unless they can be sold for a known dollar amount.

The entrepreneur can develop a false sense of security by including intangible assets in the balance sheet. In many cases, creditors will not accept intangible assets as being valuable, or will question the dollar amount placed on them.

The *liabilities* of the firm are those amounts owed to creditors of the company. They can be categorized into current and long-term liabilities, based on whether or not they are due within one year (see Exhibit 14–9).

Amounts that must be paid to suppliers and other creditors within one year are classified as *current liabilities.* Included here are accounts payable, taxes payable, the current portion of notes and mortgages that are due within a year, and salaries and commissions that are payable to employees. Accrued debts to local, state, or federal governments typically include withholding taxes on wages and salaries, Social Security

EXHIBIT 14–9

Sample Balance Sheet

(Name of Business)
BALANCE SHEET
December 31, 19__

	ASSETS			
1.	Current Assets:			
2.	Cash		$ 8,000	
3.	Accounts Receivable	$22,400		
4.	Less Allowable for Bad Debts	(1,000)		
5.	Inventory (valued at cost)		21,400	
	Total Current Assets		26,000	
6.	Fixed Assets:			$55,400
	Fixtures and Equipment	$13,000		
	Truck	3,200		
7.	Less Accumulated Depreciation		$16,200	
8.	Total Fixed Assets		(3,880)	
9.	Intangible Assets:			12,320
	Goodwill			
	Copyrights/Patents			
	Total Assets			$67,720
10.	LIABILITIES AND CAPITAL			
11.	Current Liabilities:			
12.	Notes Payable (due within 1 year)	$ 3,500		
13.	Accounts Payable	15,300		
14.	Accrued Expenses	700		
	Total Current Liabilities		$19,500	
15.	Long-Term Liabilities:			
16.	Notes Payable (due after 1 year)		2,400	
17.	**Total Liabilities**			$21,900
18.	Capital			
19.	Owner's Capital, January 1		$45,120	
20.	Profit for Period	$17,930		
21.	Owner's Withdrawal	(17,230)		
22.	Undistributed Earnings		700	
	Total Capital, December 31, 19__			$45,820
23.	**Total Liabilities and Capital**			$67,720

Source: "Financial Recordkeeping for Small Stores," Small Business Administration Management Series No. 32, 12.

payments, sales taxes collected from customers and owed to the government, and business income taxes.

Amounts owed but not payable within the year are listed as *long-term liabilities*. Mortgages payable, bank, or commercial loans, and bonds to be redeemed commonly are itemized in the balance sheet.

The difference between what is owned by the company and what is owed to creditors belongs to the owner of the firm. This is shown as the *net worth* of the business. Included here are the owner's original investment in the firm, any subsequent investments, and all profit derived from the operation of the business. From this are subtracted any losses incurred over the years, and any withdrawals made by the owner and dividends paid to stockholders if the firm is a corporation.

Income Statement

The **income statement,** commonly referred to as a *profit and loss statement,* reports on the business transactions in financial terms over a defined period of time. Although an income statement is only required at the end of a fiscal year, it is generally recommended that it be constructed monthly. By doing this on a monthly basis, the entrepreneur can easily see how profitable or unprofitable the company is before it is too late to take any necessary corrective action.

Unlike the balance sheet, the income statement reports on all sales generated and all expenses incurred over a specified time period. It is composed of two to three general parts, depending on the operations of the company: business income generated, business expenses incurred, and sometimes nonbusiness-related income and expenses (see Exhibit 14–10). For the firm that has nonbusiness-related assets that generate revenue (for example, land or building rental), it is wise to separate that from the purely business-related transactions. This provides a better method of appraising the operations on their own.

The income section of the income statement contains three important elements. The total revenues generated by the firm must be totaled from the sales and cash receipts journals. While many entrepreneurs look at total income as the all-important measure of company activity, it is not.

The net sales of the company is much more important because it reflects the true revenue generated by the firm. There are two common deductions from total sales that may be necessary. First, any merchandise returned to the firm by its customers or allowances given for defective goods or services or incorrect orders must be subtracted from total sales. Since money is returned or the buyer is not charged for the goods or services, it should not be counted as a part of sales. Second, any discounts offered to and taken by customers should also be subtracted. If, for example, a 2 percent cash discount is taken for quick payment on an $1,000 purchase, the $1,000 would be recorded in total sales, and $20 subtracted out as a sales discount, leaving net sales of $980.

A common question relating to modifications to total sales is why count them in the first place? In the cash discount example, why not simply record a sale of $980 instead of the manipulation of entering $1,000 less $20? The reason is that the amount of sales returns and allowances and sales discounts needs to be specified for management control purposes. Excessive returns and allowances may indicate bad products or services, while few discounts taken may signify a poor or ineffective discount policy. By highlighting these in the income section, the entrepreneur can see the true picture of total and net sales.

Business expenses incurred in the production and/or sale of goods and services by the firm can be grouped into two categories: *cost of goods sold* and *operating expenses.* While it may seem cumbersome to separate these expenses when dealing with a small business, such a breakdown is important for management decision making. Being able to identify

EXHIBIT 14–10 Sample Income Statement

Description of Income Statement Terms

A. **Net sales:** The dollar amount of sales made during the year, excluding sales tax and any returns or allowances.
B. **Cost of goods sold:** The cost value of beginning physical inventory plus merchandise purchased during the year (including freight costs), less discounts received from suppliers, minus the ending physical inventory.
C. **Gross profit** (gross margin): The difference between net sales and cost of goods sold.
D. **Operating expenses:** Selling, administrative, and general overhead costs involved in store operations throughout the year.
E. **Net profit before owner's withdrawal and income taxes:** This is the figure on which the owner will pay income tax, and represents his or her compensation.

(Name of Business)
INCOME STATEMENT
For the year ending December 31, 19__

				OPERATING RATIOS
A. NET SALES				
B. COST OF GOODS SOLD:			____	____
Inventory Jan. 1		____		
Purchases	____			
Less Cash Discount	____			
		____		
		____		
Less Inventory Dec. 31		____		
Cost of Goods Sold				____
C. GROSS PROFIT				____
D. OPERATING EXPENSES:				
Accounting and legal		____		____
Advertising		____		____
Bad debts		____		____
Delivery costs		____		____
Depreciation		____		____
Employees' wages		____		____
Entertainment and travel		____		____
Insurance		____		____
Interest		____		____
Maintenance and repair		____		____
Miscellaneous		____		____
Rent		____		____
Supplies		____		____
Taxes and licenses		____		____
Utilities and telephone		____		____
Total expenses			____	____
E. NET PROFIT BEFORE OWNER'S WITHDRAWAL AND INCOME TAXES			____	____

Source: "Financial Recordkeeping for Small Stores," Small Business Administration Management Series No. 32, 10.

both the direct costs of goods purchased for resale or manufacture and the operating costs gives the entrepreneur a better perspective on the firm's operations and trouble spots. This is described more fully in the next chapter.

For retailing and wholesaling firms that do not produce goods, the cost of goods sold is shown by the formula:

$$\text{Beginning inventory} + \text{Purchases} - \text{Ending inventory} = \text{Cost of goods sold}$$

Consequently, the cost of goods sold requires only an inventory check at the end of a fiscal period, and this also serves as the beginning inventory for the next fiscal period.

Manufacturing concerns, on the other hand, have more difficulty determining their costs of goods. The costs include the raw materials and direct labor involved in producing the output, plus the factory overhead (for example, utilities, foreman salaries) that can be directly attributed to the manufacture of the goods. The difficulty in determining the costs lies in deciding whether some cost should be a part of factory overhead or a part of operating expenses. Generally, costs obviously incurred in the manufacture and an estimated percentage of questionable direct costs are used for this computation.

Service industries have little in the way of cost of goods sold. Materials used to provide services usually are treated as supplies in the next section of the income statement.

Other costs incurred by the firm are considered *operating expenses.* These include such expenses as salespeople's salaries and commissions, promotion, supplies, depreciation, vehicles, insurance, and taxes. Keeping track of these on an individual basis allows the entrepreneur to maintain closer control over expenses that could severely hurt the firm's profitability.

If the small business generates income from sources not directly a part of its normal operations, these should be separated out for evaluation and control purposes. Examples include rental property and sales of unrelated goods on a one-time basis. The reason for isolating these is that profits or losses on them can grossly distort the financial picture of the firm as shown on the income statement. For instance, if the firm is incurring losses on its regular business but making an overall profit due to nonbusiness activities, the entrepreneur could be lulled into the belief that the business is a success when in fact it is not.

Cash Flow Statement

Because cash is the most liquid asset, it is to some extent the lifeblood of the company. Consequently, the inflow and outflow of cash must be monitored on a continual basis (see Exhibit 14–11).[5]

While it commonly is thought that cash flow problems are most typical of companies with poor sales levels, this is not necessarily true. It is possible for a thriving firm to experience cash flow troubles, especially if it grants credit to its customers. Assume, for instance, that a firm gives its customers 45 days to pay their bills, but it only has 30 days to pay its suppliers. Trying to match inflows and outflows will be very difficult because of the 15-day lag time.

The **cash flow statement,** sometimes called the *sources and uses of cash statement,* is mainly an internal statement used by management to keep track of cash flow over time. Like the income statement, it reflects a series of transactions over a period of time, usually three months. As shown in Exhibit 14–12, the cash flow statement is composed

EXHIBIT 14–11 **Cash Flow**

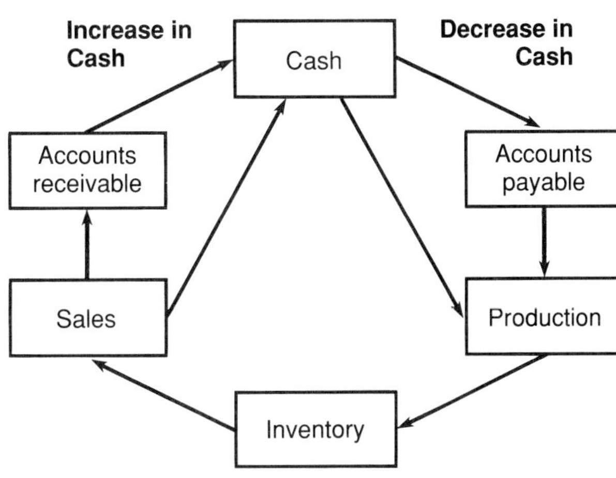

of three parts: cash receipts, cash disbursements, and the reconciliation to show cash excesses or deficiencies.

Cash inflows to the firm come from cash sales, collections on accounts receivable, sales of assets, loans to the firm, and additional investments made in the firm by the owner. Taken from the cash receipts journal, these represent the total amount of cash coming into the firm for its use. When cash receipts are too low, additional cash must be obtained through either loans or the sale of some assets of the firm, or by delaying payments to creditors.

Payments of cash by the firm will be for merchandise and raw materials, operating expenses, repayment of debt, and withdrawals of funds by the owner. All of these need to be reflected in the cash flow statement, since they act as a cash drain on the company.

As shown in Exhibit 14–12, the cash receipts and disbursements need to be reconciled to show increases or deficiencies of cash. Every firm needs some cash on hand to provide a cushion between the timing of inflows and outflows. How large this balance must be depends on the level of sales activity and the disparity between collection and payment periods.

If cash excesses exist over a prolonged time period, the entrepreneur should consider using all or part of the excess to purchase more inventory or to buy something else the owner finds potentially profitable. Otherwise, the excess cash should be invested in some highly liquid short-term securities that will pay interest on the money.

If cash deficiencies exist, the entrepreneur is faced with a potentially serious problem. Creditors must be stalled, or money borrowed, or assets sold for cash. While none of these alternatives is desirable, at least the entrepreneur will be able to recognize the oncoming problem and deal with it accordingly. This is preferable to being faced with a crisis and having to borrow or sell on unfavorable terms, or damaging credit relations with suppliers.

EXHIBIT 14–12 **Sample Cash Budget**

CASH BUDGET
(for three months, ending March 31, 19___)

	January		February		March	
EXPECTED CASH RECEIPTS:	Budget	Actual	Budget	Actual	Budget	Actual
1. Cash sales						
2. Collections on accounts receivable						
3. Other income						
4. Total cash receipts						
EXPECTED CASH PAYMENTS:						
5. Raw materials						
6. Payroll						
7. Other factory expenses (including maintenance)						
8. Advertising						
9. Selling expense						
10. Administrative expense (including salary of owner-manager)						
11. New plant and equipment						
12. Other payments (taxes, including estimated income tax; repayment of loans; interest; and so on)						
13. Total cash payments						
14. EXPECTED CASH BALANCE at beginning of the month						
15. Cash increase or decrease (item 4 minus item 13)						
16. Expected cash balance at end of month (item 14 plus item 15)						
17. Desired working cash balance						
18. Short-term loans needed (item 17 minus item 16, if item 17 is larger)						
19. Cash available for dividends, capital cash expenditures, and/or short-term investments (item 16 minus item 17, if item 16 is larger than item 17)						
CAPITAL CASH:						
20. Cash available (item 19 after deducting dividends, and so on)						
21. Desired capital cash (item 11, new plant equipment)						
22. Long-term loans needed (item 21 less item 20, if item 21 is larger than item 20)						

Source: "Is Your Cash Supply Adequate?" by Jack H. Feller, Jr., Small Business Administration Management Series No. 174, 1977, 4.

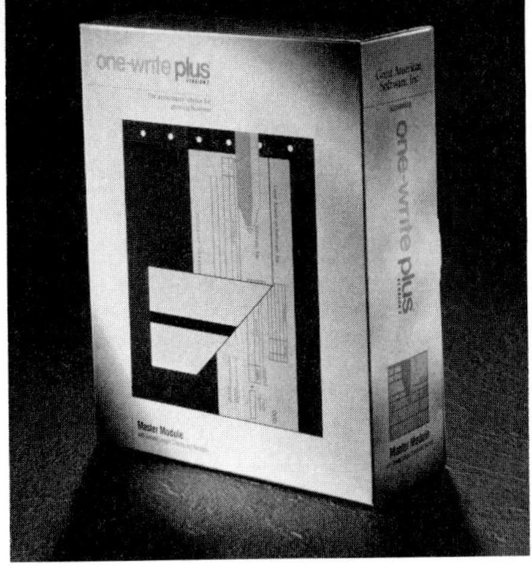

Accounting software, such as Great American Software's IBM-compatible One-Write Plus™, is available to help small businesses computerize their accounting and generate the financial information needed to help make important business decisions. (Photograph courtesy of Great American Software, Inc.)

HOW TO KEEP RECORDS

Being able to have good data available for management decision making depends on how well and how accurately the information is recorded in the journals and ledgers. Sloppy and haphazard entries usually result in inaccurate and out-of-date information.[6]

William Gladstone, chairman of Arthur Young and Co., was asked to explain the difference between being an accountant for a very large firm and a small one. His comment was, "There's a dramatic [difference] of course. One is a much more structured environment . . . and they've got lots of people who can help. . . . Dealing with an entrepreneurial company, it's more of a hand-holding, you're in most parts of the business, you're making an obvious immediate contribution to the health of that company."[7]

Recording Information

Letting invoices and receipt vouchers sit in a drawer is one way of getting the books confused. As noted earlier, the accounting equation necessitates the use of a double entry form of recordkeeping. If a payment of $100 was received from Buyer A, an entry would have to be made in the cash receipts journal to show the extra $100 in cash. Under the double entry system, another entry would have to be made to show that Buyer A paid off what he or she owed.

In order to show this more clearly, *T accounts* often are used in the ledgers of the firm. On the left side are the *debits* and on the right the *credits*. Debits reflect the assets of the company, while credits reflect liabilities and owner's net worth. In the previous example, then, the payment of $100 from Buyer A would look like that shown in Exhibit 14–13. This process must be followed for each transaction. The basic flow of entries is shown in Exhibit 14–14.

Beginning with cash receipts, a sale to a buyer on a cash basis will first be recorded as a debit in the cash receipts journal to reflect the increase of, say, $200 in cash. This will then be transferred to the cash accounts in the general ledger. When income statements and balance sheets are prepared at a later time, this $200 will be shown as part of the sales in the income statement and will be partially offset by the manufacturing costs of the merchandise sold, assumed for illustrative purposes to be $150. The excess $50 will be profit. In the balance sheet, the cash account will be increased by $200, while the inventory will decrease by $150, since the goods were taken from inventory and sold. The final entry will be a $50 increase in the owner's net worth because this

EXHIBIT 14–13

Flow of Bookkeeping Entries

TRANSACTION:

$100 received from Buyer A as payment for goods

JOURNAL ENTRIES:

Sales Journal	Debit	Credit
Buyer A	$100	
Buyer Payment		$100
Cash Receipts Journal		
Cash Payment from Buyer A	$100	

T ACCOUNTS:

Accounts Receivable Ledger
Buyer A

$100	$100

General Ledger
Cash

$100	

Accounts Receivable

	$100

FINANCIAL STATEMENT CHANGE:

Balance Sheet

Cash	+$100
Accounts Receivable	−$100

is profit that belongs to the entrepreneur. These entries in the cash flow statement will be listed as a source of funds (see Exhibit 14–15).

Cash purchases are handled in a similar way. Here, any purchase of materials, assumed to be $150 from the previous example, to be used in or by the business, is first recorded in the cash disbursements journal. This in turn is transferred to the general ledger as a decrease in cash and increase in inventory, since materials will be used to make the final product to be sold for $200 (or it may be the final product). From the general ledger, the income statement would show the increase of $150 in costs of goods sold. Entries in the cash flow statement would be listed as a use of cash.

From the general ledger, the income statement would show the increase of $150 in cost of goods sold as the partial offset to the $200 sale. Similarly, the purchase would serve to decrease the inventory by $150, as shown in Exhibit 14–16. The net result of these transactions in cash is a $50 increase in cash and a $50 increase in net worth.

The process of recording is slightly different for credit purchases and sales. A credit sale, for example $300, is recorded in the sales journal to reflect the $300 due the firm from Buyer B. This in turn is recorded as a debit in Buyer B's account in the accounts receivable ledger and as an increase of $300 in the total accounts receivable in the general ledger. At the time the financial statements are prepared, the credit sale of $300 will be reported like any other unless the entrepreneur wants to separate cash and credit sales in this statement. The only exception is in the balance sheet, where the $300 will be listed in accounts receivable instead of the cash account, as shown in Exhibit 14–17.

EXHIBIT 14–14 **Accounting Flow of Transactions**

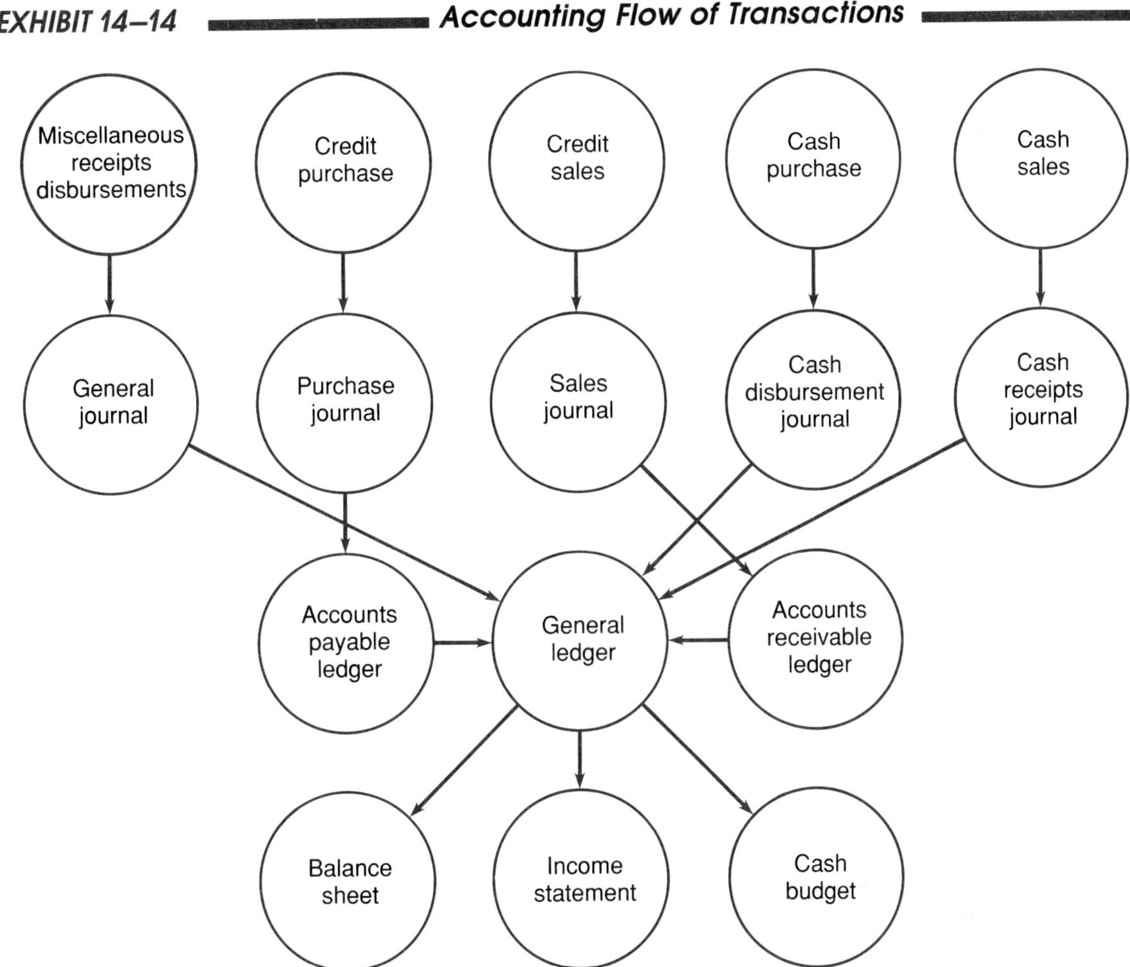

EXHIBIT 14–15 **Cash Sale Transaction**

TRANSACTION:

Cash Sale of $200

JOURNAL ENTRY:

Cash Receipts Journal: +$200

T ACCOUNTS:

General Ledger:

Cash		*Inventory*	
+$200			−$200

EXHIBIT 14–15

Cash Sale Transaction *(continued)*

FINANCIAL STATEMENT CHANGE:

Income Statement:

Sales		$200
Cost of goods sold	150	
Profit		50

Balance Sheet

Assets		*Liabilities and Owner's Capital*	
Cash	+$200		
Inventory	−$150		
		Owner's Capital	+$50
	+$50		+$50

Source: "Financial Recordkeeping for Small Stores," Small Business Administration Management Series No. 32, 70, 71.

EXHIBIT 14–16

Cash Purchase Transaction

TRANSACTION:

Cash Purchase of $150

JOURNAL ENTRY:

Cash Payments Journal: +$150

T ACCOUNTS:

General Ledger:

Cash		*Inventory*	
	$150	$150	

FINANCIAL STATEMENT CHANGE:

Balance Sheet

Assets		*Liabilities and Owner's Capital*
Cash	−$150	
Inventory	+$150	

Source: "Financial Recordkeeping for Small Stores," Small Business Administration Management Series No. 32, 70, 71.

When Buyer B pays off the debt, an entry will be made in the sales journal (these transactions are in parentheses, shown in Exhibit 14–17) and offsetting credits made in the accounts receivable ledger and general ledger. The balance sheet also will change to show the increase in cash of $300 and the corresponding decrease in accounts re-

EXHIBIT 14–17

Credit Purchase Transaction

TRANSACTION:

Credit Purchase of $200

JOURNAL ENTRIES:

Sales Journal	
Buyer B	–$300
(Payment	+$300)
Cash Receipts Journal	+$300

T ACCOUNTS:

Accounts Receivable Ledger:

Buyer B

Debit	Credit
+$300	($300)

General Ledger

Accounts Receivable		*Inventory*		*Cash*	
$300	($300)		$300	($300)	

FINANCIAL STATEMENT CHANGES:

Income Statement

Sales		$300
Cost of goods sold	$200	
Profit		$100

Balance Sheet

Assets		*Liabilities Owner's Capital*	
Cash	$300		
Inventory	($200)		
		Owner's Capital	$100
	+$100		+$100

Source: "Financial Recordkeeping for Small Stores," Small Business Administration Management Series No. 32, 71–72.

ceivable. The payment of $300 will be entered into the cash receipts journal and posted to the general ledger as a $300 increase in cash. Reflection of this will be made in the cash flow statement.

Credit purchases are recorded in much the same way as credit sales. A credit purchase of $200 in goods from Supplier A would first be posted to the purchase journal and then to the accounts payable ledger. The general ledger will show an increase in total accounts payable of $200 in goods for sale. When the merchandise is sold, it will be an addition to cost of goods sold like that shown in the income statement. If the merchandise is not paid for or sold before the financial statements are prepared, it will be recorded in the balance sheet as $200 in accounts payable and $200 in inventories (see Exhibit 14–18).

EXHIBIT 14–18

Sale of Merchandise

TRANSACTION:

JOURNAL ENTRIES:

Purchases Journal:		
From Supplier A	$200	
Payment		$200
Cash Disbursements Journal		+$200

T ACCOUNTS:

Accounts Payable Ledger:

Supplier A	
($200)	$200

General Ledger:

Inventory		*Accounts Payable*		*Cash*	
$200		($200)	$200		($200)

FINANCIAL STATEMENTS CHANGE:

Balance Sheet

Assets		*Liabilities and Owner's Capital*	
Cash	($200)	Accounts Payable	+$200
Inventory	$200		−$200

Source: Financial Recordkeeping for Small Stores," Small Business Administration Management Series No. 32, 75.

When the company pays off Supplier A, an entry will be made in the purchase journal (see Exhibit 14–18; all payment transactions are in parentheses). This will be transferred to the accounts payable ledger as a debit and to the general ledger as a debit to accounts payable and a credit to cash. Again, if the merchandise is sold it will be shown in the income statement. If not, on the balance sheet the reduction in cash and accounts payable will be indicated. Any payment will be posted to the cash disbursements journal, which in turn shows changes in cash in the cash flow statement. The last type of entry concerns miscellaneous receipts and/or disbursements, which are first recorded in the general journal and then posted to the general ledger. From here, the entries will be made to the relevant financial statements.

Maintaining the Books

The fact that the bookkeeping must be done does not necessarily mean that each transaction must be recorded as it occurs. Normally, the entries can be made daily, twice weekly, or weekly, depending on the volume of business and the needs of the entrepreneur.

One point of concern in this process is separating the recordkeeping functions from paying the bills and handling incoming cash. Giving these responsibilities to one individual makes the firm highly vulnerable to employee embezzlement. For example, a fictitious supplier may be paid for merchandise which is never received and which eventually is "lost." The fictitious supplier could be the employee or an accomplice.

Many small business owners cannot or prefer not to do the bookkeeping themselves, nor do they want them done by employees. Hiring someone else can provide the solution to this dilemma. There are several outside sources of recordkeeping available to small businesses.[8] Public accountants, certified public accountants, and bookkeeping services can provide guidance in setting up the system, and can maintain the books on an ongoing basis. Entrepreneurs who use an employee or an outside service still must understand the process in order to maximize the benefits of financial records for decision-making purposes.

SUMMARY

1. Records should be kept for internal and external reasons, as a permanent and visual basis for observing operations and for keeping records for IRS purposes and for creditors.
2. Entrepreneurs should be actively involved in the development of an accounting system that is understandable and serves their needs.
3. The basic books for recordkeeping are journals and ledgers.
4. Journals are used for initial recording of all transactions and include the general journal, purchase journal, sales journal, cash disbursements journal, and cash receipts journal.
5. After the transactions have been recorded in the journals, they are posted to the appropriate accounts in the ledgers. Ledgers provide a convenient way to systematize financial activities.
6. The three most important financial statements for internal and external use are the balance sheet, income statement, and cash flow statement.
7. The balance sheet is a statement of the firm's position at a given point in time and equates assets with liabilities and net worth.
8. The income statement is a measure of the firm's profit or loss over some particular period of time.
9. Because cash is the most important liquid asset of the firm, it is important that the inflow and outflow of cash be monitored on a continuous basis. This is the object of the cash flow statement.
10. Recording transactions should be done systematically, utilizing the proper double entry accounting procedures to ensure continued accuracy of all accounts.
11. The activities of recording entries, paying bills, and receiving cash should be separate functions, because of the possibility of embezzlement if left to one person.
12. There are several outside sources of recordkeeping available to small firms, including public accountants, certified public accountants, and bookkeeping services.

KEY TERMS AND CONCEPTS

Records for internal purposes
Records for external purposes
General journal
Double entry bookkeeping
Purchases journal
Sales journal
Cash receipts journal
Cash disbursements journal
General ledger
Accounts receivable ledger
Accounts payable ledger
Balance sheet
Income statement
Cash flow statement

QUESTIONS FOR DISCUSSION

1. Why should a firm keep records?
2. What are the uses of financial records for internal purposes? For external purposes?
3. What are the characteristics of a financial recordkeeping system for the small business owner?
4. Distinguish between a journal and a ledger.
5. Differentiate current, fixed, and intangible assets.
6. What is net worth in terms of the balance sheet?
7. Describe how costs of goods sold are determined for retailers and manufacturers.
8. What should be done in the case of cash excesses? Cash deficiencies?
9. What is the double entry form of recordkeeping?
10. Why should the entrepreneur develop some competence in recordkeeping?

SELF-TEST REVIEW

MULTIPLE CHOICE QUESTIONS

1. Which of the following is used to record cash sales?
   a. Sales journal.
   b. Purchases journal.
   c. Cash receipts journal.
   d. Cash disbursements journal.
2. A financial statement that is a report on financial conditions at one particular moment is a:
   a. Balance sheet.
   b. Income statement.
   c. Cash flow statement.
   d. Capital expenditure statement.
3. Assets that are not used up within a year and are not easily converted into cash are:
   a. Current assets.
   b. Fixed assets.
   c. Intangible assets.
   d. Prepaid expenses.
4. A financial statement that reports financial conditions over a period of time is a:
   a. Balance sheet.
   b. Income statement.
   c. Cash flow statement.
   d. Capital expenditure statement.
5. Which of the following is a debit?
   a. An increase in assets.
   b. An increase in liabilities.
   c. An increase in net worth.
   d. None of the above.

True/False Statements

1. It may be necessary to keep different records for different business purposes.
2. The purchases journal is used to record credit purchases for a business.
3. The ledger is a book of original entry.
4. Current assets generally are convertible into cash within one year.
5. Mortgages payable, bank loans, and redeemable bonds are common types of current liabilities.
6. It is recommended that income statements be constructed monthly or at least quarterly.
7. Operating expenses are not directly attributable to the production or sale of goods.
8. The accounting equation necessitates the use of a single entry form of recordkeeping.
9. A transaction that increases the amount of assets or net worth is called a credit.
10. It tends to be advantageous to have the same person receive purchase goods, pay the bills, and receive incoming cash.

G—W REMODELING

After working together for a larger builder of custom homes for eight years and a relatively small contractor for the past two years, Jack Gaines and Jerry Wilder have decided to go into business for themselves. Although their past employers had both gone bankrupt, Gaines and Wilder think they can avoid many of the mistakes they have witnessed.

Even though both are licensed contractors and have considerable experience in new home construction, they have decided to limit their work to remodeling and renovation. They see construction of new homes as too speculative and subject to sudden economic swings like those that occurred in the early 1980s. They think that remodeling carries less risk, although fewer opportunities for vast profits, because all work is done on a contractual basis. The homeowner pays for a portion of the project in advance, so G–W Remodeling has little of its own money at risk. In addition, remodeling projects and some renovations are less cyclical, and people seemingly always are altering their homes to fit their changing needs. Thus, they assume that they will have regular work even if it is on a smaller scale than building several new homes at once.

Gaines and Wilder agree that it is essential to maintain good financial records. Their previous employers had been lax in recordkeeping, and suffered because of it. The large custom-home builder had not monitored the inflow and outflow of cash, and did not watch expenses closely. The last contractor they worked for kept virtually no records—he simply used his checkbook as his books. As a result, both companies had financial problems that eventually forced them out of business.

Determined not to suffer the same fate, Gaines and Wilder want to have the best recordkeeping system possible. To ensure that everything is done properly, Gaines wants to hire an accountant to set up and maintain the records.

Wilder, however, thinks it would be best to set up and maintain the records themselves. He argues that the cost of having an accountant, approximately $500 per month, is more than they need to spend. More importantly, Wilder feels that if they learn how to do the recordkeeping and are forced to do it on a regular basis, they will gain a better understanding of G–W Remodeling's financial position. He thinks that if they turn it over to an accountant they will begin to devote less and less time to this aspect of the business.

To resolve this difference of opinion, Gaines has agreed to let Wilder explore further the possibilities of the partners doing the recordkeeping for the business. Wilder has decided to determine what type of recordkeeping system will be best for G–W Remodeling. After that is done, he thinks they can better decide whether to do the recordkeeping themselves or turn it over to an accountant.

Both agree that the remodeling will be done on a contractual basis, with a 15 percent deposit payable on signing, an additional 35 percent payable on delivery of the materials, and the last 50 percent due on completion of the project. To help them with their purchasing, they have arranged for a lumberyard to provide them with materials on 15 days' credit.

With these terms, Wilder knows that there will be payables and receivables as well as cash payments in advance. Accordingly, he thinks that an extensive set of records will be necessary in order to watch cash, receivables, payables, and profits.

QUESTIONS

1. What types of books will Wilder need in order to establish a recordkeeping system for G–W Remodeling?
2. Evaluate the differing views of Gaines and Wilder concerning recordkeeping set-up and maintenance.

NOTES

1. Based on Cable News Network's "Pinnacle," July 22, 1989. Guest: Larry Cochran, Six Flags.
2. Based on Cable News Network's "Pinnacle," April 22, 1989. Guest: Deborah Szekely, Golden Door.
3. Small Business Administration, *Financial Recordkeeping for Small Stores,* Management Series No. 32.
4. Irving M. Cooper, Small Business Administration, *Accounting Services for Small Service Firms,* Management Aid No. 1.010.
5. Bank of America, "Cash Flow/Cash Management," *Small Business Reporter,* 1985.
6. Bank of America, "Understanding Financial Statements," *Small Business Reporter,* 1980.
7. Based on Cable News Network's "Pinnacle," April 10, 1988. Guest: William Gladstone, Arthur Young and Company.
8. Bank of America, "Establishing an Accounting Practice," *Small Business Reporter,* 1985.

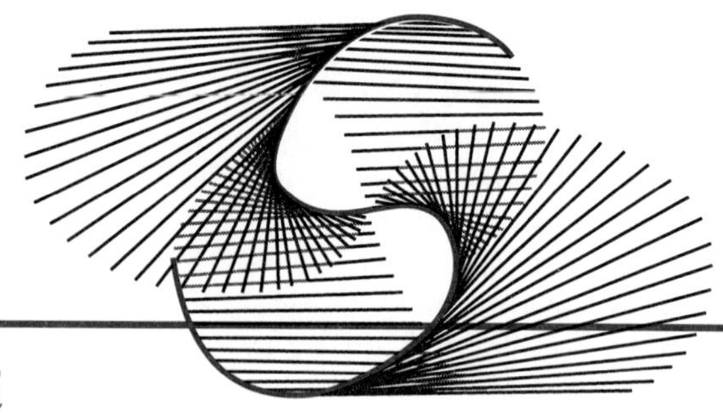

CHAPTER FIFTEEN

Use of Accounting and Financial Records

CHAPTER OUTLINE

BUDGETING
- Nature and Purpose of the Budget
- Component Budgets
- Flexible Budgets
- Budgetary Control

EVALUATING FINANCIAL CONDITIONS
- Nature of Performance Review
- Ratio Analyses
- Use of Ratios and Their Limitations

FINANCIAL REPORTS FOR AUDITS

TAXATION
- Federal Taxes
- State Taxes

SUMMARY

LEARNING OBJECTIVES *The objectives of this chapter are to assist you in understanding:*

1. What budgets are and their purposes.
2. How budgets can be used for control purposes.
3. How ratio analyses can be used to evaluate a firm's financial condition.
4. The value of financial audits.
5. The types of taxes the small business must pay.

Keeping good financial records ensures that pertinent information is available for internal and external use. For outside purposes, an accurate set of accounting records is essential for meeting the firm's tax obligations and creditor requirements. From an internal perspective, financial records can be used to help establish operating budgets for future time periods, evaluate the firm's current financial condition, and control some of the more critical problem areas in the firm (for example, cash flow discrepancies).

One person who gets good use of financial statements is Ronald Rule, chairman of U.S. Playing Card. As he noted: "I'm concerned really about the budget because if the budget's going to run higher [than] what we're doing on our sales, then we're going to have to cut it. . . ." Monitoring sales and profits indicated that costs had to be controlled, even when it meant that 300 workers and two unions went on strike over issues of benefit concessions and wage cuts. Small firms face the same issues of control, but are even more vulnerable to strikes and other work stoppages.[1]

BUDGETING

One of the most important entrepreneurial tasks is deciding where the firm should be heading and how it should get there. An integral part of this process is to develop budgets that serve to direct the firm's activities.

Nature and Purpose of the Budget

A **budget** is a quantified business plan. Although the budget is commonly referred to as a single entity, in fact the entrepreneur may develop several budgets to cover various aspects of the firm's operations. Production budgets, cash budgets, and sales expense budgets provide for efficient company control.

The budgeting process provides a mechanism through which the entrepreneur can design the firm's activities and attach dollar costs and expected revenues to their implementation. This serves to better define the details of the plan and highlight financial trouble spots—where costs will be too high and/or profits will be too low.

While preparing budgets can be a very helpful management tool, there are drawbacks to the process. It can be a time-consuming and arduous task, in that it deals with an unknown future. For example, an entrepreneur who wants to increase dollar sales may decide that extra advertising is necessary. After determining how much the firm should spend, he or she may suddenly be faced with increased media rates that go beyond the budget. Similarly, forecasting sales and production expenses can be difficult simply because of uncertainties surrounding costs and availabilities of raw materials.

Too many entrepreneurs do not realize that a budget can and should be revised periodically to meet changing internal and external conditions. As long as each change receives a thorough investigation, the purpose of budgeting is attained. Developing from the financial records of the firm and tempered by forecasts of the future, the budget provides the mechanism to direct the firm's financial reserves toward achieving its goals.

Maintaining control over costs is critical to success. For example, Nike made about 10 percent of its shoes in the United States until about 1985. The financial statements, however, showed that labor costs were hurting profitability. As a result, Nike closed all United States' factories and now produces about 90 percent of its shoes in Asia and 10 percent in Europe.[2]

While budgets need not be developed to cover every facet of the business, they should include all activities that are important—whether because of their high cost or because they are troublesome to the firm's operations. Entrepreneurs usually will develop a master budget and component budgets.

The **master budget** is an overall financial plan that looks similar to the income statement and balance sheet. This is typically developed for a one-year period to show anticipated profits or losses and the financial position of the company. It can serve as a summary of the other expected activities over the relevant time period. An example is shown in Exhibit 15–1.

Essentially, there are two methods for preparing master budgets. One involves developing an overall budget and then breaking it down into components on a monthly

EXHIBIT 15–1

Master Budget

Income Statement

	Department				
	A	B	C	D	Total
Sales	$ ______	$ ______	$ ______	$ ______	$ ______
Cost of Goods	$ ______	$ ______	$ ______	$ ______	$ ______
Gross Margin	$ ______	$ ______	$ ______	$ ______	$ ______
Operating Expenses					
Accounting and Legal	$ ______	$ ______	$ ______	$ ______	$ ______
Advertising	$ ______	$ ______	$ ______	$ ______	$ ______
Bad debts	$ ______	$ ______	$ ______	$ ______	$ ______
Delivery	$ ______	$ ______	$ ______	$ ______	$ ______
Depreciation	$ ______	$ ______	$ ______	$ ______	$ ______
Employee wages	$ ______	$ ______	$ ______	$ ______	$ ______
Entertainment and travel	$ ______	$ ______	$ ______	$ ______	$ ______
Insurance	$ ______	$ ______	$ ______	$ ______	$ ______
Interest	$ ______	$ ______	$ ______	$ ______	$ ______
Maintenance and repair	$ ______	$ ______	$ ______	$ ______	$ ______
Management salaries	$ ______	$ ______	$ ______	$ ______	$ ______
Rent	$ ______	$ ______	$ ______	$ ______	$ ______
Supplies	$ ______	$ ______	$ ______	$ ______	$ ______
Taxes and licenses	$ ______	$ ______	$ ______	$ ______	$ ______
Telephone	$ ______	$ ______	$ ______	$ ______	$ ______
Utilities	$ ______	$ ______	$ ______	$ ______	$ ______
Miscellaneous	$ ______	$ ______	$ ______	$ ______	$ ______
Total	$ ______	$ ______	$ ______	$ ______	$ ______
Net Profit before Taxes	$ ______	$ ______	$ ______	$ ______	$ ______

or quarterly basis. This is known as the *break-down method.* The other approach is to start preparing the component budgets on a monthly basis and then combine them into the master budget. This is known as the *build-up method.* While either approach can be effective, many entrepreneurs prefer the build-up method because it is easier to account for seasonal or periodic fluctuations, and because it is simpler to plan for one month than to plan for a full year.

Component Budgets

The details of the master budget are contained in a series of component budgets. Depending on the nature of the business and the need for budgetary control, there can

EXHIBIT 15–1

Master Budget *(continued)*

Balance Sheet

	Department				
	A	B	C	D	Total
Assets					
Current Assets					
Cash	$ ______	$ ______	$ ______	$ ______	$ ______
Accounts receivable	$ ______	$ ______	$ ______	$ ______	$ ______
Inventory	$ ______	$ ______	$ ______	$ ______	$ ______
Securities	$ ______	$ ______	$ ______	$ ______	$ ______
Prepaid expenses	$ ______	$ ______	$ ______	$ ______	$ ______
Other	$ ______	$ ______	$ ______	$ ______	$ ______
Total	$ ______	$ ______	$ ______	$ ______	$ ______
Fixed Assets					
Automobiles	$ ______	$ ______	$ ______	$ ______	$ ______
Equipment	$ ______	$ ______	$ ______	$ ______	$ ______
Fixtures	$ ______	$ ______	$ ______	$ ______	$ ______
Machinery	$ ______	$ ______	$ ______	$ ______	$ ______
Other	$ ______	$ ______	$ ______	$ ______	$ ______
Total	$ ______	$ ______	$ ______	$ ______	$ ______
Total Assets	$ ______	$ ______	$ ______	$ ______	$ ______
Liabilities					
Current Liabilities					
Accounts payable	$ ______	$ ______	$ ______	$ ______	$ ______
Notes payable	$ ______	$ ______	$ ______	$ ______	$ ______
Taxes payable	$ ______	$ ______	$ ______	$ ______	$ ______
Wages payable	$ ______	$ ______	$ ______	$ ______	$ ______
Other	$ ______	$ ______	$ ______	$ ______	$ ______
Total	$ ______	$ ______	$ ______	$ ______	$ ______
Long-Term Liabilities					
Notes payable	$ ______	$ ______	$ ______	$ ______	$ ______
Other	$ ______	$ ______	$ ______	$ ______	$ ______
Total	$ ______	$ ______	$ ______	$ ______	$ ______
Total Liabilities	$ ______	$ ______	$ ______	$ ______	$ ______
Net Worth	$ ______	$ ______	$ ______	$ ______	$ ______

be as many as six components focusing on all of the critical financial aspects of the firm's operations.

Sales Budget

The **sales budget** is used to forecast sales of each product line along one or more dimensions (see Exhibit 15–2). For example, if the firm operates in several geographic areas, the sales budget can be itemized by product and territory. On the other hand, if the firm sells to a limited number of customers, the budget can be broken down by product and individual client. The sales budget provides the basis for other component budgets, since all production and other activities are contingent on selling products or services.

To develop a sales budget, the entrepreneur needs to identify the company's products and forecast what the sales will be for each. If the firm sells only a limited number of products, this can be easy. One way to do this would be to use the forecasting techniques discussed in Chapter 9. For example, if the firm sold 1,000 units of Product One in the first year, and if the growth rates in sales from the preceding years averaged 5 percent, the entrepreneur might project Product One sales for the next year to be 1,050 units (1,000 × 1.05). In addition, if these sales had not experienced much seasonal fluctuation, the monthly estimate would be 87.5 units for Product One (1,050 ÷ 12).

Similar approaches can be used if the firm decides to forecast for whole product lines or departments instead of specific products. This also can work where the firm breaks down sales by territory. In this case, the firm can estimate territory sales growth based on past trends or information from the salesforce. From this, the historical mix of sales can be determined from past records to get an indication of expected sales by product or product line. For instance, assume Territory One has a forecasted sales volume of 4,200 units. If Product One historically has accounted for 25 percent of sales, the entrepreneur can estimate its sales to be 1,050 units (4,200 × .25).

Sales Expense Budget

A firm must keep its revenues and costs of selling in some reasonable proportion. Spending $200,000 to sell $150,000 in merchandise will always be a losing proposition.

EXHIBIT 15–2 **Sales Budget**

	Product				
	One	Two	Three	Four	Total
Sales Territory					
East	$ ______	$ ______	$ ______	$ ______	$ ______
West	$ ______	$ ______	$ ______	$ ______	$ ______
North	$ ______	$ ______	$ ______	$ ______	$ ______
South	$ ______	$ ______	$ ______	$ ______	$ ______
Central	$ ______	$ ______	$ ______	$ ______	$ ______
Northeast	$ ______	$ ______	$ ______	$ ______	$ ______
Northwest	$ ______	$ ______	$ ______	$ ______	$ ______
Southeast	$ ______	$ ______	$ ______	$ ______	$ ______
Southwest	$ ______	$ ______	$ ______	$ ______	$ ______
Total	$ ______	$ ______	$ ______	$ ______	$ ______

Meshing the desired sales level with the anticipated costs is a necessary step in successful financial management. Not only does this serve to allocate funds, it also provides the mechanism for assuring that selling costs do not get out of hand.

The sales expense budget should be itemized by salespeople's salaries, anticipated commissions, travel expenses, advertising, sales promotion, and other selling expenses (see Exhibit 15–3). This can be done either on a yearly basis and then reduced to a monthly one, or vice versa. From the sales budget, one will make estimates about the level of expenditure needed to cause such sales. Here again past financial data can provide some rough guidelines.

To prepare the sales expense budget, the entrepreneur needs to specify and list all expense items involved in the sale of the goods and/or services. Dollar projections can be based on such elements as historical trends and salesforce estimates.

Production Budget

Determining what processes, including labor and material, are involved in producing goods for sale is important to any business. For the small firm, with little room for financial error, it is vital that accurate cost estimates be made of production activities. Labor and material costs often are the major expenditures of firms involved in manufacturing.

Developing a **production budget** begins with the sales forecast, so that the amount of goods to be produced can be estimated. The entrepreneur will then decide how many people are needed in the production process, and how much raw material must be ordered. Care must be taken to consider any anticipated increases in prices from suppliers, and any labor or union negotiations that might affect labor costs in the relevant period.

The ability to isolate the per unit costs for labor and material is helpful. If sales are not seasonal, and/or manufacturing can occur at a relatively constant pace, the monthly costs of production will be approximately one twelfth of the annual budget. Seasonal shifts, however, can complicate this, because monthly costs must be revised to reflect these changes. Here, historical data can be most informative. Consideration also must be given to inventory levels presently held and levels deemed desirable. If inventory levels are to be adjusted, it will alter the production expense budget.

EXHIBIT 15–3

Sales Expenses Budget

	Area				
	North	South	East	West	Total
Air travel	$ ______	$ ______	$ ______	$ ______	$ ______
Automobile	$ ______	$ ______	$ ______	$ ______	$ ______
Entertainment	$ ______	$ ______	$ ______	$ ______	$ ______
Hotel	$ ______	$ ______	$ ______	$ ______	$ ______
Promotional material	$ ______	$ ______	$ ______	$ ______	$ ______
Samples	$ ______	$ ______	$ ______	$ ______	$ ______
Supplies	$ ______	$ ______	$ ______	$ ______	$ ______
Telephone	$ ______	$ ______	$ ______	$ ______	$ ______
Other	$ ______	$ ______	$ ______	$ ______	$ ______
Total	$ ______	$ ______	$ ______	$ ______	$ ______

Accounts Receivable and Payable Budget

For firms that sell on a credit basis, developing an **accounts rcccivable and payable budget** is advisable (see Exhibit 15–4). Receivables can be projected based on historical accounts of the time involved in collecting from established customers. If the company has dealt with particular suppliers and plans to continue doing so, the terms they offer for payment are known when estimating payables.

The timing of receivables and payables should be estimated as carefully as possible in order to pinpoint future trouble spots in the firm's cash flow. While it is difficult at best to schedule these inflows and outflows, projected excesses or shortages of cash can be planned for in advance.

Cash Flow Budget

The **cash flow budget** should be developed by all entrepreneurs (see Exhibit 15–5). To some extent it follows closely the receivables and payables budget just described. Monitoring the inflow and outflow of cash is essential to the survival of most small businesses. This particular budget should be prepared on at least a monthly basis, and the composite should be made into a yearly budget.

While many of the items contained in the cash budget will be determined from other budgets, it is necessary to synthesize them into a single one that clearly shows the

EXHIBIT 15–4

Accounts Receivable and Accounts Payable Budgets

Accounts Receivable Budget

	Age (Days)				
Customer	**Under 30**	**30 to 45**	**46 to 60**	**Over 60**	**Total**
A	$ ______	$ ______	$ ______	$ ______	$ ______
B	$ ______	$ ______	$ ______	$ ______	$ ______
C	$ ______	$ ______	$ ______	$ ______	$ ______
D	$ ______	$ ______	$ ______	$ ______	$ ______
E	$ ______	$ ______	$ ______	$ ______	$ ______
F	$ ______	$ ______	$ ______	$ ______	$ ______
Other	$ ______	$ ______	$ ______	$ ______	$ ______
Total	$ ______	$ ______	$ ______	$ ______	$ ______

Accounts Payable Budget

	Age (Days)				
Creditor	**Under 30**	**30 to 45**	**46 to 60**	**Over 60**	**Total**
A	$ ______	$ ______	$ ______	$ ______	$ ______
B	$ ______	$ ______	$ ______	$ ______	$ ______
C	$ ______	$ ______	$ ______	$ ______	$ ______
D	$ ______	$ ______	$ ______	$ ______	$ ______
E	$ ______	$ ______	$ ______	$ ______	$ ______
F	$ ______	$ ______	$ ______	$ ______	$ ______
Other	$ ______	$ ______	$ ______	$ ______	$ ______
Total	$ ______	$ ______	$ ______	$ ______	$ ______

EXHIBIT 15–5 ***Cash Budget***

CASH BUDGET (for three months, ending March 31, 19____)						
	January		February		March	
EXPECTED CASH RECEIPTS:	Budget	Actual	Budget	Actual	Budget	Actual
1. Cash sales						
2. Collections on accounts receivable						
3. Other income						
4. Total cash receipts						
EXPECTED CASH PAYMENTS:						
5. Raw materials						
6. Payroll						
7. Other factory expenses (including maintenance)						
8. Advertising						
9. Selling expense						
10. Administrative expense (including salary of owner-manager)						
11. New plant and equipment						
12. Other payments (taxes, including estimated income tax; repayment of loans; interest; and so on)						
13. Total cash payments						
14. EXPECTED CASH BALANCE at beginning of the month						
15. Cash increase or decrease (item 4 minus item 13)						
16. Expected cash balance at end of month (item 14 plus item 15)						
17. Desired working cash balance						
18. Short-term loans needed (item 17 minus item 16, if item 17 is larger)						
19. Cash available for dividends, capital cash expenditures, and/or short-term investments (item 16 minus item 17, if item 16 is larger than item 17)						
CAPITAL CASH:						
20. Cash available (item 19 after deducting dividends, and so on)						
21. Desired capital cash (item 11, new plant equipment)						
22. Long-term loans needed (item 21 less item 20, if item 21 is larger than item 20)						

Source: "Is Your Cash Supply Adequate?" by Jack H. Feller, Jr., Small Business Administration Management Series No. 174, 1977, 4.

movement of cash into and out of the firm. Not only will this account for the normal receipts and expenditures, it also will include any cash used to purchase capital goods such as equipment, land, and buildings. Monthly evaluations of this budget allow the entrepreneur to pinpoint times when cash balances may be too low, and necessitate short-term lending or the sale of some asset(s). In addition, periods when cash is over-abundant highlight opportunities for increasing expenditures for promotion, purchasing additional inventory, or making short-term investments.

Capital Budget

Purchases of capital goods typically require large outlays of money, and should be planned for well in advance. By developing a **capital budget,** the small business owner will be better able to identify how much money will be needed and when it will have to be spent. Sound financial management requires that the necessary funds be saved or borrowed on the most advantageous terms.

While an entrepreneur might not make capital purchases in each fiscal year, it is important that any anticipated expenditures be itemized in the capital budget. Accordingly, this budget can be developed for a one-to-three-year period (see Exhibit 15–6). The budget itself may be a simple listing of needed equipment, buildings, land, and so on, along with the anticipated cost and timing of the purchases.

Flexible Budgets

Because the future is uncertain, it is difficult for the entrepreneur to precisely project sales, expenses, and costs of capital purchases. When these variables prove to be higher or lower than expected, a budget loses its meaning as a planning and controlling device. Few entrepreneurs will turn away customers simply because their purchases will cause sales to exceed projections.

To be most effective, therefore, *flexible budgets* should be prepared for possible errors in forecasting. In this way, they can adjust to changing internal and/or market conditions and still give the firm the direction it needs to achieve the entrepreneur's goals.

For example, if actual sales exceed projections by 10 percent, it would be unrealistic to expect costs of goods and some operating expenses to remain within the original budget. If the small business owner was to try to keep costs to budgeted amounts, it could stunt growth or reduce the quality of the merchandise or services.

EXHIBIT 15–6

Capital Budget

	Department				
	A	B	C	D	Total
Automobiles	$ ______	$ ______	$ ______	$ ______	$ ______
Equipment	$ ______	$ ______	$ ______	$ ______	$ ______
Fixtures	$ ______	$ ______	$ ______	$ ______	$ ______
Machinery	$ ______	$ ______	$ ______	$ ______	$ ______
Other	$ ______	$ ______	$ ______	$ ______	$ ______
Total	$ ______	$ ______	$ ______	$ ______	$ ______

EXHIBIT 15–7

Flexible Budget

	Budget	+5%	+10%	−5%	−10%
Sales	$ ______	$ ______	$ ______	$ ______	$ ______
Costs of Goods	$ ______	$ ______	$ ______	$ ______	$ ______
Gross Margin	$ ______	$ ______	$ ______	$ ______	$ ______
Operating Expenses					
Accounting and legal	$ ______	$ ______	$ ______	$ ______	$ ______
Advertising	$ ______	$ ______	$ ______	$ ______	$ ______
Bad debts	$ ______	$ ______	$ ______	$ ______	$ ______
Delivery	$ ______	$ ______	$ ______	$ ______	$ ______
Depreciation	$ ______	$ ______	$ ______	$ ______	$ ______
Employee wages	$ ______	$ ______	$ ______	$ ______	$ ______
Entertainment and travel	$ ______	$ ______	$ ______	$ ______	$ ______
Insurance	$ ______	$ ______	$ ______	$ ______	$ ______
Interest	$ ______	$ ______	$ ______	$ ______	$ ______
Maintenance and repair	$ ______	$ ______	$ ______	$ ______	$ ______
Management salaries	$ ______	$ ______	$ ______	$ ______	$ ______
Rent	$ ______	$ ______	$ ______	$ ______	$ ______
Supplies	$ ______	$ ______	$ ______	$ ______	$ ______
Taxes and licenses	$ ______	$ ______	$ ______	$ ______	$ ______
Telephone	$ ______	$ ______	$ ______	$ ______	$ ______
Utilities	$ ______	$ ______	$ ______	$ ______	$ ______
Miscellaneous	$ ______	$ ______	$ ______	$ ______	$ ______
Total	$ ______	$ ______	$ ______	$ ______	$ ______
Net profit before Taxes	$ ______	$ ______	$ ______	$ ______	$ ______

To overcome this problem, costs of goods and operating expenses should be estimated based on several different volumes of sales. Thus, if sales rose faster than anticipated, additional funds would be allocated to satisfy the higher costs. An example of a flexible budget is shown in Exhibit 15–7.

Budgetary Control

In addition to serving as a mechanism for defining and refining company plans, the budget can be an effective control device. Since most component budgets are prepared for each month as well as for the entire fiscal year, they measure company progress toward its objectives.

To be an effective tool for control, any budgetary device must satisfy certain requirements:

- *The budget must represent a realistic set of company goals.* Idealistic budgetary figures can be detrimental, since the entrepreneur may spend considerable time and money trying to achieve the impossible.
- *The budget needs to be flexible if it is to be effective.* Conditions both internal and external to the firm may change and will require modifications to the firm's budgets. While budgets should not be subject to arbitrary revision, neither should they be considered unchangeable. Budget revisions should be rigorously questioned to

ascertain whether the modification is really necessary and what caused it to occur (for example, an inaccurate forecast of sales, or an error in identifying an important variable).

- *The master budget must have component budgets that focus on factors important to the firm's operations.* Excluding key factors from the budgetary process destroys the potential value of a control process.
- *The use of budgets as a control process must be a relatively inexpensive and quick reporting mechanism.* A control device that costs as much as or more than the amount to be saved is counterproductive. Similarly, a reporting mechanism that is slow is of little value. Many entrepreneurs therefore try to standardize the budgetary process and delegate the more routine budgeting activities.
- *For maximum effectiveness, a budget should be clearly described to those affected, and their support for its achievement should be encouraged.* The entrepreneur must recognize that by their very nature budgets are viewed as restrictive and as affecting people aversely. By helping in the preparation of budgets, employees take ownership in their implementation.

EVALUATING FINANCIAL CONDITIONS

The entrepreneur must critically evaluate the firm's past performance just as he or she must prepare it for future business activity. **Performance reviews** are a basic step in future planning, both in terms of determining the firm's existing position and in trying to learn from previous actions and events.

Nature of Performance Review

Certainly one way to evaluate the firm's operations is to compare budgeted revenues and expenses with the actual results. By simply making each budget a two-column entry, one for projections and one for actual, one can observe any significant differences. This is illustrated in Exhibit 15–8. Assuming that the budget represents the financial goals of the company, under- or over-achievement can be monitored and analyzed to discover why the disparity occurred.

In much the same manner, the entrepreneur can compare income statements and balance sheets of the past with those for the most recent period. This will allow a more enlightening view because it compares the entire firm's operations to previous periods.

For example, if company sales have remained relatively stable over a few fiscal years, but administrative costs have been increasing, it is an indication that cost controls are not being exercised. Gradual increases in inventories, bad debts, and long-term debt might not be of much concern at a given point, but such trends over time may be indicative of serious problems.

Some entrepreneurs like to graph changes of certain parts of their financial statements in an effort to visualize the changes better (see Exhibit 15–9). In particular, they tend to look at sales, costs of goods sold, administrative expenses, selling expenses, and profits from the income statements. Graphs of current assets, fixed assets, current liabilities, long-term liabilities, and net worth are drawn from the balance sheet.

This type of analysis, whether comparing actual versus projected or the current year versus past years, is just the starting point. Rigorous investigations should be made of what went wrong and why. If the firm made $1,500 less than projected, why did this

EXHIBIT 15–8 Comparative Budget: Actual to Budget

	Department A		Department B	
	Actual	Budget	Actual	Budget
Sales	$ ______	$ ______	$ ______	$ ______
Costs of Goods	$ ______	$ ______	$ ______	$ ______
Gross Margin	$ ______	$ ______	$ ______	$ ______
Operating Expenses				
Accounting and legal	$ ______	$ ______	$ ______	$ ______
Advertising	$ ______	$ ______	$ ______	$ ______
Bad debts	$ ______	$ ______	$ ______	$ ______
Delivery	$ ______	$ ______	$ ______	$ ______
Depreciation	$ ______	$ ______	$ ______	$ ______
Employee wages	$ ______	$ ______	$ ______	$ ______
Entertainment and travel	$ ______	$ ______	$ ______	$ ______
Insurance	$ ______	$ ______	$ ______	$ ______
Interest	$ ______	$ ______	$ ______	$ ______
Maintenance and repair	$ ______	$ ______	$ ______	$ ______
Management salaries	$ ______	$ ______	$ ______	$ ______
Rent	$ ______	$ ______	$ ______	$ ______
Supplies	$ ______	$ ______	$ ______	$ ______
Taxes and licenses	$ ______	$ ______	$ ______	$ ______
Telephone	$ ______	$ ______	$ ______	$ ______
Utilities	$ ______	$ ______	$ ______	$ ______
Miscellaneous	$ ______	$ ______	$ ______	$ ______
Total	$ ______	$ ______	$ ______	$ ______
Net Profit before Taxes	$ ______	$ ______	$ ______	$ ______

EXHIBIT 15–9 Sample Graph of Sales, Costs of Goods, Expenses, and Profits

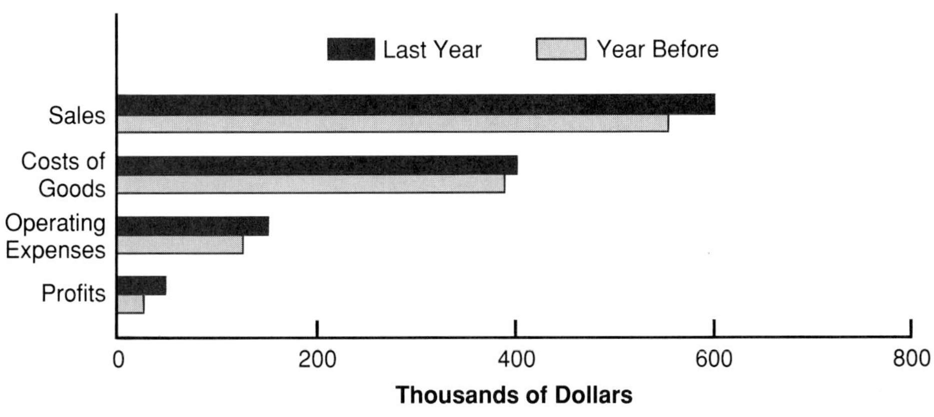

happen? Was it due to a slack period in sales, merchandise returned because of poor quality, bad-debts loss, or increased costs of production or sales? Was the projection unrealistic, and therefore should have been $1,500 less? Similar questions should be asked if the firm makes $1,500 more than anticipated. Were costs trimmed to the potential detriment of product or service quality? Has a new economy of scale been reached in production that lowered costs? Was there a flaw in the sales forecasting process?

Understanding why a variation occurred is important. Minor variances are to be expected, and some tolerance limits should be developed. However, differences beyond a 5 to 10 percent level should be examined closely.

Ratio Analyses

A more technical method for evaluating the company's financial position is through **ratio analyses.**[3] Financial ratios quantify the relationship between two or more variables. As a result, they reduce the subjectivity involved in examining the actual versus budgeted results.

Use of ratios as a means of financial evaluation can range from a cursory glance at a few key ratios to a close scrutiny of virtually countless ones. Opinions about how many and which ratios need inspection vary considerably.

The specific ratios to be used by an individual company will depend on the type of business in which it is engaged, the industry characteristics, and the financial structure of the firm. Although the needs of each company will vary, there are a number of ratios commonly used by firms (see Exhibit 15–10).

Current Ratio

The **current ratio** is a measure of the short-term liquidity of the business—the extent to which the firm can pay its short-term debt with cash or other assets easily converted to cash. It is computed as:

Current Assets / Current Liabilities

EXHIBIT 15–10 *Financial Ratios*

	Actual	Last Period	Industry Average
Current ratio	______	______	______
Acid test ratio	______	______	______
Accounts receivable to working capital	______	______	______
Average collection period	______	______	______
Average payables period	______	______	______
Fixed assets to net worth	______	______	______
Total liabilities to net worth	______	______	______
Current liabilities to net worth	______	______	______
Total liabilities to total assets	______	______	______
Cost of goods to inventory	______	______	______
Net sales to total assets	______	______	______
Net profit to net sales	______	______	______
Net profit to net worth	______	______	______

A rule of thumb is that the firm should have roughly twice as many current assets as current liabilities. If it does not, it may be forced to sell fixtures, equipment, or other fixed assets to meet demands for payment from creditors. For example, assume a company has a current asset and liability structure as shown in Exhibit 15–11. Even though it appears that the firm has sufficient current assets to meet demands for payment, this may not be the case. If all creditors demanded payment immediately ($10,000), the firm would have to sell its accounts receivable to a lender (factoring) and sell its inventory. However, it is unlikely that the entrepreneur would obtain the full value for either receivables or inventory—they would have to be sold at a discount to gain cash quickly. If the discount were 25 percent, the firm would find it still did not have adequate cash to meet creditors' demands for $10,000. At that point, the entrepreneur would have to sell some fixed assets to make the payments.

When the current ratio is too high (that is, greater than 2 to 1), it may mean that the firm has too much money tied up in current assets. If this sample company had $60,000 in current assets, it would probably have an excessive amount. Since it is unlikely that all creditors will demand payment at once, some of this cash could be invested in short-term securities, where it would generate some added income. Importantly, too, a high current ratio may mean that receivables or inventory are too high in relation to other assets. For example, if the firm can operate effectively with $5,000 in inventory, then $25,000 may be unnecessary.

Acid Test Ratio

The **acid test** (or *quick*) **ratio** is similar to the current ratio in that it measures the degree of the firm's liquidity. The main difference is in computation. Although current assets are considered to be readily convertible to cash, as a practical matter they are not. A quick sale of inventories will necessitate their being discounted, and their sale can hamper normal business operations.

Consequently, the acid test ratio is a comparison of current liabilities to the current assets most easily convertible to cash. The formula for this ratio is:

(Current Assets − Inventory) / Current Liabilities

EXHIBIT 15–11 ***Sample Current Asset and Current Liability Structure***

Current Assets		
Cash	$5,000	
Accounts receivable	3,000	
Inventory	3,000	
Total		$11,000
Current Liabilities		
Accounts payable	$6,000	
Notes payable	4,000	
Total		$10,000

A rule of thumb here is that the ratio should be at least 1 to 1. If it is not, the firm might be forced into selling inventory—incurring losses on the discounting and having to reduce production and/or sales efforts.

Accounts Receivable to Working Capital Ratio

Because many small business owners, especially at the start, strive to achieve high levels of sales, they sometimes grant credit to all potential customers. While advancing credit can stimulate sales, credit extension to risky borrowers is dangerous for the small firm with limited resources.

The ratio for this evaluation is:

Accounts Receivable / (Current Assets − Current Liabilities)

The difference between current assets and current liabilities is the firm's *working capital.* It represents the difference between what is owned and what is owed in the short term. Thus, this ratio determines the percentage of perhaps the most risky current assets relative to the money the firm has to work with. Too high a ratio may indicate a too lenient credit policy, with the potential results being high losses because of bad debts. Too low a ratio may mean that the firm is too conservative in granting credit and thereby may be inhibiting sales growth. Although there are no rules of thumb for this ratio, comparisons with industry averages (described later in this chapter) provide a helpful assessment of what this ratio should be.

Average Collection and Average Payables Periods

Entrepreneurs must also direct attention to the time it takes to collect on receivables. Even if all customers are paying, some may not be paying on time. Comparing the time it takes to receive payment from customers with the time available for paying suppliers and other creditors provides excellent insights into the firm's ability to meet its short-term obligations with its current assets.

To measure the **average collection period,** the formula to be used is:

(Accounts Receivable / Daily Credit Sales) / 365 days

This ratio provides the average number of days it takes to receive payment on credit sales.

If the average collection period is much longer than the average daily payables, it may means that the firm's policy on payment is lax or that its credit-granting judgment is poor. Stiffening up the terms by shortening the number of days a customer has to pay is one way of getting the money sooner. Another approach is to offer incentives for early payment. Such terms as "2/10, net 30" are often used to speed up payment. Here, the buyer can discount the bill by 2 percent if payment is made within 10 days; otherwise, the entire amount is due in 30 days.

Even though these cash discounts reduce the net profit per sale, they can prove advantageous. Since the funds are received sooner, they can be put to use more quickly, and thus earn more than the discount offered. Generally, too, the longer the payment is outstanding, the greater the probability that it will never be paid.

Fixed Assets to Net Worth

Another measure of the firm's liquidity is the relationship between the company's fixed assets and its net worth. The net worth is the true measure of what the entrepreneur actually owns in the firm.

The ratio is:

Fixed Assets / Net Worth

The greater the portion of fixed assets, the less liquid the company will be. Too high a proportion of fixed assets is undesirable, since they are more difficult to liquidate when cash is needed, and not likely to be sold at full value.

Total Liabilities to Net Worth

A standard measure of who owns what is the *debt-to-equity* ratio, computed by the formula:

Total Liabilities / Net Worth

This is an overall appraisal of the debt structure of the firm. As this ratio moves close to 100 percent, it means that creditors have nearly as much interest in the firm as the entrepreneur does. A high ratio may be indicative of heavy debt or the lack of much equity by the owner. In either case, future borrowing might be restricted, since the creditors already have a heavy investment in the company.

Current Liabilities to Net Worth

This is another measure comparing what is owned to what is owed creditors. The greater this ratio, the less sound the entrepreneur's investment in the firm. Short-term creditors can quickly deplete some of the ownership's net worth if current assets must be sold at large discounts to meet obligations.

The ratio is:

Current Liabilities / Net Worth

When the ratio exceeds 80 percent, it may indicate that the entrepreneur is relying too heavily on short-term debt to finance the firm's operations.

Total Liabilities to Total Assets

One of the better measures of the safety of creditor claims against the company is the *debt-to-asset* ratio:

Total Liabilities / Total Assets

It is a measure of the security of the debt, based on what assets the firm has to sell should it need to do so. As this ratio approaches 100 percent, creditors will become more concerned because there will be an insufficient value in assets to cover the debt.

Times-Interest-Earned Ratio

One of the most important ratios affecting the firm's ability to borrow is the times-interest-earned (TIE) ratio. This is given by the formula:

(Net Profit + Interest Expense) / Interest Expense

This ratio measures the firm's ability to meet its interest obligations out of profits. The importance of this ratio lies in the desire of creditors to be repaid their loans without further borrowing by the firm. As a general rule, this ratio should be at least 5 to 1, and preferably 10 to 1. At these levels, the firm should be able to pay its interest expenses out of profits, and not have to rely on additional infusions of capital just to pay interest expenses.

Costs of Goods to Inventory

Just as accounts receivable can be out of control, so too can inventory levels. Holding excess inventory is a common and serious financial problem. Not only does too much inventory tie up funds that could be used for other purposes, but also the merchandise can become obsolete and thus unsalable. On the other hand, too little inventory can mean that the firm is losing sales because of stock-outs or insufficient variety of lines.

A delicate balance must be maintained. This is done by monitoring the turnover of inventory—the number of times the inventory is sold over the course of the year. The ratio is:

Costs of Goods / Average Inventory

The result is the number of times the inventory is bought and sold. If, for example, the turnover is 12 times (for example, costs of goods = $600,000 and average inventory = $50,000), it means that the average inventory was bought and sold twelve times—or approximately every month.

While this is an important control area, the formula does have a major flaw if not interpreted properly. In the example above, it would appear that the inventory is being bought and sold with good speed. Accordingly, the entrepreneur may assume that inventory is not a problem. However, the inventory figure is the average, and not for each product line. It is quite likely, in fact, that some items are turning over too slowly (suggesting that too much inventory is being held), while others are turning over too quickly (evidence of an inventory deficiency). Because these two factors can balance each other out, the problem may never be discovered if this ratio is the only evaluation made of inventory levels.

Net Sales to Total Assets

Just as inventory should be turning over with reasonable speed, so should the total assets. Since assets generate sales volume for the firm, this ratio measures the extent to which assets are being sold. The formula is:

Net Sales / Total Assets

The result is the number of times total assets are converted into sales. If the number is low, it indicates that the money invested in the firm is not being put to good use. If it is too high, it may mean that the firm does not have the assets to take advantage of its sales potential. (For example, while it is desirable to manage accounts receivable, overly tight credit restrictions may result in lost sales and profits.)

Net Profit to Net Sales

Many entrepreneurs equate a high level of sales with success. A statement often made with considerable pride is, "My firm just passed the million-dollar sales level." But large sales volume is not necessarily indicative of high levels of profitability. Many firms could sell a million dollars' worth of merchandise if they could spend $2,000,000 on promotion and sell their products well below cost. However, firms using that strategy are not likely to survive for very long. One mark of business success is dollar profit in relation to dollar sales. The ratio for this is:

Net Profit / Net Sales

This measure will provide a clear indication of what income is to be derived from the sale of goods and services.

If this ratio is too low, it may be indicative of higher-than-necessary costs of operating the firm. This may be high costs of goods in relation to the prices the firm can charge for its merchandise and/or services, or that the operating expenses are disproportionately high.

Net Profit to Net Worth

The most critical test of the firm's success is measured by the formula:

Net Profits / Net Worth

This ratio shows how much money is being earned on the owner's investment. Sometimes called the *return on investment* (ROI), it should in time be at least as high as the amount that could be earned by purchasing a government bond, or placing the net worth into a savings account in a bank. If, for example, this ratio were to be 6 percent (for example, net profits = $3,000 and net worth = $50,000), the entrepreneur might be better off financially to sell the business, take the net worth (or whatever could be obtained for the firm), and placing it in a time deposit that earns 8 to 10 percent. Not only will the $50,000 be more secure, but it will be more profitable for the entrepreneur. However, as noted in Chapter 4, there are many reasons for going into business other than just dollar profits.

Net Profit to Total Assets

A somewhat different measure of profitability is given by the formula:

Net Profit / Total Assets

Instead of measuring profits on the owner's investment with ROI, this ratio measures the profits being generated on the funds supplied by both the owner and the firm's creditors. This ratio is sometimes called the *return on assets* (ROA), and is of greater concern to creditors than the ROI formula.

Use of Ratios and Their Limitations

The calculation of ratios provides an objective approach to assessing the financial condition of a company. Comparing the operating ratios over time provides a chronological basis for evaluation. This is very useful in monitoring the firm's progress in succeeding periods. Increases or decreases in the current ratio, for example, can be watched to ensure that adequate liquidity is being maintained or being achieved.

In addition, ratio analyses can be used to make comparisons between the firm and others within the industry. Both Dun and Bradstreet and Robert Morris Associates publish composites of ratio analyses for various industries. Each publication has its unique advantages, but both are adequate for comparative purposes.

It is important to make industry comparisons, since rules of thumb may not be practical for particular firms or industries. For example, a 2 to 1 current ratio may be too high for grocery stores, because of the volume of merchandise being carried and sold. However, the ratio may be too low for jewelry stores, which rely heavily on fewer numbers of transactions but in greater amounts. Identifying the industry norms provides a useful measure for estimating where the firm should be financially.

FINANCIAL REPORTS FOR AUDITS

One major concern of many small business owners is whether formal accounting audits should be conducted to ensure the propriety and accuracy of the financial statements being generated. Determining factors in this regard are the nature of the firm, the form of ownership, and the financial and accounting expertise of the entrepreneur.

For small business owners who are well-versed in the financial aspects of business, and who maintain close control over this function, an occasional **financial audit** may be all that is warranted. Audits are costly and can consume a considerable amount of an entrepreneur's time.

Entrepreneurs who rely on one or more employees to prepare and maintain the records, however, may need relatively frequent audits (perhaps one to two times per year). By conducting audits more often, the owner has greater assurance that the records are accurate and that employees are not stealing from the company. Corporations, of course, almost always need to have outside audits, especially if their stock is being traded in the open market.

Two key benefits of an independent audit are that it can uncover internal fraud and embezzlement, and it can spot problem areas overlooked by company management. Controlling the controller is serious business. Left unwatched, even a mediocre bookkeeper can siphon funds from the firm. All that is necessary is for the bookkeeper to create fictitious bills and pay them to a nonexistent supplier—typically a personal bank account. This can drain considerable sums from the company. Comprehensive audits usually will uncover these and other crimes. To the extent that audits are publicized, they tend to discourage such employee activity in the first place.

Another benefit of the audit is obtaining an outsider's perspective on the company operations from a financial standpoint. People involved in the day-to-day activities of the firm are likely to overlook serious problems on the horizon. The outside auditor offers fresh insights into the firm's policies and operations.

GOLDEN DOOR®

RANCHO LA PUERTA ®

Use of financial audits and records varies by the form of organization and demands of creditors. For example, Deborah Szekely, founder of the Golden Door health resort, indicates that not having a bank as a financing source allows her to do what she wants without interference.[4]

TAXATION

To meet the small business' tax obligations, accurate financial records are critical.[5] Even if the entrepreneur could mentally keep track of all the firm's transactions, it would not satisfy the Internal Revenue Service in the event of a tax audit. Consequently, any good recordkeeping system must be designed in part to document revenues and expenditures for government agencies.

The impact of taxes on small business can be significant. For example, the Tax Reform Act of 1986 restricted entertainment deductions to 80 percent of their costs. This had a seriously detrimental impact on restaurants that targeted businesspeople for lunch and dinner.[6]

The change in taxes also made it more desirable at that time for some firms to become subchapter S corporations because personal taxes were lower than corporate taxes. Since subchapter S corporation income is taxed maximum at the personal rate of 28 percent, it is more advantageous than the 34 percent maximum corporate tax rate.[7]

Federal Taxes

Although many different **federal taxes** are levied on the small business, the most common ones are income, Social Security, excise, and unemployment taxes. A worksheet for keeping track of tax obligations is provided in Exhibit 15–12, and current information on applicable taxes can be obtained from any IRS office.

Income Tax

All profit from business operations is subject to federal income taxes. The amount, method of calculation, and forms used depend on whether the firm is a proprietorship, partnership, or corporation.

As a sole proprietor, the entrepreneur treats business income as regular income, just as if he or she were an employee instead of an employer. One difference, however, is that business expenses must be itemized and deducted from the revenues generated. Federal forms for listing business income and expenses must be prepared to show these transactions. Another difference is that income must be estimated and prepayments made on a quarterly basis. A Declaration of Estimated Tax (1040 ES) must be filed on or before April 15 of each year. This is a composite of quarterly estimates of profits based on projected sales, expenses, and exemptions. Payments are made on a quarterly basis, and are due on the fifteenth of April, June, September, and January. The tax itself is the same as that for personal income of employees.

If the entrepreneur is a member of a partnership, the same income tax situation exists as for a sole proprietorship. For tax purposes, a partnership is very similar to two individual proprietorships. The only difference is that a return must be filed to show the revenues and expenses of the business and the portion of profits going to each partner. A Declaration of Estimated Tax also must be filed and prepayments of taxes sent in on the same dates as for sole proprietorships.

For corporations, the income tax laws are somewhat different. Profits of the corporation are taxed at different rates than they are for proprietorships and partnerships. In addition, any owner/manager salaries and dividends are taxed at the personal income tax rate. Since fiscal years can differ from calendar years, the due dates for different corporations will vary considerably. Quarterly payments, like those for proprietorships and partnerships, also are required.

In addition to income taxes on the business, the firm must withhold income taxes for its employees. These need to be reported, and the money sent to the IRS on a specific time schedule.

Social Security Taxes

Both the employee and the employer must contribute to Social Security. This tax is assessed on earnings as a percentage of employee wages.

EXHIBIT 15–12

Worksheet for Meeting Tax Obligations

This worksheet is designed to help the owner-manager to manage the firm's tax obligations. You may want an accountant or bookkeeper to prepare the worksheet so you can use it as a reminder in preparing for and paying the various taxes.

Kind of Tax	Due Date	Amount Due	Pay to	Date for Writing the Check
Federal Taxes				
Employee Income Tax				
Social Security Tax				
Excise Tax				
Owner-Manager's and/or Corporation's Income Tax				
Unemployment Tax				
Unemployment Taxes				
Income Taxes				
Sales Taxes				
Franchise Tax				
Other				
Local Taxes				
Sales Tax				
Real Estate Tax				
Personal Property Tax				
Licenses (retail, vending machine, etc.)				
Other				

Source: "Steps in Meeting Your Tax Obligations," SBA Small Marketer's Aid No. 142, 6–7.

As in the case of employee income tax withholding, the entrepreneur must deduct the Social Security taxes from employee wages and forward them to the government on a quarterly basis. The only significant difference between Social Security and employee income tax withholding is that the entrepreneur also must pay Social Security taxes. Certain remitting requirements vary by the nature and size of the business, and in some cases prepayment deposits are required. Entrepreneurs should check applicable regulations with their accountants, bankers, or IRS agent.

Unemployment Taxes

If the entrepreneur has employees, the firm may be liable for federal unemployment taxes, depending on the amount of wages paid in a calendar quarter, or if an employee was hired for at least some part of one day in twenty or more calendar weeks (not necessarily consecutive). In many cases, quarterly deposits must be made and all closing payments for a calendar year paid by January 31 of the following year. Federal liability is partially reduced by state unemployment taxes.

Excise Taxes

Depending on the type of business the firm is engaged in, payment of federal excise taxes also may be required. Retail liquor stores, wholesale dealers in alcoholic beverages, and sellers of diesel fuel and special types of motor oils are subject to excise taxes. Quarterly reports and in some cases monthly prepayment deposits are required. Entrepreneurs should check with their local IRS office to determine if they must pay excise taxes, and how reporting and payment should be made.

State Taxes

In addition to federal taxes, the small business may have to pay **state taxes.** These vary according to the location of the firm, but the most common types are income, unemployment, and sales taxes.

Income Taxes

In states that impose income taxes, the firm will generally have to pay taxes in a manner similar to that outlined for federal income taxes. In addition, the entrepreneur may have to withhold taxes on the wages earned by employees. State income tax rates vary considerably from state to state. Some states, like Minnesota, impose a minimum tax—irrespective of whether the firm has generated any profits.

Unemployment Taxes

While all states have unemployment taxes, the specifics on filing, charges, and qualifications vary significantly. According to the Small Business Administration, unemployment taxes often are based on the taxable wage base of a quarter. The unemployment experience of the individual business and the unemployment experience of the state in which the business is located determine the rate of tax charged.

Sales Taxes

Many states impose sales taxes on all or some retail transactions, and some local governments add a percentage to the tax to finance various civic projects. When sales taxes are used, the entrepreneur is required to collect the taxes on the transactions and remit the funds to the state. While the entrepreneur does not pay the taxes, he or she is fully responsible for their collection. Therefore, one must keep accurate records for verification purposes.

SUMMARY

1. The budgeting process provides a mechanism through which the entrepreneur can set out the planned activities and attach dollar costs and revenues to their implementation and results.
2. There are essentially two methods by which budgets can be prepared—break-down and build-up—each of which utilizes the same basic process for looking at the past and present to predict the future.
3. The primary budget for the firm is the master budget, and it contains the projections of several component budgets, including the sales budget, sales expense budget, production budget, accounts receivable and payable budget, cash budget, and capital budget.
4. Budgets can be used as effective control devices. To be effective for control, the budget must represent realistic goals, be flexible, have components covering all operational factors, be relatively inexpensive to use, offer quick reporting, and be clearly described to those affected.
5. The budget can be useful for evaluating a firm's operations by comparing budgeted revenues and expenses with actual results.
6. The use of business ratios as a means for financial evaluation can range from a cursory glance at a few key ratios to close scrutiny of seemingly countless ratios.
7. In using ratios, one can make comparisons with past ratios of the firm, industry averages, or both.
8. Independent audits can benefit the firm in two key areas: discovering internal fraud and embezzlement, and spotting problems overlooked by company management.
9. Financial reports are very important to the firm in meeting its tax obligations.
10. Federal taxes include income taxes, Social Security taxes, unemployment taxes, and excise taxes. State taxes include income taxes, unemployment taxes, and sales taxes.

KEY TERMS AND CONCEPTS

Budget
Master budget
Sales budget
Sales expense budget
Production budget
Accounts receivable and payable budget
Cash flow budget
Capital budget
Performance review
Ratio analyses
Current ratio
Acid test ratio
Average collection period
Financial audit
Federal taxes
State taxes

QUESTIONS FOR DISCUSSION

1. What are the disadvantages of budgeting?
2. What is wrong with the comment, "How can I budget when things change so quickly?"
3. Differentiate between the two methods used to prepare budgets.
4. What is necessary for preparing the sales expense budget?
5. Explain the value of historical data for internal statements or budgets.
6. Name two types of comparisons using financial statements or budgets.

7. Differentiate between the current ratio and the acid test ratio.
8. Which ratio is an overall appraisal of the debt structure?
9. What does the net profit to net worth ratio describe?
10. What kinds of ratio comparisons can be made?

SELF-TEST REVIEW

Multiple Choice Questions

1. Which of the following is the preferred method of budget preparation?
   a. Developing an overall budget only.
   b. Developing monthly component budgets only.
   c. Developing an overall budget and then breaking it down into monthly component budgets.
   d. Developing monthly component budgets and then building them into an overall budget.
2. The sales expense budget should not include:
   a. Salespeople's salaries.
   b. Raw materials.
   c. Salespeople's travel expenses.
   d. Advertising and other promotion.
3. Which of the following is not a measure of the firm's liquidity?
   a. Current ratio.
   b. Acid test ratio.
   c. Average collection period.
   d. Total liabilities to net worth.
4. The most critical test of the firm's success is measured by:
   a. Net sales to net worth.
   b. Net profit to net worth.
   c. Net profit to net sales.
   d. None of the above.
5. Which of the following is a key benefit of an audit?
   a. It protects the firm from internal fraud.
   b. It protects the firm from external fraud.
   c. It satisfies the IRS.
   d. None of the above.

True/False Statements

1. In preparing a sales budget, the entrepreneur should make as detailed an estimate of anticipated sales as possible.
2. All small business owners should develop accounts receivable and accounts payable budgets.
3. In comparing past financial conditions to present ones, a stable growth pattern is most desirable.
4. When the current ratio is too low, it may mean that the firm is holding too much in current assets.
5. The acid test ratio is a measure of the firm's ability to borrow.
6. The average collection period for a small business will always be less than the average payable period.
7. The net sales to net worth ratio is called the return on investment.
8. Comparison of ratios with industry averages is the only means of evaluating how well the firm is doing.
9. A financial audit is a method for protecting the firm from embezzlement.
10. Businesses must pay their federal income taxes in quarterly installments.

PALM PHARMACY

Richard Johnson, owner of Palm Pharmacy, has just finished reviewing his financial statements for the first half of the current fiscal year. Sales have increased nearly 7 percent over the same period last year, but profits have risen by only 0.3 percent (see Tables A and B). Despite the higher sales volume, the pharmacy has been having problems with cash—there never seems to be enough money available to pay the bills on time. On several occasions, Johnson has had to forego cash discounts and even be late in paying his suppliers. He knows that this situation must be corrected before his suppliers begin selling to him on a cash-only basis, or stop selling to Palm Pharmacy altogether.

Palm Pharmacy is a relatively large community-oriented pharmacy located in Southern California. Of its approximately 4,500 square feet of floor space, nearly 3,600 are devoted to the sale of "front-end" merchandise: over-the-counter drugs, cosmetics, greeting cards, photography equipment and sup-

TABLE A
Condensed Income Statements, Last Two Years

	Two Years Ago	*Last Year*
Net Sales		
Prescriptions	$215,800	$209,200
Front-end merchandise	310,200	353,300
Total	526,000	562,500
Cost of Goods	352,100	371,700
Gross Margin	173,900	190,800
Operating Expenses		
Owner's salary	35,000	40,400
Employee wages	75,200	79,100
Rent	25,200	27,000
Utilities	6,800	7,900
Delivery	1,900	3,200
Advertising	4,100	7,600
Bad debts	1,800	2,700
Interest expense	2,000	2,100
All other	14,300	13,100
Total	166,300	183,100
Net Profit before Taxes	7,600	7,700

TABLE B
Balance Sheet

Last Year	
Assets	
Current Assets	
Cash	$ 4,700
Accounts receivable	14,300
Inventory	61,000
Other	3,000
Total	83,000
Fixed Assets	
Net fixtures and equipment	17,200
Total Assets	100,200
Liabilities	
Current Liabilities	
Accounts payable	$ 36,000
Notes payable	7,300
Total	43,300
Long-Term Liabilities	
Notes payable	21,000
Total Liabilities	64,300
Net Worth	$ 35,900

plies, and gifts. The other 900 square feet are used for the prescription department, which accounts for 38 percent of total sales.

During the first seven years, the pharmacy's sales and profits grew slowly but progressively. There was little competition in the immediate area, and Johnson had most of the business for himself.

One year ago, however, a discount chain drugstore moved in nearby, and from that point on, sales have stagnated and profits have declined. Consequently, at the beginning of the current year, Johnson decided to compete more aggressively with the chain store by reducing prices on front-end merchandise and prescription drugs by nearly 10 percent. He has also offered more liberal credit, provided free delivery, and advertised heavily in the local newspaper.

Even though this strategy has been successful, Johnson is not happy with the resulting cash flow problems. Furthermore, he is not sure that the pharmacy's overall performance is what it should be, since profits have not risen much. He thinks that part of his cash problem and lack of profit growth are due to the price reductions and more liberal credit. Yet he is not certain that these are the sole causes.

As he looks over the financial statements for the past two years, he realizes that he does not know just what the pharmacy's financial position is, or how well it is doing compared to other pharmacies. At times, however, he wonders why it is important to evaluate the performance of the pharmacy—it has always provided him with a decent standard of living.

QUESTIONS

1. Evaluate Johnson's questioning the importance of making financial analyses. Does he really need to know the financial performance of the pharmacy? Why?
2. Evaluate the financial position of Palm Pharmacy. How good or bad is it?

NOTES

1. Based on Cable News Network's "Pinnacle," March 11, 1989. Guest: Ronald Rule, U.S. Playing Card.
2. Based on Cable News Network's "Pinnacle," March 22, 1987. Guest: Philip Knight, Nike.
3. Dennis H. Tootelian and Ralph M. Gaedeke, *Small Business Managment: Operations and Profiles,* (Glenview, Ill.: Scott Foresman, 1984).
4. Based on Cable News Network's "Pinnacle," April 22, 1989. Guest: Deborah Szekely, Golden Door.
5. Small Business Administration, *Steps in Meeting Your Tax Obligations,* Marketer's Aid No. 142.
6. Earl C. Gottschalk, Jr., "Living With Tax Reform," *The Wall Street Journal,* May 15, 1987, 38D.
7. *Ibid.*

CHAPTER SIXTEEN

Marketing Considerations

CHAPTER OUTLINE

MARKETING AND SMALL BUSINESS
MEANING AND FUNCTIONS OF MARKETING
THE MARKETING CONCEPT
- Implementing the Marketing Concept

UNDERSTANDING CONSUMER BEHAVIOR
SELECTION OF TARGET MARKETS
DEFINING MARKETING OBJECTIVES
DEVELOPING MARKETING STRATEGIES
EVALUATING MARKETING PERFORMANCE
PRODUCT CONCEPTS AND STRATEGIES
- The Product Life Cycle
- Introducing New Products
- New Product Failures
- Product Abandonment

DISTRIBUTION DECISIONS
- Choosing the Right Distribution Channel
- Direct Distribution
- Attracting Good Middlemen
- Independent Sales Agents
- Evaluating Distribution Channels

PRICE DECISIONS
- Cost-Oriented Pricing
- Demand Considerations
- Competitors' Actions
- Legal Considerations
- Retail Pricing
- Computation of Mark-up
- Pricing for Services

PRICING FOR SMALL MANUFACTURERS
- Cost-Based Methods
- The Price Ceiling

SUMMARY

LEARNING OBJECTIVES *The objectives of this chapter are to assist you in understanding:*

1. The role of marketing in small business firms.
2. The meaning of marketing and the marketing concept.
3. Basic product concepts and strategies.
4. Fundamental distribution decisions.
5. Pricing for retail firms, service firms, and manufacturers.

MARKETING AND SMALL BUSINESS

Small business owners must understand the role of marketing in order to develop effective marketing strategies for their goods and services. Unfortunately, too many entrepreneurs view marketing only in terms of selling and advertising. This indicates a misunderstanding of the broad scope of marketing. Furthermore, small business owners tend to ignore the opportunities of international marketing (discussed in chapter 1) by focusing almost entirely on the U.S. market.

Marketing, according to thirty-eight-year-old inventor Richard C. Levy, "is 90 percent of anything," including his sale of about 30 inventions ranging from toys, games, gift items, and custom-made items sold or given away to consumers to promote loyalty to a brand. "I think the blessing I have is that I am an 'imagineer,' " says Levy. "I am a smattering of the inventor, the marketer, the developer, the designer. I understand enough about how to take the idea from a seed through the negotiating contracts . . . and that is the big downfall that a lot of people have. A guy invents something and doesn't know what to do with it."[1]

Timberland®

The importance of marketing is also understood by Sidney Swartz, chairman, chief executive officer, and president of The Timberland Company. Marketing, according to Swartz, was the turning point for Timberland. He indicates that there is no definitive way to measure it, but feels that marketing played an enormous role in the company's growth.[2]

Too many small business owners are so busy with the day-to-day operations that they have no time to assess the performance of their marketing practices. And their size of operation and their resource constraints do not permit the employment of marketing specialists. That is why owner-managers of small businesses need to be knowledgeable about marketing and how to adapt basic marketing principles to an operation their size.

Competent marketing is necessary for the success of every business, and small firms are no exception. Consequently, just as basic principles of aeronautics apply equally to both jumbo jets and single-engine aircraft, so also do basic principles of marketing apply to both large and small businesses. However, such principles must be adapted according to the size and resource limitations of the firm.

It is often difficult for small business firms to compete with larger firms in marketing, since they often lack the established products and large markets that make promotion, pricing, and distribution of goods and services easier. On the other hand, small firms can be very innovative, and they can quickly adapt to changing market conditions. These strengths of small business can be exploited through effective marketing.

MEANING AND FUNCTIONS OF MARKETING

Marketing can be defined in many ways. The American Marketing Association defines **marketing** as "the process of planning and executing the conception, pricing, promotion, and distribution of ideas, goods, and services to create exchanges that satisfy individual and organizational objectives."[3] This definition has several significant implications:

- Marketing involves various functions,
- Marketing affects every organization, and
- Marketing satisfies both organizational and customer objectives.

It is important to recognize that marketing is a process, not a single activity. It is a process that attempts to establish a mutually satisfying exchange relationship between buyers and sellers.

To accomplish the **exchange process**—the process of offering someone something of value in order to acquire something of value in return—various marketing functions must be performed. These include:

- Research of markets—notably customers and competitors,
- Product conception and planning,
- Pricing,
- Distribution, and
- Promotion.

The marketing functions of product conception and planning, pricing, distribution, and promotion make up what is known as the **marketing mix.** These are the tools that a firm uses to attract and keep customers. In other words, these are the controllable marketing variables that the firm combines to satisfy customers.

THE MARKETING CONCEPT

The **marketing concept** is a management philosophy about an organization's total activities. It is a philosophy that stresses that an organization should attempt to satisfy the needs and wants of customers and thereby achieve its own goals as well. The marketing concept focuses on the customer by first identifying unsatisfied needs and wants, then developing a marketing program to satisfy them.

The marketing concept replaces the logic of the so-called production concept and the sales concept. The **production concept** is a management orientation that emphasizes efficiency in producing and distributing goods. This philosophy assumes that customers are primarily interested in the availability of quality goods at low prices. Marketing is simply viewed as an incidental sales activity. The **sales concept** is based on the premise that unwilling consumers must be convinced to buy. The most effective way to accomplish this is through high-powered personal selling and aggressive advertising.

The difference between the sales concept and the marketing concept is frequently confused. The contrast between these two orientations can be summarized as follows:

> Selling focuses on the needs of the seller, marketing on the needs of the buyer. Selling is preoccupied with the seller's need to convert his product into cash,

Stew Leonard's mission is simply . . . "To create happy customers." He often dresses in a cow costume and mingles with his customers. Here he is shown as, "Wow," the cow.

Probably no single-store proprietor has been more admired than Stew Leonard, who twenty years ago stopped delivering the milk his cows produced and opened Stew Leonard's Dairy Store to sell it. No proprietor has received more publicity. Leonard needs a clipping service just to keep track of the books that cite him and his two-step business credo: "Rule 1: The customer is always right; Rule 2: If the customer is ever wrong, reread Rule 1." (Photograph courtesy of Stewart J. Leonard)

> marketing with the idea of satisfying the needs of the customer by means of the product and the whole cluster of things associated with creating, delivering, and finally consuming it.[4]

In short, if a firm wants to implement the marketing concept, it must be customer-oriented.

Implementing the Marketing Concept

Entrepreneurs can begin implementing the marketing concept by following these basic steps:

1. *Know the business*—whatever a person's vocation, one must get to know the chosen business field very well before successfully launching and operating a small firm.
2. *Achieve customer wants satisfaction*—a crucial component of marketing includes studying buyer needs and wants, and then offering those goods and services that closely meet them.
3. *Determine who the customers will be and whether they can support a marketing effort*—potential customers should consist of people who need and want what is to be offered, are able to pay the price for the goods and services, and buy enough to cover the cost.
4. *Know customer characteristics that affect purchases*—marketing strategies should be derived from a careful study of customer characteristics, including demographic, geographic, and social factors.
5. *Identify the competition*—marketing strategies must take into consideration competitors' strategies to lure potential customers away from them.

To increase the prospect for growth and survival, small business owner-managers must consider each of these steps. They must be knowledgeable about the market and competition when implementing the marketing concept.

Here are a few examples of entrepreneurs who are implementing the marketing concept.

- *Anthony Lemme*—he is the son of a wine importer, and once tried to market some wine himself. He found his greatest success, however, when he broke the rules. What he sells is Vacu-Vin, a $19.95 resealer that keeps wine fresh after it is opened. Lemme identified an unsatisfied need and proceeded to fill it. His Vacu-Vin is sold through mail-order catalogues, gourmet shops, and department stores. Wine and liquor wholesalers sell the product to liquor stores, hotels, and restaurants.[5]
- *Tom and Kate Chappel*—founders of Tom's of Maine. These entrepreneurs knew that when a firm is small and in a mature market, it is necessary to win over someone else's customers to survive. That is exactly what they did when they discovered the market segment interested in all-natural products. The result was producing and marketing all-natural toothpaste, deodorant, mouthwash, and more. The company's advertising campaign is built around the message, "Natural is better." The campaign seems to be winning over health-conscious consumers.[6]
- *Paul J. Whiteneir*—inventor and marketer of Stroke-Master. Noting that hours of tennis practice typically fail to lead to a tennis victory, Whiteneir developed the

> Stroke-Master, which analyzes a tennis player's technique in midstroke. Worn like a backpack, the battery-powered computer, which weighs half a pound and is about the size of a Walkman, comes with sensors that are attached to joints to detect improper movements. It then sends a beep through a set of headphones when the player's technique is wrong.[7]

Small businesses that do not incorporate the marketing concept into their overall operations often fall prey to competitors who are skilled marketers or are wise enough to seek professional marketing assistance. In the past, a small firm could succeed if its sole claim to fame was a superior product or service—but not today. Competition is keen, product/service differences are often minimal, product benefits are easily duplicated, and consumers are better informed. Consequently, the small business owner who says, "We're doing all right now. We'll get into marketing later on," is doomed to failure. "Later on" might never come.[8]

UNDERSTANDING CONSUMER BEHAVIOR

Successful implementation of the marketing concept calls for an understanding of consumer buying habits and motives. In studying consumer behavior, one has to consider:

- Who buys?
- What do they buy?
- When do they buy?
- How do they buy?
- Why do they buy?

Answers to the first four questions may not be difficult to determine. They can usually be arrived at through direct observation and interviewing. On the other hand, discovering why customers buy, or why not, is a difficult task. The answers to this question will tend to vary with the assumptions made about complex relationships between buying-influence factors and purchasing responses. Unfortunately, there is no single model for analyzing consumers to provide all answers about behavior.

Determining why some people buy a product or service while others do not involves the study of motives. A motive can be defined as a mental force that induces an act, for example, an inner state that directs a person toward the goal of satisfying a felt need. The formal research technique used to discover underlying motives of consumer behavior is called *motivation research.*

Consumers are typically confronted with many unsatisfied needs that a firm tries to identify and then satisfy. For example, a security blanket might be fine for Linus, but for others it may not do the job. Some kids need to cuddle with "Pillow People," like "Squeaky Door" and " Window Rattler," to chase away their fears of the dark. In response to such needs, entrepreneur Penny Ekstein dreamed up the idea for a line of pillow-shaped dolls, called "Pillow People." The dolls represent both scary and pleasant bedtime experiences. Stores such as Macy's, Caldor, and K mart sell the pillow dolls in the home furnishings department, right next to conventional pillows.[9]

Compaq Computer's success is due to staying ahead of competitors and focusing on user needs. In other words, the company tries to do a better job than any of its competitors and understands what its users are after. The company tries to match that with the latest technology available and then apply it as quickly as possible. That has allowed Compaq Computer to get ahead of IBM in the laptop computer market.[10]

In practice, determining customers' needs and wants is not easy, because consumers themselves may not know what they are. For example, an individual may not know what really motivated the purchase of a particular product or brand—what need was satisfied by choosing brand X rather than brand Y. In short, motives can be conscious, subconscious, or unconscious. If motives are conscious, one is aware of what they are. If they are subconscious, one may be aware but hesitant to admit them. If they are unconscious, one is not aware of what they really are.

Customers are influenced by many motives simultaneously in making decisions in the marketplace. Some of the motives are rational, while others are emotional. It is unlikely that only those motives that involve conscious deliberation (rational motives) are present in a particular decision. For example, a customer may shop at a specific store for a number of reasons, including:

- Past experience with the store,
- Friendliness of store personnel,
- Short waiting lines at checkout counters,
- Short driving time from home,
- Actual and perceived price levels,
- Cleanliness and general appearance of the store,
- Accessibility and availability of parking,
- Ownership of the store,
- Loyal patronage to a neighborhood store,
- Image and atmosphere of store,
- Personal acquaintance with store personnel,
- Convenient opening and closing hours,
- Selection of merchandise,
- Acceptance of credit cards or check-cashing privileges,
- Store policy on out-of-stock specials.

This list of possible influencing factors, while far from complete, illustrates that one factor alone does not explain why a customer patronizes a particular store. At best, a single factor explains how some customers act some of the time.

To illustrate that the motivation behind a particular purchase decision tends to vary with the individual involved, findings from a flower holiday study are revealing.[11]

Profile of the Valentine's Day Wire Order Purchaser

There are two discrete wire customers on Valentine's Day: the man and the woman. Men buy flowers primarily for romantic reasons, to express love for a woman. Women buy flowers to express their feelings as well, but the fit is not romantic; the recipient is usually a female adult relative or one's mother.

Regardless of who is on the receiving end, there are two common denominators to the Valentine's Day purchase. The Valentine's Day gift is motivated by a need to personally express love or affection to another individual. It is a personal form of communication. Furthermore, arrangements of flowers appear to be the appropriate floral gift for doing this.

However, the two groups of senders are quite different in both their demographic and behavioral profiles. Yet both the male and female senders on Valentine's Day are important to the Florists' Transworld Delivery Association (FTD).

Women tend to be older, married, and more likely purchasers of flowers and plants all year long for various occasions, using local or wire orders. The female Valentine's Day sender is more similar to the Christmas and especially Thanksgiving sender in both the demographic and behavioral profiles.

In contrast, male senders have a much younger profile and, as such, are at a different stage in life. They are single, less likely to be in the work force, and when employed their earning power is less than female Valentine's Day senders. They also have less flower-buying experience. Valentine's Day may be the entry point of this customer into the wire market.

The holiday flower purchase study shows that Valentine's Day wire order purchasers tend to vary in the motivation behind the purchase. Furthermore, the study shows that the purchaser profiles differ considerably. Individual Valentine's Day advertising should address the potential buyer accordingly. For example, the message for female senders might stress the benefit of being able to express nonromantic feelings by sending a wire order. The message for male senders might stress the benefit of being able to express romantic feelings by sending a wire order.

SELECTION OF TARGET MARKETS

Owners of small businesses have limited resources to spend on such marketing functions as product conception, distribution, and promotion. Given such limited resources, small businesses should concentrate their marketing efforts on carefully selected target markets. A **target market** is the specific segment of potential customers toward which a firm directs its marketing program. Instead of marketing a product or service to everyone in a market, one should aim marketing programs at segments of the market in which the firm's offer has greatest potential appeal. The approach used to select target markets is known as *market segmentation,* and can be illustrated by Whittle Communications.

Whittle Communications' business is publishing. As with any publisher, selecting the right target market is crucial for Whittle's success. Each of its 42 publications is targeted to a specific audience, such as high school students, the target market of its Channel One news program. The company's first publication, *Knoxville in a Nutshell,* was a survival guide for college freshmen.[12]

DEFINING MARKETING OBJECTIVES

Marketing objectives are a reflection of overall company objectives. They are important to the development of marketing strategy because they define the specific marketing

Because small businesses have limited resources to spend on marketing functions, they need to concentrate their efforts on carefully selected target markets. This college bookstore aims its marketing programs at students attending the college. (Photograph © Ann M. Mason)

goals to aim for and to measure performance against. In order to be effective, these objectives should be specific enough so that performance can be measured. They should also be realistic enough that their attainment is possible.

Specific marketing objectives might be appropriate in the following categories:

- *Product sales volume*—$125,000 during next fiscal year,
- *Territory sales volume*—$35,000 in Region A during next fiscal year,
- *Market share*—15 percent of total sales for all firms in market by the end of next fiscal year,
- *Stock turnover*—three times per week for product group X,
- *Profit on sales*—15 percent net profit on sales,
- *Volume of reorders*—two reorders per customer per month,
- *Business image*—recognized as leader in customer service,
- *Advertising awareness*—80 percent of potential customers,
- *Customer satisfaction*—reduce customer complaints by 90 percent.

All of these categories should be reviewed periodically to determine whether they continue to reflect the realities of the marketplace.

DEVELOPING MARKETING STRATEGIES

The selection of target markets and marketing objectives provides specific guidelines for planning marketing strategies. Basically, **marketing strategy** answers the question, "How do we get where we want to go?" Marketing strategies consist of marketing mix decisions concerning products, price, distribution, and promotion for each target market. It is important to recognize that every marketing strategy must have a marketing mix as well as a target market.

Developing a product strategy involves making decisions regarding various features of a product—its brand, package, quality, warranty, and servicing. Product strategies also need to address problems associated with product lines, namely, expansion, contraction, alteration, and trading up and trading down. A **trading up** strategy involves adding value to a product by including more features or higher quality materials. A **trading down** strategy involves reducing the number of features, quality, or price of a product.

In developing a price strategy, one might need to consider each of the following factors: price discounts and allowances, one price versus several prices, unit pricing, geographic price policies, and the overall importance of price competition versus nonprice competition.

Distribution strategies require analysis of the advantages and disadvantages of alternative distribution methods. They are also concerned with such factors as site selection and hours of operation.

The selection of promotion strategies includes an assessment of alternative methods of communicating with the target market. The promotion strategy must have the proper blend of personal selling, advertising, and sales promotion.

In developing marketing strategies, one should keep the following points in mind:

1. Every marketing strategy must have a marketing mix.
2. Every marketing strategy must have a target market.

3. The needs and wants of the target market determine the most appropriate marketing mix.
4. The components of the marketing mix are interrelated.
5. Decisions about the components of the marketing mix should be made at the same time.
6. Generally, no one component of the marketing mix is more important than another.
7. A marketing strategy should be developed after target markets are analyzed.

A firm should constantly study the market environment to spot new opportunities. New marketing strategies must be planned frequently, because the needs and wants of target markets are always changing. Current marketing strategies must be modified to account for changing environmental conditions, competitive actions, and market needs.

EVALUATING MARKETING PERFORMANCE

The effectiveness of the various elements of the marketing mix should be evaluated on a periodic basis. This requires determination of performance standards, so that results can be evaluated against standards and corrective action can be taken if necessary. Without an evaluation of performance, there is no basis for taking corrective action when needed.

Some common methods used to evaluate performance include sales and cost trend analysis, breakeven analysis, stock turnover rates, market share analysis, and customer attitude tracking. If any of these methods are employed, sound performance data must be available. If gaps in actual performance versus standards are identified, the possible problem areas must be identified and analyzed before corrective action is taken.

An overall evaluation of marketing operations is called a **marketing audit.** In general, a comprehensive marketing audit focuses on these types of questions:

- Have appropriate target markets been selected?
- Have marketing objectives been defined?
- Are the marketing functions carried out effectively?
- Have specific marketing strategies been developed for each target market?
- How well are the strategies being implemented and controlled?

PRODUCT CONCEPTS AND STRATEGIES

A product (or service) may be viewed from two distinct perspectives. From the point of view of the seller, a product represents an offer to the target market. Such characteristics as color, features, styling, trademark or brand name, and packaging are tangible and thus readily recognized in the market. However, these product attributes may or may not be of particular importance to the target market.

From the consumer's perspective, a product consists of more than its physical attributes. When buyers purchase a product, they are actually buying the benefits and satisfactions the product provides. So the tangible attributes of the product may be of secondary importance. For example, a camera store does not sell a particular line of well-known cameras; rather, it sells the benefits of the cameras—pleasure, nostalgia, a form of immortality. The ability to recognize what benefits customers derive from a particular product or service will suggest appropriate advertising and sales strategies. Viewing the product from the customer's perspective is consistent with the marketing concept.

THE PRODUCT LIFE CYCLE

Products and brands usually go through a *life cycle:* the item is introduced in the market, then sales pass through a period of rapid growth, followed by maturity and eventual decline. Meanwhile its profits go from a negative position (loss), which is due to product development and launching costs, to a positive position. Profits peak in the latter stage of growth or early stage of maturity and decline as sales fall off. Exhibit 16–1 illustrates the course of a product's sales and profits over its life cycle.

The typical stages of a **product life cycle** and underlying reasons for those stages can be summarized as follows:

Stage 1, product introduction—new products have low consumer awareness and acceptance, and thus low sales.

Stage 2, product growth—sales increases are rapid because the target market has accepted the product.

Stage 3, product maturity—sales growth is slowing down and beginning to stabilize, because the product has achieved acceptance by most of the potential customers.

Stage 4, product decline—sales fall off because new products replace the old ones, or the need for the product has disappeared.

EXHIBIT 16–1 **Stages in a Product Life Cycle**

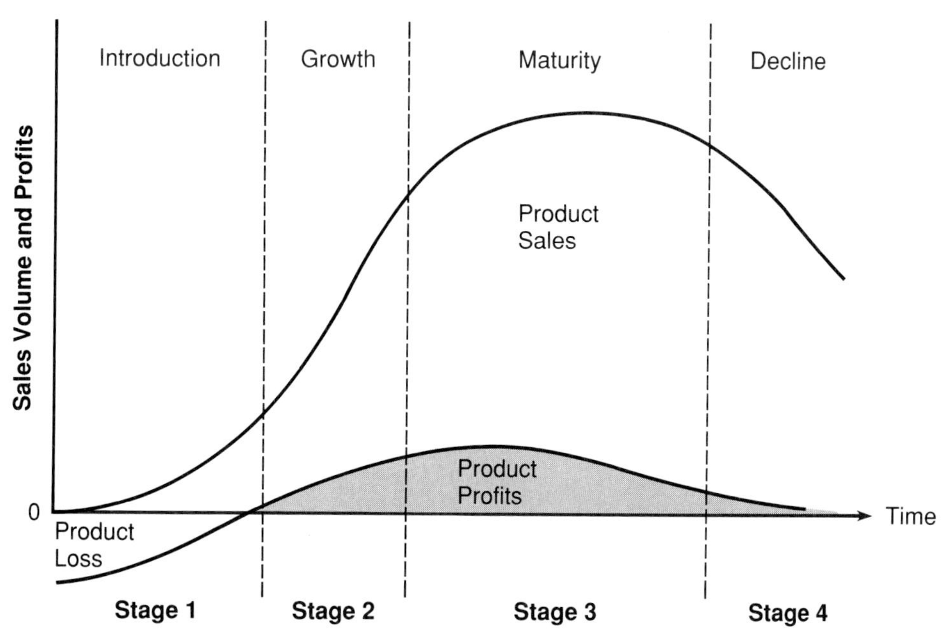

Not all products go through this cycle. Many never get out of the introduction stage because they fail to be accepted. Also, the actual length of each stage varies according to the nature of the product and market characteristics.

The concept of the product life cycle provides a useful framework for assessing marketing strategies and forecasting profits. As a product progresses through all four stages, consumer behavior toward the product can be expected to undergo dramatic changes. Innovators, those who are first to buy new products, have different needs than those consumers who will buy the product once others have adopted it. Sales changes are the result of one or more of the following factors:

- The need for the product lessens or disappears entirely,
- A better product is developed to satisfy the same need, and
- A competitive product gains an advantage through more effective marketing strategies.

Therefore, different marketing strategies are required as the product moves through the various stages of the life cycle.

Introducing New Products

The concept that products have a limited life points to the importance of developing and launching new products. All firms committed to long-term growth must be prepared to offer new or improved products and/or services to their target market(s). For example, the importance of introducing new products is recognized by Lenox China and Crystal. In the company's new product line, crystal is a very important and growing part of its business. Crystal is not only an important segment for the company, but it also is a natural adjunct to the china business.[13]

Nike is another example of a company that recognizes the importance of introducing new products. In response to customers' more balanced approach to fitness, Nike has come out with a new shoe that can be used for all activities. It is the cross-training shoe, which is a departure from anything Nike has done in the past.

Although Nike has had air shoes since 1978, only recently has the company been able to use air in its shoes to give customers better cushioning and better performance for virtually any activity. One of the great success stories for Nike has certainly been the Michael Jordan shoe. According to Philip Knight, chairman of Nike, it is a good shoe that captured the public's imagination, and that is what business is all about. One without the other does not work.[14]

Never satisfied, Nike continually investigates ways to improve upon their athletic shoes in response to the growing consumer demand for shoes designed for a wide array of athletic activities. (Photograph courtesy of Nike, Inc.)

Small manufacturers suffer in many respects when developing new products. They face the threat of competition from major firms, and are limited in their resources—cash flow, research facilities, and management experience with new products. On the other hand, they have easier access to government assistance, such as from the Small Business Administration, and, most important, they have greater flexibility than large firms. Where a major corporation can take months to approve development of a new product, a small company can do it in a day or less. This ability to move quickly extends through the entire product life cycle.

New Product Failures

There are many reasons why new products fail. Small companies commonly point to their lack of financial resources as the single major cause for product failure. A close evaluation of typical failures shows, however, that the main reasons for failure relate to the product itself, not to the amount of funds available for marketing the product. The results of a study of 87 companies by the National Industrial Conference Board point to eight major reasons for new product failure.[15] These reasons, in order of importance, are:

1. *Inadequate market analysis*—includes failure to provide a product with a substantial improvement over existing products, misreading what the market actually wanted, and poor forecasting as to the actual size of the market.
2. *Product defects*—often involves poor design, but also entails production problems, such as poor quality control.
3. *Poor cost estimates*—involves higher costs than anticipated, which lead to higher prices than anticipated, which in turn lead to smaller volume and profits.
4. *Poor timing*—failure to get the product developed before it becomes obsolete.
5. *Competition*—competitors greet the new product with price reductions and drive it out of the market, or reduce the trade's (wholesalers and retailers) incentive to stock the item.
6. *Inadequate sales force effort*—because of insufficient training or motivation, salespeople do not move the product.
7. *Weak distribution*—selection of the wrong channel of distribution for the product, or failure to stimulate the trade with appropriate introductory offers.

Product Abandonment

Companies generally develop well-thought-out strategies for products that are in the introductory, growth, or maturity stage of their life cycle. Unfortunately, this is usually not the case for products in the stage of sustained sales decline. There is both a reluctance to bury old products and the hope that somehow product sales will pick up. Unless strong reasons for retention exist, however, weak products should be abandoned. A product becomes weak when it is no longer suited to its target market.

Major reasons for dropping products are:

- To reduce the financial losses resulting from the product,
- To free company resources for more profitable products,
- To allow more management time to look for new market opportunities,

- To divert advertising and salesforce attention to making other products more profitable,
- To restore consumer confidence in the company.

Low-profit or rapidly declining products which were recently dropped include Sony's Beta format videocassette recorder, Kodak's disc camera line, and *Newsweek on Campus* and *Business Week Careers,* two magazines targeted to college students.

Perhaps the biggest cost of not dropping products at the proper time is paid in the firm's future. Weak products delay the search for replacement products, and thus weaken the firm's long-run survival. Too many firms are long on yesterday's breadwinners and short on tomorrow's breadwinners.

A product abandonment program should include a policy regarding how often products are to be reviewed. In periodic checks of each product, sales records should be used to help answer such questions as:

- Is the percentage increase in sales of this product declining? For example, compare an increase last year of 5 percent against an increase of 10 percent the year before last. What is causing this decline? If sales are remaining the same, is this a good sign in a growing economy?
- Are present territories saturated? Should one expand present territories before finding new ones?
- Did the percentage of selling expense, including advertising, increase for this product? If so, why?
- If sales, profits, or prices have slipped, why?
- Is competition now putting out a new product that is causing the decline?

If a competitor's product is causing the decline, these questions should be considered:

- Is the competitor's product of a higher quality, according to customers?
- Is the competitor's product physically more attractive to customers? Why?
- How is the competing product priced, distributed, and promoted?

It may be necessary to conduct a consumer survey to answer the first two questions. After all, the customer's perception is of greatest importance.

DISTRIBUTION DECISIONS

One key decision for an entrepreneur concerns which distribution channel to use. A **channel of distribution,** also called a trade channel, is the route taken by the goods as they move from producer to consumer. Ultimately, the distribution channel must deliver the goods and services desired by customers at the right time and at the right place.

The issue of choosing the right distribution channel is illustrated by Compaq Computers. The company sells its computers through its dealer base. It is an independent base, not captive to IBM or anyone else. As long as Compaq Computers meets the needs of its dealers in terms of their sales and profits, they are able to sell to their customers and create satisfaction. The company believes it will be able to do very well no matter who else is selling through the distribution channels. For example, Digital primarily sells direct, and one of IBM's most important sales channels is direct. The dealer channel, combined with Compaq's product leadership, put the company in a very strong position.[16]

A manufacturer can employ its own salesforce to sell the product direct to the final consumer, or it can use one or more middlemen in its distribution channel. In most cases middlemen are used because they can perform the necessary marketing functions at a lower cost than producers can.

Marketing goods and services includes basic functions that must be performed by someone, regardless of which distribution method is used. The basic distribution functions include buying and selling, transporting, storing, grading or sorting, financing, risk-taking, and providing market information. These functions can be shifted from one channel member to another, but they cannot be eliminated.

Choosing the Right Distribution Channel

When decided which type of distribution channel to use, the entrepreneur must first define the target market. Five questions become especially relevant:

1. Who are the customers?
2. Where are they located?
3. How can they be reached?
4. How would they like to be reached?
5. When do they buy?

Answers to these questions will narrow the choices regarding the right channel to use. For example, if there are many potential customers scattered over a wide area, widespread distribution is required. If the product is a low-ticket item, such as toys, it would be too expensive to employ a salesforce to sell direct to the consumer. On the other hand, it may be appropriate to sell directly through the mail.

Selection of the distribution channel that will allow a small manufacturer to reach the market profitably often narrows down to three choices:

1. To sell directly to the customer,
2. To sell to the retailer,
3. To sell to wholesalers or use independent sales agents.

The more direct the manufacturer's distribution, the more can normally be charged, but the more marketing functions must also be performed by the manufacturer. Given their limited resources and distribution expertise, small manufacturers usually rely on middlemen.

Direct Distribution

Direct distribution normally requires a salesforce. Whether it is economically feasible for entrepreneurs to hire, train, and support their own salesforce depends on a number of factors, such as:

Factors	*Characteristics*
Customers	Concentrated in a small number of regions
Products	Sufficiently broad to give the salesforce a full workload and to absorb the cost of the salesforce
Complexity	Technically complex
Prices	Per unit prices high enough to support the salesforce
Order size	Average order size large enough to support the salesforce

If the characteristics associated with the specific factors are present, selling direct may be a viable method of distribution.

Attracting Good Middlemen

One common and frustrating problem of a small business is attracting good middlemen. Middlemen are not anxious to rely on unknown sources of supply and assume the risk of buying goods that might not sell. Some firms find, therefore, that they must initially be satisfied with any middlemen they can get. If the product catches on and becomes better known, other distribution channels will open for them.

Significant promotional and selling effort is usually needed to attract good middlemen, assuming they are available. A new firm often finds, however, that the best dealers are already committed to competing products. Fortunately, there are other alternatives. One option is to use independent sales agents.

Independent Sales Agents

The independent sales agent may be the answer for owner-managers who have problems with selling.[17] In some cases, the problem may be that there are not enough prospects to justify putting a full-time salesforce on the factory's payroll. In other cases, because of heavy schedules, the sales staff may be missing opportunities to cultivate new accounts.

Selling for others is the business of **independent sales agents.** They make their money by representing several clients on a commission basis. They solicit orders for clients in agreed-upon territories. Some agents have employees who help them cover a wide area. The manufacturers, as a rule, ship and bill the customers directly. Manufacturers set prices, terms, and other conditions of sale.

Sales agents go by various names. A few examples are manufacturer's agent, manufacturer's representative, and rep. The labels vary according to industries. Also, the marketing functions that agents perform vary from one industry to another.

Whether it is better to use one's own salesforce (direct selling) or a sales agent depends mainly on cost and control. In considering the cost, one should include items such as the paperwork necessary to keep them on the road; Social Security obligations; and fringe benefits, such as vacations and health insurance. On control, the question is: What degree of control does one need to achieve one's sales objectives? When an agent represents a firm, the agent controls the approach to customers. In effect, they are the agent's customers.

Using an independent sales agent may be as good as, or better than, using one's own salesforce. For example, if the product is attractive to wholesale distributors and retailers, it may make little or no difference whether they buy from a factory salesperson or an independent sales agent. When it makes no difference, the owner-manager who insists on maintaining a salesforce for the sake of ego may be kidding himself or herself. On the other hand, when products require a special personal touch or service, the owner-manager may need to control the entire selling job.

Every sales agent, no matter how good, is not right for every manufacturer. Selecting the one that can be an extension of one's firm to the trade is not easy. To the customer, the agent is the company.

Sales agents can be found through several sources. Classified advertisements in trade papers, agent listings available from the Manufacturer's Agents National Association and directories published by industry, and recommendations from customers and sales managers or owners of noncompeting companies in one's industry can be good sources. Also, editors or salespeople from trade magazines can often offer recommendations.

Working with a sales agent starts by having a written contract with the agent. It should spell out what each party is to do. Working harmoniously with an agent is very important. Companies that work successfully with an independent sales agent accept the agent as a professional arm of their firm. Their owner-managers respect the talents of their agents.

The sales agent should be involved in various phases of marketing. For example, the agent may have constructive suggestions on packaging, sales promotion, and advertising. Many sales agents have strong ego drives and thrive on involvement. The agent's interest, challenge, and profit come from making a sale. One should not burden the agent with detail. Rather, one should help cut through to the heart of what the representative is expected to accomplish: sales.

Evaluating Distribution Channels

A firm should periodically check the distribution channels for weaknesses. Channels of distribution may be getting the product to the target market at the right time and right place, or they may be off target. In applying information about present and prospective customers to the channels of distribution, attention should be focused on:

- Changes in customers' purchasing pattern,
- Changes in customers' location,
- Changes in the marketing functions performed by middlemen, and
- Changes in the distribution strategies of competitors.

These changes are taking place with such regularity that periodic evaluation of distribution practices is necessary.

PRICE DECISIONS

Price decisions directly affect a firm's sales and profits. They should therefore be evaluated as critically as the other marketing variables. Effective pricing requires an understanding of costs, market demand, competitors' price policies, and the limitations imposed by law.

Cost-Oriented Pricing

Most pricing methods are versions of the cost-plus approach. In its simplest form, the **cost-plus approach** means that the selling price for a product is equal to the cost, plus a desired profit. Costs provide a floor below which prices cannot go in the long run, while profits provide the necessary return on investment. This is the most popular pricing method because it is simple and easy to apply.

Using cost-oriented pricing methods requires knowing the costs of producing and marketing a product or service. This is not as simple as it might appear, however, because several types of costs may have to be considered. Furthermore, as the volume of output or purchases changes, not all costs will behave the same way. The following cost concepts may need to be considered when prices are based on cost: total cost, total fixed costs, total variable costs, average total costs, average fixed costs, average variable costs, and marginal costs. Suffice it to say that there may be several costs a firm needs to calculate in using the cost approach. This is especially true for manufacturers.

Demand Considerations

Even if a firm determines its prices solely on cost, it cannot ignore consumer demand. A pricing strategy can be effective only if customers are able and willing to pay the price. For example, different price points have been established for Lenox China and Crystal products. The range of its dinnerware prices runs between $78 for a five-piece place setting all the way up to $325 for a heavily gilded pattern.[18]

Häagen-Dazs

Estimating demand for a product is difficult at best. Some of the factors that need to be considered are availability of substitutes, urgency of need, and customer satisfaction derived from the product. Indeed, the price a consumer is willing to pay may be largely a function of the perceived quality of the item. According to Mark Stevens, chief executive officer of Häagen-Dazs, people do not mind paying a little extra for whatever they love to eat, but they do not want the quality compromised.[19]

Competitors' Actions

Regardless of the pricing method used, a firm cannot ignore prices charged by competitors. If competitors offer quantity discounts, for example, and are successful in inducing customers to purchase in larger quantities, other firms will be forced to follow suit. Similarly, the competition in a market may determine what sellers generally have to offer with respect to specials, seasonal discounts, cash discounts, trade-in allowances, and transportation costs. Many small businesses thus find it convenient simply to follow the prices of competitors.

Many factors—such as costs, market demand, competitor's price policies, and the limitations imposed by law—may be taken into consideration when determining the price of merchandise. (Photograph © Ann M. Mason)

Legal Considerations

Generally speaking, a business can charge whatever it wants to charge, even outrageously high prices, but there are some legal restrictions. In particular, antitrust legislation prohibits price-fixing. This occurs when competitors get together and agree on what prices to charge.

The temptation to fix prices by collusion is at times almost irresistible, especially when rising costs put a squeeze on profits. Although small businesses may not feel as threatened by government action against price-fixing as large corporations do, they are also targets of investigation. Business owners convicted of price-fixing face stiff monetary penalties, and the individuals responsible may get jail terms.

Retail Pricing

Retailers generally try to establish guidelines or policies that help make pricing decisions simple and routine. Some common policy considerations include:

- Whether to price to cover costs,
- Whether to sell at one price,
- Whether to use price lines, and
- Whether to use special sales.

Pricing to cover costs can be accomplished by using either the cost-plus approach or the mark-up approach. Most retail prices are determined by using traditional mark-ups. Using this method, the retailer adds a mark-up to the delivered cost of the goods.

In the past, the traditional mark-ups were applied mechanically. Some merchants used the same percentage mark-up for all their goods. This seemed justifiable because almost all small retailers were using them. At minimum, they gave users assurance that if they used the standard mark-up percentages correctly, they could at least cover costs and expenses.

The competition faced by retailers from all forms of discount and chain operations today is causing merchants to reassess strict adherence to a standard mark-up percentage. It is argued that more price flexibility is needed to deal with price competition. Retailers may thus take a lower mark-up on some items to meet competitors' prices. At the same time, they may have to abandon traditional mark-up percentages because consumers will not accept them.

Selling at one price to all customers who purchase goods under essentially the same conditions is the practice of most retail stores. From a practical point of view, a one-price policy makes pricing easier than a flexible price policy. Furthermore, customers generally regard a one-price policy as being fair. Considerable ill will is often generated when customers discover that someone else was charged a lower price for the same product sold by the same store. There are exceptions, of course, such as giving senior discounts.

For some retailers, however, a flexible price policy is traditional. For example, automobile dealers and pawnshops usually bargain over price with customers.

Price-lining refers to the range of prices offered within a product line. It consists of selecting a limited number of prices at which a store will sell a line of merchandise. For example, an apparel store may sell slacks at $14.95, $19.95, and $24.95, depending on brand and quality. The range of prices offered should be based on customer buying patterns and preferences.

Special sales have become a matter of policy for most retailers today. Aggressive competition is forcing merchants to advertise specials almost every week. Indeed, customers will often postpone buying certain merchandise until specials are advertised.

Some retailers, however, maintain a policy of stable prices and emphasize other marketing aspects. This is especially common among specialty stores. In nonprice competition, emphasis might be placed on the variety, quality, and distinctiveness of merchandise and/or special services provided.

Computation of Mark-up

A **mark-up** is the amount a firm adds to its cost to obtain its selling price. As pointed out earlier, the mark-up approach to pricing is commonly used by retailers.

Mark-up can be computed as a percentage of cost or of selling price. Although many business owner-managers consider mark-up a percentage of the selling price, retailing authorities point out that figuring mark-up on the cost price is easier and less confusing in everyday pricing. The important thing to remember is that when mark-up is figured on the selling price, a different mark-up percentage must be used than when figuring the mark-up on the cost price. Otherwise the anticipated margin will not be attained.

Mark-up on price is the difference between the cost of goods and the selling price, expressed as a percentage of the selling price. An example is:

$$\frac{\text{Selling Price} - \text{Cost}}{\text{Selling Price}} = \frac{\$10 - \$5}{\$10} = 50\% \text{ Mark-up (Margin) on Selling Price}$$

Mark-up on selling price, or margin, corresponds to the gross profit figure on a profit-and-loss statement. It is the margin available to cover the costs of selling and the management of the business, as well as to provide a profit.

Mark-up on cost is also the difference between the cost of goods and the selling price, but is expressed as a percentage of cost. An example is:

$$\frac{\text{Selling Price} - \text{Cost}}{\text{Cost}} = \frac{\$10 - \$5}{\$5} = 100\% \text{ Mark-up on Cost}$$

In dollar terms, margin and mark-up figures are the same, but when put in terms of percentage, the figures are different. Some small businesses fail to make an expected profit because the owner makes the wrong assumption that the percentages of margin and mark-up on cost are the same.

Easy conversion of margin to mark-up percentages can be made by using conversion tables as shortcuts. Exhibit 16–2 represents a typical comparison of margins and mark-ups. Thus, to achieve a profit margin of 25 percent on an item, the cost mark-up is 33.3 percent. To achieve a profit margin of 33.3 percent on an item, the cost mark-up would have to be 50 percent.

Pricing for Services

Service business pricing may be more complex than retail pricing.[20] However, the end result is reached the same way—cost plus operating expenses, plus the desired profit.

EXHIBIT 16–2

Mark-up Table

Margin Percent of Selling Price	Markup Percent of Cost	Margin Percent of Selling Price	Markup Percent of Cost
4.8	5.0	25.0	33.3
5.0	5.3	26.0	35.0
6.0	6.4	27.0	37.0
7.0	7.5	27.3	37.5
8.0	8.7	28.0	39.0
9.0	10.0	28.5	40.0
10.0	11.1	29.0	40.9
10.7	12.0	30.0	42.9
11.0	12.4	31.0	45.0
11.1	12.5	32.0	47.1
12.0	13.6	33.3	50.0
12.5	14.3	34.0	51.5
13.0	15.0	35.0	53.9
14.0	16.3	35.5	55.0
15.0	17.7	36.0	56.3
16.0	19.1	37.0	58.8
16.7	20.0	37.5	60.0
17.0	20.5	38.0	61.3
17.5	21.2	39.0	64.0
18.0	22.0	39.5	65.5
18.5	22.7	40.0	66.7
19.0	23.5	41.0	70.0
20.0	25.0	42.0	72.4
21.0	26.6	42.8	75.0
22.0	28.2	44.4	80.0
22.5	29.0	46.1	85.0
23.0	29.9	47.5	90.0
23.1	30.0	48.7	95.0
24.0	31.6	50.0	100.0

Note: This table shows what the mark-up on cost must be to give the desired margin of selling price. To use this table, find the margin or gross profit percentage in the left-hand column. Multiply the cost of the item by the corresponding percentage in the right-hand, or mark-up, column. The result added to the cost gives the correct selling price.

Services can be more difficult to price, because costs may be harder to estimate or the competition might not be as easy to compare.

Every service will have different costs. Many small service businesses fail to analyze the costs involved in each service, and therefore fail to price the services profitably. Some businesses make a profit on certain services and lose money on others, not knowing which is which. By analyzing the costs associated with each service, one can set prices to maximize profits and eliminate unprofitable services.

The total cost of producing any service is composed of three parts: material, labor, and overhead. Material cost is the cost of materials used directly in the final product, such as spark plugs and gaskets in the repair of an engine. Supplies such as paper towels are part of overhead, and not materials cost. Materials costs must be determined and updated frequently. A cost list must always be used in preparing a bid or quoting a job. If there are shipping, handling, or storage costs for materials, they must be included in the total material costs that are charged.

Labor cost is the cost of work directly applied to a service, such as a mechanic's work. Work not directly applied to the service, such as cleaning up, is an overhead cost. The direct labor costs are derived by multiplying the cost of labor per hour by the number of hours required to complete the job. A time card and clock can be used for determining the number of hours of labor involved in each service.

Overhead cost includes all costs other than direct materials and labor. Overhead is the indirect cost of the service. There are many people on a company's payroll who perform support services. These are not charged to direct labor, but must be included as a cost. Some examples of these employees are: clerical, payroll, legal, janitorial, and supply. Insurance, taxes, depreciation, rent, accounting, advertising, office supplies, utilities, and transportation are also part of the overhead cost. A reasonable amount of the overhead costs must be allocated to each service performed. The overhead rate can be expressed as a percentage or as an hourly rate.

PRICING FOR SMALL MANUFACTURERS

Basic to good pricing practices is a recognition that there is more to pricing than internal costs.[21] Two factors are important in developing prices for small manufacturing companies. First, it must be recognized that it is the market, not the costs, that determines the price at which the product will sell. Second, it must be recognized that costs and desired profits only establish a price floor below which one cannot sell to make a profit.

The area between the price ceiling, established by the market, and the price floor, determined by costs and desired profits, is the relevant price range. Only if one can produce at a cost that will permit recovery of costs and the desired margin at the price the market determines can one expect to conduct business profitably.

Manufacturing companies are confronted with the same problems that face retailers and service providers—their pricing practices can get out of date quickly. Market conditions change rapidly, so that pricing strategies successful a year ago may no longer be appropriate. For example, inflation, strict environmental regulations, wide swings in the economy, and increased foreign competition may affect the market. Consequently, pricing practices need to be reviewed frequently and necessary changes initiated accordingly.

Cost-Based Methods

There are several methods of developing price floors based on costs. One should keep in mind that each of these methods is designed to meet specific pricing objectives under different conditions.

Mark-Up on Cost Method

The most basic and frequently used method for developing price floors is the mark-up on cost method. This involves identifying the various types of costs and adding an additional percentage of those costs as a mark-up. Exhibit 16–3 provides examples of the various mark-up on cost approaches.

EXHIBIT 16–3 Mark-up on Cost Pricing

Mr. Smith, president of ABC Manufacturing Co., develops a new product and wants to determine at what price he should sell it. With the help of his accountant, he develops the following cost information:

Direct Labor (DL)	$.10 per unit
Direct Materials (DM)	.20 per unit
Overhead (OH)	.06 per unit
Total Cost (TC)	.36 per unit

Mr. Smith is considering three pricing methods, outlined below, to establish his price floor:

Method 1		Method 2		Method 3	
Full Cost Pricing		**Incremental Cost**		**Conversion Cost**	
P = TC + M(TC)		P = (DL + DM) + M(DL + DM)		P = (DL + OH) + M(DL + OH)	
Therefore, price is:		Therefore, price is:		Therefore, price is:	
Total Cost	.36	Direct Labor	.10	Direct Labor	.10
Margin (50%)	.18	Direct Materials	.20	Overhead	.06
Price	.54	Direct Costs	.30	Conversion Cost	.16
		Margin (100%)	.30	Margin (200%)	.32
		Price	.60	Price	.48

Mr. Smith has selected the margin he wants in each of the three pricing methods and has come up with three different prices for his new product. By looking carefully at each, he sees that if he changes the desired margin in any of the three, the price would change. He must now say to himself, "These are price floors developed on the basis of my costs and desired margins. Can I sell the product at any of these prices?" If so, he obviously would want to receive the highest price he could and would select the $.60 price for his product. If he could not sell for even $.48, he would have to either accept lower margins or somehow reduce costs in order to stay in business.

Source: Small Business Administration, *Pricing for Small Manufacturers,* Management Aid Number 226 (1976).

Full Cost Base

This method is designed to recover all costs plus a margin. It is computed by adding up all costs and adding to them a mark-up, or some fraction of those costs. The formula for full-costing is:

$$P = TC + (M)(TC)$$

or, price (P) equals total cost (TC) per unit plus a mark-up (M), or percentage, of that total cost. (See Method 1 in Exhibit 16–3). This method's main advantage is that it is simple and easy to use. Its biggest disadvantage is that profit may be foregone because of arbitrary overhead allocation. In all cost-based pricing approaches, careful treatment of overhead is important.

Incremental Cost Base

This method uses direct labor and direct material as its base and emphasizes the incremental cost of producing additional units. Because it is normally a larger mark-up on a smaller base than in the case of full-cost, it shifts sales emphasis toward products that absorb more overhead. The formula for incremental costing is:

$$P = (DL + DM) + M(DL + DM)$$

or price equals direct labor (DL) plus direct materials (DM) plus a mark-up on the sum of direct labor plus direct materials. (See Method 2 in Exhibit 16–3).

Conversion Cost Base

Conversion cost basing emphasizes the value added or direct labor plus overhead in developing the price floor. It shifts sales emphasis toward products with high materials costs and economizes on company labor and machines. The formula for conversion cost base is:

$$P = (DL + OH) + M(DL + OH)$$

or price equals direct labor plus overhead (OH) plus a mark-up on the sum of direct labor and overhead. (See Method 3 in Exhibit 16–3). Its obvious disadvantage is that overhead allocation must be based on a clear rationale, because the allocation of overhead will influence the price so heavily.

Other cost-based approaches to pricing include methods designed to determine prices required to accomplish either a desired margin objective or a desired rate of return on investment. The first is target margin on sales, and the second is target return on investment.

Target Margin on Sales

If the objective is to establish a price that will return a desired margin on sales, one can use target margin on sales. This method is illustrated in Exhibit 16–4. The formula is:

$$P = \frac{\text{Total Cost per Unit}}{100\% - \%SA - \%PM}$$

or price equals total manufacturing cost per unit divided by 100 percent minus the percent of sales and administrative costs (SA) minus the percent of desired profit margin (PM).

This method will identify what price must be charged to achieve a desired margin on sales. As with all the methods discussed, one can vary the factors and see what price must be charged to accomplish different returns, or what price must be charged based on various cost figures. The target margin on sales requires accurate information on sales and administrative costs.

Target Return on Investment

This method determines what price must be charged to achieve a desired return on investment. Exhibit 16–5 illustrates this method. The formula is:

$$P = \frac{(ROI)\ I/Y + FC + VC\ (Q)}{Q}$$

or price equals desired return on investment (ROI) times the ratio of investment (I) in dollars over the desired payback period in years (Y), plus fixed costs (FC), plus variable costs (VC) times quantity sold (Q), all divided by the quantity sold.

EXHIBIT 16–4 ***Target Margin on Sales***

Mr. Jones, president of XYZ Manufacturing Co., has developed a new product and wants to determine at what price he should sell it. Mr. Jones has many products in his product line, and through experience has learned that if he can get a 25 percent margin on sales, he can make a satisfactory return. He also knows that his selling and administrative costs usually run around 15 percent. By using the Target Return on Sales method he can determine at what price he should sell. Mr. Jones' accountant has developed the following cost figures:

Direct Labor (DL)	$ 4.50 per unit
Direct Materials (DM)	8.00 per unit
Overhead (OH)	12.50 per unit
Total Cost Per Unit	$25.00 per unit

Mr. Jones calculates his price floor in the following manner:

$$\text{Price} = \frac{\text{Total Cost per Unit}}{100\% - 15\% - 25\%} = \frac{25.00}{1.00 - .15 - .25} = \frac{25}{.60} = \$41.67$$

Mr. Jones must now determine whether his product will sell at $41.67. If it will not, he must either accept a lower profit margin or reduce costs if he is going to be able to sell his product.

Source: Small Business Administration, *Pricing for Small Manufacturers,* Management Aid Number 226 (1976).

The target return on investment method is only as accurate as the estimate of the quantity that will be sold. Often, where sales volume is sensitive to price, only a rough estimate of how much will be sold at a given price is possible. Therefore this method should not be considered an exact method for determining price just because a formula has been developed to compute the price with this method.

After determining the price using this formula, one should ask, "How many can I sell at this price level?" If anticipated sales at this price level are not at least equal to the unit volume used in the pricing formula, the Q in the formula, either costs must be reduced or a lower ROI must be accepted in order to reduce the price of the product.

If lower costs are possible or low ROI is acceptable, the formula needs to be reworked to determine the new price. Only when the volume that one can actually sell equals or exceeds the quantity (Q) used in the price formula will the desired return on investment be attained.

The Price Ceiling

The forgoing methods of determining the price floors based on cost are only half the pricing problem. They tell what price is required to cover costs and earn a return. But they are accurate only if the market will accept the required volume at the resulting price. The **price ceiling,** determined by the market, is the other half of the pricing problem. Determining the price ceiling is usually difficult. Economic, market, competitive, customer, and other factors can influence it. Two approaches can be used to determine the price ceiling: hit or miss and market research.

EXHIBIT 16–5 ***Target Return on Investment Pricing***

Mr. Green, president of JKL Manufacturing Co., has developed a new product and wants to determine at what price he should sell it. Because this new product will require a substantial investment, he wants to be sure that he can get a satisfactory return for his investment. His requirement is a 30 percent return before taxes. Since he is in the 48 percent tax bracket, this will give him approximately a 15 percent return after taxes. Mr. Green's accountant has estimated the following costs for the new product:

Required Investment	\$100,000.00
Fixed Costs	\$ 20,000.00
Variable Costs	\$ 200.00 per unit

Mr. Green also requires that his investment be paid back within five years and estimates that he can sell 500 units per year. He can use the Target Return on Investment formula to develop his price.

$$\text{Price} = \frac{(\text{ROI})\frac{I}{Y} + FC + VC(Q)}{Q} = \frac{(.30)\frac{100{,}000}{5} + 20{,}000 + 200(500)}{500} =$$

$$\frac{(.30)20{,}000 + 20{,}000 + 100{,}000}{500} = \frac{6{,}000 + 20{,}000 + 100{,}000}{500}\ \frac{126{,}000}{500} = \$252$$

Mr. Green must now ask himself if he thinks he can sell 500 units at \$252 in each of the next five years. If he cannot, he must either accept a lower ROI or reduce costs in order to make his investment pay.

Source: Small Business Administration, *Pricing for Small Manufacturers,* Management Aid Number 226 (1976).

The hit-or-miss approach requires that the product be produced and put on the market. One principle should be kept in mind when using this approach: It is easier to lower prices than to raise them.

Therefore, for new products it is better to put the product on the market with a little extra margin than with not enough. If the market will accept the product at the price with the extra margin included, more rapid recovery of costs will occur. If it will not, the price can be reduced to see if that will stimulate sales. Lowering the price from a high margin is much more acceptable to the market than introducing the product, finding that the price was too low, and then raising it.

The market research approach offers the benefit of not having to risk finding out that the market will not accept the product at the required price before an investment is made in producing the product. But usually this requires the use of outside experts, and it can be costly. The choice between the hit-or-miss approach and market research should be based on the cost to manufacture a small amount of the product and put it on the market, compared to the cost of market research.

The principle to remember is that products are bought on the basis of perceived value in the minds of the buyer and not on the basis of what it costs to produce and market them. Only if one can produce and market at a cost permitting sale of the product at a price equal to or below the buyer's perceived value will a manufacturer make the sale.

Perceived value pricing works to assign a price to a product based upon its price ceiling, that is, its value to the customer in the use of the product. For example, the popular 3M Corporation's Post-it Notes and Nintendo's "Super Mario Brothers," "Legend of Zelda," and "Megaman" are priced high relative to their cost. However, these prices are consistent with the value that the end-user places on the products.

SUMMARY

1. Marketing attempts to establish a mutually satisfying exchange between buyer and seller. The functions involved in this process include research, product planning, pricing, distribution, and promotion. The marketing mix is made up of the latter four functions, which are the controllable marketing variables that a firm combines to satisfy customers.
2. The marketing concept replaces the traditional sales concept. The sales concept involves persuasion of the customer in purchasing a given product. The marketing concept seeks to identify customer needs and develop products that will satisfy those needs.
3. The study of consumer buying behavior is a study of buying habits and motives. Motives may be conscious, subconscious, or unconscious, thus making determination of consumer needs and wants difficult.
4. Target markets should be selected to maximize marketing strategies in areas of high potential appeal. This selection of target markets is known as market segmentation.
5. An important phase in marketing strategy is defining measurable and realistic marketing objectives.
6. Developing marketing strategies involves setting the marketing mix and identifying the target market(s).
7. The marketing strategy and its various components need periodic evaluation. An overall evaluation of marketing activities is a marketing audit.
8. The product life cycle is made up of four stages: introduction, growth, maturity, and decline. All stages have their own characteristic marketing strategies.
9. New product failures are primarily a result of problems with the product itself rather than lack of financial resources.
10. Generally there is no well-developed strategy for products in the decline stages of their life cycles.
11. Distribution decisions involve the use of direct or indirect distribution of products. Middlemen are typically used because they can perform certain marketing functions at a lower cost than can producers.
12. In choosing the distribution channel, one must define the target market and select the type of channel. If a middleman is to be used, there can be difficulty in finding a good one. With direct distribution, the firm must maintain its own salesforce.
13. Independent sales agents may be the answer for small businesses that have problems with selling and distribution.
14. The most popular pricing method for retailers is the cost-plus method, in which the price for a product equals the cost plus a profit, with the cost acting as a floor for prices.
15. Several cost concepts, such as variable cost and fixed cost, must be considered when prices are based on cost.
16. Many retailers develop pricing guidelines based on general company policy, such as pricing to cover cost, selling at one price, using price lines, and special sales.
17. Mark-up is the amount a firm adds to its costs to obtain its selling price. It can be computed as a percentage of sales or of cost.
18. In developing pricing practices, small firms should consider not only internal costs but also such influences as competition, technology, and the general business environment.
19. Service business pricing, which may be more

complex than retail pricing, needs to take into consideration the same factors considered in retail pricing.

20. Mark-up on cost pricing methods used by manufacturers can be based on full cost, incremental cost, conversion cost, target margin on sales, or target return on investment. These methods determine the price floor.
21. The price ceiling, determined by market characteristics, can be calculated on a hit-or-miss basis or on a market research approach.

KEY TERMS AND CONCEPTS

Marketing
Exchange process
Marketing mix
Marketing concept
Production concept
Sales concept
Target market
Marketing strategy
Trading up
Trading down
Marketing audit
Product life cycle
Channel of distribution
Independent sales agent
Cost-plus pricing
Mark-up
Price ceiling

QUESTIONS FOR DISCUSSION

1. What is the definition of marketing?
2. Which marketing functions make up the marketing mix?
3. Why does the marketing concept reverse the logic of the sales concept?
4. The difficult question in the study of consumer behavior is, "Why do people buy?" In attempting to determine this, what must be studied?
5. What is the value of target marketing for the small business?
6. Why should a firm have marketing objectives?
7. What is a marketing audit?
8. Differentiate between the two perspectives from which products may be viewed.
9. What four stages comprise the product life cycle?
10. As a product moves through its life cycle, consumer behavior toward the product can be expected to undergo dramatic changes. Why is this so?
11. What are the advantages of using independent sales agents rather than a salesforce?
12. Why do most firms rely on middlemen to reach their customers?
13. What are some considerations in using a cost-oriented pricing strategy?
14. What are some common pricing policies that help make retail pricing decisions relatively simple and routine?
15. What are some common methods of pricing used by small manufacturers?

SELF-TEST REVIEW

Multiple Choice Questions

1. The functions of product planning, pricing, distribution, and promotion make up the:
   a. Marketing concept.
   b. Marketing research.
   c. Marketing mix.
   d. None of the above.
2. Which of the following is the most difficult question to answer about consumer behavior?
   a. Who buys?
   b. When do they buy?
   c. How do they buy?
   d. Why do they buy?
3. The typical product life cycle consists of four stages: 1) introduction, 2) decline, 3) maturity, and 4) growth. Which of the following is the correct order for these stages?
   a. (1), (4), (3), (2).
   b. (1), (3), (4), (2).
   c. (1), (4), (2), (3).
   d. Could be any of the above.
4. Which of the following must be considered in making price decisions?

a. Cost.
b. Customer demand.
c. Prices of competitors.
d. All of the above.

5. If an item costs $10 and sells for $15, the mark-up on cost is:
   a. 33.3 percent.
   b. 50 percent.
   c. 100 percent.
   d. None of the above.

True/False Statements

1. Marketing is a process that attempts to establish a mutually satisfying exchange between buyers and sellers.
2. Under the marketing concept, a firm makes a product and then uses various methods to persuade customers to buy it.
3. Once developed, marketing strategies require little if any modification.
4. From the customer's perspective, the physical attributes of a product are always the most important consideration when deciding whether or not to buy the product.
5. Different marketing strategies are required for different stages of the product life cycle.
6. The main reasons for new product failures relate to the amount of funds available for marketing them:
7. Direct distribution normally requires the employment of a sales force.
8. Most pricing methods are versions of the cost-plus approach.
9. Mark-up on cost is the difference between the cost of goods and the selling price expressed as a percentage of the selling price.
10. The price floor is determined by the market.

THE ORIGINAL KLIP JOINT

The Original Klip Joint was purchased by Philip Bellings three years ago under the name "Gay 90's Barber Shop." At the time of purchase, Bellings was a full-time employee at the shop. The shop has a prime location, and until two years ago it catered to a specific target market: males. Realizing the trend toward more up-to-date styles and blow-cuts, Bellings converted the Gay 90's Barber Shop to a unisex hairstyling salon, and named it the Original Klip Joint.

In order to create a new image, the shop was attractively remodeled and modernized with individual styling booths, creating a professional customer-to-stylist atmosphere. Bellings hoped to attract both male and female customers. The hairgrooming services offered by Bellings and his two employees are precision haircuts, styling, permanents, hair coloring, bodywaves, shampoo sets, and trims.

To promote the Original Klip Joint, Bellings advertises in the yellow pages and has specials every Tuesday and Wednesday. The promotion expenditures are 3.5 percent of sales, a figure that falls within the range of the 3 to 5 percent suggested by the National Hairdressers and Cosmetologists Association. The goal of the promotion effort is to increase the number of customers by 10 percent annually.

The current prices charged for precision haircuts and haircuts plus styling by the Original Klip Joint and its competitors within a two-mile radius of the shop are:

	Precision Haircuts		*Haircuts plus Styling*	
	Men	Women	Men	Women
Figaro's	$10.00	$14.00	$16.00	$16.00
Kim's Hair Styling	9.00	8.50	14.00	14.00
Original Klip Joint	10.50	15.00	16.00	18.00
Pompani's	12.00	12.00	19.50	20.50
Sir Richard's	12.00	12.00	21.00	21.00
Supercuts	8.00	8.00	15.00	15.00

In reviewing the store's performance and clientele for the past two years, Bellings is disappointed to find that sales have increased by only 20 percent and that only 12 percent of his customers are new ones. The average number of customers per day is 35. These customers can be classified as 90 percent male, aged 35 and older, with an annual income of $28,500. The other 10 percent consists primarily of wives of regular customers and girls from a nearby high school.

The breakdown of customers does not represent the target markets Bellings tried to appeal to when he changed the store two years ago. Ideally, he would like to attract males and females aged 20 to 45. This market is viewed as being very concerned with up-to-date styles and the unisex salon atmosphere. A second target market consists of swinging singles. This group is seen as spending more on hair care and related products than any other group, and follows current fashion trends closely. The neighborhood where the Original Klip Joint is located consists largely of white collar workers.

QUESTIONS

1. How can Bellings determine what factors influence individuals to become regular customers of a specific shop?
2. What changes might Bellings make in his marketing mix to attract the target markets he is aiming for?

NOTES

1. "Secret to Inventor's Success Is His Marketing Know-How," *Sacramento Bee,* April 4, 1986, C2.
2. Based on Cable News Network's "Pinnacle," August 30, 1987. Guest: Sidney Swartz, The Timberland Company.
3. "AMA Board Approves New Marketing Definition," *Marketing News,* March 1987, 1.
4. Theodore Levitt, "Marketing Myopia," *Harvard Business Review,* July–August 1960, 45–56.
5. "Entrepreneur Fills Hole in Wine Industry," *USA Today,* August 26, 1988, 10B.
6. "Natural-Toothpaste Firm Bites into Market," *USA Today,* May 6, 1988, 9B.
7. "A Tennis Teacher on Your Back," *Venture,* January 1989, 12.
8. "Small Firms: Try These 10 Techniques to Increase Sales," *Marketing News,* March 15, 1985, 3–4.
9. "Pillow People," *Venture,* February 1989, 8.
10. Based on Cable News Network's "Pinnacle," October 4, 1987. Guest: Rod Canion, Compac Computer.
11. Florists' Transworld Delivery Association, *Flower Business Fact Book,* 1977, 63–64.
12. Based on Cable News Network's "Pinnacle," March 4, 1989. Guest: Christopher Whittle, Whittle Communications.
13. Based on Cable News Network's "Pinnacle," February 27, 1988. Guest: Safford Sweatt, Lenox China and Crystal.
14. Based on Cable News Network's "Pinnacle," March 22, 1987. Guest: Philip Knight, Nike.
15. "Why New Products Fail," *Conference Board Record,* October 1974, 11–18.
16. Based on Cable News Network's "Pinnacle," October 4, 1987. Guest: Rod Canion, Compac Computer.
17. Excerpted from Small Business Administration, *Is the Independent Sales Agent for You?* Management Aid Number 4.005 (1985).
18. Based on Cable News Network's "Pinnacle," February 27, 1988. Guest: Safford Sweatt, Lenox China and Crystal.
19. Based on Cable News Network's "Pinnacle," November 14, 1987. Guest: Mark Stevens, Häagen-Dazs.
20. Excerpted from Small Business Administration, *Pricing Your Products and Services Profitably,* Management Aid Number 4.014 (1988).
21. Adapted from Small Business Administration, *Pricing for Small Manufacturers,* Management Aid Number 226 (1976).

Chapter Seventeen

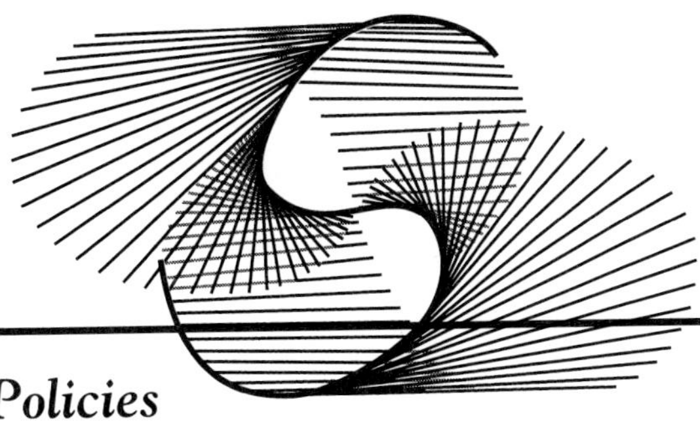

Promotion and Credit Policies

Chapter Outline

Learning Objectives *The objectives of this chapter are to assist you in understanding:*

1. The role of promotion in small business.
2. Factors to consider in establishing an advertising program.
3. The nature and objectives of sales promotion.
4. What is involved in creative personal selling.
5. Credit practices and ways to reduce bad debts.

PROMOTION IN SMALL BUSINESS

The three widely used methods of promotion are advertising, sales promotion, and personal selling. **Advertising** is any paid form of nonpersonal communication about an organization, product, or service by an identified sponsor. **Sales promotion** is a short-term inducement offering added value or incentive for the product to consumers, resellers, or salespersons. **Personal selling** is oral presentation in a conversation with one or more prospective buyers for the purpose of making sales. Personal selling usually occurs face-to-face, but also takes place over the telephone and through video teleconferencing.

The term "sales promotion" should not be confused with "promotion." Sales promotion is only one component of the more comprehensive area of promotion. Sales promotion tools, such as coupons, rebates, sweepstakes, and free samples provide an incentive to buy, whereas advertising provides a reason to buy.

Compared to advertising and sales promotion, personal selling has both advantages and limitations. While advertising and sales promotion are directed at a relatively large number of customers, personal selling is aimed at one or a few individuals. The impact on customers resulting from personal selling efforts is usually greater than through advertising and sales promotion, but so is its cost.

ADVERTISING

Recent surveys show that the average consumer is bombarded with about 2,500 advertising messages every 24 hours. This shows that competition for the listener's ears, the viewer's eyes, and the reader's mind is fierce.

There is no magic formula to successful advertising. To hear some people tell it, all one has to do is spend a lot of money to ensure success. With experience, the businessperson will come to realize that this is nonsense. It is not how much is in the advertising budget, but rather how effectively the advertising dollars are spent. To be an effective advertiser requires critical planning, implementation, and evaluation of an advertising campaign.

Advertising can literally be fun and games. When entrepreneur Eric S. Medney calls on corporate advertising offices, there is no haggling over advertising rates. Companies pay a flat $25,000 to put their logos on a square on Medney's new board game, Condomoneyum. "The game exposes their names to consumers for a longer time than a 30-second TV spot or print ad," says Medney. According to executives who have paid to put their companies' logos on the board game, Condomoneyum is a great, innovative way to promote their companies.[1]

Creation of an advertising campaign should begin with a thorough assessment of the business, its products or services, its competitors, and perhaps most important, its customers. Who are they? What do they know about the products, services, and prices? What is their current image about the business? Where are they located? What are their shopping habits? What newspapers do they read? What radio stations do they listen to? Answers to these types of questions will provide needed insights on which to base advertising objectives and to plan advertising strategies.

Objectives of Advertising

The objective of advertising is to sell something: a product, an idea, a service, an image. Such objectives are too broad, however, and need to be made more specific to be carried out effectively. Examples of specific advertising objectives are:

- To obtain immediate buying action from 10 new customers,
- To introduce a new product or service,
- To increase sales by 25 percent during the next two months,
- To help obtain 10 additional dealer outlets in six months,
- To reach people who are inaccessible to the salesforce,
- To increase daily store traffic by 10 percent,
- To enter a new geographic area,
- To keep the business's name before the public,
- To tie in with a manufacturer's national advertising campaign,
- To promote a new store location.

After specific objectives have been determined, advertising budgets should be prepared.

Establishing the Advertising Budget

"How much should be spent on advertising?" is a question faced by all organizations. There is no single answer to fit every situation. The best answer is that the size of the advertising budget is not as important as how the budget is viewed. Professionals in the field agree that advertising expenditures should be viewed as a necessary part of marketing strategy, not as a luxury to be given up when sales or profits decline.

Sidney Swartz, chairman, chief executive officer, and president of The Timberland Company, believes one must make an up-front investment in advertising. Indeed, Timberland is doing something that was traditionally totally unheard of in the industry. The company was spending between 8 and 10 percent of total sales on marketing, mainly on advertising. Swartz indicates that if you really want to catch the wave, you have got to paddle out and get ready to be on it, and Timberland was willing to do that. The company was actually spending more money than it could afford, according to the balance sheet, but it had faith in an idea, and the idea really worked.

Having positioned itself at the top level of rugged outdoor boots and shoes, Timberland began a television advertising campaign with the objective of making Timberland a national brand in its industry, because the shoe industry has few national brands. Outside of athletic shoe companies, not too many national footwear companies use television as a medium to help establish a national brand.[2]

Advertising should be viewed as a sales-building investment, and not simply as an element of business expense. When advertising is well planned and well executed, it can be an important factor in the growth of a business, as the following example illustrates.

Entrepreneur Robert Gamm recognized a problem that many people face: not knowing what to do with pocket change and keys while jogging or playing tennis. Having had experience designing shoes, Gamm was inspired to design KangaRoos, an athletic shoe with a zippered pocket on the side and a logo of a bounding kangaroo with a baby in its pouch.

KangaRoos introduced Robert Gamm to the world of marketing. First, he recognized an unmet need in the market and went about designing a product to meet that need. To gain visibility for the shoes among Nike, Adidas, and numerous other athletic shoes, Gamm invested $300,000 in an advertising budget and placed four-color advertisements in running magazines. This brought the product to the attention of customers and retail outlets alike, and soon orders started to pour in. Sales have been phenomenal, reaching a level that has attracted numerous competitors.[3]

There are four major methods commonly used in deciding the size of the advertising budget:

1. The percentage-of-sales method,
2. The competitive-parity method,
3. The affordable method,
4. The objective-and-task method.

Percentage-of-Sales Method

The **percentage-of-sales method** involves setting advertising expenditures at a specified percentage of sales. For example, bars and cocktail lounges typically spend 1.0 to 1.2 percent of net sales for advertising purposes, while gift stores allocate an average of 1.5 to 2.5 percent of net sales, as illustrated in Exhibit 17-1. This approach to advertising is used more often than other methods because:

- It is simple and easy to use.
- It gives the business owner a sense of control over the budget.
- It means that advertising expenditures are likely to vary with what the business can afford.
- It encourages competitive stability in advertising expenditures.

In spite of these advantages, this approach has major weaknesses, namely:

- It treats advertising as the result of sales, rather than sales as the result of advertising.
- It is not forward-looking.
- It does not provide a basis for allocating the advertising budget on a product-by-product and territory-by-territory basis.

Competitive-Parity Method

When using a **competitive-parity method,** one sets the advertising budget according to what competitors spend. An argument for using this method is that it prevents costly advertising wars.

Trying to match the advertising expenditures of competitors is a defensive rather than an aggressive approach. It tends to result in blind imitation and ignores the needs of the business. Furthermore, sufficient information may not be readily available from sources such as the media and advertising agencies to estimate competitors' advertising budgets. Such information is more completely reported in secondary sources for some products than for others. When only incomplete information can be obtained, competitive parity can be misleading.

Affordable Method

Many small business firms set the advertising budget on the basis of what they think the business can afford. The **affordable method,** a "this-is-all-we-can-afford" approach, treats advertising as a luxury. It is a financial rather than a marketing approach to advertising. It ignores what advertising can and should accomplish. Furthermore, this method leads to a fluctuating advertising budget that makes it difficult to achieve long-run objectives.

EXHIBIT 17–1 ***Advertising Budget Guide***

Type of Business	Average Advertising Budget (Percent of Net Sales)
Apparel stores	2.5–3.0
Appliance, radio, TV dealers	2.3
Auto supply stores	0.5–2.0
Bakeries	0.7
Bars and cocktail lounges	1.0–2.0
Bookstores	1.5–1.7
Children's and infants' wear stores	1.4
Coin-operated laundries	0.6–2.0
Drugstores (independents)	1.3
Dry-cleaning shops	1.7
Eating and drinking places	5.6
Florists	2.1
Furniture stores	5.0
General job printing	0.4–1.0
Gift stores	1.5–2.5
Grocery stores	1.4
Hardware stores	1.6
Hairgrooming/beauty salons	2.5–3.0
Health food stores	1.1–2.8
Jewelry stores	4.4
Liquor stores	0.9
Lumber and other building materials	2.2
Mail-order houses	6.6
Menswear stores	2.4–2.8
Music stores	1.8
Office supplies dealers	0.6–1.1
Personal services	3.7
Shoe stores	1.9
Sporting goods stores	3.5
Travel agents	5.0
Women's ready-to-wear stores	2.7

Sources: Bank of America, "Advertising Small Business," *Small Business Reporter,* 1976, 1978, 1981, 1982; Newspaper Advertising Bureau, "The 'I Wonder How To Set Up an Advertising Program and How Much To Budget' Book," 1981, 20–26; and "Advertising and Promotion Expenditures as a Percentage of Net Sales," *Sales and Marketing Management,* February 20, 1989, 44.

Objective-and-Task Method

The **objective-and-task method** is the most logical approach to determining the advertising appropriation. In using this approach, the budget is decided by:

- Defining the specific advertising objectives,
- Determining the tasks that must be performed to achieve these objectives,
- Estimating the cost of performing the tasks.

A major problem with this approach is that it does not indicate whether the cost of attaining the objectives is justifiable. The main difficulty with trying to implement the approach is the problem of estimating how much advertising effort is actually needed to achieve the objective.

Message and Copy Development

The effectiveness of advertising depends not only on the amount of the advertising budget but, also, and more important, on how the advertising dollars are spent. Specifically, what appeals are used? How and where are they communicated? How frequently are they presented? Determining the right message involves finding effective things to say to the target market.

Creating the right message sometimes involves a bold imagination, as illustrated by advertising agency Della Femina, Travisano and Partners' memorable singing Meow Mix cat concept. The singing cat is proof that it is sometimes better to be lucky than to be smart or prepared. The company found a piece of footage of a cat choking while trying to swallow a piece of cat food. By putting music to this, they made it almost look as though the cat was singing. (People who hear the story always ask, "Did the cat die?" The cat is alive, collecting residuals.)[4]

Advertisers can get help preparing the advertising message and meeting copy requirements by using some of the following sources:

1. Many media have salespeople who are helpful in copy preparation, artwork, layout, placing of ads, and general promotion.
2. Manufacturers supply point-of-purchase and advertising materials free, grant advertising discounts, and provide co-op advertising (the manufacturer pays half the cost of the ad if its product is featured).
3. Direct mail and advertising agencies provide some of their services at minimal cost. They can be helpful in advising the retailer on how to round out an advertising program.
4. Trade associations, the Better Business Bureau, and the local chamber of commerce can provide information on advertising and advertising ethics.
5. Trade magazines and newspapers that deal with the retailer's particular line of business provide information on different types of advertising campaigns available.

Jerry Della Femina, with his advertising firm Della Femina, McNamee WCRS, has earned a reputation as a creative boutique with the knack for developing ingenious commercials with the right message to the right target audience. (Photograph by Deborah Feingold, reprinted courtesy of Della Famina, McNamee WCRS, Inc.)

Advertising Media

Choosing the best advertising medium for carrying the message is not easy. The effectiveness of a particular medium depends on:

- The advertising objective,
- The requirements of the message,
- The cost of the medium, and
- The customer's media habits.

If the objective is to advertise a special sale at the last minute, for example, newspapers or radio may be used. If the objective is to inform newcomers, the yellow pages might be most appropriate.

Requirements of the message will limit the use of certain media. If a product is best presented through a demonstration, television may be appropriate. If a very brief message can be used, billboards may be best.

The cost of the advertising medium must also be considered. Television is a relatively expensive medium, whereas radio and newspaper advertising are comparatively inexpensive. The funds available and the reach of the media limit the available alternatives.

The medium should never be selected until the advertiser knows the target market to be reached. This is the most important step in selecting a medium. The medium chosen must be read, heard, or seen by the target market.

Each medium has individual characteristics that should be kept in mind. Daily newspapers, which receive the major share of the advertising dollars in the United States, are appropriate for advertising within limited geographical areas, to people of both sexes and all ages, to people with different incomes, educational levels, and lifestyles, and

Because this small business attracts customers from a limited geographical area and must advertise prices on a weekly basis, the local weekly newspaper is the ideal medium for its message. (Advertisement reprinted courtesy of The Farmer's Wagon)

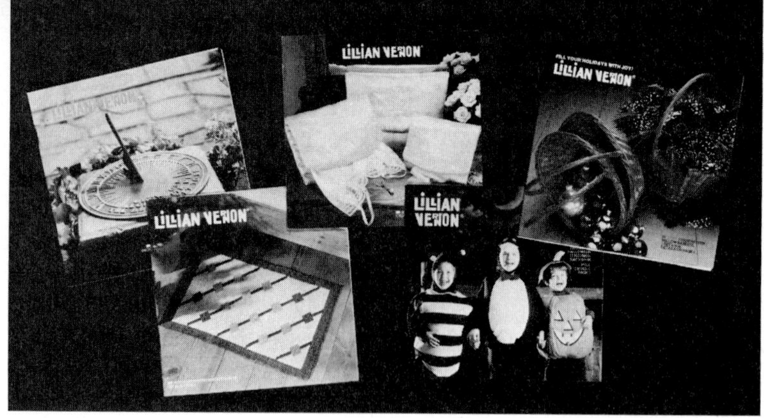

Direct mail, such as these Lillian Vernon catalogues, is an effective way for a small business to reach a target market at minimal cost. (Photograph courtesy of Lillian Vernon Corp.)

with varied interests. Radio, on the other hand, is more fragmented, with different stations appealing to different audiences because of distinctive programming.

Direct mail can provide a personalized advertising approach to reach prospective customers. Mailing lists of prospects with specified demographic characteristics, such as age, income, sex, occupation, or ZIP code, can be purchased for fees as low as $30 per 1,000 names. Direct mail is especially suitable for new businesses and those using coupons or other sales incentives.

Television, notably cable, which reaches a definable market area, is increasingly used by small businesses. The increase in the number of available local and regional television stations is decreasing the cost of television advertising time. The dramatic impact of television makes this medium especially suitable for highly personal, owner-oriented businesses.

Other media include weekly newspapers, which are especially suitable for retailers who service local markets; weekly shoppers, which are used by neighborhood retailers and service businesses; telephone directories (Yellow Pages), which reach active shoppers for goods and services; and billboards targeted toward drivers.

In addition to conventional media, there are other rather innovative advertising methods. Here are some recent examples:

Since most brochures mailed end up in the garbage pail, entrepreneur Paula George offers an alternative by putting sales spiels on floppy disks. The interactive software, which runs on any personal computer, gets more attention than catalogues. Clients use mailing lists to target computer users.[5]

Entrepreneur Eric Clarke figured out that to hit a home run over the left-field fence, you first need a fence. So he developed a portable fence, priced at $3,795, which can convert an athletic field into a regulation ballpark in just 15 minutes. To avoid striking out with team sponsors concerned about the fence's price, Clarke delivers a winning sales pitch: The cost of the fence can be absorbed by selling advertising on it.[6]

Entrepreneur Richard Weisman found a truly clever way to direct advertisements to a captive audience. He has been placing advertisements inside stall doors in public restrooms![7]

Timing of Advertising

Timing is an important consideration in planning effective advertising. It involves adjusting advertising plans over the seasons, the months, and even the days, with careful consideration of delays in impact. The actual advertising timing patterns can be concentrated at the beginning of each month, intermittently throughout the month, or on a continuous basis. Exhibit 17–2 illustrates what a well-timed advertising approach for a retail store might be. Exhibit 17–3 shows a sample worksheet representing one retailer's approach to scheduling advertisements in a newspaper.

Cooperative Advertising

Cooperative advertising is a program in which advertising costs are shared between retailers and manufacturers. The rationale for cooperative advertising is this: A manufacturer advertises brand name products regionally or nationally to persuade consumers to buy them. In order to tell consumers where to buy, manufacturers then offer to share with retailers the cost of local advertising. For the retailer, cooperative advertising makes it possible to expand the promotional effort without increasing costs.

Working with cooperative advertising can be simple and effective. The following procedure can be used:

1. Identify key supplier accounts.
2. Assemble co-op promotion data.

EXHIBIT 17–2 A Well-Timed Advertising Approach

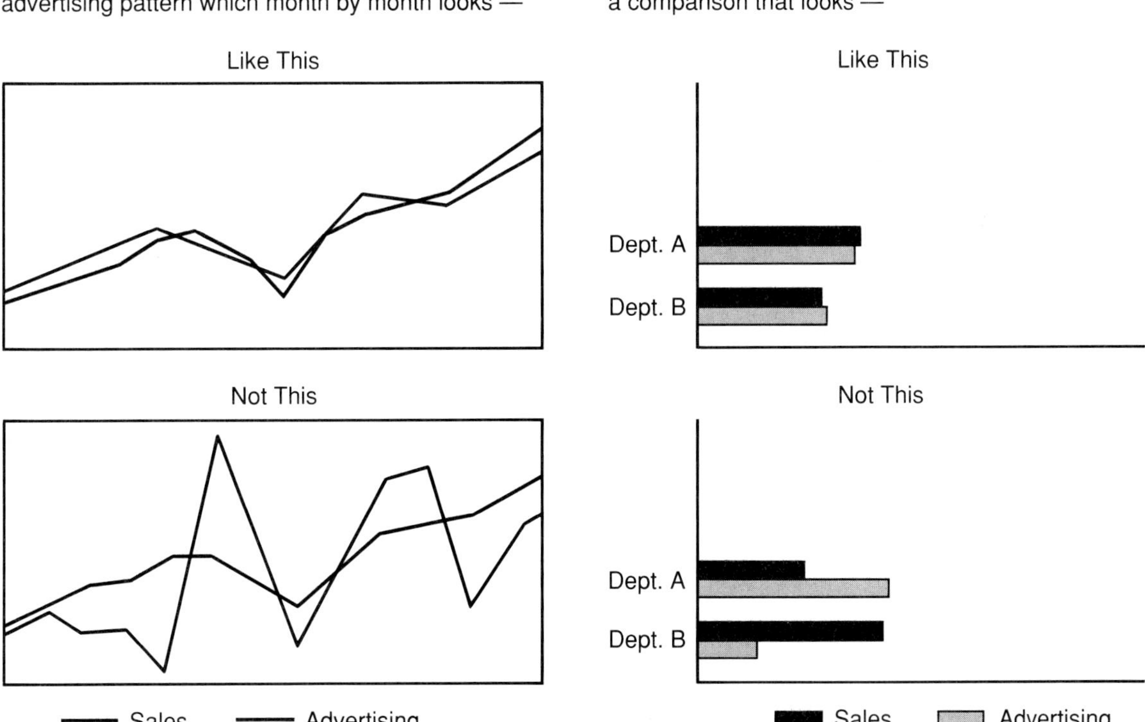

Source: The *Sacramento Bee,* "1982 Sales Planbook," (1982), 4. Reproduced with permission from the *Sacramento Bee.*

EXHIBIT 17–3 Sample Worksheet Representing One Retailer's Approach to Scheduling

His city's newspaper is published evenings and Sunday

1. Set a sales goal

Department	Sales Goal	% of Goal
....	$______	______%
....	$______	______%
....	$______	______%
....	$______	______%
....	$______	______%
....	$______	______%
....	$______	______%
....	$______	______%
....	$______	______%
Totals	$______	______%

2. Decide how much advertising

______________________ % of sales
______________________ dollars
______________________ rate
______________________ linage

3. Decide what to promote

Write in percent of month's sales which each department contributes. Allot percent of month's advertising on an equivalent basis. Calculate the linage for each department.

Department	% of Sales	% of Advertising	Linage
....	______	______	______
....	______	______	______
....	______	______	______
....	______	______	______
....	______	______	______
....	______	______	______
....	______	______	______
....	______	______	______
....	______	______	______
Total	100%	100%	______

4. Fill in this day-by-day schedule

Sunday	Monday	Tuesday	Wednesday	Thursday	Friday	Sataurday
1	2	3	4	5	6	7
8	9	10	11	12	13	14
15	16	17	18	19	20	21
22	23	24	25	26	27	28
29	30	31				

Source: The *Sacramento Bee,* "Sales and Marketing Planbook," (1979). Reproduced with permission from the *Sacramento Bee.*

3. Calculate co-op money available.
4. Allocate co-op money month to month.
5. Integrate co-op money into the regular advertising budget.
6. Create effective product-moving advertising.
7. Merchandise the advertisments to customers and employees.
8. Collect money from manufacturer.

To collect from the manufacturer, the dealer must present proof of advertising and a copy of the invoice. For newspaper advertising, a tearsheet of the page on which the advertisement appears is generally required. For radio and television, an affidavit that the advertising was broadcast is normally required.

Measuring Advertising Results

Measuring advertising effectiveness is not easy. Generally there is no simple analysis of sales that can be used to determine the results of advertising. This is because all elements of the marketing mix are responsible for sales, not only advertising. The exception to this is mail-order advertising, where given units of sales can be related to a specific advertisement or campaign.

Most measurement of advertising effectiveness is done by advertising agencies when pretesting and posttesting a given advertisement or campaign. These tests evaluate consumers' reactions to specific advertisments and the effect they have on buyers' awareness and feelings. Posttesting includes readership, recognition, and recall tests, designed to measure communication effectiveness.

For retailers, there are some techniques available to measure immediate consumer response. Using coupons that must be redeemed within a limited time period is one popular technique. Another approach is keeping track of particular sale items or limited-time offers. Generally, however, retailers recognize that the links between advertising and sales may be too uncertain even with these techniques to permit measuring the direct impact. They recognize that the effect of advertising is long term in nature.

Tests for Immediate-Response Advertisements

Immediate-response advertising is designed to cause the potential customer to buy a particular product within a short time—today, tomorrow, this weekend, or next week.[8] An example of such decision-triggering advertising is an advertisement that promotes regularly priced merchandise with immediate appeal. Other examples are advertisements that use price appeals in combination with clearance sales, special purchases, seasonal items, and "family of items" purchases.

Such advertising should be checked for results daily or at the end of one week from appearance. Because all advertising has some carryover effect, it is a good idea to check also at the end of two weeks from advertising runs, three weeks from runs, and so on to ensure that no opportunity for using profit-making messages is lost.

In weighing the results of immediate-response advertisements, the following devices are useful:

- *Count coupons brought in.* Redeemed coupons usually represent sales of the product. When the coupons represent requests for additional information or contact with a salesperson, were enough leads obtained to pay for the ad? If the coupon is dated—which it should be—the number of returns for the first, second, and third weeks can be determined.

- *Requests by phone or letter referring to the advertisement.* A hidden offer can cause people to call or write. Include, for example, in the middle of the advertisement, a statement that on request the product or additional information will be supplied. Results should be checked over a one-week through six- or twelve-month period because this type of advertisement may have considerable carryover effect.
- *Testing advertisements.* Prepare two different advertisements and run them on the same day. Identify the advertisements—in the message or with a coded coupon—so it can be determined which is more effective. Ask customers to bring in the coupon or to use a special phrase. Run two broadcast advertisements at different times or on different stations on the same day with different "discount phrases." Ask a newspaper to give a *split run*—that is, print Ad A in part of its press run and Ad B in the rest of the run. Count the responses to each advertisement.
- *Sales made of particular items.* If the advertisement is on a bargain or limited-time offer, consider that sales at the end of one week, two weeks, three weeks, and four weeks came from the advertisement. It may be desirable to determine how many sales came from in-store displays and personal selling.
- *Check store traffic.* An important function of advertising is to build store traffic that results in purchases of items not advertised. Pilot studies show, for example, that many customers who were brought to a store by an advertisement for a blouse also bought a handbag. Some bought the bag in addition to the blouse, others instead of the blouse.

Testing Image Advertising

Image advertising is advertising used to keep a store's name and merchandise before the target market.[9] Some people think of this as image-building advertising. With it, people are reminded week after week about regular merchandise or services or told about new or special services or policies. Such advertising should create in the minds of customers the image a store owner wants them to have about the store, its merchandise, its service, and its policies. To some degree, all advertising should be image advertising. It is a reputation-builder for the business.

Image advertising is more difficult to measure than immediate-response advertising because a specific sale cannot always be attributed to it. Sales are usually created long after the advertisement has appeared. For example, an advertisement or a series of advertisements that announce the exclusive franchise for a particular brand start to pay off when customers who want that brand only and ask no questions about competing brands begin to come in.

Because image advertising is spread out over an extended period of time, measurement of results is difficult and not very accurate. Some image advertising, such as a series of advertisements about the brands the store carries, can be measured at the end of one month after the appearance of the advertisements, or at the end of the campaign.

One approach is to make comparisons on a weekly basis. If an advertisement is run each week, for example, at the end of the first week after the advertisement appears or is broadcast, one should compare that week's sales with sales for the same week a year ago. At the end of the second week, one should compare sales with those at the end of the first week as well as the figures for a year ago.

At the end of the third week, one month, three months, six months, and twelve months from the running of the advertisement, one should repeat the process, even though additional advertisements may have appeared or been aired in the meantime. For each of these advertisements, one should make the same type of comparison. The momentum of all of the advertisements, as well as the results of a single advertisement, will thus be measured.

Legal Considerations in Advertising

Regulations on advertising exist at federal, state, and local levels. As a result, small business owner-managers must be aware of what is legally permissible and what types of advertisements violate the law.

Nationally, the Federal Trade Commission, the Food and Drug Administration, and the Federal Communications Commission are among the regulatory bodies that are most concerned about advertising practices. At the local level are such mechanisms as state departments of consumer affairs, local bureaus of consumer affairs, and the Better Business Bureaus.

Among the regulations of the greatest importance to retailers are those concerning the use of false or misleading advertising in *bait-and-switch* practices, in which the advertiser offers an alluring but insincere retail offer to sell a product or service that is not intended to be sold. Its purpose is to switch a buyer from buying the advertised merchandise or service to buying something costlier.

Advertising is a very visible or audible medium easily subject to supervision and criticism from both legal and consumer standpoints. Therefore, care should be taken when making statements and claims for products or services advertised. Advertisements must always conform to the various federal, state, and local regulations and the standards of good taste. As a general guideline, one should always be able to substantiate anything stated in an advertisement.

SALES PROMOTION

Sales promotion has become a popular promotional tool for business firms. As stated earlier in this chapter, sales promotion is designed to provide an incentive to the target market. The range of sales promotion methods is large: coupons, free product samples, cents-off promotions, premiums, sweepstakes, in-store demonstrations, point-of-purchase displays, frequent purchase programs, conventions, trade shows, and many others.

There are several reasons underlying the increased spending for sales promotion. Primarily, however, it is due to the fact that results can easily be measured, and they accomplish specific objectives.

Objectives of Sales Promotion

Sales promotion objectives will vary with the nature of the target market: consumers, the trade, the salesforce, or some combination. Sales promotion directed at consumers might involve increasing brand awareness, encouraging product trial, introducing new products or services, stimulating product usage, or maintaining brand loyalty. Common consumer sales promotions include coupons, cents-off offers, free samples, premiums, money-refund offers, contests and sweepstakes, demonstrations, and point-of-purchase displays.

Sales promotion targeted for the trade (channel members) might have the following objectives: obtaining more extensive product distribution, inducing retailers to participate in cooperative promotional efforts, introducing new products, or obtaining more shelf space. Sales promotions directed at channel members include display allowances, *slotting allowances* (payments made to retailers to stock a new product), cooperative advertising, *push money* (cash payment for each unit sold), conventions, and trade shows.

When sales promotions are directed toward the salesforce, the objective is to motivate the salespeople. Incentives such as sales contests and special bonuses are often provided to help fulfill sales quotas or other objectives.

Sales promotion can, and frequently does, have both a trade objective and a consumer objective. For example, a trade promotion designed to help introduce a new product frequently consists of retailer incentives in the form of display allowances and push money, and consumer incentives in the form of free product samples and/or cents-off coupons.

PERSONAL SELLING

Personal selling is the major promotional method used in business, as measured by total expenditures and by number of people employed. It is especially important for small business because a good personal selling effort provides a valuable competitive edge over larger competitors.

The relative deemphasis of personal selling by large-scale retailers and other businesses has left a gap in customer service that a small business is in a good position to fill. By emphasizing the role of personal selling and developing a good personal sales program, a small firm can gain a competitive advantage not easily matched by larger operations. It is more difficult for small businesses to compete with the big firms on things like merchandise assortment, price, and promotion.

Effective selling does not happen by accident. The small entrepreneur must work to achieve a high level of sales effectiveness in his or her business. In order to achieve this goal, the owner-manager should be aware of the different types of salespeople, the selling process, and the attributes of effective salespeople. Applying such knowledge to a business situation should result in the desired goal of effective sales personnel—the competitive edge.

Elements of the Personal Selling Process

The activities involved in the personal selling process vary among salespeople and will differ for various selling situations. As a general rule, however, the sales process can be broken down into the following separate stages: prospecting and qualifying, the preapproach, the approach, the sales presentation, handling objections, closing the sale, and postsale follow-up. These stages are illustrated in Exhibit 17–4.

1. *Prospecting and qualifying*—developing a list of potential customers is called **prospecting.** This is the first and perhaps most important step in the selling process.

EXHIBIT 17–4 **Steps in the Selling Process**

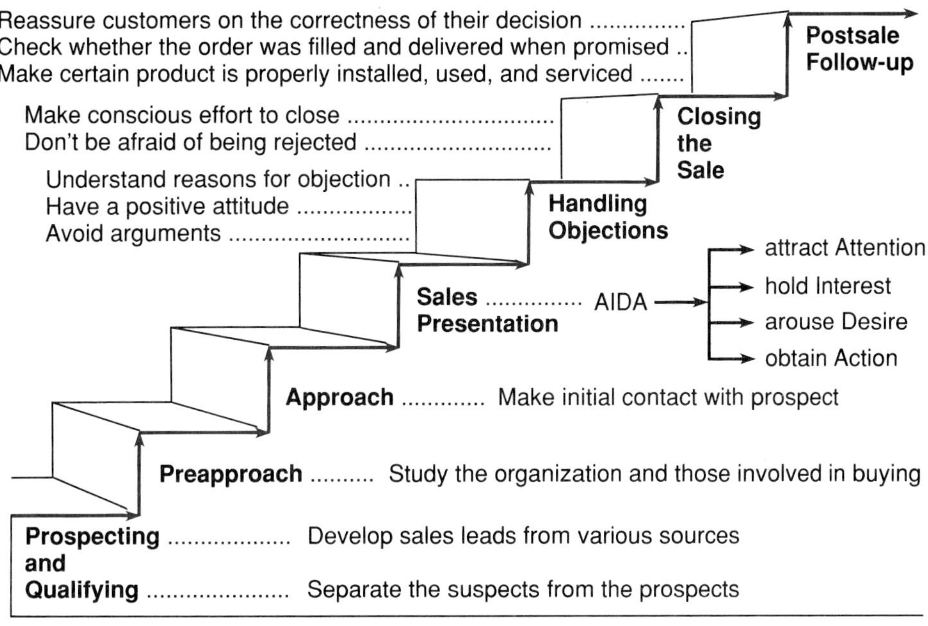

Without a regular flow of potential prospects, the salesperson will have few, if any, potential sales. Prospective customers have to be qualified to separate the "suspects" from potential customers.

A list of prospects can be developed from several sources, including present customers who suggest new leads; public records; newspaper announcements of weddings, births, deaths, graduations, newcomers, and so on; and telephone directories.

2. *Preapproach to individual prospects*—before calling on prospects, the salesperson attempts to obtain as much precall information as possible. For example, a salesperson should obtain and analyze information regarding the prospect's current needs and use of products, as well as his or her feelings about them. The more information obtained about a prospect, the easier the task of tailoring an effective presentation.
3. *Approaching the prospect*—several approaches can be used to contact a potential customer. One type of approach is based on referrals, in which the salesperson explains that a friend, associate, or colleague has suggested the call. Another approach is simply to greet the prospect and state what is being sold. Regardless of the approach used, it is critical that a favorable impression be made and the stage be set for making the presentation.
4. *Making the sales presentation*—during the sales presentation, the salesperson must attract the prospect's attention, hold his or her interest, and stimulate a desire for the product. If possible, the salesperson should demonstrate the product in some way. This will usually stimulate greater interest.

5. *Handling objections*—a salesperson should always expect to hear some objections. A good way to overcome them is to anticipate what they might be and counter them before they are raised. A skilled salesperson actually welcomes objections, because they provide information about where additional sales emphasis is needed.
6. *Closing the sale*—the closing step involves the salesperson actually asking the prospect to buy the product. This is often the most difficult step in the selling process, because there is no one best closing technique. Another reason why closing the sale is difficult is because many salespeople do not attempt to close for fear of being rejected. The so-called *trial close* is probably used as much as any other technique. Using this technique, the salesperson assumes the prospect is going to buy and asks such questions as, "What model have you decided on?" or "Is this going to be cash or charge?"
7. *Follow-up*—an effective selling job does not end when the prospect buys the product or signs the order. Instead, the salesperson should follow up the sale to make certain that any services promised, such as delivery and installation, were fulfilled. The follow-up stage helps insure repeat business and can provide leads to new prospects.

Attributes of a Creative Salesperson

In addition to having personnel who understand and apply the creative selling process, an organization should try to have salespeople who possess certain attributes that can make them more effective in their jobs.[10] These attributes, which can be grouped into mental and physical categories, merit further discussion.

Judgment

Common sense, maturity, intelligence—these and other terms are used interchangeably with judgment. A salesperson knows that it does not pay to argue with a customer. The salesperson also knows that the firm should never be criticized in front of the customers. These situations reflect the use of good judgment on the part of the employee. Please note that the term "maturity" is sometimes used in place of "judgment," but that it is not necessarily a function of age. Many older people do not use good judgment, while some young employees will have a high level of common sense.

Tact

If an employee has a keen sense of what to say and do, many problems can be overcome before they are created. Many employees give little thought to the impact of

The development of a good personal selling program is especially important for small business in order to compete with larger firms. Through his presentation, this salesperson hopes to stimulate a desire for the product and close the sale. (Photograph © Ann M. Mason)

their actions. A child playing with toys in the toy store is told in a blunt manner to "quit playing with the toys and go find your mother." While all this is going on, the mother is standing behind the salesperson. Was a confrontation with the child necessary? No. Could it have been handled differently? Yes. How do the child and mother feel about the store? The feeling is not good. This salesperson lacked the knowledge of what to do and say in order to maintain good customer relations. Be tactful.

Attitude

A good salesperson will have a positive attitude toward customers, merchandise, services, and the business. A good attitude means that an employee is willing to accept suggestions, to learn and to apply the steps in the creative selling process, and to work hard. A salesperson with a bad attitude can create unnecessary problems. A bad attitude is contagious. If an employee is otherwise competent, management should work with him or her to develop a positive attitude. Positive attitudes can result in sales.

Selected Physical Attributes

To be a success, the salesperson must physically belong in the firm's particular environment. Personal appearance and personal hygiene are important in the selling environment. In terms of personal appearance, a slim salesperson would be more appropriate than a larger person in a sales position at a health spa. Equally inappropriate in terms of personal appearance is a clothing salesman who wears last year's styles. He will have difficulty in selling the latest fashions to his customers. Personal appearance does count in the selling equation.

As for personal hygiene, body odor, bad breath, dirty hair, soiled clothes, scuffed shoes, and unkept hands are all reasons why a sale may be lost. Obviously, one needs to be tactful when handling the problem of personal hygiene. An observant owner-manager should keep a watchful eye out for hygiene problems among the staff and, when necessary, counsel the offending employee in private about improving his or her appearance. If he or she does not feel physical attributes are important, ask if he or she would like to buy low-calorie health foods from an overweight salesperson with body odor. Sound funny? It isn't! Customers will usually react unfavorably to this and similarly inappropriate selling situations.

Word of Caution

Mental and physical attributes of salespeople are important. Management must continue to observe sales personnel in regard to the desired traits. Mental or physical attributes of individuals can change over time. Management must be aware of this possibility and attempt to correct any deviations from desired norms before problems are created.

A business can greatly enhance its probability of success by stressing the creative selling process, giving special attention to the desired mental and physical attributes of a creative salesperson. Good creative selling can provide the competitive edge.

Improving Personal Selling

Developing a program for improving the creative selling skills of salespeople is the essence of building an effective personal selling effort. A framework for such a program should consist of the following basic elements:

1. Selecting people who are suitable for particular sales positions.
2. Providing regular and frequent training.
3. Devising an appropriate compensation plan.

If a business is willing to develop a program based on these three elements, a more effective and rewarding selling program should emerge.

Selection

Finding good salespeople is a problem for managers of both large and small firms. Both frequently claim that it is hard to find good people, especially today, in light of the shrinking labor pool. What they fail to realize is that much of the problem is of their own making, because they do not define clearly what they mean by "good" salespeople. They do not specify what qualities they want in the salespeople they are seeking. It is no wonder, then, that they are not satisfied with many of the people they hire.

An effective way to help avoid this problem is to use job specifications (or job descriptions). This device has been used successfully for many years by large firms, and it can be used with equal effectiveness by small firms. A job specification is basically a written statement, typically no longer than one or two paragraphs, delineating the requirements for a particular job. For example, a job specification for a retail sales position in a sporting goods store might appear as follows:

> This job involves mainly in-store sales of a full line of sporting goods, ranging from items of low-unit value (such as golf balls) up to higher-priced merchandise (such as complete sets of golf clubs and skiing equipment). The emphasis is on big-ticket items. Telephone follow-up selling is expected, and there is occasional stock work.

The value of writing a job specification is that it forces the firm to be more explicit about what the job requires and thereby provides a guide for appraising the abilities of prospective employees. For example, since the job described above emphasizes the big-ticket items, the retailer should look for people who have this kind of experience. Many salespeople can do an excellent selling job on low-unit value merchandise but have trouble closing sales on the big-ticket items. Job specifications help avoid such problems.

Training

When the word "training" is mentioned, the small firm typically associates it with the formal programs conducted by large firms. However, sales training by the small operator does not have to be a formal and structured program. Any conscious effort the business owner-manager makes that is aimed at improving the basic skills needed for effective selling is a form of sales training.

Compensation

There is no one best way of compensating salespeople. Compensation plans depend on the nature of the product sold, the position of the salesperson (training or post-training), and common practices in the industry. There is, however, a general principle that should be observed in any type of compensation plan: Compensation should be closely linked to performance. That is why the most common compensation plan is one that consists of salary plus commission.

The key to gaining a real understanding of the principle and being able to apply it to a compensation plan lies in how performance is defined. Performance does not necessarily mean simply sales volume. While the importance of sales volume cannot be overemphasized, other factors such as providing information to customers, creating goodwill for the business through friendly and courteous service, and a willingness to help out with nonselling tasks are also important and should be rewarded. Failure to recognize these other aspects of performance is a mistake too many businesses make. They tend to reward only the salespeople who make the most sales and neglect others who have acceptable sales volumes but do a better job in the other aspects of performance. Of course, if a salesperson does well in nonselling work and not in sales, this weakness must be dealt with through increased sales training.

Thus, if salespeople are doing a good job regardless of the volume they produce, they should be praised. For example, a retailer developed an ingenious approach using repeat business as a reflection of customer goodwill. This retailer developed an increasing schedule of commissions for sales to the same customer. This encouraged salespeople to treat customers so well that they would come back and ask for them by name.

CREDIT POLICIES

Buying goods and services on credit has become an accepted part of everyday living in the United States. "Buy now, pay later" allows consumers to buy what they want when they want it and to pay for it from future earnings. The widespread availability and use of retail credit in the nation's economic system helps maintain a balance among production, distribution, and consumption of goods and services. In short, credit sales are an indispensable part of business today. Few retail establishments sell on a cash-only basis.

Credit is indispensable not only for the retailer, but also for almost every other business. But offering credit poses several problems. Businesspeople must decide whether to offer credit, what type of credit to offer, and how to reduce bad debts. Like any powerful marketing tool, credit must be managed.

LILLIAN VERNON®

Like most other mail order firms, Lillian Vernon Corp. realizes the importance of credit cards. The company also recognizes that credit cards can create problems with cash flow and defaults. To deal with these problems, Lillian Vernon clears the credit cards before filling an order. The company now has an instant clearance, so that it does not have many uncollectable credit card sales. In the past, most sales were in cash and money orders, because the company was selling to young women through *Seventeen* magazine. Not many women had checking accounts in the 1950s. With today's use of credit cards, the average order is larger. Now, all of the company's telephone orders are credit card orders, and this method has helped the business to grow.[11]

Types of Retail Credit

Retail credit can be offered in various forms, including 30-day charge accounts, revolving credit, bank credit cards, and installment credit.

Through the **30-day charge account,** or ordinary open account, a customer usually arranges for credit services on a short-term basis of 30 days. Customers with this type of account can charge merchandise in almost any amount, although a review by the store's credit department may be required for very expensive items. This type of credit requires that payment be made in full within 30 days after the billing date. The customer generally does not pay any interest for this credit privilege. When payment is not made on time, a small penalty is often charged.

Under the **revolving credit account,** a customer agrees to pay a fixed amount in equal monthly payments. Unlike the open account, in which there is usually no interest payment, the revolving credit account involves an interest charge levied against the unpaid balance. If the customer pays off the entire balance at the end of the billing period, no interest charge is made.

The retail revolving credit plan allows the customer to make a series of purchases with no down payment. The individual customer's credit line is based on the store's judgment of the customer's ability to pay.

Bank credit cards have had a dramatic effect on the various categories of consumer credit. The Visa Card, MasterCard, Discover Card, and American Express Card are four universally known and accepted credit programs. Today these cards are even accepted in some grocery stores and fast-food outlets. Customers are allowed to charge goods and services at any participating firm up to a predetermined ceiling. Purchases are then billed through the local bank or through the issuer of the credit card.

The popularity of bank credit cards is widespread among retailers. In return for paying a percentage of charged sales (usually 2 to 6 percent) to the bank or issuing agency, participating retailers receive immediate repayment and are relieved of credit investigation, billing, bookkeeping, and collection. If they maintain their own credit departments, these costs could be in excess of 6 percent. Because it is seldom practical to open store charge accounts when the average sales ticket is about $10, credit card sales are commonly the only type of credit extended.

Installment sales credit is used primarily for financing high unit-value goods and services, such as cars, boats, and physical health and fitness programs. A customer must make periodic payments, which are divided into parts called *installments.* These payments are based on the amount of time needed for repayment and the customer's ability to repay the loan.

Installment credit differs from revolving credit in that a written contract called an *installment purchase contract* is used. This is a legal and binding agreement that contains information such as the total amount to be financed, the interest rate, the repayment period, and a *security agreement* that provides the seller with rights of repossession in case the purchaser fails to make the required payments.

An installment sales credit transaction generally has two parts. If the customer is buying a car, for example, he or she would first arrive at an agreement about the price with the car dealer. Because the amount of cash required is usually unavailable, the customer must borrow the money needed for the transaction. This may be borrowed directly from a consumer finance or sales finance company, or the dealer may handle the financing.

In either case, the consumer will soon be making the installment repayments to a consumer installment credit company, since most dealers eventually sell credit contracts they write to a sales finance company or bank. The sales finance company or bank pays the dealer for the item purchased by the customer, providing the dealer with capital to buy more merchandise. The finance company collects the finance charge (carrying or service charge) for the use of its money from the customer.

Extending Credit

A retailer's decision to extend credit depends on a number of factors. The decision is often based on what competitors are doing. Business survival can force a retailer to extend credit in order to meet competition. Another reason for extending credit may be the kind of merchandise sold. As previously mentioned, credit is almost mandatory for stores selling high unit-value goods.

The most important reason for offering credit is that customers demand and expect it. Today's shoppers view credit purchases as the standard way of buying goods and services. This involves not only those items that are high priced but also many of those that carry low price tags and were traditionally paid for in cash.

Providing retail credit requires considerably more cash than is necessary in a cash-and-carry business. The cost of merchandise, not to mention the profit, is not returned to the credit retailer for at least one month, and in some instances not for one to six years. For example, under certain conditions, it is estimated that a merchant will need $35,000 to $40,000 to carry installment sales credit amounting to $10,000 a month. However, the additional income produced through a finance charge will eventually warrant the extra cost of offering credit. The offering of credit also generates additional sales.

The extension of credit has disadvantages, especially if the customer fails to repay on time or in full. When collections begin to fall off on accounts receivable, capital reserves must be drawn on in order for the company to continue in business. Attempts to recover unpaid accounts through professional collectors may help, if made in time. Unfortunately, as the accounts receivable age, chances for collection decline rapidly. Because of these disadvantages, credit experts often advise that small retailers should not extend credit except through bank credit cards.

Ways to Improve Credit Controls

It is common practice to write off a percentage of sales to bad debts.[12] In most businesses, the write-off or charge-off rate runs from one half of 1 percent on low-profit transactions to 5 percent on high-profit sales and services. But a business does not need to accept excessive losses as part of doing business. When the charge-off rate exceeds 5 percent, it is not only possible but also necessary to find ways to improve controls over bad debt losses.

Fundamentals of establishing and maintaining effective controls over bad debts are comparatively simple, regardless of the way credit is extended. When extending credit, the three most important requirements are:

1. A clear understanding of terms when a credit transaction is initiated,
2. A systematic and diligent follow-up of every account, and
3. A periodic age analysis of every outstanding account.

The first requirement, establishing a clear understanding of payment terms, is the most neglected. When payment terms are not fully understood in the beginning, this results in problems that are difficult and costly to overcome. This weakness must be corrected quickly and systematically so that bad debts can be controlled.

The second requirement, systematic follow-up, makes it necessary for the creditor to decide what techniques best fit the particular situation. Communication techniques are oral (person-to-person or by phone) and written. Oral communication must be controlled by the creditor. Written communication is most effective when it is brief and aimed at a single purpose.

The third requirement, age analysis, can be accomplished by using a simple, inexpensive form listing the name, amount owed, and age of account (30 days, 60 days, 90 days, over 90 days).

Credit-Reporting Agencies

If a credit applicant has used credit before, there is probably a credit file at a local credit bureau or credit-reporting agency. This credit file will include facts about the applicant's identity, occupation, employer, income, dependents, and spouse's name. It also includes information on public record such as tax liens, judgments, and bankruptcy; who has extended credit before; and how the bills were paid. Each individual credit file is continually updated, and thus constitutes a fairly permanent record of a person's credit activity.

There are more than 2,500 credit-reporting agencies in the United States. Creditors who subscribe to these services are usually required to provide information on their own customers to the agency. This information becomes part of a reference bank for other subscribing creditors. Because of the sensitive nature of credit-report information, legal safeguards are provided by the federal Fair Credit Reporting Act. This act indicates that an individual is entitled to know the nature and substance of the information in the credit file and to dispute the accuracy of any information believed to be erroneous.

Through membership in the Associated Credit Bureaus, a creditor has available current file information for most customers. Should a customer move, a request can be made to have the credit record sent to the credit bureau in the new community in advance so that credit will be readily available on arrival. Through the medium of electronics, local credit bureaus are currently being tied into several networks so that information on any consumer can be made available at a moment's notice. For the customer who has a good credit record, credit extension is an almost routine matter.

Reducing Bad Debts

At a time when combined corporate and consumer debt in the United States exceeds $2.4 trillion, businesses are facing an alarmingly high number of "skips," or accounts that are delinquent because the customer has vanished.[13] Coping with credit problems, according to industry experts, requires that a company take measures to protect itself.[14]

The collection industry's experts estimate that bad debts range from 3 to 5 percent of consumer accounts and 2 to 4 percent of commercial accounts. Good collection procedures, by most estimates, can reduce unpaid debts to 2 to 3 percent on consumer accounts and 1 percent or less on the commercial side.[15]

Paying habits of customers are quickly revealed when fundamental procedures become part of the daily business routine. Following these procedures is important in avoiding unnecessary losses.

Assuming there is a regular billing, most credit users will pay as agreed. A certain number will pay after a mild reminder. Some will have had changed circumstances, such as unexpected illness or loss of a job. But after a regular follow-up, they will voluntarily give good reason for nonpayment, promise future payment, and then fulfill their promise.

Beginning with the first signs of delinquency, the following steps should be taken:

1. *Resell the payment terms*—determine the reason for the communication breakdown between the customer and the creditor, and use the best method possible to show the customer the benefits of reestablishing a payment schedule. Use this opportunity to its fullest and select the most effective sales medium. The telephone and a personal interview may be the best ways to accomplish this job. Unusual friendliness and firmness can be combined best through oral communication. However, written appeals or "reselling" letters have been used with good results. Some debtors do not respond favorably, however. Such accounts now are definite delinquency problems, and it is time to take the next step.
2. *Insist on a firm payment agreement*—whether this is done orally or by mail, less time can be devoted to this step than to the previous collection procedure. More objective techniques are required. The communications will be based on appeals to fairness, pride, and desire for a good credit reputation, and will attempt to set up a definite and clearly understood payment program, regardless of the circumstances of the individual cases. Long-term as well as short-term extensions must be pegged to definite dates. Indefinite promises, protestations of honest purpose, and nebulous payments are usually worthless. The debtor who honestly intends to pay seldom resents having a definite payment schedule set up for a delinquent obligation. Anyone unwilling to cooperate needs stronger action.
3. *Demand settlement in full within a specified time*—the term *settlement in full* is preferred to *payment in full* because it is more flexible, and gives both the creditor and the debtor greater opportunity to dispose of the debt satisfactorily. Whatever term is used, it should be brief and concise. A common error at this stage of collection is to review the whole history of delinquency. This should be avoided. It only causes additional delaying arguments. It should be emphasized that the money must be received on or before a certain date. This should be stated briefly and only once. Repetition at this point is deadly. If this procedure is followed closely, there will generally be good results. Unsuccessful cases will require the final action.
4. *Take final action*—for some debtors, the older a debt becomes, the more reasons there are for not paying it. The value of efforts at this stage is questionable. Often time spent by the creditor is not productive, and only occasionally are there returns. But final demand—supported by positive reasons for payment—sometimes brings positive results. At this stage of collection, past attempts at collection when constructive appeals failed should be remembered. If the debt is not paid by a certain date, nothing remains to be done but to state to the debtor that decisive action will begin, such as placing the account elsewhere for collection. One should fully intend to carry out any action mentioned to the debtor. This type of collection action should be planned and used carefully. Much of it has little value, and some of it could be illegal. A notice of intent that is sent by certified mail will do the best job at the least risk.

Because risk is a part of the extension of credit, there will be unpaid accounts even when the collection procedures just summarized have been followed. A certain percentage of these bad debts can be recovered, and it is important to identify this type of account. There is more to identifying potential bad debts than merely considering the age of the account.

Potential bad debts should be identified early so they can be kept to a minimum and have the best chance of recovery. Action at this point in the credit collection process is important. It may mean the difference between recovery or loss. Normally, the more time debtors get, the less they pay.

The owner-manager should look for help in collecting bad debts when any of the following symptoms are present:

1. The new customer does not respond to the first reselling notices. The reason may be that the customer will not or cannot pay. Potential losses can be kept to a minimum by prompt collection agency referral.
2. Payment terms fail for no valid reason. In these cases, irresponsible debtors pay if and when they decide to. This group is responsible for 25 to 50 percent of the cost of collection. This cost and potential losses are reduced by quick action.
3. Repetitious, unfounded complaints occur. Such debtors usually are handled better by those experienced in collection techniques.
4. There is a denial of responsibility. Without immediate professional help, these can be written off as total loss.
5. Delinquency coexists with serious marital difficulties. This is the same situation as the previous one, with the added urgency of obtaining payment before the disappearance of one or both responsible parties.
6. Repeated delinquencies are concurrent with frequent changes of address and/or occupation. It is from this group that 90 percent of all "skips" originate. The wise creditor seeks help from a professional collector when the location of this type of debtor is still known, before he or she becomes a "skip."
7. Obvious financial irresponsibility is found. In such cases, there is no hope for voluntary payments.
8. The debtor is a "skip." The farther such debtors get away and the longer they stay away, the harder it will be to find them and recover the account.
9. There is an unauthorized transfer or disposal of goods delivered on a conditional sales contract. Only prompt professional assistance can make any recovery. (A conditional sale is the sale of goods for which the buyer obtains possession, but the seller retains title until the purchase price is paid.)
10. The delinquent debtor fails to keep in contact. Such a debtor is in one of the above groups. Using a professional collector is the only hope of obtaining any part of the indebtedness.

There are other situations that need prompt attention in specialized fields. Department store credit managers will be concerned about unauthorized charges. Creditors doing business in a large trading area may find debtors relying on distance to avoid payment.

Owner-managers determined to maintain close control over bad debt losses should review the 10 categories, based on their own experience. This should convince them that they will need help in collecting such accounts.

SUMMARY

1. The three most widely used methods of promotion are advertising, sales promotion, and personal selling.
2. Success in advertising involves critical planning, implementation, and evaluation of programs. Through analysis of the firm's needs, specific advertising objectives can be developed, and from these objectives a determination of the appropriate budget should be made.
3. Advertising budgets are commonly decided through the use of the percentage-of-sales method, the competitive-parity method, the affordable method, or the objective-and-task method.
4. Advertising effectiveness involves not only the budget but also the message—when, where, and how it is communicated.
5. The best advertising medium is limited by the type of message to be transmitted and, most important, by the target market—the audience—to be reached.
6. Cooperative advertising is a sharing of advertising costs by retailers and manufacturers.
7. Measuring advertising effectiveness is not easily accomplished, because all the elements of the marketing mix affect sales, not just advertising. Measurements by advertising agencies involve pretests and posttests.
8. Immediate-response advertising can be evaluated by measuring the number of coupons returned, the number of requests made, the test results of two different advertisements run on the same day, the sales of advertised products, or store traffic generated by an advertisement.
9. Measuring image advertising results requires making comparisons over regular time intervals, such as on a weekly basis.
10. Advertising regulations exist at the federal, state, and local levels.
11. Sales promotions are directed at consumers, the trade, or the sales force.
12. Personal selling holds certain advantages for the small firm. It is easier and less costly to compete on the basis of a strong personal sales program than in the areas of product assortment, advertising, and price.
13. The personal selling process consists of these steps: prospecting, the preapproach, the approach, the sales presentation, overcoming objections, closing the sale, and postsale follow-up.
14. Effective personal selling involves knowing everything there is to know about the product or service, and being able to convince customers that the product or service fulfills their needs.
15. Attributes of a creative salesperson include judgment, tact, attitude, and physical characteristics.
16. A program for developing good salespeople should consist of: selecting people suitable for the particular sales program, providing regular and frequent training, and devising an appropriate compensation plan.
17. Almost all goods and services move through the channels of distribution on credit.
18. Retail credit may take several forms, including 30-day charge accounts, revolving credit, bank credit cards, and installment credit.
19. The extension of credit often depends on competitors and the types of merchandise sold, but the most important factor is that customers demand and expect it.
20. When providing retail credit, a firm needs more cash and runs the risk of late payments and lack of full payment, but these extra costs should be offset by the revenue from finance charges and the generation of additional sales.
21. Firms often write off a percentage of sales to bad debts. When this percentage become excessive, it is necessary to find ways to improve controls over bad debt losses.
22. Many firms set their own criteria for extending credit, often using such factors as customer stability, income, and age.
23. Credit-reporting agencies are valuable sources of credit information available to subscribing firms.

24. To keep bad debts at a minimum, a collection schedule containing the following elements should be used: resell the payment terms, insist on a firm payment agreement, demand settlement in full within a specified time, take final action.
25. It is important to identify bad debts early and to act quickly to minimize these losses.

KEY TERMS AND CONCEPTS

Advertising
Sales promotion
Personal selling
Percentage-of-sales method
Competitive-parity method
Affordable method
Objective-and-task method
Cooperative advertising
Image advertising
Prospecting
30-day charge account
Revolving credit account
Bank credit card
Installment sales credit

QUESTIONS FOR DISCUSSION

1. The three most widely used methods of promotion are advertising, sales promotion, and personal selling. What is the meaning of each of these terms?
2. In creating an advertising program, what areas should be evaluated?
3. What are the four methods used to determine advertising budgets, and what are the weaknesses of each?
4. Where can an advertiser get help in preparing advertising messages and meeting copy requirements?
5. Why is advertising's effectiveness difficult to measure?
6. What is image advertising and how can it be measured?
7. Why can a small business gain a competitive edge by emphasizing the role of personal selling and developing a good personal sales program?
8. What are the steps in the selling process?
9. What are the attributes of a creative salesperson?
10. Under what conditions are physical attributes of a salesperson important?
11. What are three basic elements for improving personal selling?
12. What fundamental questions should be considered before a decision is made to extend credit?
13. What are the three most important requirements for extending credit?
14. Why should a firm attempt to resell the payment terms at the first signs of delinquency?
15. In demanding settlement in full, what should be stressed and how should it be stressed?

SELF-TEST REVIEW

Multiple Choice Questions

1. Which of the following should be the first step in developing an effective advertising campaign?
   a. Establishing the budget.
   b. Choosing the media.
   c. Choosing the message.
   d. None of the above.
2. Which of the following is the most important consideration in selecting the advertising medium?
   a. The advertising objective.
   b. Requirements of the message.
   c. Cost of the medium.
   d. Customers' media habits.
3. The sales process can be broken down into the following stages: (1) prospecting, (2) the approach, (3) handling objections, (4) the sales presentation, (5) the preapproach, (6) closing the sale, and (7) postsale follow-up. Which of the following is the order in which these stages should be carried out?
   a. (1), (5), (2), (6), (4), (3), (7).
   b. (1), (4), (5), (3), (2), (6), (7).
   c. (1), (5), (4), (2), (3), (7), (6).
   d. (1), (5), (2), (4), (3), (6), (7).
4. Which of the following is the most important reason for offering credit?
   a. Competitors are offering credit.
   b. The type of transaction requires credit.

c. Customers demand and expect it.
d. To increase profits.

5. The procedure to follow in reducing bad debts is: (1) insist on a firm payment agreement, (2) take final action, (3) resell the payment terms, and (4) demand settlement in full within a specified time. Which of the following is the order in which these procedures should be carried out?
   a. (3), (1), (2), (4).
   b. (3), (1), (4), (2).
   c. (3), (4), (1), (2).
   d. (1), (3), (4), (2).

True/False Statements

1. The most popular method used in setting the advertising budget is the affordable method.
2. Advertising expenditures should be viewed as a necessary part of the marketing strategy.
3. Sales promotion is only a part of the more comprehensive area of promotion.
4. The most logical method used to set the advertising budget is the objective-and-task method.
5. Cooperative advertising is a program in which advertising costs are shared between manufacturers and the media.
6. Emphasis on personal selling by large firms has closed the gap that small firms used to fill.
7. A skilled salesperson welcomes objections because they provide feedback about where additional sales emphasis is needed.
8. The most important reason for offering credit is because customers demand and expect it.
9. Providing retail credit requires less cash than is necessary in a cash-and-carry business.
10. The longer a firm keeps an account receivable, the greater the chance that the debt will be collected.

THE RICHARDSON COMPANY

The Richardson Co. manufactures and markets a line of unfinished furniture through furniture, home improvement, and building-supply stores. Richardson's annual sales volume is $3.5 million. The company traditionally budgets an amount equivalent to 10 percent of sales to advertise its products in newspapers and consumer magazines. This amount is in accord with the industry's rule of thumb regarding advertising expenditures. What Richardson does not know is whether these expenditures are effective in generating sales volume. Although the company has never analyzed the effectiveness of its advertising program, management considers it a necessary part of marketing strategy.

Richardson's new marketing manager, Darrell Young, believes that the company can get much more for its advertising dollar. When he realized that the corporate objective of 10 percent annual sales growth volume was not being met, he analyzed the costs and results of the advertising program and made a number of discoveries.

Young has learned that although the media portion of the advertising expenditure was divided about evenly among two newspapers and three magazines, inquiries generated by one of the newspapers outnumber inquiries generated by each of the other media by more than two to one. So he has increased the advertising in the most effective publication and has stopped using the others. In the process, media expenses have been cut to 7 percent of company sales, while the number of inquiries generated has decreased by only 8 percent.

New ads have stopped stressing price and quality and have begun to emphasize user benefits. By carefully charting sales over a six-month period, Young has seen that the products advertised have shown substantial sales volume increases, almost offsetting the sales volume declines among the already low-volume items for which advertising has been discontinued. While this approach has shown promising results, sales volume still has not met sales objectives.

As part of Young's analysis of the effectiveness of the new advertising campaign, he has conducted interviews with the store managers of some furniture outlets, and has discovered that managers are not generally aware of Richardson's advertising program. Consequently, Young has developed a campaign that not only keeps furniture store managers advised of the company's advertising campaign, but also provides them with point-of-purchase posters and the opportunity to engage in cooperative advertising.

Under the cooperative advertising program, Richardson pays 50 percent of the furniture store's advertising costs, provided the advertised items are featured in conjunction with Richardson's advertising campaign. (Furniture stores account for 75 percent of Richardson's sales).

QUESTIONS

1. How sound is Young's new promotion campaign?
2. What are the strengths and weaknesses of Richardson's current advertising budgeting method?

NOTES

1. "Advertising Can Be Fun and Games," *Venture,* August 8, 1986, 2.
2. Based on Cable News Network's "Pinnacle," August 30, 1987. Guest: Sidney Swartz, The Timberland Company.
3. Based on David P. Garino, "Zippered Pocket Gives Firm Niche in Crowded Shoe Market," *The Wall Street Journal,* November 22, 1982, 27.
4. Based on Cable News Network's "Pinnacle," May 7, 1988. Guest: Jerry Della Femina, Della Femina, Travisano and Partners.
5. "Sales Pitches on Software," *Venture,* March 1987, 11.
6. "Fences Create Instant Ballparks," *Venture,* February 1986, 13.
7. "Ad Space Is Where You Find It," *Venture,* August 1987, 12.
8. Extracted from Small Business Administration, *Do You Know the Results of Your Advertising?* Management Aid Number 4.020, 2–3.
9. *Ibid.*, 2–4.
10. Excerpted from William H. Bolen, Small Business Administration, *Creative Selling: The Competitive Edge,* Management Aid Number 4.002, 5–6.
11. Based on Cable News Network's "Pinnacle," December 18, 1988. Guest: Lillian Vernon, Lillian Vernon Corporation.
12. This section is extracted and adapted from "A Collection Guide for Creditors," by the American Collectors Association. Reproduced with permission from the American Collectors Association, Inc.
13. *Ibid.*
14. Charles A. Jaffe, "Bad Debts Are Worth Collecting," *Nation's Business,* May 1989, 53.
15. *Ibid.*

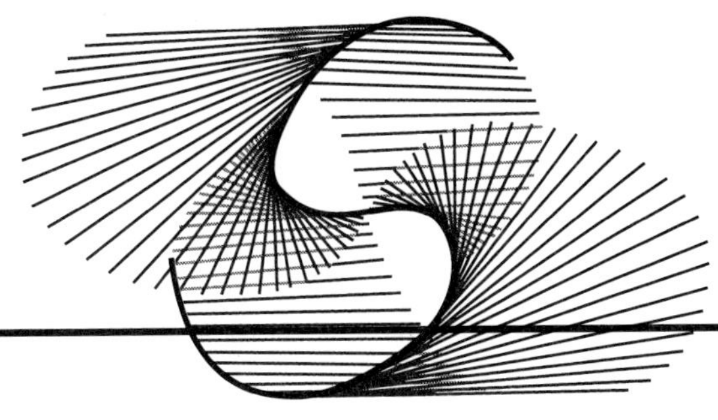

Chapter Eighteen

Employee Orientation, Training, and Compensation

Chapter Outline

EMPLOYEE ORIENTATION
- The Orientation Process
- Employee Handbook

EMPLOYEE TRAINING AND DEVELOPMENT
- Scope of the Training Program
- Training Methods
- Employee Advancement

WAGE AND BENEFIT PROGRAMS
- Establishing Wage Levels
- Internal Alignment of Wages
- Benefit Programs

SUMMARY

Learning Objectives *The objectives of this chapter are to assist you in understanding:*

1. The employee orientation process.
2. The scope of the employee training program and the various training methods.
3. How promotions within the firm can be decided.
4. How wage levels are established.
5. What benefits a small business can offer its employees.

The search and selection process for hiring an employee is just one part of the overall staffing process. To some entrepreneurs the process is complete once an individual is hired, when in fact it is just beginning. They fail to realize that it also is imperative for the new employee to be oriented to the company and position, trained so that the work will be done properly, and told that future advancement within the firm will be based on job performance. If the new employee is not taken care of at this point, the chances of advancement are slim at best.

There are some differing views on how to get employees to share the values of the entrepreneur. Joseph Baum, a restaurant entrepreneur, holds this view of instilling the concepts of innovation and perfection, "I don't think you can explain to people. You can encourage people to commit themselves, but it lies within themselves to love what they do, to sense the standards for being the best."[1]

EMPLOYEE ORIENTATION

Anyone who has ever held a job probably remembers the ordeal of the first few days. New employees will be concerned about what the job will be like, whether they will be able to perform their tasks satisfactorily, how well they will fit in with other employees, and whether that nice interviewer will be a nice boss. There can be little doubt that questions, concerns, and fears, while normal, will affect new employees' initial performance. In fact, these concerns may well affect their relationships with the firm over the long term.

Consequently, the entrepreneur must strive to acclimate new employees to the company, the job, and the other personnel. Such an **employee orientation** process is also critical for existing employees who are moving to different positions within the firm.

The Orientation Process

For new employees, an orientation program can span several days, weeks, or even months, depending on the job and the company. Certainly the first few days will be the most traumatic, and the entrepreneur or whoever is providing the orientation should spend as much time as necessary with the individual. On the first day, the new employee

Joseph Baum's collection of luxury restaurants includes Windows on the World and The Rainbow Room. Baum knows that in order to implement his ideas, he must have the help of the people who work for him. Baum tries to challenge the people who work for him to join his visions for the firm and to develop an understanding of mutual goals. (Photograph courtesy of Joseph Baum)

should meet other employees, learn about the physical facilities and the firm's processes and policies. During this time, the new employee should become familiar with the plant or shop and understand what the job entails and how it fits into the firm's total operations.

Special emphasis should be placed on the human aspects of employment—meeting and fitting in with fellow employees. If this is not handled properly, the new employee might not be accepted by other people. Frequently, the result of this is employee turnover. Thus, new and current employees should understand where they all fit with respect to each other.

Also of great importance is a new employee's understanding of company policies and procedures. If these are not clear, it is unlikely that the individual will perform well. The policies and procedures should be fully specified in an employee handbook.

Employee Handbook

It is best to give each employee a personal copy of an **employee handbook.** This is a document that contains the goals, policies, and procedures relevant to the employee and the job he or she is assuming.[2] The composition of an employee handbook is outlined in Exhibit 18-1.

It is possible to familiarize the new employee with company policies and procedures through a simple explanation during the first day or two of employment. Most likely,

EXHIBIT 18–1 *Sample Employee Handbook: Table of Contents*

1. Welcome Message
2. History of the Company
3. This Is Our Business
4. You and Your Future
5. What You Will Need to Know:
   Working hours
   Reporting to work
   Time clock
   Rest periods
   Absence from work
   Reporting absences
   Employment record
   Pay period
   Shift premiums
   Safety and accident prevention
   Use of telephones
   How to air complaints
6. These Are Your Benefits:
   Vacations
   Holidays
   Group insurance
   Hospitalization and surgical benefits
   Free parking
   Training program
   Christmas bonus
   Savings plan
   Profit-sharing plan
   Suggestion awards
   Jury duty
   Military leave
   U.S. old age benefits
   Unemployment compensation
   Service awards
7. These Special Services Are for You:
   Credit union
   Education plans
   Medical dispensary
   Employee purchases
   Company cafeteria
   Monthly magazine
   Annual outing
   Bowling league
   Baseball team
8. Index or Table of Contents

Source: "Pointers on Preparing an Employee Handbook," Small Business Administration Management Aid No. 197, 3.

however, this method will result in some aspects not being explained by the employer or forgotten by the employee. An employee handbook can be of considerable value in case of future labor disputes. Employees who have received these documents have less opportunity to claim that they did not know the firm's policies and procedures.

The sample employee handbook outlined in Exhibit 18-1 has seven parts, plus an index or table of contents. Parts One, Two, and Three serve to acquaint the new employee with the company and what it does. By providing an overall picture of its history and purpose, it helps the employee to understand the policies and procedures. Part Four concerns the employee's future with the company. This is a critical component, since an individual will want to know what the company can offer over the long term. Part Five contains the mechanics of day-to-day operating procedures. These should be described clearly and in great detail. After reading this section, the new employee should have a reasonable understanding of the daily processes.

Parts Six and Seven deal with employee benefits and special services available to employees. Benefit programs, described later in this chapter, are especially important to employees because they can represent significant savings from what they would have to pay if they were to acquire these benefits for themselves. Special services typically are made available to employees, but are not paid for by the firm. Examples would include opportunities to join credit unions, obtain favorable terms for credit cards, and purchase memberships and event tickets at discounts.

EMPLOYEE TRAINING AND DEVELOPMENT

Whether a new employee is brought into the company to fill a position or the job is being staffed by a current employee, some degree of training will be necessary. Training is important to the employee's and the firm's success because an individual who is not well prepared for a job will most likely do unsatisfactory work and never reach full potential.[3] An extensive checklist for developing a training program is presented in Exhibit 18-2.

Timberland®

The Timberland Company, maker of rugged outdoor boots, shoes, apparel, and accessories, started as a family-owned business, but still used a training period for the children. Its chairman, chief executive officer, and president, Sidney Swartz, discussed this situation.

> Family businesses had a lot of built-in disadvantages and the fact is you really can't get too mad at your own family. . . . I still have black and blues from my father in the early days. He never thought any of his children could measure up. . . . It was very difficult, and we had a very difficult training period. My father expected us to learn the business from the ground up and we did.[4]

Scope of the Training Program

One key initial decision the entrepreneur must make with respect to training is whether any employees are to be prepared for advancement in the future. If particular individuals have been earmarked for later promotion, it is important that they be developed early on in the training process. The training program for these people will be considerably different from that used for employees who do not have those opportunities.

EXHIBIT 18–2

Checklist for Developing a Training Program

A. What is the goal of the training program?
   1. Will you improve your employees by training them to perform their present tasks better?
   2. Is training needed to prepare employees for promotion?
   3. Is the goal to orient new employees to their jobs?

B. What does the employee need to learn?
   1. Are there standards of quality that trainees can be taught?
   2. Are there certain skills and techniques that trainees must learn?
   3. Are there performance standards that employees must meet?

C. What type of training?
   1. Can you train on the job so that employees can produce while they learn?
   2. Will a combination of scheduled on-the-job training and vocational classroom instruction work best?

D. What method of instruction?
   1. Does the subject matter call for a seminar or series of seminars?
   2. Does the subject matter lend itself to demonstration?
   3. Can the instructor direct trainees while they perform the job?

E. What audio-visual aids will you use?
   1. Will a manual of instruction—including job instruction sheets—be used?
   2. Can outside textbooks and other printed materials be used?

F. What about the timing?
   1. Should the training be conducted part time or during working hours?
   2. Should the sessions be held after working hours?

G. Who will be selected as instructor?
   1. Can you fill in as an instructor?
   2. Should a skilled employee be used as the instructor?

H. What will the program cost?
   1. Will the wages of trainees be included?
   2. Will the time you and others spend in preparing and administering the program be part of the costs?

I. What checks or controls will you use?
   1. Can you check the results of the training against the goal or objective?
   2. Can data on trainee performance be developed before, during, and after training?
   3. Will records be kept on the progress of each trainee?

Source: Adapted from "Checklist for Developing a Training Program," Small Business Administration Management Aid No. 186, 2–7.

A Dallas woman, for example, owned five small businesses with a total of 29 employees and sales of $6 million. Having often worked until 10 P.M. and on weekends, she realized the importance of hiring and developing managers to insulate her from the daily operations. In this way, she could focus her energies on more overall management activities. As a result, her businesses grew rapidly.[5]

A critical question, therefore, is whether the entrepreneur wants to classify employees in this manner and in a sense create two career paths—one for future managers and the other for nonmanagement personnel. Because of the relatively high costs of management training, the small business owner cannot justify this type of training for all employees.[6]

On the other hand, preparing only one individual is risky, because that person might become incapacitated, leave the company, or simply not turn out to be as promising as originally thought. In many cases, it is wise to prepare a few potential managers with the understanding that all might not be promoted at once.

Expecting all employees to be similar and fit into a mold can be dangerous. Rod Canion, cofounder of Compaq Computer, responded to critics who claimed that there is little room in the company for loners or those who come up with exotic ideas by saying, ". . . from a personality standpoint, they go off in all directions. The one thing they do have in common is that they're nice people and they know how to work together as a team, and to that degree, I welcome that homogeneity."[7]

Whether individuals are being groomed for management or nonmanagement positions, it is important in a small firm that employees be able to assume other duties on reasonably short notice. To some extent, therefore, training should not be confined to the immediate job. Employees who can perform a range of different jobs effectively are a great asset to the small business in particular. Most entrepreneurs can afford to hire relatively limited numbers of employees, and each will have a substantial impact on the firm's activities. Being able to fill in for others ensures some continuity to the operations.

Training programs also show the employees that the small business owner is concerned about them and their development. Rather than being viewed as "warm bodies" or "pieces of meat," they are considered a real part of the firm for which the entrepreneur is willing to invest both time and money. Such a perspective does much to solidify long-term employer–employee relationships.

Training Methods

The kind of training program used will depend on the type of job and whether the employees are being prepared for management or nonmanagement positions.

Management Training and Development

While a number of approaches to management development are available, none will be of much benefit unless certain guidelines are followed:

- *Development must be action-oriented.* Unless the trainee is allowed to do something, and in most cases that means decision making, the individual will never fully develop. It is difficult to imagine a manager doing well after being thrust into a high-level job without having made actual business decisions.
- *Development must be an ongoing process.* One-shot, short-term training programs tend not to be especially effective. The training needs to be continuous, even after a promotion has occurred. Since technology and management methods change, the individual must be updated periodically so his or her ideas do not become obsolete.
- *A management development program must provide room for mistakes.* Trainees who are not allowed to make errors without severe penalties will feel stifled and will not achieve their full potential. Small business owners need to encourage the blending of a degree of creativity and innovation with cautious decision making.
- *The development process must be flexible enough to be geared to the needs of individual employees.* Recognition should be given to the unique strengths and weaknesses

of each new employee, and to the need to develop a training program oriented to individual characteristics.

- *All phases of the development process must be closely controlled and monitored.* Trainees' errors need to be corrected quickly and their performances appraised periodically. Employees like to know how well they did, where they made mistakes, and how to better prepare themselves for the future.

The most common types of management development programs are:

- *On-the-Job Training (OJT)*—very small businesses need to hire individuals who can make immediate contributions. Because of this, **on-the-job training** offers a distinct advantage. While the employee may not be working to full capacity, at least some productivity is gained during the training period.

  For this method to be effective, however, it must be carefully planned and supervised. Training involves demonstrating the job and letting the employee actually perform the tasks. Too often, whoever is doing the training maintains excessive supervision and creates an improper learning environment. The employee must be free to learn by doing without the boss breathing down his or her neck. Proper supervision means showing how to do the job and then standing back and assisting only when necessary. It involves rapid feedback on how well the individual is doing.
- *Job Rotation*—**job rotation** in small businesses can be used where there are a number of positions for middle managers. Here, employees trade jobs on a relatively frequent basis during the training period, so that each individual has an opportunity to manage a whole spectrum of positions. Not only do employees gain a broader perspective, they develop expertise in every major aspect of the firm's operations.

  This approach, however, has a serious flaw. By changing jobs periodically, one creates some instability within the company. Lower-level employees are forced to work for different superiors. The trainees often do not have time to become fully comfortable with a given job before being rotated. Job rotation must be carefully explained to both lower-level employees and the trainees if this approach is to be successful. Otherwise, it will create unnecessary turmoil.
- *Creation of "Assistant To" Positions*—if the entrepreneur is training an individual to assume a top-level position, it may be practical to make the trainee an "**assistant to.**" While similar to OJT, this differs in that the trainee is not fully vested with specific responsibilities. Rather, the individual does odd jobs and essentially watches

On-the-job training (OJT) that is done by supervisory personnel can save the firm time and money because at least some productivity is accomplished during the training period. (Photograph © Ann M. Mason)

and learns the various processes and procedures and performs in a staff or advisory position.

For jobs critical to the firm, this "assistant to" approach may be better than OJT because it reduces the possibility of error. The dangers of this approach are that the trainee may be overly influenced by the manager and stifled in bringing new ideas to the firm. In addition, the individual may be used incorrectly—running errands and handling unimportant tasks rather than learning the ins and outs of managing.

- *Off-the-Job Training*—in some instances, the employee development process may include training off company premises. **Off-the-job training** includes seminars, college courses, and the like, which may prepare individuals to serve the firm's needs better. These usually are paid for by the company and can be taken during working hours. Although they are seldom used as the sole source of training, it some cases employees are given less significant jobs until their educations are complete. While expensive, the off-the-job training approach does serve to bring new ideas to the firm.

Nonmanagement Training

New employees in nonmanagement jobs also must be trained. While this process may be less time-consuming, complex, and costly than training managers, it certainly is no less important. After all, nonmanagement people are the mainstays of the firm. If they are ineffective or inefficient in the performance of their tasks, so will be the entire firm's operations. Consequently, in many respects the five guidelines described in the preceding section (Management Training and Development) apply here too.

The most common techniques for training nonmanagement employees are on-the-job training and apprenticeships.

- *On-the-Job Training*—this is the most frequently used training method for nonmanagement positions. These jobs tend to be routine, and entrepreneurs typically do not want to invest considerable sums of money in training. Although OJT does demand entrepreneurial time, or the time of some other supervisor, it does not require much in the way of cash outlays.
- *Apprenticeships*—jobs that require extensive training and practice often are handled on an apprenticeship basis. Frequently, such preparation takes several years and utilizes both on- and off-the-job training. Typical of this approach are apprenticeships for electricians, plumbers, and other jobs that have trade unions. Whether the entrepreneur should bring an employee into the firm in need of this kind of preparation, or simply hire someone already well versed in the field, depends on how urgently the employee is needed and the relative costs of skilled versus unskilled labor.

Employee Advancement

Two critical aspects of any staffing process involve decisions about whether to promote from within or from the outside, and informing employees and prospective employees where they stand and where they can hope to end up with the firm. The issue of promoting from within or not is important to both the entrepreneur and the employees. Promotions from within offer several advantages. To some extent the selection process is simplified because the employees and their backgrounds, performance records, and abilities are known to the entrepreneur. In addition, it provides an incentive for individuals to work hard and do well. A disadvantage is that it fosters inbreeding and may result in promoting from a group of mediocre people.

Promotions from outside the firm offer the entrepreneur a chance to bring in fresh ideas. Furthermore, there are more people to choose from, which makes it possible that a better individual can be found. Unfortunately, this approach can cause severe employee problems. Bringing in somebody new not only creates some degree of instability but also causes employee resentment and stifles the extra effort some would otherwise exert to get the advancement.

A common approach to this issue is to try to promote from within if there is a qualified individual. Only if one cannot be found will a search outside the firm be initiated. This blends the advantages of both approaches and eliminates many of their respective weaknesses.

Whatever technique is used, it is important that decisions be made about where each position can lead. Is a particular job a stepping stone to top management? Is it a dead-end position with no place to go? The entrepreneur must decide these issues in order to gauge the depth and breadth of training needed. All these considerations need to be discussed with job applicants so that they fully understand what they can expect in the future.

Designating a position as a stepping stone means that training and development must focus not only on the present job but also on a future one. The job itself becomes a training program for the next. Thus, the entrepreneur should be willing to invest time and money in the process. Supervision and performance reviews also should be oriented to the future.

Dead-end jobs usually do not require this extensive an effort. Training and performance reviews are exclusively oriented to the present job. The amount of time and money spent on this may be considerably less, assuming the position is neither highly specialized nor critical to the firm. These jobs often require different types of control throughout the training and posttraining periods. With nothing to aspire to, employees can quickly lose motivation and become lax in their efforts.

WAGE AND BENEFIT PROGRAMS

Wage and benefit considerations are a necessary part of any staffing process. As is described in the next chapter, however, these may not be the sole or even the main issues of importance to present or prospective employees. Concerns for advancement possibilities and the amount of responsibility and authority provided may be of greater significance to some individuals.

Nevertheless, the wages offered and benefits provided usually will have a significant impact on both the number and quality of people willing to work for and stay with the firm (see Exhibit 18–3). Few top-notch individuals are attracted to companies offering low wages and no benefits—nor are they likely to stay if they find it difficult to live on their levels of compensation.

In establishing wage and benefit programs, therefore, the entrepreneur needs to discover the relatively narrow line between paying too little and paying too much. Too

EXHIBIT 18–3 Components of a Compensation Package

Direct Pay
- Wages
- Salaries
- Commissions
- Incentives
- Premiums:
  - Overtime
  - Shift differentials
  - Holiday, call in

Employee Benefits

Legally Required
- Social Security
- Workers' compensation
- Unemployment insurance
- State temporary disability

Pensions
- Defined benefit:
  - Fixed benefit
  - Unit benefit
  - Flat benefit
- Defined contribution:
  - Money purchase
  - Profit sharing:
    - Thrift plan
    - Employee Stock Ownership Plan (ESOP)
- Individual Retirement Account (IRA)

Group Insurance
- Life
- Medical
- Dental
- Vision care
- Prescription drugs
- Major medical
- Short-term disability
- Long-term disability
- Health Maintenance Organizations (HMOs)

Supplementary Insurance
- Term life
- Ordinary life
- Travel–accident
- Accidental death and dismemberment
- Homeowners
- Automobile

Payment for Time Not Worked
- Personal business
- Severance–layoff
- Military duty
- Lunch period
- Vacations
- Holidays
- Bereavement
- Jury duty
- Clean-up allowance
- Supplemental unemployment
- Guaranteed annual wage
- Relief break

Employee Services
- Employee meals
- Social–recreational programs
- Legal services
- Christmas bonus
- Employee suggestion program
- Membership in professional trade associations
- Travel clubs
- Credit unions
- Discount purchases
- Credit cards
- Income tax services
- Preretirement counseling
- Relocation expenses
- Food services
- Work–study programs
- Scholarships for dependent children
- Matched donations—universities and colleges
- Preretirement planning

Source: John B. Hanna, "Managing Employee Benefits," Small Business Association Management Aid No. 5.008.

low a rate of pay draws few good workers, while too high a wage may drain the firm of its profits. The most pressing questions faced by entrepreneurs are:

- What wage levels should be established?
- To what extent should wages be aligned internally within and between management and nonmanagement personnel?
- What benefits should be provided, and how should the costs of these benefits be allocated?

Establishing Wage Levels

To some extent, wage decisions have already been decided for the entrepreneur by the Fair Labor Standards Act of 1938 and its subsequent amendments of 1966, 1974, and 1989. This statute was enacted at the federal level to eliminate *sweatshops* in certain industries in large cities, which exploited workers and allowed employers to treat them as independent contractors and thereby escape employment laws that precluded payment of very low wages and no benefits. In addition, many states have established their own regulations regarding wage rates, work hours, overtime pay, and wage discrimination. The small business owner should check with the Wage and Hour Division of the U.S. Department of Labor to see if the firm falls within the provisions of this law.

In general, most entrepreneurs can expect to pay at least the federal minimum wage to hourly workers for a 40-hour work week. In 1989, legislation was passed to raise the hourly pay rate by 45 cents to $3.80 on April 1, 1990, and by another 45 cents a year later. It created, for the first time, a subminimum training wage, which employers may pay to workers aged 16 to 19. The training wage will be 85 percent of the minimum wage for a three-month period, and could be extended an additional three months if the youths were in a certified training program.[8] This training wage can have a significant impact on some firms. For example, Six Flags theme park employs about 2,500 people who are in either high school or college, ranging in age from 16 years to about 20.[9]

SIX FLAGS

Overtime pay may be one and one half times the hourly rate for hours in excess of 40. Furthermore, the employer should adhere to the *equal pay for equal work* rule and be especially careful in the administration of wages, hours, and working conditions for child labor.

Although the federal minimum wage serves as a guideline, it is common for the entrepreneur to pay well above the rate and/or to provide additional forms of compensation, as shown in Exhibit 18–4. Of first concern, however, is whether the wage is to be based on straight salary, hourly rate, piece rate, or commission.

Straight Salary

The **straight salary** approach to establishing wages is the most common. Its simplicity and ease of administration are attractive advantages to the small business owner. Although it can be used for management and nonmanagement personnel alike, it is more frequently used for the former group.

Overall, salary levels for managers will depend on the:

- Industry,
- Size of the company,
- Geographic location of the company,

EXHIBIT 18–4 **Sample Benefits Provided to Employee Pharmacists**

	1980	1981	1982	1983	1984	1985	1986	1987	1988	1989
Number of respondents	703	818	1463	1126	750	622	688	711	520	495
(response rate)	26.0%	30.0%	51.0%	42.0%	28.6%	23.5%	26.8%	30.4%	18.9%	17.3%
Average age	42	43	42	43	43	43	43	42	44	45
Average years employed in present position	9	9	9	8	8	9	8	8	9	10
Average years in practice	17	18	17	18	17	19	18	17	19	19
Average monthly income	$2,279	$2,537	$2,761	$2,941	$3,171	$4,108	$3,416	$3,530	$3,874	$4,190
Average hours worked per week	44	45	44	41	41	41	40	41	42	42
Average number of paid vacation days										
after 1 year	9	8	8	—	14	12	14	12	12	14
after 2 years	11	10	11	—	—	—	—	—	—	—
after 5 years	15	14	15	—	—	—	—	—	—	—
after 10 years	17	16	17	—	—	—	—	—	—	—
after 15 years	19	18	19	—	—	—	—	—	—	—
Hospitalization insurance paid for at least partially by employer	79%	80%	82%	78%	78%	79%	70%	79%	68%	69%
Cost of living provision	28%	25%	27%	37%	32%	34%	30%	34%	40%	32%
Periodic review	63%	61%	61%	65%	68%	88%	57%	64%	58%	56%
Association dues paid at least partially by employer	12%	18%	19%	30%	26%	30%	21%	84%	25%	24%
Professional meeting expenses paid at least partially by employer	27%	31%	33%	52%	45%	50%	38%	52%	41%	36%
Employee professional liability insurance paid at least partially by employer	59%	56%	64%	74%	54%	52%	44%	47%	42%	43%
Overtime compensation (straight time, time-and-a-half)	82%	96%	69%	59%	50%	49%	48%	54%	46%	62%
Average sick days paid	—	—	—	—	—	—	10	10	6	9
Average number of weeks employed	—	—	—	—	—	—	48	50	50	51

Source: Dennis H. Tootelian, "1989 Socioeconomic Survey," *California Pharmacist,* August 1989, 36. Reprinted by permission of the California Pharmacists Association.

- Responsibilities of the job,
- Growth potential of the company, and
- Pay method and whether bonuses are used.

The level of pay must be reasonably close to salaries paid to others in comparable positions within the industry. Although the entrepreneur may elect to offer a bit more or less than competitors, gross differences may either waste company funds or make it difficult to attract competent people. Of course, salary levels vary widely depending on the geographic area. The cost of living is a critical factor, in that high-cost areas usually necessitate higher pay levels. Consequently, the salary offered someone in Phoenix may be considerably less than what is offered in New York City.

While the salary level must be reasonable, it should not be more than the company can afford or more than commensurate with the duties of the job. Establishing the salary should include a process of examining what comparable people are making and what the firm can afford to pay. Competitive salary data can be obtained from local or national reports and surveys as well as the entrepreneur's contacts within the industry and community. Even a look through the help-wanted section of the local newspaper can be useful. Company resources can be examined from the firm's financial statements, with different salary levels inserted into projected income statements to see how much impact they have on the firm's profitability.

Once competitive wages have been researched, and the company's ability to pay has been determined, the entrepreneur can begin to design a salary structure. Generally, a system of salary ranges is most effective. The Small Business Administration suggests a variety of ranges for upper-, middle-, and lower-level managers (see Exhibit 18–5).[10] Typically, the competitive salary is in about the middle of the range. Lower salaries tend to be reserved for training periods or less critical individuals, while higher salaries are provided to outstanding personnel. Salaries should be reviewed at least once a year to see if they remain in line.

Bonuses based on company profits frequently are used in small firms that cannot afford large salaries. By developing a bonus system for employees, an entrepreneur can provide higher overall incomes if the company prospers. A bonus system, however, should be tied to profits and be applied to the extent possible in relation to contributions to profits. In addition, the salary plus bonus usually is higher than a straight salary offered by a competitor. If, for example, a firm can only afford to pay a manager $35,000 while managers for competitors are offered $40,000, the potential bonus should be at least $5,000, and more likely between $7,000 and $10,000. Not only does this protect the company from excessive salaries, it also serves to motivate the manager to better levels of operating performance.

Hourly Wage

Most nonmanagement personnel are paid an hourly wage. This is due partly to tradition and partly to the fact that some people are affiliated with labor unions. Hourly wages provide a relatively easy way to pay employees for their efforts, especially when their performance cannot be directly related to output.

These rates usually are set on the basis of those offered by competitors, with the same stipulations relating to geographic location and affordability described for straight salaries. When dealing with labor unions, the small business owner will have to reckon not only with competitive rates, but also with the firm's profitability. If the company is quite profitable, the union may use this as an argument for paying higher-than-competitive wages.

In addition to union issues, the entrepreneur will have to contend with federally established minimum wages, overtime pay, and other matters. Despite these potential problems, the hourly wage offers flexibility in paying for the time spent working. Since many firms use this approach, identifying competitive levels along with minimum requirements provides a reasonably simple method for setting wage levels.

Piece Rates

In instances in which employee efforts can directly be tied to output, a **piece-rate system** offers many advantages. Most important, the wage level can closely coincide with units and/or sales and can serve as an incentive for the work force. This approach will work for a salesforce as well as for production employees. When used for a salesforce, the piece-rate system is known as a *straight commission program.*

EXHIBIT 18–5

Establishing a Salary Structure for a Small Business

To provide incentive with competitive salaries an owner-manager should set up a salary range, adjust present salaries to that range, and periodically review his or her compensation plan.

Establish a Salary Range

The spread of a salary range from minimum to maximum depends on (1) the amount of time it takes a person to be fully effective in the job, (2) the impact that different levels of a person's performance can have on company success, and (3) the amount of time an effective manager would normally remain in that job.

Each factor increases as the level of responsibility in the company increases. Therefore, responsibility determines the required spread in a range rather than the dollar amount of salary. For example, at the vice-presidential level, a spread of 60 percent will be needed. This percentage also allows for the limited opportunities for promotion a vice-president has. The vice-president may have none unless he or she takes your job. At the lower management levels, a 40 percent spread should be sufficient.

In setting up a salary range, the competitive salary is the midpoint; it is halfway between the minimum and the maximum of the range. The percentage spread is between the minimum and the maximum dollar amounts as in the following examples:

Percentage Spread	*Range Minimum*	*Midpoint*	*Range Maximum*
40	$ 8,300	$10,000	$11,700
50	$12,000	$15,000	$18,000
60	$15,400	$20,000	$24,600

Adjust Present Salaries

Once the owner-manager sets up salary ranges, he or she should compare the salaries being paid to the ranges. The objective is to adjust present salaries to the ranges, provided the work performances merit adjustment.

The upper part of a range—above the midpoint to the maximum—should be paid to managers whose performances are better than the owner's standard for good performance. Salaries around the midpoint should be paid to managers whose performance just meets the standard. Salaries from the minimum to the midpoint should be paid to those managers whose performances are below standards, possibly because they are new in their jobs.

Review the Plan Periodically

Because pay levels and practices are constantly changing, the owner-manager should check the compensation plan against competitive practices on a periodic basis—at least annually. When this is done, the most recent available information on executive pay practices should be used.

Source: "Setting Pay for Your Management Jobs," Small Business Administration Management Aid No. 195, 4–5.

A common method for establishing a piece-rate system is to calculate both the normal and maximum potential output of an average employee. By timing the various aspects of a job, for example, it may be determined that the average time would be twenty minutes per unit of output. Thus, an employee doing a normal job should produce three units per hour (60 minutes divided by 20 minutes), or 22.5 units per day (hours per day minus one-half hour of break time, times three units per hour). From this point, the entrepreneur can assess the costs and profit margins on the product. These data, coupled with an evaluation of daily wages for reasonably similar types of work, can determine a piece rate. If, for instance, comparable jobs pay about $6.00 per hour, the piece rate could be set at $2.00 per unit ($6.00 per hour divided by three units per hour). Faster or more efficient efforts would result in greater output, and thereby greater income—one of the key objectives of this approach.

Commissions

Straight **commission,** or a combination of salary plus commission, often are used as a means of directly linking employee income to sales. Typically, this form of compensation is designed to motivate the salesforce to maximize its selling efforts.

Commissions can be computed as a flat percentage of overall sales, or can be staggered to different tiers of sales. The percentage also can be varied to focus selling efforts on special products or types of customers. For example, a small manufacturer may use a straight 4 percent commission on all sales, or 3 percent on replacement parts and 8 percent on new items. The commission ultimately should be established to focus the efforts of the salesforce to the desires of the entrepreneur. Commission selling is described further in Chapter 17.

Internal Alignment of Wages

The entrepreneur must not only establish reasonable wage levels, but must also make them internally consistent. At times these can be contradictory requirements. For example, a middle-level manager may receive a salary of $40,000, which is deemed comparable to the required skills and to competitive offerings. The firm's truck driver, however, may earn $50,000 or more due to overtime pay, union membership, and so on. Another illustration of this is that a new employee may have to be paid nearly the same amount as an individual who has worked for the company for several years due to prevailing wage conditions. Internal increases in wages often do not keep pace with market conditions, meaning that there is little difference between wages paid to new versus established employees.

Thus, the entrepreneur must strive not only to make sure that income within both management and nonmanagement groups is fair, but also must seek to align income levels between groups. Income within groups should be based on such things as skills needed, importance of the job to the firm's success, job conditions (for example, danger, physical exertion), responsibility, and experience. The wage program should reward those who have greater skill, more years of service, greater responsibility, and more difficult work conditions.

Similarly, it usually is assumed that managers should make more money than nonmanagement personnel. This may or may not be fair. Nonmanagers who work very long hours or are exceptionally skilled on a piece-rate system may well deserve high levels of income. Nevertheless, any time this group makes more than management, the likelihood of personnel problems increases.

Benefit Programs

Most entrepreneurs mistakenly view wages as being the only significant cost in the staffing process. Employee **benefit programs** can be very costly if not closely administered.

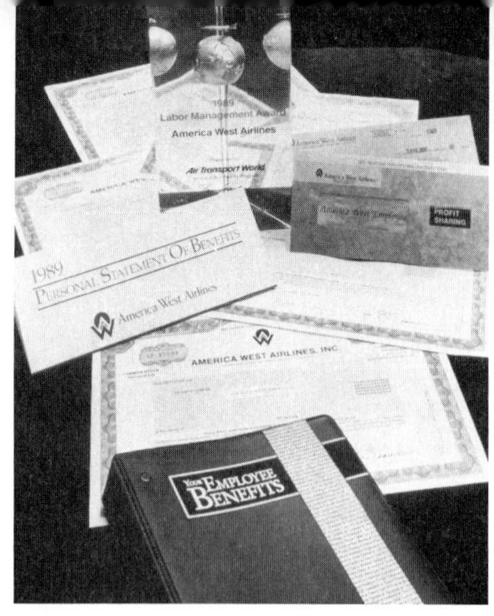

America West Airlines provides its employees with a compensation plan, including stock purchase plans and a profit sharing program, designed to tie individual success to the success of the company. The management of America West Airlines believes that this compensation plan creates an "ownership attitude and increases employees' understanding of corporate goals and encourages teamwork." (Photograph courtesy of America West Airlines)

The benefits offered employees must be carefully decided upon.[11] A sample of some benefits that are provided one group of professionals was shown in Exhibit 18–4.

Vacations

All employees need time off if they are not to become stale or fatigued. Although paid vacations are expensive, they are necessary. Usually based on length of service, they tend to begin with one to two weeks and increase over time to four to six weeks per year. Vacations should be scheduled to take advantage of slower periods in the firm's operations and be spread out so that all employees cannot take them at one time.

Holidays

Some holidays are established by state and federal law, while others are discretionary. Of particular concern here is what other companies are doing. It is difficult, for example, to get good work from employees when comparable workers have the day off. Conventional holidays include New Year's Day, Presidents' Day, Easter, Memorial Day, Independence Day, Labor Day, Thanksgiving, and Christmas. Most geographic areas also recognize Martin Luther King, Jr.'s, birthday. Additionally, many companies provide employees with one or more personal holidays to be taken at certain times or at their discretion (for example, their birthday).

Sick Leave

There will be times when employees will not report to work due to illness. The number of these days to be allowed as paid sick days and whether they will accumulate over time should be established.

Group Insurance

Hospitalization and other medical and health benefits can be made available, although the employer is not required to provide most of this type of insurance.[12] Not only does this type of benefit protect employees and their families from the high cost of illness, but it also is a selling point for the firm in attracting qualified personnel. Many insurance companies have special programs covering life, medical, dental, vision, disability, and professional liability insurance.[13] The costs of these can be paid by the employer, split with the employee, or paid fully by the worker. This is an entrepreneurial decision that must be based on what the firm can afford and what competitors are offering.[14]

Christmas Bonus

This is a good morale-builder and need not be overly expensive. Once established, however, it is difficult to terminate because employees come to expect the bonus irrespective of whether the company is achieving its financial goals.

Savings Plan and Profit Sharing

Some of the more common plans are described in Exhibit 18-6. In a 1989 study of firms with fewer than 250 employees, 36 percent offered 401(K) retirement plans (in which a percentage of profits can be set aside in a special account and not be taxed until retirement)—this is up from 8 percent in 1984.[15]

Before adopting any of these, however, the entrepreneur should consult with a financial advisor to make sure they enroll in the best plan for the firm as well as for the employees.

EXHIBIT 18–6 Savings Plans

Points of Comparison	Keyman Deferred Compensation	Thrift Plan	Keogh Plan	Profit Sharing	Money-Purchase Pension Plan	Pension Plan
Purpose	Motivate and retain key employees	Provide employee incentive through tax-deferred savings	Provide employee incentive through participation in profits and tax-deferred savings	Provide employee incentive through participation in profits and tax-deferred savings	Generally provide incentive through retirement income	Generally promote well-being through fixed retirement income
Incentive value	High	Average	High	High	Average	Low
Contributions by company	Definite amount	Percent of employee contribution—can depend on profits	Depends on earned income	Depends on profits	Fixed annual dollar amount	Fixed on formula basis
Contributions as percent of wages						
By company	No limit (usually 5 to 10%)	Up to 10%	10% to limit of $2,500	Up to 15%	No limit (must be reasonable)	No limit
By employee	Not applicable	Up to 6%	10% to limit of $2,500	Up to 10%	Up to 10%	Not applicable
Benefits	Depends on performance of investment or agreement	Depends on performance of investment	Depends on performance of investment	Depends on profits and performance of investment	Depends on performance of investment	Definitely determinable
Allocation of contributions and earnings	Not allocated until retirement unless otherwise agreed	Allocated to the account of each employee	Allocated to the account of each employee	Allocated to the account of each employee	Allocated to the account of each employee	No allocation required

EXHIBIT 18–6 Savings Plans (continued)

Points of Comparison	Keyman Deferred Compensation	Thrift Plan	Keogh Plan	Profit Sharing	Money-Purchase Pension Plan	Pension Plan
Vesting (employee's nonforfeitable share of employer's contributions)	All at retirement or as agreed	All after a reasonable period of time (usually 10 years)	Immediate	All after a reasonable period of time (usually within 10 years)	All after a reasonable period of time (usually within 10 years)	No later than specified retirement age
Disposition of amounts forfeited (unvested portion)	Firm retains	Allocated to account of remaining employees	None—immediate vesting	Allocated to account of remaining employees	Allocated to account of remaining employees	Must be used to reduce employer's cost of maintaining plan
Ownership	Firm owns	Employee credited with his contributed portion plus any vested amount	Employee credited with entire balance in his account	Employee credited with his contributed portion plus any vested amount	Employee credited with his contributed portion plus any vested amount	Employee has right to pension payments if he qualifies
Method of payment of benefit	Lump sum or systematic withdrawal	Lump sum or systematic withdrawal	Lump sum or systematic withdrawal	Lump sum or systematic withdrawal	Lump sum or systematic withdrawal	Life annuity payout
Receive payments before retirement	No, except as agreed	Yes	Yes	Yes, when vested	Yes, when vested	No, except incidental benefits
Tax advantage	If firm is corporation, yes; otherwise, no	Yes	Yes	Yes	Yes	Yes
Ease of						
Establishment	Easy	Not too difficult	Easy	Not too difficult	Not too difficult	Difficult and complex
Administration	Easy	Not too difficult	Easy	Not too difficult	Not too difficult	Difficult
Understanding	Easy	Easy	Easy	Easy	Easy	Easy
Cost (legal, accounting, and so on)						
Establishing without prototype	Under $200	Under $200	Under $200	Under $750	Under $750	Over $1,000
Establishing with prototype	Not applicable	No cost	Under $25	No cost	No cost	Cost not available
Administration (per year)	None	Under $200	Under $200	Under $500	Under $500	Over $500
Average age of participants	Generally under 50 years	Generally under 50 years	Generally under 60 years	Under 55 years	Over 50 years	Over 55 years

Source: "Selective Employee Programs," Small Business Administration Management Aid No. 213.

The IRS has issued an 179-page set of regulations based on the Tax Reform Act of 1986 pertaining to employee benefits. The purpose is to ensure that employers do not provide some employees with disproportionately greater benefits than others. Unfortunately, it also estimated that compliance with this set of regulations will add 9 billion hours of paperwork to employers.[16]

In some cases, tax laws have significantly affected compensation plans. Sanford Weill, former chief executive officer of Primerica Financial Services, commented on the implications of eliminating the tax-deferred status of many Individual Retirement Accounts, "This was something that got tens of thousands of people to make a positive investment decision which led not to just putting $2000 in an account every year but to thinking about investing on their own rather than having a company do it for them or having it done in a 401(K) plan. . . ."[17]

Stock Options

One of the benefits of being incorporated and issuing stock is that there are opportunities to give stock as part of compensation plans or as incentives for good work. The concept of this was described by Sanford Weill of Primerica: " . . . we've come up with a new plan in our company to really make people feel like partners. . . . For [some employees] . . . part of their compensation every year will be in company stock so they will all become shareholders and all be interested in what we are doing for the whole."[18]

A relatively new approach to providing employees benefits and protecting a corporation is the **employee stock ownership plan,** better known as an ESOP. While not used for very small businesses, this benefit allows employees to purchase stock in the company and have the shares administered by the management. It is attractive for employees of companies that are growing in size and financial strength, because it is conceivable that they could someday own the business.[19] For the current owner, it is a way of distributing shares rather than cash, and provides a means of selling his or her shares without losing operating control over the firm until retirement.

Special Services

Occasionally, companies receive special offers from financial institutions, retail stores, and others to provide patronage discounts to their employees. For example, banks may offer advantageous checking account plans, direct deposits, favorable lending rates, discounts on credit card memberships, and so on. Retail stores may provide special discounts to the firm's employees or in-store credit that is not available to the general public. Typically, these special services are not an expense to the company, but are benefits offered by other companies and passed on to employees.

SUMMARY

1. The orientation process should emphasize meeting and fitting in with fellow employees, and understanding company goals and procedures.
2. An employee handbook can be valuable in answering employee questions and making certain that all policies and procedures are outlined and written down.
3. Training is a necessary ingredient in the development of an employee. The entrepreneur must make decisions as to who will receive training and how much training will be provided.
4. Management training involves development that is action-oriented, ongoing, flexible, controlled, and allows for mistakes.
5. The most common types of management development programs are on-the-job training, job rotation, "assistant to" positions, and off-the-job training.
6. Nonmanagement training is of equal importance, though less time-consuming and less costly than management training. The two most common techniques are on-the-job training and apprenticeships.
7. In promotion decisions, the question usually is

whether to promote from within or hire from the outside. Each has advantages and disadvantages. Often the procedure involves looking for a qualified applicant from within the firm and only seeking outside applicants if none are found internally.
8. In establishing wage and benefit programs, the entrepreneur must find that narrow range between paying too little and paying too much.
9. Wages are paid on a straight salary, hourly wage, commission, or piece rate. Care must be taken that these different methods are consistent within the organization.
10. Benefit programs should be assessed in conjunction with the wage programs, since they can be very costly if not administered properly. Some of the common benefits are vacations, holidays, group insurance, bonuses, savings plans, profit sharing, stock options, and special services.

KEY TERMS AND CONCEPTS

Employee orientation
Employee handbook
On-the-job training
Job rotation
"Assistant-to" positions
Off-the-job training
Straight salary
Hourly wage
Piece-rate system
Commission
Benefit programs
Employee stock ownership plan

QUESTIONS FOR DISCUSSION

1. Discuss the importance of job orientation.
2. What is the value of an employee handbook?
3. What considerations should be given to the task of conducting a successful employee training program?
4. Describe the benefits provided by an effective training program.
5. Describe the important guidelines to follow for employee training.
6. List the common types of management development programs.
7. What are the advantages and disadvantages of promoting from within?
8. What pressing questions face the entrepreneur in establishing wage and benefit programs?
9. Name the two factors in determining a salary level.
10. Describe various benefit programs that the firm may offer its employees.

SELF-TEST REVIEW

Multiple Choice Questions

1. The process of job orientation should emphasize:
   a. Meeting other employees.
   b. Learning about the physical facilities.
   c. Understanding company policies and procedures.
   d. All of the above.
2. Which of the following is an advantage of on-the-job training?
   a. It can be used with virtually all kinds of jobs.
   b. It requires little planning and supervision.
   c. It provides high levels of productivity during all of the training period.
   d. All of the above.
3. The most frequently used training technique for nonmanagement positions is:
   a. On-the-job training.
   b. Off-the-job training.
   c. Apprenticeships.
   d. Job rotation.
4. Which of the following is a true statement?
   a. The entrepreneur should always promote from within the company.
   b. The entrepreneur should always promote from outside the company.
   c. The entrepreneur should try to promote from within the company and then turn to outside sources if necessary.

d. The entrepreneur should try to promote from outside the company and then turn to inside sources if necessary.

5. The most common payment plan used by small businesses is:
   a. Hourly wages.
   b. Straight salary.
   c. Piece rate.
   d. Bonus plan.

True/False Statements

1. An employee handbook contains statements about company policies and procedures.
2. A management development program should allow trainees to participate in decision making.
3. Trainees tend to resent evaluations during the development process.
4. On-the-job training is limited to positions in which work is somewhat repetitious and not overly complex.
5. Off-the-job training is seldom used as the sole source of training.
6. Employee advancement is not a major consideration in the initial staffing process.
7. In using a straight salary approach, the entrepreneur should set levels of pay reasonably close to those of competitors within the industry.
8. Any bonus system should be independent of profits.
9. When employee efforts cannot be tied directly to output, a piece-rate system of establishing wages offers many advantages.
10. Vacations are an expensive but necessary type of employee benefit.

SOUTHERN LEATHER IMPORTS

Henry Wilkes, owner of Southern Leather Imports, has just completed plans to expand his import business geographically and now must train the new personnel he has hired to fill the positions he created. As an importer of high-quality leather coats and jackets and leather accessories, Wilkes has been quite successful in selling his products to fine clothing stores in selected parts of California and Arizona. Wishing to capitalize on his formula for success, he has decided to attempt to market his merchandise in limited sections of the Midwest and South. To do this, he has had to hire a salesperson in each area.

Southern Leather Imports was started by Wilkes nearly 10 years ago to import leather handbags and wallets from South America for resale to small clothing stores in California. As he quickly discovered, however, there was an abundance of such items already available, and the price competition was keen. Accordingly, he made some changes in his plans and began to import only the highest quality men's and women's leather coats and jackets he could find. In this way, he believed he could concentrate on the finer specialty shops and avoid the intense price competition.

Although there is considerable competition within his current market, Wilkes carries consistently good products and has offered to do some merchandising for stores that carry his line of products. As a result, these specialty stores have learned how to display their merchandise better—especially Southern Leather Imports' items—and sales are strong. Not having expertise in store layout and merchandise, many owners welcome the advice Wilkes provides and make his assistance part of the agreement to carry Southern Leather Imports lines.

In expanding his business, Wilkes knows that he cannot do all of the selling himself, nor can he provide merchandising assistance to every new customer. He believes that if the attempt was made to build sales in the Midwest and South, it would take the efforts of full-time salespeople located within these areas. In this way, more stores could be reached and those buying from Southern Leather Imports could receive the best service and merchandising assistance possible.

Currently, Southern Leather Imports has full-time salespeople situated in Northern California, Southern California, and Arizona. These people have been with the company for at least five years, and were the original ones hired to cover their respective territories. All three had experience in selling to retail clothing stores, did not need much training, and have performed up to Wilkes' expectations. However, they do not consider themselves to be experts in merchandising.

Wilkes pays them a small base salary of $200 per week plus a 15% commission on all sales. In addition, they are provided automobiles and given credit cards for gasoline and hotel/motel accommodations. The salespeople are expected to pay for their own meals. Although there are no dollar limits on the use of the credit cards, Wilkes examines all of their charges and never feels that they abuse their charges to the firm.

The new employees that Wilkes has hired have some experience in retail sales and merchandising. Nevertheless, he feels that they need to be trained to sell to clothing stores and to sell leather products. Furthermore, Wilkes wants to finalize their salary and commission structures, and thinks it may be necessary to develop more stringent procedures for controlling credit card use.

QUESTIONS

1. What should the training program for the new employees at Southern Leather Imports consist of?
2. How should Wilkes structure the salary and commission for the new employees? How should controls be established for use of credit cards, and to whom should these controls apply?

NOTES

1. Based on Cable News Network's "Pinnacle," March 19, 1988. Guest: Joseph Baum, Restaurateur.
2. Small Business Administration, *Pointers on Preparing an Employee Handbook,* Management Aid No. 197.
3. Small Business Administration, *Checklist for Developing a Training Program,* Management Aid No. 186.
4. Based on Cable News Network's "Pinnacle," August 30, 1987. Guest: Sidney Swartz, The Timberland Company.
5. Michael Totty, "When the Cat's Away," *The Wall Street Journal,* May 15, 1987, 39D.
6. "To Cut Service Costs, Train the Customer," *The Wall Street Journal,* May 10, 1989, B1.
7. Based on Cable News Network's "Pinnacle," October 4, 1987. Guest: Rod Canion, Compaq Computer.
8. "President Signs Minimum Wage Bill," *The Small Business Advocate,* Small Business Administration, December, 1989, 1.
9. Based on Cable News Network's "Pinnacle," July 22, 1989. Guest: Larry Cochran, Six Flags.
10. Small Business Administration, *Setting Pay for Your Management Jobs,* Management Aid No. 195.
11. Small Business Administration, *Managing Employee Benefits,* Management Aid No. 5.008.
12. Small Business Administration, *Health Maintenance Programs,* Management Aid No. 16.
13. "Universal Insurance Recommended," *California Hospitals,* Volume 3, Number 3 (May/June, 1989), 7–10.
14. "Patient Data May Reshape Health Care," *The Wall Street Journal,* April 17, 1989, B1.
15. Buck Brown, "Enterprise," *The Wall Street Journal,* March 22, 1989, B1.
16. "Employee Benefit Rules Issued in 179 Pages," *Insight,* March 27, 1989, 46.
17. Based on Cable News Network's "Pinnacle," June 11, 1989. Guest: Sanford Weill, Primerica.
18. *Ibid.*
19. "ESOPs: Are They Good for You?" *Business Week,* May 15, 1989, 116–124.

Chapter Nineteen

Personnel Relations

Chapter Outline

MANAGING THE WORK FORCE
- Employee and Company Goals
- Employee Morale and Motivation
- Organizational Communication

EMPLOYEE PERFORMANCE APPRAISAL
- Methods of Appraising Performance
- Use of Employee Appraisals

IMPROVING EMPLOYEE RELATIONS
- Handling Employee Grievances
- Employee Discipline and Dismissal
- Union–Management Relations

SUMMARY

Learning Objectives *The objectives of this chapter are to assist you in understanding:*

1. How entrepreneurs can mesh employee and company goals.
2. How employee motivation and morale can be improved within the small business.
3. The role of organizational communication within the firm.
4. How entrepreneurs can discipline or dismiss employees.
5. The role of employee performance appraisals in the small business.

One of the most valued of all assets in any small business is one that does not appear on the balance sheet—the firm's employees. The quality and loyalty of personnel often make the difference between a company's success and failure.[1] Individuals who can be trusted and relied on not only ease many of the burdens placed on the entrepreneur, but also increase the firm's productivity and opportunity for profitability.

In the early 1800s, Robert Owen discussed the need to foster good employee relations. After noting that the firm must maintain its *innate machinery* by keeping it clean, well oiled, and in good repair, Owen posed a significant question: If the owner should take such good care of innate machinery, shouldn't the same be done for the firm's human machines? Owen argued that these machines were certainly more complex than the metal ones and that they needed at least as much care and feeding.

MANAGING THE WORK FORCE

Modern management recognizes the need to foster good employee relations. Simply hiring individuals is no guarantee that they will contribute much to the firm. Even training cannot ensure high levels of employee productivity. Concerted efforts must be made to provide a work environment conducive to success (see Exhibit 19–1). This involves cultivating high morale, developing appropriate leadership styles, making a continuous effort to motivate employees to do their best, and constructively evaluating their performance.

Unfortunately, many entrepreneurs prove to be poor managers. The very desire to be involved in all aspects of operations makes it difficult for small business owners to allow others to play a role in the firm's success. Examples include Nolan Bushnell, founder of Atari, who as head of Axion (a toy company) avoided bringing in skilled talent. The reason, according to Mr. Bushnell: "ego."[2]

EXHIBIT 19–1

Tips on Managing People

1. Periodically review each position in the company. Take a quarterly look at the job. Is work being duplicated? Is it structured so that it encourages the employee to become involved? Can the tasks be given to another employee or employees and a position eliminated? Can a part-time person fill the job?
2. Play a private mental game. Imagine that the company must get rid of one employee. If one person had to go, who would it be? How would jobs be realigned?
3. Use compensation as a tool rather than viewing it as a necessary evil. Reward quality work. Investigate the possibility of using raises and bonuses as incentives for higher productivity.
4. Remember that there are new ways of controlling absenteeism through incentive compensation plans. For example, the owner/manager could eliminate vacations and sick leave and instead give each employee 30 days annual leave to use as he or she sees fit. At the end of the year, the employees could be paid at regular rates for the leave they didn't use.

Source: Jack H. Feller, Jr., "Keep Pointed Toward Profit," Small Business Administration Management Aid No. 1.003.

EXHIBIT 19–2 **What Employees Want from a Job**

Ranking by Employees	What Employees Want	Ranking by Management
1	Credit for all work done	7
2	Interesting work	3
3	Fair pay	1
4	Understanding and appreciation	5
5	Counsel on personal problems	8
6	Promotion on merit	4
7	Good physical working conditions	6
8	Job security	2

Source: "Human Relations in Small Business," Small Business Administration Management Series No. 3, 35.

LILLIAN VERNON®

Another example was Lillian Vernon, founder of Lillian Vernon Corp. She realized that her strong suit was entrepreneurial skills, and only after 31 years in the business did she hire professional managers to help her and her two sons run the business. The company has become a leader in catalogue sales, with a growth pattern of 10 to 15 percent increase in sales annually.[3]

Too many entrepreneurs leave this function to chance. Caught up in the flurry of day-to-day activities, they often neglect this facet of their jobs. Consequently, employee relations either deteriorate or never fully develop.

Employee and Company Goals

One error commonly made by small business owners when it comes to employee relations is that they forget the workers have goals too, or they assume that they know what their workers want in their professional and personal lives. In many instances, however, small business owners do not understand, as shown in Exhibit 19–2.

Employees are working for reasons, be it to earn a living, pass idle time, or simply to meet the challenge of a difficult job. Whatever the case, employees expect to accomplish something through their employment. Whether their goals are similar to or even compatible with company goals varies according to the type of individual and the firm. Nevertheless, if an individual views company goals as counter to personal goal achievement, it is most likely that the firm will suffer. If they complement each other, the firm will prosper with respect to its personnel relations.

Goal Congruence

The shaded area in Exhibit 19–3 shows that the firm and an employee will likely have at least some commonality of goals. Although there may be many different areas of mutual interest, the common desire for the firm to survive is one of the most important. If the firm ceases to exist, the employee will be out of a job.

What motivates a founder of a business? According to Christopher Whittle, chairman of Whittle Communications:

EXHIBIT 19–3 Company Goal Congruence

(A) Company–Employee Goal Congruence

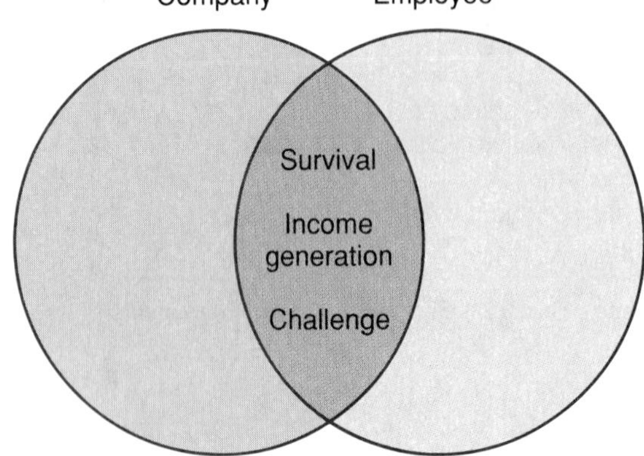

(B) Company–Employee Goal Incongruence

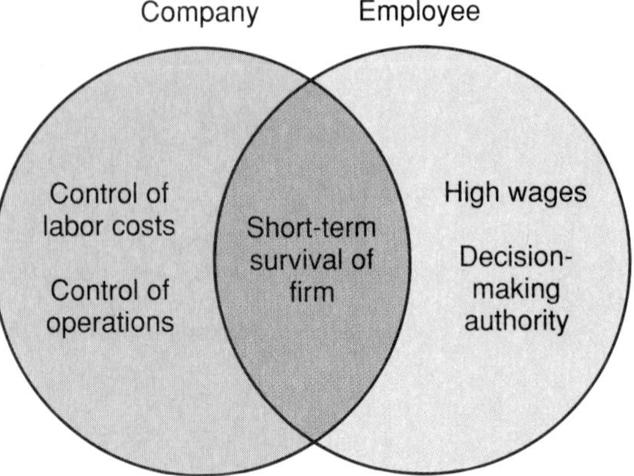

> I've been motivated by fear. . . . Fear of bankruptcy, fear of failure at times, and particularly early in my business career, I was frightened by being kind of overextended. I've been motivated by obligation and periodically am still motivated. If investors put a lot of money into things, I pay attention to that, and even though it's other people's money, I feel like they're supposed to get something back. I've been motivated with financial reward.[4]

Other areas of mutual interest could include profitability, if the employee views personal income as being directly related to the firm's financial success, and interest in the firm's products and/or services. The entrepreneur must capitalize on these areas of mutual interest to develop good relations with the firm's personnel.

Some aspects of motivation can lie simply in security. Earl Graves, the publisher of *Black Enterprise* magazine, summed it up this way:

> I'm . . . looking forward to the security of what it is I think we've achieved in our business for our employees. I would like to see them know that we have and will continue to have a stable, ongoing company which will grow, which will give them an opportunity to grow within our company, and an opportunity to retire if they should choose to do so, and also to know that there's an opportunity to move up in the company and to grow within the company.[5]

In some cases, however, there may be virtually no mutual interest (see Exhibit 19–3). Individuals hired for the short term may not have sufficient time to develop much interest in the firm or have much concern for its survival. Similar circumstances apply to an employee who takes a position on an interim basis. Finally, personal conflicts between the small business owner and employees can result in the latter working in a manner counterproductive to the firm's goals. Slowdowns and production errors frequently arise on these occasions.

The best interests of the entrepreneur are achieved when the goals of the firm become those of the employee. To accomplish this, however, the small business owner must set goals that also provide benefits to the firm's personnel (see Exhibit 19–4). This sounds easy, but what do employees want? How do their goals change over time? The complex nature of goals makes answers to these questions not always easy to obtain.

Personal Goal Structures

Employees bring aspirations to the firm in the hope that they will be satisfied. Although these goals can be classified in many ways, the grouping advanced by Abraham

EXHIBIT 19–4 Entrepreneur–Employee Expectations and Trouble Spots

1. *What the worker expects from the supervisor:*
   Proper job instruction
   Impartial treatment and loyalty
   Fair production standards
   Good working conditions
2. *What the supervisor expects from the worker:*
   Cooperation
   Standard production
   Attendance
3. *What the supervisor expects from the management:*
   Clear line of authority
   Nonconflicting rules and regulations
   Reasonable production schedules
   Decisions backed by management
4. *What management expects from the supervisor:*
   Trouble-free leadership
   Carrying out company rules
   Meeting production quotas
   Keeping adequate records
5. *Is the supervisor "turnover conscious"?*
   The effect of turnover on production costs
   The effect of turnover on department morale
   Are the reasons given for discharges or quits sufficiently detailed to allow for complete analysis of trouble spots?
   Are grievances heard privately and are they resolved promptly?
6. *The worker as an individual:*
   What makes the worker different from others? (Temperament, education, outside interests, and so on)
   What outside conditions affect the worker? (Finances, marital troubles, transportation, children, and so on)
   Age and how it affects the worker
   Reasons for working? (Support self, supplement spouse's earnings, buy clothes, and so on)
7. *How to get the most out of a worker:*
   Gain respect
   Let the worker know what is expected
   Be fair and impartial
   Be patient and understanding at all times
   Make each worker feel a part of your team
8. *The problem worker:*
   Lack of respect for supervisor
   Inefficiency
   Carelessness
   Rumor monger
   Time and material waster
   Privilege abuser
9. *Causes of problem employees*—The common denominator of all problem cases is the failure of the employees to adjust themselves to the work situation. Principal causes for problem employees are:
   Poor selection and placement
   Inadequate training
   Incompetent supervision
   Failure to enlighten workers on management's attitude on matters of promotion, grievances, and so on
   Unsound personnel practices
   Off-the-job problems

Source: "Personnel Management Guides for Small Business," Small Business Administration Management Series No. 26, 36–37.

EXHIBIT 19–5 **Maslow's Hierarchy of Needs**

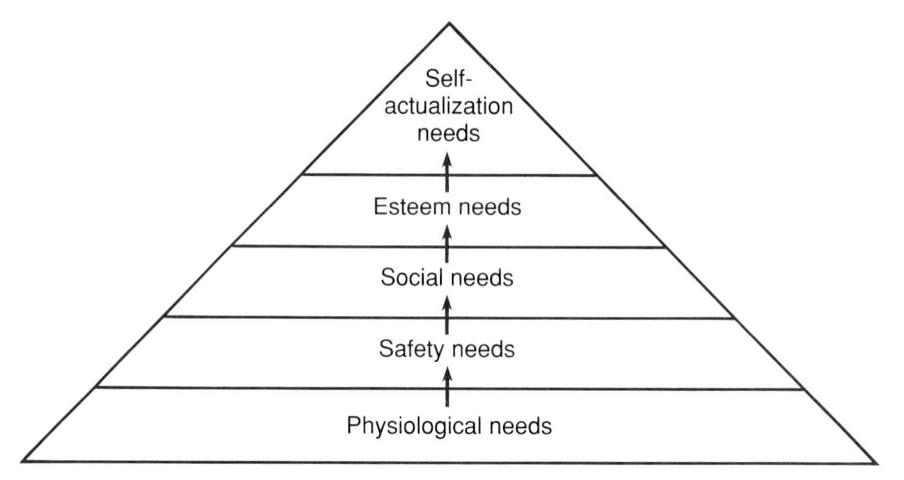

Maslow in 1943 still is one of the most frequently cited. Suggesting that there are five different sets of needs, Maslow sees them as arrayed in a hierarchy, beginning with physiological needs and moving through safety, social esteem, and self-actualization needs (see Exhibit 19–5). Thus, one set of goals does not become of much importance until more basic, lower-level goals are satisfied.

The most elementary of all needs are those essential for survival. For the entrepreneur, it is important that the employee earn enough to survive economically. Wages below the levels needed to purchase food and shelter will make it necessary for the employee to work elsewhere.

Once the employee's physiological needs are satisfied, the desire for safety and security takes on added importance. Assuming that they are physically safe, most individuals work more productively when they feel secure in their positions. The fear of being fired or laid off is not conducive to high levels of productivity. By maintaining rigorous standards in hiring and by continually training employees, the owner makes it less likely that employees will need to be fired. Building a stable work environment can be a mutually desirable goal.

After the individual achieves reasonable fulfillment of the physiological, safety, and security needs, social needs become more prominent. The desire to belong and be accepted by others, especially by a peer group, is important. Accordingly, the small business owner should make developing a cohesive work force a priority issue. Here, effective orientation and training can be of great value. The employer must make sure that both the individual and the work group understand the role and position of the new employee. Neither party should feel uncertain or threatened. Rather, their mutual acceptance should be cultivated to establish the type of working environment that will satisfy the social needs of all.

A fourth need, according to Maslow, is that of ego fulfillment. Everybody likes to feel independent and self-confident, and wants to be recognized and appreciated from time to time. The extent to which the entrepreneur allows employees freedom to undertake important jobs and also recognizes their accomplishments is of critical importance to how emotionally involved in their work employees will become. If the opportunity for ego satisfaction is not present, employees will certainly look elsewhere. The job may simply become a vehicle to generate money so that other personal activities can be undertaken. For example, an employee may use the job to get money to enjoy skiing, boating, stamp collecting, and so on. When the employer provides the opportunity for individuals to achieve their ego needs through the work experience, jobs take on added personal value. Consequently, the entrepreneur should offer employees the chance to do something important and reward them accordingly.

The ultimate goal of most individuals is that of self-actualization—doing all that one is capable of. While few ever really achieve this, it is important that people have the opportunity to try. Chances for advancement, more challenging assignments, or perhaps part ownership in the firm through stock ownership programs (ESOPs) are options deserving consideration. When employees feel they have gone as far as they can with a company, but still are not fully satisfied, they either look to other opportunities for employment or lose interest in their jobs.

Employee Morale and Motivation

The extent to which an employee can achieve personal needs affects motivation on the job. When personal goal achievement is closely intertwined with that of the company, the stage is set for high levels of employee motivation and productivity. But how does the entrepreneur tell when the employee perceives that personal goals coincide with those of the firm? How can the small business owner strengthen the employee's desire to perform well?

One well-known study on employee motivation was conducted by Frederick Herzberg in the 1950s on groups of accountants and engineers. Although these were atypical employees, two sets of factors that may play a critical role in many issues of employee motivation were identified: maintenance factors and motivation factors. Herzberg found that the lack of some variables would cause employee dissatisfaction, but that their presence would not cause them to try to excel. These were the **maintenance factors,** including money, working conditions, and company policies and administration. Other

This employee's need for ego fulfillment is partially met by his employer's recognition of his outstanding achievement by designating him "Editor of the Year" and awarding him a plaque. (Photograph by Carol Alper and Lisa Feder)

variables, called motivation factors, could cause employees to strive for improved job performance, but their absence would not cause dissatisfaction. **Motivation factors** included recognition, challenging work, and opportunities for advancement and personal growth.

SIX FLAGS

One interesting comment from Larry Cochran, chief executive officer of Six Flags theme park, perhaps best sums up the role of management with respect to motivation: "I think that my motivating strategy is for me to get what I want from you and make you think it was your idea. It is give and take. It is giving people praise for what they do. It is directing them and I think correcting them when they are wrong."[6]

Employee Morale

Attitudes that individuals and groups have on the job usually directly impact their work performance. Known as **employee morale,** these attitudes can be either favorable or unfavorable to the job and the work environment. Since attitudes can be defined as predispositions to behave in certain ways, favorable morale tends to result in employees performing at their best, while unfavorable morale results in poor or perhaps counterproductive performances.

Because attitudes cannot be seen or heard directly, the small business owner must be alert to symptoms of poor morale. Many entrepreneurs believe that if employees are unhappy with something they will say so, or that their dissatisfaction will be readily apparent. Usually this is not true. Employees fearful of losing their jobs or simply too shy to complain often resort to subtle ways of expressing their displeasure.

An obvious symptom of poor morale is increased numbers of complaints or grievances from one individual or a group of employees. Whether the complaints are valid is not as important as the fact that they are being made. The entrepreneur should not only try to correct any real problems but should also probe for deeper issues not being discussed. Unanswered complaints decrease productivity.

A high number of employee turnovers indicates intolerable work conditions or mismatching people and jobs. When turnover is not concentrated among a few jobs or within a single department, it is most likely that a more general morale problem exists. A full evaluation of personnel policies and the work environment typically is necessary to determine the problems.

A third symptom is an increase in absenteeism and tardiness. Some employees will not go to the extreme of quitting, but will become lax in coming to work. Increasingly

After Victor Kiam's acquisition of the faltering Remington Corp., his plan to put the company back on its feet included a large lay off of many longtime employees. Kiam knew that if he wanted to keep the remaining employees, he would have to raise company morale and convince people that their jobs were secure. He instituted a number of changes designed to turn the company into a cohesive unit—eliminating executive washrooms, eliminating company perks, and adding incentive programs for employees in all areas of the firm. (Source: *Going for It,* Victor Kiam. William Morrow and Company, 1986; photograph courtesy of Victor Kiam, Remington Products, Corp.)

frequent incidents of employees calling in sick, simply not showing up, or arriving late are indications that they are not eager to work for the firm. Since these symptoms can be costly in terms of lost productivity, the entrepreneur should determine their causes.

Another hint of low morale is production of an increasing number of defective parts. Whether this indicates a deliberate attempt to hurt the firm, or simply a lack of care and concern, the results are about the same—decreasing profitability. In situations in which there is considerable antagonism between entrepreneur and employees, it is not unusual to find worker sabotage. Manufacturing defective products, mixing up merchandise on retail shelves, and other actions serve to vent the frustrations of employees on their jobs.

Finally, there may be an increase in the number of accidents. Perhaps this is the ultimate in carelessness. Often when people dislike some aspects of their jobs, they direct their attention elsewhere to mentally escape the unpleasantness. Unfortunately, their physical beings remain, and they make errors. In some instances, too, bad working conditions jointly affect morale and the accident rate. Factors such as loud noises and uncomfortable working conditions serve to disorient people and cause them to make mistakes they would not otherwise have made.

To be an effective manager, the entrepreneur must be able to recognize possible symptoms of poor morale and take corrective action before valuable employees are lost or costly errors are made. Some suggestions on keeping morale high include:[7]

- Accept the fact that management and employees do not always see things similarly.
- In any differences of opinion, consider the possibility that the employee might be right.
- Show employees that management is interested in them and that it wants their ideas on how conditions can be improved.
- Treat employees as individuals rather than dealing with them impersonally.
- Insofar as possible, give explanations for management actions.
- Provide information and guidance on matters affecting employees' job security.
- Make reasonable efforts to keep jobs interesting.
- Encourage promotion from within.
- Express appreciation publicly for jobs well done, and offer criticism privately in the form of constructive suggestions for improvement.
- Train supervisors to be concerned about the people they manage, the same as they would be about merchandise, materials, or equipment.

While many small business owners watch for problems in employee morale, others rely on extensive personal interviews, open sessions with employees, and/or anonymous surveys in which workers provide written responses to general questions about their jobs and work conditions. Another useful approach is to use an employee suggestion system along the lines described in Exhibit 19-6. Such a method provides a confidential means for workers to air their complaints and make positive recommendations for company improvement.

Interviews and surveys tend to be a little more expensive to develop, and may be inaccurate if employees perceive any danger in being honest. Nevertheless, they are useful in spotting troubles before they reach the stage of being counterproductive to the firm. In addition, the simple fact that the small business owner cares enough to ask employees often bolsters morale by itself.

EXHIBIT 19–6

Employee Suggestion System

The idea behind the suggestion plan is simple. The employees spend most of their workday performing one or more specific tasks. They know the details of their jobs better than anybody else, including the plant manager, engineer, or supervisor. Certainly, they look at the job from a different point of view. They may, and in practice often do, have ideas that nobody else would think of about better ways to do the job.

Workers may have many good ideas for improving the production or sale of the company's products, services, equipment, or facilities, but they may be reluctant to suggest them because:

- They fear that the supervisor will think it a reflection on him or her for not having thought of the idea.
- They believe that the company will get all the benefit from the suggestion and they will get none.
- Since there are no recognized channels for making suggestions, they are afraid that suggesting a new and untried idea will make them appear peculiar in the eyes of fellow workers and supervisors.

If, however, all employees are encouraged to submit suggestions by providing a formal suggestion plan, this reluctance can in most cases be overcome and valuable ideas obtained.

Inviting workers to make suggestions about that phase of the business with which they are most familiar—primarily, their own jobs and surroundings on the job—is in effect asking them to lend a hand in planning plant processes and procedures. And you are providing them with a channel by which they can go right to "topside" with ideas.

There are five elements of an employee suggestion system:

1. A suggestion box to keep employees reminded of the plan and to receive their ideas,
2. An administrator to gather suggestions, obtain evaluations from operating officials concerned, and otherwise see to the smooth functioning of the suggestion system,
3. A committee to consider suggestions and approve rewards,
4. Recognition and rewards for ideas that are accepted and suitable explanations for those that are not,
5. A follow-up system to see that good ideas are put to use, either immediately or whenever changing conditions make them applicable.

Source: "An Employee Suggestion System for Small Companies," Small Business Administration Management Series No. 1, 2.

Leadership Style

Leadership style refers to the approach the manager uses to direct the actions of employees. How the small business owner views and treats employees will have significant impacts on worker morale and motivation. Perhaps the two most important aspects of leadership style concern the degree to which the small business owner allows employees to share in the management of the company, and the extent to which the entrepreneur is concerned about the human versus production management of the firm.

Management style has a significant impact on how well the company operates. Rod Canion, cofounder of Compaq Computer, responded to a question about what he does best by saying:

> The role I try to play at Compaq is a leader and moderator. We have an excellent team of people who plan our products and I participate in the consensus

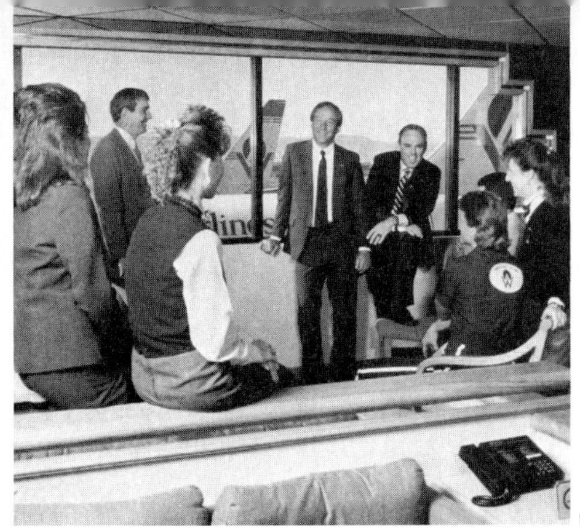

A democratic leadership style, employee participation in determining management goals, is one of the unique characteristics of America West Airlines. Edward R. Beauvais, founder and chief executive officer, is shown here with a group of employees. Beauvais puts great emphasis on two-way communication. Employee advisory boards representing pilots, technicians, and customer service representatives meet regularly with all levels of management to discuss work-related issues and share ideas for improving operations. (Photograph courtesy of America West Airlines)

> process we use. . . . I believe also that a company tends to follow the example set by the leaders of the company . . . so I think how we act and how we interact with each other in the company is an important role for me.[8]

The type of approach used by the small business owner can be autocratic, democratic, or something in between. An **autocratic leadership style** means that the entrepreneur retains absolute control by not allowing employees to make decisions or provide any input into the decision-making process. Some entrepreneurs have little confidence in their employees' abilities to make decisions. In addition, this type of owner feels, since all the risks are taken by the owner, why should anyone else determine the firm's fate? In many very small businesses, too, there is little need for numerous decision makers. Coordination and communication problems often are not worth the trouble involved.

Contrary to the autocratic style, some small business owners are more comfortable with a **democratic leadership style.** Here, decision making within the firm is fully shared between the owner and employees. The entrepreneur must have great confidence in the employees and their ability and desire to make decisions in the best interests of the firm. The democratic style tends to get employees ego-involved in the firm and serves to improve their morale and motivation. Sharing decision making can complicate coordination problems, but at the same time improve the quality of decisions, since they are being made more quickly and closer to the scene.

Although many small business owners are either autocratic or democratic, most are somewhere in between. They may seek the input of employees before making a decision, or they may allow them to make the actual decision within certain specified limits. In some instances, the entrepreneur will announce a tentative decision and ask employees for their opinions so as to provide them with an opportunity to voice concerns or support. In other cases, the entrepreneur will provide employees with the authority and responsibility to make management decisions outright.

The style of leadership selected by a small business owner depends on several factors, including:

- The degree of self-confidence the small business owner has,
- The degree of confidence the entrepreneur has in subordinates,
- The importance of the decisions to the survival or success of the firm, and
- The extent to which workers want decision-making responsibilities.

The small business owner who has ample self-confidence will feel more secure in delegating decision-making authority. In addition, confidence in the work group, coupled with their desire to make decisions and a reasonably secure business climate, will be more conducive to democratic management. However, if the decision has a major impact on the firm's survival, most entrepreneurs will make the ultimate decision themselves.

Such retention of decision-making authority can also be found among entrepreneurs who have retired and turned operations over to their offspring. During difficult times or when critical decisions have to be made, founders often return to "their" companies. An Wang, for example, reportedly had his son removed as president of Wang Laboratories due to losses the computer maker incurred and differences of opinion on strategic issues. Having founded and built the company, he was thought to be dissatisfied with the direction the company was taking.[9] This frequently occurs in smaller firms in part because the founder may continue to have a great financial interest in the company.

Although there is no one right style of leadership, it is highly important that the entrepreneur take into consideration the desires of employees. An autocratic approach may frustrate more creative employees who want some decision-making responsibility. Similarly, a democratic style may be unacceptable to employees who like structure and do not want extra responsibility.

One interesting theory on leadership style was advanced by Fredrick Fiedler in 1965.[10] Arguing that it was difficult and costly to try to change a manager's leadership inclinations, Fiedler suggested that the job be changed to fit the individual. For example, an entrepreneur who wants to control all aspects of the business and not delegate any decision-making authority should look for employees who prefer not to make decisions.

Production versus Personnel Orientation

Related to the issue of autocratic versus democratic management is whether the entrepreneur is more concerned about employees or the firm's output. Explored by Blake and Mouton, this issue highlights some common pitfalls of managing a business.[11]

Their *Managerial Grid®* identifies two extremes of entrepreneurial concern, for production or for workers. The small business owner may be a *production manager* who is totally concerned about the production aspects of the firm and has no regard for the employees or their working conditions. Even though the entrepreneur should never lose sight of the production goal, such disregard for the workers usually will hinder achievement of company goals.

The opposite of the production manager is the *personnel manager.* This entrepreneur is concerned with employees and their working conditions. It is a true paternalistic approach to management. It is assumed that if the employees are well cared for, the productive effort will follow naturally. Unfortunately, pampering the work force will not always lead to greater production. Indeed, some workers resent this parental approach. In other cases, this attention might impede the employees' own self-development.[12]

Organizational Communication

One of the most critical factors in the area of personnel relations is **organizational communication.** Perhaps nothing creates more problems and destroys employee morale and motivation faster than a breakdown in the communication process within the firm. Not knowing what is going on results in disruptions in the productive process and uneasiness among workers. Employees need accurate and timely information if they are to avoid missing assignments and making preventable errors.

Lapses in communication lead to rumor, innuendo, and general distrust. Since people typically fear the unknown, such gaps within the organization have a definite unsettling effect. In addition, without a formal communication process it is probable that an informal one, the *grapevine,* will develop. Although the grapevine can be an effective vehicle for communication, it generally is outside the entrepreneur's control.

To minimize potential problems with the grapevine, the small business owner should be sure to set up at least a simple communications network so that rumors will not go unchallenged. The key to this process is identifying what information employees need in order to do their jobs properly.

Communication processes can flow either one or two ways. One-way communications move from the top down and do not allow for much dialogue between the entrepreneur and the employee. In a pure sense, the entrepreneur would give orders and the employee would accept them or quit. There would be no interchange. While one-way flow can be expedient, it often leads to employee dissatisfaction because employees are not involved in the management process. This approach also does not gain the perspectives of employees who are closer than the owner to the firm's basic operations.

Two-way communications allow information to move from the entrepreneur to the employee and from the employee to the entrepreneur. This is generally preferred since it involves and utilizes employees to a greater extent.

The formal line of communication can be used to pass along information in nonproductive areas when desirable. Information on the general success of the firm, possible changes in the future, and social factors can be effectively communicated.

One of the major advances in communication technology within organizations in the late 1980s was *voice mail.* Used mostly by larger companies to reduce paperwork and speed up the communications process, telephone messages within the company are deposited into employee *electronic mailboxes.* A sender can leave a message for one or several employees at once, and the receiver can get his or her messages by dialing a number either from within the company or from an outside telephone. Variations in the design of voice mail systems have made them cost effective even for smaller firms. Voice mail makes it possible to stay in close contact with employees, customers, and suppliers. Overall, it improves the quality and speed of the communication flow.

Coupled with the formal lines for passing oral and written information, the small business owner also must recognize such factors as mannerisms and body gestures. Entrepreneurs, for example, often tell employees that they have an *open door policy*—that they are accessible; then they proceed to walk into their offices and close their doors—making it very difficult for employees to believe in the policy.

EMPLOYEE PERFORMANCE APPRAISAL

A critical element in any personnel relations program is the **employee performance appraisal.** Not only can such an evaluation improve the quality of labor, it also holds important implications for employee motivation and discontent. When used effectively, the appraisal identifies the individual's strengths and weaknesses and provides the entrepreneur with information relative to the worker's capacity for retention and promotion.

Methods of Appraising Performance

There are many methods available for evaluating effort and ability. For management positions in particular, the **management by objectives** (MBO) approach is most valuable. This is one of the most commonly used and desirable techniques available, since it involves a joint effort and evaluation by both the owner and the employee. The key to its use lies in having employees establish objectives, developing action-oriented plans for achievement, and periodically reviewing performance. Because it is an interactive approach, communication concerning performance is assured.

For nonmanagers, a host of evaluation techniques have been prepared. Two samples are presented in Exhibit 19–7. The advantage of either of these is that they are reasonably comprehensive, yet easy to administer and understand. To the extent possible, the form used should be made available to employees at the time they are employed. In this way, they will know the criteria to be used to evaluate their performance and the method by which the evaluation will take place.

The desirability of any method of performance appraisal can be assessed on the basis of its ability to make a complete yet simple evaluation. Although the content will vary by the type of job and company needs, some of the more common attributes to be measured include:

1. *Units of output*—this can be measured on a per-hour, per-day, per-week, or per-month basis. For sales positions, sales per amount of time can be measured.
2. *Quality of work*—based on number of defective amounts produced, or number of complaints, some assessment of the employee's quality of efforts should be made.
3. *Dependability*—measured in terms of coming to work on time, one assessment will be dependability. Another dimension is the extent to which the individual can be counted on to do a good job. This is an intangible factor that is hard to measure.
4. *Job knowledge*—an individual's knowledge of the job, company policies, and so on, can be measured through objective testing techniques if desired. Informal questioning of the employee also can be used to assess this.
5. *Ability and willingness to work with others*—since the small business relies on relatively few people, it is essential that they be willing and able to work in a cooperative spirit. This, however, is very difficult to measure quantitatively. Observation of the employees' interaction as well as monitoring any conflict, grievances, fights, or other hostilities will provide several bases for rather subjective approaches.
6. *Initiative and ability to handle ambiguity*—the extent to which individuals can work on their own and perform relatively unstructured tasks is a definite asset to the firm. Measurement of these factors is difficult, short of psychological testing. Most small business owners do not want to take the time or spend the money to conduct such tests. Thus, observation of the employees' work and the extent to which they take command is all that can be viewed. This is a crude measure and must be recognized as such.

The first three of these factors can be measured quantitatively with reasonable accuracy. The last three are qualitative factors subject to considerable judgment and error.

Use of Employee Appraisals

The employee appraisal process is not complete until it has been personally discussed with the individual. Secret evaluations whose results are not conveyed to the worker

EXHIBIT 19–7

Sample Job Evaluation Forms

Employee Rating Scale

Name ______________________ **Date** __________
Dept. ______________________ **Job** __________
Rated by ______________________

This Rating Scale is an aid to measuring—with a reasonable degree of accuracy and uniformity—the abilities of one of your employees and his or her skill in his present job. It will help you to appraise present performance as compared with previous performance in the same job, and it may indicate promotion possibilities. Because the rating requires your appraisal of the employee's actual performance, snap judgment must be replaced by careful analysis. The following instructions may be helpful.

Instructions

1. Disregard your general impression and concentrate on a single factor at a time.
2. Read all four specifications for each factor before determining which one closely fits the employee.
3. In rating an employee, make your judgment on instances occurring frequently in his or her daily routine. Don't be swayed by isolated incidents that aren't typical of his or her work.
4. Don't let personal feelings govern your rating. Make it carefully so that it represents your fair, objective opinion.

Factor	1	2	3	4
a. Quality of work	Poor; often does unacceptable work; is careless; requires constant supervision.	Fair; needs supervision and frequent checking.	Generally good; makes only occasional mistakes; requires little supervision.	Excellent; work is A-1 most of time; makes very few mistakes; needs supervision only very occasionally.
b. Quantity of work	Very slow; almost never does complete job in time assigned for it.	Erratic; sometimes fast and efficient; other times slow and unskillful.	Steady worker; does job consistently, and occasionally does more.	Exceptionally fast; does work quickly and well; does extra work to stay busy.
c. Flexibility	Does not adapt readily to new situations; most of the time, instructions must be repeated frequently.	Adequate; requires thorough, complete instruction before taking on new duties or new type of work.	Quick; learns new assignment in short time if given some instruction.	Very adaptable; fast learner, quickly meeting needs of new situation or assignment.
d. Job knowledge	Limited knowledge of job; shows little desire to improve.	Passable knowledge of job; needs frequent instruction and continuing supervision.	Well informed about job; rarely needs instruction or assistance.	Full knowledge of job; able to proceed alone on almost all work.
e. Responsibility	Irresponsible in attendance; seldom carries out orders without being prodded.	Some absences; occasionally needs reminder to do work assigned.	Attendance record good; reliable in work.	Excellent attendance record; most reliable in doing work assigned; can always be depended on.

➤

EXHIBIT 19–7

Sample Job Evaluation Forms (continued)

Factor	1	2	3	4
f. Housekeeping and safety	Never cleans working area; is reckless in behavior.	From time to time, cleans work area; is occasionally negligent about safety.	Keeps work area clean; is careful about safety.	Keeps work area spotless; is unusually careful about safety.
g. Attitude	Uncooperative; often complains, is a disruptive influence among other employees.	Some cooperation, but is often indifferent both to fellow workers and to quality of own work.	Usually cooperative; attentive to work; gets along well with others.	Exceptionally cooperative; very interested in work; always helpful to others and considerate of them.

Source: Small Business Administration, *Personnel Management, Administrative Management Course Program. Topic 6.* (Washington, D.C.: Government Printing Office)

Sample Performance Evaluation

Employee Name: ____________________
Department: ____________________
Job Title: ____________________
Evaluation Date: ____________________
Evaluator: ____________________

Rate the employee identified above on the basis of each of the criteria listed below. Restrict your evaluation to matters related to job performance.

Criteria	Very Good	Good	Average	Poor	Very Poor
1. Speed of dispensing	____	____	____	____	____
2. Frequency of patient consultation	____	____	____	____	____
3. Quality of patient consultation	____	____	____	____	____
4. Knowledge of new medications (Rx)	____	____	____	____	____
5. Ability to work with prescribers	____	____	____	____	____
6. Ability to work with other personnel	____	____	____	____	____
7. Maturity	____	____	____	____	____
8. Enthusiasm for the job	____	____	____	____	____
9. Initiative	____	____	____	____	____
10. Appearance	____	____	____	____	____

Other

11. Number of Rx dispensed per day: ____________________
12. Number of days late (unexcused): ____________________
13. Number of days absent (unexcused): ____________________

I, ____________________, have received a copy of this evaluation.

SIGNATURE OF EMPLOYEE: ____________________
DATE: ____________________

will be of no value for improved performance, and in fact will be viewed negatively by employees. Not knowing where they stand or how they are rated has a destabilizing impact on the work force.

Used properly, the evaluation form will be reviewed at a meeting between the entrepreneur and the employee. Each aspect of the individual's performance should be discussed in terms of strengths and weaknesses, and how the latter can be improved. Many large firms require employees to sign the evaluations, stating that they have seen and discussed them with their managers. This assures that such a meeting actually took place. As a positive assessment, this approach can do much to improve overall employee performance.

In addition to its use for strengthening employee performance, the assessment process also can be a vehicle for motivating people and an input to the promotion process. By showing employees how they can improve, and by identifying any possibilities for advancement, one can expand the benefits of evaluation. Most important, these evaluations over a period of time will show how well an employee is doing and where he or she is headed with respect to a career within the firm. Such an assessment of the firm's most valuable asset—its employees—is essential to the development and maintenance of sound personnel relations.

IMPROVING EMPLOYEE RELATIONS

No matter how careful the small business owner is in developing employment plans and practices, it is likely that employees will at times become dissatisfied. In some cases, this might be the result of poor working conditions or the job itself. In others, employees may be having personal problems that they unavoidably bring to work. Finally, there will be some bad days for both the entrepreneur and the workers—days when they wake up in bad moods that get progressively worse.

While these problems are to be expected when human personalities are involved, they should be dealt with quickly yet cautiously to avoid long-term problems. When handled properly, these difficulties can be resolved and in many cases used to solidify a strong bond between the owner and the work force. When mishandled, the result typically is intense labor problems.

Handling Employee Grievances

To get the best from employees, it is important to give them opportunities to voice their opinions. Christopher Whittle, chairman of Whittle Communications, uses retreats to take five to seven people away for several days at a time just to brainstorm. The company has approximately 50 such retreats a year, with about 10 of them at his Vermont farmhouse.[13]

Successful handling of employee dissatisfaction revolves around several processes:

- Recognizing problems quickly,
- Allowing grievances to be vented, and
- Equitably resolving the problem(s).

Quick Recognition

Whether a complaint is serious, valid, or resolved to the employee's satisfaction, the longer it lingers before being treated, the more it strains the long-term employer–employee relationship. If nothing else, a long recognition time is viewed as evidence of entrepreneurial insensitivity to the cares and needs of the work force. In addition, one irritant often sets the stage for other complaints that might never have arisen.

Consequently, the small business owner needs to be alert for signs of employee discontent—slowdowns, tardiness, accidents, excessive waste. By identifying and focusing on those areas where problems are most likely to occur, the entrepreneur will increase the chances of early detection. Although these areas vary by firm and type of industry, in many instances they include jobs that are highly routine and those in adverse working environments (for example, too hot or too cold, noisy, highly stressful).

Airing Complaints

Closely related to this early recognition is the need for an outlet for discontent. When employees have no established means of airing complaints, they often resort to counterproductive measures that are more difficult to recognize.

Since everybody needs to "blow off steam" at some time, the small business owner should establish a mechanism through which employees can voice their complaints. This may act to some extent as therapy, and some small business owners regularly schedule open sessions with employees, during which they are encouraged to say what they like and dislike about the firm and its management.

Other entrepreneurs use *grievance boxes,* which are similar to suggestion boxes. Not only can employees submit complaints, but they can maintain their anonymity, which is impossible to do with the open-session approach.

While there are many approaches to bringing **employee grievances** to light, the success of any such process depends on the atmosphere created by the owner and manager. There must be a genuine concern conveyed to employees, and an assurance that grievants are free from management reprisal. If employees are not encouraged to be free and open with the owner, they will likely conceal their complaints and get even through various means.

Equitable Resolution

Even if the small business owner makes every effort to identify problems quickly and creates an open employer–employee atmosphere, it will be of little value if grievances are not resolved equitably. Not eliminating the conflict will certainly damage this relationship.

This does not mean that the entrepreneur must give in on all areas of conflict. Rather, the owner should try to maintain an open mind and try to understand the problem from the perspective of the employee(s). By openly discussing the problem and methods of resolving it, the entrepreneur can probably find a solution that is fair and acceptable to all. In many cases, the true problem will be a personal one due to emotional, financial, or health difficulties. Simply being willing to listen to the troubled employee and showing concern and sympathy may be all that is necessary. When employment-related issues are involved, the entrepreneur needs to assess the costs and benefits to be derived from all possible options.

The critical point is whether or not the employee views the solution as equitable. When no changes or only partial changes are made, the individual should be told why complete action was not taken. In this way, the employee will at least understand the reasons and go away with the belief that the owner was being honest and trying to be fair.

Employee Discipline and Dismissal

Over the life of any business it is likely that there will be a need for employee discipline and dismissal. In some cases, it will simply be a result of an error in hiring—the employee did not fit the needs of the job or the personality of the organization. In others, it will be due to evolutionary changes in the business—including its objectives and the types of jobs to be accomplished—that make the firm different from what it was and what it needs in terms of personnel. Similarly, the needs of employees change over time, and the firm may not be in a position to satisfy those and still accomplish its own objectives.

Eliminating personnel can place great strains on a company, and is seldom a pleasant experience. Philip Knight, chairman of Nike, attested to this after reducing the company's labor force by 10 percent: "It's awful. It's the worst part of any business. It's just a terrible thing you have to do. You justify it because that's what's needed. You prune the tree to make the tree more healthy but it's certainly the least fun of any decision that you have to make in any business."[14]

Whatever the cause, the small business owner must be ready to deal with the fact that discipline or dismissal may be called for. Such actions must be based on a clear understanding of the ground rules for employment. This necessitates identifying and publicizing actions like theft, fighting, continued tardiness, or other infractions that will result in discipline or dismissal.

Disciplinary actions should be prompt, commensurate with the violation, and clearly explained to all affected. Lengthy delays between the time of the employee action and the resulting disciplinary steps usually are viewed as indecisive. Similarly, management over- or under-reaction generates little employee confidence and respect.

To be effective, therefore, employee practices calling for discipline or dismissal should be well communicated, and management actions properly taken. Some of the more common grounds for discipline or dismissal are:

- Refusal to work or take direction,
- Disorderly conduct,
- Tardiness and absenteeism,
- Poor treatment of customers,
- Stealing from the company or other employees,
- Destruction of company property,
- Violation of safety practices,
- Alcohol or drug abuse, and
- Gambling while on the job.

What is most important is that the discipline be positive in nature and not a personal attack that embarrasses or destroys the employee's sense of self-worth. Thus, corrective action should be oriented toward improving future performance rather than punishment for past mistakes. Similarly, any discipline should be directed toward the mistake and not used to make an example of the individual being disciplined. If the ground rules are well known, there should be no need to make anybody the "classic case." The process may begin with a verbal warning, followed by a written warning the next time, and ultimate dismissal. From a legal standpoint, however, all such actions should be documented for future reference.

While dismissing employees is seldom a pleasant experience, it may be necessary. Incompetent workers are a drain on the already limited resources of a small business. Insubordinate workers who have already been disciplined two or three times add another headache to the already overworked entrepreneur's life. Neither can be tolerated for long if the firm is to survive and have a chance to prosper.

Perhaps the most difficult termination is the one in which there is insufficient work for all employees, or there is a change in the direction of the firm's efforts. At this point, a good employee's job must be eliminated. Some actions can be taken to ease the damage this causes. First, the individual can be given sufficient notice so that he or she might find employment elsewhere before leaving. Second, the entrepreneur can assist the worker in finding other employment through business contacts and letters of recommendation, making the employee's search for a new job more tolerable.

Disciplining or dismissing employees is a particularly sensitive activity in a small business, since there are fewer people and they tend to know one another better than in a larger organization. However, the entrepreneur must take action when necessary or the firm may not survive.

Union–Management Relations

The inability of management to resolve employee grievances is one of the more common reasons cited for unionization within small firms. Other reasons include employee desires for higher wages, greater job security, and a voice in the overall management of the firm. To be sure, many small business owners believe "It won't happen to me—my employees are my friends!" More often than not, this is a naïve perspective. It frequently transcends the question of employer–employee friendship. In many cases, this is a simple question of economics. Union representation provides employees with some degree of security, protection from arbitrary management actions, and the hope of higher wages.

Since employees do have the ability to unionize, the entrepreneur must decide whether to fight it or encourage it. Some consider unionization a fate worse than death. These entrepreneurs adopt exotic policies and practices designed to keep employees happy, and they avoid hiring union instigators. Other entrepreneurs actually prefer to deal with one representative entity rather than try to negotiate with individual employees one by one.

Although small business owners at times can deter or delay unionizing, in most cases it is best to recognize the union's right to exist and strive for a rational and harmonious relationship. Interfering with employee rights to organize can violate federal law, the National Labor Relations Act. In addition, such a fight creates a poor basis for building future relationships.

The chief executive of a small family-owned glass company based in New England, for example, was training his son to take over the company by having him heavily involved in collective bargaining. He felt this would teach his son how to deal with employees and work with them to better the company.[15]

SUMMARY

1. Good employee relations are as necessary as the care and upkeep of a firm's machinery.
2. Entrepreneurs should set company goals that also provide for the benefit of the employees.
3. Personal goals of employees are related to Maslow's hierarchy of needs, which move from survival to self-actualization.
4. The extent to which personal goals are intertwined with company goals affects the levels of employee motivation and productivity.
5. The entrepreneur must be aware of morale problems. Some of the symptoms may be increased complaints, high turnover, tardiness and absenteeism, defective products, and accidents.
6. Not only should symptoms of morale problems be corrected, but efforts also must be made to find the deeper problems manifested by the symptoms.
7. The leadership style of the entrepreneur can have a significant effect on employee relations. Two general styles are autocratic and democratic.
8. Related to the autocratic/democratic distinction is whether the entrepreneur is more concerned with production or personnel.
9. The communication process within a firm has a decided effect on the morale and motivation of a firm's employees. It is important for them to have accurate information on a timely basis.
10. Successful handling of employee dissatisfaction revolves around several processes: recognizing problems quickly, allowing grievances to vent themselves, and equitably resolving the problems.
11. When disciplining or dismissing employees, the entrepreneur should take action that is prompt, commensurate with the violation, and clearly explained to all affected.
12. The entrepreneur should maintain a positive attitude with unions. It is better to seek a more rational, harmonious relationship than to cause a fight that may affect future cooperation.
13. Effective job evaluations are important to both employer and employee because they identify the strengths and weaknesses of the individual and his or her capacity for retention and promotion.
14. Job evaluations can be important aids to strengthening employee performance, motivating people, and contributing to the promotion process.

KEY TERMS AND CONCEPTS

Goal congruence
Maintenance factors
Motivation factors
Employee morale
Leadership style
Autocratic leadership style
Democratic leadership style
Production versus personnel orientation
Organizational communication
Employee performance appraisal
Management by objectives
Employee grievances
Union–management relations

QUESTIONS FOR DISCUSSION

1. What is the most common employee relations error committed by small business owners?
2. How can the entrepreneur use employee goals and company goals to create a more effective organization?

3. Discuss Maslow's hierarchy in relation to the individual's employment goals.
4. Describe maintenance and motivation factors.
5. Explain the symptoms of poor employee morale.
6. Identify several measures the entrepreneur can take to improve human relations within the firm.
7. What are the two most important aspects of developing a leadership style? Give examples of the type of leadership styles these factors create.
8. Explain some of the problems that commonly occur with a breakdown in the communication process. How can the entrepreneur overcome these problems?
9. Relate the importance of the three processes that lead to successful resolution of employee grievances.
10. List reasons for discipline or dismissal of an employee.
11. Briefly describe management by objectives.
12. What common attributes should an evaluation attempt to measure?
13. What step must be included to complete the evaluation process?

SELF-TEST REVIEW

Multiple Choice Questions

1. In what order are the needs of an employee satisfied?
   a. Survival, social, safety, ego-fulfillment, self-actualization.
   b. Survival, safety, social, ego-fulfillment, self-actualization.
   c. Social, survival, safety, self-actualization, ego-fulfillment.
   d. Survival, safety, ego-fulfillment, social, self-actualization.
2. The leadership style that allows employees no voice in decision making is:
   a. Totally autocratic.
   b. Totally democratic.
   c. Partly autocratic and partly democratic.
   d. Contingency management.
3. The leadership style that allows employees to be pampered is:
   a. Totally production-oriented.
   b. Totally personnel-oriented.
   c. Partly production- and partly personnel-oriented.
   d. Contingency management.
4. Grievances should be handled:
   a. Quickly.
   b. Only after a "cooling off" period.
   c. Only after two or more complaints have been filed.
   d. By a grievance committee.
5. When appraising performance, which of the following cannot be measured quantitatively?
   a. Quality of work.
   b. Dependability.
   c. Initiative.
   d. Units of output.

True/False Statements

1. Areas of mutual interest for employees and the firm could include profitability and interest in the firm's products and/or services.
2. According to Maslow's hierarchy, the most basic need is ego-satisfaction.
3. The dissatisfaction of employees will usually be readily apparent to the entrepreneur.
4. Anonymous employee surveys can spot morale problems even before symptoms appear.
5. An autocratic style of leadership allows the employee to have input in decision-making processes.
6. Most small business owners have a totally democratic style of leadership.
7. Effective management typically requires an intermediate position between concern for production and concern for the workers.
8. Informal channels of communication should closely parallel formal ones.
9. The easiest termination is one that results from insufficient work.
10. Employee appraisals should always be discussed with employees.

GENERAL BOOKKEEPING SERVICES

General Bookkeeping Services (GBS) is a small bookkeeping and tax service located in a town of 89,000 people in the northeastern United States. Started over six years ago by Elmer Robbins, GBS has grown into a nine-person office complete with computerized bookkeeping and general tax service for small- and medium-sized businesses.

Although both revenues and profits have increased significantly over the years, Robbins thinks he has had his share of problems. In the early years, GBS had a difficult time becoming established as a reliable and competent service. Since Robbins is a Public Accountant (PA) and not a Certified Public Accountant (CPA), he was viewed with skepticism by many business owners who had come to rely on CPAs to do their accounting and bookkeeping. Only after providing high-quality service for several years did Robbins and GBS gain the necessary credibility to prosper.

With the prosperity, however, have come another set of problems. To keep up with the growing demand for his services, Robbins has had to hire additional employees, including five Public Accountants on either full-time or part-time bases, two full-time secretaries, and one computer operator-secretary. Because personnel costs are very high, Robbins feels he should closely supervise their activities to be sure that they are kept busy and that their work is of the highest quality.

Although the secretaries and two of the accountants do not seem to mind close supervision, the other three accountants have voiced some dissatisfaction. The accountant who has been with the company the longest (three years), is especially resentful of what he considers Robbins' distrust of his work habits. On several occasions he has threatened to quit and take his clients with him. Since he has a large number of clients, Robbins is reluctant to let him leave.

Even though Robbins has no reason to believe that the accountants are not performing their duties in a professional manner, he wants to maintain a close watch over them for two reasons. First, they are the most costly personnel and a highly visible part of the company's operations. He believes that if they did not perform up to the highest standards, GBS would fail. Second, he is afraid that if he does not monitor the accountants' work closely, he will have problems with the other employees in the company who would view his close supervision of them as unfair. Thus, he reasons that he has to exercise the same amount of supervision over all employees regardless of their positions in GBS.

As the pressures on the employees mount because of greater business, the issue of supervision is becoming critical. The senior accountant has become adamant about being given greater freedom, and this is disrupting the work of everyone else. Robbins has discovered that the senior accountant and the two other unhappy accountants have met to discuss forming their own company—possibly taking 40 to 45 percent of GBS's business with them.

Robbins does not want to give in to their demands, but he is concerned about losing such a sizeable portion of his total revenues. He knows, however, that the problem must be resolved soon so that this will not happen.

QUESTIONS

1. Evaluate Robbins' belief that all personnel should be supervised equally, regardless of position within the company.
2. Should Robbins give the accountants more freedom so that they will not leave GBS?

NOTES

1. "Companies That Compete Best," *Fortune,* May 22, 1989, 36–38.
2. Carrie Dolan, "Entrepreneurs Often Fail as Managers," *The Wall Street Journal,* May 15, 1989, B1.
3. Based on Cable News Network's "Pinnacle," December 18, 1988. Guest: Lillian Vernon, Lillian Vernon Corporation.
4. Based on Cable News Network's "Pinnacle," March 4, 1989. Guest: Christopher Whittle, Whittle Communications.
5. Based on Cable News Network's "Pinnacle," May 23, 1987. Guest: Earl Graves, *Black Enterprise* magazine.
6. Based on Cable News Network's "Pinnacle," July 22, 1989. Guest: Larry Cochran, Six Flags.
7. Small Business Administration, *Human Relations in Small Business,* Management Series No. 3, 14–16.
8. Based on Cable News Network's "Pinnacle," October 4, 1987. Guest: Rod Canion, Compaq Computer.
9. Udayan Gupta and Mark Robichaux, "Handing Down Power Can Tear at Relationships," *The Wall Street Journal,* August 9, 1989, B1.
10. Fredrick E. Fiedler, "Engineering the Job to Fit the Manager," *Harvard Business Review,* Vol. 43, No. 5, 1965, 115–122.
11. Robert R. Blake and Jane Srygley Mouton, *The Managerial Grid,* (Houston: Gulf Publishing, 1964).
12. "ESOPs: Are They Good for You?" *Business Week,* May 15, 1989, 116–123.
13. Based on Cable News Network's "Pinnacle," March 4, 1989. Guest: Christopher Whittle, Whittle Communications.
14. Based on Cable News Network's "Pinnacle," March 22, 1987. Guest: Philip Knight, Nike.
15. "Handing Down Power Can Tear at Relationships."

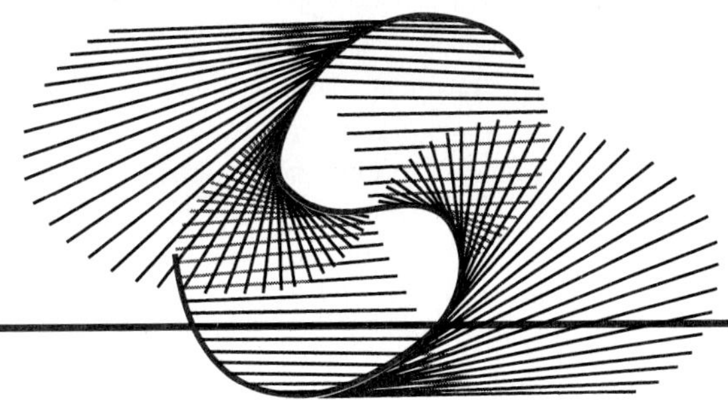

CHAPTER TWENTY

Purchasing and Inventory Control

CHAPTER OUTLINE

PURCHASING CONSIDERATIONS
- Importance of Effective Purchasing
- Purchasing Policies and Procedures
- Objectives and Activities of Purchasing
- Working with Suppliers
- Number of Suppliers
- Sources of Supplier Information
- Types of Purchase Discounts

PURCHASING FOR OWNERS OF SMALL PLANTS

RELATIONSHIP BETWEEN PURCHASING AND INVENTORY CONTROL

SUCCESSFUL INVENTORY MANAGEMENT
- Objectives of Inventory Control
- Valuing Inventory
- Computation of Inventory Turnover Rate
- Economic Order Quantity

INVENTORY CONTROL METHODS
- Manual Recordkeeping Methods
- Using Computers in Inventory Management

JUST-IN-TIME INVENTORY MANAGEMENT

SUMMARY

LEARNING OBJECTIVES

The objectives of this chapter are to assist you in understanding:

1. The role and considerations of purchasing in small firms.
2. Purchasing considerations for owners of small plants.
3. What is necessary for successful inventory management.
4. The different types of inventory control methods.
5. Recent developments in inventory management.

Small business manufacturers, wholesale distributors, and retailers are all involved in inventory procurement and management. A large share of their investment consists of inventory: supplies, raw materials, parts, and merchandise. Firms often carry thousands of different items, and must therefore be knowledgeable about inventory management.

Unlike most factors in business, inventory is a controllable variable. The firm decides from whom to purchase and how much inventory investment to make. If owners do not apply inventory control techniques, the firm faces lost sales and customers, work stoppages and interruptions, overinvestment, obsolete merchandise, and crisis management. Stated positively, sound purchasing and inventory management greatly increases profits.[1]

PURCHASING CONSIDERATIONS

Purchasing is a term that describes the business activity of securing goods or merchandise. The scope of purchasing includes buying materials, supplies, and equipment for manufacturing; buying merchandise for customers; buying materials for maintenance and repair; and buying custodial services and supplies. Anything a business must obtain from an outside source generally falls under purchasing.

Purchasing includes such activities as selection of suppliers, inspection of incoming shipments, coordination of purchasing with other operations of the firm, and follow-up procedures necessary to ensure continuous delivery service. The smaller the business operation, the more likely it is that these purchasing activities will require a great portion of the owner-manager's time.

There are two basic types of purchasing: purchasing for resale and purchasing for consumption or conversion. Purchasing for resale is performed by wholesale distributors and retailers. Purchasing for consumption or conversion is performed primarily by industrial buyers—manufacturers. *Industrial purchasing* is the term that describes the latter activity.

Wholesale distributors and retailers determine what their customers need and want, purchase it at a price to which they can add the necessary mark-up, and then resell it at a profit. Industrial buyers, on the other hand, help determine what products the firm should manufacture and what should be purchased from outside suppliers. However, most of the basic purchasing tasks are faced by all buyers, regardless of the business. These tasks include inventory control and buying merchandise or materials and supplies of the right quality, in the right quantity, at the right time, at the right price, from the right source, with delivery at the right place.

Importance of Effective Purchasing

The purchasing function plays a vital role in all business firms, and its significance is steadily increasing as the number of suppliers increases, as customers become more choosy and critical, and as more and more new products are developed. The importance of purchasing for resale has frequently been underscored by small business owner-managers.

Buying is the elusive art of second-guessing customers. Determining what merchandise to buy for resale involves an insight into the type, kind, quality, brand, size, color, and style that will sell best. Successful buying requires close attention to sales personnel, trade journals, trade shows, catalogues, and any other signs pointing to the likes and dislikes of potential customers. The small business owner-manager acquires a "feel for

Skillful buying is essential to a profitable business operation. Participation in a trade show is one of the ways to help the entrepreneur locate and acquire the merchandise demanded by consumers. (Photograph © Ann M. Mason)

it," as one retailer puts it. Knowing what customers want, where to buy it, and how much to buy are the crux of the purchasing task. If one does not buy enough, disappointed customers leave frustrated. If one overbuys, one has too much money tied up in inventory.

Skillful buying is essential to a profitable operation. This is true for every business firm. The potential for profit that exists through proper purchasing no longer escapes the attention of managers in most modern companies. A number of studies have shown that approximately 50 percent of every dollar received in sales by a firm is expended on the purchase of goods and services. This is generally the most important category of expenditure in the firm.

The profit potential resulting from effective purchasing can be demonstrated this way: Assume that a company is making a profit of 10 percent on net sales, and that its cost of purchased supplies and materials is 50 cents of the sales dollar. Through more effective purchasing, profits can be increased by 10 percent (11 cents per dollar) if 2 percent (one cent) savings can be realized on every 50 cents spent on supplies and materials.

Purchasing Policies and Procedures

In order to derive maximum benefit from the purchasing function, it is necessary to assess the firm's purchasing policies and procedures on a periodic basis. Questions such as those listed in Exhibit 20–1 point to some important areas to consider.

Purchasing policies should be flexible and reflect the company's objectives and plans. They must leave room for discretion to allow the company to respond to such unanticipated events as strikes, unusual demand fluctuations, and special price incentives offered by suppliers.

Objectives and Activities of Purchasing[2]

If one were to ask those responsible for purchasing in a company to describe their responsibilities, the response from almost everyone would be: to buy merchandise or materials of the right quality, in the right quantity, at the right price, from the right supplier, and at the right time. These are basic objectives of sound purchasing.

Buying the Right Quality

The term *quality* as used in the field of purchasing carries a meaning quite different from that usually associated with the word. In common usage, when the term is not

EXHIBIT 20–1 Assessing Purchasing Policies and Procedures

1. **Do you have specific policies and procedures regarding who is authorized to purchase goods or services? Receive salesperson's calls? Place requisitions? Process records?**
   In a small firm the manager will usually do all the purchasing, but this may not always be possible. Therefore the manager must control the purchasing function to prevent possible deception or fraud. The first step toward control is to carefully select the person authorized to do the buying. Then records to indicate need, receipt of purchase, and subsequent payment should be maintained.
2. **Have you ever reviewed existing purchasing procedures to see if they meet your needs?**
3. **Have you ever discussed your purchasing function with other firms or with local trade associations to obtain suggestions and/or techniques?**
   An easy way to develop a working purchasing method is to review your needs. An extremely sophisticated procedure is not necessary if you purchase only a few or relatively inexpensive outside products or services. Good sources of data or ideas are the local purchasing association, a business similar to your own, and trade or craft associations.
4. **Do you request prices from several vendors for each product or service you purchase?**
   Prices do differ from vendor to vendor because of their cost structure, quality of materials and services, location, and so forth. To obtain the best price consistent with quality and service, shop around.
5. **Have you ever visited or investigated your existing or potential vendors to verify that they can meet your requirements in terms of price, quality, quantity, and service?**
   Your commitments to your customers are quite often, if not entirely, based on the promises your vendors make to you. Therefore, it is essential for you to know your vendors' limitations and strengths. If they continually delay or provide inferior-quality products, this will reflect on your services and must be corrected.
6. **Does your volume of purchasing for any particular item warrant your dealing directly with its manufacturer?**
   If the key ingredient to the service you offer is some manufactured product, you might consider direct buying to reduce the costs associated with middlemen. Communications with regard to technical problems may also be made easier.
7. **Do your vendors have regular and competent sales personnel?**
   Salespeople are more than just nice guys. If they know their products, they can be an aid to you and make recommendations when you encounter special problems. They will not waste your time either, but will make themselves available when you need them by helping you with expediting and order follow-up.
8. **Have you had problems with suppliers in regard to shortages? Backdoor selling? Delivery delays? Unsolicited favors and gifts?**
   Ethical suppliers will rarely ship shoddy merchandise intentionally. But on occasion they may ship substandard material due to error or failure of internal production processes. On the other hand, if your supplier makes a habit of questionable or unethical selling practices, you can also be certain that you are paying for it in the form of inferior goods or services, inflated prices, or some other similar fashion.

Source: Small Business Administration, *Management Audit for Small Service Firms,* Small Business Management Series No. 38.

further modified, it refers to the excellent features of the subject. In purchasing, this term refers to the suitability of a product for its intended use.

Buying the Right Quantity

There is but one right quantity to purchase for any given transaction, but since there are many different kinds of transactions, determination of the correct quantity is a complicated matter. Similarly, there is only one right time to purchase this right quantity. The issue is an important one because if too small a quantity is purchased the unit cost will usually be higher, shortages are likely to increase, expediting work will be greater, and the relationship between supplier and purchaser will probably suffer. On the other hand, if too large a quantity is purchased, the excess inventory will raise costs, obsolescence will become a more serious problem, and the need for additional storage facilities will create investment problems.

Buying at the Right Price

The right price is the price that is reasonable and fair to both buyer and seller. Buying personnel have always insisted on paying a fair price for any item bought. This insistence has been incorporated into the policy manuals and codes of purchasing practice for most well-run purchasing departments.

But what is a fair price? This concept involves an allowance of profit to the supplier. How much profit? Certainly a supplier is entitled to enough return to justify remaining in business. However, even this cannot be allowed if the buyer's competitors are able to buy from other sources at lower prices. Purchasers must maintain their own company's competitive position above all else.

Buying from the Right Source

The selection of the source of supply is the acid test of sound purchasing. A purchaser may describe the quality of the desired product accurately and completely, establish the precise quantity needed, estimate the exact price that will be demanded, and clearly determine and specify the exact time and place of delivery. But all this careful planning on these points can be jeopardized and even nullified by poor selection of a supplier. Some suppliers will not be capable of producing to the desired quality specifications; others will not be able to furnish the amounts needed at the time when they are needed; still others, who may be able to meet the quality and quantity requirements, will not sell at the right price. The purchaser must find the supplier who will furnish the optimum combination of these factors.

Buying at the Right Time

Proper buying involves buying without loading warehouses with inventory. It also involves buying judiciously so as to minimize the unfavorable effects of price changes.

Timing orders in connection with price changes involves study of the present supply and demand situation in the market and forecasts of future conditions. Since markets are dynamic, those responsible for purchasing must constantly study all the varied factors that affect the markets for materials, goods, and supplies in order to buy at the right time.

Working with Suppliers

Selecting and working with capable suppliers is a significant function of purchasing. Probably no one is more important to the operations of manufacturers, wholesale distributors, and retailers than suppliers. Yet many purchasing executives and small business owner-managers have not recognized that good supplier relationships result in supplier goodwill. Instead, suppliers are often treated in a suspicious and even ill-mannered fashion. It is mutually advantageous to have a positive buyer–seller relationship. There have been numerous instances when an unexpected customer problem or emergency was solved with the help of a friendly supplier. Purchasing people must have suppliers who are motivated by goodwill to cooperate with them in such situations.

Number of Suppliers

The question of how many suppliers to use has no definitive answer. As is true for so many business decisions, it depends. Many buyers have found it advantageous to spread purchases among many suppliers to gain the advantage of the most favorable prices, best delivery schedules, and promotional material offered. Another reason for relying on several suppliers is that it gives buyers an opportunity to continually evaluate alternative sources of supply, to have greater assurance of supply reliability, and to keep suppliers competitive with one another.

On the other hand, several distinct advantages of concentrating purchases with as small a number of suppliers as possible can also be cited. For example, the argument for doing the bulk of buying from a single source is that in times of shortage suppliers will take better care of their primary customers. Other possible advantages include:

- Receiving more attention and help from the suppliers who know they are receiving most of the firm's business,
- Having a smaller inventory investment,
- Having larger purchase orders, which may permit larger discounts,
- Simplifying credit problems,
- Becoming known in the community as the seller of a certain brand or line of merchandise, if a business is buying for resale, and
- Maintaining a fixed standard in product, if a firm is buying materials to be used in making other goods.

These advantages are convincing arguments as to why it is often better for a small business to concentrate its purchases and work closely with a few suppliers.

Sources of Supplier Information

There are many useful sources of information concerning suppliers. For any business, both personal contacts and published materials are available. Through contacts with local purchasing associations, such as local chapters of the National Association of Purchasing Management, information concerning suppliers with whom purchasing agents in other local companies have dealt can be obtained. Attendance at trade shows provides excellent opportunities to learn about new products and their suppliers. Among the types of published materials available are supplier catalogues, trade journals, trade registers and directories, and the Yellow Pages.

Types of Purchase Discounts

Purchase discounts represent reductions in price given by suppliers. Because they may not be identified in price lists, it is wise always to ask whether discounts are available. Two common types of discounts are quantity discounts and cash discounts.

Quantity discounts are reductions in price allowed for buying certain quantities. They are generally expressed in terms of total dollar value purchased (value) or number of units (quantity) ordered. For example, a supplier might offer a 5 percent quantity discount for orders over $500 or 100 units. Sometimes these discounts are graduated, for example, over $500 or 100 units, 5 percent discount; over $1,000 or 200 units, 7 percent discount; and over $5,000 or 1,000 units, 10 percent discount.

Another variation on quantity discounts is cumulative discounts. These represent discounts calculated at the end of specified time periods. For example, a 10 percent discount may be offered if a firm's purchases total over a certain dollar amount or units of merchandise purchased during a year. These discounts tend to build loyalties to a single supplier.

Cash discounts are reductions in price offered to those who pay their bills promptly. They are offered by suppliers because it saves them money by reducing credit risks and losses from bad debts. They also permit suppliers to reinvest the money from early payment of bills or use it to pay their own bills.

It is prudent to deal with suppliers who offer the best cash discounts. Supplier credit terms normally vary from 30 to 90 days and up to six months in special cases. Cash discounts are usually available if a bill is paid within 10 days.

A sales term quoted as "2-1-, net 30" or "2/10 n/30," means the supplier gives a cash discount of 2 percent if the bill is paid within 10 days of the invoice date. The 30 represents the number of days within which payment must be made. A sales term quoted '2/10 E.O.M. n/30" means that the dating period does not begin until the end of the month (E.O.M.) of the date shown on the invoice. If the buyer has cash available, payment should be made within 10 days of the invoice date or the E.O.M., because the approximate cash discount value is 36 percent a year. Other examples of the approximate cash discounts available on an annual basis are:

1% in 10 days, net 30 days . . . . . 18% a year
2% in 10 days, net 60 days . . . . . 14% a year
2% in 30 days, net 60 days . . . . . 24% a year
3% in 10 days, net 30 days . . . . . 54% a year
3% in 10 days, net 60 days . . . . . 21% a year

These examples show why every effort should be made to take advantage of cash discounts. If a buyer is considered a credit risk, suppliers will normally require C.O.D. (cash on delivery).

PURCHASING FOR OWNERS OF SMALL PLANTS

One of the most important aspects of managing a small plant is industrial purchasing, which is the process of securing materials, supplies, and capital stock inputs required for production operations.[3] An effective industrial purchasing program can have a vital impact on profits. For example, it has been shown that a 1½ percent savings on purchasing can translate into as much profit as a 10 percent increase in sales.

Purchasing considerations for owners of small plants should take into consideration the following factors: specifications, promoting purchasing savings, considering leases versus purchases, systems contracting, cash discounts, and inventory control. The advantages of taking cash discounts were discussed earlier in this chapter and inventory control will be considered later in the chapter. The other factors are briefly discussed next.

Specifications

Specification-writing provides a common basis for bidding. Well-written specifications should leave little room for error or misunderstanding and ensure that the company obtains the materials needed. In writing specifications, one should consider the following elements:

1. One should not request features or quality that are not necessary for the items' intended use.
2. Descriptions should be included explaining any testing to be performed.
3. Procedures should be included for adding optional items.
4. Quality of the items should be described in clear terms.

Promoting Purchasing Savings

There are several actions that can help save money during purchase operations, namely:

1. Substitution of less costly material without impairing required quality.
2. Improvement in quality or changes in specifications that would lead to savings in process time or other operating savings,
3. Developing new sources of supply,
4. Greater use of bulk shipments,
5. Quantity savings due to large volume,
6. A reduction in unit prices due to negotiations,
7. Initiating make-or-buy studies, and
8. Application of new purchasing techniques.

Lease versus Purchase

One may wish to consider leasing rather than purchasing capital equipment. It could save money. Leasing permits a more effective timing of capital expenditures and a greater potential return. The value of conserved capital will vary from company to company and will be dependent on the particular company's ability to employ capital productively.

For example, a dollar in an accounting machine earns little for a retail store, but the same dollar, kept turning in merchandise by leasing the accounting machine, generates a profit. Leasing also conserves capital by offering 100 percent financing, since it often requires no down payment. Additionally, there are frequently included in the lease certain expenses such as installation and freight charges that allow such costs to be amortized over the life of the lease. There are also a variety of lease and related equipment financing methods that can be tailored to the terms, conditions, and services required by the user.

Leasing is a fast, easy way to acquire needed equipment, even when normal money lines are closed. This enables companies to obtain use of modern equipment and remain competitive.

Systems Contracting

Simply defined, **systems contracting** is a purchasing technique that enables a company to acquire repetitively used materials and services from suppliers so that the cost of these items is at the absolute minimum at their point of consumption. There should be a written contract with clear and precise descriptions so that there will be no misunderstanding.

Where properly implemented, systems contracting will greatly reduce the amount of paperwork. Additional benefits include the reduction of inventory shrinkage, reduction of obsolescence, improved expense control, reduction of inventory levels with a corresponding gain in usable floor space, and often a significant reduction in the true costs of items covered. The main objectives of systems contracting are: reduced costs, improved service, and increased profits.

RELATIONSHIP BETWEEN PURCHASING AND INVENTORY CONTROL

Sound purchasing and inventory control are separate but closely related elements. The first, knowing the right quality and quantity of items to order, when to order, at what price, and from what source has already been discussed. Inventory is simply the result of this buying. Some kind of inventory control system is essential to carry out the purchasing function effectively. For example, one must know how much of a given item is in stock at a given time in order to decide whether it is time to reorder or schedule another production run.

SUCCESSFUL INVENTORY MANAGEMENT

"Inventory" to many small business owners is one of the more visible and tangible aspects of doing business.[4] Raw materials, goods in process, and finished goods all represent various forms of inventory. Each type represents money tied up until the inventory leaves the company as purchased products. Likewise, merchandise stocks in a retail store contribute to profits only when their sale puts money into the cash register. In short, every business should have an inventory control system. The importance of such a system is illustrated by U.S. Playing Card Co.

U.S. Playing Card is the world's largest and oldest card maker. In the United States, the company has about 65 to 70 percent market share and worldwide approximately 45

U.S. Playing Card requires, as does any business firm, a system to maintain proper inventory control. When Ronald Rule joined the company in 1986, U.S. Playing Card had a $2.2 million operating loss. Part of the problem included unacceptably large inventory costs because inventory was stacked everywhere. Rule brought the situation under control by instituting an inventory production control system. (Photograph courtesy of The United States Playing Card Co.)

percent. Worldwide, the company makes about 220,000 decks of cards a day. Between its plants in Cincinnati and Spain, it makes about 75 million decks annually. Needless to say, such inventory involves high costs. Indeed, the company's inventory costs were much too high until managers looked at its system of inventory control. Until recently, the company did not have an inventory production control system. Inventory was stacked everywhere. With a new inventory control system, U.S. Playing Card saw company profits rebound and the once-ailing company go from bad times to good.[5]

In a literal sense, **inventory** refers to anything necessary to do business. These stocks represent a large portion of the business investment and must be well managed in order to maximize profits. In fact, many small businesses cannot absorb the types of losses that arise from poor inventory management. Unless inventories are controlled they are unreliable, inefficient, and costly. In attempting to control inventories, managers often lean toward keeping inventory levels on the high side, yet this greater investment (given a constant amount of profit) increases risk and yields a lower return on the dollar invested. This is one of the contradictory demands made upon the manager with respect to keeping inventory. Others include:

1. Maintaining a wide assortment of stock—but not be spread too thin on the rapidly moving items,
2. Increasing inventory turnover—but not sacrifice service level,
3. Keeping stock low—but not sacrifice service or performance,
4. Obtaining lower prices by making volume purchases—but not end up with slow-moving inventory,
5. Having an adequate inventory on hand—but not get caught with obsolete items.

Successful inventory management involves simultaneously attempting to balance the costs of inventory with the benefits of inventory. Many small business owners often fail to appreciate fully the true costs of carrying inventory, which include not only direct costs of storage, insurance, taxes, and so on, but also the cost of money tied up in inventory. The total annual cost in inventory may amount to between 15 and 25 percent. Inventory also ties up capital, which can strain a business and lead to a severe cash crisis. Good inventory management improves customer service, increases sales, increases profit, and increases working capital without the need to borrow money.

Objectives of Inventory Control

The importance of inventory control is illustrated by Lenox China and Crystal. The fine china and delicate crystal company manufactures about 2,300 different pieces each year. To manage such inventory, the company must forecast demand for each of its products targeted to specific market segments, such as newlyweds and collectors. Given customers' continuous changes in style preferences, this is no small feat.[6]

There are several objectives of inventory control:

1. Minimize the inventory investment,
2. Determine the appropriate level of customer service,
3. Balance supply and demand,
4. Minimize procurement costs and carrying costs, and
5. Maintain an up-to-date inventory control system.

Unfortunately, it may be impossible to achieve these goals concurrently. For example, conflict exists within the firm concerning the appropriate level of inventory stock. In a manufacturing firm, production tends to encourage overstocking to ensure that there will be no disruption in the production process. Similarly, salespeople prefer abundant merchandise to protect against stock-outs. In addition, the purchasing department's activities may have the same effect when advantage is taken of available quantity discounts. All these situations can easily lead to overstocking and thus excessive investment in inventory.

Achieving the desired level of customer service requires sufficient amounts of inventory to maintain customer goodwill. Since there are normally short- and long-range variations in demand for goods and services, it is necessary to plan an inventory position that keeps stock-outs at an acceptable level. This means that sufficient safety stock must be kept to attract repeat customers. In today's business climate of high interest rates, intermittent product shortages, and rapid product innovations, there is constant pressure to improve inventory turnover rates, reduce inventory, and eliminate slow-turn items. But customers expect to find the right assortment of products in stock at all times, and will not hesitate to shop elsewhere if they encounter stock-outs too frequently.

Balancing supply and demand is an important and difficult responsibility when a great deal of time elapses between production and consumption. For example, when seasonal demand is concentrated during a few weeks, or even days, manufacturers and distributors are forced to order inventory far in advance of the peak sales period. Many Christmas orders, for example, must be planned by retailers six to 10 months prior to the holiday season. If in early December it turns out that the sales forecast is far off the mark, it is often too late to cancel, reduce, or increase the order.

Minimizing the various costs associated with inventory requires a proper balance between the size of inventory on hand and its effect on customer relations. The major costs of inventory are procurement costs and carrying costs.

Procurement costs include costs of making requisitions, writing orders, receiving and inspecting goods, completing the purchase transaction, and maintaining inventory records. These costs are normally fixed, regardless of the size of the order.

Carrying costs include such items as interest, insurance, taxes, deterioration, spoilage, obsolescence, handling, and warehousing. Interest payments in particular can be major cost items if there are large sums of money tied up in the inventory stock. As indicated earlier, for a typical business firm, 15 to 20 percent of its working capital is tied up in inventories, so a small reduction in inventory investment can result in a significant increase in working capital, reducing the amount of money the firm needs to borrow. Even if a firm does not borrow to finance its inventory, it would be advantageous to reduce inventory levels, since the money can be invested elsewhere.

Obsolescence costs represent risks that are increased in direct proportion to the amount of inventory in stock. Goods are subject to obsolescence due to model or fashion changes or an overall decrease in demand.

Valuing Inventory

Valuing inventory is a major factor in the measurement of taxable income, and adopting a sound valuation policy is of prime importance. There are two bases of calculation commonly used by business concerns using the first-in-first-out (FIFO) inventory method: (1) cost and (2) cost or market, whichever is lower.

A new business may use either the cost or the cost or market, whichever is lower, basis of valuing the inventory. But if the last-in-first-out (LIFO) method of identification is used, valuation must be on the cost basis. Whichever basis is adopted, it must be applied to the entire inventory and may not be changed without the permission of the Internal Revenue Service.

Several pricing methods recognized for tax purposes may be used to arrive at the cost basis of inventory. The dollar value resulting from the method selected is the cost basis of the inventory. The following are several commonly used methods.

Specific Cost Identification Method

The cost of merchandise purchased during the year is ordinarily invoice price less appropriate discounts. If the specific cost identification method is used in arriving at the inventory value of merchandise, materials, or supplies, cost means:

1. For goods on hand at the beginning of the year, the inventory price of the goods;
2. For goods purchased during the year, the invoice price less appropriate discounts.

A firm may or may not deduct cash discounts at its option, but it must follow a consistent policy. If it does not deduct cash discounts, it must include them in business income.

Full Absorption Method

All taxpayers engaged in manufacturing or production operations must use the full absorption method of valuing inventories. This method requires including both direct and indirect production costs in the inventory valuation. Direct production costs are generally costs incident to and necessary for production or manufacturing operations or processes, and are components of the cost of either direct material or direct labor. Indirect production costs include other expenses incident to and necessary for the production process, such as repairs, rent, utilities, maintenance, and supervisory wages.

Cost or Market Method

The lower-of-cost-or-market means that the market value of each item on hand at the inventory date is compared with the cost, and the lower valuation is used as its inventory value. Thus, if at the end of the tax year a firm had the following items on hand, the value of its closing inventory would be $600:

Items	*Cost*	*Market*	*Whichever is Lower*
A	$300	$500	$300
B	200	100	100
C	450	200	200
Totals	$950	$800	$600

If a firm uses this method, it must value each item in the inventory. It may not value the entire inventory at cost ($950) and at market ($800) and use the lower of the two results. If it used the cost basis of valuation, the value of the closing inventory would be $950.

Unsalable Goods

Any goods in inventory that are unsalable at normal prices or unsalable in the normal way because of damage, imperfections, shop wear, changes of style, odd or broken lots, or other similar causes, including secondhand goods taken in exchange, should be valued at selling prices less direct costs of disposition, whether the firm uses the cost or cost or market, whichever is lower basis of valuing inventory. If the goods consist of raw materials or partly finished goods held for use or consumption, they must be valued on a reasonable basis, considering the usability and condition of the goods, but in no case shall they be valued at less than scrap value.

Perpetual or Physical Inventories

Perpetual or book inventories, maintained in accordance with sound accounting practices, are acceptable for determining the cost of goods on hand. Inventory accounts, however, must be charged with the actual cost of goods purchased or produced and credited with the value of goods used, transferred, or sold. Credits must be calculated on the basis of actual cost of goods acquired during the year and the inventory value at the beginning of the year.

Physical inventories must be taken at reasonable intervals, however, and the perpetual inventory accounts must be adjusted to conform. If a firm uses the lower-of-cost-or-market basis of valuation of book inventory, cost so adjusted at the close of each tax year must be compared with the market value of each article on hand at the inventory date.

Computation of the Inventory Turnover Rate

One commonly used, simple measure of managerial performance is the **inventory turnover rate.** This rate indicates the number of times inventory is sold and replaced during a given time period. In most trade and professional statistics, the time period used is one year.

Inventory turnover rates give a rough guideline by which managers can set goals and measure performance, but it must be realized that the turnover rate varies with the function of inventory, the type of business, and how the ratio is calculated (whether on sales or cost of goods sold). For example, on a cost of goods sold basis, the average inventory turnover rate for manufacturers of paperboard containers ranges from 4.5 to 21.0. Values such as these are published periodically by trade associations and professional organizations.

Retailers can calculate inventory turnover rate by using either cost or retail figures, but not a mixture of the two. The following formulas can be used to determine turnover rates:

$$\text{Rate of Turnover at Retail Value} = \frac{\$\text{ Annual Net Sales}}{\$\text{ Average Inventory at Retail}}$$

$$\text{Rate of Turnover at Cost} = \frac{\$\text{ Cost of Goods Sold in One Year}}{\$\text{ Average Inventory at Cost}}$$

Average inventory equals inventory on January 1 plus the following 12 months' ending inventory figures, divided by 13.

Economic Order Quantity

Many companies seek to balance two types of costs involved in inventory:

1. Inventory holding costs (such as storage expenses, interest charges, insurance, taxes, and pilferage),
2. Order costs (such as filling out orders, computer utilization, and merchandise handling).

Inventory holding costs increase with the addition of more inventory, while processing costs decrease as the quantity ordered increases. The **economic order quantity (EOQ)** is the order volume corresponding to the lowest sum of inventory holding costs and order costs.

The following formula is used to determine the economic order quantity:

$$EOQ = \sqrt{\frac{2DS}{IC}}$$

where

EOQ = economic order quantity (in units)
D = annual demand (in units)
S = cost of placing an order (in dollars)
I = annual inventory carrying costs (as a percent of unit costs)
C = unit cost of an item (in dollars)

In this formula, D is an estimate based on the demand forecast for the item; S is calculated from the firm's cost records; and I is an estimate based on the cost associated with carrying inventory.

To illustrate the use of this formula, consider a firm that used 10,000 units ($10 per unit) of Product X last year. It cost $5 to issue a purchase order; 15 percent of the inventory value is the carrying cost of storage, interest, insurance, taxes, and pilferage. Inserting these figures into the formula yields an EOQ of 258 units.

$$EOQ = \sqrt{\frac{(2)(10{,}000)(5)}{(.15)(10)}} = \sqrt{\frac{100{,}000}{1.5}} = 258$$

The EOQ makes three basic assumptions:

1. The firm knows with certainty the annual usage of a particular item of inventory,
2. The rate of usage of inventory does not vary over time, and
3. Orders placed to replenish the inventory are received at exactly the point in time when inventory is zero.

These highly restrictive assumptions greatly limit the usefulness of the formula.

INVENTORY CONTROL METHODS

Two commonly used inventory control methods are manual recordkeeping methods and using computers in inventory management.[7]

Manual Recordkeeping Methods

At a very basic level, business inventory records provide the information needed to make decisions about inventory management. But the number and kinds of records maintained, as well as the type of control system needed, depend upon the type and size of inventory.

In very small businesses where visual control is used, records may not be needed at all or only for slowly moving or expensive items. But in a larger organization where many items from various suppliers are involved, more formal inventory records are appropriate. In such a case, regardless of the type of records maintained, the accuracy and discipline of the recording system are critical. It is important to remember that in many cases attempts to improve management and reduce costs fail, not simply because of insufficient records, but rather because of inaccurate and carelessly recorded inventory data.

Many small manufacturers, wholesalers, and retailers with relatively few items in inventory use a manual inventory control system. They use card records, inventory tags, and accounting data to capture the historical information necessary to establish economic order quantities (EOQ), order points, and other parameters for effective inventory control. However, as the number of items, suppliers, and general importance of inventory increases, it is often desirable to consider use of a computerized system for inventory control.

Using Computers in Inventory Management

Today, the use of computer systems to control inventory is far more feasible for small business than ever before, both through the widespread existence of computer service organizations and the decreasing cost of small-sized computers. Often the justification for such a computer-based system is enhanced by the fact that company accounting and billing procedures can also be handled on the computer.

Most computer manufacturers offer information on the inventory management systems available for their computers. In addition, computer service companies often have

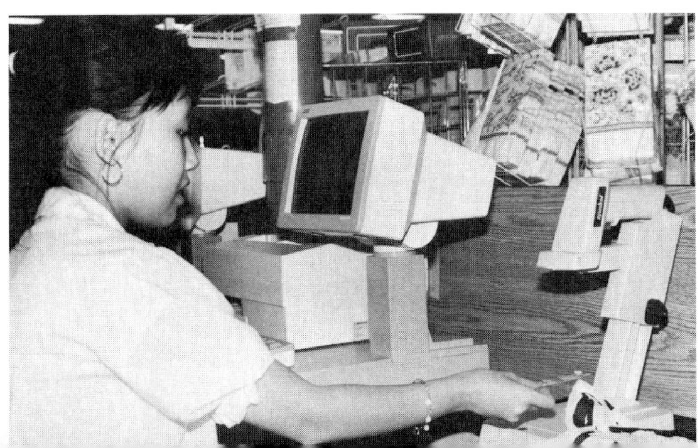

By using a scanner to monitor each sale, a firm can computerize many aspects of the business such as inventory control and sales levels. (Photograph © Ann M. Mason)

material readily available describing the use of their particular computer software programs for inventory management. These companies provide a good source of information on general descriptions of particular inventory management techniques, as well as help on specific inventory management problems.

JUST-IN-TIME INVENTORY MANAGEMENT

Just-in-time (JIT) inventory management is an approach that works to eliminate inventories rather than optimize them.[8] The inventory of raw materials and work-in-process falls to that needed in a single day. This is accomplished by reducing set-up times and lead times so that small lots may be ordered. Suppliers may have to make several deliveries a day or move close to the user plants to support this plan.

The development of just-in-time inventory systems is ushering in far-reaching changes for thousands of distributors, most of which are small companies with under $5 million in sales and fewer than 30 employees. It requires distributors to work more closely with manufacturing customers in planning inventory needs. The manufacturers are reducing the number of suppliers they buy from to make closer planning more workable. This may require distributors to hold larger inventories, thus increasing inventory costs. As a logical step, distributors have to turn to their own suppliers and insist that their own deliveries arrive closer to the time when they have to move goods out the door.[9]

Without proper information from the requesting firm, suppliers cannot meet the fast delivery times required for an effective JIT system. The most common approach in viewing the time from order placement to order receipt is the order cycle concept. **Order cycle time,** from the seller's viewpoint, is the time required to transmit, process, prepare, and ship an order. While this concept still retains a great deal of validity, the timing of the various operations will be unacceptable with JIT.[10]

Two examples of small companies that have responded to JIT follow.

Fireplace Manufacturers, a maker of prefabricated metal fireplaces, was having cash-flow problems because it needed to carry $1.1 million in inventory to support annual sales of about $8 million. Using a JIT consultant, the company shortened the assembly line by eliminating some tasks and recombining others. By devising ways to standardize components, management made it possible to produce parts in smaller quantities. This, in turn, reduced the firm's inventory of raw materials and work in process to $750,000, although sales have doubled.[11]

Polycom Huntsman built its newest plan just 1,500 feet from General Motor's Harrison Radiator Division, and then connected the two factories by a pneumatic conveying system. Now, when the GM plant starts to run low on the plastic compounds that Polycom supplies, a computer-controlled system automatically begins shipping material from Polycom's silos to Harrison's.[12]

As these examples illustrate, good inventory management has become increasingly critical in recent years. The improvement of inventory management requires record-keeping systems and then improved decision making based on the information. Quite simple systems can contribute greatly in the beginning. Later, when people have gained the discipline to make these systems work, more advanced systems and computers can add to performance. Some companies improve their inventory management to increase their own profitability; others have to do better to keep their more demanding customers. But all must bring about an improvement in a major company resource, inventory.

SUMMARY

1. Purchasing describes the business activity of securing goods or merchandise.
2. There are two basic types of purchasing: purchasing for resale and purchasing for consumption and conversion.
3. Purchasing plays a vital role in all businesses, with skillful buying essential to profitable operations.
4. Purchasing policies and procedures should reflect the objectives and plans of the firm. They should be reassessed periodically.
5. The objective of purchasing is to buy materials or merchandise of the right quality, in the right quantity, at the right price, from the right supplier, at the right time.
6. Small firms will usually find it advantageous to purchase from a few suppliers, because in times of shortage suppliers take better care of their own customers.
7. Purchase discounts may take the form of quantity discounts or cash discounts.
8. Purchasing considerations for owners of small plants include specifications, promoting purchasing savings, considering leases versus purchases, systems contracting, cash discounts, and inventory control.
9. Sound purchasing and inventory control are separate but closely related issues.
10. Inventory control is essential to good business management. It entails a balance between the costs of inventory and the benefits of inventory.
11. The objectives of inventory control involve minimizing inventory investment, determining the appropriate level of customer service, balancing supply and demand, minimizing procurement and carrying costs, and maintaining up-to-date inventory control systems.
12. Common methods of valuing inventory are the specific cost identification method and the lower-of-cost-or-market method.
13. The inventory turnover rate is a commonly used measure for merchandise inventory control.
14. The EOQ is economic order quantity that minimizes the total cost of placing an order and holding the item in inventory.
15. Two commonly used inventory control methods are manual recordkeeping methods and computers.
16. The use of computer systems to control inventory is far more feasible for small business than ever before.
17. Just-in-time inventory management is an approach that works to eliminate inventories rather than to optimize them.

KEY TERMS AND CONCEPTS

Purchasing
Systems contracting
Inventory
Procurement cost
Carrying cost
Obsolescence cost
Market value
Perpetual inventories
Physical inventories
Inventory turnover rate
Economic order quantity
Material requirements planning
Just-in-time inventory management
Order cycle time

QUESTIONS FOR DISCUSSION

1. What is included in the scope of purchasing?
2. Why is effective purchasing significant for a firm's profit potential?
3. Why should purchasing policies be flexible?
4. What is meant by "buying the right quantity?" How does this relate to "buying at the right time?"
5. What are the advantages and disadvantages of dealing with many suppliers?

6. What is the objective of offering cumulative discounts?
7. What is meant by "3/10, net 60," and what is the approximate annual cash discount value?
8. Why is inventory control a logical extension of a good purchasing system?
9. How can excessive inventory or the wrong assortment of inventory disrupt a firm's operations?
10. What are the accepted methods of valuing inventory for tax purposes?
11. How can a firm keep stock-outs at an acceptable level?
12. What are inventory turnover rates, and what are they based on?
13. What is the formula for determining the rate of turnover at retail value? At cost?
14. What are the shortcomings of EOQ?
15. What is the objective of just-in-time inventory management?

SELF-TEST REVIEW

Multiple Choice Questions

1. Which of the following is important for a firm making purchasing decisions?
   a. Right quantity.
   b. Right price.
   c. Right supplier.
   d. All of the above.
2. An advantage of buying from one supplier is:
   a. Having greater assurance of supply reliability.
   b. Receiving more attention and help.
   c. Both a and b.
   d. Neither a nor b.
3. Which of the following is not an objective of inventory control?
   a. Minimizing carrying costs.
   b. Balancing supply and demand.
   c. Maximizing inventory investment.
   d. Maintaining an up-to-date inventory control system.
4. An inventory control system that allows a firm to know how much of any item is in inventory at any given time is a:
   a. Physical system.
   b. Perpetual system.
   c. Both a and b.
   d. Neither a nor b.
5. An inventory control system that allows a firm to identify shortages is a:
   a. Physical system.
   b. Perpetual system.
   c. Both a and b.
   d. Neither a nor b.

True/False Statements

1. Purchasing policies should be flexible enough to allow the company to respond to unanticipated events.
2. In purchasing, quality refers to the suitability of a product for its intended use.
3. It is better for a small business to spread purchases among many suppliers.
4. Purchase discounts may not always be identified in price lists.
5. An inventory control system is essential in order to carry out effective purchasing.
6. The major costs of inventory are procurement costs and carrying costs.
7. Computer inventory systems are today more feasible for small businesses.
8. A turnover rate that is greatly out of line with industry averages may indicate symptoms of sluggish sales.
9. Just-in-time inventory management works to eliminate inventories.
10. Just-in-time inventory systems are seldom applicable to small businesses.

A & B WAREHOUSE LIQUORS

Tom Williams owns and operates a warehouse liquor store in a rapidly growing West Coast city. The store, opened three years ago, has experienced an annual sales growth of 25 percent. This growth can be attributed to the following factors: knowledgeable, helpful, friendly salespeople; the most extensive selection of liquor, wine and beer in the city; being located next to a regional shopping center; and A & B's advertising promise, "We Will Match Anybody's Price."

Williams uses the perpetual inventory method to keep track of stock on hand. Although it is time-consuming, he believes that this method is very efficient because any one of his seven employees can and does count stock on a daily basis during slack business hours. The employees are paid $4.50 per hour and together devote between 25 and 35 hours per week taking inventory. Their other duties are operating the cash register and stocking shelves.

A & B Warehouse Liquors' inventory consists of 275 liquor varieties, 156 brands of domestic and foreign wines, 115 brands of domestic and foreign beer, 30 brands of cigarettes, 22 brands of soft drinks and mixers, and 5 racks of potato chips and snacks. Based on weekly inventory summaries, Williams decides which items should be reordered or dropped. He estimates that $180 in monthly sales is lost because a requested item is out of stock. Williams does not know the turnover rates for individual items, but he has a feel for what they are. "This is a basic business, no matter how sophisticated my competitors might be at inventory control," says Williams. "If you keep a fully stocked store most of the time and can get employees to help customers and smile at all times, you do all the business you can handle."

Frequent customer requests for delicatessen items, ice, glassware, contemporary cards, and collectors' decanters prompted Williams to stock the following additional items last month: 8 varieties of meat, 14 varieties of cheese, 6 prepackaged salads, 5 types of bread and rolls, 7 varieties of glassware, 3 racks of contemporary cards, and 25 different collectors' decanters.

Williams decided to use visual inventory control for the new items in order to minimize the additional paperwork. He considers inventory control to be too time-consuming with all its "worthless" paper shuffling. He feels that his casual approach to controlling inventory is good enough. After all, he has experienced 25 percent annual sales growth.

QUESTIONS

1. What are possible advantages of Williams's inventory control methods?
2. Does a computerized inventory control system appear to be feasible for A & B's Warehouse Liquors?

NOTES

1. Warren Rose, "Inventory Control," in Walton Beacham, Richard T. Hise, and Hale N. Tongren, *Beacham's Marketing Reference* (Washington, D.C.: Research Publishing, 1986), 430.
2. This section is adapted from the National Association of Purchasing Management, *Purchasing as a Career*, 4th ed., 1976. Reproduced with permission from the National Association of Purchasing Management.
3. Excerpted from Small Business Administration, *Purchasing for Owners of Small Plants*, Management Aid No. 2.030 (1987).
4. Portions of this discussion are excerpted from Small Business Administration, *Inventory Management*, Management Aid No. 3.005 (1987).
5. Based on Cable News Network's "Pinnacle," March 11, 1989. Guest: Ronald Rule, U.S. Playing Card.
6. Based on Cable News Network's "Pinnacle," February 27, 1988. Guest: Safford Sweatt, Lenox China and Crystal.
7. Excerpted from *Inventory Management*.
8. *Ibid.*
9. Steven P. Galante, "Distributors Bow To Demand of " 'Just-In-Time' Delivery," *The Wall Street Journal*, June 30, 1986, 25.
10. James H. Bookbinder and David M. Dilts, "Logistics Information Systems in a Just-In-Time Environment," *Journal of Business Logistics*, Volume 10, No. 1, 1989, 56.
11. Steven P. Galante, "Small Manufacturers Shifting to " 'Just-In-Time' " Techniques," *The Wall Street Journal*, December 21, 1987, 25.
12. "Beyond Just-In-Time," *Inc.*, February 1989, 21.

Chapter Twenty-One

Operations Management and Computerizing the Small Business

Chapter Outline

PRODUCTION MANAGEMENT
- The Planning Process
- Deciding Whether to Make or Buy
- Converting the Sales Plan to a Production Plan

METHODS OF PRODUCTION
- Methods Development
- Work Scheduling

CONTROLLING THE PRODUCTION PROCESS
- Production Control
- Quality Control

COMPUTERIZING THE SMALL BUSINESS
- The Advantages and Disadvantages of Computerizing
- Elements of a Computer System
- Acquiring a Computer

SUMMARY

Learning Objectives *The objectives of this chapter are to assist you in understanding:*

1. How entrepreneurs convert sales plans to production plans.
2. How work is scheduled to achieve an efficient production process.
3. How the production process and quality are controlled.
4. What role computers can play in the small business.
5. The process the small business owner would use to acquire a computer system.

Entrepreneurs engaged in the manufacture of goods face the dual problem of producing and selling their products. While any firm is essentially involved in the production or buying of goods or services and selling, those that manufacture face a more complex task. In the production process, raw materials must be accumulated, machinery readied for use, and a competent labor force gathered. The merging of these costly activities can be a challenging task even for large firms that employ specialists in these endeavors.

PRODUCTION MANAGEMENT

Before the firm ever reaches the production stage, plans must be formulated for how the goods will be produced, what varieties and how much of each will be made, and when each will be manufactured. Since inefficient operations and unnecessarily high costs will all but destroy a firm's chances of survival, the production activity is of great importance in the overall management process.

Manufacturing to meet consumer demand can be a challenging process. For example, Mortimer Levitt, Custom Shop founder and owner, described the complexities of the process of making custom-made shirts to an interviewer:

> . . . we make it [the collar] in five different back heights to begin with, depending on the length of your neck; we make it in four different front heights depending upon your age (I'm an older man, and I need a higher front to cover the wrinkles) and your posture. 4 back heights times 5 front heights makes twenty variations of that collar. We also make it in three different point lengths. That means sixty variations. But we also make it in three different spreads and three different point lengths and that makes 180 variations of a basic collar style. And unless you understand that every one of those variations is not for kicks but to make you look better, then for the first time you begin to understand why you look better in custom made."[1]

The Planning Process

Successful manufacturing is the result of deliberate and detailed planning of the entire process of converting raw materials into finished goods—at least finished from the firm's perspective. Specific areas of focus are shown in Exhibit 21–1.

Product Development and Design

Determining what product(s) are to be produced is a prerequisite to any further planning. This involves delineating a full set of specifications. The product design will in many cases dictate the type of production possible as well as most other facets of the manufacturing process.

For example, Compliment Vans developed a customized van that is targeted to the busy executive who does not want (or cannot afford) a limousine.[2] The firm customizes vans to be mobile offices that include a desk, upholstered chair, television, compact disc player, telephone, fax machine, hide-away bed, and other comforts of an office. The customized van sells for approximately $25,000 less than comparable limousines. Tailoring each to the specific needs of the customer, however, is a complex production problem.

EXHIBIT 21–1 **The Production Planning Process**

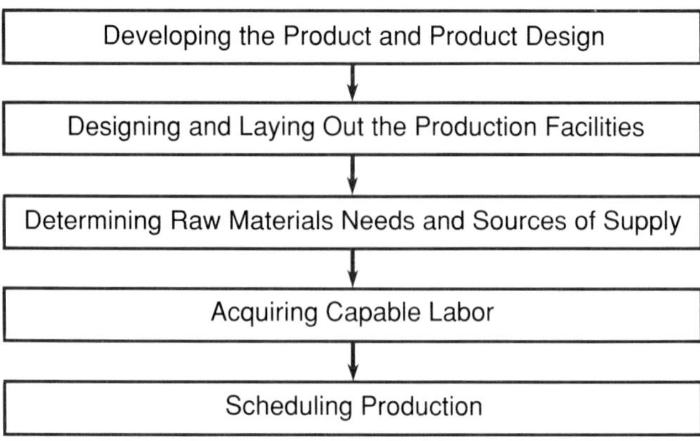

Timberland

Keeping technologically current is critical to any business, and the small business owner must invest time and personnel to do this. In looking to the future of The Timberland Co., Sidney Swartz, its chairman, chief executive officer, and president, stated: "I believe the future of this business will be driven by the new designs and new technology that we can develop. We have some of the finest designers in the world working for this company. . . . That's going to keep us in the marketplace for years to come." He noted that their time is allocated to 80 percent technical aspects of product function and 20 percent design.[3]

Production Facilities and Layout

Once the particular products are defined in terms of their technical specifications, the entrepreneur can begin to assess the firm's needs for various types of machinery and equipment. In addition, the physical spacing and general layout of work stations and machinery will directly affect the firm's ability to maximize output of high-quality goods. If the work space is not arranged in an orderly manner, workers will either be bumping into each other or making unnecessary movements that create delays and reduce output.

Raw Material Needs and Acquisition

Proper machinery and excellent layout will be of little value if raw materials are not available. Similarly, the finest machinery and equipment will not make good products out of poor quality materials. Consequently, obtaining the right materials at a reasonable price and at the right time is critically important. The entrepreneur should give high priority to developing a dependable source of supply.

Acquiring Capable Labor

Even in the most highly mechanized firms, there is still a need for a workforce that can skillfully operate, maintain, and repair the machinery. Capable labor ensures that the equipment will be put to its best use, will manufacture high quality products, and will not break down or wear out prematurely.

Johnny Imerman, owner of Mindis Recycling Co., is able to supply materials for his recycling plant by relying on a system of regional collection points which feed into a centralized facility. (Photograph courtesy of Johnny Imerman, Mindis Recycling)

Scheduling Production

Once all of the productive resources are accumulated—design, equipment, material, and labor—they should be scheduled to provide an orderly process of converting inputs into outputs. When a plant is producing only a single product, the scheduling can be a relatively simple task. If many products are to be manufactured, however, decisions must be made as to which is produced first, second, and so on. In addition, it must be decided how many of each should be produced at one time before the process is shut down and converted to the manufacture of other goods. Demand, economies of scale in production, and many other considerations will enter into this decision.

Deciding Whether to Make or Buy

In many cases, the small business owner will elect to purchase all or some of the products needed rather than produce them directly. Some components, for example, might be too difficult or too costly to make. In other cases, the entrepreneur may prefer to assemble a variety of component parts into a finished product.

The entrepreneur should fully evaluate the issue of whether it would be better to make or buy the components needed by the firm. Specific issues in this **make or buy decision** include:

- The quality of product needed,
- The quantity of product demanded,
- The availability of raw materials or component parts,
- The manufacturing requirements for producing a component.

Quality of Goods

Many entrepreneurs believe that "if you want it right, do it yourself." Applying this philosophy, they quickly decide that the only way to get high quality parts is to manufacture them outright. While in some instances this may be true, in many others it is not. Since a multitude of firms specialize in the development and production of component parts for resale to other companies, it often is possible to find a supplier who can provide a better quality product than could be produced by the entrepreneur.

There are, however, instances in which highly technical and unique parts cannot be purchased from other manufacturers. They may not have the right equipment and/

or technical expertise needed to make products, or they may simply not have adequate quality control standards and controls. Under these circumstances, the small business owner has little choice but to engage in the production process.

Quantity Needed

The quantity of component parts needed frequently will be the deciding factor in the make or buy decision. When relatively few units are needed, it usually is not feasible to go into production directly—especially if the part is available from reputable suppliers.

On the other hand, where very large quantities are needed, it is more likely that the entrepreneur will find it feasible to manufacture the part(s). In this instance, needed equipment will be utilized to capacity and economies of scale in production will reduce per unit costs substantially.

Coupled with the question of sheer numbers needed is the added dimension of when the units are needed. If they are used on a seasonal basis, it might be best to buy parts when needed rather than have idle equipment consuming space during nonpeak periods, and having to hire and then lay off workers. When component needs are continuous, it may be advantageous to produce them outright.

Availability of Supply

In many instances, the issue of whether to make or buy will be decided on the basis of whether the supply of raw materials or component parts is dependable. Interruptions in availability can cause serious delays in the overall production process. Lacking one critical part may result in an inability to complete the firm's products. This means lost sales, excessive unfinished inventory, and possibly the layoff of the work force.

The simple unavailability of supplies is not the only concern. The timing of delivery also is important. Either early or late delivery can be costly in terms of having excess inventory on hand or delays in being able to produce products. Thus, concern over any aspect of supply can affect the decision to make or buy the part.

Manufacturing Requirements

Closely linked to the supply issue are the manufacturing requirements involved in producing the part. Of particular concern is the investment needed to obtain the machinery, the costs of raw materials, and the overall cost per unit of output.

Factors such as physical space additions and disruptions to other operations also need to be examined. Similarly, the costs per unit must be of concern. Here, the costs of buying from specialized suppliers may be less than making the product directly. Special machinery, skilled labor, and economies of scale in mass production often make purchase decisions more advantageous. On the other hand, some components might easily fit into the firm's normal production process. Taking up slack time or being a natural byproduct of some other process may prove a definite advantage in the decision to make the product. Thus, any decision must be based on unit costs as well as overall costs.

Converting the Sales Plan to a Production Plan

The interaction between sales and production often is a source of serious concern to the small business owner. Essentially, there are two main issues to be resolved. First, the entrepreneur must ensure that the products demanded are the same as those being produced. Second, scheduling production must be done in such a way as to minimize delays both in filling orders and in building up inventory.

Products Demanded Should Be the Same as Those Produced

To the frustration of many customers and producers alike, there often are differences between what customers want and what manufacturers want to or do produce. If viewed from a purely economic standpoint, there would have to be a divergence. Consumers want the most for their purchasing dollars, while producers want to give the least. In addition, consumers may well expect certain attributes or features that the manufacturer may find too difficult or costly to include in the finished product.

One of the most significant issues concerns product quality. How much quality should be built into the product design? While consumers want a high level of quality, they are at times unwilling to pay for it.

A second issue relates to the variety of products needed. While wide variations in color, style, and size will appeal to a larger number of consumers, they create immense challenges in manufacturing. Not only will there be added purchasing and scheduling complexities, there will almost always be build-ups in inventory. All of these factors can translate into higher production costs. Here again, the entrepreneur must try to reconcile demands for variety with the realities of production.

Production Scheduling

Although specific scheduling techniques are described later in this chapter, there are some major decisions to be made in advance. The most pressing question concerns how production is to be related to the sales plan of the firm. Should the small business produce to order or produce in anticipation of orders? Assuming that several items are manufactured, how are they to be scheduled relative to one another?

One key to successful production is to have a reasonably accurate sales forecast. Knowing well in advance what needs to be produced and when it will be demanded greatly reduces the complexities of planning the productive effort. Unfortunately, in most industries this is not possible. International Mobile Machines Corp., for example, produces a product called "Ultraphone"—a telephone that sends and receives calls through radio waves.[4] It is best used for areas that are too isolated for telephone lines. Despite great interest in the product, the large telephone companies only purchase units as they need them, making it very difficult for the firm to close sales and schedule production.

Since there are uncertainties about when consumers will demand the firm's products and in what quantities, the entrepreneur must try to arrive at a method of scheduling that is both conducive to sales and reasonably inexpensive. This is no simple task. When consumers want something, they typically want it instantly. If one firm cannot provide the item at that point in time, consumers will go elsewhere if there are alternatives available. For the small business, it may be too costly to hold large quantities in inventory just in case some customers come calling. Not only can considerable sums of money be tied up this way, but it increases the risks of obsolescence and damage during storage.

Because of the risk involved in producing to order, many small business owners produce in anticipation of sales. They are willing to tie up some funds in inventory and accept the risk that the items might become obsolete or otherwise undesirable. The costs of lost sales are greater than the costs of building inventory.

If it is decided that holding inventory is more desirable, the next question is whether to use **batch production** or maintain a continuous level of production. Although the types of products and the firm's production capabilities often will decide which method to use, these options are important to consider at least once each year.

Most entrepreneurs will produce in batch lots and try to schedule them in advance of sales. If there are seasonal variations, these should be accounted for so that production will be sequenced to meet demand as well as fit into the firm's overall production process.

METHODS OF PRODUCTION

Any production process essentially is one of converting inputs into outputs. Raw materials, labor, management time, facilities, utilities, and other factors are turned into finished products ready for sale. Even though the basic conversion process is much the same whether the product is complex or simple, many entrepreneurs mistakenly assume there is only one right way to manufacture a product. Too often, small business owners do not recognize that their manufacturing methods are a basic process on which adaptations are built.

Methods Development

For an entrepreneur to get the best results from a production process, consideration must be given to possible **methods of production.** Of particular concern should be the type and quality of machinery available, how equipment is spatially arranged within the physical plant, and whether employees are working efficiently or wasting time and effort. Decisions relating to these issues must be directed to maintaining an appropriate quality of output while attempting to reduce the time and costs of production.

Machinery Considerations

In many instances, small business owners cannot afford to buy the newest and the best equipment available. Their limited resources force them to utilize more dated equipment or equipment whose quality is not of the highest caliber.

Modern machinery can improve performance, but knowing how to use the equipment to the best advantage is certainly of equal and perhaps greater importance. Many small business owners wrongly shrug off their inefficiencies by blaming the equipment.

Manufacturing competence and ingenuity can make the production process sufficiently workable so that the firm can remain competitive. What it takes is a thorough

Even a small business needs to be technologically current if it is to compete with large firms. This flexible "factory of the future" produces high-quality custom Bravo pagers in minutes instead of several days. Robots are controlled by an integrated computer network. (Photograph courtesy of Motorola, Inc.)

examination of each step in the production process, and an analysis of how well each piece of equipment can and should work. Equipment not up to capacity should be modified if it can be done at a reasonable cost, or earmarked for quick replacement when funds permit.

Even if the firm had the financial resources to buy ideal machinery, this might not be advisable. Just because new equipment is brighter and shinier does not mean it will work better. A new pair of shoes, for example, does not necessarily protect the feet any better than an older pair, nor do they necessarily make the feet walk faster or straighter. All they really do is look better.

Machinery Investments

One major question in deciding whether to purchase a machine is, "How long will it take for the machine to pay for itself?" Calculating the **payback period**—the time it will take for increased revenues or reduced costs to pay for the machine—provides a means of evaluating the wisdom of making a major purchase. The formula for this is:

$$\text{Payback Period (in Years)} = \frac{\text{Total Costs of Purchase}}{\text{Yearly Cost Savings or Profit Increases}}$$

Although there is no set rule as to how quickly the equipment or other fixed asset should pay for itself, it certainly should do so before its useful life is over. Thus, if a machine has a five-year life and the payback period is seven years, it is likely that it will never pay for itself. Consequently, the philosophy regarding payback periods is the sooner the better. Typically, firms look for a payback within two to three years, depending on the useful life of the equipment.

Plant Layout

The entrepreneur also must be sure that the appropriate machinery is arranged for an orderly flow within the overall production process. Spatial considerations are important in improving operating efficiency.

Of particular concern here is to ensure that the flow is efficient in that it eliminates unnecessary movements and backtracking. A few of the innumerable layout possibilities are presented in Exhibit 21–2. The entrepreneur should be especially careful when selecting a site to ensure that both the overall size and the shape conform to the needs of the manufacturing process.

The layout shown in Exhibit 21–2–A is quite common either when four unique products are being manufactured, or when the products are interrelated (as shown with the dotted lines). When using four separate processes to produce one product, starting at point A and ending at point P may prove advantageous in that transit between the work stations is minimized and the inflow and outflow of materials and finished goods are located on the same side of the building. In this situation, supplies should be at the center point.

Exhibit 21–2–B is a diagram of another layout conducive to an orderly flow in the processing of one product. Beginning at point A and progressing through point P, the same advantages as in Exhibit 21–2–A are evident. The only real problem is that of locating supplies, which would have to be near the south (that is, A–H–I–P) or north (that is, D–E–L–M) and could result in some inefficiency. This approach works best when producing four unique products. Here, all processing would start at A–H–I–P and

EXHIBIT 21–2 **Variations in Plant Layout**

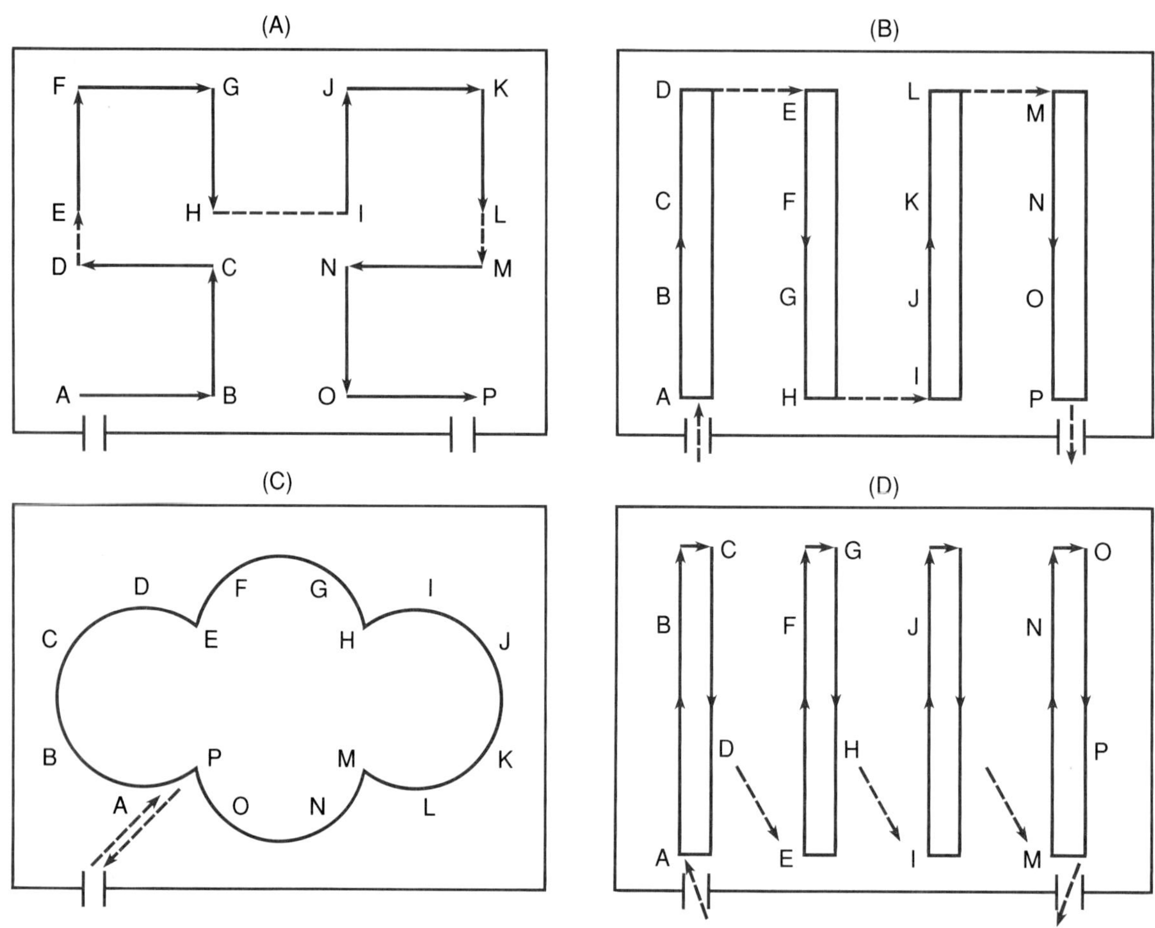

work toward D–E–L–M. Raw materials would arrive at the south end of the building and exit as finished goods at the north end.

Another common approach, and one that is most applicable to the manufacture of one product through a series of separate processes, is shown in Exhibit 21–2–C. The central input and output at points A and P provide efficiency in the receipt of raw materials and shipment of finished products. In addition, supplies can be stored at the center point and be convenient to everyone.

A final possibility, although not as common as the other three, is shown in Exhibit 21–2–D. Following a single product from point A through point P does provide a logical flow of work with a reasonably small amount of transit between tables. Of course, supply stations still are a problem, as they were in Exhibit 21–2–B. For separate products, this layout has the advantage that all work begins and ends at one side of the plant. This allows for a centralized inflow and outflow of materials and goods.

The key to efficient plant layout is to maintain some degree of flexibility in the overall design. As the business changes, so will the need for particular space and physical layout. The Small Business Administration has identified five factors that a plant should provide for:

1. *Adequate land*—the small firm must have a sufficient amount of land on which to operate. If the entrepreneur uses all the land available at the beginning of the venture, the firm may soon be forced to move. Coupled with sheer size should be considerations of proximity to natural resources and transportation facilities.
2. *Modular construction*—the essence of modular design is that walls of the plant may be moved to allow for building redesign without destroying the overall structure. Interior layout can be modified relatively quickly at a reasonably low cost.
3. *Shell structure*—the small business owner who elects to build a plant should consider future expansion possibilities before the plant is erected. If it appears likely that expansion will be required within two to three years, it may be more economical to have a shell built and left unfinished until needed. Unused space which is built as part of the initial unit will be less costly than trying to reconstruct the building at a later time.
4. *High ceiling*—increasingly, firms are having plants built with high ceilings—up to 20 feet instead of the more conventional 12 to 14 feet—because it facilitates overhead transport of materials and placement of utility lines. This increases the flexibility of the plant layout, since electricity can be established at virtually any spot within the building.
5. *Underground ducts*—for small entrepreneurs the need for a neat and unobstructed physical layout may be of great importance. In these instances, underground ducts providing the necessary utilities (water, electricity, gas) can be valuable. This approach also reduces the hazards of exposed pipes and wires.

Work Scheduling

Once the most effective methods of production are determined and the physical layout is made conducive to efficient manufacture, the work must be scheduled appropriately. Confusion in scheduling the various elements of the production process typically results in delays in deliveries and lost sales, as well as costly changeovers and down times.

Before raw materials are placed in machinery and before any output is obtained, the entrepreneur should fully schedule the entire process. **Production scheduling** involves determining each step of the process for each product, the time it will take to complete each step, and the overall capacity of the equipment and labor in terms of output per hour or day or month.

Identifying Each Step

Even though the entrepreneur may believe that he or she knows the production process fully, each step needs to be laid out individually for inspection and analysis. This might begin with an examination of the finished product in terms of each component to be made or bought. For those to be bought, the lag time between order and delivery must be determined so that a sufficient number will be available when needed.

One of the most useful tools in defining the production process is the **operations process chart,** which is a graphic representation of the various operations, time allowances, and materials used in a manufacturing process. This chart clearly delineates each step so that none will be forgotten or ignored. In graphic form, this approach allows the entrepreneur to visualize each aspect of production and each decision point in the overall process. A sample operations process chart for producing a slingshot is shown in Exhibit 21–3.

Timing the Process

An important aspect of planning the production process is determining how much time each part in the overall operation will take. Since timing affects the sequencing and scheduling of activities, it must be done with accuracy. Providing too little time for process completion will result in frequent bottlenecks or efforts to hurry up the process and cause quality to suffer. Making too much time available will result in lost production capabilities and higher costs per unit of output.

Determining Production Capacity

Closely related to task timing is determination of production capability. Since a piece of machinery often is used in the completion of a task, its normal and maximum speed and output are of great significance. In most instances, the manufacturer of the equipment will provide information on the capabilities and speed of the machinery.

Even with this information, the entrepreneur should test the machinery and time the operation at slow, normal, and high speeds. By clocking the speed at which inputs can be readied, outputs transported, and other processes completed, one can assess the overall capacity per hour of operation. For nonmachine operations the techniques discussed earlier can be used. Time also must be allotted to normal maintenance, repairs, and employee breaks.

Scheduling the Productive Effort: PERT/CPM

Once the methods of production have been decided, the plant laid out in a facilitating manner, and all facets of the production process identified and timed, the entrepreneur is ready to actually schedule production. To be effective, scheduling must be done for each aspect of the process and based on blocks of time.

Although there are a number of techniques available to help the entrepreneur in scheduling, the most common are PERT (Program Evaluation and Review Training) and CPM (Critical Path Method).[5] Taking the list of activities as developed from the operations chart and detailing out the operations even further, the small business owner can construct the operations chart. With this, the entrepreneur can add in the completion times of each facet of the production process.

CONTROLLING THE PRODUCTION PROCESS

Controlling the production process is necessary to the success of any business involved in manufacturing. When the process gets out of control, production costs become too high, there are delays in delivery, and the quality of output tends to suffer.

EXHIBIT 21–3 Operations Process Chart

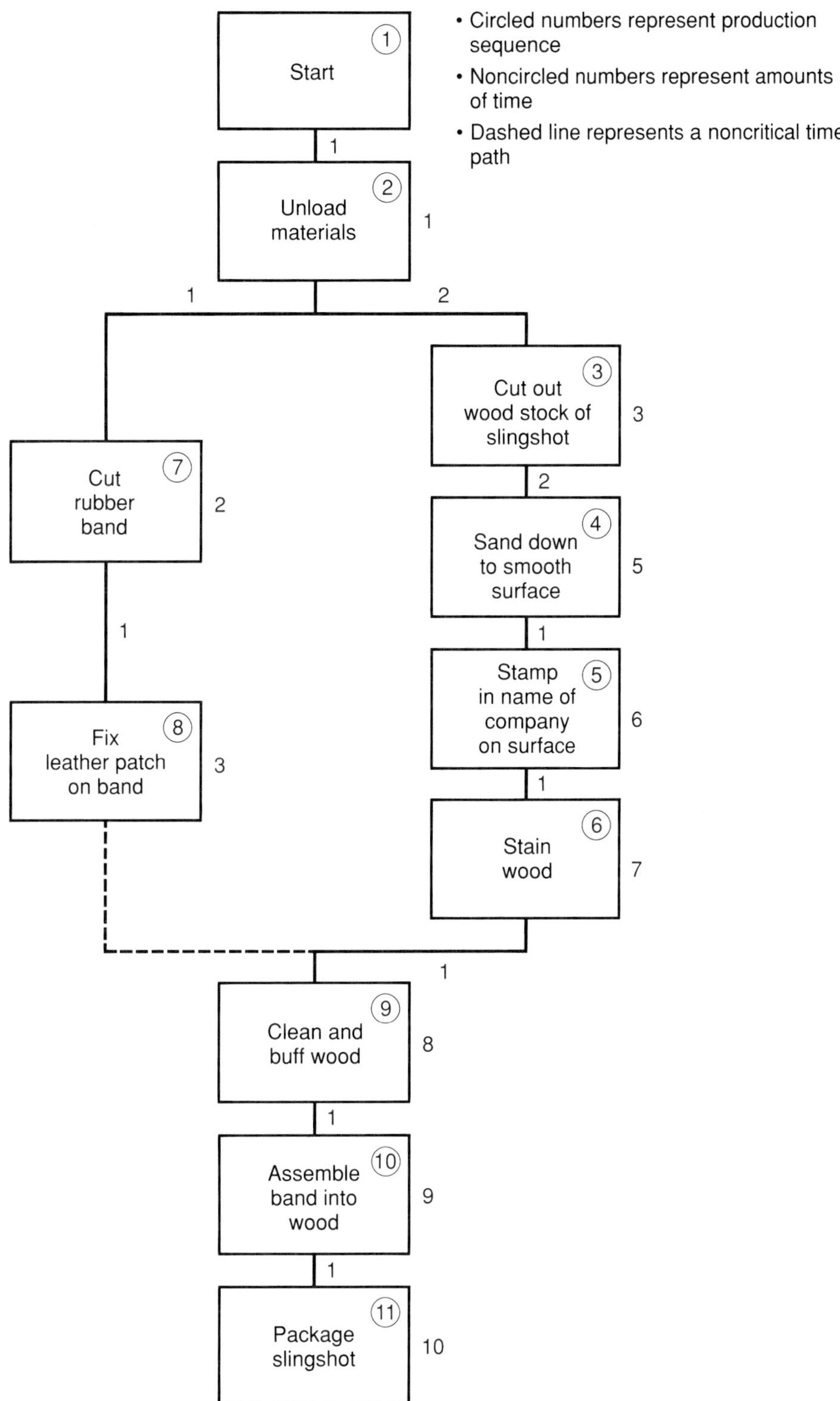

Production Control

The issue of what goods to manufacture involves marketing and make or buy decisions. Determining what quantity to produce is of greater concern in the production process itself. For firms making only one or a few products on a manufacture-to-order basis, the quality decision is relatively simple. But what if the business produces 15 to 20 products—all of them in anticipation of orders? How much of each should be made? When?

Timberland®

The importance of a well-run manufacturing operation cannot be overstated. One example of this came from Sidney Swartz, chief executive officer, chairman, and president of The Timberland Company, the maker of rugged outdoors boot and shoes. In commenting on how the company has progressed, Mr. Swartz stated:

> We felt that as long as we controlled the manufacturing floor and we made only for ourselves, we could control the quality, and that was the most important thing that we could do, plus the shorter turnaround times. I guess that's what's really driving the company right at this moment. We get a lot of credit as a marketing company. We're a better manufacturer than a marketer.[6]

The answers to these questions strike at the heart of the scheduling process. Not having enough goods available may result in lost sales or rushed production. Hurried efforts often are more costly because of disruptions to normal scheduling, rush orders for raw materials, and so on.

Economies of Scale

As levels of production increase, the costs per unit of output tend to decline. This is partly the result of continuous manufacture—no stoppage or down times plus the increased skill of the work force. Getting full use of the equipment and having the labor force achieve high levels of competence generally leads to greater levels of output, reduced waste, and higher overall levels of efficiency. These **economies of scale** give the firm a greater profit margin as output increases.

As illustrated in Exhibit 21–4, the full economy of added production is not achieved until the firm reaches Output Level A. Between Levels A and B, the firm can maintain the lowest cost per unit of output possible. After Point B, the firm starts to reach a state of **diseconomies of scale.** This is due to demands for output that are greater than the normal capacity of the firm's equipment and labor. In many respects, therefore, Point B can be considered the level of maximum capacity under normal operating conditions.

The entrepreneur may elect not to limit sales, and instead opt for increasing overall plant capacity. This can mean a larger building, added equipment, and more employees. Perhaps more importantly, it may require an added investment of capital by the entrepreneur or considerably higher levels of debt. A *step increase* in fixed cost, like that shown in Exhibit 21–5, indicates that if the entrepreneur wishes to produce past output Level B, fixed costs per unit will go from Y-1 to Y-2.

The essence of this consideration is that if needed output is not at least to Level A in Exhibit 21–4, it may be advantageous for the entrepreneur to buy rather than manufacture the product directly. If demand is sufficiently great, then batch runs of at least quantity A would probably be wise. Similarly, if output requirements are higher than

EXHIBIT 21–4

Economies and Diseconomies of Scale in Production

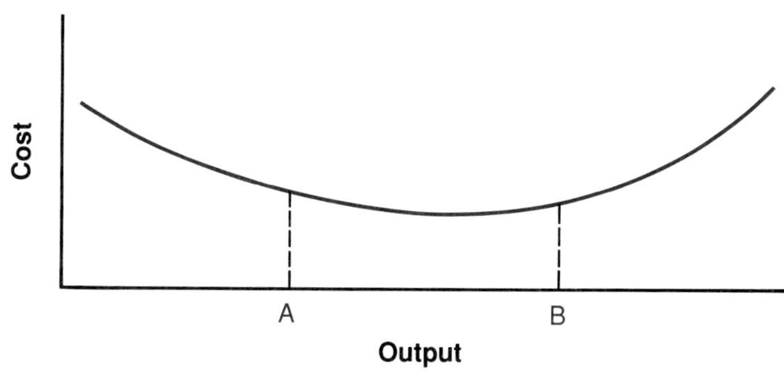

Level B in Exhibit 21–4, the entrepreneur may consider manufacturing up to Level B and buying the rest of the volume needed.

Inventory Levels

Production levels should be designed to achieve economies of scale in the manufacturing process and maintain a desired inventory level. Keeping some inventory on hand usually is advisable, since it guards against stockouts and lost sales as well as reducing the need for short production runs. On the other hand, there is a fine line between holding too much inventory and holding too little.

The costs of maintaining certain levels of inventory must be correlated to the cost savings of larger production runs and the increased likelihood of being unable to fill incoming orders. Regulating the inventory levels for each product is a focal point for production control. Economic order quantities can be calculated using the formula shown in Exhibit 21–6.

EXHIBIT 21–5 **Fixed Cost Curve in the Production Process**

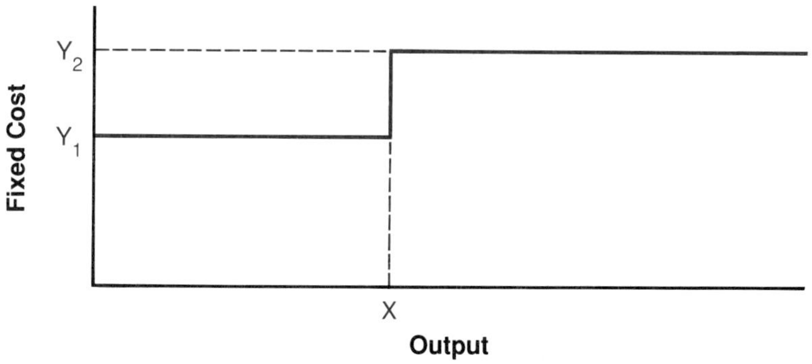

EXHIBIT 21–6 **Economic Order Quantity**

Formula: Economic Order Quantity $= \sqrt{\frac{2\ LM}{W}}$

where: L = Annual purchases in dollars
M = Dollar cost of issuing a purchase order
W = Cost of capital or carrying inventory (interest rate on borrowed funds)

Graphic Illustration: Known Demand

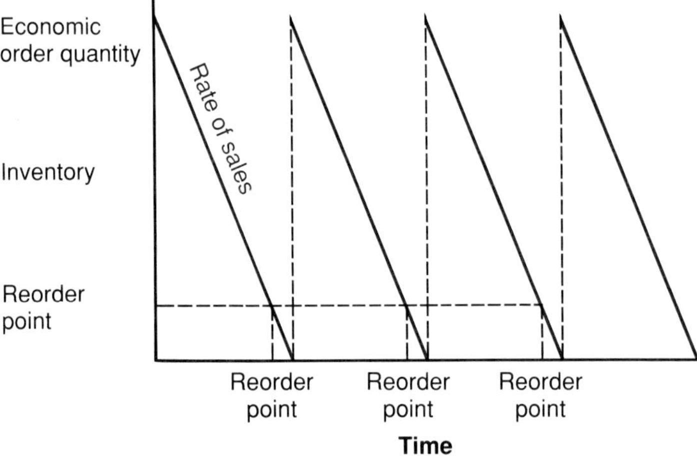

Quality Control

Control of the production process includes not only the number and type of products produced, but also the quality of the output. It makes little sense to manufacture a large quantity of shabby products efficiently. However, making sure that each unit meets a high quality standard will be prohibitively expensive. Thus, the small business owner must develop a **quality control** process that effectively regulates the quality of output at reasonable costs.

Manufacturing products is not all skill. When Robert Mondavi, founder of Robert Mondavi Winery in Napa, California, was asked whether wine making was an art or a science, his response was, "Believe you me, it's an art . . . [science is] very helpful, but it's an art. . . . You can make sound wine. It's difficult to make truly fine wine." Mr. Mondavi indicated that they watch every detail, starting with the soil, adjusting for the climate, and focusing attention on the grape, " . . . the finer the grape, the finer the wine."[7]

Quality Control Points

Ideally, the control system should ensure that any production problems that result in defective output are corrected instantly and that all defective units are removed from

To make a truly fine wine it takes total dedication, total involvement, and quality control of every detail. The quality control begins by checking the soil and climate conditions and continues as the grapes grow to maturity and are finally bottled as wine. The bottles are checked every few weeks throughout the aging process so that the winemaker knows the quality of the product. (Photograph courtesy of Robert Mandavi Winery)

finished goods. To do this, checkpoints need to be established within the production process so that materials can be monitored as they are being converted into final products. Although the specific points will vary depending on the type of manufacturing done, the points should all have the following characteristics:

- *They should fit easily within the process.* If quality control is disruptive to the manufacturing process itself, the costs of monitoring will be high.
- *They should be directly related to some aspect of production.* The inspection must identify the cause of product defects if it is to be effective in maintaining a given quality standard.
- *They should be quick to identify any production problems.* Lengthy delays will become quite costly in terms of the manufacture of defective products.
- *They should be closely tied to critical aspects of production.* Some parts will be more important than others and more likely to create quality problems. Controlling insignificant aspects of production or those least likely to cause defects can be a costly waste of time and money.
- *They should be reasonably inexpensive to use.* The entrepreneur must keep an eye on the costs of maintaining a quality control system to ensure that the costs of controlling production do not exceed possible losses from defective merchandise.

Product Inspection

Individual units of output also must be examined. In any production process, there will be some level of defective merchandise. However, in most cases the production process itself should not be stopped in an effort to achieve zero defects. Instead, the entrepreneur should try to minimize the number of defects through a checkpoint system of **product inspection.**

Although quality inspections can be simple for some types of products, it can be difficult for others. Checking the quality of oak tables, for example, involves looking for flaws in the wood and/or finish. Since tables are large and contain no internal components, the process can be comparatively easy.

Examining canned foods, on the other hand, is much more complex, since the product must be chemically examined for foreign matter and the product is thereby destroyed. Interestingly, the Food and Drug Administration sets standards on the extent to which undesirable items can be contained in food.[8] For example, packaged mushrooms are allowed to contain up to 20 maggots per 3.5 ounces, and 3.5 ounces of peanut butter can have as many as 30 insect fragments and one rodent hair.

In some instances, all units can be examined relatively easily and economically. Generally, however, entrepreneurs do not have to inspect all units and cannot do so without incurring high costs. Consequently, most small manufacturers must rely on a method of selecting samples for quality inspection. How many units to sample depends on the normal level of defective production and the costs of both quality control and of letting bad products pass by unnoticed. For example, food processors often purchase metal cans from independent companies. Any defective metal cans are returned to the can manufacturer and the processor is given credit not only for the defective can itself but also for the can's contents. Bad products also carry an intangible cost—the ill will generated in the firm's customers.

The entrepreneur also must establish some minimum level of quality as the standard against which each sample unit can be compared. The small business owner must decide how much variability there should be in product quality.

COMPUTERIZING THE SMALL BUSINESS

Electronic technology has rapidly become a critical element to the success of small businesses. While every entrepreneur does not need to computerize, most find that computers and commercial programs have become so easy to use and so low in price that their integration into the firm's operations should at least be evaluated. By the end of 1988, 44.2 percent of small businesses with fewer than five employees had at least one computer, and the percentage increased to 76 for those with 20 or more employees.[9]

Bill Gates, the founder of Microsoft Corp. and a billionaire by the age of 31, described the benefits of computers:

> I think personal computers have already had a very positive impact on productivity. . . . I think that five years off when you get . . . companies having a workstation on almost every desk, that it's going to allow them to do business planning, change their products so much better than they do today that it'll have a major impact. . . . Right now the computers require some skill to get the benefit out of them. . . . As we're making the machines easier to use and they become educational devices, hopefully anybody who has a little bit of curiosity can get involved . . . [10]

Bill Gates, founder of Microsoft Corporation, believes that although it will take some time, eventually there will be a personal computer in every home and every office. (Photograph courtesy of Microsoft Corporation)

There are many uses for computers in small businesses. They can help process accounts receivable, generate mailing lists, assist in telecommunications to transmit information rapidly to suppliers and customers, play "what if" games to measure possible impacts of price changes on sales and profits, track sales by customer or sales territory, monitor inventory levels, and assist in most facets of word processing.

While there are applications for computers in manufacturing, most computers are used to process data. For example, a salesperson in a small hardware store fills in a sales slip and the sales slip is recorded by hand in a sales journal. At the end of the month, sales can be summarized in a sales journal and reported on the store's monthly income statement—also prepared by hand.

If the hardware store had processed its transactions on a computer, at the end of the month the owner could automatically produce a sales journal and an income statement and balance sheet, accounts receivable and payable lists, cash flow statement, and an updated inventory status report. With such computer-generated reports, the small business owner would have accurate information to help operate the business without the burden of a large clerical staff.

This is not to say that computers can operate without people. Computers can do only what humans have told them to do. They must be directed in each step by people-produced programs. Some clerical effort will always be needed, but the amount can be greatly reduced as more functions are computerized. While this will result in a savings in labor costs, it is not always as great as expected—people involved with the computer process tend to be higher-paid individuals. It is the faster and more complete reporting and greater efficiency that justify the use of computers in many businesses.

The Advantages and Disadvantages of Computerizing

Computerizing the firm's operations offers many advantages. No routine activity is immune to the influence of the computer. However, computers are not a panacea—they will not make an otherwise poorly managed business into a successful one; and there are some drawbacks to computerizing.

There are a number of reasons why small business owners acquire computers. According to one survey of small business owners, the benefits derived from computers were (in descending order): improved business information, improved productivity, improved work quality, made work easier, improved organization of the business, and reduced labor costs.

Computers can help a small business such as this video store keep customer records, catalogue available titles, project sales, and determine rental trends. (Photograph © Ann M. Mason)

A computer allows the manager to maintain a personal grasp on what is going on in the firm since better information and analyses can be made of internal operations. For example, by knowing what is held in inventory on a continual basis, dollar investments can be controlled more precisely with fewer stock-outs. Employee morale can improve when the mundane tasks are handled by computers. Slow-paying customers can be identified quickly, allowing the manager to be more aggressive in collecting on accounts receivable and thereby improving the firm's cash position.

In manufacturing plants, computers can control the production process to ensure that the best use of people and material is being achieved. In 1988, for example, computers were available for computer-aided design (CAD) and computer-aided manufacturing (CAM) systems that allowed firms to more precisely design and cut their products. This made it possible for them to seek business that demanded high precision, which they otherwise could not produce.[11]

Despite these and other possible benefits, there are some disadvantages that at times outweigh the advantages. At least initially, computers will make more demands on an organization, especially if the firm does not have people who are knowledgeable in the use of computers. To be most effective, computers require a structured, formal operating process. Jobs and needed reports must be well defined if the computer is to be helpful. Computers usually do not exactly fit the firm's present methods of operation.

Conversions from manual to computer systems, and even from one computer system to another, can be traumatic for the firm. It will take time, and the firm may operate inefficiently until the system is well in place. Additionally, a computer is capable of generating large amounts of information, some of which will prove to be of little value to managers in their decision-making processes. The volume of information that can be generated can overwhelm the manager if it is not limited.

Elements of a Computer System

One of the important aspects of computerizing a small business is to ensure that those who work with or are affected by computers understand the elements of a computer system. Listed below are the components of a computer system:[12]

- *Central processing unit (CPU)*—this is the heart of the computer system. The central processing unit **(CPU)** performs calculations, manages the flow of data, and executes program instructions. The CPU is the core of the computer's **hardware**—the parts of the computer other than the software described below.
- *Software*—these are programs used to tell the CPU what to do with the data it has. **Software** programs are available for such purposes as word processing, spreadsheets, statistical analyses, graphic presentation, and keeping accounting records. Many software programs are predesigned and sold in retail stores, but specially written ones can be made to fit the specific needs of the small business owner.
- *Memory*—there are two types of memory within the CPU. *ROM* is *read-only memory,* which is built into the system and can be read but not erased when the computer is turned off. The more important memory for the small business user is *random access memory,* or *RAM.* The amount of RAM determines how much information or the number of calculations the computer can work with at one point in time. Normally, at least 512K (or 512,000 bytes) of RAM are desired,

with one byte equal to a single letter or number. If the computer has less than this, it may not be able to run some of the software available. When the computer is turned off, the RAM is erased.

- *Storage*—to store data so that it can be used in the future, computers use *disk drives* and *hard disks*. Disk drives are attached to the CPU so that external information can be transmitted into the system, and sent from the internal processing system to diskettes that store the information in the form of *files*—names given by the computer operator to specific groups of data being processed. Diskettes may be either 3.5 or 5.25 inches in size, and usually store from 360K to 1.2MB (one megabyte equals one million bytes). The hard disk is installed within the internal operating system and can store from 10MB to over 80MB. Conceptually, hard disks are not much more than a much larger diskette. However, because they are linked directly to the processing unit, hard disks can store and retrieve data much more rapidly than can be accomplished by disk drives.
- *Workstations*—this is the equipment used by the computer operator to run the computer. It consists of a keyboard and monitor. The *keyboard* is similar to a typewriter, although there may be considerably more keys to use. The *monitor,* or cathode ray tube (CRT), is the screen which is used to visually operate the system. The monitor may be either color or monochrome (for example, green on black or amber on black).
- *Printer*—this is an electronic device that prints information based strictly on commands given by the CPU. Printers typically are *dot matrix, letter quality,* or *laser.* As their names imply, dot matrix printers form letters and numbers through a series of dots, letter quality printers are similar to typewriters in the way they form letters and numbers, and laser printers form letters and numbers using an electrically charged and rotating metal drum.

Acquiring a Computer

Not every small business needs a computer in order to operate successfully. The most important rule for computerizing a business is to have specific tasks in mind for the system before making a purchase or entering into a lease. A computer should not be acquired unless tasks are well defined, and analyses completed to determine if the benefits of a system outweigh the costs. Unfortunately, many owners feel they need to own computers even though they have no real uses for them.

The steps involved in acquiring a computer can be grouped into the series of six activities described below.[13] Ordinarily, these steps should be undertaken in sequence.

Step One: Prepare a Job Description for the Computer

The most important step in the process of acquiring a computer is to determine just what it is to do, what benefits it will provide, and who is to operate the system. Deciding on these factors is very similar to preparing a job description for a new position within the firm. This job description should be developed with the focus on not only the immediate needs of the firm, but also for one to two years in the future. To the extent possible, a system should be acquired that will—with possible modifications—serve the firm for a period of two to three years.

Additionally, computers are costly, and they become technologically obsolete relatively quickly. Accordingly, the small business owner must consider whether it is best to purchase or to lease a system. Purchasing can be less expensive over the long run, but leasing reduces the initial expenditure and provides more flexibility in replacing a system when the current one is no longer adequate.

Advances in computer technology are always a concern when deciding whether to acquire a new system. According to Rod Canion, the co-founder of Compaq Computer:

> [The pace of change, technological change] . . . certainly has been rapid for a long time, but I believe it's even accelerating today. We're seeing new advances in many of the key areas that relate to personal computers, the processor, integration of chips, the storage areas . . . because we have had . . . industry standard[s] now for the last five years, old computers really don't have to be thrown away or gotten rid of. They can be used somewhere else in the company very efficiently.[14]

Step Two: Select the Software

Some small business owners mistakenly select hardware (Step Three) before software. Because hardware tends to be a more expensive element in computerizing, owners tend to focus their attention on this component. Unfortunately, the hardware is of little value without the proper software—and some programs will only work with certain types of hardware.

Since the software tells the computer what to do, the small business owner should find the programs that will perform the desired tasks as specified in Step One.[15] In some instances, it may be necessary to combine Steps Two and Three when the choice of software will have a major impact on the type and cost of hardware to acquire. For example, if the small business owner has the choice of two software programs that will perform the needed tasks adequately, consideration should be given to the type and costs of hardware each would need. One software alternative may require hardware that is more costly or configurations that limit the use of the hardware for other purposes.

Generally, the small business owner has three alternatives in the selection of software: purchase predesigned programs, have special programs written, or use a combination of the two.

There are many predesigned programs readily available to do many of the tasks needed in the small business. According to one source, there are more than 15,000 software packages available for IBM and IBM-compatible computers.

Word processing programs have become quite sophisticated, and many have desktop publishing capabilities. Spreadsheets can be used to prepare financial statements, make financial and market analyses, and so on. A variety of programs is available for data management, and most of those also are capable of generating mailing lists. Similarly, there are numerous programs for basic accounting processes, handling payrolls, and monitoring inventory levels.

Generally, there are sufficient numbers of predesigned programs available to satisfy the basic needs of most businesses. The advantages of using these programs are that considerable resources are available to help the small business owner learn how to use the programs, and they are less costly than having programs written specifically for the firm. The major disadvantage is that these programs are not tailored to the individual firm's operations. Accordingly, the small business owner must adjust to the software's requirements by altering the firm's operations.

Programs can be written to satisfy the owner's specific needs for information or perform certain business functions. Programmers are available to design software applications and assist in their implementation. The advantage is that the needs of the small business owner can be better accommodated. Disadvantages include the costs of having programs written and the reliance on one or a few programmers. Usually, the costs are considerably higher than purchasing predesigned programs, and the programmer may not be readily available if problems occur and/or adjustments need to be made in the software. Accordingly, it is generally recommended that specially written programs only be used if predesigned ones cannot satisfactorily meet the owner's needs.

The ultimate evaluation of software includes answers to the following questions:[16]

- To what extent will it require changes in current business practices?
- Will it provide accounting and management information?
- How easy is it to use?
- How easy will it be to change? To expand?
- What control and security features does it incorporate?
- If the software is being written for the firm, who will own the program(s)?
- How well is it documented (that is, have written descriptions of what it does)?

Step Three: Select the Hardware

Selection of hardware should be based on the needs of the software. One of the decisions to be made at this point concerns whether to acquire hardware that is IBM- or Apple-compatible. In many instances, this will be decided by the type of software to be used. However, there are times when software will be available for either type of system, and the small business owner will have to choose one or the other. Advantages and disadvantages of each should be carefully evaluated based on cost, expandability, graphics capabilities, and so on.

A second decision concerns whether to acquire a brand name or *clone*. Brand-name hardware tends to be more expensive, but may offer some advantages in quality, servicing and repair, life expectancy, and trade-in value. Clones are computers that do not carry a national brand name, and often are assembled by individual retail stores or purchased from another company. They vary considerably in terms of their component parts and configurations, and therefore may need to be serviced by the sellers. Servicing of national brands tends not to be so limited. There has been considerable debate about the relative advantages and disadvantages of brand names versus clones. The ultimate decision often depends on budget, availability, and convenience of service.

A third set of decisions will center on the components of the system in terms of computer speed, the number of disk drives, the number and size of hard disks, and so on. The components of the hardware will be influenced by a variety of factors, including the software to be used, how fast the system must operate, the number of workstations to be used, and cost.

Step Four: Select the Vendor

In addition to assessing software and hardware alternatives, the small business owner must evaluate the vendors. Of critical concern here will be price, support service capabilities, amount and speed of service available, and stability and reliability.

Generally, it is best to acquire both the software and the hardware from the same vendor to ensure their compatibility. When this is not possible, or where there are substantial cost differences between using one versus multiple vendors, the small business owner must be sure that the software and hardware are integrated into a single overall system. If the owner does not have the technical expertise to do this, consideration should be given to hiring a consultant who will assemble the total system and install the unit and train the individual who will be using the computer.

Because of the complexity and importance of the process of computerizing, many small business owners send requests for proposals (RFPs) to several possible vendors and invite them to prepare plans detailing which software and hardware they recommend, and how they would go about installing and implementing the system. Components of the RFP, criteria for evaluating proposals, and what should be contained in a contract are shown in Exhibit 21–7.

EXHIBIT 21–7

Acquiring a Computer System: Preparing a Request for Proposal

Since most first-time users get turnkey systems with custom software, the following guidelines apply to RFPs for this method.

1. Give a brief description of the company as a whole.
2. Describe the business operation to be computerized.
3. For each application:
   a. Describe how the system is to function.
   b. Specify the minimum, average, and maximum number of transactions of each type which must be processed, and any monthly, weekly, or daily peaking. Provide a growth factor so the firm will not outgrow the system's capacity before it is installed.
   c. Specify relevant master file information, such as the number of products at each inventory location, the number of sales, the number of customers, or the number of suppliers, and number of employees on the payroll.
   d. Describe the input documents or, if input is to be through a terminal, specify the screen format.
   e. Describe the layout of all hard-copy accounting, management information, and control reports.
   f. Describe the frequency and number of copies for each report.
   g. Describe required inquiry capability.
   h. Include special processing requirements; for example, if cost must be accounted for on both average cost and LIFO basis.
4. Describe the criteria that will be used to evaluate proposals and request a response for each criterion (for example, maintenance, technical support, training).
5. Specify which requirements must be met exactly and which must be met only in substance. Distinguishing between discretionary and nondiscretionary requirements is important when dealing with software packages.
6. Request a detailed price quotation that includes all charges, including one-time charges for equipment, set-up training, applications and systems software, and ongoing charges such as maintenance and technical support. Request financing alternatives such as purchase and direct or third-party lease.

Source: Edward C. Kramer, "Can You Use A Minicomputer?" Small Business Administration Management Aid No. 2.015, 5–7.

Step Five: Install and Implement the Computer System

Converting from a manual operation to a computer system, or from one type of system to another, can be an arduous task. Old methods of conducting day-to-day operations will change, and this conversion process will take time and generate at least short-term inefficiency.

Of particular concern in this process is whether the conversion will be phased in overtime, installed at an instant in time (for example, over a weekend), or undertaken in parallel. Phasing in the computerization over a period of three to six months allows management time to become accustomed to the system, and may be the least disruptive to daily operations. However, this means that the benefits of computerizing will not be achieved for a longer period. If the system is to be installed within a very short period, some degree of pretraining will have to be completed so employees will know how the new system works before it is on line.

A parallel conversion involves continuing the old methods of operation while also initiating the new computer system. This means that the work is being duplicated, but it reduces the impact on the firm's customers and provides a method for checking the accuracy of the computer system. While this approach is more costly to the firm because of the extra work involved, it helps illustrate the benefits of the new system, since direct comparisons can be made.

To ensure that the implementation of the system causes minimum disruption to the firm's operations, the small business owner should:

1. Set target dates for key phases of the implementation,
2. Assign responsibilities and train personnel (or designate who should be trained by the company doing the installation),
3. Prepare the installation site so that it is convenient and secure,
4. Monitor and test the implementation at designated stages to ensure that the software and hardware are performing as intended, and
5. Run parallel operations to evaluate the system and check its accuracy.

Step Six: Establish Systems for Back-up and Security

No computer system is foolproof and completely secure. Because erasures of files, power failures, and other computer disasters do occur, some back-up must be built into the system. For example, what happens if the files containing the names of the firm's customers and amounts they owe are mistakenly erased? What will a supermarket do if its electronic scanning system fails?

Businesses that rely heavily on computers to continue daily activities must have some alternative means of remaining operational when the computer is out of service. This may involve having a manual back-up system ready, contracting with a company that supplies back-up services, or some other alternative. At minimum, data on a computer system should be backed up daily to ensure that if the system fails that information will not be lost. This may involve copying the data on the hard disk to another hard disk outside the CPU or copying files onto diskettes to be stored in a place physically removed from the system.

In addition to back-up procedures, the firm should have some process for ensuring the security of the system. Access to the system should be limited to designated individuals, and files should be inspected every one to three months to ensure that payroll figures, customer accounts, and so on, have not been altered. Risks of embezzlement and other business crimes have been described in Chapter 12. Additionally, care must be taken to maintain the confidentiality of the firm's operations. Computer records must be secured so that they are not passed on to competitors, disgruntled employees, or others.

SUMMARY

1. In planning the production process, specific areas of focus include product development and design, production facilities and layout.
2. In converting the sales plan to a production plan, two main issues must be resolved: ensuring that the products demanded are the same as those produced, and scheduling production so as to minimize delays in filling orders and buildups in inventory.
3. To ensure the best results from a production process, it is critical that full consideration be given to each method and how it might be improved upon.
4. In maximizing facility use and minimizing costs, it is necessary to sequence and schedule each aspect of producing one or more products.
5. The work schedule should be fully planned before production begins. This involves determining each step of the process for each product, the time it will take to complete each step, and the overall capacity of the equipment and labor.
6. In controlling the production process, the small business owner should control both what is produced and how it is produced.
7. Quality control systems should ensure that any production problems resulting in defective products are corrected instantly and that defective units are removed from the finished products available for sale.
8. The entrepreneur must establish some minimum level of quality as the standard against which each sample unit is compared.
9. Computers can be helpful to many small businesses, but they are not right for every firm.
10. Computers will cause some inefficiency during the early stages of their installation.
11. The first step in acquiring a computer is to develop a job description for what the computer is to do for the firm.
12. The software is usually acquired before the hardware, but occasionally it is necessary for software and hardware to be purchased together.

KEY TERMS AND CONCEPTS

Make or buy decision
Batch production
Methods of production
Payback period
Plant layout
Production scheduling
Operations process chart
Production control
Economies of scale
Quality control
Product inspection
CPU
Hardware
Software
Workstation

QUESTIONS FOR DISCUSSION

1. What planning must be done before the firm reaches the production stage?
2. What specific issues determine whether a firm should make or buy products?
3. What does the basic production process involve?
4. What are the particular concerns of plant layout?
5. What does controlling the production process mean?
6. Describe the common characteristics of quality control points.

7. Explain why the entrepreneur might not always strive for zero defects in the delivered output.
8. Describe the advantages and disadvantages of computerizing the small firm.
9. What should a small business owner look for in computer software? In hardware? In a vendor?
10. Describe the steps in the process of acquiring a computer system.

SELF-TEST REVIEW

Multiple Choice Questions

1. In planning production, which of the following should come first?
   a. Facilities and layout.
   b. Development and design.
   c. Raw materials acquisition.
   d. Labor acquisition.
2. An advantage of production after sales is:
   a. Not carrying unnecessary inventory.
   b. Infrequent changeovers in machinery.
   c. Ability to buy supplies in bulk.
   d. Economies of scale.
3. Which of the following machines is the best buy?
   a. Five-year life, 10-year payback period.
   b. Five-year life, one-year payback period.
   c. Ten-year life, 10-year payback period.
   d. Ten-year life, 20-year payback period.
4. Which of the following is not a hardware component?
   a. Central processing unit.
   b. Disk drive.
   c. Hard disk.
   d. Computer program.
5. Which of the following is not a criterion for evaluating software?
   a. How easy it is to use.
   b. How easy it is to change or expand.
   c. What control and security features it incorporates.
   d. All of the above are useful criteria.

True/False Statements

1. The most pressing issue of production schedules concerns how production is to be related to the sales plan.
2. The payback period of a piece of machinery is the time it takes to pay off a loan on it.
3. The small business owner must establish as logical and convenient a plant layout as possible.
4. The production process should be broken down into individual steps.
5. A key element of quality control is determining when product inspections should be made.
6. The entrepreneur should always strive for zero defects in the actual manufacturing operations.
7. Hardware refers to the set of programs that control the computer's operations.
8. A disadvantage of a computer system is that it usually does not exactly fit the firm's present methods of operation.
9. A small business owner should acquire the computer hardware before the software.
10. Generally, it is best to purchase or lease a computer system from a single vendor if possible.

CENTRAL WINDOW COVERINGS

Central Window Coverings is a relatively new producer of uniquely designed louvered window coverings for homes and offices. Despite intense competition from department and specialty stores, Denise Granger, the owner of Central Window Coverings, has survived and prospered in her first two years of business. Sales have grown at an annual rate of nearly 78 percent, and profits have increased approximately 23 percent each year.

The rapid growth, however, has begun to cause some potentially serious problems. During the first two years, Granger was able to complete her custom orders within 10 days, giving her a significant advantage over competitors who took from three to seven weeks to fill an order. Now, the same process is taking sixteen days, even though she has more than doubled the number of employees.

With a 16-day delivery period, Central's time advantage is only marginal. Furthermore, since both department and specialty stores are offering ever-wider ranges of styles of coverings, Granger doubts whether the uniqueness of her window coverings will continue to be much of a competitive advantage over the next two to three years.

Because speed is such an important selling point, Granger thinks she has taken the necessary steps to ensure fast and high-quality work. She does all of the creative designing and then assigns an employee to complete an order, doing all the steps shown in Exhibit A. The plant layout is shown in Exhibit B.

When she first started, she had wanted to have one employee complete an entire order so that the quality and time could be controlled more easily. While Granger is not getting any complaints from customers about the quality of products, there are problems when an order is not filled within the guaranteed time of 10 to 14 days. In two recent instances, customers have refused delivery, and in another case the customer had wanted a price discount for having to wait an extra week.

In trying to resolve the scheduling problems, Granger knows that the employees are working with reasonable speed and care. But somehow there always seem to be delays, especially with the use of the saws and painting equipment.

Even with more workers to handle the greater volume, the problem of delays is not resolved. Granger is now wondering whether she needs to add more workers or whether the problem is in the work flow she had first established for the plant. She thinks that if the problem is not solved soon, she will face the prospect of providing an average delivery time or having to turn away business in order to keep the time factor as a competitive advantage. Neither of these alternatives seems satisfactory.

EXHIBIT A
Present Work Process for Central Window Coverings

Tasks in Order Completed	Task Description	Time to Complete Task (Mins.)
1	Design covering	40
2	Measure and cut frame	20
3	Measure and cut inserts	30
4	Assemble inserts	20
5	Attach hardware to frame	10
6	Attach inserts to frame	10
7	Sand assembled covering as needed	15
8	Apply first coat of paint/stain	10
9	Allow covering to dry	120*
10	Sand covering as needed	10
11	Apply final coat of paint/stain	10
12	Allow covering to dry	120*
13	Touch-up as needed	5
14	Package for delivery	5
Total job time per order (excluding Tasks 9 and 12)		185 mins.

*Other orders would be worked on during these times.

EXHIBIT B
Central Window Coverings' Plant Layout

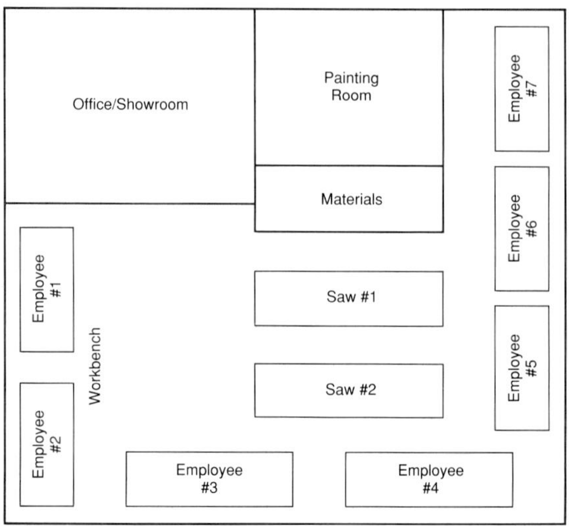

QUESTIONS

1. Evaluate the work process and plant layout as originally developed for Central Window Coverings. Is it set up well?
2. Other than taking more time and turning away business, what options does Granger have if no further improvement can be made in work scheduling?

NOTES

1. Based on Cable News Network's "Pinnacle," June 11, 1988: Guest: Mortimer Levitt, The Custom Shop and direct information from Mortimer Levitt.
2. "Office on Wheels for Execs on the Go," *Insight,* May 8, 1989, 48.
3. Based on Cable News Network's "Pinnacle," August 30, 1987. Guest: Sidney Swartz, The Timberland Company.
4. "A Hot Phone Maker that Cooled Off Fast," *Business Week,* June 12, 1989, 104.
5. Small Business Administration, *PERT/CPM Management System for the Subcontractor,* Management Aid No. 86, 3.
6. Based on Cable News Network's "Pinnacle," August 30, 1987. Guest: Sidney Swartz, The Timberland Company.
7. Based on Cable News Network's "Pinnacle," November 21, 1987. Guest: Robert Mondavi, Robert Mondavi Winery.
8. "A Little Gross Stuff in Food is OK by FDA," *Insight,* May 22, 1989, 25.
9. Jeffrey A. Tannenbaum, "For Many, Road to the Right PCs Paved with Glitches," *The Wall Street Journal,* July 24, 1989, B2.
10. Based on Cable News Network's "Pinnacle," July 12, 1987. Guest: Bill Gates, Microsoft Corporation.
11. Ralph E. Winter, "Small Machining Firms Get Boost from Computers," *The Wall Street Journal,* April 17, 1989, B2.
12. Bank of America, "Business Computers from A to Z," *Small Business Reporter,* 1986, 5–52.
13. *Ibid.*
14. Based on Cable News Network's "Pinnacle," October 4, 1987. Guest: Rod Canion, Compaq Computer.
15. Myron Karasik, "Selecting a Small Business Computer," *Harvard Business Review,* January–February, 1984, 26–30.
16. Edward C. Kramer, Small Business Administration, *Can You Use a Minicomputer?* Management Aid Number 2.015, 5.

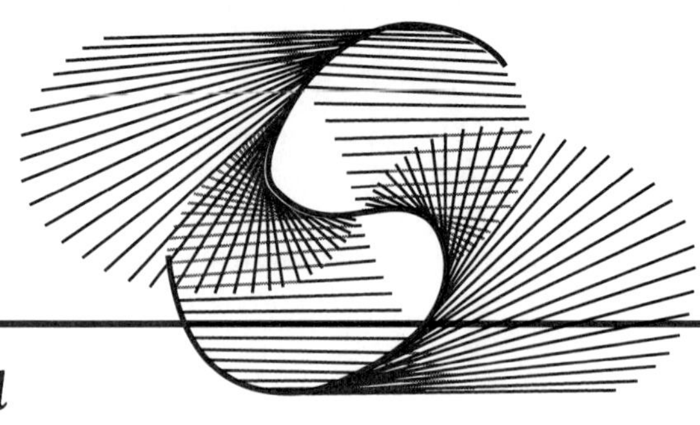

CHAPTER TWENTY-TWO

Government and Small Business

CHAPTER OUTLINE

LEARNING OBJECTIVES *The objectives of this chapter are to assist you in understanding:*

1. The rationale and foundations of government control over business environments.
2. Which regulations affect business practices.
3. The role the government plays in helping small businesses obtain needed capital.
4. How the government contracts with small businesses to provide various products and services.
5. How the government provides management assistance to small businesses.

Every business, large or small, must deal with government. City, county, state, and federal agencies exert some degree of control or influence over the actions of all firms. Government regulations prohibit businesses from engaging in certain types of activities, and require them to undertake or comply with others. Government can protect small firms from predatory tactics of larger companies, while simultaneously entangling them in a seeming nightmare of taxes and paperwork that raises their costs of doing business.

For example, a senior executive of a car-leasing company located in Boston reportedly spent 20 percent of his time complying with state insurance laws and regulatory agencies. A business service provided to farms in California spent $25,000 per year reviewing employee manuals to ensure that they comply with the law. And an owner of a public relations firm in New York stated that yearly changes in federal benefit laws add 15 to 20 percent to her accounting bill.[1]

Entrepreneurs are protected from severe price cutting by larger companies that could drive them out of business. However, businesses in some industries are required to have between five and 15 licenses and permits to operate, and may pay as much as 20 percent of their revenues out for employment and other business taxes (excluding income tax).

Government regulation, while at times restrictive and cumbersome, is designed to equalize opportunities and prevent unfair methods of competition that over time could destroy the free enterprise spirit. This helps to preserve the economic system and protect the public from unscrupulous business practices.

Government assistance programs are partly the result of a historic perspective that the United States is the land of opportunity, in which people can progress from rags to riches. They also are the result of the belief that one way to guarantee an efficient allocation of resources is to create a competitive economy that gives small firms an opportunity to remain afloat so that they can grow and prosper.

The principal federal agency created to oversee small business development and success is the Small Business Administration (SBA). Established in 1953, the SBA "by the direction of Congress, has as its primary goal the preservation of free, competitive enterprise in order to strengthen the nation's economy.[2] As is described in this chapter, the SBA is engaged in a wide variety of activities, including financing, procurement, and management assistance.

The number and type of state and local agencies oriented to assisting small business varies significantly by geographic area. Nevertheless, most levels of government have expressed objectives to help create small business opportunities and preserve the well-being of entrepreneurs (see Exhibit 22–1).

Although frequently considered a necessary evil, government regulation serves to protect the competitive environment for small business. However, this is not achieved just through regulatory actions. Various federal, state, and local agencies have embarked on small business assistance programs. By providing funding, contracts to bid on, and management assistance, these programs give small businesses opportunities to compete among themselves and with larger firms.

Funding typically is made possible when small business owners cannot obtain loans from other sources. One nationwide study of entrepreneurs who received loans through the SBA found that about 30 percent of the borrowers believed that without the SBA program, they could not have received loans.[3]

EXHIBIT 22–1 The Role of Government in Small Business

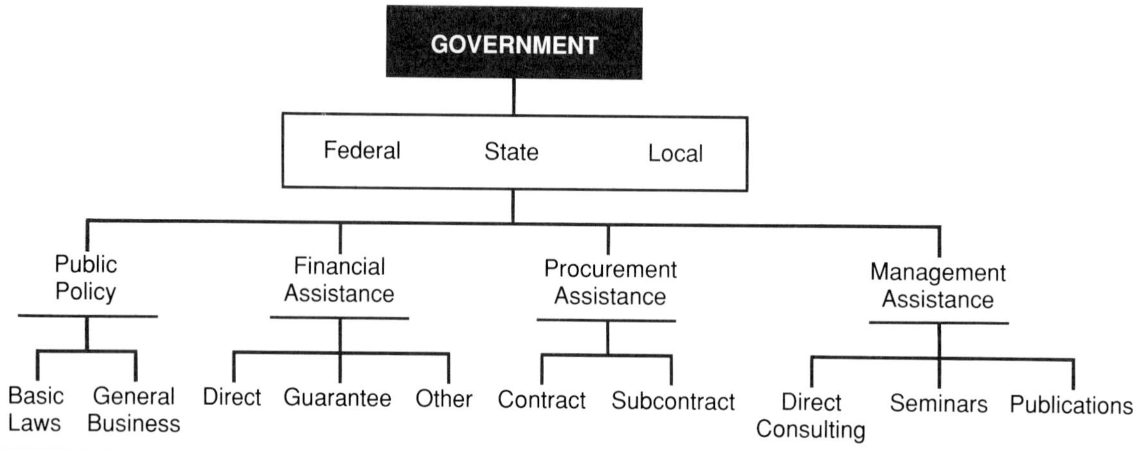

Some contracts for government projects are set aside for small businesses, and others require large firms to subcontract certain portions of their government work to small and/or minority-owned businesses. In fiscal year 1986, for example, the federal government alone purchased more than $60 billion in goods and services from small firms.[4]

Consultants, made available through various government programs, provide entrepreneurs with technical management assistance to better manage their businesses. The advice is provided free or at low cost, and would not otherwise be affordable to small business owners.

GOVERNMENT REGULATION

At the foundation of the American economic system is the concept of **free enterprise,** first proposed in 1776 by Adam Smith in his book, *The Wealth of Nations.* Smith argued that the public good is best served when many firms are competing among themselves for the public's business. In a competitive environment, only efficient companies can survive as prices are driven down and higher-cost operations are forced out of existence. Thus, the public as a whole is well served: Prices are as low as possible, and the nation's resources (for example, minerals, lumber, labor) are used only by firms that can operate efficiently.

The theory of firms fighting it out for the consumer's dollar is appealing. However, it is unrealistic to assume that all competitors will start or remain equal. Eventually, firms in better locations, with more astute managers, greater financial resources, and more skilled personnel will gain the potential to drive their rivals out of business. While Smith's concept of a free enterprise system would work in the short term, over time monopoly positions could be achieved that would allow a firm to charge higher prices and work less efficiently. The public good, therefore, may need some protection so that *many* firms rather than just a few can remain competitive.

Further concerns for the public good involve protecting the buying public from some actions and practices used by businesses. For example, the adulteration of food and drugs and the lack of sanitary working conditions for processing foods have continually been scrutinized by agencies at many levels of government. Periodic inspections of meat and poultry processing plants, restaurants, and so on, provide a measure of consumer protection.

Protecting the public from deceptive business practices has long been regarded as a necessity. In part, it serves to keep inefficient firms from defrauding customers in order to remain in business, and prevents others from preying on those who are disadvantaged or uneducated.

In addition to unscrupulous business practices, there are concerns about the products offered for sale. In Adam Smith's time, the products were simple and the variety was more limited. Increasing numbers and sophistication of products over time have made it more difficult for consumers to make evaluations. For example, few people have the ability to knowledgeably analyze differences between brands of home computers, compact disc players, automobiles, or microwave ovens.

To help consumers in an era of product complexity, government regulations have been created to ensure that products are correctly labeled so that at least rudimentary evaluations become possible. A question, however, is the extent to which consumers need to be protected from their own ignorance. For instance, do microwave oven manufacturers need to tell potential buyers not to use their ovens to dry their household pets? Do producers of cigarette lighters really need to tell users to take the lighters out of their pockets before igniting them? Consumers have done both.

Promoting the public good is a multifaceted concern. On the surface, the public good may seem easy to determine. But, since the public is such a large group, satisfying the needs of some will almost certainly be detrimental to others. For example, the added precautions manufacturers and retailers must take to inform consumers of potential dangers in using their products are costly and not easily passed on to the buyer in competitive markets.

FOUNDATIONS OF GOVERNMENT CONTROL

Although many thousands of laws affect business activity, only a few act as cornerstones of government control. Enacted many years ago, these statutes serve as bases for government policy with respect to the promotion of the public good (see Exhibit 22–2).

Sherman Antitrust Act of 1890

During the mid- to late-1800s, great concentrations of wealth and power accrued in the hands of a few individuals and families. In some instances, this was the normal conclusion of sound investments and proper business dealings. In many cases, however, it was the result of unscrupulous tactics. Whichever the case, these accumulations grew to the point where they threatened to destroy competition in many industries.

Reaction to this threat to the free enterprise spirit was the **Sherman Antitrust Act of 1890.** The essence of this law is that "contracts, combinations, or conspiracies in restraint of trade are illegal." This law applies not only to business transactions involving interstate commerce but also to individuals, subjecting them to possible fines and prison sentences for violations. Although this act falls within the jurisdiction of the U.S. Department of Justice, people or businesses competitively injured can seek recourse through civil proceedings.

EXHIBIT 22–2 Public Policy Laws

Pro-Competition	Consumer Protection
Sherman Antitrust Act—Prohibits monopolies or attempts to monopolize	*Clayton Act*—Prohibits bait-and-switch advertising
Clayton Act—Prohibits substantial lessening of competition, and specific business practices	*Federal Trade Commission Act*—Investigates fraudulent business practices
Federal Trade Commission Act—Prohibits unfair methods of competition	*Pure Food and Drug Act*—Prohibits adulteration of foods and drugs
Robinson–Patman Act—Prohibits injury to competition, and specific business practices	*Consumer Product Safety Act*—Regulates product design and safety
	Specific Products Regulation—Regulates such products as fur, clothing, children's products, and so on

Historically, the Sherman Act has been of little consequence in protecting small businesses. The courts initially were not very sympathetic to the Justice Department's actions. At times accused of being bribed by big business, and at other times of lacking any business knowledge, the courts established stringent conditions for proof of monopoly. Because of these high standards of proof, few of the early giants were found guilty.

During the 1980s, the Sherman Act was used at times to block mergers of larger firms that might jeopardize the survival of smaller businesses. Additionally, this statute on occasion has served as the basis for splitting up large companies. The 1984 breakup of American Telephone and Telegraph is an example of this.

Even though the Sherman Act did little to reduce the looming threat of big business, it was the ground-breaker for other antitrust legislation and statutes against predatory and unfair practices. Subsequent legislation was designed to strengthen this act and rectify problems and misconceptions that had not been anticipated in 1890.

Clayton Act of 1914

One piece of legislation designed to strengthen the Sherman Act was the **Clayton Act.** Because proving that a firm had a monopoly or attempted to monopolize was extremely difficult, the Clayton Act made "substantial lessening of competition" illegal. The evidence need not prove that a firm had an overwhelming share of the market or was engaged in predatory practices. It only had to be shown that competition had been reduced substantially.

Defining "substantially," however, has been a problem. How a firm defines its market (for example, by type of buyer, geographical boundaries) can significantly affect the decision as to whether it has violated this act.

In addition to easing antitrust requirements, the Clayton Act contains provisions that make certain business practices illegal. Of particular significance are tying contracts, exclusive dealing arrangements, and interlocking directorates, which are described later in this chapter.

Generally, it is very unlikely that small businesses would violate provisions of the Clayton Act. However, this statute has been of value in protecting smaller businesses from the actions of larger companies. Since penalties emanating from this law carry the possibility of treble damages, big companies have been more careful about engaging in activities that might lessen competition or violate any of its key provisions.

Federal Trade Commission Act of 1914

The **Federal Trade Commission Act** was passed in the same year as the Clayton Act. Its purpose was multifaceted and stemmed largely from court rulings on lawsuits brought under the Sherman Act. Although the courts frowned on unfair methods of competition, they did not render them illegal. Furthermore, it became apparent that a body of specialists was needed to assist the courts and other governmental agencies in overseeing competitive business practices.

The result was that the Federal Trade Commission Act made "unfair methods of competition" illegal and established the Federal Trade Commission (FTC) as the regulatory agency to monitor business practices. Some of the specific practices considered illegal, such as bait-and-switch advertising, are described later in this chapter. Importantly, however, these practices apply to small business actions as well as those used by larger companies.

Perhaps one of the most significant aspects of this law is that the FTC has the authority to investigate and issue cease-and-desist orders directly. Small business owners who believe unfair practices have been used by large or small competitors can file complaints with the FTC rather than engage in expensive lawsuits.

Robinson–Patman Act of 1936

Of all the basic laws for the public good, the **Robinson–Patman Act** was the most controversial. This act amended the Clayton Act and reduced the more stringent antitrust standards of "substantial lessening of competition" to "injury to competition." Unfortunately, the courts at times have interpreted this as "injury to competitors," which would make all competitive practices used by large and small firms illegal.

Under more recent usage, however, the Robinson–Patman Act has been used to prevent large buyers from pressuring sellers into granting unreasonable price and promotional allowance concessions. Specific provisions regarding charging different prices or offering different promotional allowances are described later in this chapter.

Importantly, the Robinson–Patman Act offers small sellers some degree of protection from the demands of large buyers. However, if the small firm does discriminate in its pricing or promotional allowances, it will be in violation of the law.

According to this law, a seller is prohibited from selling its products at different prices to buyers who are competing unless the different prices can be justified. For example, different prices can be charged to one buyer if the costs of selling are less or if the seller is matching prices offered by other sellers. Promotional allowances provided to one buyer to encourage it to advertise the products must be offered to its competitors on proportionally equal terms.

REGULATION OF BUSINESS PRACTICES

The four laws described above form the foundation for government policy in regulating business activity for the public good. However, they do not cover the entire spectrum of the law as it concerns the regulation of business practices. Entrepreneurs and managers of large companies must adhere to a wide range of laws emanating from these and other laws relating to entry into business, marketing activities, contracts, employment law, and so on.

Regulation of Business Entry

In most states, specific laws govern how and under what circumstances prospective entrepreneurs can enter into business. Requirements, of course, vary from state to state, and even between cities and counties.[5] Examples of some of the licenses and permits for business entry are described below, and are illustrated in Exhibit 22–3.

At the federal level, the entrepreneur will have to apply for an employer identification number from the Internal Revenue Service. This number is used for such matters as submitting federal income and Social Security taxes, and opening retirement programs. Patents, copyrights and trademarks must be applied for at the federal level.

Many states require business owners to obtain a seller's permit. This essentially is a vehicle for filing with the state a notice of intent to engage in business, and forms the

EXHIBIT 22–3 **Regulation of Business Entry: Sample Types of Permits Needed to Open a Business**

Zoning Check: Ensure that location does not have restricted commercial use.

Building Permit: Need when planning to make physical or cosmetic changes in building.

Sign Permit: Need if planning to have an exterior sign.

Home Occupation Permit: Need if setting up business in home.

Health Permit: Need if planning to dispense food to public, clean pools, clean septic tanks.

Weights and Measures Device Registration: Need if using commercial weights or measuring equipment.

City Insurance and Bond Requirements: May need to show proof of liability insurance or bonding.

Special Permits to Operate Specific Businesses: Need if business is in one of a number of specified categories requiring special permits.

Fictitious Business Name Statement: Need if using a business name other than that of the owner.

Employer Registration: Need if hiring employees.

Seller's Permit/Sales and Use Tax Permit: Need if business will be selling personal property.

Business Tax Certificate: Need in some cities that tax businesses.

Transportation Permit: Need if business uses large vehicles or vehicles with heavy loads.

Fire Inspection Permit: Some businesses need permit from Fire Inspector.

Hazardous Materials Permit: Need if business uses or handles hazardous materials.

basis for payment of state taxes and the collection of applicable sales taxes. If a business is to be formed as a corporation, articles of incorporation must be filed with an appropriate state agency.

Cities and counties typically require business licenses, which must be renewed annually. If the firm is to prepare food or beverages for sale, it typically will need a permit to operate from the local health department. That agency then will make inspections of the premises to assure cleanliness and adherence to building codes.

One of the more common licenses is the fictitious business name statement. Entrepreneurs usually have to file for a fictitious name if they intend to use names other than their own to identify their businesses. For example, a James Smith would have to file such a registration if he wanted to open a pharmacy under the name Central City Pharmacy. This would not be necessary if it were to be named Smith's Pharmacy. Coupled with this, entrepreneurs will have to publicize the fact that they will be operating businesses under fictitious names in newspapers of general circulation for a specified period of time.

Certain occupational categories may need specialized licenses and/or certifications. Bars and cocktail lounges, for example, will need a retail liquor dealer's stamp from the Internal Revenue Service. Pharmacies will need a Drug Enforcement Administration registration number for carrying controlled substances (narcotics). Hairstyling salon owners may need special licensing and certifications from a state board of cosmetology.

An entrepreneur may be faced with obtaining many licenses and permits to meet federal, state, and local statutes. It is not uncommon, for example, to find anywhere from 5 to 15 such permits required. As a result, it also is common to find new businesses operating without all of those that are required.

Regulation of Marketing Activities

Based partly on the Clayton, Federal Trade Commission, and Robinson–Patman Acts, many marketing practices come under close scrutiny because of the potential to injure competition. Potentially illegal practices can be classified into five main groupings: competitive tactics, product strategies, promotional strategies, distribution strategies, and price strategies.

Competitive Tactics

It is expected and required that firms will compete and try to improve their market positions. However, there are some activities that are not allowed in the pursuit of those positions: interlocking directorates, collusion to fix prices, and collusion to split markets.

Interlocking directorates, individuals serving on the boards of directors of competing companies, are illegal under the Clayton Act when the effect could be a substantial lessening of competition. The concern is that overlap of boards creates opportunities for collusive practices. For this law to apply, the firms must have assets of at least $1 million, and banks and common carriers are excluded from this statute since those businesses are regulated by the Federal Reserve Board and the Interstate Commerce Commission, respectively.

The most common cooperative dealings involve **price-fixing** and **splitting markets.** Efforts by large or small firms to avoid price competition by agreements to fix price levels are in direct violation of antitrust laws. For example, two food processors cannot agree to charge the same or even different prices for their canned fruits or vegetables. While each processor is likely to evaluate competitors' prices and set its own accordingly, these firms cannot work together to price their products. Similarly, two small pharmacies operating within the same general geographic area cannot agree to set particular prices for their prescriptions or over-the-counter medications.

Agreements to divide up markets so that firms will not compete against one another also are violations of antitrust laws when the effect is to lessen competition. An example of this would be if two firms agree that one will stay west of the Mississippi River while the other will remain to the east. While smaller firms are not likely to violate this law, they may be affected if large companies concentrate their efforts in certain areas.

Some competitive tactics are illegal if they take a predatory twist and serve to reduce competition. Examples include attempting to cut off a competitor's source of supply, or selling products below cost to drive other firms out of business.

In addition, even if a small or large business grows and captures a very large share of the market through entirely legal tactics, it may violate antitrust laws. Since the objective of these regulations is to protect free enterprise, lessening of competition is illegal—irrespective of how it is achieved.

Product Strategies

Laws related to the products the firm sells tend to focus on protecting the rights of firms that create new products and protecting the consumer from products that are potentially harmful. These laws apply to large and small firms.

Patents are designed to protect the rights of firms to make and sell products they developed (or have purchased the rights to make). While patents do offer a degree of protection, they do not work as well as is often presumed. Unless unique processes are patented, such as Polaroid achieved with instant film processing, it is likely that competitors will make relatively minor changes in product design and receive patents.

Brandmarks and trademarks are legally protected portions of brands and trade names. Large companies such as Coca-Cola, Xerox, and Sony expend considerable effort to make sure other firms do not copy them in any way. These laws also protect smaller firms, but most entrepreneurs do not have the money and legal expertise to continually watch for infringements.

From a public policy perspective, regulations to ensure product safety are a major concern. Manufacturers are required, for example, to clearly specify the contents and quantity of their products, and to provide addresses of their offices. Product usage and net weights must be clearly marked, and contents must be delineated, beginning with the predominant ingredient. Food and drug items must comply with very precise regulations emanating from the Food and Drug Administration in terms of quality and usefulness.

In 1972, the Consumer Product Safety Act created a Consumer Product Safety Commission to establish standards for product safety. Furs, clothing, and a host of other products come under various specific federal regulations. For producers of children's products, there are specific laws prohibiting the sales of items that are potentially dangerous or contain electrical or mechanical hazards. Packages containing dangerous substances must be child-resistant.

There are two other Acts that must be considered by the small business owner. The Consumer Product Safety Act of 1972 provides for the Consumer Product Safety Commission to set standards on products, require warning labels, make product recalls, and so on, for about 15,000 product categories. The Federal Hazardous Substances Act of 1977 revised the 1960 Act to provide proper warning labels or ban substances that can cause injury or illness as a result of normal handling and use.

Promotional Strategies

Many of the laws governing marketing strategies relate to promotion. Generally, a firm cannot engage in false or misleading advertising. It is illegal, for example, to state that products will do more than they are capable of or are designed to do, promoting nonexistent attributes (for example, "all wool" when the product is all cotton), or portraying products as being on sale when in fact they are not.

Of all the promotional violations, **bait-and-switch advertising** is probably the most common. Here, the entrepreneur advertises products for sale at ridiculously low prices—the bait—to get customers interested, and then promptly tries to switch them to other higher-priced items once they enter the store. While an entrepreneur is not required to have sufficient inventory available for all potential buyers, the true measure is whether the seller really intends to sell the promoted merchandise or is simply using the advertisement to lure customers into the store. An example of this would be a furniture store that advertises a complete bedroom set for $159, with the intent of switching prospective buyers to more expensive sets when they respond to the advertisement.

Distribution Strategies

Most small firms are not likely to violate laws relating to distribution. It is much more common for them to be the injured party as a result of efforts by larger companies to restrict the availability of competing products. The four most common problems faced by smaller firms in distribution are tying contracts, exclusive dealing arrangements, territorial restrictions, and cooling-off laws.

Tying contracts occur when a seller forces a buyer to agree to purchase goods or services other than what is desired as a condition for providing what the buyer wants. Without the Clayton Act, large manufacturers could use their power to force entrepreneurs to purchase items they would not otherwise buy.

For example, an apparel manufacturer cannot force a small retail clothing store to carry all of its products as a condition for carrying one or two of the most desirable lines. Smaller businesses may not have the capital to invest that much money in inventory, and might go out of business if they were forced to carry lines they could not sell.

Exclusive dealing occurs when a seller agrees to sell to a buyer only if the buyer does not carry products of the seller's competition. As with tying contracts, larger producers could force entrepreneurs into such agreements by threatening to withhold merchandise needed by the buyer to stay in business. An example of this would be an apparel manufacturer demanding that a small retail clothing store carry only its lines and not those of other manufacturers.

One distribution strategy that has raised important legal questions relates to attempts to limit middlemen (that is, wholesalers, retailers) to certain geographic areas. Can, for example, a manufacturer limit its wholesalers and retailers to operating within particular geographic areas? Can a wholesaler do this to the retailers it supplies? Being restricted to selected areas can injure competition, and generally is illegal. Fundamentally, when a product is sold, the seller loses control over the merchandise in terms of how and where it is distributed, what price is charged for the product, and how it is promoted.

A fourth distribution strategy relates to methods by which products are sold. The so-called **cooling-off laws** place certain constraints on sellers of items sold direct to homes.[6] Generally, buyers of higher-cost products sold under a purchase contract door-to-door have three business days in which to rescind their purchases. The rationale for this law is that buyers cannot escape from situations where purchases are made at home. Accordingly, cooling-off laws provide the buyer time to reconsider the wisdom of his or her purchase. The impact of this law on small businesses can be profound. Many entrepreneurs sell their products direct to home, and sell their sales contracts to finance companies so they can obtain cash. When buyers have several days to cancel their purchases, sellers cannot convert their contracts to cash until the cooling-off time has expired—forcing them to keep more cash in their businesses.

Pricing Strategies

Pricing products and services is one area in which entrepreneurs need to be especially careful. These are closely monitored by regulatory agencies. Most laws related to pricing focus on strategies used by larger companies to injure competition, and small firms are more likely to be injured parties than the ones violating the laws.

Most efforts, however, to fix prices among competing firms are considered illegal. Even smaller firms are at risk here because entrepreneurs within the same industry often know each other, and it is not unusual for them to talk about their businesses. If they discuss their pricing strategies and agree to set prices at some levels, they are likely to be guilty of conspiring to fix prices.

Small manufacturers and wholesalers also must be careful not to discriminate on the basis of price when selling to competing firms. Even if there is no lessening of competition by charging different prices to competing firms, complaints about price differentials are likely to cause investigations that can be time-consuming and expensive to the seller.

Large and small retailers in most states are required to sell their merchandise above cost. While entrepreneurs can charge prices as high as they like, states have enacted **Unfair Trade Practices Act** that require businesses to mark up their products at least a minimum percentage above cost—commonly 2 percent above cost at the wholesale level, and 6 percent at the retail level. The objective of these laws is to protect smaller firms from predatory pricing by businesses that are willing to sell below cost and drive out competition.

Other laws prohibit deceptive pricing strategies that partly fall into the realm of promotion. One of the most common violations of deceptive pricing is to create artificially high price lists and then reduce actual prices to make it appear as if the items were being put on sale. Another is for a firm to use *closeout pricing* when the seller has no intention of going out of business or eliminating the product line. Finally, if credit sales are involved, the interest and carrying charges must be fully delineated and explained to borrowers.

Contracts

Many firms use business **contracts** as a normal part of their operations. They rent warehouses, offices, and storefronts; enter into agreements with suppliers, labor unions, and customers; and hire consultants and other business professionals. Accordingly, entrepreneurs should recognize the attributes of a valid contract.

Although complex agreements frequently require the services of an attorney, many legal contracts are verbal and quite casual in nature. Each contract should be in writing. Even though verbal contracts may be held enforceable by a court, most verbal agreements are between the two parties and lack corroborating evidence (witnesses). When there are problems, the result usually is a standoff, with both parties offering conflicting testimony. There are five requirements for a valid contract:

1. *It must be in proper form*—while rules vary from state to state, some types of contracts—such as real estate contracts—must be written and in a specific format. If the contract is completed only verbally, or is not in the proper format, it will be ruled invalid.
2. *It must be fully agreed to by both parties*—contracts made under fraud, duress, undue influence, or by mistake are not enforceable. Contracts are valid only when the parties involved willingly agree to all the terms and conditions set forth in the contract.
3. *It must involve competent parties*—persons who are intoxicated, insane, or under the legal age cannot be held by the terms of a contract. Generally, all parties must be of legal age and capable of understanding the implications of what they are doing. In instances where only one party is competent, that person is held to the conditions of the agreement, while the incompetent one is not.
4. *It must be legal in terms of purpose*—contracts to perform or engage in unlawful acts or practices are not enforceable. Thus, a contract between two individuals to fix prices or use deceptive advertising will not be binding if one backs out and the other sues for breach of contract.
5. *It must involve consideration by all parties*—for a contract to be valid, all parties involved must give something of value. This can be money, time, or a product or service.

Employment Law

Some of the most complex laws affecting both large and small business are related to hiring, retaining, and dismissing personnel. Many entrepreneurs believe that laws relating to employment apply solely to large organizations. This, however, is not the case. Although some statutes vary based on the size of the firm and the number of people it employs, all businesses are subject to some regulation.

There are several key regulations affecting the overall issues of employment. The Equal Pay Act of 1963 required that equal pay be given for equal work. An employer cannot discriminate in pay due to an employee's gender.

The Civil Rights Act of 1964 prohibited **employment discrimination** based on race, color, sex, religion, national origin, and other factors. It was amended by the Equal Employment Opportunity Act of 1972, which established the Equal Employment Opportunity Commission to settle complaints of discrimination in employment.

The Age Discrimination Act of 1967 and 1978 prohibited discrimination based on age. This applies to those between the ages of 40 and 70 years.

EXHIBIT 22–4 **Discrimination Factors**

Name	Sex	Religion
Age	Marital status	Arrest record
Citizenship	Family status	Military service
National origin	Race	Economic status
Nonjob-related physical description	Color	Nonjob-related activities

Employment law has become of great concern because of the potential for discrimination and abuse of what some legislative bodies and courts considered to be fundamental employee rights. Of particular interest were violations of laws related to hiring women and minorities. While there are some variations between states, generally large and small employers cannot fail to hire an individual based on such factors as sex, age, race, religion, and other factors shown in Exhibit 22–4. Entrepreneurs cannot ask applicants questions that will provide information upon which to discriminate. Some sample questions that employers can and cannot ask are shown in Exhibit 22–5.

An additional issue of concern to employers is the right of an employee to continued employment within a firm. Known as **employment at will,** the major question is whether an employer has the ability and right to terminate an individual's employment for any reason whatsoever. Generally, employers have begun using employment contracts which specifically state that employment is not guaranteed, and that an employee may be dismissed with or without cause.

Other Legal Considerations

Not all of the legal issues affecting business activities have been described in this chapter. For example, the Environmental Protection Act of 1970 created the Environ-

EXHIBIT 22–5 ***Employment Questions That* Cannot *be Asked***

Maiden name
Own or rent a home
Age, date of birth, dates attended school
Birthplace, whether has citizenship
Nationality, ancestry, national origin
Sex
Marital status
Family status, number of children, ages of children
Pregnancy, child bearing, birth control
Height, weight
General medical condition
Religion
Military service record
Arrest record
Membership in nonjob-related organizations
Current or past assets, liabilities, credit rating

mental Protection Agency to set standards for and enforce standards of quality for air, water, and so on.

Because of the extent, complexity, and variability of laws from state to state, the entrepreneur should consult with an attorney licensed by the state within which the firm is based. The time and cost savings over the long run may well be worth the attorney fees paid. To the extent that small business owners are capable of understanding and applying the law, they should keep basic business law books handy to resolve some of the simpler issues that arise from time to time.

In addition, the entrepreneur should find an accountant who can assist in tax law matters. Since these laws are of a specialized nature and change frequently, most small business owners are not able to get the maximum benefits from tax legislation without expert advice. Tax planning should ensure that income taxes are legally minimized, and that management decisions relating to all facets of the firm's operations are evaluated on the basis of future tax considerations.

Taxes are a serious, and sometimes mystifying, issue for all businesses. William Gladstone, chairman of Arthur Young and Company, commented on the Tax Reform Act of 1986: " . . . our clients would say it's a curse. It's certainly one of the most complicated pieces of legislation ever passed. And we and the IRS are still sorting that out [in 1988]."[7]

GOVERNMENT ASSISTANCE

As described earlier in this chapter, not all government action is designed to regulate business practices. Federal, state, and local government agencies seek to assist entrepreneurs to go into business, bid for and obtain government contracts, and strengthen their management skills.

Government support for business can come from city as well as state and federal levels. Mathias DeVito, chief executive officer of Rouse Co., a real estate developer, described the type of assistance cities provide to developers:

> The question is whether or not they understand the amount of commitment it takes on the part of the city, the amount of political risk that it takes on the part of the chief executive of the city, to do all the things that it takes [for example, condemn property, relocate tenants, fix streets, provide parking] to do a major renovation of a dying area. . . . Some cities understand that and come in and really take leadership as Mayor Koch did in New York, Donald Shaeffer did in Baltimore, Kevin White did in Boston. . . . Other cities just haven't been willing to bite the bullet, and in those cases the projects just haven't been able to get off the ground.[8]

Many of the activities of government agencies are also directed to assisting minority- and women-owned businesses. In the late 1980s these groups comprised 6.4 percent and 28.1 percent, respectively, of all small businesses.[9]

Certainly the most well-known and organized effort to assist entrepreneurs is conducted through the **Small Business Administration.** The SBA has a series of programs that also are linked to state efforts to help small business owners obtain needed capital, build their revenue bases, and improve the quality of their management. Because it is such a potent force in small business assistance programs, it is the focal point of this discussion.

Financing

Although financing small business is described in Chapter 11, an overall perspective of government programs for funding is presented here. The SBA is the principal lending agency, but various state and local governments have established programs to provide funds to particular groups. Minority loans and funds for disabled persons, for example, are frequently handled by state agencies. These programs vary considerably, however, not only in content, but also with respect to the availability of funds on a year-to-year basis.

Over the years, the SBA has increased its financial support for small businesses with an effort to create and assist small firms in deprived areas, improve minority enterprise opportunities, and increase small business contributions to economic growth. The magnitude of government financial assistance is illustrated in Exhibit 22–6.

Support from government agencies also has been directed to the development of some high-cost technologies. For example, Thermo Electron Corp. is a maker of a variety of instruments used by the federal government. According to its founder, George Hatsopoulos, ". . . the government has been very useful because we address some exceedingly difficult technologies that require a lot of basic R&D to be done. . . . The budget constraints have gone up and down over the last 30 years . . . [but this] . . . never affected us very much because we're dealing with such critical technology."[10]

By law, the SBA cannot loan money to small business owners if they can obtain funding from local banks or other lending institutions. In cities of 200,000 people or more, entrepreneurs must be rejected by two banks before they can apply for SBA financing. Other factors that make potential borrowers ineligible for government-assisted financial aid are presented in Chapter 11.

Types of SBA Loans

There are two main types of funding available to entrepreneurs who are in need of financing.[11] These are oriented to assisting small businesses to start, remain active, or

U.S. government contracts are a major source of business for Thermo Electron Corporation, a scientific research and development firm specializing in scientific instrumentation, cogeneration systems, and biomedical products. George Hatsopoulos, owner and founder of the company, says that although federal budget constraints go up and down, they have very little effect on the firm because Thermo Electron provides extremely critical and specialized technology for the government. (Photograph courtesy of Thermo Electron Corporation)

EXHIBIT 22–6 **Financial Assistance to Small Businesses 1980–1987**

Year	Total (in millions)	SBICs	Minority and Disadvantaged
1987*	$512.80	$402.20	$110.60
1986	$620.80	$475.90	$144.90
1985	$542.30	$434.60	$107.70
1984	$513.90	$425.50	$ 88.00
1983	$468.80	$412.90	$ 55.90
1980	$337.40	$295.20	$ 42.20

*January through September
Source: State of Small Business (Washington, D.C.: U.S. Government Printing Office, 1988), 172.

grow when they have no place else to turn for funding. The most frequently used type of loan is the **guaranteed loan,** made through the SBA. In this program, the SBA will guarantee as much as 90 percent of a loan under $155,000, and 85 percent up to $750,000, to a small business owner or prospective owner. The lending organization still makes the loan, but its risks are substantially reduced because of the guarantee. This is the most common form of SBA financing, since the agency does not loan actual funds. More loans can be supported in this way than if cash was given to the entrepreneur.

If entrepreneurs cannot find lending institutions that will provide funding, they can apply to the SBA for **direct loans.** In these instances, the SBA can lend up to $150,000 directly to a borrower. Because of the higher risks involved, and the limited resources the SBA has available, however, these loans are made infrequently and more often to certain types of borrowers such as businesses located in high-unemployment areas, handicapped individuals, Vietnam-era veterans, or disabled veterans.

Aside from guaranteed and direct loans, the SBA has a series of special lending programs. Each of these affects smaller businesses in different ways. Some of the more significant programs are:

- *Local development company loans*—made to groups of local citizens whose aim is to improve the economy of their area. Loan proceeds may be used to assist specific small businesses with plant acquisition, construction, and expansion.
- *Small general contractor loans*—used to assist small construction firms with short-term financing.
- *Seasonal line of credit guarantees*—used to provide short-term financing for small firms with cyclical loan requirements due to seasonal increases in business activity.
- *Handicapped assistance loans*—provided to physically handicapped small business owners and private nonprofit organizations that employ handicapped persons and operate in their interests.
- *Surety bonds*—provide guarantees of up to 90 percent of losses incurred by small emerging contractors under bid, payment, or performance bonds issued on contracts valued up to $1 million.
- *Small business investment companies*—offer financial assistance to privately owned and operated Small Business Investment Companies, which make *venture* or *risk*

investments by supplying equity capital and extending unsecured loans to small enterprises.

As is evident from these lending programs, federal loans are made to small businesses in general, and to specific types of firms. Additionally, many of the financing programs arranged through state governments are based on funding provided by the SBA and a few other federal agencies.

Terms of the Loans

Typically, SBA loans are for no more than 7 to 10 years, with 20-year loans provided on new construction. Interest rates on direct loans are based on statutory formulas relating to the cost of government money. Banks and other lending organizations are allowed to set interest rates on guaranteed loans within some preestablished limits.

Collateral for SBA-funded loans usually consists of mortgages on land, buildings, and/or equipment; assignment of warehouse receipts for marketable merchandise; guarantees or personal endorsements; or assignment of current receivables. Mortgages on inventories generally are unacceptable to the SBA unless the inventory is stored in bonded warehouses.

Procurement

In addition to providing sources of financing, government agencies at all levels help small businesses obtain government contracts. They require that some portions or entire contracts go to smaller firms, and that larger companies subcontract some of their work to smaller ones. During the 1986 fiscal year, for example, small businesses provided $36.3 billion in services to the federal government—18.2 percent of its purchases. Smaller firms also subcontracted for $24.3 billion in additional federal contracts through larger companies. Overall, approximately 46 percent of all contracts under $25,000 and 15.5 percent over $25,000 went to entrepreneurs.[12] Amounts of **procurement** contracts and sources of those contracts are illustrated in Exhibits 22–7 and 22–8.

One example is Pauline Smith, owner of P. Precision Electronic Manufacturing. The company produces printed circuit parts for the aerospace industry, but reportedly had trouble obtaining contracts. In 1980, her company was provided an opportunity to bid for federal government contracts, and her business went from $556,000 in that year

EXHIBIT 22–7 ***Procurement Contracts to Small Business, 1980–1986***

	FY 1980	FY 1986
Total	100.0%	100.0%
Large Business	74.0%	74.3%
Small Business	15.2%	15.5%
Educational Institutions, Nonprofit Organizations, Other Government	6.0%	5.5%
Foreign Recipients	4.8%	4.7%

Source: State of Small Business (Washington, D.C.: U.S. Government Printing Office, 1988), 188.

EXHIBIT 22–8 Procurement Contracts to Small Business by Government Agency (Top Ten Agencies)

	Total (in millions)	Small Business Share	1986 Percent
Total	$183,010	$28,362	15.50
Department of Agriculture	$ 2,066	$ 1,041	50.39
Department of Defense	$145,961	$21,459	14.70
Department of Energy	$ 13,931	$ 389	2.79
Department of Interior	$ 888	$ 407	45.83
Department of Transportation	$ 1,483	$ 479	32.30
Environmental Protection Agency	$ 606	$ 157	25.91
General Services Administration	$ 2,065	$ 798	38.64
NASA	$ 7,327	$ 584	7.97
Tennessee Valley Authority	$ 2,271	$ 1,345	59.23
Veterans Administration	$ 1,843	$ 618	33.53
Other	$ 4,569	$ 1,085	—

Source: State of Small Business (Washington, D.C.: U.S. Government Printing Office 1988), 190–191.

to more than $2 million by 1989. According to government reports, not one of P. Precision's more than 750,000 circuit parts has been returned in eight years due to defects.[13]

Although many government contracts can be quite attractive to smaller firms, bidding on and winning one is a complex process. Agencies that offer contracts may have special requirements for insurance, bonding, and so on. They also have specific methods for promoting and awarding contracts which are different from those found in the private sector.

Consequently, designated local, state, and federal organizations were created to inform small businesses of government agencies who will buy their products, help them get on agencies' bidders lists, and assist them in obtaining drawings and specifications of purchases to be made by the agencies. This gives small firms greater opportunities to bid and get business that they would otherwise not have.

In many instances, these contracts can be lucrative and may mean the difference between success and failure. Contractors can be either prime contractors or subcontractors. Since many jobs are too large for small firms, they often are more capable of subcontracting for only a portion of the total.

One of the responsibilities of the SBA in the area of procurement is to work with other federal agencies to identify and earmark certain contracts for the **set-aside program.** These are contracts which can only be bid for by smaller firms, and they allow entrepreneurs to compete among themselves for some government business. Determination of which contracts are to be set aside is made jointly by SBA representatives and those of the various agencies.

Closely related to the set-aside program is the **breakout program.** When selected procurement orders are too large for a small firm to handle, efforts are made to break certain jobs out of the overall contract. Small businesses then are allowed to bid on the various portions.

EXHIBIT 22–9 **Management Assistance Programs**

Direct Counseling
- Service Corps of Retired Executives
- Active Corps of Executives
- Small Business Institute Counseling
- Small Business Development Center

Seminars (examples)
- Workshop for Prospective Entrepreneurs
- Seminars on Finance
- Seminars on Marketing
- Seminars on Business Organization
- Seminars on Business Site Selection
- Seminars on Working Capital Needs
- Seminars on Business Forecasting

International Trade Counseling and Training
- Individual Counseling
- Seminars on Exporting

Management and Marketing Publications
- Free Publications
- For-Fee Publications

Management Assistance

According to federal and private estimates, nine out of ten business failures are the result of management deficiencies. The SBA and some state and local agencies offer a variety of **direct management assistance** programs designed to strengthen entrepreneurial skills.[14] These programs include direct counseling, seminars, and published monographs. State and local governments tend to focus their efforts on seminars and monographs, while the SBA offers a broad array of all types of assistance, as shown in Exhibit 22–9.

Direct Management Assistance

The SBA is one of the few government agencies that makes specialists available to work with entrepreneurs on a one-to-one basis. Since most small business owners cannot afford to hire experts, the SBA enlists help from volunteers who provide their services on a free basis. However, for a few programs, the agency pays preestablished fees to consultants to work with entrepreneurs. All programs are free to the small businesses. They include the following programs.

Service Corps of Retired Executives (SCORE)

Working on a volunteer basis to assist entrepreneurs, retired business executives donate their time to strengthen management capabilities within small firms and help them solve specific problems. In many instances, the vast experiences of SCORE counselors provide a much-needed resource to entrepreneurs who cannot afford to hire this type of expertise.

SCORE chapters are located in many cities across the United States, and usually are composed of individuals with a wide variety of backgrounds. When requests for assistance from SCORE counselors are received, an effort is made to match the business need with the expertise available. In some cases only one counselor will be needed, while in others a team approach might be used.

Active Corps of Executives (ACE)

The SBA has developed a group of business executives who, like SCORE counselors, donate their time free to small business owners. Since they are active executives, the time they have available is limited, and often is used to complement and supplement SCORE to provide knowledge of modern management techniques to the entrepreneur. These executives represent a broad range of professions from both large and small firms.

Small Business Institute (SBI)

Operating in many of the nation's university and college business schools are Small Business Institute counseling programs. SBI was established in a cooperative venture between business schools and the SBA. Faculty and college students serve as consultants to owners who request management assistance. This increases the availability of counseling, and serves as part of the educational program for students, giving them opportunities to gain real-world experience and acquainting them with the problems of small business.

The SBI program is funded by the SBA, and clients do not pay for the services. Typically, student teams work with clients as part of their class assignments over a quarter or semester.

406 Counseling

With the 406 Counseling program, the SBA contracts with professional consultants to provide management assistance to entrepreneurs. Within each of the 10 SBA regions, contracts are awarded through competitive bidding and negotiation. These 406 counselors are called in by SBA field representatives to provide whatever expertise is necessary. Often, these contractors are used when time is limited and other forms of counseling cannot be scheduled. The 406 program also is used in difficult-to-reach geographic areas and for problems not within the capabilities of the other programs.

Management Training

In addition to providing specific consultations with entrepreneurs on an individual basis, the SBA also sponsors a variety of courses, conferences, and clinics to prepare entrepreneurs to solve their own problems. Courses range from general survey classes in several areas of management to more detailed courses on particular topics, such as export trade and crime prevention. One-day conferences are used to prepare and/or keep entrepreneurs abreast of modern business practices and topics of concern. One of the more successful of these training programs is the Workshop for Prospective Small Business Owners, which focuses on the issues of critical importance in starting and managing a venture.

Management Publications

The SBA and a variety of state and local agencies offer a host of instructional material to prospective and current entrepreneurs. Since many small business owners have neither the time nor the background to read textbooks on management, the SBA has developed a series of over 300 publications dealing with a wide range of business issues. Presented in a concise and easy-to-follow form, these can be used to supplement or act as substitutes for other management assistance programs.[15] The types of materials available include:

- *Management Aids for Small Manufacturers*—this is a series dealing with functional problems of small plants, with the emphasis placed on subjects of interest to executives.
- *Small Marketers Aids*—these are guides for retail, wholesale, and service firms.
- *Technical Aids for Small Manufacturers*—these are leaflets for top technical personnel in small firms, or technical specialists who supervise that part of a company's operations.
- *Small Business Bibliographies*—this is a series of reference sources for the more common management problems faced in operating a small business.

State and local agencies commonly publish booklets on requirements for licensing and permits, how to bid on government contracts, where to obtain management assistance, employment law, and so. In addition, most state and local agencies that regulate particular industries or professions (for example, Board of Pharmacy, Alcoholic Beverage Control) publish manual designed to assist current and prospective owners to conform to their statutes.

SUMMARY

1. While somewhat restrictive and at times cumbersome, government action is designated to equalize opportunities and prevent unfair methods of competition.
2. Concern for the public good involves protection of the marketplace to keep *many* firms competitive, and of the buying public from bad business practices and unsafe or useless products.
3. The foundations of government control are based on a few statutes: the Sherman Antitrust Act, the Clayton Act, the Federal Trade Commission Act, and the Robinson–Patman Act.
4. Most states have regulations governing entry into business.
5. Regulation of marketing activities falls under five main categories: competitive tactics, product strategies, promotional strategies, distribution strategies, and price strategies.
6. Contracts are an important part of most business operations. As such, they must be valid, which requires proper form, agreement by both parties, competency of parties, legal purpose, and consideration.
7. Employment law applies to large and small firms alike, and focuses on discrimination in hiring and terminating employees, and on the issue of the right of employment.
8. The government tries to foster the development and growth of small businesses through the Small Business Administration.
9. The principal functions of the SBA are to help prospective entrepreneurs borrow the funds they need to go into business, to help current owners obtain additional capital, to procure government contracts for small firms, and to provide technical management assistance.
10. Entrepreneurs are eligible for SBA loans only if they cannot obtain loans elsewhere. In most instances, the SBA will guarantee loans rather than provide money.
11. Terms of loans vary according to use, and interest rates on SBA guaranteed loans are based on statutory formulas relating to the cost of government money.
12. The SBA and many state and local agencies are involved in procuring government contracts for

small business, helping to get them on agency bidder lists, and assisting them in obtaining drawings and specifications of proposed government purchases.

13. Smaller firms may either bid on government contracts as primary contractors, or can subcontract for parts of contracts in conjunction with other small or large firms.
14. The SBA is the primary source of direct management assistance to smaller firms through its SCORE, ACE, SBI, and 406 Counseling programs.
15. The SBA and state and local agencies publish a wide range of manuals on how to manage a small business.

KEY TERMS AND CONCEPTS

Free enterprise
Sherman Antitrust Act of 1890
Clayton Act of 1914
Federal Trade Commission Act of 1914
Robinson–Patman Act of 1936
Interlocking directorates
Price-fixing
Splitting markets
Bait-and-switch advertising
Tying contract
Exclusive dealing
Cooling-off laws
Unfair Trade Practices Act
Contract
Employment discrimination
Employment at will
Small Business Administration
Guaranteed loans
Direct loans
Procurement
Set-aside program
Breakout program
Direct management assistance

QUESTIONS FOR DISCUSSION

1. Why is promoting the public good a multifaceted concern?
2. What were the effects of the Sherman Antitrust Act?
3. What practices were made illegal under the Clayton Act?
4. Describe what impact the Federal Trade Commission Act had on the protection of small businesses.
5. What restrictions are imposed on firms under the Robinson–Patman Act?
6. Describe bait-and-switch advertising.
7. Describe the cooling-off law and its effect on small business.
8. Describe the types of SBA loans available to small business.
9. What is the role of the SBA in small business procurement programs?
10. What management assistance programs are available to smaller firms?

SELF-TEST REVIEW

Multiple Choice Questions

1. Which of the following laws prohibits tying contracts?
   a. Sherman Antitrust Act.
   b. Clayton Act.
   c. Federal Trade Commission Act.
   d. Robinson–Patman Act.
2. The most common violation of laws relating to promotional strategies is:
   a. Stating that the product will do more than is true.
   b. Promoting attributes that are nonexistent.
   c. Falsely portraying a product as being on sale.
   d. Bait-and-switch advertising.
3. Functions of the SBA include all but which one of the following?
   a. Competing with financial organizations in offering loans to small businesses.
   b. Assisting small businesses to obtain contracts to provide products and services to government agencies.
   c. Helping minority- and women-owned enterprises.
   d. All of the above are functions of the SBA.

4. Under what circumstance would a firm have to file a fictitious business name statement?
   a. All firms must file this statement.
   b. Only when the name of the firm is not the name of its owner.
   c. Only when it employs more than 20 people and is a corporation.
   d. Only when it receives a contract from a government agency.
5. Which of the following is a management assistance program offered to small businesses through colleges and universities?
   a. ACE.
   b. SBI.
   c. SCORE.
   d. None of the above are offered through colleges and universities.

True/False Statements

1. Government regulation is not important to small firms because it is intended to apply only to large ones.
2. The concept of free enterprise as initially proposed by Adam Smith is somewhat unrealistic in modern times.
3. The increased sophistication of consumers has made government regulation of products almost unnecessary.
4. The Sherman Antitrust Act has been effective in breaking up monopolies.
5. The Small Business Administration is the primary federal agency responsible for assisting smaller firms.
6. Small firms are not included in antidiscrimination laws concerning hiring personnel.
7. All legally binding contracts must be in written form.
8. The Small Business Administration cannot lend money to small business owners who can obtain funding elsewhere.
9. The breakout program helps small businesses by setting aside certain contracts for them exclusively.
10. Management assistance programs include direct assistance, seminars, and publications.

HELEN'S FINE FASHIONS

Helen Garr started Helen's Fine Fashions nearly six years ago with a loan guarantee from the Small Business Administration. After struggling for the first two years, her business began to grow, and now has achieved annual sales of over $600,000 and before-tax profits of approximately 15 percent of sales.

Helen's Fine Fashions is located in a small shopping center in a town of about 40,000 people. Garr carries only expensive product lines of formal evening wear, career attire, casual evening wear, and accessories (for example, earrings, necklaces, belts, scarfs). The markets for her products are women in upper-income categories, and those who are pursuing careers that require finer and stylish clothing.

To appeal to these customers, Garr offers them appointments for reviewing merchandise, and overnight tailoring. She believes that these women have limited time to spend on shopping, want the finest clothing available, and do not like having to wait for alterations. Accordingly, a client can make an appointment, privately examine the merchandise available with a salesperson, and have the garments altered and available the next day.

Although the town is relatively small, it has a large percentage of upper-income households. There are over 30 stores that carry women's apparel, and of these, 6 cater to higher-income groups.

One of the most important suppliers of merchandise to Helen's Fine Apparel recently approached Garr and requested that she carry some of the company's other lines. These are less expensive dresses and pantsuits that are targeted to women in middle-income households.

Initially, Garr rejected the lines, because they do not fit the market to which her store caters. However, the supplier has continued to pressure Garr, and has even indicated that its other lines may be pulled from her store and given to a competitor if Helen's Fine Apparel does not stock these other lines. The supplier has suggested that these lines be offered as "closeout specials" in hopes of gaining impulse sales. There are enough variations in seasons and in the lines so that the specials could be offered almost continually without receiving undue attention.

Although Garr is enraged by the manner in which the supplier operates, she is somewhat reluctant to refuse the lines again. This supplier's products account for nearly 40 percent of her sales, and are by far the most popular. If the supplier takes the lines to another store, Garr thinks she might lose a considerable portion of her clientele, who are very brand conscious.

QUESTIONS

1. Should Garr take the other lines of the supplier? What are the implications of doing or not doing this?
2. Assuming that she does take the lines, how should she try to sell them?

NOTES

1. Udayan Gupta, "Red Tape Tangling Those Least Suited to Handling It," *The Wall Street Journal*, October 25, 1989, B1.
2. Small Business Administration Act, 1953, U.S. Government Printing Office.
3. Dennis H. Tootelian and Dale Pletcher, "S.B.A. Loan Benefits—A Survey of Borrowers," Unpublished Study.
4. *The State of Small Business: A Report of the President* (Washington, D.C.: U.S. Government Printing Office, 1988) 173.
5. "One-Stop Checklist," Office of Economic Development, City of Sacramento, Calif., July, 1987, 5–24.
6. "An Examination of the Potential Impact of the 'Cooling-Off' Law on Direct-to-Home Selling," *The Journal of Retailing*, Vol. 51, No. 1 (Spring, 1975), 61–70, 114.
7. Based on Cable News Network's "Pinnacle," April 10, 1988. Guest: William Gladstone, Arthur Young and Company.
8. Based on Cable News Network's "Pinnacle," July 5, 1987. Guest: Mathias DeVito, Rouse Company.
9. *The State of Small Business: A Report of the President*, 40, 44.
10. Based on Cable News Network's "Pinnacle," December 6, 1987. Guest: George Hatsopoulos, Thermo Electron Corporation.
11. Small Business Administration, *Business Loans from the SBA*, U.S. Government Printing Office, June, 1987.
12. *The State of Small Business: A Report of the President*, 173–174.
13. Susan S. Engeleiter, "Promoting Minority Enterprise," *Network*, Small Business Administration, September–October, 1989, 1.
14. Small Business Administration, *Your Business and the SBA*, U.S. Government Printing Office, February, 1987.
15. Small Business Administration, *Directory of Business Development Publications*, U.S. Government Printing Office, 1987.

COMPREHENSIVE CASES

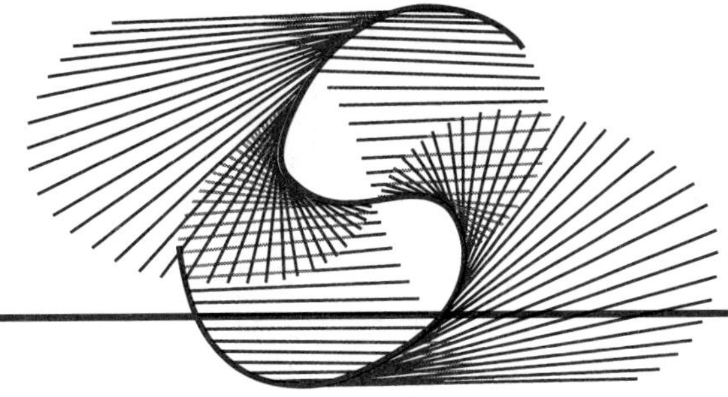

NORTHERN MAMMOTH EQUIPMENT CO.

Harold Walton, office manager of Northern Mammoth Equipment Co., at the request of the board of directors, was trying to decide what should be done with respect to company sales. Mammoth's profits had been declining steadily for the last three years because, as Walton stated: "There simply isn't much construction business in the area now, and we have to wait for contractors to obtain business before we can sell equipment to them."

COMPANY PRODUCTS

Northern Mammoth sold and serviced heavy equipment used in large construction projects. They handled several makes of well-known equipment. Equipment the company sold included various sizes of end-dumps, crawlers, front-end loaders, scrapers, bell-dumps, shovels, cranes, backhoers, miners, and paving equipment. The prices for Northern Mammoth's equipment ranged from $10,000 to about $250,000.

In addition to selling and servicing new equipment, Northern Mammoth rented equipment, sold parts, and sold and serviced used equipment. The sale of new equipment and parts accounted for approximately 68 percent of the company's total sales.

Cases were prepared by Professor Dennis H. Tootelian, California State University, Sacramento. All company names, names of individuals, and facts and figures have been disguised to assure anonymity.

HISTORY

Northern Mammoth Equipment Co. was founded in 1958 in northern California as a franchised dealer for Mammoth Equipment Co. located in Cleveland, Ohio. Mammoth Equipment Co., in turn, is owned by General Equipment Co., one of the largest contractors in the world.

The board of directors for Northern Mammoth was composed of its general manager (Eugene Rayburn) and office manager (Harold Walton), two representatives from Mammoth Equipment Co., and three representatives from General Equipment Co.

Northern Mammoth maintained a relatively stable market within the area almost from its inception. The main reason for this was that it handled equipment and parts which were well accepted in the construction industry. Thus, although it still had to compete with other equipment lines, its main product was already established. Mammoth had a franchised dealer in every state, and through them it also conducted foreign operations.

THE MARKET

In northern California, the relevant market area for Northern Mammoth, competition was very keen. Northern Mammoth competed with other companies that also sold well-known brands. For the most part these were, like Northern Mammoth, franchised dealers which had the exclusive rights to sell their respective brands. While franchise agreements placed restrictions on territorial expansion and types of products handled, no restrictions were placed on foreign operations.

Although Northern Mammoth had not made a study of its market position, the management felt that it was the second largest dealer in northern California. Management assumed that Northern Mammoth's largest and most important competitor was the Caterpillar dealership located in San Francisco. As one company member put it: "We are probably the second largest dealer in northern California, but CAT is way ahead of us."

San Francisco was considered to be the most important market area for heavy equipment, primarily because there were a large number of construction contractors located in and around the city. In general, contractors would bid for public and/or private contracts for construction projects. The winning bidder would then purchase whatever equipment and parts he or she needed from one of the dealers. Most dealers, such as Northern Mammoth, attempted to establish good working relations with as many contractors as possible to make them "established" customers.

ORGANIZATION

Northern Mammoth had 48 employees, including eight salespeople. The salespeople were located in various regions of northern California, and each maintained a small office there. For the 48 employees, there were four department managers plus a general manager who coordinated the entire operation (see Exhibit 1). The departments were broken down into a sales department, service department, parts department, and an office department; and there was a manager for each of these departments. With the exception of the parts manager, all of the managers had been in their respective positions since the company began its operations.

Sales Manager

The sales manager, James Farrell, forty-eight years old, was responsible for supervising the eight salespeople. He had been in the heavy equipment business for almost 17 years. Before coming to Northern Mammoth, Farrell worked as a sales manager for another company that sold heavy equipment. That company, however, did not sell lines that competed with Northern Mammoth.

Farrell was responsible for maintaining control over selling activities. Not only did he have to hire and fire salespeople, but he also had to approve all new and used equipment sales made for Northern Mammoth. In addition, he handled some of the company's larger accounts.

Service Manager

The service manager, Harold Wilman, was in charge of the service department where all repair and maintenance work was done. Although he ordinarily did not work on equipment himself, he was qualified to make repairs. Furthermore, he was directly in charge of customer relations for sales and service areas. Wilman, fifty-six years old, had been in the heavy equipment business for 32 years, 14 of which were with Mammoth. Before Wilman came to work for Northern Mammoth, he worked as a shop foreman in the same company that previously employed Farrell.

Parts Manager

The parts manager, William Borely, ordered and controlled all parts inventory, including shipping and receiving. In addition, he took care of all telephone orders for equipment for northern California. Borely, forty-one years old, had been in this field for 21 years and with Northern Mammoth for 13 years. Borely was a parts manager for an automobile dealership before he came to Northern Mammoth. He worked for Northern Mammoth for four years in the parts department before becoming the parts manager 9 years ago.

EXHIBIT 1 Northern Mammoth Equipment Organizational Chart

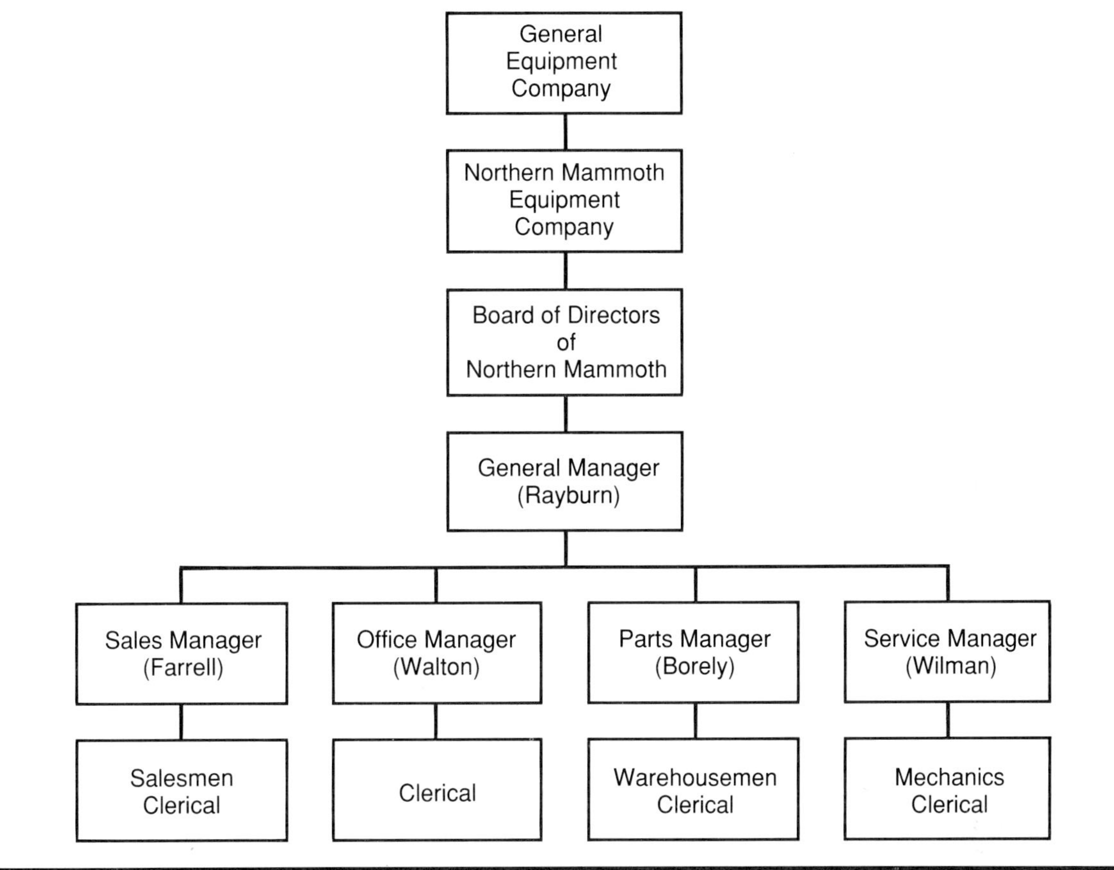

Office Manager

The office manager, Harold Walton, was the secretary-treasurer for the company. He controlled the accounting, credit, and clerical work for day-to-day operations. Because he had been in this field for 28 years, mostly with the Northern Mammoth company, he had been instrumental in setting company policy. He was also considered by most of the employees of the company to be the most knowledgeable about the product line. He was sixty-two years old.

General Manager

The general manager, Eugene Rayburn, fifty-one years old, coordinated all company operations. He was primarily concerned with establishing goodwill with clients and potential customers. Seldom did he concern himself with the day-to-day operations of the company; he left that to Walton. Rayburn had an engineering degree and 20 years of experience in the business. He was the only one of the five managers who had a college education. When Northern Mammoth was founded, Rayburn became the General Manager after leaving one of Mammoth's principal competitors.

SALES

The market for Northern Mammoth extended from Eureka in the north to the Fresno and Monterey areas in the south. Although this total area had been quite busy with construction work, Walton felt that it was beginning to tail off: "We have been involved in some of the largest projects in northern California, but now there doesn't seem to be much construction taking place."

Normally, Walton and others forecasted the potential demand for the area by reading about the contracts that were open for bid. They would try to determine who would bid for each contract, and who would make the winning bid. Since many of the bidders were established customers of one dealer, the company could frequently determine if they would be selling any equipment for the contract. They considered all contracts for the northern California area as potential sales.

Domestic Sales

To cover this area, Northern Mammoth employed eight salespeople who had, on the average, been with Northern Mammoth for eight years. Each lived in their respective area and conducted business from a small regional office located in that area. The regional offices for these salespeople were in Modesto, San Jose, San Francisco, Martinez, Santa Rosa, Sacramento, Yuba City, and Eureka.

Each salesperson worked for a salary plus a commission on sales. While the salaries varied with the individual salesperson, the commissions were fixed. On new equipment sales, the commission was 1½ percent of the *actual* sale price; and, on used equipment the commission was 3 percent of the sale price. If there was a trade-in with the sale, however, the commission was reduced to compensate for any overallowance given on the equipment turned in.

In addition to the salary and commission, the salespeople were given expense accounts and the use of a rented car. The expense accounts ranged between $300 and $450 per week for meals, gas, and lodging. Except for unusual conditions, the salespeople were not required to turn in any receipts except for gasoline. As Walton stated: "The cost of handling all the paperwork would be higher than it's worth." On the average, a salesperson made about $35,000 each year.

The sales manager, Farrell, and the equipment salesperson accounted for all of the new and used equipment sales and rentals, and about 10 percent of the domestic parts sales. (Note: Northern Mammoth rents out both new and used equipment, although this accounts for a small part of their total sales.) The remainder of the parts sales were made by the parts department manager, either over the telephone or by mail orders.

Northern Mammoth had about 300 steady customers which accounted for about 85 percent of their sales for both equipment and parts. Their orders were not definitely timed, nor were they for the same equipment or parts each time. Most customers did not stock parts, since Northern Mammoth was close by and stocked the parts for them. Even though orders varied considerably, sales over the years have tended to remain stable, except for the decline over the last three years. As Rayburn put it: "If our sales change very much on a yearly basis, the factory representatives who come by every so often want to know why." (See Exhibits 2, 3, 4, and 5.)

Export Sales

In addition to domestic sales, Northern Mammoth exported parts and equipment to the Philippines, Indonesia, Ghana, Mexico, and Guatemala. The company did not keep records of the breakdown of domestic and foreign sales, but estimated that foreign sales accounted for about 50 percent of the company's parts sales. The amount of export sales of equipment was estimated to be about 10 percent of total equipment sales. These sales were not solicited.

Advertising

As far as other marketing aspects are concerned, Northern Mammoth did a little advertising in trade publications such as *Local Construction.* Their total advertising budget ran around $18,000 annually, and had not changed much over the years. When Northern Mammoth advertised their main brand, they received a promotional allowance from the manufacturer which was set at a maximum of $1500 per year. The only other advertising that Northern Mammoth did was to buy a spot in the Yellow Pages of the telephone directory. The management as a whole felt that the main method of promoting the company's products was by personal contact with the prospective contractors and with other cus-

EXHIBIT 2 Comparative Profit and Loss Statements (in thousands)

	1990	1989	1988	1987	1986	1985	1984	1983
Sales								
Equipment								
New	$2,038	$2,141	$2,196	$2,204	$2,187	$2,072	$1,939	$1,900
Rental	406	427	438	452	463	426	378	379
Used	1,031	1,103	1,093	1,130	1,001	1,013	989	904
Service								
Customers	158	162	171	182	170	163	150	138
Other	183	199	208	216	193	180	186	192
Parts	2,013	2,092	2,111	2,187	2,081	2,000	1,893	1,630
Total	$5,829	$6,124	$6,217	$6,371	$6,095	$5,854	$5,535	$5,143
Cost of Goods Sold								
Equipment								
New	$1,824	$1,863	$1,868	$1,871	$1,863	$1,792	$1,671	$1,620
Rental	377	397	404	409	413	404	347	330
Used	951	1,015	997	1,063	978	998	979	900
Service	161	187	190	194	187	205	207	212
Parts	1,496	1,536	1,595	1,667	1,560	1,390	1,293	1,150
Total	$4,809	$4,998	$5,054	$5,204	$5,001	$4,789	$4,497	$4,212
Gross Profit	$1,020	$1,126	$1,163	$1,167	$1,094	$1,065	$1,038	$ 931
Other Expenses								
Sales' Salaries	$ 315	$ 298	$ 291	$ 269	$ 257	$ 230	$ 213	$ 213
Other Operating Expenses	380	367	374	369	372	368	379	386
Fixed Expenses	109	109	109	109	109	109	109	109
Total	$ 804	$ 774	$ 774	$ 747	$ 738	$ 707	$ 701	$ 708
Net Profit Before Income Tax	$ 216	$ 352	$ 389	$ 420	$ 356	$ 358	$ 337	$ 223

EXHIBIT 3 Comparative Balance Sheets (in thousands)

	1990	1989	1988	1987	1986	1985	1984	1983
Current Assets								
Cash	$ 549	$ 567	$ 526	$ 575	$ 538	$ 498	$ 502	$ 478
Receivables	845	874	836	931	875	926	872	799
Inventory	1,751	1,646	1,701	1,662	1,741	1,599	1,638	1,621
Other	78	58	71	47	26	37	49	19
Total Current Assets	$3,223	$3,145	$3,134	$3,215	$3,180	$3,060	$3,061	$2,917
Fixed Assets	82	89	96	103	110	117	124	131
Total Assets	$3,305	$3,234	$3,230	$3,318	$3,290	$3,177	$3,185	$3,048
Current Liabilities	$ 678	$ 698	$ 702	$ 808	$ 825	$ 818	$ 831	$ 824
Notes Payable	372	372	372	372	372	372	372	372
Other Liabilities	45	11	20	36	50	9	46	23
Stockholders Equity	343	343	343	343	343	343	343	343
Retained Earnings	1,867	1,810	1,793	1,759	1,700	1,635	1,593	1,486
Total Liabilities	$3,305	$3,234	$3,230	$3,318	$3,290	$3,177	$3,185	$3,048

EXHIBIT 4 Common Size Profit and Loss Statements

	1990	1989	1988	1987	1986	1985	1984	1983
Sales								
Equipment								
New	35.1%	35.0%	35.4%	34.2%	35.9%	35.6%	35.2%	37.1%
Rental	7.0	7.0	7.0	6.2	7.5	7.2	6.7	7.2
Used	17.6	18.3	17.5	17.0	16.5	17.3	17.8	17.5
Service								
Customers	2.6	2.5	2.7	2.4	2.8	2.5	2.7	2.7
Other	3.1	3.1	3.3	6.2	3.2	3.1	3.2	3.7
Parts	34.6	34.1	34.1	34.0	34.1	34.3	34.4	31.8
Total	100.0%	100.0%	100.0%	100.0%	100.0%	100.0%	100.0%	100.0%
Cost of Goods Sold								
Equipment								
New	31.4%	30.5%	30.1%	29.2%	30.5%	30.1%	30.0%	31.8%
Rental	6.5	6.5	6.5	6.4	6.8	7.0	6.3	6.5
Used	16.4	16.6	12.8	16.6	16.0	17.2	17.8	17.6
Service	2.8	3.1	3.1	3.0	3.1	3.5	3.8	4.2
Parts	25.8	25.1	25.7	25.6	25.6	24.0	23.5	22.5
Total	82.9%	81.8%	78.2%	80.8%	82.0%	81.8%	81.4%	82.6%
Gross Profit	17.1%	18.2%	21.8%	19.2%	18.0%	18.2%	18.6%	17.4%
Other Expenses								
Sales' Salaries	5.4%	4.9%	4.7%	4.2%	4.2%	4.0%	3.9%	4.2%
Other Operating Expenses	6.6	6.0	6.0	5.8	6.1	6.3	6.9	7.6
Fixed Expenses	1.9	1.8	1.6	1.7	1.8	1.9	2.0	2.1
Total	13.9%	12.7%	12.3%	11.7%	12.1%	12.2%	12.8%	13.9%
Net Profit Before Income Tax	3.2%	5.5%	9.5%	7.5%	5.9%	6.0%	5.8%	3.5%

EXHIBIT 5 Common Size Balance Sheets

	1990	1989	1988	1987	1986	1985	1984	1983
Current Assets								
Cash	16.6%	17.6%	16.2%	16.9%	16.3%	15.6%	15.7%	15.9%
Receivables	25.6	26.3	26.0	27.3	26.5	28.7	27.5	26.5
Inventory	53.2	51.3	52.6	51.3	53.1	50.8	51.4	52.8
Other	2.2	2.1	2.2	1.4	.8	1.3	1.5	.6
Total Current Assets	97.6%	97.3%	97.0%	96.9%	96.7%	96.4%	96.1%	95.8%
Fixed Assets	2.4	2.7	3.0	3.1	3.3	3.6	3.9	4.2
Total Assets	100.0%	100.0%	100.0%	100.0%	100.0%	100.0%	100.0%	100.0%
Current Liabilities	20.6%	21.8%	21.9%	24.2%	24.7%	26.2%	26.4%	27.2%
Notes Payable	11.4	11.5	11.5	11.4	11.4	11.5	11.5	12.3
Other Liabilities	1.2	—	.1	1.0	1.5	—	1.5	.6
Stockholders Equity	10.3	10.4	10.4	10.3	10.3	10.4	10.4	11.2
Retained Earnings	56.5	56.3	56.1	53.1	52.1	51.9	50.2	48.7
Total Liabilities	100.0%	100.0%	100.0%	100.0%	100.0%	100.0%	100.0%	100.0%

tomers who bought their parts from Northern Mammoth.

Pricing

Although the company had manufacturer's suggested retail price lists, they rarely used them except as a starting point for negotiations. Sales contracts were negotiated on an individual basis; and in almost every case a discount was given on the retail price of the new equipment. In many cases, too, an overallowance was given on the equipment that was traded in; and sometimes both discounts and overallowances were given.

However, even with discounts and/or overallowances, Northern Mammoth had a policy of pricing their equipment somewhat higher than their competitors. As Farrell put it: "Our prices are a little higher because we feel that our equipment is of a better quality, and this is what we try to stress to the contractors." In conjunction, Walton added: "Our main products are sort of like the 'Cadillac' of the heavy equipment lines and most contractors know this. We don't want to sell lower quality lines."

Discounts and Credit Policies

Sales discounts on new and used equipment varied in size and type with each sale. Sometimes a straight percentage was taken off the list price, or payment periods were lengthened, or both. Since each sale was negotiated independently, the discount depended on what was needed to make the sale. As for parts, no discounts were given except for export sales. In these cases, usually a 5/10/net 30 discount was offered.

As for the credit policies, contracts for new and used equipment were made for each sale. Ordinarily either Mr. Farrell or Mr. Walton made an investigation of the credit rating of the potential buyer. Basically, Mr. Farrell or Mr. Walton checked Dun and Bradstreet reports, the Retail Credit Associations, and the relevant banks. On some occasions the investigator would analyze the buyer's financial statements before making the final decision on granting credit for the purchase; however, there was no set policy. By being quite cautious, company management felt that they had a very low bad debt loss, averaging approximately 0.9 percent of total sales, and 6.0 percent of the total accounts receivable.

Profitability

The profit on new and used equipment sales was set by the terms of the negotiation and contract. For new equipment, Northern Mammoth tried to make between 12 percent and 24 percent on their main lines, and between 7½ percent and 20 percent on the other lines. The company maintained specific mark-ups on its parts sales ranging from 24 percent to 30 percent. Overall, their main line parts accounted for about 65 percent of the total parts sales with all others making up the balance. In Northern Mammoth's parts department they had arranged their inventory into two separate divisions, one for their main line and one for other parts.

CUSTOMER SERVICE

Even though their prices were high, Northern Mammoth offered some services that were specifically designed to assist their customers. Two programs have been instituted in the last few years, the Exchange Component Program and the Temporary Warehouse Program. Although none of the managers knew what these programs cost, they admitted that they were expensive. They agreed, however, that they were justifiable expenditures.

Exchange Component Program

Under the Exchange Component Program, if a customer bought a tractor or any other piece of equipment from Northern Mammoth and the machine broke down in the field, Northern Mammoth would send a boom truck and a team of mechanics to the construction site to pull out the engine, transmission, differential, or other defective part, and replace it with a rebuilt one from the company's inventory. The broken part would then be returned to Northern Mammoth and repaired. The contractor paid only for parts and labor and kept the rebuilt part that was put in by the team of mechanics; the company kept the repaired part. It should be noted that the contractor was not charged for the service call. Wilman felt that the cost to Northern Mammoth to send a boom truck and a team of mechanics out to replace a broken part, was anywhere from

$100 to $400, depending on the distance and part(s) replaced.

Temporary Warehouse Program

The second service, the Temporary Warehouse Program, was essentially a temporary parts warehouse set up at the site of a large construction project if the contractor(s) bought some of Northern Mammoth's equipment. Ordinarily, the warehouse was something like a large trailer with one or two employees from Northern Mammoth operating it. In addition, there were usually two or three field mechanics who moved from one site to another to assist in the repair of any Northern Mammoth equipment.

Both of these services normally were run at a loss, but were used to provide "a little extra" for the customers. All of the managers seemed quite pleased with the two programs, and considered them to be two of the most important actions they had initiated. As Walton explained, "These two programs are somewhat expensive to the company but they are needed. We couldn't meet competition without them."

PURCHASES

Northern Mammoth bought its equipment primarily from their plant in Cleveland, Ohio. Northern Mammoth also had set up depot areas across the country. For northern California, there were depots in Denver, Portland, Dallas, and Los Angeles. Although Northern Mammoth had made purchases from each of these, it more frequently bought from Denver or Los Angeles. These depots, for the most part, only handled parts, although some equipment was available at times. It should also be noted that Northern Mammoth maintained its own parts warehouses at San Leandro and Arcadia, although both warehouses were quite small.

On the average, Northern Mammoth tried to stick to making regular weekly orders, which averaged about $30,000 apiece. Northern Mammoth did not receive discounts on parts or equipment purchases; however, the shipping expenses from Cleveland were prepaid although the shipping expenses from the depots were not. When ordering equipment from Cleveland, Northern Mammoth usually had to wait one month. Delivery from there was most commonly by rail (piggyback). Although the company could order parts from Cleveland, this was done quite infrequently. The parts usually came from one of the depots by a special-order truck. In either case, when the shipments arrived they were unpacked immediately and inspected for damage, usually by a member of the parts department.

Special Orders

Because there are so many parts in this type of business, Northern Mammoth did not carry all of the parts that were desired by its clients and ran out of parts quite frequently. In these cases, they faxed their orders to one of the depots and usually received delivery within two days. One employee in the parts department stated that the company made special orders on the average of four to five times a day, accounting for approximately 12 percent of its parts purchases. The cost of making a special purchase order was the costs of the fax, a 5 percent emergency charge from the depot, and the extra freight costs involved since special orders were usually sent by bus or airplane. On the whole, management figured that they lost about 10 percent of their profits on a purchase order of this sort.

Regular Ordering

Since Northern Mammoth did not have a purchasing department, the parts manager signed all order forms. He was not held to a maximum limit (dollarwise) on what he could order. Ordinarily, he was the only one who made out purchase orders. In most cases, Borely tried to order so as to maintain a stock for about 90 days. All purchases were automatically insured by an insurance policy that the company carried.

INVENTORY

Although sales tended to be highest between May and December, Northern Mammoth kept extra inventory on hand over and above the estimated 90-day supply during the January to April period. On the average, then, they tried to maintain a parts inventory valued at approximately $800,000, and an equipment inventory of approximately $1,200,000.

Northern Mammoth carried about 15,000 different parts which they classified as their "active" parts in their parts list system. They also handled about 5,000 parts which were "inactive" and not always carried in the supply room. Of the $800,000 in parts, approximately 10 to 15 percent were considered to be either extremely slow-moving or obsolete. Some of this inventory included specially ordered parts which were not used and could not be returned (specially ordered goods could not be returned at any time). All of the extremely slow-moving and obsolete parts were kept in a loft above the supply room. A few of these parts were used occasionally in repairing old machines. However, since management did not feel that they needed the extra space, no attempt had been made to dispose of them. No one in the company had investigated whether they could be sold.

Inventory Control

Inventory control was handled primarily by the parts manager, but occasionally Walton assisted in this area. All inventory information was maintained by the use of a Cardex file. Each active part type was listed on a card with the minimum and maximum quantities to keep on hand as well as the actual inventory available. Although this system gave a rough idea as to how much inventory was on hand, Northern Mammoth only made one actual inventory count per year. It was estimated by Walton that it cost Northern Mammoth about $8,000 a year to maintain its inventory control system.

Pilferage

Although management did not make estimates of pilferage, losses of this sort were thought to be considerable. As one employee stated: "A lot of these parts and tools can be used on cars and other trucks. This place gets robbed of everything from neon light filaments to engine parts." Management caught several of its mechanics stealing in the past and in most cases fired them.

ASSESSMENT

In assessing the company's development to date, Walton felt that on the whole Northern Mammoth had been fairly successful: "Sales have been somewhat steady except for 1975, 1976, and 1977. The factory representatives complain that we don't have enough penetration into different market areas, but the companies we buy from don't always have the size of equipment that the contractors need, and we do no product research and development ourselves."

Another member of the management team felt that Northern Mammoth could do considerably better if the factory left them alone. He stated: "They have training schools for each department and they make us use various accounting forms which just don't fit into our operations. The representatives are always coming around and questioning us; if they would let us run the company the way we wanted to, we would be much better off."

Although they did have to use specified accounting procedures, other managers did not feel that the factory was being overly domineering. The general consensus was that Northern Mammoth had done reasonably well, but they didn't know what actions they should take to increase sales and profitability.

PARK PHARMACIES, INC.

INTRODUCTION

After losing their third manager in four years, Jerry Smith and Jeff Montgomery were reassessing their operating practices for Park Pharmacies, a holding company for three drugstores they owned and managed. The corporation had remained profitable over the years, but it seemed to Smith that although they were working harder, company sales and profits were stagnating. And, with the personnel problems in their third store, the frustrations were becoming tiresome. As Smith noted:

> We have been in business for over 15 years now, and have done reasonably well. But I'm getting tired of all the work, the crises, and the frustrations of third-party billing (where payments were made by insurance companies and the government). Worst of all, I don't think that I'm getting any richer.

HISTORY

Park Pharmacies was founded nearly 16 years ago in a relatively large community in the northeastern United States. Smith, president of Park Pharmacies, and Montgomery, its vice-president and treasurer, initially began working together as partners of Smith's Drugs, their first community-oriented pharmacy, soon after graduating from pharmacy school together. Three years later, they purchased Medico Pharmacy, a medical pharmacy, and incorporated Park Pharmacies as a holding company for both stores. For the next nine years, Smith managed Smith's Drugs while Montgomery managed Medico Pharmacy.

After accumulating a sizable net worth, Park Pharmacies, at Smith's insistence, purchased a third pharmacy and called it Jay's Drugs. This store was located in a less desirable area of the community and had been previously owned by a friend of Montgomery's. Although the store had been reasonably successful before acquisition by Park Pharmacies, the previous owner had let the business deteriorate in the few years preceding his retirement. While Montgomery was content with two stores and did not want the added burdens of rejuvenating this pharmacy, Smith was eager for the challenge and the opportunities for added growth and profits.

ORGANIZATION

The organizational structure of Park Pharmacies is shown in Exhibit 1. Smith served as president of the corporation and manager of Smith Drugs; Montgomery served as the corporation's vice-president and treasurer, and as manager of Medico Pharmacy. They believed that the duties of the president would be about as time-consuming as those of the vice-president and treasurer, therefore balancing out their work.

Because neither man wanted to manage two stores at once, they hired a manager for Jay's Drugs. Ron Karle was the last of a series of managers they had employed in that capacity. After the owners fired the first manager because they caught him taking merchandise from the store, the next manager (Ames) and the next (Karle) quit due to what they considered to be undesirable working conditions.

Karle was especially vocal about what he thought to be the problems in managing this pharmacy:

> Even though my duties as manager and pharmacist were fairly clear, either Smith or Montgomery would occasionally stop by and check what I was doing. Quite often they would make conflicting recommendations and I really did not know what to do then.
>
> For example, Jerry would want me to promote the store more aggressively, using fliers and in-store sales programs and to have my staff use more aggressive selling techniques. Jeff would come in and see this and hit the roof. He would tell me that such practices were unprofessional and should be stopped immediately. You'd think that after all the years they have been in business together, they would understand each other's methods of operation. Instead, they would come in, tell me different things, and evidently never talk about it to each other.
>
> I became very frustrated trying to balance their orders. I can make almost the same amount of money as an employee pharmacist, actually only about $2,000 less, and it's just not worth the headaches. Besides, this store tends to cater to very low-income clientele. These people are hard for me to deal with, especially with all the Medicare claims processing (the state-operated health care program for welfare recipients). Each store does its own billing to insurance companies and to the state under the Medicare program. We also had considerable problems with shoplifting, and we were robbed twice this year by drug addicts. It just wasn't worth the additional $2,000.

As Karle noted, each pharmacy was managed independently of the others. Since they were nearly seven miles apart, Smith and Montgomery felt that they were not competing with one another for customers, so they would operate autonomously. By

EXHIBIT 1 Park Pharmacies Organizational Chart

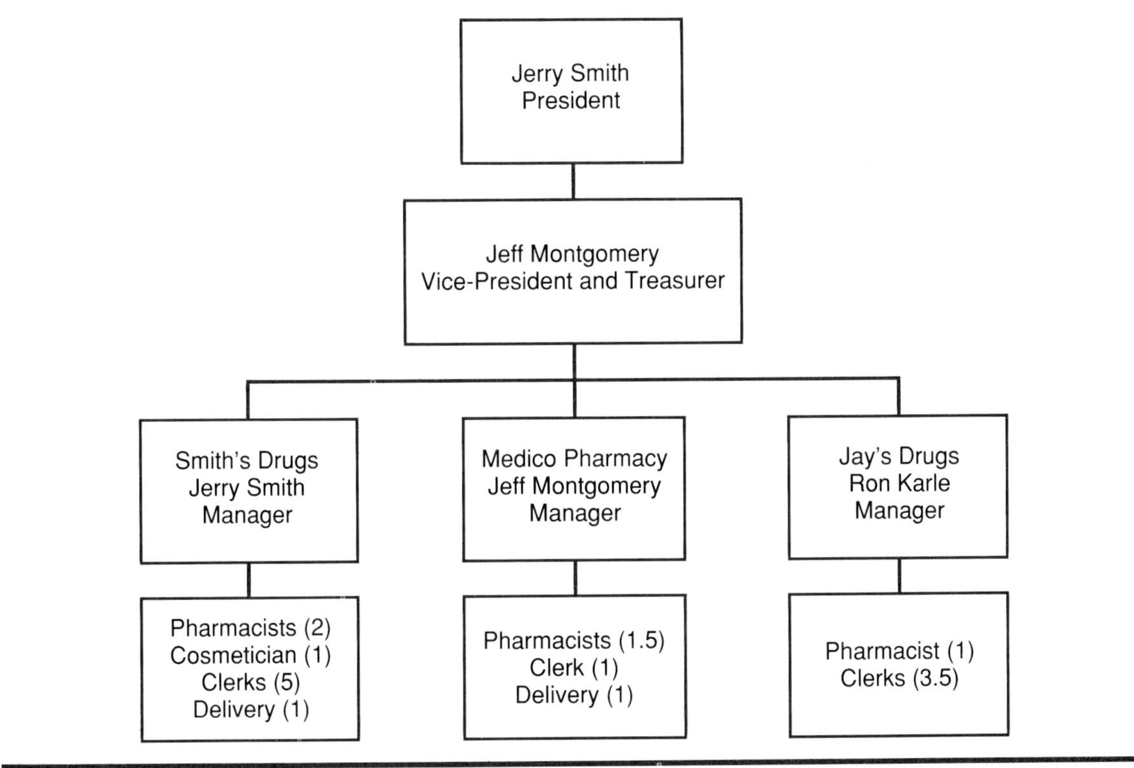

doing this, they could each run their store as they saw fit, avoiding some of the common problems associated with partnerships. Not wanting to cause any new troubles, they agreed when they purchased Jay's Drugs that each would take an interest in overseeing its operations on a time-available basis. They left the day-to-day operations to the pharmacist-manager. Normally, Smith would stop by the store once a week, and Montgomery once very three weeks.

THE MARKET

Located in a city of nearly 350,000 people, the three pharmacies faced moderate to intense competition from both chain and independent drugstores located nearby. Within the city there were 17 chain drug outlets, over 40 independent pharmacies, and out-patient pharmacies in the four local hospitals (see Exhibits 2 and 3).

Smith's Drugs faced the greatest amount of competition, since three chain stores and two independent pharmacies were located within two miles of the store. Being well established, however, the pharmacy was thought to have a loyal clientele, who were older and had higher incomes. Accordingly, these customers were not considered to be especially price sensitive or overly concerned with comparing chain store prices with those of Smith's Drugs. Smith believed that his customers were primarily interested in service and in-store credit rather than price. Although the store's growth had slowed down as new competition entered the area and the total population in the immediate area declined, both Smith and Montgomery thought that the store was doing very well.

EXHIBIT 2 Selected Demographics of the Market Area

	Smith's Drugs	Medico Pharmacy	Jay's Drugs
Age			
Under 21	9%	12%	16%
21 to 35	17	23	31
36 to 50	24	28	19
51 to 64	31	26	18
over 64	19	11	16
Income ($000s)			
Under 10	5%	9%	16%
10 to 20	11	23	35
21 to 35	29	33	32
36 to 50	33	21	15
over 50	22	14	2
Sex			
Female	56%	49%	59%
Male	44	51	41
Employment			
Blue collar	19%	24%	39%
White collar	47	42	21
Professionals	21	25	10
Unemployed	5	4	14
Other*	8	5	16

*Includes retired

Medico Pharmacy was situated in a medical center located near one of the larger hospitals in the city. Being the only pharmacy in the center gave Medico Pharmacy a significant advantage. However, there were four other independent pharmacies and one chain outlet located within 1.5 miles. While Montgomery considered convenience to be a critical factor in selecting a pharmacy among those operating within his area, other pharmacies had been competing more on price since the chain store moved into the area. Montgomery, however, refused to do this because he considered price cutting to be unprofessional. As he noted:

> If customers are going to patronize Medico Pharmacy strictly because we offer the lowest prices, I don't want them. After all, how long will they remain our customers? I'll tell you—just until one of the other pharmacies offers them a better deal. There's no future in that type of activity. I offer my customers good service and convenience, and I expect them to pay for it. And they do!

Jay's Drugs was located on the outskirts of the city in a relatively depressed area, along with one chain and two independent pharmacies. Incomes tended to be lower and a significant level of unemployment was evident. A greater percentage of this store's customers were under the Medicare and other third-party programs than in either Smith's Drugs or Medico Pharmacy. As Karle commented:

> Under third-party programs, our fees are limited to the ingredient cost of the drug plus a set fee. Prescriptions that are not under these programs earn us considerably more money, about double the fee paid by the insurance companies and the state. With all of the paperwork I have to do for this, and the delays we often have in receiving payments (averaging 40 days on third-party claims), we have a tough time making a profit. These programs only account for about 25 percent of Smith's Drugs' total revenues, and 40 percent of those for Medico Pharmacy. For us, they represent about 80 percent of total revenues. Even though we have a lot of floor space, our nonprescription sales represent only 20 percent of total revenue. These people do not buy our merchandise. I think they prefer to go to the chain stores instead, where they think they can get lower prices.

MARKETING

The marketing programs used in the three pharmacies differed greatly, reflecting the attitudes of the store managers. The most consistently aggressive efforts were conducted by Smith for Smith's Drugs. Of the 3,800 square feet of floor space, approximately 2,500 square feet were devoted to nonprescription merchandise. Smith made certain that he carried a wide range of merchandise, and used weekly newspaper advertising with specials on selected nonprescription items. The full-time cosmetician and all other personnel were well trained in personal selling. Accordingly, Smith felt that he could compete with both the independent pharmacies and the chains in terms of both products and services (see Exhibit 3). However, he thought that the chains

EXHIBIT 3 Competitor Profile

	Store	Chains			Independents			
A. For Smith's Drugs	**Smith's**	**1**	**2**	**3**	**1**	**2**	**3**	**4**
Product Offerings								
Prescriptions	X	X	X	X	X	X		
Nonprescription drugs	X	X	X	X	X	X		
Cosmetics	X	X	X	X		X		
Greeting cards	X	X	X	X		X		
Gifts and notions	X	X	X	X	X			
Photographic		X		X				
Service Offerings								
Medication records	X	X		X	X	X		
Consultations	X	X	X	X	X	X		
Emergency prescriptions					X	X		
In-store credit	X							
Delivery	X				X	X		
B. For Medico Pharmacy	**Medico**	**1**	**2**	**3**	**1**	**2**	**3**	**4**
Product Offerings								
Prescriptions	X	X			X	X	X	X
Nonprescription drugs	X	X			X	X	X	X
Cosmetics		X			X		X	
Greeting cards		X			X	X		X
Gifts and notions		X					X	
Photographic								
Service Offerings								
Medication records	X	X			X	X	X	X
Consultations	X	X			X	X	X	X
Emergency prescriptions					X		X	
In-store credit	X					X		
Delivery	X					X		X
C. For Jay's Drugs	**Jay's**	**1**	**2**	**3**	**1**	**2**	**3**	**4**
Product Offerings								
Prescriptions	X	X			X	X		
Nonprescription drugs	X	X			X	X		
Cosmetics		X			X	X		
Greeting cards	X	X			X			
Gifts and notions	X	X						
Photographic	X							
Service Offerings								
Medication records	X	X			X	X		
Consultations	X	X			X	X		
Emergency prescriptions						X		
In-store credit								
Delivery								

could offer lower prices if they were willing to take lower profit margins.

To complement his other marketing efforts, Smith also was involved in various civic activities. Although he did this partly for personal enjoyment, he also felt that the publicity and goodwill he generated for the store were quite important:

> If I want the community to support my store, I have to support the community. It's important for people to get to know me, and for me to get to know them.

In contrast to Smith's Drugs, Medico Pharmacy received almost no marketing effort. With only 1,000 square feet of space, 400 of which were available for nonprescription merchandising, Montgomery did not think it was wise to aggressively promote the pharmacy. Since nearly 80 percent of the pharmacy's revenues came from prescription sales, he preferred to maintain a highly professional image—which meant no marketing effort other than a well-maintained store. Nearly all of Montgomery's marketing efforts were directed to cultivating good relations with physicians in the medical center. He believed that good rapport with the physicians would prompt them to recommend Medico Pharmacy when they wrote prescriptions. Medico Pharmacy's product and service offerings are shown in Exhibit 3.

The most sporadic of all marketing efforts was undertaken by Jay's Drugs. In the 14 months that Karle managed the store, he implemented several marketing programs that Smith had used successfully for Smith's Drugs. However, these were only moderately successful. While the store had nearly 4,500 square feet of floor space, not all of the 3,500 square feet of nonprescription space was stocked. Karle had suggested that the store seek a postal station for the unused area, but neither Smith nor Montgomery could decide whether it was worth the money and effort.

COMPANY OPERATIONS

Since Smith and Montgomery ran their own individual stores, there was very little in the way of standardized procedures. Montgomery worked closely with the corporation's accountant, and insisted that there be separate financial statements for each of the three stores, so that they could evaluate individual performance. Smith and Montgomery met formally on the third Thursday of every other month to review store activities. Aside from this, they managed their stores as if they were not under central ownership.

Smith's Drugs employed two pharmacists, a cosmetician, three clerks, and one part-time delivery person. Although Smith felt that he did not always need two pharmacists, his community service work often kept him away from the store. Accordingly, he preferred to be free from those duties except during peak times. On those occasions when he was not in the store, the pharmacist on duty would be in charge. During the evening hours, the senior clerk would have such duties since no pharmacist would be working. Store hours were 9 A.M. to 9 P.M, Monday through Saturday. The pharmacy was open 9 A.M. to 6 P.M., Monday through Friday. Since all employees were paid straight hourly wages, there were no financial incentives for managing the store during the times when Smith was away. He believed that the prestige of being store manager was adequate.

Store operations at Medico Pharmacy were much simpler. The pharmacy was open from 9 A.M. to 6 P.M., Monday through Friday. Montgomery ordinarily remained in the store throughout that time, even during normal lunch hours. He employed a delivery person on a part-time basis, and a semi-retired pharmacist during the time he had to be away from the pharmacy.

Jay's Drugs employed a pharmacist-manager, one full-time pharmacist, and three clerks. Because so many of its prescriptions were third-party (and therefore carried low profit margins), delivery service was not offered. Both Smith and Montgomery felt that the costs of delivery (estimated to be $2.50 to $3.50 each) were too high to justify this service, and that delivery costs could not be passed on to store customers as an added charge. Store hours were 9 A.M. to 7 P.M., Monday through Saturday. The store manager, unlike other employees, was paid a straight salary. In addition to the management responsibilities for hiring and firing, the manager was expected to fill in as a backup pharmacist during

EXHIBIT 4 Park Pharmacies Income Statement by Pharmacy (for the current year)

	Smith's Drugs	Medico Pharmacy	Jay's Drugs
Sales			
Prescription	551,900	645,000	325,000
Nonprescription	598,000	72,000	108,300
Total	1,149,900	717,000	433,300
Cost of Goods	781,900	496,450	272,900
Gross Margin	368,000	220,550	160,400
Expenses			
Manager's Salary	50,000	50,000	33,100
Employees' Wages	160,500	63,800	81,400
Advertising	31,000	4,000	7,500
Rent	26,700	32,500	19,600
All Other	53,700	38,500	13,100
Total	321,900	188,800	154,700
Net Profit Before Taxes	46,100	31,750	5,700

peak times. Typically, the manager would work 5.5 days per week and receive $2,000 more in salary than the employee pharmacist earned in hourly wages for a month.

FINANCIAL POSITION

As Smith and Montgomery reviewed the financial statements for each pharmacy (see Exhibits 4, 5 and 6), it became apparent that the businesses had not grown to the extent that Smith had hoped. Although both Smith's Drugs and Medico Pharmacy had always been profitable, the former generated considerably more sales and profits than did the latter. Nevertheless, the owners divided the profits equally, and tried to maintain a policy of retaining 20 percent of the net profits before taxes in the company. Believing that the acquisition of Jay's Pharmacy would increase their sales to $3 million and profits to about $125,000, Smith expected Park

EXHIBIT 5 Park Pharmacies Condensed Income Statement (for the last three years)

	This Year	Last Year	Two Years Ago
Sales			
Prescription	1,521,900	1,425,000	1,267,000
Nonprescription	778,300	690,000	680,500
Total	2,300,200	2,115,000	1,947,500
Cost of Goods	1,551,250	1,395,400	1,277,600
Gross Margin	748,950	719,600	669,900
Expenses	665,400	614,500	608,000
Net Profit before Taxes	83,550	105,100	61,900

EXHIBIT 6 Park Pharmacies Balance Sheet

	Smith's Drugs	Medico Pharmacy	Jay's Drugs
ASSETS			
Current Assets			
Cash	30,600	30,500	9,000
Accounts receivable	42,900	51,000	44,000
Inventory	163,300	96,700	107,200
Other	4,000	6,000	3,000
Total	240,800	184,200	163,200
Fixed Assets			
Furniture, equipment	36,700	16,600	21,300
TOTAL ASSETS	277,500	200,800	184,500
LIABILITIES			
Current Liabilities			
Accounts payable	70,200	50,400	60,800
Notes payable	19,500	5,000	5,900
Accrued expenses	33,300	7,200	17,500
Total	123,000	62,600	84,200
Long-Term Liabilities			
Notes payable	30,800	16,000	26,500
Total Liabilities	153,800	78,600	110,700
Net Worth	123,700	122,200	73,800
TOTAL LIABILITIES AND NET WORTH	277,500	200,800	184,500

Pharmacies to continue to grow, possibly with the purchase of another pharmacy.

Montgomery, on the other hand, seemed quite content with the level of sales and the income he was receiving. Although he agreed that the profitability of the corporation was not up to expectations, he noted that the business still provided him with a comfortable living. However, he did express one major concern:

> Despite the fact that I am happy with my income from the business, I am worried about the future need for more money. Smith's Drugs is getting pretty old, and will need some extensive modernization within the next two years. I expect that this will cost approximately $70,000. And I would like to have a new computer for my store. Jerry has a new one, and I would like to put the present one I have in the other store and get a new one for myself. This may cost somewhere around $25,000. When we take these expenditures into account, we don't have all the money we think we do. Neither of us particularly likes to borrow money, so we could have some trouble here.

THE FUTURE

In considering Smith's comments regarding the problems they were facing, Montgomery was both concerned and amused:

> Jerry was the one who wanted to jump into the Jay's deal. I was reluctant to change the good thing we had going; I just wanted to keep everything the way it was. He wanted to grow and get rich and be the big businessman. Unfortunately, I don't think that

we can sell Jay's Drugs without losing a lot of money.

Before even considering the possibility of selling Jay's Drugs, Smith wanted to review the entire operation of Park Pharmacies. He knew that the poor operating performance of Jay's Drugs over the past four years would make it very difficult to sell the store. Furthermore, he did not want to give up, feeling that there must be ways to solve the problems they faced:

I don't think we have done all that we could to make Jay's successful. Our advertising hasn't been consistent and the store is not well merchandised. Some of the strategies I have used in my store should work well in Jay's, but Jeff has not agreed. The effect has been a sporadic effort and the operating results show this to be true.

Subject Index

Company Index